THE EMERGENCE OF FILM ART

Second Edition

Also by Lewis Jacobs
The Documentary Tradition
Second Edition

THE EMERGENCE OF FILM ART

Second Edition

*The evolution
and development
of the
motion picture
as an art,
from
1900 to the present*

LEWIS JACOBS

W · W · Norton & Company
New York   London

Library of Congress Cataloging in Publication Data
Jacobs, Lewis, editor
    The emergence of film art, 2nd ed.
    Includes index.
    1. Moving-pictures—Addresses, essays, lectures.
I. Title.
PN1994.J24   1979   791.43'09   79–13908
ISBN 0–393–95049–2

1 2 3 4 5 6 7 8 9 0

For
Danny,
Adam,
Jonathan,
and
Caryn,
who at this moment
are unconcerned
with the medium
or the message.

Contents

PREFACE—*Lewis Jacobs*

PART ONE: THE SILENT FILM (1900–1930)
4. Introduction: *A New Medium, A New Art*

I. CREATIVE PIONEERS
10. *Georges Méliès: Artificially Arranged Scenes*—Lewis Jacobs
20. *Edwin S. Porter and the Editing Principle*—Lewis Jacobs
36. *D. W. Griffith: New Discoveries*—Lewis Jacobs

II. THE SUPREMACY OF TECHNIQUE
58. The Birth of a Nation: *The Technique and Its Influence*—Seymour Stern
80. *D. W. Griffith: Social Crusader*—Richard Watts, Jr.

III. TOWARD A SILENT FILM ESTHETIC
85. *The German Film*—Paul Rotha
111. *The French Avant-Garde*—George Morrison
118. The Passion of Jeanne D'Arc—Harry Alan Potamkin
122. *Eisenstein, Pudovkin and Others*—Dwight Macdonald
147. *The Composition of* Potemkin—Sergei Eisenstein

PART TWO: THE SOUND AND COLOR FILM (1930–1950)
158. Introduction: *An Expanding Art*

IV. NEW PLASTIC ELEMENTS
170. *The Sound Film*—Alberto Cavalcanti
187. *Camera and Microphone*—John Howard Lawson
198. *The Composer and the Motion Picture*—Hanns Eisler
206. *The Problem of Color*—Robert Edmond Jones
210. *The Man Who Was Colorblind*—Len Lye

V. ORIGINALITY AND STYLE
215. *Nanook*—Robert Flaherty
222. *The Films of René Clair*—Maurice Bardeche and Robert Brasillach
230. *The Method of John Ford*—Lindsay Anderson

246. *The Animated Cartoon and Walt Disney*—William Kozlenko
254. *Cartoons as Art*—Aline Saarinen
258. *Movies Without a Camera*—Harold Benson
262. *The Study of a Colossus:* Citizen Kane—Peter Cowie
275. *The Course of Italian Neorealism*—Arthur Knight

PART THREE: THE CREATIVE PRESENT (1950–)
286. Introduction: *New Realities, New Visions*

VI. PATTERNS OF INVOLVEMENT

296. *Why I Make Movies*—Ingmar Bergman
305. *The Literary Sophistication of*
      François Truffaut—Michael Klein
315. *A Movie Is a Movie Is a Movie Is a*—Andrew Sarris
321. *Movie Brutalists*—Pauline Kael
330. *Dostoevsky With a Japanese Camera*—Donald Richie
338. *Director of Enigmas: Alain Resnais*—Eugene Archer
343. *Fellini's Double City*—Eric Rhode
355. *The Event and the Image*—Michelangelo Antonioni
358. *Shape Around a Black Point*—Geoffrey Nowell-Smith
370. *Richard Lester*—Philip French
384. *Saul Bass*—Raymond Gid

VII. THE SEEDS OF CHANGE

386. *Cinema of Common Sense: A View of*
      Cinéma-Vérité—Colin Young
394. *The Auteur Theory Re-examined*—Donald E. Staples
402. *Free Cinema and the New Wave*—Jonas Mekas
422. *Film Happenings*—Jonas Mekas
425. *The Film Generation*—Stanley Kauffmann
440. *A Minor Masterpiece—Dušan Makavejev's* WR:
      Mysteries of the Organism—Lawrence Becker
443. *The Zen Artistry of Yasujiro Ozu*—Marvin Zeman
459. *Jancsó Plain*—Gideon Bachmann
470. *Politics and Poetry in* Two or Three Things I
      Know About Her *and* La Chinoise—James Roy
      MacBean
480. *The Dark Night of the Soul of Robert Bresson*—
      Colin L. Westerbeck, Jr.
494. *The Ideological Foundations of the Czech New*
      Wave—Robin Bates
506. *Luis Buñuel: An Integral Vision of Reality*—
      Randall Conrad

519. Merchant of Four Seasons: *Structures of Alienation*
     —Barbara Leaming

525. Acknowledgments

529. Index

The idea of this book is to show what has been learned about the art of the motion picture through a step-by-step study of the medium's development as a new form of creative expression.

The creative engagements of film history, like those of any art, flowed from the continuous urge to refine, deepen, and personalize experience, and to endow it with that deeper meaning which can only come from artistic excellence.

The uniqueness and distinction of directors from Méliès to Bergman is not due to the fact that they paid so much attention to artistic qualities, though they did, but to the fact that whenever they attended to them most, their films achieved a deepening of subject matter.

As a result of the formal discoveries and advances of a Griffith, an Eisenstein, a Welles, a Resnais, the very character of the film medium changed and took on greater significance. Such changes in turn brought changes in the very conception of motion pictures and the recognition of motion pictures as a new art capable of profound expression.

Lev Kuleshov, the Russian director and theoretician, was one of the first to define the art of film. In the early 1920's he told a group of young directors in the new Soviet film industry: "Every art has a basic material and a particular method of composing that material. In the art of film, the basic material is represented by separate shots, and the latter by the arrangement of the shots in a form by which the apprehension of the world is enriched or revealed."

In his own way, Kuleshov was explaining how the film maker could use his medium to discover, develop, and manipulate his experience, creating a personal form or structure which would at the same time objectify his subject, give it meaning, and, finally, value.

This approach to film art demonstrates itself in the wide spectrum of critical and analytical essays presented here.

The purpose of this book is two-fold: first, to provide insight into creative film expression, and second, to present an historical overview of the medium's artistic development. It is hoped that the multiple character of the art of the motion picture— as it was formed and reformed under the impact of technological advances, new ideas, creative film makers, and man's changing outlook on the world—will be better revealed when placed in the perspective of time. The essays, moreover, gain in meaning as they illuminate the medium's outward thrust, from its beginnings as a commercial novelty to its maturity as a new art form, with its own distinguishing characteristics, canons and standards, and an ever mounting body of creative works.

Because of the book's over-all purpose, the essays tend to vary in style, method and approach. *Part One* is largely an account of the efforts made to achieve a technique indigenous to the new medium, and a mode of composition derived from its nature and materials. The contributions of various directors and schools of film making are described, and the esthetic theories and doctrines as they grew up around the silent film are traced and evaluated.

For *Part Two* I have favored essays focusing attention on attempts to achieve a greater completeness of expression, equal to the enlarged physical and technical resources of the motion picture medium made possible by the addition of sound and color. Other articles evaluate certain film makers who creatively absorbed the broadened means of expression, and explain the distinctiveness of their artistic works.

Part Three, I hope, fulfills the task of conveying a sense of the creative present and the preoccupation with new subject matter and form. It begins with an examination of the aims of today's most distinguished directors and their predilection for various new areas of film engagement. The latest selections openly question the traditional foundations of film art, vigorously defend new explorations, and raise the standard for an esthetic more suitable to the changing ethos and spirit of the time.

Although the book's central concern is with creative expression, with originators and innovators, it does not purport to be a definitive study of all the film makers who have achieved artistic distinction or international reputation. The aim, rather, is to strike a balance between the pioneers who explored the special qualities and values intrinsic to the medium and those creative film makers who came later and, building upon this body of knowledge, developed original works of personal expression and esthetic dimension.

Lewis Jacobs

Preface to the Second Edition

The original edition of *The Emergence of Film Art* appeared in 1969. Today, a decade later, the book is still a valuable commentary on the historical development of creative film expression as evidenced by its repeated adoption as a textbook by colleges and universities.

In preparing this new edition, I have not altered the original text. The primary change has been the addition of a new body of material dealing with recent European cinema, particularly the work of those filmmakers who have assumed a first-rate importance in the 1970s. These new articles, by a variety of critics writing from different perspectives, have been incorporated into the final section, "The Seeds of Change." Their inclusion broadens and deepens the scope of the entire volume.

Lewis Jacobs

Part One

The
Silent
Film
(1900-1930)

THE BIRTH OF
A NATION
(1915)
DIRECTED BY
D. W. GRIFFITH

Introduction
A New Medium, A New Art

The major concern of the motion picture maker during the first period of movie development (1900–1930) was the search for an idiom indigenous to the new medium. From the very beginning, at the turn of the century, when movies were limited to literal reproduction, turning the cameras on vaudeville skits or scenery and seldom more than a minute or two in length, there were attempts to explore creative possibilities. At first such efforts were haphazard and improvisational, but soon accidental discoveries made about the special characteristics of the motion picture camera led to visual manipulation, which extended the boundaries of the medium and made it possible for movies to apprehend and interpret reality in new ways.

Then the revolutionary form of composition peculiar to screen art was discovered and developed. Professionally called "editing," this was a method of organization which linked a series of shots or scenes together, and by combining and arranging them in a specific order, created a specific meaning. This discovery set the movies upon a course fundamental to its own nature and pointed the way by which its latent powers could be released to affect the minds as well as the emotions of a mass audience. Technological improvements led to the deepening and extension of camera and editing technique, so that by 1910 movie making had advanced from a scientific curiosity to a creative enterprise, involving planning, selecting and organizing subject matter and technique into compositions with esthetic interest.

The next years saw a constant striving on the part of film makers to treat more and more significant subject matter with more and more individuality. The most inventive among them, David Wark Griffith, created almost single-handed a large variety of camera devices, a rich body of technique and new elements of composition that enabled motion picture expression to achieve greater unity, clarity, and effectiveness. The climax of his efforts were two masterworks, *The Birth of a Nation* (1915) and *Intolerance* (1916). Both pictures were

4

distinguished by a bold and imaginative grasp of camera usage for psychological, dramatic, and poetic effects, and by structural innovations in editing that generated powerful forces in their impact upon audiences. High points in the progress of motion picture creativity, these pictures propelled the medium into an artistic peak that earned for the screen the status of an art, and became the sources of inspiration and study for many of the great films that were to follow.

New refinements in technique and form came after World War I, largely in pictures made in Germany, Sweden and France. Between 1920 and 1925 a number of European pictures were produced that exhibited extraordinary virtuosity, high imagination and psychological depth. Setting off in individual directions, these films reflected strong, artistically ambitious personalities for whom creative film expression was of paramount importance. For the first time, artists and intellectuals, who had been indifferent to the screen before, became attracted to what they praised as an entirely new art form with great potentialities and a brilliant future.

In the late Twenties the European innovations were eclipsed by a powerful wave of Soviet productions that aroused even more excitement and controversy. The revolutionary zeal expressed in the subject matter of these films, their deeper purpose and stress on reality, combined with a profound grasp of cinematic form, set new standards for film creativity and disclosed realms of artistry until then unsuspected in the movie medium. The Russian movie makers approached film with the analytical attention of revolutionary artists, scholars and scientists—studying, theorizing and experimenting to discover the unique values and basis of their medium—rather than as businessmen. They consolidated the results of their research and experimentation in a body of formal principles and artistic doctrines which, underlying their own productions, placed them in the vanguard of film art. The summary of their credo was the concept of *montage*—a method of shooting and relating shots "to scientifically force the spectator to think in a certain direction and to create a given impression on an audience."

Montage made clear that the art of movie making need no longer lack a methodology or flounder for an idiom. The film's singular method of expression became clarified, and distinct

5

from that of all other media. Thirty years of artistic progress had evolved a body of creative pictures from which could be derived an intrinsic tradition with its own canons and standards that elucidated the medium's own esthetic roots.—*L.J.*

1. TRIP TO THE MOON
   (1902)
   DIRECTED BY
   GEORGE MELIES

2. DREAM OF A
   RAREBIT FIEND
   (1906)
   DIRECTED BY
   EDWIN S. PORTER

3. UN CHIEN ANDALOU
   (1928)
   DIRECTED BY
   LUIS BUNUEL
   L'AGE D'OR
   (1930)
   DIRECTED BY
   LUIS BUNUEL

4. METROPOLIS
   (1926)
   DIRECTED BY
   FRITZ LANG

5. THE CABINET OF
   DR. CALIGARI
   (1919)
   DIRECTED BY
   ROBERT WIENE

6. BALLET MECHANIQUE
   (1923)
   DIRECTED BY
   FERDINAND LEGER

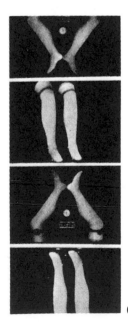

6.

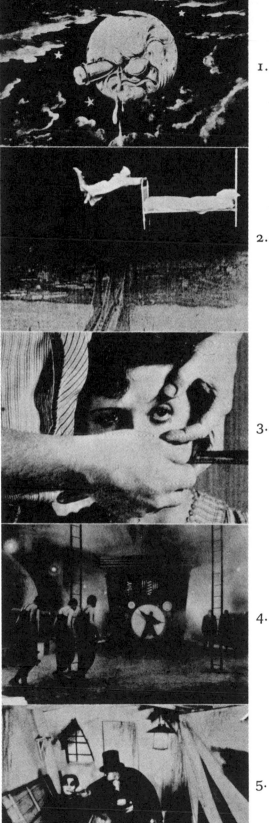

1.

2.

3.

4.

5.

7.

8.

9.

10.

11.

THE MAY IRWIN- 7.
JOHN C. RICE
KISS,
A POPULAR AMERICAN
FILM OF 1896

D. W. GRIFFITH 8.
DIRECTING
DONALD CRISP,
OWEN MOORE,
LILLIAN GISH AND
ROBERT HARRON
IN A REHEARSAL (1914)

THE BIRTH OF A NATION 9.
(1915)
DIRECTED BY
D. W. GRIFFITH

THE SECRETS OF 10.
THE SOUL
(1926)
DIRECTED BY
G. W. PABST

THE LAST LAUGH 11.
(1925)
DIRECTED BY
F. R. MURNAU

THE GREAT TRAIN 12.
ROBBERY
(1903)
DIRECTED BY
EDWIN S. PORTER

12.

13.

13. POTEMKIN
(1926)
DIRECTED BY
SERGEI EISENSTEIN

14. MAN WITH THE CAMERA
(1928-29)
DIRECTED BY
DZIGA VERTOV

15. 10 DAYS THAT SHOOK
THE WORLD
(1927)
DIRECTED BY
SERGEI EISENSTEIN

16. THE END OF
ST. PETERSBURG
(1927)
DIRECTED BY
V. PUDOVKIN

17. SOIL
(1930)
DIRECTED BY
ALEXANDER DOVZHENKO

18. THE PASSION OF
JOAN OF ARC
(1928)
DIRECTED BY
CARL DREYER

14.

15.

16.

17.

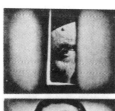

18.

Georges Méliès: 'Artificially Arranged Scenes'
by Lewis Jacobs

This chapter appeared originally in "The Rise of the American Film," first published in 1939.

It is with a Frenchman that the film as an art begins. The first to exploit the medium as a means of personal expression, Georges Méliès started movies on a new course, broadened their scope, and focused attention upon their creative potentialities. Imported into America when American movies, derisively nicknamed "chasers," were simply pictures of events, his innovations were revolutionary. Georges Méliès, imaginative, resourceful, skillful, was the movies' first great craftsman and the father of its theatrical traditions.

Méliès discovered magic in the motion picture camera. He turned its lens away from reality—from mere reporting—to fantasy and genuine creation. He also brought to movie making, with his system of "artificially arranged scenes," a conception of organization which was to change the haphazard, improvisational methods of the Americans and fertilize their technique. He enriched movies by introducing many theatrical elements: costuming, settings, professional actors. To these formal elements he added a new source of subject matter, literature, which widened the range of film subjects.

In 1896 Georges Méliès, thirty-four years old, was a jack-of-all-trades—caricaturist for an anti-Boulangist paper, theatrical producer, actor, scenic painter at the Théâtre Houdin, and professional magician. This was the year in which he turned to moving pictures. From then until the outbreak of the World War he devoted himself to his adopted art. "Film making," he wrote, "offers such a variety of pursuits, demands such a quantity of work of all kinds, and claims so sustained an attention, that I did not hesitate to proclaim it the most attractive and fascinating of all the arts."

At first Méliès roamed the streets with his camera, shooting people, trains, soldiers—anything that moved—for the mere pleasure of it. One day while he was photographing a Paris street scene his camera jammed; the film had caught inside the aperture gate. Méliès cleared the gate, readjusted the film, and resumed shooting. When the film was projected later, he was surprised to see on the screen a bus suddenly turn into a hearse. The bus he had been photographing when the camera jammed had gone its way while he was readjusting the camera, and in its place a hearse had appeared. When Méliès had started shooting again, the camera had taken a picture of the hearse on the same bit of film and in the same place where the bus had been photographed.

Being a professional magician, Méliès was greatly excited by the coincidence. He at once visualized the superior "supernatural" capacities of the moving picture as compared to the ordinary magician. Investigating camera possibilities further, he discovered many more devices for trick effects—effects that were to astound the movie world for many years.

He now went into movie making in earnest. By 1900 he had made over two hundred "magical, mystical and trick films," each a minute or two long. Imported into the United States, these unique and amazing movies were immediately singled out by the public and became the most popular of all screen entertainments. So popular were they, and so unmatchable, that American manufacturers made copies or "dupes" and sold them under new names as their own.

Méliès' aim in these films was to mystify and startle. His prowess as a magician found curious expression in his earliest efforts: *The Vanishing Lady, The Haunted Castle, The Laboratory of Mephistopheles, A Hypnotist at Work, Cagliostro's Mirror, The Bewitched Inn, Conjurer Making 10 Hats in 60 Seconds.* These films showed people disappearing magically, cut in half, flying through the air; apparitions taking horrible shapes; animals turning into human beings, and human beings into animals. Typical of his method was his 185th film, *The Devil in a Convent,* a religious fantasy

to illustrate the Triumph of Christianity over Satan . . . While it is quite fantastical and religious, there is not the least action in the film which would be obnoxious or shock the most sensitive audience.

The movie opened by showing the Devil, followed by an imp, jumping from the font of holy water in the interior of a convent.

Both are transformed into a priest and choir boy. They then summon the nuns to service and while preaching change themselves back to their natural shapes, frightening the nuns out of their wits. The Devil then transforms the church to resemble Hell and the nuns flee for their lives. Many imps appear and dance wildly round the Devil, but are finally driven off by the ghosts of departed nuns, leaving only the Devil. Suddenly an apparition of St. George appears and in a struggle with His Satanic Majesty overcomes him, driving him off to Hell and ending the film with a cloud-burst of smoke.

Picture-card sermon though it was meant to be, the film displayed Méliès' ingenious and individual flair for the unreal and his unusual perception of the camera's capabilities. Like all other films of that day, its entire action was confined within a single scene, as if it were a stage presentation. Unlike others, however, it was distinguished by the camera tricks that only Méliès had mastered: double exposures, masks, stop-motions, reverse shootings, fast and slow motion, animation, fades, dissolves. Such effects, which made American producers sigh with envy, were not to become generally understood until years later.

His skill developing, Méliès undertook ever more elaborate and more ambitious enterprises. From single scenes he turned to stories, written by himself or adapted from literature, and including multiple scenes. Such undertakings required preliminary organization of the subject matter: scenes had to be planned and staged in advance so as to tell a story logically. Méliès himself called the method he devised "artificially arranged scenes." A novel and advanced approach to movies, it was to work profound changes in the methods of American film makers, who had as yet neglected prearrangement of the scenes and, in fact, boasted that none of their subjects was "faked."

Méliès' first outstanding and successful realization of his new method, *Cinderella*, appeared at the close of 1900. This picture was an unprecedented accomplishment, a remarkable advance beyond the formlessness of other current films. Highlights of the fairy tale, in a series of twenty "motion tableaux," as Méliès labeled the scenes, had been selected, staged, and photographed progressively. Following is Méliès' original plan:

1. Cinderella in the Kitchen
2. The Fairy
3. The Transformation of the Rat
4. The Pumpkin Changes to a Carriage
5. The Ball at the King's Palace

6. The Hour of Midnight
7. The Bedroom of Cinderella
8. The Dance of the Clocks
9. The Prince and the Slipper
10. The Godmother of Cinderella
11. The Prince and Cinderella
12. The Arrival at the Church
13. The Wedding
14. Cinderella's Sisters
15. The King
16. The Nuptial Cortege
17. The Bride's Ballet
18. The Celestial Spheres
19. The Transformation
20. The Triumph of Cinderella

This effort of Méliès illustrated rather than re-created the fairy tale. Yet, primitive though it was, the order of the scenes did form a coherent, logical, and progressive continuity. A new way of making moving pictures had been invented. Scenes could now be staged and selected specially for the camera, and the movie maker could control both the material and its arrangement. Movie making, heretofore an unselective process, became with "artificially arranged scenes" a creative enterprise, involving planning, selection, direction, and control of material and instruments, and the fusing of all to produce a single effect. Possible material which had heretofore been ignored was now recognized as being within the movies' range.

Cinderella introduced, moreover, devices of the stage. Elaborate settings, special costumes, carefully composed tableaux, professional acting, and many "dissolving scenic effects, ballets, and marches" gave the film a theatrical grandeur that distinguished it above all its competitors.

In America *Cinderella* was received enthusiastically. The public, rejoicing in the familiar rags-to-riches fable, was enthralled by its elegant backgrounds, spectacular staging, and magical camera effects. Vaudeville managers ran the movie again and again on their programs. Even better-grade theatres which had stopped showing "living pictures" exhibited *Cinderella* with pride. American manufacturers hastened to "dupe" the film and sell it as their own. The unusual success of the picture, in fact, not only spurred American movie makers to improve their own product, but, at a time when movies needed encouragement, to improve their reputation.

Success made Méliès more ambitious. He busied himself with a variety of stories with more elaborate "artificially arranged scenes," more imaginative conceptions of theatrical values. *Joan of Arc* was in twelve scenes, with "500 persons enacting the tableaux, all superbly costumed." *The Christmas Dream* had twenty scenes, "dissolving effects, tricks, spectacular tableaux, snow scenes, ballets, night effects and marches." *Off to Bloomingdale Asylum* was a fantastic tale that might have come out of a surrealist's anthology:

An omnibus drawn by an extraordinary mechanical horse is driven by four Negroes. The horse kicks and upsets the Negroes, who falling are changed into white clowns. They begin slapping each other's faces and by the blows become black again. Kicking each other, they become white once more. Suddenly they are all merged into one gigantic Negro, and when he refuses to pay his carfare, the conductor sets fire to the omnibus, and the Negro bursts into a thousand pieces.

The Seven Deadly Sins, Bluebeard, Red Riding Hood, The Maiden's Paradise, were other pictures with picturesque content, imaginative camera treatment, and theatrical effects.

Unique and effective though these films were, Melies in 1902 produced another that surpassed any of his previous achievements. This movie, called *A Trip to the Moon*, established him conclusively as the dominant creative force in motion pictures. His 400th film, it was 825 feet long, twice the length of *Cinderella* and at least three times the length of the average movie of the day. It was advertised in his "Star" Catalogue of 1902–1903 as "Ten extraordinary and fantastical cinematographic series in thirty scenes." Certainly it was an eloquent display of his fertile imagination and the graphic possibilities of the motion picture camera for fantasy and satire.

Based on *From the Earth to the Moon and Around the Moon*, the Jules Verne story, *A Trip to the Moon* charmingly lampooned the scientific and mechanical interests of the new century. Méliès' experience as a caricaturist enabled him to depict wittily the lunar dream world of the professors and the fantastic hopes of some of the scientific societies. The astronomers who take the journey to the moon are foppish; their preparations are ridiculous. The start from their textbook world with solemn ceremonies, their entry into the moon—right into its eye—and their meeting with the Selenites were nonsense of a high order. Their inglorious return to earth and their reception as heroes—they are crowned and decorated—ends the extravaganza, dispelling the dream atmosphere that has been carefully created.

The scenario for *A Trip to the Moon*, written by Méliès himself, indicates his order of "artificially arranged scenes," but the bald listing hardly suggests his imaginative intent, the film's rich visual effects, the ingenuity of the camera devices, or the quality of the film's unique style. The scenario follows:

1. The scientific congress at the Astronomic Club.
2. Planning the trip. Appointing the explorers and servants. Farewell.
3. The workshops. Constructing the projectile.
4. The foundries. The chimney-stacks. The casting of the monster gun.
5. The astronomers enter the shell.
6. Loading the gun.
7. The monster gun. March past the gunners. Fire!!! Saluting the flag.
8. The flight through space. Approaching the moon.
9. Landed right in the eye!!!
10. Flight of the shell into the moon. Appearance of the earth from the moon.
11. The plain of craters. Volcanic eruption.
12. The dream (the Solies, the Great Bear, Phoebus, the Twin Sisters, Saturna).
13. The snowstorm.
14. 40 degrees below zero. Descending a lunar crater.
15. Into the interior of the moon. The giant mushroom grotto.
16. Encounter with the Selenites. Homeric flight.
17. Prisoners!!!
18. The kingdom of the moon. The Selenite army.
19. The flight.
20. Wild pursuit.
21. The astronomers find the shell again. Departure from the moon.
22. Vertical drop into space.
23. Splashing into the open sea.
24. At the bottom of the ocean.
25. The rescue. Return to port.
26. The great fête. Triumphal march past.
27. Crowning and decorating the heroes of the trip.
28. Procession of Marines and the Fire Brigade.
29. Inauguration of the commemorative statue by the manager and the council.
30. Public rejoicings.

In every respect *A Trip to the Moon* towered above the standard production of the day. American pictures, despite two years of competition with Méliès' films, were still absurdly poor. Porter's efforts for the Edison Company were still confined to reproductions of vaudeville skits and scenes of local interest. Blackton of Vitagraph, when not turning out comic-strip novelties, was continuing to make his fake news events; Bitzer and McCutcheon of Biograph were shooting similar subjects. In comparison with such "camera copying," Méliès' films were monumental, quite unmatched for style, ingenuity, and imagination.

Some idea of the intricate creative labor that went into *A Trip to the Moon* can be gathered from a letter Méliès wrote in 1930 to Jean LeRoy, who asked for details:

> I made myself the model sculptured terra cotta and the plaster moldings. . . . The entire cost was about 10,000 francs, a sum relatively high for the time, caused especially by the mechanical sceneries and principally by the cost of the cardboard and canvas costumes made for the Sélénites . . . all those articles being made especially and consequently expensive. . . .
>
> There were not yet stars amongst the artists; their names were never known or written in bills or advertisements. The people employed . . . were entirely acrobats, girls and singers coming from the music halls, the theatrical actors having not yet accepted to play in cinema films, as they considered the motion pictures much below the theatre. They came only later, when they knew that music hall people gained more money in performing films than themselves in playing in theatres. . . . Two years after, my office was, every night, full of theatrical people asking to be engaged. I remember that . . . the Moon (the Woman in the Crescent) was Bleuette Bernon, music hall singer, the Stars were ballet girls, from Théâtre Du Châtelet —and the men (principal ones) Victor André of the Cluny Théâtre, Delpierre, Farjaux-Kelm-Brunnet, music hall singers, and myself. The Sélénites were acrobats from Folies Bergère.

Not only had Méliès rewritten Jules Verne's story, designed and painted the sets, acted the principal character, directed and organized the film, but he had personally taken care of the business problems. He had hired the cast, designed the costumes, overseen the developing and printing of the film, and financed and sold the production. A prolific and original worker, Melies was also a precise and forward-looking one.

American manufacturers, pouncing on *A Trip to the Moon*, "duped" it over and over again. Méliès tried to halt such infringements by publishing in his 1903 catalogue to the trade the following warning:

Georges Méliès, a proprietor and manager of the Théâtre Robert Houdin, Paris, is the originator of the class of cinematographic films which are made from artificially arranged scenes, the creation of which has given new life to the trade at a time when it was dying out. He conceived the idea of portraying magical and mystical views, and his creations have been imitated without success ever since.

A great number of French, English and American manufacturers of film who are searching for novelties, but lack the ingenuity to produce them, have found it easier and more economical to advertise their poor copies, that is, duplicate prints of Méliès' original film, as their own original conceptions. This accounts for the simultaneous appearance in several issues of a well-known New York paper of advertisements of the celebrated *A Trip to the Moon* by four or five different concerns, each pretending to be its creator. All these pretensions are false. . . .

This modest enough document sheds light on Méliès' awareness of his importance in the motion picture world and spotlights the brazen practices of his competitors.

For the next two years Méliès continued to startle moviegoers with similar "fantastical fantasies." *Gulliver's Travels, Beelzebub's Daughters, The Inn Where No Man Rests, Fairyland or The Kingdom of the Fairies*—the first movie to have a musical score at its opening—and the amazing *Damnation of Faust*, inspired by Berlioz's celebrated song poem, were among the most imaginative and resourceful of the hundreds of distinguished films Méliès produced. Still emphasizing artificially arranged scenes as his unique style, these pictures intensified the envy among American movie makers and stirred them to scrutinize their own pictures more closely.

In 1904 Méliès' most ambitious and costliest ($7,500) undertaking, *The Impossible Voyage*, appeared. This film, like his *A Trip to the Moon*, was a satire on scientific societies, but it was far more self-conscious. In forty "motion tableaux" and 1,233 feet of film—Méliès' longest to date—its incredible story told of "The Institute of Incoherent Geography and how they discussed the proposed voyage of a new machine which must surpass in conception and invention all previous expeditions of the learned world." Its farcical intent is apparent not only in the names Méliès gave his savants but in their ludicrous adventures. "Under the Presidency of Professor Polehunter, assisted by Secretary Rattlebrains, and Vice-President Humbug, the Institutes plan a trip of the world."

The conception is in the best Disney fashion, with the scientists poring madly over maps, studying fantastic charts, and examining machines in "Engineer Crazyloff's machine shop." With a great flourish, the learned group finally takes off, "employing all the known devices of locomotion—automobiles, dirigibles, balloons, submarines, boats, rockets, etc." And now their adventures begin. "At three hundred miles an hour," they visit the rising sun and the aurora borealis, pass through a solar eruption, get frozen in a heavenly embankment, are thawed out by an explosion, and eventually land on earth again to receive decorations for their brilliant voyage.

This film expressed all of Méliès' talents. In it his feeling for caricature, painting, theatrical invention, and camera science became triumphant. The complexity of his tricks, his resourcefulness with mechanical contrivances, the imaginativeness of the settings, and the sumptuous tableaux made the film a masterpiece for its day.

Though superior to his former efforts, *The Impossible Voyage* was overshadowed by the debut of a far more revolutionary film, Edwin S. Porter's *The Great Train Robbery*, which had come to the screen some months earlier but was still commanding the attention of the public. This American film, itself inspired by Méliès' contributions, was more vigorous in both style and content than any of the Frenchman's pictures, and its subject matter was more intrinsically interesting to Americans. Méliès' position as the leader in motion pictures was now taken by Porter. The Frenchman's films, until now enormously popular, began to fall behind the more dramatic productions of the American.

Méliès continued to make pictures until the outbreak of the World War. But each year after 1904 saw his reputation failing before new techniques, new men, new ideas. He was gradually all but forgotten. Struggling to meet a growing American competition, he turned away from his own unique style and subject matter to imitate, futilely, those of the Americans. *Humanity Through the Ages*, made in 1907 at the time of the Hague Peace Conference, and *The Conquest of the Pole*, made in 1912, were among his last distinguished efforts to regain some of his former prestige.

Méliès was defeated not only by innovations in movies themselves but by innovations in their distribution. The rental method of distribution was proving its efficiency. Méliès, who still sold his films outright to exhibitors, found it difficult to recoup even his costs. An added burden fell upon him when his branch in America was robbed of three hundred negatives.

Everywhere competition forced Méliès to the wall. Disdaining American business methods, he failed to keep up with them. By 1914, retiring more and more from the main scene of competition, he had become just a novelty- and travel-picture producer. When war broke out later, his place of business in France was commandeered by the government. He was now in a desperate plight. Too poor to rent a new office or to move his stock of negatives, he was forced to sell his films to a junk dealer and quit the business.

For fourteen years thereafter no one heard of Méliès. Then in 1928 he was recognized in the streets of Paris selling newspapers. Friends bought him a tobacco-and-candy kiosk. In 1933, when he was too old to run his small stand any longer, the Chambre Syndicale Française du Cinématographe, which he had founded in 1897 and of which he had been president for ten years, sent him to a home for destitute actors. He died January 22, 1938, at the age of 77. The expenses of his funeral were defrayed by French and English film workers.

The significance of Méliès in the life of the motion picture industry can hardly be exaggerated. His discovery of the camera's unique resources and his "artificially arranged scenes" freed the movie art from the slavery of dull imitation. He was the dean of motion picture directors, the pioneer in film organization, the first movie artist. He brought new subject matter and many theatrical devices to films, endowing everything he touched with individuality and flavor. Never low or cheap in appeal, his films never exploited the off-color gag or the vulgarities of the "embarrassing situation," favorite resorts of his competitors. He was the first artisan in the industry to merit serious attention; his efforts earned for the motion picture respect and admiration, and were to exert for years an elevating influence on American productions. It was through this ingenious Frenchman's achievements that American movies in 1903 could begin to take on the qualities of an art.

Edwin S. Porter and the Editing Principle
by Lewis Jacobs

This chapter appeared originally in "The Rise of the American Film," first published in 1939.

If Georges Méliès was the first to "push the cinema toward the theatrical way," as he claimed, then Edwin S. Porter was the first to push the cinema toward the cinematic way. Generally acknowledged today as the father of the story film, he made more than fictional contributions to movie tradition. It was Porter who discovered that the art of motion pictures depends on the continuity of shots, not on the shots alone. Not content with Méliès' artificially arranged scenes, Porter distinguished the movies from other theatrical forms and gave them the invention of editing. Almost all motion picture developments since Porter's discovery spring from the principle of editing, which is the basis of motion picture artistry.

Significant for his genius for structural technique, Porter is equally noteworthy for his eye for content. Unlike Méliès, who made fantasies, Porter turned to the real world for subject matter. He dramatized what he saw, reflected and commented on contemporary American life, illuminated many of the issues and interests of his time. His efforts to make real occurrences dramatic by means of editing widened the scope of movies, educated its technique, and through the introduction of the story film made the industry boom.

In 1896 Porter, a mechanic with an enthusiasm for machinery, had come to the Edison Company as a general handy man, wondering whether or not he should have gone instead into the newfangled business of making horseless cars. Even after he had become a cameraman for Edison, he still seriously considered quitting the movies, for like most others he felt that popular interest in "living motion photography" would soon subside. He remained with Edison simply because he needed a job.

Porter's career in motion pictures lasted seventeen years. It was within four years that he transformed motion picture art. During the years 1902 to 1906, he discovered the principle of editing (*The Life of an American Fireman*) and developed its methods to include direct story construction (*The Great Train Robbery*), contrast construction (*The Ex-Convict*), and parallel construction (*The Kleptomaniac*). In these years also he reached out daringly for new social subject matter (*White Caps, The Miller's Daughter*), explored more carefully the use of camera devices (*Dream of a Rarebit Fiend*), and enlarged the scale of production (*Uncle Tom's Cabin*).

Superseding Méliès with these innovations, Porter became the dominant figure in the industry. Film makers imitated him zealously until 1908, when D. W. Griffith, bringing still greater talent to filmdom, became the most admired of movie celebrities.

By 1902 Porter had a long list of films to his credit. But neither he nor other American producers had yet learned to tell a story. They were still busy with elementary, one-shot news events (*President McKinley's Inauguration, McKinley's Funeral Cortege, The Columbia and Shamrock Yacht Races, The Jeffries-Ruhblin Sparring Contest, The Galveston Cyclone*), with humorous bits (*Grandma and Grandpa* series, *Happy Hooligan* series, *Old Maid* series), with vaudeville skits (cooch dancers, magicians, acrobats), scenic views (*A Trip Through the Columbian Exposition*), and local topics (parades, fire departments in action, shoppers in the streets). None of these productions stood out from the general; literal and unimaginative, they are significant today mainly as social documents. Porter himself made such pictures for six years without showing any notable signs of originality.

It was his contact with Méliès' fairy-tale films that struck the spark in Porter. He would probably have continued his prosaic, unenthusiastic career had he not been startled by the Frenchman's unusual pictures. In the laboratory Porter had the opportunity to handle and examine the "magical films" of this French director at first hand. Impressed by their length and arrangement, he scrutinized them closely, noting that they contained more than one scene or camera shot and that the scenes were strung together progressively to illustrate a story. Porter hit upon the idea that he also might make stories by cutting and joining, in a certain order, scenes that he had already shot.

Excitedly he determined to try, and his employers, seeing a chance to increase the sale of their product, encouraged him.

Porter rummaged through the stock of Edison's old films, searching for suitable scenes around which to build a story. He found quantities of pictures of fire-department activities. Since fire departments had such a strong popular appeal, with their color and action, Porter chose them as his subjects. But he still needed some central idea or incident by which to organize the scenes of the fire department in action.

Now Méliès' pictures were all "magical," "mystical," "fantastic," often seasoned with humor and whimsey. The realism of fire engines and firemen had nothing to do with fantasy and humor. Porter therefore concocted a scheme that was as startling as it was different: a mother and child were to be caught in a burning building and rescued at the last moment by the fire department.

Tame though such a plot sounds to us today, it was then revolutionary. No film of a dramatic nature had yet been made in this country. Movies to date had been mere reports of events. The incident as shown on the screen lasted no longer than in real life. Porter was now about to attempt a drama of more than one scene, covering a longer period of time in real life than on the screen. The scheme not only involved a new application of the movies but necessitated a new kind of form.

Porter's next step was to stage such additional scenes as his plot demanded. Having completed them, he set about assembling all the shots into a dramatic arrangement. First there was exposition: a fire chief dreams of an imperiled woman and child. Then came an incident: the fire alarm is rung. Action was next: firemen, hearing the call, rush off to the fire. Suspense was created: will the firemen get there in time? A crisis was depicted: the burning building. The climax is reached: the helpless fire victims are about to expire. And, finally, there is resolution: the rescue. Joining the scenes together in this order, Porter created the dramatic continuity which he called *The Life of an American Fireman.*

This first American dramatic film was unique, depending for meaning upon its combination of shots into scenes. The scenes had two functions: to communicate the action and, more important, to relate it to the next action so that a meaning was given to the whole. The scene thus became a unit dependent upon all the other units; to be fully understood, it was inseparable from them. This process of cutting film, recombining and rearranging its units, is now known as editing, and is what makes a film expressive.

The scenario for *The Life of an American Fireman*, published in the Edison Catalogue of 1903, after the film was completed, reveals the dramatic arrangement of its scenes and the new-born technique of editing. The advance over Méliès' artificially arranged scenes is evident. Méliès merely listed scenes and roughly described their content, but Porter specified for the first time not only a full description of the dramatic action, but details of location, camera position, and transition. Porter's script, which follows, is the primitive of the continuity form used to this day in Hollywood:

THE LIFE OF AN AMERICAN FIREMAN

Scene 1: THE FIREMAN'S VISION OF AN IMPERILED WOMAN AND CHILD

The fire chief is seated at his office desk. He has just finished reading his evening paper and has fallen asleep. The rays of an incandescent light rest upon his features with a subdued light, yet leaving his figure strongly silhouetted against the walls of his office. The fire chief is dreaming, and the vision of his dream appears in a circular portrait on the wall. It is a mother putting her baby to bed, and the impression is that he dreams of his own wife and child. He suddenly awakens and paces the floor in a nervous state of mind, doubtless thinking of the various people who may be in danger from fire at the moment.

Here we dissolve the picture to the second scene.

Scene 2: CLOSE VIEW OF A NEW YORK FIRE-ALARM BOX

Shows lettering and every detail in the door and apparatus for turning in an alarm. A figure then steps in front of the box, hastily opens the door and pulls the hook, thus sending the electric current which alarms hundreds of firemen and brings to the scene of the fire the wonderful apparatus of a great city's Fire Department.

Again dissolving the picture, we show the third scene.

Scene 3: SLEEPING QUARTERS

A row of beds, each containing a fireman peacefully sleeping, is shown. Instantly upon the ringing of the alarm the firemen leap from their beds and, putting on their clothes in the record time of five seconds, a grand rush is made for a large circular opening in the floor through the center of which runs a brass pole. The first fireman to reach the pole seizes it, and, like a flash, disappears through the opening. He is instantly followed by the remainder of the force. This in itself makes a most stirring scene. *We again dissolve the scene to the interior of the apparatus house.*

Scene 4: INTERIOR OF ENGINE HOUSE

Shows horses dashing from their stalls and being hitched to the apparatus. This is perhaps the most thrilling and in all the most wonderful of the seven scenes of the series, it being absolutely the first moving pictures ever made of a genuine interior hitch. As the men come down the pole and land upon the floor in lightning-like rapidity, six doors in the rear of the engine house, each heading a horse-stall, burst open simultaneously and a huge fire horse, with head erect and eager for the dash to the scene of the conflagration, rushes from each opening. Going immediately to their respective harness, they are hitched in the almost unbelievable time of five seconds and are ready for their dash to the fire. The men hastily scamper upon the trucks and hose carts and one by one the fire machines leave the house, drawn by eager, prancing horses.

Here we again dissolve to the fifth scene.

Scene 5: APPARATUS LEAVING ENGINE HOUSE

We show a fine exterior view of the engine house, the great door swinging open and the apparatus coming out. This is the most imposing scene. The great horses leap to their work, the men adjust their fire hats and coats, and smoke begins pouring from the engines as they pass our camera.

Here we dissolve and show the sixth scene.

Scene 6: OFF TO THE FIRE

In this scene we present the best fire run ever shown. Almost the entire fire department of the large city of Newark, New Jersey, was placed at our disposal, and we show countless pieces of apparatus, engines, hook-and-ladders, hose towers, hose carriages, etc., rushing down a broad street at top speed, the horses straining every nerve and evidently eager to make a record run. Great clouds of smoke pour from the stacks of the engines, thus giving an impression of genuineness to the entire series.

Dissolving again we show the seventh scene.

Scene 7: ARRIVAL AT THE FIRE

In this wonderful scene we show the entire fire department as described above, arriving at the scene of action. An actual burning building is in the center foreground. On the right background the fire department is seen coming at great speed. Upon the arrival of the different apparatus, the engines are ordered to their places, hose is quickly run out from the carriages, ladders are adjusted to the windows, and streams of water are poured into the burning structure. At this crucial moment comes the great climax of the series. We dissolve to the interior of the building and show a bed chamber with a woman and child enveloped in flame and suffocating smoke. The woman rushes back and forth in the room endeavoring to escape, and in her desperation throws open the window and appeals to the crowd below. She is finally overcome by the smoke and falls upon the bed. At this moment the door is smashed in by an ax in the hands of a powerful fire hero. Rushing into the room, he tears the burning draperies from the window and smashes out the entire window frame, ordering his comrades to run up a ladder. Immediately the ladder appears, he seizes the prostrate form of the woman and throws it over his shoulders as if it were an infant and quickly descends to the ground. We now dissolve to the exterior of the burning building. The frantic mother having returned to consciousness, and clad only in her night clothes, is kneeling on the ground imploring the fireman to return for her child. Volunteers are called for and the same fireman who rescued the mother quickly steps out and offers to return for the babe. He is given permission to once more enter the doomed building and without hesitation rushes up the ladder, enters the window and after a breathless wait, in which it appears he must have been overcome with smoke, he appears with the child in his arms and returns safely to the ground. The child, being released and upon seeing its mother, rushes to her and is clasped in her arms, thus making a most realistic and touching ending of the series.

Two scenes are of particular significance because they reveal a feeling and a striving for an extension of structure to be achieved later. In Scene 2 a close-up is used for the first time, dramatically and logically, to advance the story. It preceded by at least five years Griffith's use of the close-up and the establishment of the close-up as an integral part of movie technique. The last scene also is noteworthy, for it actually comprises three different shots: (1) the arrival at the fire, (2) the imperiled woman and child, (3) the descent down the ladder. This is one of the earliest signs of a realization that a scene need not be taken in one shot but can be built by a number of shots. It was not until ten years later, however, that the shot as a single element in a scene of many elements was to be fully understood and used by film makers.

Porter himself, having had no background or experience in art, was aware of few of the implications of what he had attempted. Unacquainted with either literature or the theatre, he would have been shocked to learn that he had combined elements of both to create another art.

The Life of an American Fireman aroused excitement wherever it was shown. Audiences, as if viewing a real crisis, could not remain passive. They identified themselves with the fireman and the rescue on the screen. The fire engines simply *had* to get to the fire in time! The mother and child *must* not perish! Such intense personal reactions to a movie were unprecedented.

The immediate influence of *The Life of an American Fireman* upon other film makers was, nevertheless, negligible. Since nickelodeons did not yet exist at the time the film was released, its success was limited and its importance was overlooked by the trade. But Porter suspected that he had hit upon something novel, and he wanted his next film to develop his dramatic idea even further. He reasoned that if he could build a good story out of edited stock scenes, he could make a much better one if he planned it beforehand and photographed scenes specifically for it.

Porter's hunch was to make history. When a friend suggested making a picture similar to a popular road show of the day, "The Great Train Robbery," Porter was impressed by the timeliness of the subject: train robberies were being reported in the newspapers almost daily. The robust and provocative title, moreover, stirred his imagination. He saw at once what an admirable chance the theme presented for dramatic effects: a daring train holdup, a brave and desperate pursuit, and a thrilling last-minute capture.

But his next film was not to be *The Great Train Robbery*. Edison assigned Porter to numerous other films, among which was an adaptation of the play "Uncle Tom's Cabin." This film turned out to be the largest and most expensive picture yet made in America, running the extraordinary length of 1,100 feet and including fourteen scenes and a prologue. His heart being set on *The Great Train Robbery*, however, Porter did *Uncle Tom's Cabin* perfunctorily, without any of the originality displayed in *The Life of an American Fireman*.

Uncle Tom's Cabin followed the Méliès pattern, with scenes arranged in logical order and photographed one after the other just as they are played on a stage. The advertisement made a virtue of the method: "The story has been carefully studied and every scene posed in accordance with the famous author's version." What the advertisement went on to call "a departure from the methods of dissolving one scene into another by inserting announcements with brief descriptions" was in reality a return to the lecture-slide method.

Finally in the fall of 1903 Porter made *The Great Train Robbery*, the primitive classic for which he is venerated today. This film has been called the first story film made in America; it was, more accurately, the most successful and influential of early story films. Nickelodeons, which were to spring up a year and a half later, opened with *The Great Train Robbery* as their initial attraction. For years *The Great Train Robbery* was the nickelodeon's most widely exhibited picture, and it is said to have insured the permanence of the movies. It became the bible for all film makers until Griffith's films further developed Porter's editing principle. The efforts of all movie makers to imitate its form and content stimulated the industry as nothing—not even Méliès' films—had ever done before.

In the script of *The Great Train Robbery* one sees improvements over the cruder editing that distinguished *The Life of an American Fireman*. There is a scene-by-scene construction of a dramatic narrative in straightforward style. Longer by 250 feet than the earlier film, *The Great Train Robbery* had more room for supplementary scenes, for more shots. It is therefore not so brusque and jerky as Porter's earlier work. Each scene is more skillfully conceived in relation to its neighbor; the narrative is closer-knit and flows more smoothly. Above all, the story is executed from the sum of its edited parts. This unifying conception characterizes every shot except the last, Scene 14, a close-up of the outlaw leader taking aim and firing point-blank at the audience. Tacked on to the film for no other purpose than to startle the movie-goer, this scene was recommended to exhibitors as an opening or closing stunt for the performance. The other scenes as a group show excellent editing, and established that operation as the basis for future motion picture development.

The scenario is taken from the Edison Catalogue of 1904:

THE GREAT TRAIN ROBBERY

Scene 1: *Interior of railroad telegraph office.* Two masked robbers enter and compel the operator to get the "signal block" to stop the approaching train, and make him write a fictitious order to the engineer to take water at this station, instead of "Red Lodge," the regular watering stop. The train comes to a standstill (seen through window of office); the conductor comes to the window, and the frightened operator delivers the order while the bandits crouch out of sight, at the same time keeping him covered with their revolvers. As soon as the conductor leaves, they fall upon the operator, bind and gag him, and hastily depart to catch the moving train.

Scene 2: *Railroad water tower.* The bandits are hiding behind the tank as the train, under the false order, stops to take water. Just before she pulls out they stealthily board the train between the express car and the tender.

Scene 3: *Interior of express car.* Messenger is busily engaged. An unusual sound alarms him. He goes to door, peeps through the keyhole and discovers two men trying to break in. He starts back bewildered, but, quickly recovering, he hastily locks the strong box containing the valuables and throws the key through the open side door. Drawing his revolver, he crouches behind a desk. In the meantime the two robbers have succeeded in breaking in the door and enter cautiously. The messenger opens fire, and a desperate pistol duel takes place in which the messenger is killed. One of the robbers stands watch while the other tries to open the treasure box. Finding it locked, he vainly searches the messenger for the key, and blows the safe open with dynamite. Securing the valuables and mail bags, they leave the car.

Scene 4: This thrilling scene shows the tender and interior of the locomotive cab, while the train is running forty miles an hour. While two of the bandits have been robbing the mail car, two others climb over the tender. One of them holds up the engineer while the other covers the fireman, who seizes a coal shovel and climbs up on the tender, where a desperate fight takes place. They struggle fiercely all over the tank and narrowly escape being hurled over the side of the tender. Finally they fall, with the robber on top. He seizes a lump of coal, and strikes the fireman on the head until he becomes senseless. He then hurls the body from the swiftly moving train. The bandits then compel the engineer to bring the train to a stop.

Scene 5: *Shows the train coming to a stop.* The engineer leaves the locomotive, uncouples it from the train, and pulls ahead about 100 feet while the robbers hold their pistols to his face.

Scene 6: *Exterior scene showing train.* The bandits compel the passengers to leave the coaches, "hands up," and line up along the tracks. One of the robbers covers them with a revolver in each hand, while the others relieve the passengers of their valuables. A passenger attempts to escape, and is instantly shot down. Securing everything of value, the band terrorize the passengers by firing their revolvers in the air, while they make their escape to the locomotive.

Scene 7: The desperadoes board the locomotive with this booty, compel the engineer to start, and disappear in the distance.

Scene 8: The robbers bring the engine to a stop several miles from the scene of the "hold up," and take to the mountains.

Scene 9: *A beautiful scene in a valley.* The bandits come down the side of a hill, across a narrow stream, mounting their horses, and make for the wilderness.

Scene 10: *Interior of telegraph office.* The operator lies bound and gagged on the floor. After struggling to his feet, he leans on the table, and telegraphs for assistance by manipulating the key with his chin, and then faints from exhaustion. His little daughter enters with his dinner pail. She cuts the rope, throws a glass of water in his face and restores him to consciousness, and, recalling his thrilling experience, he rushes out to give the alarm.

Scene 11: *Interior of a typical Western dance hall.* Shows a number of men and women in a lively quadrille. A "tenderfoot" is quickly spotted and pushed to the center of the hall, and compelled to do a jig, while bystanders amuse themselves by shooting dangerously close to his feet. Suddenly the door opens and the half-dead telegraph operator staggers in. The dance breaks up in confusion. The men secure their rifles and hastily leave the room.

Scene 12: Shows the mounted robbers dashing down a rugged hill at a terrific pace, followed closely by a large posse, both parties firing as they ride. One of the desperadoes is shot and plunges headlong from his horse. Staggering to his feet, he fires at the nearest pursuer, only to be shot dead a moment later.

Scene 13: The three remaining bandits, thinking they have eluded the pursuers, have dismounted from their horses, and after carefully surveying their surroundings, they start to examine the contents of the mail pouches. They are so grossly engaged in their work that they do not realize the approaching danger until too late. The pursuers, having left their horses, steal noiselessly down upon them until they are completely surrounded. A desperate battle then takes place, and after a brave stand all the robbers and some of the posse bite the dust.

Scene 14: A *life-size [close-up] picture of Barnes*, leader of the outlaw band, taking aim and firing point-blank at the audience. The resulting excitement is great. This scene can be used to begin or end the picture.

The limitations of *The Great Train Robbery* were those of youth. The action of every scene was told in one shot instead of a number of shots. Every shot, moreover, was a long shot, its action being confined to the proscenium-limited stage area. With the exception of the scenes in which the passengers are lined up outside the train, the robbery of the mail car, the hold-up of the engineer, and the battle between the posse and the bandits, the action was played in profile before the camera. Foreground and middle ground were equally ignored, the background alone serving as the acting area. The camera never moved from eye level. Tension and excitement were achieved by a quickening of the players' movements rather than by variation of the lengths of the shots. Within this simple framework, however, the kinetic possibilities of the new technique were convincingly demonstrated.

The success of *The Great Train Robbery* established Porter at once as the outstanding figure in the movie world and initiated an American film style of vigor, movement, and melodrama. A series of similar films, all utilizing the editing technique and similar subject matter, flooded the market. The heretofore unrivaled Méliès and his "magical" films fell back to second place.

Despite the success of *The Great Train Robbery*, Porter

was still regarded as a mechanic by his employers. Held to a rigid production schedule, in the next three years he made hundreds of films patterned more or less on *The Great Train Robbery*.

In 1905 he made two further contributions to motion picture technique. To the editing principle as evolved in *The Life of an American Fireman* and *The Great Train Robbery*, Porter now added the corollaries of contrast and parallel construction, as if instinctively he was applying to the movie certain principles that had long been established in other arts.

Like the discovery of the editing principle, these innovations were prompted by the needs of the subject matter. In *The Ex-Convict*, for instance, a wealthy manufacturer refuses to give an ex-convict work. It was necessary to contrast the two men's life situations in order to emphasize for the audience the drama of their encounter. Porter therefore employed the formal device now known as contrast editing. Scenes of the poverty-stricken home of the ex-convict were opposed to scenes of luxury in the manufacturer's household, and thus by implication the sympathy of the audience was directed. This new application of editing, not straightforward or direct, but comparative, pointed to future subtlety in film expression. Not until years later, however, was contrast editing to be properly valued and developed.

Although Porter himself could not have explained what he had done, he believed that he had significantly extended his editing technique. After *The Ex-Convict* he made another film in which he refined his contrast editing and ventured into a third kind of technique: parallel editing. This new film, *The Kleptomaniac*, like *The Ex-Convict*, protested against social injustice. The story told of two women, one poor and the other rich, who are caught shoplifting and arrested. The rich one is freed; the poor one is jailed. The story's effectiveness depended on the paralleling of the causes of the actions and fates of the two women. The picture was perhaps Porter's most interesting achievement, and in technique and content it was the most advanced picture yet produced.

Porter divided the story into three parts: two parallel sequences and a resolution, to which was added his own ironic comment in an epilogue. The first sequence showed a wealthy woman shoplifting some trinkets from a department store, and then her arrest. In the second sequence a poor woman stealing a loaf of bread to keep from starving is likewise arrested. The third part brings the two women together, arraigned in a police court. The judge orders a chair for the rich woman, who is placed away from the crowd; the poor woman is herded with other arraigned unfortunates. When the poor woman is called before the judge, she pleads in vain for mercy; he sentences her to jail. In the meantime the rich woman's husband, a banker, has come in with a lawyer. When they appear for her, the judge ignores the evidence offered by the store detective and discharges her.

Porter could have ended his film there, as in *The Ex-Convict*, leaving the audience to draw its own conclusions. But he added his own comment in an epilogue which served to sum up all three sequences. A figure of Justice, blindfolded, is shown holding a scale. On the one side of the balance is a bag of gold; on the other, a loaf of bread. The balance moves in favor of the gold. Then the bandage over the eyes of Justice is removed, revealing her with only one eye—a glittering eye, fixed on the gold.

Original and highly expressive, *The Kleptomaniac* revealed further possibilities of film technique. Movies could now appeal to the minds of the audiences as well as to the emotions. Contrast and parallel editing not only heightened the movies' dramatic values but made it more than just a story. The picture was an interpretation of one aspect of life in society, and became in itself an agency of protest against that aspect of life.

From ramifications of editing, Porter turned to examine the camera more thoroughly. In 1906 he made what might have been a trivial picture but was actually a most imaginative one through his intelligent manipulation of camera devices. *The Dream of a Rarebit Fiend* pictured the fanciful nightmare of a man who, before going to sleep, has Welsh rarebit and a few bottles of ale. We see the man asleep. His shoes mysteriously creep out of the room; then his table and chair become animated and quickly disappear. From the dreamer's head a large, steaming chafing dish appears, and three devils jump out to beat a lively tattoo on his head. Soon the bed comes to life and, after a lively dance, spins through the room like a top, then shoots through the window and sails high above New York, past bridges, rivers, skyscrapers, with the dreamer clinging desperately to the bedposts. A sudden wind capsizes the bed and the sleeper spins through space, at last catching on a weather vane atop a church steeple. There the wind blows him around and around until he loses his balance and falls again. He crashes down through the ceiling of his own room and lands on his bed, awake, and realizing that he has been dreaming.

As Edison Company advertised, "Some of the photographic stunts have never been seen or attempted before, and few experts will be able to understand how they were done." The technical tricks which Porter put into this film did lift it to a level which no similar film had attained. The picture still looks fairly good today despite more recent mechanical and technical progress. Obviously stemming from Méliès' magical films, *The Dream of a Rarebit Fiend* had a cinematic style more advanced and distinguished than the Frenchman's. Both men used a variety of camera devices—stop-motion, double exposure, masking, moving camera, dissolves—but Porter's knowledge of editing gave his effects a fluency and rhythm lacking in Melies' work.

After 1906 Porter did little to advance either his reputation or the movie medium. Still the leading director in the industry, he continued to turn out some of the most spectacular films and participated actively in an industry enjoying its first boom. The demand for pictures increased a hundredfold during the mushroom growth of nickelodeons. It was all Porter could do to keep pace with production requirements, though his company had given him two new assistants. There was neither time nor need to experiment for the enthusiastic movie-goer. Thus the hundreds of pictures Porter turned out became more and more routinized. Film after film repeated the dramatic method crystallized in *The Great Train Robbery*. Porter's urge for social criticism, moreover, waned as his personal fortunes flourished.

In the next two years other movie makers rapidly assimilated Porter's contributions and, following the editing principle, flooded the market with story films. Turning out a movie became a formula, followed with little imagination or enthusiasm; speed and quantity of production were deemed more necessary.

Not until about 1910, when D. W. Griffith came to the

fore, did the industry take a new turn. Outrivaled by the experimenting Griffith but still securely established, Porter left Edison in 1911 to head Rex, his own company, and he became a leader of the independents. After competing more than a year with his former employer, he pioneered with Adolf Zukor's Famous Players Company, directing its first feature picture. To have been selected for such a momentous venture was a signal honor and indicates the rank and respect Porter commanded.

His first feature film for Zukor, *The Count of Monte Cristo*, was not released; a rival company beat it to the market with a similar picture. With his second feature, *The Prisoner of Zenda*, Porter distinguished himself anew. W. Stephen Bush, critic of The Moving Picture World, paid tribute to his craftsmanship:

> The skill of a talented and ardent master of the cinema silent drama is apparent at every turn. Mr. Porter knew the possibilities of his instrument and made the conquest quite complete. He has disarmed and delighted the most captious critics by the daring but entirely successful use of all those advantages which are peculiar to the motion picture.

For three years Porter remained with Famous Players as Director-General. An influential figure in the broadening screen world, he formulated the production policy of the company and directed many of its biggest stars, including Mary Pickford (*Tess of the Storm Country*), John Barrymore (*The Dictator*), Pauline Frederick (*Sold*). When the Italian film *Quo Vadis* made Americans spectacle-conscious, Porter, with a company of players, went to Rome to produce what was America's second big film spectacle, the first having been Griffith's *Judith of Bethulia*. The film Porter returned with, *The Eternal City*, was his last. After its presentation in 1915, he retired from the industry, wealthy and with an honorable career behind him.

Porter's flexible inventions endowed movies with new capabilities of technique and form, opening the way for other craftsmen to follow. The movie would have remained a novelty with little social or artistic significance had not Porter, or someone else, discovered the film's adaptability to being cut up and rejoined for narrative and interpretive purposes. During the past thirty-odd years of movie making, the principle of editing has remained fundamental and peculiar to the motion picture art. It has been developed, enlarged, and reinforced by the application of other arts—theatre, painting, literature, music—but has not been essentially altered. It is the method by which the latent power of photography is released, by which a series of pictures can become impressive, eloquent, and significant. Without editing a film is dead; with it, alive. The intensity and subtlety of a director's editing are the indices of his craftsmanship.

Pointing the way to a cinematic *art,* the content of Porter's films was seasoned with a strong social feeling. Porter's interest in the streets and their humanity affected his technique and accounted partly for the popularity of his productions. Alert and sharply critical, he sympathized with the poor (*The Miller's Daughter, A River Tragedy*), consciously agitated for social justice (*The Ex-Convict, The Kleptomaniac*), and awakened the populace to a better understanding of America in the new century (*White Caps, Desperate Encounter, Capture of the Yegg Bank Burglars*). By accenting the bravery and courage of firemen and policemen, by dramatizing the hardships and misery of the poor, by showing the personal maladjustments that lead to crime and the difficulty of rehabilitation, Porter made his audiences aware of heroism in their lives and stimulated the already growing interest in the common man.

To the non-theatre-going audience, movies had to be physically compelling, melodramatic. Images on the screen had to suggest the slang and profanity of back streets. Stories had to elucidate, criticize, or acclaim their own narrow settings. Porter understood these things earlier and better than anyone else, and his films had a forthright style adapted both to theme and to audience. His technique and choices of content introduced the movies to the great task of dramatizing reality.

D. W. Griffith: New Discoveries

by Lewis Jacobs

This chapter appeared originally in "The Rise of the American Film," first published in 1939.

David Wark Griffith, the third major figure in the early development of film art, did not want to make motion pictures. No contradiction proved more ironic for, in the entire history of the American screen, no other director achieved greater success, none won more esteem. This "enigmatic and somewhat tragic" figure, as Gilbert Seldes describes him, secretly cherished the ambition to become famous as an author and counted the moments until he should have sufficient money to quit the "flickers" and write. Ashamed of "selling his soul," he changed his name on entering the movies, only later to retrieve it and make it as familiar as the term "movie" itself.

Griffith further developed the art of Méliès and Porter, contributing devices of his own that made for greater unity, clarity, and effectiveness. Sensing from the beginning the need for a body of technique to catch and control the emotions of the spectator, he did more to realize a method and a viewpoint than any other man of his day. Although he was himself a former actor and playwright, he repudiated theatrical conventions and evolved a method of expression peculiar to the screen.

Griffith came to films at that propitious moment when they were in the plastic beginnings of artistic development. To them he brought new elements of form and a variety of resources, and added at least two great productions to American motion picture achievement. The most revered and influential movie creator of his day, and perhaps of all motion picture history, he justified the new medium to the world. His productions became models for directors wherever films were made, and to this day stand not only as important achievements in themselves but as the source of central motion picture developments.

In temperament Griffith was a conventional product of his origins and upbringing. Born into an impoverished family in Kentucky in 1880, nicknamed "Sugar," he was inculcated in his earliest years with Southern prejudices, Victorian sentiments, and a local social viewpoint which he never outgrew.

His father, a former Confederate colonel known as "Thunder Jake," because of his roaring voice, filled him with tales of Johnny Reb, the old chivalrous South, and Confederate bravery, subjects romantic enough to fire a boy less imaginative and emotional than Griffith. This grand mural of a departed glory was later to appear time and again in Griffith's one-reel cameos of plantation life, Civil War battle episodes, and vignettes of Southern chivalry, and finally to culminate in that powerful film of secessionist bigotry, *The Birth of a Nation*.

The sentimental bias implanted in Griffith by his father was reinforced by the boy's love of poetry in the Victorian manner. His adolescent dallying with the works of Browning, Kingsley, Tennyson, and Hood was later to be recalled and readapted for the screen in such films as *The Taming of the Shrew, Sands of Dee, Enoch Arden* and *Song of the Shirt*. Griffith's romantic values and poetic ideals persisted even after the rest of the world had abandoned them. Many of his films were saturated with the saccharine sentiments and homilies characteristic of Godey's "Lady's Book." Even when on occasion he took up the cause of justice, tolerance, and sympathy for the downtrodden, he could not refrain from becoming maudlin. Whether as fictioneer or pamphleteer, Griffith was a man of sentimentality. That accounts in part for his phenomenal pre-war success and his swift post-war eclipse.

Griffith's romanticism determined not only his choice of subject matter but his choice of players. His persistence in casting mere slips of girls, fifteen or sixteen years old, blond and wide-eyed, was due as much to Southern ideals of femininity and his immersion in Victorian poetry as to the camera, always absolute in its demands for pulchritude. All his heroines—Mary Pickford, Mae Marsh, Lillian Gish, Blanche Sweet—were, at least in Griffith's eye, the pale, helpless, delicate, slim-bodied heroines of the nineteenth-century English poets.

But Griffith had a strong creative urge that could divert attention from his weaknesses. This quality of his character was in evidence long before he came to movies. Sent to work at an early age, he was dissatisfied with his short experience as a dry-goods clerk and bookstore salesman; he aspired to become a writer. At seventeen he got a job as newspaper reporter on The Louisville Courier. Soon he became ambitious to write plays, and following the advice of a friend who told him that all great playwrights had been actors, he left home to join a traveling stock company.

During the next few years, while acting, Griffith wrote continually, sending out poems, plays, and short stories to various editors and occasionally making a sale. Once, when both acting and writing failed to give him a living and he was stranded in California, he became a hop-picker. This experience he immediately turned into a drama of an itinerant laborer, called *A Fool and a Girl*, which in October 1907 played for two weeks in Washington and Baltimore. Lukewarm though the newspaper criticism was, it throws light on the outlook in the play later to appear in his films:

> . . . If one wants to tell the old and beautiful story of redemption of either man or woman through love, it is not necessary to portray the gutters from which they are redeemed.*

The little money and slight public recognition that the play gave him made Griffith more determined than ever to win fame as a writer. Some of his poems and short stories were published in Leslie's Weekly, Collier's Weekly, Good Housekeeping, and Cosmopolitan. He finished another play called "War," based on soldiers' diaries and letters which he diligently studied at the 42nd Street Library in New York City. The play proved to be unsalable, but years later the material was put to use in his screen drama, *America*.

His creative urge is confirmed by his wife, who recorded that he tried to make every minute in his life count. When he was not acting or writing he was inventing things. With his restless temperament and experimental turn of mind, he would astonish his wife time and again with ideas for "non-puncturable" tires, schemes to harness the energy of the sea, methods of canning cooked foods—inventions that he thought might make him suddenly rich. This flair for attempting the impossible, or the improbable, later led him to discover new methods and devices in film making, to thrust aside the objections made by technical men and to open up new resources of the film medium.

Original and profound as a craftsman, Griffith, however, was never to outgrow his Southern sentiments and Victorian idealism. When his creative genius was most vigorous, it could

* Quoted by Mrs. D. W. Griffith, "When the Movies Were Young," p. 26.

lift him from sentimentality to dignity and art; when he surrendered to his emotional impulsiveness, his films became orgies of feeling. This accounts for the incongruity between the discipline of his structure and the lack of restraint in his sentiment that mars even the best of his works.

Griffith's screen career falls into three periods: development, maturity, and decline. His years at the Biograph Company, which he began with *The Adventures of Dolly* (1908) and continued through some hundreds of films to *Judith of Bethulia* (1914), can be characterized as his apprenticeship period. He was then alert and active, displaying a critical and fertile mind. He not only learned all there was to know about the technique of motion pictures, but added to the existing technique a host of new elements. His quick intuition discovered the camera as a dramatic tool and developed its devices as integral properties of film language: the full shot, the medium shot, the close-up, the pan shot and the moving camera. In addition, his employment of such narrative transitions as the cut, the spot-iris, the mask, and the fade contributed importantly to the art of continuity in films. But even more important than such integral devices was his contribution to editing: an awareness of tempo and the device of parallel and intercutting, which greatly expanded and enriched the internal structure of movie art.

It was in 1907, when he was out of work in New York City, that Griffith first learned of the opportunities in movies. An actor friend, Max Davidson, advised him to apply to the American Mutoscope and Biograph Company for work to tide him over during the slack spring and summer months. Griffith applied for employment and found that he could make $5 a day for acting and $10 to $15 for story suggestions. Working hard, he acted and wrote a number of Mutoscope films. Among these were *Old Isaacs the Pawnbroker*, a bitter diatribe against the amalgamated association of charities then being muckraked; *The Music Master*, strongly reminiscent of Belasco; *At the Crossroads of Life; The Stage Rustler*, and *Ostler Joe*. At this time he appeared also in several Edison pictures. But like other movie craftsmen of that day, Griffith was ashamed of his occupation and attempted to conceal it from his friends.

Poet, playwright, actor, inventor—a more fitting background for a motion picture director would be hard to define.

Yet when an opportunity came to direct, Griffith debated with his wife:

"In one way it's very nice . . . but you know we can't go on forever and not tell our friends and relatives how we are earning our living."

He argued with his employers:

"Now if I take to this picture directing and fall down, then, you see, I'll be out of an acting job."

The vice-president of Biograph, Henry Marvin, reassured him:

"If you fall down as a director, you can have your acting job back."

With this promise to hearten him, Griffith accepted the assignment, continuing with the name he had taken for stage purposes, Lawrence Griffith. He had told his wife that he would only use his real name, David Wark, when he became famous.

His plan was to make enough money in movies to enable him to quit them and return to his real interest, writing. But Griffith never was to leave the movies. From June 1908, when he undertook to direct his first picture for Biograph, he was to remain in the field for more than twenty years. Commenced apathetically, almost unwillingly, his directorial career was to bring to him personal fame and fortune, and to the movies, fresh respect and importance. Medium and master had at last discovered each other, although neither suspected it.

Griffith took his first directorial job, *The Adventures of Dolly,* seriously. Before going to work on it he asked Henry Marvin to run off a few films to study. What he saw was not very impressive, and he left the projection room confident that he could do better.

His talent for innovation was revealed at once. Stopping a stranger on Broadway because he recognized in him the type he wanted, Griffith selected his first leading man off the street. His intuition was later vindicated. The stranger, Arthur Johnson, became one of America's first screen idols. For the leading female role Griffith chose his wife, Linda Arvidson, who had been playing background bits; and for the role of a villainous gypsy he persuaded a stage actor, Charles Inslee, to play in the "flickers." Having selected his cast with more care than was customary, he went to work.

The film that began Griffith's career as director was 713 feet long, a naïve tale picturing "kind providence thwarting the gypsies' attempt to kidnap a child for revenge" (all films of the day had to point a moral lesson). A synopsis of *The Adventures of Dolly* in the Biograph press sheet (July, 1908) reveals its quaint story as typical of contemporary productions:

On the lawn of their country residence sport mamma, papa, and baby Dolly. Near them flows a picturesque stream where mamma and Dolly watch the boys fishing. A band of gypsies . . . whose real motive is pillage, offers mamma some goods for sale. Her refusal rouses the ire of the gypsy and he attempts to steal her purse. Papa is attracted by her screams and comes on the scene with a heavy snake whip, lashing out at the gypsy unmercifully, driving him away with revengeful venom in his heart.

Later the gypsy gets his chance and kidnaps Dolly. Hiding her in a water cask, [the gypsies] put it on their wagon and speed away. As they pass over a stream, the cask falls off the wagon and into the water, where it is carried by a strong current downstream, over a waterfall, through seething rapids, finally to enter the quiet cove of the first scene. Fishing boys hearing strange sounds from the cask break it open and discover Dolly. Soon she is safe in the arms of her overjoyed papa and mamma.

In discussing *The Adventures of Dolly* years later, Billy Bitzer, the cameraman, said:

He showed it to me and I told him it was too long. Too long! In the light of a completed scenario today, I can readily say that Griffith was years ahead of us.

Novice though Griffith was, *The Adventures of Dolly* compared favorably with the Biograph productions by more experienced directors. The company must have liked the picture, for they quickly had him sign a contract at $45 a week and a royalty of one mill for every foot of film sold.

Feeling his way in the new medium, Griffith turned out five pictures in the next four weeks, each within a reel: *The Red Man and the Child, The Stage Rustler, The Bandit's Waterloo, The Greaser's Gauntlet* and *The Man and the Woman*. All were in the conventional style and showed no deviation from the form initiated by Porter. Whatever distinction they may have had was due to greater care in the selection of the casts and in execution, for Griffith insisted on rehearsing scenes before shooting them, a procedure then uncommon and considered a waste of time. Dubbed the "once-again" idea, it was later to be taken up by others.

The experience of directing these pictures and learning the rudimentary principles aroused Griffith to an awareness of the movies' limitations. He saw the need for a means whereby action could be developed and emphasized, characterizations built, atmosphere evoked, the whole story expressed with more fluidity and variety.

But it was one thing to be aware of a need and another to fill it. Resolved to experiment with his next assignment, Griffith chose Jack London's "Just Meat," changing its title to *For Love of Gold*.

The climax of the story was the scene in which the two thieves begin to distrust each other. Its effectiveness depended upon the audience's awareness of what was going on in the minds of both thieves. The only known way to indicate a player's thoughts was by double-exposure "dream balloons." This convention had grown out of two misconceptions: first, that the camera must always be fixed at a viewpoint corresponding to that of a spectator in a theatre (the position now known as the long shot); the other, that a scene had to be played in its entirety before another was begun (this was a direct carry-over from the stage).

Griffith decided now upon a revolutionary step. He moved the camera closer to the actor, in what is now known as the full shot (a larger view of the actor), so that the audience could observe the actor's pantomime more closely. No one before had thought of changing the position of the camera in the middle of a scene. Simple as this solution appears now, it was daring then.

The innovation was portentous, for it introduced the exploitation of camera mobility and the custom of breaking up a scene into separate shots. Such new methods would further the movie on its own course and free it from its crippling reliance on the stage. A closer view of the actor would make extravagant gestures, thought necessary on the stage, unnecessary—not to say unnatural and ludicrous—in the movie. Realizing this wonderful advantage of the full shot, Griffith saw that henceforth the movie must be weaned from the stage and given independence for self-development.

Excited at the effectiveness of his experiment and what it

foreshadowed, Griffith employed the full shot throughout the many films he made in the next three months. Of these the most outstanding were *The Heart of Oyama, The Barbarian, Ingomar, The Vaquero's Vow, Romance of a Jewess* and *Money-Mad.* Gradually the full shot became a regular device in the director's yet limited repertory.

The next logical step was to bring the camera still closer to the actor in what is now called the close-up. With this in mind, in November, 1908, Griffith had Frank Woods, soon to come known as the film's major critic, make a screen adaptation of Tennyson's "Enoch Arden." Biograph opposed the story on the ground that it had neither action nor a chase, the two conventional requisites for all films. But the company's arguments were of no avail. Griffith was aiming for something which to him was more important than gross action. In the quiet ballad he saw the chance to use his new device, the close-up. His hunch, bringing a new concept into the technique of editing, made movie history.

Not since Porter's *The Great Train Robbery,* some five years before, had a close-up been seen in American films. Used then only as a stunt (the outlaw was shown firing at the audience), the close-up became, in *Enoch Arden,* the natural dramatic complement of the long shot and full shot. Going further than he had ventured before, in a scene showing Annie Lee brooding and waiting for her husband's return, Griffith daringly used a large close-up of her face.

Everyone in the Biograph studio was shocked. "Show only the head of a person? What will people say? It's against all rules of movie making!" With such naïveté was the close-up greeted.

But Griffith had no time for arguments. He had another surprise, even more radical, to offer. Immediately following the close-up of Annie, he inserted a picture of the object of her thoughts—her husband, cast away on a desert isle. This cutting from one scene to another, without finishing either, brought a torrent of criticism down upon the experimenter.

"It's jerky and distracting! How can you tell a story jumping about like that? People won't know what it's all about!"

Griffith was ready for all dissenters.

"Doesn't Dickens write that way?"

"Yes, but writing is different."

"Not much. These stories are in pictures, that's all."

But Biograph was greatly worried. It renamed the film *After Many Years*, sent it out, and watched its reception closely. To the company's surprise it was immediately singled out as a masterpiece and proved to be among the first American films honored by foreign markets as worthy of importation.

Griffith's instinct had been right. In the close-up he had made use of one of the most valuable attributes of the moving picture camera, and in "cutting" from Annie Lee to her husband thousands of miles away, he had broken away from the rigid one shot per scene continuity, and disclosed a more fundamental method of film construction. Not only was the scene made up of several shots, but one scene followed another without waiting for it to end. Not connected by time, separated in space, the shots were unified in effect by the theme. Thus Griffith proved not only that the basis of film expression is editing but that the unit of editing is the shot, not the scene.

Before the year was over Griffith had introduced other innovations. Ever since movies had been made in studios, the use of electric light had been considered a necessary evil. A scene was always lit from above, and it was considered bad taste and amateurish to leave any portions of a scene shadowed. There was no regard for any possible tonal or dramatic value that lighting might provide. To his two cameramen, Marvin and Bitzer, Griffith complained of the haphazard and disastrous results of lighting. The cameramen did not know what could be done, since the raw film was both "slow" and "color-blind"; very strong light was needed to make any image on the film emulsion. The clumsiness of the lighting apparatus —mercury-vapor lamps—complicated the problem.

Griffith deliberately chose a story that involved a problem in lighting, *The Drunkard's Reformation*. In one scene the actors were to be illuminated by a fireside glow. The cameramen protested that the film would not take an image if they followed Griffith's directions—or that the peculiar lighting would cast ugly shadows on the players' faces. But Griffith disdained all their objections, and Marvin and Bitzer photographed the scene under his direction. Projected the next day in the studio, the scene was greeted with a murmur of admiration, and the cameramen were perhaps the most surprised and approving of all. From then on lighting was regarded more

44

seriously as a means of enhancing the dramatic effect of a film story.

Aiming above the obvious and absurd "chase" melodramas of the day, fighting repeatedly for the privilege of making films that would force the stage, the critics, and the discriminating public to approve of the young art, Griffith realized that pictures could become significant only if their content was significant. He therefore led a raid on the classics for his material. Before his first year as a movie director was ended, he had not only adapted works by Jack London and Tennyson but boldly brought to the screen Shakespeare, Hood, Tolstoy, Poe, O. Henry, Reade, de Maupassant, Stevenson and Browning. Among the hundred or so pictures of this first year were *The Taming of the Shrew, The Song of the Shirt, Resurrection, Edgar Allan Poe, The Cricket on the Hearth, The Necklace, Suicide Club* and *The Lover's Tale.*

Griffith soon saw that acting must be more natural, less a matter of "artistical attitudes." He canvassed theatrical agencies for fresh talent which could adjust itself to a more realistic style. Since it was not easy to persuade better-grade actors to appear before the camera, he paid as high as $10 a day for the services of such professionals as Frank Powell (later famed as the director and discoverer of Theda Bara), James Kirkwood, and Henry Walthall, a triumvirate which became, under Griffith, America's earliest anonymous screen idols. When $10 did not prove to be enough to attract Broadway talent, Griffith raised the offer to $20. Pitifully small though this salary appears today, it was then ridiculously high. In a matter of months, however, Griffith's pictures were being pointed out for their "more natural" performances as well as for their better stories and originality.

The climax of his early efforts was the film he directed just about a year after he came to Biograph: *The Lonely Villa.* In this he extended the editing method initiated in *After Many Years* and added to his technique the innovation of intercutting. The story of *The Lonely Villa,* in a last-minute rescue, offered a more complex development of the chase pattern. To thwart a robbery and save his wife and children, a husband rushes home in a race against time. Griffith built suspense by prolonging the situation, intercutting from the helpless family and burglars to the speeding husband in ever-shortening intervals. The effect of such back-and-forth movement was to prolong the suspense and create a mounting tension in the audience, as they experienced by turns the fears of the family and the anxiety of the husband. Their relief at the rescue was therefore all the more pronounced.

So effective was this intercutting that it was immediately taken up by other directors, who honored its discoverer by calling it the "Griffith last-minute rescue." (Technically, the device became designated as "the cross-cut," "the cut-back," "the switch-back.") It solved a major problem of story-telling in films. Heretofore, to depict two actions taking place simultaneously at different places, directors had resorted to the double-exposure "dream balloons," or they had given up the attempt to present any such simultaneous action at all. Griffith's *After Many Years* had been a step toward freedom from such a rigid method. Now, cutting back and forth before a scene was completed solved the space problem and, moreover, brought in the element of time to aid the director.

Until now the duration of a shot had been determined by the time the action would take in real life. *The Lonely Villa* proved that the duration of a shot need not be dependent upon its natural action but could be shortened or lengthened to heighten its dramatic effect. This manipulation of the time element not only increased the story's effectiveness but enabled the director to give his shots pace and rhythm.

Having within one year accomplished important innovations in technique, extended the scope of movie content, and improved motion picture acting, Griffith was regarded with mounting admiration in Biograph and in the industry generally. Everyone at Biograph now hastened to carry out his directions, wondering what great new thing he was now evolving, glad to have a hand in it. Rival directors would slip into theatres to watch his pictures and then hurry back to their studios to imitate them. Audiences and critics as well were seeking pictures with the "AB" trade-mark, the only distinguishing insignia of Griffith's films (as yet no individual credits were being given). In The Moving Picture World (July 3, 1909) the high regard for Griffith's pictures was expressed this way:

The other afternoon when I sat in my accustomed seat at the Bijou Dream on 14th Street and the title of the Biograph subject, *The Way of a Man,* appeared on the screen, there was a sudden hush. . . . Now this picture held the attention of the audience right up to the very last foot of film because the Biograph Company have got down to the root idea of a moving picture. . . . Their photographs are not mere snap shots or rapidly taken groups of small parties of puppets moving about on the stage. No. They are active photographs of thinking men and women. . . . Now all of this is indicative of progress in the making of moving pictures, in which the Biograph Company prominently shines. It is clear as day that all the other manufacturers will also have to advance. . . . The photographer does his work to perfection. He puts his camera near the subjects and the lens and you see what is passing in the minds of the actors and actresses. The total combination is that you get as perfect a picture play from the Biograph studio as it is possible in the present stage of moving-picture making to get.

Signing his second contract with Biograph in August, 1909, Griffith little realized that all he had achieved so far was only a preparation for what he was yet to do. From the outset his second year with Biograph was triumphant.

For months he had been trying to convince his employers to let him make a film based on Browning's poem "Pippa Passes." But it was not until a month after his new contract was signed —a busy month in the pastoral atmosphere of Cuddebackville, New York, where he made two mementos to the Revolutionary era, *Hessian Renegades* and *Leather Stocking*—that permission was granted him to film *Pippa Passes*.

Production began in mid-September, 1909. Griffith at once turned to experiments with lighting. No doubt the success of his lighting effects in *The Drunkard's Reformation* had motivated his desire to do *Pippa Passes*, for the latter presented a complex lighting problem. Divided into four parts, Morning, Noon, Evening, Night, the film involved a more organic and dramatic use of lighting than Griffith had yet attempted. To his staff Griffith explained the problem and the kind of lighting effects he wanted. Cameramen Bitzer and Marvin were once again dubious, but Griffith—neither cameraman nor mechanic in his own right—laid out the procedure they were to follow for the first sequence, Morning. In her book "When the Movies Were Young," Mrs. Griffith records her husband's plan:

He figured on cutting a little rectangular place in the back wall of Pippa's room, about three feet by one, and arranging a sliding board to fit the aperture much like the cover of a box sliding in and out of grooves. The board was to be gradually lowered and beams of light from a powerful Kleig shining through would thus appear as the first rays of the rising sun striking the wall of the room. Other light stationed outside Pippa's window would give the effect of soft morning light. Then the lights full up, the mercury tubes a-sizzling, the room fully lighted, the back wall would have become a regular back wall again, with no little hole in it.

Marvin, remembering Griffith's past successes, was half inclined to give the new lighting scheme a try. Bitzer was wholly skeptical. Griffith, expecting more enthusiasm, exclaimed, "Well, come on—let's do it anyhow. I don't give a damn what anybody thinks about it."

The cameramen followed his orders grudgingly.

During the projection of the rushes there was great tension. "At first the comments came in hushed and awed tones, and then when the showing was over, the little experiment in light effects was greeted with uncontrolled enthusiasm."

This was another victory for Griffith's imagination. When *Pippa Passes* reached the public in October, 1909, The New York Times, which rarely noticed motion pictures, commented:

Pippa Passes is being given in the nickelodeons and Browning is being presented to the average motion picture audiences, who have received it with applause and are asking for more.

This unsolicited praise had an immediate effect upon Griffith. His earnest struggles to master the medium were being recognized and approved by the world at large. No approbation could have been more heartening, nor could it have appeared at a better moment. It marked the turning point in Griffith's attitude toward the movies. Formerly oppressed by the thought that the motion picture had little future and that his attempts to better it would never bring him renown as an artist or writer, he now felt that his endeavors must have some significance after all.

Griffith's new hopes, however, were not quite free from doubts. When he went to a stage play, his new optimism and deepening conviction about the future of movies would be dissipated. He would go home in a temper, his high resolves about movies shattered. Even the sweet success of *Pippa Passes* did not rid him of nostalgic yearnings to be an author. He would reproach himself for giving up the only thing he really cared about, and became embittered at his own inability to leave the movies. Finally he would console himself with the money he was making and the secret thought that when be became a famous author, nobody would know that David W. Griffith, the author, was once Lawrence Griffith of the nickelodeons.

Griffith was never to free himself from the labor of movie making. The more money he made, the more he seemed to need. Before the end of his second year he was earning $900 to $1000 a month in royalties alone, but he kept putting off his intention to quit the business. The more he worked, the more obstacles he saw to be overcome and the more willing he became to accept their challenge. Mechanical crudities, the lack of good stories, untrained and inexperienced actors—these, and the prevalent unconcern for quality and good taste, made his prospects dismal, but he kept on. Perhaps he was more suited to the new medium than he cared to admit even to himself.

About this time California had become the mecca of the independent movie makers. Griffith, seeing the pictures made there, was impressed with the landscapes and pictorial possibilities the state offered. Upon investigation he learned that not only mountains and beaches but historic missions, tropical vegetation, and deserts were easily accessible. His love for the picturesque, his eye for the sweep of scenery and his enthusiasm for "artistic" backgrounds, urged him to leave New York and go West. Weather conditions, moreover, always a serious problem in the East, seemed better in California; they would help him to meet his expanded production schedule.

In the winter of 1910 Griffith took his company of Biograph players to California, and on the outskirts of Los Angeles he improvised a studio. Wanting for his initial production a theme that would impress the Biograph office back in New York, he wrote a religious story about the old San Gabriel Mission. This film, *The Thread of Destiny*, proved notable for three reasons. It featured Mary Pickford, it employed a new lighting effect that was both "dim" and "religious," and, most important, its editing demonstrated conclusively that the shot is the basis of scene construction.

Griffith desired to imbue the film with as much of the Mission atmosphere as possible. He photographed the Mission in great detail, with its weatherbeaten walls, decorative interiors, stairways, choir loft, and cemetery—shots which were not called for in the plot but which, when carefully edited, created an atmosphere and background that greatly reinforced the narrative and action of the story. No one, not even Griffith himself, had as yet taken shots of the various details of a setting to build a scene. Any shot which did not present a major phase of the scene's action had always been regarded as impeding, even intruding upon, the flow of the story; it was "a waste of footage" in the usual one-reel film. Griffith's realization that the details of a background could not only enhance a scene's mood and strengthen its action, but could also be basic in a scene's construction, was a daring step forward in the refinement of movie technique.

It was now clear to Griffith that the director must use the camera not only to take the total content of a scene, but to select details within the scene that bear relations to the content of the film as a whole. This meant that a shot need not be regulated and restricted by an imaginary proscenium. Freed from this spatial bondage, the camera could be stationed at any point, according to the director's desire to select details and angles of the content that would lend strength to a scene's structure and intensify its interest. This liberty to direct attention to a vital element of a scene, to vary time and space relationships for the sake of emphasis or contrasts, gave the director a powerful means of stimulating the spectator's responses. Griffith suddenly understood how the art of the movie director differs from that of the stage director: in movie making, guiding the camera, even more than directing the actor, is the trick.

Acceptance of this new principle meant that hereafter the screen story would have to be conceived from a new point of view. Griffith had hit upon a truth with implications that all motion picture directors since then have been trying to command. It is that the primary tools of the screen medium are the camera and the film rather than the actor; that the subject matter must be conceived in terms of the camera's eye and film cutting; that the unit of the film art is the shot; that manipulation of the shots builds the scene; that the continuity of scenes builds the sequences; and that the progression of sequences composes the totality of the production. Upon the composition of this interplay of shots, scenes, and sequences depends the clarity and vigor of the story. Here Griffith saw the epitome of motion picture method.

50

Working under commercial pressure and producing pictures at a steady pace in California throughout the winter of 1910, Griffith strove to apply what he had divined about camera composition, lighting, shot details, scene construction, transitions, and other phases of film technique. He constantly tried, moreover, to weld these elements into a personal style. The pictures he turned out during this period were *The Converts, The Way of the World* and *The Two Brothers*, utilizing the missions and topography of California; semi-historical pieces such as *In Old California, Love Among the Roses, The Romance of the Western Hills* and *Ramona*, romanticizing dons, señoritas, and Indians.

Ramona provoked the most public excitement. For the privilege of adapting it Griffith had paid $100, an extraordinary sum for a story in those days. Biograph issued a specially illustrated folder which declared proudly that *Ramona* was the most expensive picture ever made. In this film appeared what Griffith subsequently was to call "the extreme long shots." These were shots of vast, distant panoramas and were intended to emphasize the spaciousness of the scene as a dramatic foil to the close shots.

Ramona was followed by a series of film sermons told in the idiom of the day: *Gold Is Not All, Over Silent Paths, The Gold Seekers, Unexpected Help, A Rich Revenge, As It Is in Life* and *The Unchanging Sea*. The last is remembered as the "first masterpiece" of Griffith's West Coast series.

Returning to New York in the spring, Griffith set himself to work so industriously that Biograph's president, Arthur Marvin sighed, "He'll die working." Besides editing his Western-made pictures, Griffith kept up with a production schedule more ambitious than ever. *In the Season of Buds, A Child of the Ghetto, What the Daisy Said, The House with the Closed Shutters, The Sorrows of the Unfaithful, The Call to Arms* and *The Usurer* led a colorful array of dramas too numerous to list. The hard-working director's activity was constantly spurred by the increased attention of the trade papers to his pictures. The growing demand of exhibitors for Biograph products and the new phenomenon of fan letters indicated his increasing ability to outshine his contemporaries.

In the summer of this year Griffith signed his third contract with Biograph. This contract stipulated the relatively high salary of $75 per week and one-eighth of a cent per foot royalty on all films sold. What made this agreement significant for Griffith was not so much the raise, however, as the fact that in it he abandoned his pseudonym "Lawrence" and for the first time used his real name, David. At last he was wholeheartedly accepting his career.

In 1911, again in California, Griffith produced *The Last Drop of Water, Crossing the American Prairies in the Early Fifties, The Lonedale Operator, The White Rose of the Wilds* and *The Battle of Elderberry Gulch*, the last being released under the shortened title *The Battle*. All these films were distinguished from the general run of contemporary pictures by their content, careful attention to detail, and freshness of treatment. But in these pictures Griffith was seeking to master something new: movement of the action. Without knowing it, all he had discovered thus far had been an approach to it. Now he set about deliberately to create it by all the means he knew, and in *The Lonedale Operator* he was most successful. This was the usual last-minute rescue type of story, stemming from *The Lonely Villa*. A girl held captive in a train depot telegraphs her father and sweetheart, railroad men, for help, and they commandeer a train and speed to her rescue. In filming the scenes Griffith seized every opportunity for emphasizing movement. Not only was there action within the shot, but the camera itself moved—not as in a pan shot, but by being placed on the moving train. The cutting back and forth from the speeding train to the captive gave momentum to the whole. The fluency of action he achieved brought a new kinetic quality to the screen.

Now Griffith began to chafe under the arbitrary limitation of a picture to one reel. One reel was hardly adequate to unfold a complete story; the limitation hindered development, curtailed incidents, and proved a general barrier to the choice of deeper themes. If the movie was ever to become a vital medium, reasoned Griffith, its length would have to be increased. But just as Porter in 1903 had had to convince his doubting employers that the public would sit through a picture a full reel in length, Griffith now had to struggle with Biograph's reluctance to lengthening films to two reels.

Finally, disregarding protests, he made a two-reel picture, another version of the story which had already proved successful in one reel, *Enoch Arden*. Biograph refused to release the film as a whole; it was sold in two parts. But the movie audiences, unsatisfied after viewing only one reel, forced exhibitors to obtain both reels and show them one after the other. Biograph in turn had to comply with the requests of the exhibitors, and so the two-reel film was introduced.

The American two-reeler appeared none too soon, for almost immediately two-reelers from European studios appeared. Their reception by audiences was anxiously watched by American producers. So enthusiastic was it that by 1912 two- and even three-reelers were acknowledged by the trade as inevitable.

Now allowed to expand his stories whenever he felt that they demanded more length, Griffith early in 1912 made two films which, for size and content, were his most ambitious efforts up to that time. Unlike any of his previous pictures, the first of these, *Man's Genesis*, was produced by a definite esthetic urge, not a commercial one. The seriousness of its theme, "a psychological study founded upon the Darwinian Theory of the Evolution of Man," indicated Griffith's lack of concern for so-called entertainment values and his desire to do something "worth-while." Needless to say, his employers were strongly opposed to the undertaking.

The philosophical and scientific aspects of the theme were dramatized in the conflict between the intelligence of "Weakhands" and the body of "Brute-force." In the struggle brain finally conquers brawn. Though the film seems naïve to us today, it was then considered very advanced. The picture turned out to be one of the most discussed films of the year, provoking Vachel Lindsay to declare in his book "The Art of the Moving Picture":

It is a Griffith masterpiece, and every actor does sound work. The audience, mechanical Americans, fond of crawling on their stomachs to tinker their automobiles, are eager over the evolution of the first weapon from a stick to a hammer. They are as full of curiosity as they could well be over the history of Langley or the Wright Brothers.

Griffith's intuitive choice of such a serious subject was proved sound, for it inspired deeper respect for the screen.

Encouraged by this response, Griffith next ventured an ambitious historical re-creation of Custer's last stand, called

The Massacre. Like *Man's Genesis*, this film was to be more than another program picture. Griffith went far beyond his budget in the production, paying no attention to the pained protests from Biograph's Eastern offices. He was determined to turn out a film greater than any he had yet done. With its cast, costumes, and sets on an unprecedentedly lavish scale, with its "hundreds of cavalrymen and twice as many Indians," the production forced Griffith to reach a new high in his series of technical triumphs. The film abounded in mass scenes, detailed shots of close fighting, vast panoramic pan shots, all skillfully blended and given a rapid continuity in a manner that presaged his later style in *The Birth of a Nation*. *The Massacre* was, in a sense, America's first spectacle film; for Griffith it was the beginning of a new and profounder turn of his talents.

But before the picture was released, the American film world was disconcerted by a sudden and unexpected influx of European pictures of such dimensions that everything which had preceded them faded into insignificance. These foreign pictures, three, four, and even five reels in length, elaborately produced, with classics for subject matter, and starring such world-famed figures as Sarah Bernhardt, Helen Gardner, Asta Nielsen, Mme. Réjane, stirred America deeply. *Queen Elizabeth, Camille, Cleopatra, Gypsy Blood, Mme. Sans Gene*, in their length and power of conception, dwarfed contemporary American productions. The American companies, particularly those in the motion picture patents-trust group, regarded the invasion with mixed feelings of contempt and jealousy. Trade papers uneasily exhorted American producers to oust the foreigners. The aloof legitimate theatre itself turned a fearful eye upon these new threats of celluloid. But the climax came with the startling announcement that a young arcade and nickelodeon upstart, Adolph Zukor, had signed a contract to feature "Famous Players in Famous Plays," all to run the foolhardy length of four reels. The industry was aghast.

In the midst of this excitement Griffith's *The Massacre* was released. Much to Griffith's chagrin, it was overlooked. Other events of momentous meaning had caught the attention of the movie world. In some quarters the anxiety over the rising popularity of long features, the foreign productions, and Zukor's Famous Players verged on hysteria. Everyone was wondering and fearing what would happen next. Griffith himself wanted to return to New York to view the foreign "miracles," but Biograph's winter production schedule kept him in California.

Smarting with the realization that foreign producers had thrust him into the background, Griffith set to work angrily on the production of what he called his masterpiece, *Mother Love*. His impatient disregard of time and money threw Biograph into a panic, but he insisted on having his way. This new film was to be his answer to the European invaders. His personnel sensed his anxiety; they worked like demons, hoping to make the production come up to Griffith's expectations. But their industry was in vain. Like *The Massacre, Mother Love* was scarcely acknowledged in the sweeping course of events. Even before the picture was completed, word reached Griffith of a new sensation, the Italian picture *Quo Vadis*, by far the most elaborate and best motion picture made to date. The news was a shock to Griffith. Twice now, with staggering suddenness, he had been outclassed.

His ambition reinforced by intense envy, Griffith now resolutely planned a reprisal that would force the world to acknowledge his supremacy. His new production would be of such dimensions as the world had never seen. To prevent rumors of his vast undertaking from spreading to the rest of the industry, he took his company to the town of Chatsworth, miles from the Los Angeles picture center. Not unnaturally, everyone working with Griffith was highly curious. What was he up to? Never before had he taken so many shots or been so exacting; never before had there been so much activity and so little known of its nature. He was rehearsing scenes over and over again, photographing and rephotographing unceasingly. How many pictures was he making, anyhow? What had inspired his new meticulous firmness? What was he driving at? Why was he so secretive? But to all questions Griffith maintained an unbroken reserve. Bitterness and envy rankled deep in him. His only concern was to achieve a triumph so outstanding that every movie ever seen before would, in comparison, seem like trash.

Finally, in 1913, the secret production was completed—the first American four-reel picture, *Judith of Bethulia*. And once again the coincidence of events interfered with Griffith's hopes for an overwhelming success. *Judith of Bethulia* was not released until almost a year after its completion, when, ironically, Griffith had already forgotten it in an undertaking of far greater consequence.

As it turned out, *Judith of Bethulia* became Griffith's Biograph swan song. When it did appear in 1914, it proved to be an extravagant treatment of the Bible story rewritten by Thomas Bailey Aldrich, and without question the ablest example of movie construction to date. Though it appeared too late to overshadow *Quo Vadis*, it was a far better film. Even if Griffith had done nothing beyond *Judith of Bethulia*, he would still be considered a sensitive and outstanding craftsman. A comparison of the usual puny American film of 1913 with the opulent and vigorous *Judith of Bethulia* proves Griffith's stature conclusively.

The unusual form of *Judith of Bethulia*, modeled on the four-part pattern of Griffith's earlier *Pippa Passes*, presaged the form of Griffith's future masterpiece, *Intolerance*. The four movements were in counterpoint not unlike a musical composition; they reacted to each other simultaneously, and the combination produced a cumulative, powerful effect. The individual episodes had a tight internal structure. The imagery was not only lavish in detail but fresh in camera treatment and enhanced by expert cutting.

The picture was produced in a deliberate effort to surpass the splendors of the Italian spectacle *Quo Vadis*, which, in fact, Griffith himself had not seen. *Judith of Bethulia* was crammed with colorful mass scenes and tremendous sets in a style that was later to be embraced by other American directors, notably Cecil B. DeMille. Such episodes as the storming of the walls of Bethulia, the chariot charges, and the destruction of the Assyrians' camp by fire "out-spectacled" any movie yet produced in America.

Satisfied with his completed achievement, Griffith returned to New York to learn that Biograph, now in a new and modern studio in the Bronx, had contracted with the theatrical firm of Klaw and Erlanger to film their successful stage plays after the policy introduced by Zukor. During Griffith's absence a new tempo had been felt in the industry; the air was full of exciting predictions that the stage and the screen were henceforth to work together. European features had made America conscious of her own movie and stage talent and had started a craze for stage names and plays. All the Eastern companies were negotiating for stage alliances.

Griffith was now notified by Biograph that, because of his reckless extravagance with *Judith of Bethulia*, he would in the future supervise production instead of direct. Angered at his employers, bitter at being misunderstood, envious of the acclaim given the foreign pictures, Griffith decided to leave Biograph. He saw in a new company, Majestic-Reliance (Mutual), the opportunity to carry out a fresh and more elaborate artistic offensive.

After getting his bearings and studying the foreign pictures for a time, he dramatically announced his break with Biograph. The announcement, listing all his technical discoveries, appeared as a full-page advertisement in The New York Dramatic Mirror on December 31, 1913.

Asked at this time by Robert Grau, film and theatre critic, whether he thought a knowledge of stagecraft was necessary for a command of motion picture direction, Griffith replied:

No, I do not. . . . The stage is a development of centuries, based on certain fixed conditions and within prescribed limits. It is needless to point out what these are. The moving picture, although a growth of only a few years, is boundless in its scope and endless in its possibilities. . . . The conditions of the two arts being so different, it follows that the requirements are equally dissimilar. . . .

Griffith perceived what so many producers have since often forgotten: in the theatre, the audience listens first and then watches; in the movie palace the audience watches first and then listens.

"The task I'm trying to achieve," said Griffith, "is, above all, to make you see."

Griffith's apprenticeship had ended. Only five years before he had entered the industry, skeptical and even contemptuous of it; now he was America's ablest film craftsman. He stood sure of himself, eager for new achievements and a still higher reputation in the industry to which he had already made such remarkable contributions.

The Birth of a Nation:
The Technique and Its Influence
by Seymour Stern

*Mr. Stern, who has taught motion picture history and film
technique at the University of California at Los Angeles
and the University of Southern California, is the authorized
biographer of David Wark Griffith and has done voluminous
research on his life and work. This chapter appeared originally
in August, 1965, in the first part of the book, "GRIFFITH:
I—The Birth of a Nation", as published by Film Culture.*

The Birth of a Nation is of primary importance in the cinema
as a work of art in its own intrinsic and independent right.
The qualities of the film as a conscious creative work are many
and definite. Structurally, it exhibits a singular clarity, symmetry, and proportion of parts. There is a wonderful flexibility
and coherence in the pattern of the action. Episode and sequence are interwoven admirably—with a fluent naturalness
and simplicity—in a moving and breathingly natural story.

No full, let alone complete, record of its influence will
ever be known, because to trace this would make it necessary
to examine every film that has been made, the world over,
since it first appeared. But the important formative impact it
has had on the serious works of outstanding creative directors
and even of the commercial directors is already a matter of
record. These will be indicated here but will not be examined
in depth because many of the esthetic policies and technical
devices that appear in *The Birth of a Nation* received more
complex treatment and wider application in Griffith's later
films, from *Intolerance* through *America* and *Isn't Life Wonderful.* The successive volumes of GRIFFITH unfold in considerable detail a document of the application and evolution
of each of the technical devices at the point at which it attains
its maximum effectiveness in his work. Only one technical
device is so examined here—the still. It reaches the high point
of its use as an expressive device in the vast and motionless
comment it makes on "War's peace" (*subtitle*)—the motionless
shots of the Civil War dead.

The inestimable importance, also, of Griffith's special use of the subtitle, which in many instances is actually a verbal extension of visual imagery, is indicated but not detailed here. A segment of a later volume is devoted to an examination of the use of subtitles through at least 25 of Griffith's films.

Mastery of cinematic expressiveness here reaches the heights.

Creatively and technically, *The Birth of a Nation* represents a triumph, a mature fulfillment, of the primitive experiments in directing, photography, lighting, and editing, which Griffith, as director for Biograph and later for Aitken's Reliance-Majestic, had struggled for seven years to attain. And the creative influence of the film is not less than the technical.

It fathered the spectacle film. *The Birth of a Nation* was the first super-spectacle—far bigger than Griffith's own *Judith of Bethulia* (1913) and bigger than the two Italian productions, *Cabiria* and *Quo Vadis?*, which were the immediate cause and motivation of its being made.

It furnished the blueprint for the creative approach to the cinema and for the technique of the Soviet cinema in its "golden age". Eisenstein, Pudovkin, Ilya Trauberg, and other Soviet directors have testified to its influence on their work.

It introduced an important new use for the motion picture: namely, the dramatic teaching and dramatization of history. It was the forerunner, and in some cases the inspiration, technical, exploitative or otherwise, of many historical and spectacle films which followed it: e.g., in Griffith's own later work, the Babylonian and the Medieval stories of *Intolerance*; *Orphans of the Storm*; and, in an ultimate degree, *America*; James Cruze's *The Covered Wagon*; King Vidor's *The Big Parade*; Wesley Ruggles' *Cimarron*; Raoul Walsh's *The Thief of Bagdad* (Douglas Fairbanks, Sr.) and *The Big Trail*; Gance's *Napoleon*; Eisenstein's *Potemkin*, *Ten Days That Shook the World* and *Alexander Nevsky*; and Pudovkin's *Storm Over Asia*, as examples. There were also, in similar vein, Grune's *Waterloo* and King Vidor's *War and Peace*, but the influence on each of these is traceable, I believe, more completely and stylistically to *America* than to *The Birth of a Nation*.

By crystallizing the basic principles of film technique, which Griffith himself created or discovered, *The Birth of a Nation* gave birth to the film as an art.

NIGHT PHOTOGRAPHY

Night photography was used for the first time in motion pictures in *The Birth of a Nation*. Three sequences were photographed at night with the aid of magnesium flares: (1) fireballs streaking through the night-sky as the bombardment of Fort Sumter begins; (2) street-bonfires during the military ball in Cameron House, and (3) the attack and bombardment which follow the *subtitle*: "The battle goes on into the night." [*Note*: The Cameron House ball was left intact, but the firing on Fort Sumter was eliminated, for no accountable reason, from Aitken's sound-print of 1930].

NATURAL LANDSCAPES

Important, and typical of Griffith, is the use of natural landscapes as backgrounds. The battle scenes, with their vast scope, action four miles from the camera, and their panoramic scale of movement—none of these was studio-made; all were taken outdoors.

The sequence of the rape and the death of the pet sister, *Flora*, likewise was photographed amid natural backgrounds. The girl's flight through the pine forest; *Gus's* pursuit; the scramble up the cliffs—these scenes feature no interiors or artificial sets; they are actual exteriors, taken at Big Bear Lake. The sweeping vistas of countryside (the "land of Dixie"), viewed across the treetops, as the girl leaps to her death, add emotionally through their naturalness to the inflammatory horror of the action.

Natural backgrounds also are used for the creation of mood. Some examples: the pine forest in the love-scenes between *Ben* and *Elsie*, immediately following the *subtitle*: "The love strain is still heard above the land's miserere"; the flaming valley and corpse-strewn sand-washes of Georgia in Sherman's march to the sea; the silvery river, low moon, and dream-like landscape, after the *subtitle*: "The double honeymoon"; and, perhaps most striking of all, the majestic vistas of Southern country, unfolded in a group of long shots, in the sequence in which *The little Colonel* brooding "in agony of soul over the ruin and degradation of his people" (*subtitle*) gazes from a hillside overlooking the river, far across the stricken land . . . There are other examples of this category.

Finally, the stupendous sequences of The Ride of the Klansmen were photographed, as already mentioned, [in a section entitled *Production*] in the hills and fields, and on the rivers and country roads, of Los Angeles, Orange and Ventura counties.

Far more extensive use by Griffith of the natural landscape either as background or as an active element of the drama itself came later in *Hearts of the World, The Greatest Question, Way Down East, The Idol Dancer, A Romance of Happy Valley, The White Rose, America* and other of his films. Of these, *Way Down East* (1920) offers perhaps the most instructive and certainly the most spectacular example in films of how a natural landscape can not only dominate but even shape story and action.

The picturization of old-time rural America, however, which Griffith achieved in a degree outclassing that of all other directors undoubtedly reaches its apogee in the melancholy pastoral landscapes of *The Greatest Question* (1919).

THE STILL

Here as mentioned the still-shot, or still, assumes its definitive usage in the motion picture. Following the *subtitle*: "War's peace", Griffith cuts to still-shots of trenches, piled with dead. The death-imagery is held for measured seconds, like a musical pause, as though the entire film had come to a dead stop, and reveals in silent judgment exactly what the subtitle states.

We of course recall that Griffith had used the still, and with telling effect, as early as 1909, in *A Corner in Wheat*, a Biograph "short" based on Frank Norris' muckraking novel, "The Pit". As the wheat-capitalist corners the market, the price of flour rises and the scene suddenly cuts to a line of poor people waiting to buy bread at a bakery. Then, as the storekeeper changes the price-sign in front of the cash register and announces the inflation, the line of people "freezes": the people, unable to meet the higher cost, stand as though struck dead. They suddenly look like corpses. By stop-action the moving image is changed into a still, and the succeeding cut back to the wheat-capitalist, gratified by the new wealth his greed has won for him on the stock market, fulfills the imagery of effect and cause.

Griffith with this scene established himself, one year after he had started directing films, as a wizard. For the device was not only esthetically and technically sophisticated: it was twenty years ahead of its time. And the most significant aspect of it is the fact that it was not used to create an "effect" or to project a clever exhibition or trick, but *to express an idea.* Twenty years later, the Soviet director Alexander Dovzhenko, in his Ukrainian masterpiece *Arsenal* (1930), duplicated both Griffith's device and the idea it was invented to express, when he showed a mass of people on a breadline, "freezing" by stop-action into a still, in just the same type of situation caused by capitalistic manipulation of the stock market. Both scenes, twenty years apart, are classic examples of the creative-expressive use of the still for projecting ideas rather than stories; both are filmic definitions of, and studies in, cause and effect; both are "portraits" of capitalism in practice—the rapacity of Profit.

Griffith's use of the still as a dramatic and ideological image-symbol bore still further fruit, from the joint parentage of *A Corner in Wheat* and *The Birth of a Nation.* This can be seen in the opening sequence of *Arsenal* (without, however, stop-motion, since there was no movement, anyway)—the unburied corpses, the broken guns, the cadavers and mangled horses' legs of a deserted battlefield: a motionless sum-image of devastation. It can be seen, again, in the opening sequence to Eisenstein's *Old and New.* Like so much else of power and value in the golden age of the Soviet film, this, too, stems from *The Birth of a Nation.*

THE IRIS

It was Griffith who conceived the idea of having the camera "open up" and "close down" on a scene in the same manner as the eye. It was Bitzer who wrestled with the problem of how to obtain this effect either with the camera directly or with the aid of auxiliary devices. The iris became famous here for the first time among millions of spectators, who did not know it by name, but knew it by sight from its stunningly dramatic use as the opening shot of Sherman's invasion of Georgia, immediately following the *subtitle*: "While the women and children weep, a great conqueror marches to the sea."

The screen is dark. A combination fade-in and iris opens it to view. A woman and her children, who cluster about her and clutch onto her skirt, are seen in the left foreground, slightly below camera. They look as though they had fallen exhausted at our feet. They are huddled amid the ashes of what may have been a shack or house; the charred frame, with cross-beam, of a window is beside them—the embers of war. Now, slowly, the camera "pans" from left to right, revealing that the group is on a hilltop, and lets us see, at last, the savage drama from which the refugees had fled: far below, in a deep, sandy valley, marches Sherman's army, burning and shooting its way through Georgia.

First, the effect; then, the concealed cause. The entire action and its historic horror are communicated in a single shot which fades-in on a dark screen and ends in a camera-"pan" that reveals the startling sight of what the iris had hidden.

TINTING

Tinting for either dramatic or psychological effect was used extensively in *The Birth of a Nation*. A classic example is the sequence of the death of the two youngest sons of the Southern (*Cameron*) and Northern (*Stoneman*) families, at the second battle of Bull Run. Another, and brilliant, example (in more than one sense) is the vista of the action which in the original prints was said to be flashes of Cold Harbor and Antietam that cut directly (without narrative connection) into the final offensive at Petersburg. The entire bloc of separate sequences forming this episode is introduced by the *subtitle*: "The battle goes on into the night", and is followed by the night-photography action, ending in flare-lighted carnage. But the best example in the film is the burning of Atlanta, which in the prints made prior to 1930 appears in flaming-red tint. The crowds of fleeing citizens are limned in black against the red, like the creatures of a nightmare. When they are seen the next morning, streaming by the thousands up distant hillsides, the red tinting is gone, and the sharp black-and-white gives the impression of a harsh and bitter dawn.

The tinting which became most widely identified with Griffith, however, was that of the pastoral and love scenes— a rich twilight-blue with a soft base and edge of sun-yellow.

MOVEMENT

The study of usages of movement and movement-forms on the screen could be almost completed from an examination of this one film.

63

The moving camera is used in both parts: e.g., Part One—camera preceding *The little Colonel*, as he charges down the road at the head of his troops; Part Two—camera preceding the horde of Klansmen during the climax of The Ride.

"Panning" shots are familiar from the opening shot of Sherman's march and the "panning" camera over the battlefield at Petersburg. A brief example also occurs near the beginning of the story proper, when the camera "pans" down to a kitten and two puppies playing in the *Cameron* household (after the humorous *subtitle*, "Hostilities").

Of far greater importance, however, and more difficult to copy or duplicate, are the multiple movement-forms and counter-movements within the single frame: for example, the street massacre in Piedmont during the guerrilla attack; the Confederate charge at Petersburg, and the scenes of the gathering of the Clans immediately prior to The Ride.

One of the classic examples in all cinema of the conjoining of two complementary but opposite movements, seen at a tangent to each other, occurs in the sequence of the pursuit of *Gus*, directly before his capture. *Gus*, after shooting a white man (*Jeff*) in the back, dashes out of *"White-arm" Joe's* gin-mill and flees for his life to a nearby field or corral. White townsmen see him and give chase, *Gus* leaps on a horse and spurs it. The townsmen run from right to left toward the field after him and take aim.

At this instant the film cuts to *Ben Cameron* and a friend hurrying down a path toward camera past a small tiger-bush. The scene is some distance from the field and lasts but an instant. The two men suddenly hear distant shooting and begin running toward and below camera on the cut.

The business of cutting into their movement down-screen from the previous movement of the townsmen in a different direction (right to left) is accomplished in a flash. The effect is to create a sense of unleashed activity from all directions in the pursuit of the Negro and to step up the tempo of imminent violence.

As a policy combining agitative dynamics with suspenseful drama, Griffith's direction of movements in this scene achieves ultimate dramatic power and cinematic beauty in the climactic moments of the incident. The white townsmen, still running, fire wildly at *Gus* and miss him each time. Then one of them

64

pauses, holds his gun at a steady level, takes cool and careful aim, fires. The bullet kills the horse. The horse buckles, sinks to its knees. *Gus* leaps to the ground and starts running. On the cut, the townsmen and the other two men, *Cameron* and his friend, burst simultaneously into the scene from opposite directions and swarm into the field. *Gus* is trapped. As he runs blindly toward them, in a last futile attempt to escape, the pursuers close in on him with lightning speed, seize him by the collar and drag him off. The counterpointed whirlwind movements are at rest. The sequence quickly fades out and cuts directly to *Gus's* trial by the Klan.

CLOSE-UPS

The close-up approaches full-screen dimension in *The Birth of a Nation*, although the first close-ups actually filling the total screen-area, coming into camera, do not appear until *Broken Blossoms* (1919). But the close-up becomes both a dramatic action and a tactical weapon here. Examples: the guard's eye at the peephole in the door at *Lynch's* headquarters; the huge close-up of *Gus*, framed in claw-like white branches of dead bramble, as he watches *Flora* playing with a squirrel from his hiding-place in the underbrush. The most impressive and technically advanced close-up of this type, however, no longer appears in the regular release-prints: it was an enormous close-up of *Gus's* face during the deleted scenes of the castration, with side-lighting that accented the whites of the eyes, rolling in agony, and the mouth, belching blood. (For a further account of this action, see "The Storm Over Censorship", in Part II of GRIFFITH).

Close-ups of *Lydia Brown* (*Stoneman's* sex-healthy mulatto housekeeper), *Stoneman, Elsie Stoneman, Flora Cameron, The little Colonel*, Lincoln, Booth, *Jeff*, "*White-arm*" *Joe*, and *Gus*, attain an effect of portraiture.

Griffith also uses the close-up to emphasize a single detail which summarizes a multiplicity: e.g., the close-up of parched corn (kernels in a pan) as the symbol of dwindling food rations for the retreating Confederate armies.

Further use of the close-up is seen in the reproduction of documents, letters, newspapers, and warnings from the Klan.

CAMEOS, VIGNETTES

From Griffith came the cameo and the vignette. The vignette,

65

in particular, distinguishes his films from those of his American contemporaries. French directors of the silent-film era used it effectively, however. The other American directors for self-evident reasons failed to appreciate the beauty of the form. The vignette occurs times without number through Griffith's films. It is recorded here only in passing because of more extended treatment in later volumes.

A good example of the cameo-profile, which combines a medium close-up or close-up of either face or object in a form of vignette and against a blurred background, is the shot of *Margaret Cameron* (Miriam Cooper) in the garden with her lover, *Phil Stoneman* (Elmer Clifton). *Subtitle.* "Bitter memories will not allow the poor bruised heart of the South to forget." As *Phil* approaches good-humoredly through the foliage and affectionately tries to engage her in conversation, *Margaret* draws away and stares stonily ahead. The profile close-up of her at this point sets off her face in high relief from the blurred background of foliage: the effect is that of a face on a cameo.

The same scene also includes a good example of the vignette: as *Margaret* moves to another part of the garden, she sees in her imagination the death of her second brother, *Wade* (André Beranger), killed during the bombardment of Atlanta. A "balloon" vignette of *Wade* appears, as he lies prostrate on the earth near a fence, refugees streaming past him, and closes his eyes in death. [*Note*: in the prints from 1915 through 1921, the vignetted "balloon," similar to the "dream-image" later used in German silent-films, appeared in the upper left-hand corner of the screen, while *Margaret's* embittered face appears in close-up to the right. The double printing of the two shots on one frame was successful but, unfortunately, not permanent. As the years passed, the vignetted "balloon" began to fade before it was actually due to fade out, and after 1921 Griffith had the shot of *Margaret's* face, alone, reprinted. Then a vignetted close-up of *Wade's*, as in the "balloon", was intercut as a separate shot—the way it appears today. As the vignette fades off, the continuity cuts back to *Margaret*].

LAP DISSOLVE

The lap dissolve (dissolving one image into another instead of direct cutting) was introduced to the screen by the pioneer French director Georges Méliès purely as a device and as a trick effect. Griffith here used it for a dramatic purpose: namely, to bring an historical facsimile to life. It is seen in one of its finest applications in the opening scene of the House of Representatives in the State House, Columbia, South Carolina, 1868. The chambers and galleries are shown, empty. A *subtitle* explains: "An historical facsimile of the actual photographed scene". The legislators and the gallery-visitors now dissolve into their seats and standing positions, respectively; the whole scene "comes to life". This meaningful, purposeful use of the dissolve is one of the best examples on record.

CAMERA ANGLES

There are a few camera angles but Griffith did not develop the form until *Intolerance*. High-angle shots of the battlefields and of landscapes are not camera angles in the sharply defined sense in which we understand the term. The nearest approach to one is the high-angle shot, taken from a moving camera, of *The little Colonel* leading his troops down the road in a charge. This shot has more angular definition than any other of its kind in the film. There are several low-*placement* rather than low-*angle* shots of the onrushing Klan, and contrary to popular misconception, there are no close-ups (only close shots) of the hoofs of the Klansmen's horses.

LONG SHOTS

The dominant scheme of the camera placements throughout the film is the abundant use of long shots. The long shot is here seen to advantage and is developed to a point of perfection. The immense perspectives of the battlefields and of the far-flung line of Klansmen during the height of The Ride are more than long shots, more, even, than perspective shots: they are *vistas*. This type of *panoramic* imagery was introduced to the screen in *The Birth of a Nation*.

COSTUMES

The Birth of a Nation, in addition to being an historical epic, is also a costume-spectacle.

The Prologue features costumes of colonial America.

Part One features (1) the manner of dress of the Southern small-plantation middle-class before and through the Civil War, and during Reconstruction; (2) in the White House scenes of Lincoln, the official dress and headgear of foreign diplomats and military attaches (some of them helmeted); and (3) the uniforms of both the Confederate and the Union armies.

Part Two has no colonial and no foreign costumes but introduces a new one not seen in Part One—the white-and-scarlet robed-and-hooded regalia of the Ku Klux Klan and of the Klan's horses. Two distinguishing features of the Klan's awesome uniform are the Cross of St. Andrew, embroidered on the breasts of the robes of both rider and horse, and the eighteen-inch spike rising from the center of the Klansman's helmet.

The Epilogue prophesies the coming of the "Prince of Peace" (*subtitle*) and shows throngs of people in flowing robes and mantles that have often, and for unaccountable reasons, been referred to as "Korean" and "Roman". The togas worn by many of the crowds may account for the Roman reference, though the style is nondescript, and the Korean reference is inexplicable.

The regalia of the Ku Klux Klan in Griffith's film held the greatest fascination and appeal for Eisenstein and other directors.

The Teutonic knights in Eisenstein's *Alexander Nevsky* are garbed in a regalia so suggestive of the Klan's that in many of the shots the knights look like Klansmen. They too wear large embroidered crosses, in keeping with a similar Christian mission, but there are no spikes stemming from the helmets.

Raoul Walsh, who plays John Wilkes Booth in *The Birth of a Nation*, directed Douglas Fairbanks, Sr., in the original version of *The Thief of Bagdad* (1924). He patterned the costumes of the magic army, which Fairbanks conjures into being through explosive powder-balls of mysterious power, after the white-and-scarlet garments of the Klansmen—and with spikes rising from the helmets.

However, we are now ready to consider a deeper and more far-reaching influence of the Klan regalia on the esthetic development of the screen.

LINEAR DOMINANTS

Besides night photography, *The Birth of a Nation* brought another "first" to the screen, along esthetic and pictorial rather than technical lines.

The costume-design of Griffith's Klan became the basis for something more than a school of costuming. It introduced to the screen the use of *line* as a dominant graphic element in the composition of the image. The line may be solid or it may consist of a myriad of individual units, such as the Klansmen, but in sequences of spectacle or vast scope, it becomes, in effect, the axis of the image, and thus dominates the image in its entirety.

The principle here is the same as that of other dominants, such as mass or light, but for the first time in film history, because of the linear nature of The Ride of the Klansmen, line became the dominant.

The consequences of this esthetic, pictorial innovation can hardly be overstated. Only a glance is needed to trace the evolution of the startling new visual motif through some of its radiant re-emergences in other films.

The linear dominant first appears on the screen in the climactic vista-image of The Ride of the Klansmen. The line of riders is viewed from a field, seemingly "stretched out" for miles along a country road. Other shots of the Klansmen are taken "head-on"—that is, with the camera photographing the first row of riders and from this vantage looking "up" the road at the assemblage as far as can be seen. But the dominant of such shots is the mass.

The dominant of the penultimate shot, on the other hand, is the line, which necessarily has to be filmed from either a horizontal placement (as in photographing a train crossing a landscape from left to right or right to left) or from a sufficiently diagonal angle to avoid emphasizing the mass and instead show it as a thin straight line in motion. The diagonal placement is the one used in this famous revolutionary shot. The impression created is that of the line of Klansmen traveling "out of" the interior depths of the landscape on a cubical axis.

Griffith himself again used line as the dominant in the shot of a railroad train speeding across an American landscape in the climax to the Modern Story of *Intolerance*, but here the train is shown crossing the screen (from right to left) on a horizontal axis.

Griffith, it should be added, was deeply influenced by the topographic pattern of Southern California, which has avenues, boulevards, highways, and roads, especially those running north and south, that unfold in vast perspectives of twenty to fifty miles without a curve or linear variation—a study in straight lines and timeless space.

The first adoption, and without adaptation, of the new motif in a non-Griffith film was the line of covered wagons, "stretched out" across the prairies, in James Cruze's spectacle, *The Covered Wagon* (1923). Here not only the pictorial scheme of The Ride of the Klansmen but the color motif—white—also bore fruit. Cruze's wagon-train is photographed from a diagonal placement, and the endless line of prairie-schooners appears to be coming "out of" the engulfing prairie as the Klansmen come "out of" the invisible background of land and forest, on a cubical axis. Cruze, whose cameraman was Karl Brown, one of the cameramen on *Intolerance* and a product of Bitzer, also has shots of the wagon-train on a straight horizontal axis, moving from right to left.

Two further adoptions of the motif appeared on the screens in 1924. Chaplin's *The Gold Rush* exploited the linear dominant very spectacularly in the scenes of long lines of prospectors winding like thousands of ants up the snow-banked slopes of the Klondike. And Walsh's *The Thief of Bagdad* patterned not only the costumes, as mentioned, of the magic army, but the linear treatment as well on the penultimate image of The Ride of the Klansmen.

The following year, 1925, King Vidor adopted the basic visual patterns of The Ride in spectacular scenes of the big parade of troop-trucks moving across France to the front. But Vidor made an interesting adaptation. In *The Birth of a Nation*, The Ride of the Klansmen follows a straight line, true as an arrow, except in a few shots in which the first rows of onrushing Klansmen are seen rounding a bend in the road; in *The Big Parade*, on the other hand, Vidor at first used the straight line but later introduced a series of circular lines, when the big parade snakes its way across the distant landscape of northern France. This was the first departure from the straight-line pattern of *The Birth of a Nation*.

The next emergence of the linear dominant does not occur in an important form until 1935, ten years after *The Big Parade*. Then, unexpectedly, the motif appears, full-blown, of all places, in a cartoon. This was *The Parrotville Fire Depart-*

70

ment—a Van Beuren Color Cartoon, one of a series named *Rainbow Parade*. It is a visual treasure, a rewarding study in the evolution of formal patterns on the screen. It consists of four colors—red, blue, black, and white, and is remarkable for its many superb designs, each of them a masterpiece of symmetrical conflicting movements. The parrot-firefighters turn their hose on the flames. The linear shafts of high-pressure water cause gigantic tongues of flame to break up into hundreds of little flames or flamelets. These as if by magic instantly appear with miniature legs attached to their bodies, and start dancing. Now the symmetrical designs of regimented masses of dancing flamelets give chase to the firefighters. As a spectacle, the complex mass of conflicting designs ranks among the finest compositional achievements of the American screen. The ever-growing masses of flamelets, like the multiplying laboratory of Dukas' "The Sorcerer's Apprentice", seem to devour infinity. As they increase to the screen horizon, they chase the firefighters down the street, running after them with incredible speed, the speed of fantasy. At this point, with almost paralyzing suddenness, the swift, whirling, wild motion of the oncoming panorama of flamelets magnetizes itself into virtually the identical line of motion that dominates the climactic image of The Ride of the Klansmen! As linear dominants go, this one is beautiful, and not the least measure of its fascination is the homogeneous preservation of its basic pattern of symmetrical whirling motion when the myriad-mass of designs changes qualitatively into a line. If an abstract were made of the two movement-lines—the one from *The Birth of a Nation*, the other from this installment of the *Rainbow Parade*, it would be found that both had been fashioned from the same conception of the use of line as dominant.

Alexander Nevsky reflects the influence of Griffith's film, besides the costumes, in the same use of line as dominant, but Eisenstein's line is adapted to a horizontal axis, with the knights placed across the horizon from screen-border to screen-border. The dominant of line in *Alexander Nevsky* quickly changes, moreover, to dominant of mass.

SUBTITLES

Through the decades Griffith has been persistently criticized for the alleged "sentimentality" of his subtitles. The criticism would have been justified if it had applied to a few subtitles or captions which by almost any standard would no doubt be correctly adjudged as sentimental in thought or wording, or both. But as the records of film criticism show, the complaints have invariably been of a general or sweeping nature, so phrased as to create among the lay readers an impression that sentimentality applies to all of the captions. In fact, it characterizes only a few.

His subtitles, in general, separate and apart from their literary qualities, are of the utmost technical and dramatic importance. The style of phrasing is traceable to the style of writing in his early, unpublished plays (e.g., "A Fool and a Girl", "War", and the others). The style is later reflected in articles and statements. It is his style, no one else's, and is well within the reach of illustrative analysis.

There was a school of thought during silent-film days which held to the doctrine that a true film should have no captions whatever and should consist only of the photographed images. Murnau's *The Last Laugh* (1924) was widely hailed as an example, on a high plane of directorial artistry, of this principle. But a word, printed or written, is also an image—a "picture" in letters. And in the case of certain of Griffith's subtitles, the words themselves conjure up imagery as either a dramatic additive or a thematic identification to the photographed image.

They identify characters in the story, and establish their relationships before the main action begins.

Sometimes, they serve to indicate place-changes or time-lapses, or other transitions.

Sometimes, they herald in broad strokes an action about to be unreeled, giving point in advance to its fundamental significance as an argument for the theme or as a link in the story.

Other times, again, a subtitle of vivid and pithy wording may follow an action and summarize its bearing on entire sequences of events, both past and to come, or its significance in relation to the film itself or to actuality. There are many subtitles in many of Griffith's films that highlight a given segment of action in the manner of a social comment.

The outstanding characteristic, however, of the subtitles written by Griffith, which are not either time or place transitions, or dialogue, is their quality of *verbalized imagery*.

Consider a few such subtitles from *The Birth of a Nation*:

1. In the Southland. Piedmont, South Carolina, the home of the Camerons, where life runs in a quaintly way that is to be no more. [*Note*: in some prints, "quaintly quiet way"].

The words, "quaintly way", foreshadow before we even see it a way of life, its pace, its rhythm, its social grace. All the scenes in the reels that follow are linked, until the beginning of the Civil War, by, to, and with the overtonal imagery of the words, "quaintly way".

2. The gathering storm. The power of the sovereign states threatened by the new administration.

"The gathering storm" is a complex of images, good for hundreds of feet of scenes that burst like a volcano from the vortex of the dramatically conjuring words. Winston Churchill was so much impressed with this subtitle, that he used "the gathering storm" for the title of one of his volumes of war memoirs (published in 1948).

3. The thunder of the impending conflict echoes throughout the land.

"Thunder", "impending conflict", and "echoes", individually and collectively, are sound-images and images dark with foreboding. The idea of looming disaster impregnates the spectator at least 500 feet before the first scenes of military conflict appear on the screen. The scenes which immediately follow the subtitle trace the growing political conflict that culminates in civil war.

4. While youth dances the night away, childhood and old age slumber.

Personification in reverse. "Youth" here refers both to the older sister, *Margaret Cameron* (Miriam Cooper), and the entire younger set, attending the military ball in the Cameron Hall living-room. "Childhood" refers to *Flora, the pet sister*, as a child (Violet Wilkey). "Old age" refers to the elder *Cameron* (Spottiswoode Aitken). Both *Flora* and her father are asleep in an adjoining bedroom. As in so many other scenes and subtitles, here, too, Griffith applies a universal term to an individual example and associates the example with the experience, universal in fact.

> 5. While the women and children weep
>   a great conqueror marches
>   to the sea.

The imagery projected in this one is self-evident and needs no elucidation. It anticipates the scene that follows, which thrillingly transcends the grandeur and the grimness of the words. [*Note*: this subtitle has appeared in some prints in a variant form—without the word "the" between "While" and "women". There is no comma on the screen after "weep"; the space after "weep" replaces the comma, and "a great conqueror marches to the sea" appears on separate lines].

> 6. The torch of war against the breast of Atlanta.
>   The bombardment and flight.

This is one of the great captions of the motion picture—a subtitle-image that transforms a flat statement into a powerful metaphor.

It is also an example of a style which Griffith introduced in *The Birth of a Nation*: that is, a main-line subtitle in standard type, followed by an appended or subsidiary subtitle in smaller type, as above.

> 7. The mortars
> 8. The masked batteries
> 9. The field artillery

Each of these three separate, identifying subtitles is good for the entire bloc of images that follows it.

> 10. In the red lane of death others take their places and
>   the battle goes on into the night.

This subtitle is a vivid, rich compound of both apocalyptic and realistic reference. "Night", "battle", and "red lane of death" are quintessential word-elements that form a Poesque imagery of horror and annihilation. "The red lane of death" in itself suggests imagery of separate theme and subject, quite apart from its application to this specific carnage. Only in *Intolerance* and in *The Idol Dancer* did Griffith again attain the same degree and quality of mixture of salient detail with universal metaphor.

> 11. The last gray days of the Confederacy. On the battle
>   lines before Petersburg. Parched corn their only ration.

In this one, the word "gray" evokes the image. It is the keyword that transforms the description from flat statement to drama. "Parched corn" and "battle lines" are additives to "gray": they are among the specific conditions to which "gray" refers, they complete an image of desolation and despair. Robert Selph Henry, in his book, "The Story of the Confederacy" (1956), entitles the final chapter: "The Last Desperate Days." But Griffith's "gray" is better: it includes "desperate" and more—the color of doom and the shadow of imminent defeat for a lost cause. The defeat is foreshadowed here, without being affirmed, by combining "gray" with "last".

12. War's peace

This is one of the great subtitles of the screen. It is both a statement of fact (as "war's end" would be) and a social comment (as "war's end" would not be). It both foreshadows and summarizes the ensuing bloc of shots—Civil War trenches piled with the dead.

13. "And then when the terrible days were over and the healing time of peace was at hand" . . . came the fated night of April 14, 1865.

The "healing time of peace", with "peace" and "healing" in apposition to each other, signals a change in both the mood and the tempo of the film. Since the action which follows this subtitle takes place in Washington, D.C., the scenes of the interim period in the South, after the Civil War but before Reconstruction, are unavoidably deferred. The "healing time of peace" covers the transition for history and scenario alike in advance of the visual appearance of the "healing time" and thus makes its introduction later unnecessary.

14. The love strain is still heard above the land's miserere.

The word "miserere" reflects and summarizes, both retroactively and ahead, the innumerable scenes of the terror and trouble into which the South has been plunged.

15. Sowing the wind.

A subtitle-image that presages a multitude of scenes that follow, depicting *Stoneman's* grip on the South, *Lynch's* rise to power, and the passage of an intermarriage law by the Black legislature of South Carolina.

16. The new rebellion of the South.

Another subtitle-image which synthesizes verbally whole sequences that follow of the rise of the Ku Klux Klan and its terroristic counter-attacks. Another subtitle, reels later, extends the same image in the words, "the new revolution".

These examples will serve our purpose here of illustrating the highly effective uses to which Griffith put the more significant of his subtitles. The wording is brief; the imagery, graphic and simple. And the style, though pithy and vivid, is un-self-conscious. None of the verbal imagery has been created for the sake of creating imagery in words. All of it relates, concretely and realistically, to the scenes that precede or follow.

Griffith instituted other new uses for the subtitle in this film. Here for the first time footnotes appear to the main part of the subtitle, bearing annotation and documentation: as, in the citations from Nicolay and Hay's "Lincoln: A Biography"; and again, in references to facsimiles or replicas of historic scenes and sites. On the other hand, citations or quotations from Woodrow Wilson and Judge Tourgee on the Reconstruction Period and the Ku Klux Klan appear as full-length subtitles (in the original, undeleted prints), at considerable length.

He was fond of the paragraph-symbol as a form of visual emphasis for captions of salient point or reference, or of sudden dramatic impact or humorous interplay (e.g.: "¶Hostilities"), although rarely for the footnotes.

Subtitles of the original, undeleted prints of *The Birth of a Nation* totalled to more than 7,000 words—the largest amount of letterpress in any film ever made, except *Intolerance.*

We return later, in a broader volume, to a more comprehensive study of Griffith's subtitles and subtitle-techniques, embracing the more illustrative ones from 25 of the other films.

THE CLIMAX

The Ride of the Klansmen is the greatest climax in all the history of the theatre.

As expected at the time, he extended the editorial methods, policies, principles, and techniques introduced here into his later works. A full examination of the basic conception of Climax, as evolved by Griffith, appears after the study of *America*, in a separate segment entitled, "The Philosophy of Climax".

The essence of his policy is to build cumulative dramatic and pictorial power in geometric progression.

The gathering of the Klansmen foreshadows The Ride itself. It begins, suddenly, with the appearance of two Night Hawks at a lonely crossroads near a barn. There is no introduction of the two stationary, ghoul-like figures, until the shot is intercut with a *subtitle*, "Summoning the Clans", which establishes the action and the sequences flowing out of it. One of the figures puts a reed-whistle to his lips and blows a signal on it. As this brief but ominous scene follows directly upon a sequence of terror and rioting in Piedmont, the effect is electric, and the anticipation of the ride to come approaches the satanic in thrill and fury.

The two Night Hawks ride with lightning-speed through the Southern countryside, through forest and stream. In successive shots, mounted Klansmen appear as though from space itself, and add their numbers to the two. At one point the Night Hawks, plunging and rearing on their wonderfully trained steeds, wheel about, brandishing the Fiery Cross; then disappear, leaving the scene empty. For a moment, there is only a landscape on the screen, but they suddenly return from offscreen with a squadron of other Klansmen. Other scenes in kind follow. Soon the original two are a numerous band.

More intercutting, back to the saturnalia in Piedmont, brings fresh impact to the next shots of the steadily massing Klansmen.

Now the original groups form a mass.

When the Klans, as a *subtitle* advises, are "fully assembled", a full-screen shot of an immense field, filled with the white-and-scarlet host, appears like a pictorial outburst upon the screen: it is both the dramatic and the visual climax to all the flashes, glimpses, and smaller scenes of organizational operations that preceded it. An image of apocalyptic splendor, as a spectacle it surpasses the battle scenes. And as The Ride itself begins, a new series of dramatic crises is set in motion, but on a larger scale, and with a still more powerful and thunderous climax ahead.

Vachel Lindsay, in his book, "The Art of the Moving Picture", describes The Ride of the Klansmen as the spectacle of an "Anglo-Saxon Niagara", pouring down the road. Simultaneously, assaults on white girls and the rising reign of Negro-carpetbagger terror in Piedmont are intercut; and, in addition, supplementing this material are scenes of the plight of a party of white refugees in a little cabin in the marshes, belonging to two Union veterans and now besieged by Negro militiamen. Thus Griffith builds a structure from which he can engineer three-way cutting at will and unleash the maximum emotional potential from each of the three separate but converging dramas. The pattern of suspense suggests a spiralling series of interlocking triangles, mounting toward a common apex—an "extraordinary composition" of film technique and editing.

The Klan rounds the final bend in the road and masses before the church at the end of the main street. Then, re-grouping, it opens fire and charges into a pitched battle with Negro troops in the town of Piedmont. After bloodshed and casualties on both sides, the Klan triumphs and restores white power. So great, however, is the torrent of emotion unleashed by The Ride, that Griffith, a supreme dramatist, launches a "run-off", or double climax; that is, he cuts to the besieged party in the distant cabin and has the Klan reassemble for a second ride, more urgent than the first, because it is timed to a Negro break-through at the cabin.

The policy of organizing a climax is here seen at its maximum effectiveness. It starts with a low number and multiplies, geometrically, into a new quantitative class. This has proved thus far on the screen the most potent way to touch off emotional explosions in audiences. Of course, other ingredients enter into the formula and form the progression—it is not all geometry, filmic or otherwise, or the results would be flat. But the other elements we shall examine later, together with the ultimate ones, in "The Philosophy of Climax".

The influence of the creation of Climax here, on Eisenstein in *Alexander Nevsky,* and earlier, and more so, on Pudovkin in *Storm Over Asia,* is film history. It was particularly strong on Pudovkin. His horde of Mongolian pony-riders suddenly appears as if by magic (a la *The Thief of Bagdad*) in the steppes of central Asia and drives out the foreign imperialists. But the ride of the Mongolians, though it has thrust, lacks force as a climax for two reasons: (1) The build-up is inadequate—the ride begins with the Mongolian revolutionary hero alone, but the steppes fill fast, too fast, with hundreds of other riders, who dissolve into the scene, in keeping with its symbolic-prophetic character; consequently, though the action is momentarily thrilling, it is not really climactic, because there is almost no cumulative effect; it is all accomplished, and is over, within seconds, and without tension. Pudovkin's climax, splendid as it is, lacks the force, the volume, the complex dynamics of Griffith's. (2) The ride of the Mongolians is not an historic event or even a legend of something that happened "once upon a time" but an imaginary prophecy of a future possibility, "things to come". As such it has the quality of fantasy, which detracts psychologically from the sense of reality in what is an otherwise bitterly realistic story.

Griffith's grand climax is greater, because its unfolding has been prepared well in advance through a mounting series of cumulative dramatic crises, out of which the climax itself flows logically and organically, like a dam-burst.

Author's Note: One technique, in particular, of major importance, which Griffith introduced in *The Birth of a Nation*, was not included in this chapter. This was the editing of certain blocs of imagery to coincide with, and thus intensify, the rhythm and emotional build-up of certain passages of classical music, planned as symphonic orchestration for these scenes—as, the repetition of climactic shots of the burning of Atlanta with the parallel repetition of climactic motifs from Grieg's "In the Hall of the Mountain King", selected as the musical accompaniment to this episode. An analysis of this technical innovation and tour de force may be found in the second chapter on "The Film's Score", in GRIFFITH: I—*The Birth of a Nation*, Part I", "Film Culture" edition of 1965.

D. W. Griffith: Social Crusader
by Richard Watts, Jr.

*Mr. Watts is drama editor of The New York Post. He wrote this
for the November 1936 issue of The New Theatre.*

David Wark Griffith is not only the father of every technical device known to cinema direction, but is also the pioneer
in the conception of the screen as a medium for social ideas.
It is not that he was invariably the inventor of these directorial
methods. For example, he is set down in film history as the
introducer of the close-ups, but the classic pre-Griffith photoplay, *The Great Train Robbery*, closes with a scene in which
a bandit shown from the waist up aims his pistol at the audience and fires. It is distinctly a close-up and it is not the work
of Griffith. Nevertheless he is the man who was responsible
for the use of that celebrated device as a method for dramatizing an emotion and concentrating on the reaction of a
character to a situation. In a word he took the close-up, which
had been used merely as a new way of photographing a scene,
and gave it some psychological point.

In the same way, you are likely to find that every other
method of camera manipulation now employed in Hollywood
or any other photoplay manufacturing center was either devised or was developed along its proper dramatic channels by
D. W. Griffith. That, however, is well known and is generally
recognized by reasonably careful followers of the cinema. His
status as a social crusader, however, is certainly at least
equally important and it has not been as frequently con-
templated.

The Griffith crusades have been many and they have been
of varying degrees of intellectual value. On the whole, I should
say that the trouble with them has been that they were based
on a sympathetic and easily aroused emotionalism that had
much to do with sentimentality and not always a great deal
with any hard-headed sense of reality. In a word it was a kind
heart, rather than a keen intelligence, that guided him in his
soul-searching among ideas. But whatever the validity of his
ideas he has always been on the side of a cause that he has
regarded with burning-eyed zealousness as a cause of justice.

80

He has never been smart or clever or brittle. Always he has been in earnest and he has proved that a frank earnestness of viewpoint can be of tremendous dramatic effectiveness. He is the father of many things in the cinema and not the least of them is this conception of the screen as the vehicle for a viewpoint.

His most famous film is, of course, *The Birth of a Nation*, and even after all of these years it remains a powerful and impressive photoplay. The scene of the little Colonel's return to his ruined home remains to this day touching and poignant, one of the great episodes among motion picture episodes. His hysterical picture of the horrors of reconstruction and his ecstatic cheering for the glories of the Ku Klux Klan unfortunately reveal the extent to which his emotionalism could carry him, but there is no disputing the enormous, if decidedly over-wrought, dramatic effectiveness of this section of the work. As a completely partisan account of a particularly ugly chapter in American history, *The Birth of a Nation* still possesses a certain stunning power. But its cruel unfairness to the Negro is an inescapable blot upon it.

Being an essentially fair, if hysterical man, Griffith was not altogether oblivious to that fact, and it worried him. I do not think it is fair to say that he was merely worried because he felt that he had alienated an entire national group of paying filmgoers. What he did was to include in a happily forgotten war picture called *Hearts of the World*, a scene in which a dying Negro soldier cried for his mother and a white comrade in arms kissed him as he perished. It was a shamelessly senti-mental scene—Griffith has always loved the shamelessly senti-mental—and it was a pretty shoddy and futile effort to make up for what he had done in *The Birth of a Nation*. In all of its intellectual implications it is far from being to Griffith's credit, and to this extent it is indefensible. For a man to believe that such a tear-jerking and rather patronizing scene should make up for an insult to a race is not a vast tribute to his intellect. My only point is that it was a sincere and honest gesture and had no box office purposes behind it. The proof of that is not a tribute to the American public of those days, for indignant audiences snarled at the scene and at the director as a traducer of racial purity.

The Birth of a Nation was a great financial success and

Intolerance was not, but I still think that *Intolerance* remains the greatest monument to the directorial genius of D. W. Griffith. In it the director told four parallel stories at once; one taking place in Babylon at the time of the fall, a second in Palestine during the crucifixion of Christ, a third in Paris during the St Bartholomew's Day massacre and the fourth in modern America. Instead of narrating these episodes one after another Griffith presented them all at once, leaping from one century to another from scene to scene, until all of the climaxes arrived at one time and you were kept busy darting between an automobile racing to Sing Sing with a reprieve from the governor and the escape of a Huguenot girl from the sword of the Guises. It was, I must say, all just a trifle confusing.

It is the Babylonian episode that is the magnificent achievement of the work. There still is nothing as superbly beautiful and exciting in film spectacle as the pictorial account of the greatness of Babylon and the tragedy of its fall. To this day film directors with much larger sums of money to spend strive without avail to equal its cinematic excellence. Mr. DeMille's vain efforts to equal its visual grandeur in such things as *The Sign of the Cross* and *The Crusades* have seemed embarrassingly puny beside it, not because the Babylonian chapter had more lavishness and a greater number of extras, but because Griffith had a far greater talent for superb visual effects and the dramatic power of cinematic movement.

Intolerance, however, is not notable merely because of its spectacle. It is deservedly famous because it was a pioneer effort to dramatize, not merely another story of young love and its trials, but a social theme. As the title suggests, Griffith was concerned with preaching the evils of intolerance and the fatal effect on both people and nations of widespread national or religious bigotry. It can hardly be said that such a theme is even outmoded at the present day. But the remarkable thing about the film's editorial viewpoint was that intolerance in modern America was shown in the framing of labor leaders and in the persecution of workers. Griffith was preaching social justice in the modern episode and even though he preached in a conventional and overly melodramatic narrative—in story the American episode is the weakest of the four—there could be no doubt of his earnestness and his integrity.

As I have said, *Intolerance* was not a financial success. In fact, monetary difficulties have long dogged Mr. Griffith's footsteps, interfering with his plans and keeping him from carrying out all of his conceptions. But I doubt that economic worries are entirely responsible for the slow disintegration of his undeniable genius for a cinema production. A mind more emotional than searching and stalwart has not always been of help to him, although it provided him with the romantic zealousness that was so important in both *Intolerance* and *The Birth of a Nation.* A certain lack of taste, a frank excess of sentimentality and a curiously sadistic urge have been, I think, the chief causes of his troubles.

As proof of this, there is the case of one of the most famous of his pictures, *Broken Blossoms.* In that dramatization of one of Thomas Burke's Limehouse stories, all of the defects of the director, as well as some of his greatest virtues, are to be found. The tale of the girl whose father tortured her to make her commit a murder and of the young Chinese who loved her possessed all of the pictorial skill and sense of melodramatic effectiveness that have gone into Griffith's best works. At the same time it was overwrought in its amorous romanticism, given to scenes so extravagant in their sentimentality as to suggest that the man who made them was curiously lacking in critical sense, and filled with episodes of torture that were almost pathological in their joy in sadism. It was over the scenes in which the heroine was being whipped by her brutal father that the picture seemed chiefly to linger, and while those scenes were filled with a great sympathy for the tortured girl, there was the suggestion that a certain relish for contemplating cruelty was not lacking. The result is that *Broken Blossoms* was a sadistic spree, as well as a beautiful and poignant motion picture.

There was also to be found in that picture a tendency that has never been one of Mr. Griffith's most admirable traits. That was his propensity for making his heroines seem slightly half-witted in their passion for fluttering about. Giggling sweetly, running around in pretty little circles and merrily chasing birds about a field were the chief occupations of the Griffith heroines, when they were not being pursued by lecherous monsters. In *Broken Blossoms* Miss Lillian Gish was forced to be so fluttery that it has taken many years and performances, in such stage works as "Hamlet" and "Within the Gates," to make people forget it.

The other Griffith films have seemed to me less important. *America*, a chronicle of the Revolutionary War, dramatized Paul Revere's ride with unequalled effectiveness, but was only a good, average historical picture the rest of the time. *Isn't Life Wonderful?* dramatized the immediate post-war days in Germany with sensitivity but without the great Griffith dramatic sense in its best form. *Orphans of the Storm* again showed the director's genius for spectacle, but revealed his defects as clearly as it did his virtues. *Sally of the Sawdust* and *That Royle Girl* were hokum melodramas even though *Sally* introduced the incomparable W. C. Fields to the cinema. With the coming of sound Mr. Griffith has offered us but two works. His *Abraham Lincoln* was an interesting romantic chronicle of the most popular American hero, demonstrating that Lincoln never recovered from the death of Ann Rutledge, and *The Struggle* was a simply terrible drama about the evils of drink.

It is undeniably true that in his later days Mr. Griffith, who seems to have retired permanently from film making, saw the procession pass him by. He saw directors with no fraction of his talents sweep on to success, while the course of social and esthetic ideas rushed on beyond him. Yet it can never be forgotten that it was he who first made motion picture direction an art; that, for better or for worse, he is the father of the motion picture as it exists today. In any possible record of the cinema, he must stand at the head, as the man who molded the photoplay quite surprisingly into his own image and likeness. With all of his defects, he remains the outstanding figure in the development of the screen.

The German Film
by Paul Rotha

Paul Rotha, a leading documentary film maker and historian, is the author of two classic books, "Documentary Film" and "The Film Till Now." The latter, published in 1930, is the source of this chapter.

In surveying the German cinema from the end of the first World War until the coming of the American dialogue film, the output may roughly be divided into three groups. First, the theatrical costume pictures; second, the big middle period of the studio art films; and third, the decline of the German film in order to fall into line with the American "picture-sense" output. These three periods naturally overlap one another, and there have been isolated exceptions to the general trend. Such distinguished films as *The Cabinet of Doctor Caligari, The Student of Prague, Vanina, The Last Laugh,* and the films of G. W. Pabst stand apart from the general run of production, in certain cases being advance examples of the type of film to come.

The easily recognizable characteristics of the earlier German films were their feeling for studio representation, for simplicity of story and treatment, for a consciousness of camera fluidity, and for a dramatic, psychological understanding of events. The German film was born and bred in an atmosphere of studio structure, for seldom did the German director go outside for his exterior material. The outstanding feature of all the greater of the early German films was their decorative sense of architecture. At an elementary stage in their cinematic development, the Germans revealed a strong and not unwanted tendency towards filmic craftsmanship. An instance of this is the perfection to which German cameramen have taken the technical qualities of their photography. It was in Germany that the camera was first freed from its tripod, that it was first given the movement and life of a human being. But although they used their camera to its full capacity, the Germans still largely retained their studio-mind, approaching at times the artificiality of the theatre. They seemed unable to accept the possibility of the free spirit of the cinema, which is so important in later Soviet and French productions.

Germany was unable to produce an *En Rade* or a *Battleship Potemkin*, but she did bring to the screen *The Student of Prague* and *The Last Laugh*. There is little doubt, however, that the studio-mind, with its love of craftsmanship and structural work, imposed limitations on the choice of theme and treatment, restrictions that have damaged the recent films of Erich Pommer: *Nina Petrovna, Homecoming,* and *Asphalt.* While it is admitted that studio architecture is absolutely necessary for certain exterior settings, which cannot be achieved on actual location (such as the creation of special streets and landscapes), nevertheless this artificiality is in opposition to the real aim of the cinema. Material that serves for filmic creation in the process of constructional editing has need to be the nearest approach to actuality, if not actuality itself.

The German film has contributed many valuable attributes to the cinema of the world. From the studio film there has been learned the complete subordination of acting material, revealed so well in *The Student of Prague;* the pre-organization of studio floor-work, including the composite set which allows for the taking of scenes in their correct sequence; the unification of light, setting, and acting material (the central part of *Tartuffe,* and *The Last Laugh*); and the freedom of the camera as an instrument of expression, assuming the status of an *observer* and not of a spectator. The German cinema has taught discipline and organization, without which no film can be produced as a unified whole.

The Cabinet of Doctor Caligari was the first significant attempt at the expression of a creative mind in the new medium of cinematography. It broke with realism on the screen; it suggested that a film, instead of being a reality, might be a possible reality; and it brought into play the mental psychology of the audience. There has been a tendency of late to look back with disdain at the theatrical character of Wiene's film. It has been objected that *The Cabinet of Doctor Caligari,* in its structural co-ordination of light, design, and players, in its cubist-expressionist architecture, was pure stage presentation. It needs but little intelligence to utter this profound criticism, but it must be realized that *The Cabinet of Doctor Caligari* was produced under extraordinary circumstances. It is simple to look back now and diagnose the crudities of Wiene's work, with the most recent progress of the Soviet film and the American "compound" cinema fresh in mind, but in 1919 all theory of the cinema was extremely raw. It is only through such experiments as that of Wiene, *Warning Shadows, The Street,* and *The Last Laugh,* that advance has been at all possible. The narrow-minded film critics of today blind themselves to the traditional development of the cinema. They seize upon Dziga-Vertov and deny the existence of Carl Dreyer; they saturate their minds with the sound film and forget the intrinsic structure of visual images. It has been said that the admirers of *The Cabinet of Doctor Caligari* are usually painters, or people who think and remember graphically. This is a mistaken conception, for the true *cinéaste* must see and recognize its importance, as well as that of *La Passion de Jeanne d'Arc, The Last Laugh, Tol'able David, Finis Terrae, Jeanne Ney,* and *Turksib.* Each of these films is related, each overlaps in its filmic exposition of thought. It is absurd to deny their existence on the grounds of theatricalism, expressionism, individualism, or naturalism. Without the creation of *The Cabinet of Doctor Caligari,* much that is admired in the cinema of today would be non-existent. It bore in it a suggestion of the fantasy that was to be the prominent characteristic of the art film. Some short time later, Kobe's *Torgus,* or *The Coffin Maker,* again with expressionist architecture, was another indication of the mystical fantasy which was to be the underlying motive of *Warning Shadows, The Student of Prague, Waxworks,* and others of a similar type.

The essence of the middle period German film was simplicity of story value and of actional interest that eventually led to a completeness of realization fulfilled in *The Last Laugh.* Many of the themes were simple experiments in film psychology. Karl Grune's *The Street* was a reduction of facts to the main development of one character during a short period of time. It obtained its mood by the co-ordination of light and camera psychology rather than by the acting, which was crude and mannered. Arthur Robison's *Warning Shadows* was again a simplification of detail, a centralization of incident into small units of space and time, decorated by a fantastic touch. *Waxworks* was yet another example. Nearly all these films contained the fantastic element. They were seldom wholly tragic or wholly comic. They were often melodramatic, as in the case of *Doctor Mabuse.*

Earlier than this middle period of simplicity and fantasy, there had been a wholesale production of theatrical costume films that made use of the German's natural love for spectacle and the property room. These served as a foundation for the stylized school of German film acting. At all periods of the German cinema, the actors have exerted a stabilizing influence on the fluctuation of the various types of films. Their restraining presence helped towards the establishment of the film as a whole. One recalls, in this respect, the numerous films of Conrad Veidt, Emil Jannings, Alfred Abel, Werner Krauss, Bernard Goetzke, Julius Falkenstein, Albert Steinrück, Alexander Granach, Asta Nielson, Henny Porten, Lydia Potechina, etc., in which the actors themselves steadied, and even, in some cases, dominated the direction.

With the German feeling for studio-craftsmanship came the decorative architecture and freedom of camerawork that were brought to a head in the big production of *Faust*, foreshadowed by Lang's *Destiny* and *Siegfried*, Robison's *Warning Shadows*, Murnau's *Tartuffe*, and Ludwig Berger's *Cinderella*. The decorative setting, based on traditional design with modern fantastic motives, played a large part in the German middle period. These fantastic productions began and ended with themselves. They carried no universal meaning, as did Karl Grune's *The Street* or *At the Edge of the World*. To this completeness, already partially achieved by the maturity of the traditional acting material, the splendid settings of Walther Röhrig, Robert Herlth, Otto Hunte, Erich Kettlehut, Karl Vollbrecht, Albin Grau, Rudolph Bamberger, Herman Warm, and others, added a final binding force. Their plastic columns, bulging mouldings, great flat expanses, simply decorated architecture formed an admirable background, never obtruding, for the acting material and simplicity of treatment of the period. It is of the utmost importance to grasp the significant part played by the architect and designer in the development of the German cinema. Indeed, it may be said without detriment to their directors, that two-thirds of the aesthetic success of *Warning Shadows, Siegfried*, and *Cinderella* lay in their design. The first part of the *Nibelungen Saga* has never been equalled for sheer decorative beauty; the complete charm of *Cinderella* came from the decoration of Rudolph Bamberger. *Destiny, The Golem, Sumurun*, and *Waxworks* were equally superb in their creative architecture. This natural feeling for decoration, for simple but rich design, in the Düreresque and Baroque styles, was the real basis of the German studio-mind. Even in films of a popular type this wonderful sense for good design was prevalent. Unlike innovators in other countries, the experimentalists in the German cinema were able to embody their revolutionary ideas in films of general practicability.

Towards the gradual decline of the decorative film, brought about by its own inbreeding, there arose a new type of cinema, less fantastic and more in touch with reality, but incorporating even more strongly the psychology of human emotions in the thematic narrative. This new form had been heralded to some extent by the appearance, in 1922, of Von Gerlach's *Vanina*, adapted from Stendhal, with Asta Nielson, Paul Wegener, and Paul Hartmann. In consideration of its date, *Vanina* was unique in its un-German feeling for fluidity of thematic conception. *Vanina* had breadth and space outside the customary studioisms of the period. Three years later there came *The Last Laugh*, which laid down the elementary principles of filmic continuity. It was, perhaps, an unequalled example of the co-ordination of production personnel. Murnau, Freund, Mayer, and Jannings worked collectively to produce a film that was a complete realization in itself. (Carl Mayer actually wrote *The Last Laugh* for Lupu Pick to act and direct, and expressed himself to me as never wholly happy with Janning's performance.) It expressed a simple, universal theme, unrelieved by incidental detail and cross purposes. It was a centralization of environment, of setting, of atmosphere, of players, to one dominating purpose. It had a plastic fluidity that was made possible by a titleless continuity. It had a completeness that for once was achieved by the architecture of the studio. It was the final outcome of the German craftsman's studio-mind. In the same year, as well as *The Last Laugh*, there were to come Dupont and Pommer's celebrated *Vaudeville*, Grune's *The Two Brothers*, Lupu Pick's *The Wild Duck* and *New Year's Eve*, and Pabst's *The Joyless Street*. With the exception of the last, these were all films with moral themes, close to the reality of modern life, treated with a new technique of moving camerawork and unusual angle of viewpoint. *Vaudeville* was, of course, the outstanding film that staggered the American producing companies when shown to them in the States. It was *Vaudeville* that took Pommer, Dupont, and Jannings to Hollywood.

Speaking broadly, for there are several notable exceptions, the German film entered into a decline after that date. The new productions, having lost the spirit and craftsmanship of the best German period (from 1921 to 1925) were constructed along the box-office lines of the American cinema. They were in the nature of a reaction from the work of the highest filmic intelligences in Europe at that time, because Soviet Russia was then but an unknown quantity, experimenting with theatrical pictures. There followed for some years a great number of second- and third-rate German movies made to supply the *Kontingent* law, which required every German distributor to buy one home production for every American film. Directed by such men as Richard Eichberg, Joe May, and Willi Wolff, they featured players like Harry Liedtke, Paul Richter, Mady Christians, Ellen Richter, Harry Halm, Liane Haid, Willy Fritsch, Lia Maria, Lilian Harvey, and Jenny Jugo.

During recent years there has been an increased commercial co-operation between Germany and other European film-producing countries. The technical studio organization of the German film industry was recognized as the most efficient in Europe, if not in the world, and both Britain and France interchanged production units with Germany. Many foreign firms were anxious to combine in joint productions because of German technical resources. These pictures were an attempt to rival the constant flood of American picture-sense movies. Amid this heterogeneous mass of German films, however, there were still several individual works by pre-eminent directors who retained some intelligent interest in the cinema. Fritz Lang's *Metropolis* and *The Spy;* G. W. Pabst's *Secrets of the Soul and Jeanne Ney;* Fritz Wendhausen's *Out of the Mist;* the films of Elizabeth Bergner's Poetic Film Company, *Donna Juana* and *The Violinist of Florence;* and Walther Ruttmann's *Berlin*, were evidence that there still remained progressive *cinéastes* in Germany.

But generally speaking, German film production was rapidly becoming like that of Hollywood in external appearances. Many of the big pictures of 1928, for example, might have been the product of American studios. They were made for an international market, and little of the old German feeling for psychology and simplicity of treatment remained. Erich

Pommer, on returning from Hollywood, attempted to combine the merits of the old German school with a new outlook of international picture-sense. Of his four pictures recently produced, *Nina Petrovna* and *Homecoming* were of better quality than the average American or German movie. They were not, I admit, good films in the sense that they were masterpieces of filmic expression, but they contained certain aspects of camerawork and architecture that were reminiscent of past achievements. There has been a tendency also towards the filming of melodramatic thrillers, light and artificial in story value, but constructed with a great deal of technical skill. Of such may be mentioned Fritz Lang's excellent *The Spy*, perhaps one of the best pictures of its kind; and Tourjanski's *Manolescu*. Pabst's *Jeanne Ney*, also, was melodramatic in action. There have also been a number of good, middle-class comedies made, of general entertainment value, such as *The Bold Sea Rover* (in Britain, *Hurrah! I'm Alive*), with that delightful comedian, Nikolai Kolin, and *Love's Sacrifice*, a light, polished picture of youthfulness, directed with admirable skill by Hans Schwartz. The old fondness for the spectacular historical film, which seems ever present on the Continent, has resulted in the large but quite unconvincing production of *Waterloo*, directed by Karl Grunc, originally a simplist director; the same director's ill-conceived *Marquis d'Eon;* the sensational and theatrical film of *Martin Luther* (which revealed clearly the fallacy of the pageant picture); Ludwig Berger's version of *The Meistersingers*, a late example of the studio-mind; and *Schinderhannes*, made by the young director, Kurt Bernhardt.

G. W. Pabst is theoretically the great director, but he has failed to justify fully his immense reputation since his second and sixth films, *The Joyless Street* and *Jeanne Ney*. Although this is adverse criticism of a director who has given many instances of his rare knowledge of the probing power of the camera, nevertheless I feel that there is a general tendency to overestimate any and every instance of Pabst's undoubted ability. But Pabst at his best, unhampered by limitations, uncut save by himself, is perhaps the one genius of the film outside Soviet Russia, approached, though in an entirely different manner, by Carl Dreyer, Chaplin, and René Clair. Both esthetically and technically, his work is of the first importance in the European cinema. Investigation of his methods is difficult, complex, and hard to express in words. Pabst possesses a power of penetration into the deepest cells of human behavior, and succeeds in psychologically representing the traits of his characters by filmic exposition. He is principally concerned with the development and understanding of the intricacies of the minds of his characters, and lays open their mentality by employing every resource available to the medium in which he works. It has been written in criticism that Pabst delights in the sheer use of technical accomplishment, as if he were simply a Monta Bell or a Mal St. Clair, but no more unwarranted statement has been made since the beginning of film journalism. It is impossible to witness the showing of a film by Pabst without marvelling at his unerring choice of camera angle for the expression of mood, or his employment of the moving camera to heighten tension. Pabst, probably far more than any other director (outside the Soviet cinema), understands the complete value of his instruments. *Jeanne Ney* has already been cited as a superb example of the uses of the camera as a means of dramatic expression; *Crisis*, although not revealing Pabst to full advantage (I have only seen the cut British version), was exceptionally interesting in its use of reverse shots and camera mobility.

Before he became interested in the cinema, Pabst was in the theatre, and it was not until 1924 that he opened his film career with *The Treasure*. This was followed by the tempestuous and badly received *The Joyless Street* in 1925. Since that date he has made eight films, *Don't Play With Love*, *Secrets of the Soul*, *Jeanne Ney*, *Crisis*, *Pandora's Box*, *The White Hell of Pitz Palü*, and *The Diary of a Lost Girl*.

It seems simple enough to write that *The Joyless Street* succeeded in showing the devastation that war conditions wreaked on the inhabitants of a small dark street in post-war Vienna, for there have been so many films which have dealt with similar circumstances. But with the genius of Pabst this film was different, for it tore away the American glamor, destroyed the romanticism, and exposed the stark reality of hunger and passion under distorted conditions. No film or novel has so truthfully recorded the despair of defeat, and the false values of social life that arise after war, as *The Joyless*

Street. With unerring psychology by which he caused the smallest actions of his characters to convey meaning, Pabst brought to his picture moments of searing pain of mental anguish, of sheer unblemished beauty. His extreme powers of truthfulness, of the understanding of reality, of the vital meaning of hunger, love, lust, selfishness and greed, rendered this extraordinary film convincing. Like *Greed*, its significance went below the artificial surface of everyday life, turning up the deepest emotions. It was, perhaps, too true for the entertainment of the masses. Like *Greed*, it was too real, too devastating in its truth. It is recorded that Pabst himself once said, "What need is there for romantic treatment? Real life is too romantic and too ghastly." Appearing in this film was Greta Garbo, and here one recognizes her beauty and ability. In Hollywood, this splendid woman has been wantonly distorted into a symbol of eroticism. But Greta Garbo, by reason of the sympathetic understanding of Pabst, brought a quality of loveliness into her playing as the professor's elder daughter. Her frail beauty, cold as an ice flower warmed by the sun, stood secure in the starving city of Vienna, untouched by the vice and lust that dwelt in the dark little street. Not only Greta Garbo, but the other players in this film were fascinating. I recall Asta Nielson, superb as the woman who murdered for her lover, slowly realizing the horror of her action, her eyes expressing the innermost feeling of her heart; Valeska Gert, the blatant, avaricious woman, who, under the thin guise of a milliner, kept the house patronized by the *nouveaux-riches;* Werner Krauss, the sleek-haired, wax-moustached butcher, secure in his pandering to the wealthy, with the great white dog at his side; Jaro Furth, the intellectual Councillor Rumfort, unable to understand the new conditions; Robert Garrison, the vulgar little speculator; and the others, Agnes Estherhazy, Henry Stuart, and Einar Hanson. When viewed more recently, the technique and technical qualities of *The Joyless Street* seemed faded (it was made in 1925), but the vital force of Pabst's direction was still present.

Of Pabst's psycho-analytical film, *Secrets of the Soul,* I can write but indifferently, for the copy reluctantly shown in Britain was badly mutilated in order to meet censor requirements; insomuch that its continuity straggled, gaps and interruptions that could not possibly have occurred in the original copy were painfully apparent. It had little story to relate, but was a simple demonstration of the theory of psycho-analysis. It was, for those sufficiently interested, a key to the working of Pabst himself. From the doctor's treatment of the patient with the knife-complex, and from the dream sequence, it was possible to discern the manner in which Pabst himself dissects his film characters. The picture was beautifully photographed, and was of interest for the scene when Werner Krauss recalled his thoughts and actions of the previous day, the incidents being isolated from their local surroundings and placed against a white background.

It took several years for the value of *The Joyless Street* to be appreciated, but when *Jeanne Ney* made its dramatic appearance in 1928, there were those who were eager to receive this new film by Pabst. It was, it is true, badly mutilated in Britain, and actually presented by the British renters, Wardour, under the fantastic title of *Lusts of the Flesh. Jeanne Ney*, which was based on the novel by Ilya Ehrenburg, was produced by Ufa, in Berlin, and apparently Pabst had difficulty in making the film in his own way. It was the time when the Americanization of the German studios was in progress, and Pabst was told to make the picture "in the American style." Fortunately, Pabst had courage, and in *Jeanne Ney* he made a more subtle, a swifter, less tragic, and more dynamic film than *The Joyless Street*. At first glance, *Jeanne Ney* was a melodramatic spy story of communists, adventurers, a typist, a blind girl, with a murder and a diamond robbery. It is curious, at this point, to remark that all the stories chosen by Pabst are melodramatic, almost novelettish in incident. *The Joyless Street* was adapted from a serial story by Hugo Bettauer, in the Vienna Neue Freie Presse, and the narrative incident of *Crisis* was not much better. Instead, however, of this being detrimental, it proves conclusively how important is filmic treatment in relation to story value. The interest of *Jeanne Ney* was not in its actional incident, but in the individuals concerned, their thoughts, emotions, and reasons for behaving as they did. From the superb opening sequence of the orgy, beginning with a close-up of the *émigré's* shabby boots, and the camera slipping away and tracking into every corner, *Jeanne Ney* developed from sequence to sequence with breathtaking power. Mood succeeded mood, each perfect in

94

its tension and its understanding. The shooting of the consul, Jeanne's father, the restless curtains caused by the draught from the opening door, the quick-cut reverse shots; the inimitable, likable kindness of the smiling Communist *attaché*, with his kippers, and the wan smile of Jeanne; the parting in the drenching rain, the mud, the anguish of the farewell, the stark trees; the superbly conveyed atmosphere of the detective bureau, the types of the sleuth hounds, the dislike of Jeanne for her new work; the reunion of the boy and Jeanne, in the warm sunlight walking through the poor streets of Paris, the flowers, the sheer beauty of love and youth; the brilliant scene where little bald-headed Raymond Ney counts his imaginary money, the murder; the tremendous scene between the blind girl and the murderer; the hotel, its sordid shabbiness overcome by the love of Jeanne, the peace of their night, unsoiled by the contagious atmosphere of the house. . . .

The cutting of *Jeanne Ney* was executed with such skill that it seemed unnoticeable. Every cut was made on actual movement, so that at the end of one shot somebody was moving, and at the beginning of the next shot the action was continued. The eye was thus absorbed in the movement and the actual transposition from one shot to another became unnoticeable. Instinctively one recalled the overlapping cutting of *Battleship Potemkin,* and recognized the similar aims of Eisenstein and Pabst in this respect. For this reason it will at once be seen how disastrous can be the effect of the censor's scissors. Pabst cut *Jeanne Ney* to a definite length; every shot had its place and meaning. The removal of only a few feet of such a film damages its balance, design, and *emotional* effect.

The photography of *Jeanne Ney,* by Fritz Arno Wagner, has been remarked on elsewhere, and it is sufficient to add that technically, for smoothness of panning and travelling shots, and for perfectly natural light values, it has never been surpassed. At Pabst's will, Wagner's camera nosed into the corners and ran with the players; photographed from below eye-level and down stairways; yet not once was the instrument misused. Every curve, every angle, every approach of the lens was controlled by the material that it photographed for the expression of mood. Sadness, joy, uplift, depression, exuberance, fear, morbidness, delight, were achieved by the position and mobility of the camera. Its viewpoints were regulated by the logic of the action. *Jeanne Ney* was a unified individual work. From start to finish it was conceived, controlled, and created by one sensitive but dominant mind—Pabst.

As a film, after the brilliance of *Jeanne Ney, Crisis* was a disappointment. As the expression of the character of a woman, a single individual, it was of passing interest. The story was a conventional plot of a misunderstood marriage; many of the same type have been manufactured in Hollywood. It is understood that once again the British version was considerably cut, while in Germany, Pabst refused to put his name to the production because of the editing. The film, as shown in this country, lacked stimulus. The direction again revealed Pabst's technical brilliance for angles and pictorial composition, occasional moments rising to heights of intensity. The wife's hysterical collapse in the night club; the discovery of her brooding husband when she returns home; the vicious undercurrents of atmosphere that lay behind the cabaret scenes—these were handled with a technique that was equal to *The Joyless Street*. The center of interest, however, was the compelling fascination of Brigitte Helm's Myra. Pabst was the first director to reveal the rare side to this actress, a quality that was not apparent in *A Daughter of Destiny, Metropolis, At the Edge of the World, L'Argent*, and her other pictures. In *Jeanne Ney*, Pabst was interested in the playing of Brigitte Helm as the blind girl. In *Crisis*, he became absorbed in the personality of Miss Helm herself. He succeeded in making her every movement exciting. Her strange latent power and underlying neurosis were here given their freedom. Her vibrant beauty, her mesh of gold hair, her slender, supple figure were caught and photographed from every angle. The intensity of her changing moods, her repression and resentment, her bitterness and cynicism, her final passionate breakdown in the Argentine club—these were constructed into a filmic representation of overwhelming psychological power. Pabst analyzed and dissected the remarkable character of Miss Helm and built up out of the pieces a unified, plastic personality. Her curious, fascinating power has never been exploited with such skill.

In each of his films, with the sole exception of the psychoanalytical essay, *The Secrets of the Soul*, Pabst has been concerned with some aspect of the character of women. His stories have been but a framework of incident on which to wind the theme of feminine character development. Every woman of Pabst's synthetic creation has had a curious, unnameable and hopelessly indefinable quality about her. He seems, in the building up of their filmic personalities, to be able to bring to the surface the vital forces of their being. Each actress employed in the films of Pabst assumes a new quality, not actually but filmically. He contrives by some unknown force to invest his characters with a quality of intense feeling, with strangely complex sexual or mental significance. In each of his succeeding films, he has sought more and more to express the motives that lie behind a woman's impulsive thoughts and actions. He appears to have the power of discovering a hidden quality in an actress, whatever her career may have been before she came under his direction. Like Greta Garbo— Asta Nielsen, Edith Jehanne, Brigitte Helm, Hertha von Walther, and Louise Brooks are almost ordinary when appearing in other films under other directors. But Pabst has an understanding, an appreciation of the intelligence, that builds the actual personality into a magnetic, filmic being.

It was, it seems, this hidden quality, this deeper, hitherto uninvestigated, side of feminine character that induced Pabst to choose, after long searching, Louise Brooks to play Lulu in *Pandora's Box*. Lulu was the theme of Wedekind's two tragedies, "Erdgeist" and "Die Büchse der Pandora," one being the sequel to the other, around which Pabst built his concept. Lulu was the final essence of the sexual impulse of woman, charged to the fullest extent with physical consciousness. The spring of her life was the attempted satisfaction of this insatiable impulse, and the power of man was the possible means of that satisfaction. She loved spasmodically, but with the strongest sensuality, until, sickening of her exhausted companion, he was indifferently destroyed. She was unable, moreover, to comprehend the ruthlessness of her devastation in her search for sexual satisfaction. She loved for the moment the man to whom she surrendered her body, but that love died like a flash when his exhaustion was complete. Her sentiment was hardened by the monotonous recurrence of the events which she had caused. She remained untouched by the death of her masculine stimulants. She had no interest in the vastness of life save sexuality and its accompaniments. She was childlike in her centralization of material purpose. She was the essence of youth, with the eyes of a child, beautiful in appearance, and utterly attractive in manner. Her ultimate and only possible ending was her destruction by the passions which she aroused, killed by the lust-murderer, Jack-the-Ripper, in London.

Neither of Pabst's last two pictures has been generally seen. The one, *The White Hell of Pitz Palü*, with its series of mountaineering catastrophes, is set in the Alps; the other, *The Diary of a Lost Girl*, concerns the revolt of a number of girls against the rigid rules of a reformatory. Both are stated to be notable for the camerawork of Sepp Allgeier, and they both have settings designed by Ernö Metzner, who made *Ueberfall*. The former film is co-directed by Arnold Fanck and Pabst; the first-named director being remembered for his beautifully photographed mountain film, *The Wrath of the Gods*.

There is a tendency, obscure but nevertheless real, to regard Fritz Lang as a more intelligent Rex Ingram. They are both expert showmen. But whereas Ingram's faculty seldom rises above a certain level of Hollywood picture-sense, Lang has definitely produced work that is of value. *Destiny*, *Siegfried*, and *Metropolis* were sufficient evidence of the fertility of his imagination and his sense of decorative design. Lang is further to be admired for his bigness of outlook and his power of broad visualization. Both *Metropolis* and *The Woman in the Moon* were magnificently big cinematic conceptions, accomplished with every technical perfection of the cinema. It is impossible not to admire Fritz Lang in this respect. On the other hand, one regrets his entire lack of filmic detail, of the play of human emotions, of the intimacy which is so peculiarly a property of the film. Only on rare occasions, notably in the tea-party scene between Gerda Maurus and Willy Fritsch in *The Spy*, has Lang revealed interest in human beings as such. As a rule, his characters are meaningless men and women (heroes, heroines, and villains) swept hither and thither by the magnitude of his conception. And yet he has an instinctive feeling for types, for there is seldom an individual part in his films that is not distinctive.

Lang is accustomed to utilize the best film technicians in Germany for his vast studio conceptions. Karl Hoffman, Freund, Fritz Arno Wagner, Gunther Rittau, the cameramen; and Otto Hunte, Erich Kettlehut, Oscar Werndorff, Karl Vollbrecht, the architects, have all worked in Lang's production unit. All Lang's scenarios have been conceived and written in collaboration with his wife, Thea von Harbou.

Both *Destiny* and *Siegfried* were supreme examples of the German art film. They were entirely studio-made, and in each the decorative value of the architecture was the binding force of the realization. They were fantastic in that they were concepts of the imagination; they were decorative in that they employed a series of visual images, designed in black and white and intervening tones of gray, in a two-dimensional pattern. For sheer pictorial beauty of structural architecture, *Siegfried* has seldom been equalled because no company could afford to spend money as did Decla-Bioskop in 1922-23. No expense can have been withheld on that extraordinary production, but in comparison with the cost, little money could have been made in return. *Siegfried* was far from being pure film, far from the naturalism of the Soviets or the individualism of Pabst, but it was restrained, simplified pageantry, rendered with a minimum of decoration to gain the maximum of massed effect. Who can ever forget the tall, dark forests; the birch glade, bespattered with flowers where Siegfried was slain; the procession of Gunther's court, seen distantly through the mail-clad legs of the sentinels; the calm, silent atmosphere of the castle rooms, with their simple heraldic decoration; and above all, the dream of the hawks, a conception by Ruttmann. *Destiny*, also, was finely created, using every contemporary resource of trick photography and illusionary setting. Unlike *Siegfried*, which was a straightforward narration of story, *Destiny* was an interplaited theme of three stories, "The Three Lights," each connected symbolically with the main modern theme of the two lovers. The film was magnificently conceived and realized, played with unforgettable acting by Bernard Goetzke as Death the Stranger, Lil Dagover as the Girl, and Walther Janssen as the Boy. It was a production that has been too soon forgotten and deserves revival.

Lang has made also two melodramatic thrillers of spies, gamblers, disguises, crooks, and police. *Doctor Mabuse, the Gambler*, was produced in 1922; *The Spy*, an improved version on the same lines, in 1927-28. In its original form, *Doctor Mabuse* was over 17,000 feet in length, and was issued both in Germany and in Britain in two parts. It was the first German film to reach England (about the same time as Lubitsch's

Dubarry, renamed *Passion*) and was regarded as remarkable in film technique by the American-influenced minds of British audiences. The story was of the usual *feuilleton* type, with murders, a Sidney Street defense of Mabuse's house against the police and the army, and fainting women, with a strong spell of hypnotism and psycho-analysis. The action, unlike Lang's other work, was rapid in pace and startling in incident, and was therefore preferred by some critics to his slow-moving pageant films. In certain respects it was interesting also as linking the pre-war long shot and chase elements with the tentative methods of the newer school. Six years later, Lang repeated his success twofold in *The Spy,* a story, not unlike *Doctor Mabuse,* of an international crook, with secret papers, a railway smash, complex disguises, and another final street battle. It was all splendid entertainment, superbly done. It was quick moving, thrilling, and melodramatic. Lang used again as his criminal genius the versatile Rudolf Klein-Rogge, who improved on his early Mabuse part. Technically, the production was brilliantly efficient, notably in Wagner's wonderful camerawork. In minor incidental effect, Lang had pilfered from far and wide. An excellent scene on diagonal steel-girder staircases looked as if it was taken from a Soviet film, but his "plagiarism" was justified.

Of *Metropolis,* more abuse has been written than praise, partly because the version shown in Britain was unhappily edited, many sequences being deliberately removed. The British copy was "arranged" by Channing Pollock, author of *The Fool.* The film, when it made its London appearance, was not enthusiastically received. H. G. Wells, among others, damned it as "quite the silliest film . . ." As a matter of fact, *Metropolis* was very remarkable, based on a brilliant *filmic* conception. Had it been shown in its entirety, it might have afforded a wonderful exposition of cinematography. As with all of the German studio-films, the dominant keynote of the picture was its amazing architecture. It is not until we compare *Metropolis* with a British picture on the same lines, Maurice Elvey's *High Treason,* that it is possible to recognize its value. There is not one member of the production units or executive committees, not one critic or film journalist in this country, who can afford to sneer at Fritz Lang's conception. *High Treason,* with its arts-and-crafts design by Andrew Mazzei, revealed only too clearly how poorly Britain produces a film of this kind. Though neither a great film, nor an example of pure filmic expression, *Metropolis* contained scenes that for their grandeur and strength have never been equalled either by Britain or America. Who, for example, could have handled the sequence when Rotwang transfers life and the likeness of human form into the steel figure with such brilliant feeling as Fritz Lang? *Metropolis*, with its rows of rectangular windows, its slow-treading workers, its great geometric buildings, its contrasted light and shade, its massed masses, its machinery, was a considerable achievement. Its actual story value was negligible; the architecture was the story in itself. Lang's recent production, *The Woman in the Moon*, a film purporting to show the journey of a rocket to the moon and the adventures of the crew there, has not yet been shown in London. From its still-photographs and conception, it appears to be quite as remarkable as Lang's other productions.

It is easy, perhaps, to call Fritz Lang a showman, but he is to be reckoned also as a director of decided film intelligence, of broad views, of rare imagination, of artistic feeling, who is not afraid to put his amazing conceptions into practical form using every technical resource of the studio to do so. Lang is to be admired and studied for his courage and self-confidence. He has not, it is true, any knowledge of constructive editing in the Soviet sense, but he has initiative and a sense of bigness. His work is primarily architectural, essentially the product of the film studio.

Much has already been written regarding the work of Murnau. Of his earlier films, *Phantom*, adapted from Hauptmann's story, and the pirated version of Bram Stoker's *Dracula* are known. The latter, produced in 1922, was possibly crude in its melodramatic acting, but nevertheless it contained much of considerable interest. There was a very definite feeling for camera angle in the establishment of a macabre mood, and effective use was made of projected negative and one-turn—one-picture camera devices for the suggestion of eeriness. Fritz Arno Wagner's camerawork was notably good, particularly a scene of frightened horses in the twilight and the close-ups of the architecture of the Count's castle. Murnau's *The Last Laugh* has been discussed earlier, and his *Tartuffe*, a production by the same team, is memorable for its superb simplicity. The scenario was again by Carl Mayer; the camera-work by Karl Freund, and the architecture by Walter Röhrig and Robert Herlth.

From the acting standpoint *Tartuffe* was a remarkable example of harmonious talent, typical of German complete-ness. The spectator felt that there was an underlying current of humor running throughout each sequence, a humor that was not without its vital dramatic moments. One recalls the crystal tear of Elmire that fell like a liquid pearl on the minia-ture of Orgon, the relationship of the figures one to another; the symbolic black figure of Tartuffe, with silhouetted thin ankles and clumsy square-toed shoes; the exquisite subtle beauty of Elmire, with curled wig, fragile dress, and gentle mien. Clever contrast was made between the closely held Bible of Tartuffe, its minute size symbolic of his hypocritical nature, and the open frankness of Orgon. *Tartuffe* constituted Jan-nings' third portrayal of comedy (former occasions being in *Waxworks,* in the final part of *The Last Laugh,* and later, of course, in *Faust*). It is difficult to forget Tartuffe descending the curved staircase—Tartuffe espying the image of Orgon's reflection in the teapot—Tartuffe listening, watching, suspi-cious, leaning on the handrail. The Elmire of Lil Dagover was fragrantly beautiful. I recollect her seduction of Tartuffe on the first occasion; her very gestures were fragile. Werner Krauss was as good as he can at times be bad.

The atmosphere that surrounded the characters enveloped the spectator. It was an atmosphere of simplification, of grace-ful curves, and wonderful detail of plaster and ironwork. There was no customary over-decoration. Unnecessary detail was eliminated to the better effect of the mass. I remember the beauty of the lace *négligé* in the final bedroom scene, the pattern of the bed covering, the porcelain clock on the fire-place, the reality of the square-toed shoes, the emphasis given to them in the scene of the hammock (a touch of genius), the design of Orgon's ring, and a hundred other points. All these were in perfect harmony, perfect taste, and of the high-est tone. Every detail and every mass was the result of creative forethought. It was this tone that was spread over the whole. No matter where the characters moved or how they gestured, the composition remained perfect. Molière, Watteau, Boucher, and the French engravers of the eighteenth century were embodied in the spirit of this film, which was only marred by the unnecessary modern prologue and epilogue.

Murnau's last film in Germany, before he accepted the Fox contract in Hollywood, was *Faust*. This film may again be taken as a consummate example of German craftsmanship. Every detail, every mass, every contrast of light and shade, emphasized the medieval atmosphere. Mention may be made of Murnau's use of the art of Dürer and of Brueghel in his psychological establishment of the period. Again, Karl Freund's photography was superb, and the production was a notable instance not only of trick camerawork but of the Scheufftan process of illusionary architecture. The Mephisto of Jannings was completely delightful, the essence of refined, subtle humor, of mischievous trickery and inimitable devilry; the Marguerite of Camilla Horn, pure and flowerlike; the Faust of Gosta Ekman, a Swedish actor, thoroughly competent, and Yvette Guilbert's playing as Marguerite's aunt was an ever-memorable piece of sheer artistry. The drinking scene between Jannings and Yvette Guilbert stands as one of the finest sequences of humor in the history of the screen. That such an artist as Murnau should have gone to Hollywood to devote his filmic, philosophic mind to such banalities as *Sunrise* and *The Four Devils* is infinitely regrettable.

In the two architectural productions of Murnau, *Tartuffe* and *Faust,* his direction was closely bound up with the design of Walter Röhrig and Robert Herlth, the acting of Jannings and the camera craftsmanship of Karl Freund. In the same way, the four outstanding films by Dr. Ludwig Berger—*Cinderella, A Glass of Water, The Waltz Dream,* and *The Burning Heart*—were the realization of the Ludwig Berger—Rudolph Bamberger team of workers. Bamberger was also the designer to Berger's version of *The Meistersingers, The Master of Nürnburg,* a Phœbus production, with Rudolph Rittner, Max Gulstörss, Gustav Fröhlich, Julius Falkenstein and Elsa Wagner in the cast. It is by *Cinderella,* however, that Ludwig Berger is best known. Made in 1923, when the German cinema was at the height of its middle and best period, *Cinderella* was a film of the most beautiful fantasy, delicately conceived and consummated with a perfection of decorative pictorialism. The touch of Ludwig Berger seemed magical, so completely entrancing was the subtle fabrication of this exquisite work. Bamberger, for his design, centred his theme around the charm of Southern Baroque art, making full use of the plastic moulding in which the German studio workers seem to excel. Technically, the "magic" in this film was brilliantly accomplished, for it was essentially cinematic. It was curious to note that Berger's design of pictorial composition was nearly always symmetrical throughout this picture—for he obviously centered his movement of acting material around a feature of the architectural composition. Thus it was observed that doorways, windows, gateways, alleyways, etc., were always set in the center of the screen, the remainder of the composition moving around them. In the same year, Ludwig Berger made *A Glass of Water*, a film that nominally concerned Queen Anne of England, but actually there was no idea of historical accuracy for that would have been antagonistic to the decorative motive as well as to the environment of the picture. Once more Rudolph Bamberger's setting was in the spirit of South German baroque, and Helga Thomas, Mady Christians, and Lucie Höflich were again in the cast, with Rudolph Rittner and Hans Brausewetter. Although it did not have the charm of *Cinderella*, this film was nevertheless pleasing, tending perhaps to overlength. Berger's later picture, *The Waltz Dream*, made in 1926, was one of the few German films to meet with success in America. It ran in New York for several weeks, appreciated by American audiences as "something different." Actually, it was a charming comedy—as one would expect from Berger—sentimental and harmless, but not to be compared with the earlier *Cinderella*. Again, Mady Christians played with graceful comedy, supported by Willy Fritsch, who was at that time practically unknown, and the soft photography of Werner Brandes and the subdued richness of the Bamberger settings contributed to the atmosphere which Berger sought to achieve. This director has made yet another German picture with Mady Christians and Bamberger, *The Burning Heart*, which has recently been synchronized, and in Hollywood he has directed *The Sins of the Fathers* with Emil Jannings, and a version of the operetta, *The Vagabond King*.

The name of Arthur Robison is at once associated with *Warning Shadows*, a film that by now is well known to all familiar with the development of the cinema. Actually, the credit for this unique work should be given equally to all the production unit, to Fritz Arno Wagner, the cameraman; to Albin Grau, the architect; and to Dr. Robison; as well as to the brilliant playing of Fritz Körtner, Gustav von Wangenheim, Ferdinand von Alten, Fritz Rasp, Max Gulstörss, Alexander Granach, and Ruth Weyher. The film was made without the use of titles, save at the opening for the introduction of the characters, but several quite ridiculous and totally discordant captions were inserted for its British presentation. At the time of production, in 1922 *Warning Shadows* was a remarkable achievement. Its purely psychological direction, its definite completeness of time and action, its intimate ensemble were new attributes of the cinema. It was a rare instance of complete filmic unity, with the possible exception of the unnecessary roof-garden scene. The continuity of theme, the smooth development from one sequence into another, the gradual communication of the thoughts of the characters, were flawlessly presented. It carried an air of romance, of fantasy, of tragedy. Every filmic property for the expression of mood, for the creation of atmosphere, that was known at the time was used with imagination and intelligence. Its supreme value as an example of unity of purpose, of time, of place, of theme cannot be over-estimated. Of Dr. Robison's other pictures, mention need be made only of *Manon Lescaut* (1927), *Looping the Loop* (1928), and *The Informer*, for British International Pictures of Elstree. For the production of *Manon Lescaut*, faithfully adapted from the immortal romance of the Abbé Prévost, Robison had the advantage of the design of Paul Leni, better known as a director. The acting material was well chosen, no easy task with a costume picture of this type. The Manon of Lya de Putti and the Chevalier des Grieux of Vladimir Gaiderov were admirable, and the supporting cast, particularly Siegfried Arno, Frieda Richard, and Lydia Potechina, were exceptionally competent. Robison succeeded in establishing an air of intimacy, of dramatic relationship between one character and another, of the deep passion that linked the two lovers, by a continual use of close-ups. The decorations of Leni gave to the film a reality that is lacking in the vast majority of costume pictures. His tendency to continue scenes through doorways and along passages lent a depth that prevented artificiality, a customary characteristic of such productions. The costumes, designed with a wealth of accurate detail that was fully revealed by the close penetration of the camera, were more faithful to their period, both in cut and wear, than any others that have been seen in historical film reconstruction. On the other hand, *Looping the Loop*, a curious contrast to Robison's earlier work, was a circus film—an environment which was popular at the time. It was not of especial interest, being a straight-forward rendering of the usual circus story: a clown with a broken heart, a girl's flirtations, and an unscrupulous philanderer. The photography of Karl Hoffman was good, the settings of Walter Röhrig and Herlth consistent, and the acting of Werner Krauss as accomplished as usual. In brief, the production unit was worthy of better material. I have been given to understand, however, that the original negative was destroyed by fire and that the copy generally exhibited was made from an assembly of leftover "takes." Of Robison's British picture, *The Informer*, Liam O'Flaherty's story of gunmen and betrayal, it is hard to write, for although it obviously contained the elements of an excellent film, the silent version shown to the public was so badly edited that little of Robison's technique could be appreciated. In order to meet market requirements at the time, a version with added dialogue sequences was presented, but this does not enter into consideration.

Karl Grune has made one outstanding film, *The Street,* and a number of others that will be forgotten in the course of time. Made in 1923, Grune's *The Street* was again typical of the German studio-mind. Its chief value lay in its unity of theme, its creation of mood by contrasted intensities and movements of light, and its simplicity of treatment. Apart from these significant features, it was acted with deplorable melodrama, and its studio structure setting was hardly convincing. Nevertheless, for its few moments of filmic intensity, such as the celebrated moving shadow scene in the opening and the cleverly handled game of cards, it must rank as important. Grune's other films include *The Two Brothers,* with Conrad Veidt in a dual role; *Arabella,* with Fritz Rasp; *Jealousy,* with Werner Krauss and Lya de Putti; *At the Edge of the World,* an unconvincing pacifist theme, distinguished only for the settings by A. D. Neppach and the playing of Brigitte Helm; *Marquis d'Eon,* a depressing historical film, with Liane Haid badly miscast as the chevalier, notable only for the camera craftsmanship of Fritz Arno Wagner; *The Youth of Queen Louise,* a Terra production with Mady Christians; and *Waterloo,* the Emelka tenth anniversary spectacle film, badly staged at great expense, foolishly theatrical and lacking conviction. Karl Grune may have made *The Street,* but he has failed as yet to develop the cinematic tendencies displayed as long ago as 1923, becoming a director of the commercial type. The same may be said of Robert Wiene, who will, of course, long be remembered as the director of *The Cabinet of Doctor Caligari,* but who, since that achievement, has done little to add to his laurels. *Raskolnikov,* made in 1923 from Dostoevsky's "Crime and Punishment" with a band of the Russian Moscow Art Players, was an essay in the same vein as *The Cabinet of Doctor Caligari,* but less successful. The following year, Wiene made *The Hands of Orlac,* with Conrad Veidt, for the Pan Film Company of Austria; a singularly dreary, melodramatic film, interesting only because of a few tense moments of Veidt's acting, and some cleverly contrasted lighting.

Henrik Galeen is yet another director who has to his credit but one pre-eminent accomplishment, *The Student of Prague.* Galeen was first associated with the cinema as a scenarist, having been connected in this capacity with Paul Leni's *Waxworks,* Wegener's *The Golem,* and Murnau's *Dracula.* It will have been noticed by those interested in films of the past, that very frequently it is difficult to discern who exactly was responsible for the merits and demerits. Galeen, for example, probably had a great deal more to do with *The Golem* than the scenario, and similarly the complete production unit of *The Student of Prague,* including Herman Warm, Gunther Krampf, and Erich Nitzschmann, all well-known technicians, should receive credit. This remarkable film, almost un-German in its character, stands out during the transition period, when the decorative art film was being succeeded by the naturalistic film. Expressionist themes and cubist settings, so marked in the first German period, had developed into motives of mysticism and Baroque design, to give place again to the naturalness of the street, the town, and the individual. *The Student of Prague* combined both of these two latter periods. It had open spaciousness and dark psychology, wild poetic beauty and a deeply dramatic theme. Beyond this, it had Conrad Veidt at his best; a performance that he never equalled before or since.

It was, possibly, theatrical—but it was, also, filmic in exposition. From the beginning of the students' drinking scene to the final death of Baldwin, this film was superbly handled. The conflict of inner realities, the sadness and joy of changing atmospheres, the storm emphasizing the anguish of Baldwin, the rendering of the depths of human sorrow and weakness, the imagination and purity of treatment, the intensely dramatic unfolding of the theme—all these entitled this film to rank as great. The interior design was admirable, lit with some of the most beautiful lighting I have observed. As a film that relied for its emotional effect on the nature of the material, the lighting and pictorial composition, it was unparalleled. Two other productions go to the credit of Galeen, *Mandrake* (*A Daughter of Destiny*) and *After the Verdict*, a British production; but little can be said in praise of them, although it is only fair to add that the British version of the former film was completely mutilated in order to meet the censor's requirements.

Paul Leni's *Waxworks* was a typical example of the early decorative film, revealing, as would be expected from an artist of this character, a strong sense of painted, rather theatrical, architecture. As is probably known, the film purported to tell three episodic incidents of three wax figures in a showman's tent, developed by the imagination of a poet, the figures being Ivan the Terrible, Haroun-al-Raschid, and Jack-the-Ripper. The parts were played by Conrad Veidt, Emil Jannings, and Werner Krauss, respectively, and it was the only occasion on which these three celebrated actors have appeared together in the same film. Their individual performances were magnificently acted in the theatrical manner. Leni's decorations were simply conceived, but *Waxworks*, certainly a film of exceptional interest, was not by any means great from a filmic point of view. Its significance lay in its exemplary methods of simplicity both in treatment and in design. Leni also made *Prince Cuckoo*, a film about which there is little on record and, as already mentioned, designed the settings for Robison's *Manon Lescaut*. His career in Hollywood, where he went in 1926, was marked by two good melodramatic thrillers, *The Chinese Parrot* and *The Cat and the Canary*, which he followed with a travesty of cinematic methods, *The Man Who Laughs*. He died in 1929, having just completed an all-sound-and-dialogue picture for his American employers, Universal.

The work of Lupu Pick has tended to become over-praised and over-estimated. He played, it is true, a part of some importance in the gradual dawn of the German naturalistic school, with the production in 1923 of *New Year's Eve*, but this film itself was dreary. It was over-acted, in the worst German manner, by Eugen Klöpfer, a stage actor who knew little of the film, and it was made without titles. Pick's direction is principally characterized by a slow, deliberate development of plot and character, depending wholly on the acting value and narrative situations for dramatic effect. Apart from *New Year's Eve* (the English renaming of *Sylvester*), he is known chiefly by his dull version of Ibsen's *The Wild Duck; The Last Cab*, in which he played the lead; *The Rail*, and *La Casemate Blindée*. He came to Elstree in 1928, and made for the Louis Blattner Film Corporation *A Knight in London*, a light comedy with camerawork by Karl Freund. His interest, therefore, really lies in the transitional nature of his earlier films. Dr. Arnold Fanck is associated principally with that superb mountain film, *The Wrath of the Gods*, a picture of great pictorial beauty. Recently he joined G. W. Pabst in the Alpine film, *The White Hell of Pitz Palü*.

The German cinema has been a great cinema. It has produced principles and processes that have made important contributions to the cinema of the world. From its individual development there have come the freedom of the camera, the feeling of completeness, and the importance of architectural environment as part of the realization. These have been brought about by the national aptitude for craftsmanship, for structure, for studioism. They have been a means to an end that in itself has not yet been discovered. It has been well said that the German film begins and ends in itself. This, with certain reservations, is true.

In recapitulation, it has been seen how the years immediately after the war gave rise to the historical costume melodrama, commercial products of the property room and Reinhardt (*Dubarry, Anne Boleyn, Othello, Merchant of Venice*). There was then *The Cabinet of Doctor Caligari*, with its decorative environment and its use of psychology, to be followed by other expressionist films, *Torgus, Raskolnikov, Genuine*, and later, *The Stone Rider*. From these there developed the decorative film, increasing in pictorial beauty to the culminating *Faust* (*Siegfried, Waxworks, Destiny*). Then began the feeling for reality, still by studio representation, with *Scherben* and *The Street*, followed in time by the work of Lupu Pick, Murnau, Czinner, Pabst, Dupont (*New York's Eve, Last Laugh, Nju, Joyless Street, Vaudeville,* and *Baruch* [1924]); later by Rahn and Bernhardt; until there came the surrender to the American cinema—resulting in commercial melodrama, to be relieved only by the isolated films of Pabst, the large-scale studio-films of Lang, and the childlike psychology of Hans Behrendt's *Robber Band* and *Die Hose.* Finally, there is the crisis presented by the advent of the dialogue and sound film, the result of which has yet to be seen.

The French Avant-Garde
by George Morrison

*Mr. Morrison, historian and journalist, has written extensively
on films for European publications. He wrote this chapter
for the Fall 1948 issue of the magazine Sequence.*

From the early Twenties onwards, the output of experimental films in France showed a remarkable increase; all of them were made with very limited means, and hardly any received distribution outside film societies and a few specialized cinemas. With no chance of reaching a wide public, one might have thought that the *avant-gardists* would have aimed at an exclusive minority appeal, but apart from the lively, gifted dilettantes—most of whom, headed by Man Ray, made abstract films—many directors grounded their work in common reality. There were, of course, films of fantasy—*La Coquille et le Clergyman, Le Chien Andalou*—mostly with a strong sexual motive, in line with surrealist explorations in the other arts; but in this period also Grémillon, Autant-Lara and Cavalcanti produced their first work, and drew their material from contemporary life—the city, the port, the music-hall, the sea.

In 1923 Marcel L'Herbier and Pierre MacOrlan wrote a scenario called *L'Inhumaine*, the story, slight but unexpected, of a young opera singer who treats all her lovers with disdain until, poisoned by a jealous maharaja, she is rescued from death through a highly dangerous experiment carried out in the laboratory of an engineer. The actress Georgette Leblanc cautiously agreed to play the lead, after the rewriting of certain scenes, and *L'Inhumaine* was produced the following year, with camerawork by Specht and Roch, and a brilliant team of art-directors—the architect Robert Mallet-Stevens, who was interested in the development of architectural design in the cinema, and the painter Fernand Léger, with Autant-Lara and Cavalcanti as assistants. Incidental music was by Darius Milhaud.

The film's main interest lies not in the laboratory experiment, which is remote, nor in L'Herbier's typically frigid treatment, but in the sets, Mallet-Stevens' designs and the charming, decorative scenes of Léger. The influence of these may be seen in *Metropolis*, made by Lang and Werndorff in 1926.

In 1924 Claude Autant-Lara made his first film, *Fait-Divers*. His training as set-designer to L'Herbier is apparent in all Autant-Lara's work, from the beautifully observed Paris backgrounds of *Fait-Divers* to *Douce* and *Le Diable au Corps* twenty years later. The subject here is daily happenings in the life of a city, with special emphasis on the story of a woman—played by the director's mother, Mme. Lara of the Comédie Française—who, after being married for twenty years, meets an old lover; this part was taken by Antonin Artaud, author of *La Coquille et le Clergyman*. The film ends with a *crime passionel:* the woman's husband, becoming jealous, murders the lover. The tale is not very distinguished, but *Fait-Divers* is remarkable for the way Autant-Lara combined it with the general background, of which L'Herbier wrote: "Autant-Lara has tried to blend, in a very musical rhythm, and with some interesting experiments in camerawork, the life of a great city and the daily, commonplace *fait-divers* which make its drama." The film contains the elements of a "city symphony," a long line of which was to follow.

Also concerned with the city, but much more abstract in its approach, was Henri Chomette's sophisticated *Jeux des Reflets et de la Vitesse*, which contained "cineportraits" of social and literary personalities of the day, the poetess Comtesse de Noailles, Princess Bibesco, Mrs. Fellowes and Lady Abdy, photographed by Man Ray. Estheticism flirts with fashion as abstract, optically distorted forms gradually coalesce and resolve themselves into the faces of these contemporary beauties, dissolve again into distorted reflections of light, and are followed by "symphonic" views of Paris and the Seine, in quickening tempo. The film is elegant and entertaining in a rather forced manner, and lacks the satirical humor of *Le Ballet Mécanique*, and the genuinely irresponsible gaiety, the sense of the ridiculous, which characterized *Entr'acte*, directed in the same year by Chomette's brother, René Clair.

Entr'acte, based on a scenario by the painter Picabia, was produced for Rolf de Mare's Swedish Ballet, to be shown during a performance of the ballet "Relâche." A young man has spent the evening at a fair, and afterwards all the images of a carnival—dancers, illusionists, side-shows, pantomime landscapes—spin through his mind. Clair traces them with completely irrational, irresponsible fantasy, and conjures up a kind of apotheosis of the harlequinade and *bouffonade*, with touches of poetry and of macabre wit. Cigarettes stand up like cylinders from their box and change into pillars of the Parthenon, the ballerina's whirling skirt seen from a low angle becomes a flower opening, an egg on a jet of water suggests the target at a shooting-gallery, the target suggests the idea of death, appropriately conveyed by a funeral procession with a hearse drawn by a camel and this in its turn plunges down an endless hill as a frantic chase develops. . . . Besides this, a number of artists made unexpected appearances—Man Ray and the painter Duchamp on a rooftop, playing chess—Eric Satie, who wrote the music, Milhaud, Mlle. Friis and Jean Borlin of the Swedish Ballet. The film was full of that delightfully laconic, visual satire that Clair was later to bring to a more familiar territory which he made peculiarly his own in *Sous les Toits de Paris* and *Le Quatorze Juillet*.

The year 1924 also saw the opening of the first specialized cinema in France, the Vieux Colombier. No film achieves its end until it is seen, and up to this time the *avant-garde* had been allowed by not unnaturally timid exhibitors no more than a very occasional showing of its work. The first program of the Vieux Colombier in October consisted of Robison's *Warning Shadows*, a film without titles, *L'Horloge*, by Marcel Silver, and extracts from *La Roue* made by Abel Gance himself, under the title *Selection des Rhythmes*. A few months later the now well-known Studio des Ursulines opened with Pabst's *Joyless Street* and *Fait-Divers*. A few others were encouraged to spring up, and for a time there was an outlet for the small independent productions of the new movement; also, several *avant-garde* films were shown at the Exposition des Arts Decoratifs in 1925.

A minor result of this was that one producer was actually moved to make an experimental film himself, as an indirect compliment to the new cinema. Louis Nalpas, who had previously managed to get Gance's *La Folie du Docteur Tube* a restricted distribution, directed in 1925 a comedy called *Hands and Feet*, in which the entire story was conveyed by shots of these parts of the body; and there, really, its interest ends.

From 1926 onwards the *avant-garde* was greatly strengthened by the lyrical documentaries of Grémillon and Cavalcanti. The abstract experiments continued—Chomette made *Cinque Minutes de Cinéma Pur,* a photographic study of growing crystals, Man Ray alternated optically distorted light and dancers in *Emak Bakia,* achieved a kind of impressionistic effect by taking shots of figures through mica screens in *L'Etoile de Mer* (with a scenario by Antonin Artaud), a film of considerable visual beauty, and in the curious, inconsequential *Mystères du Château du Dé* showed gymnasts playing with huge medicine balls in an old castle, juxtaposing some remarkable landscape shots; and the painter Duchamp, with *Anaemic Cinema* (1927) contrived some interesting patterns of abstract movement. Earlier films of this kind had been animated frame by frame from individual drawings, but here, by placing eccentrically on the surface of gramophone turntables a number of different patterns of concentric circles and spirals, Duchamp produced a variety of changing abstract designs, which he alternated with moving titles in verse. But it was in two wholly different films, *Rien Que les Heures* and *Tour au Large* that the *avant-garde,* perhaps, showed a more substantial development.

Cavalcanti's *Rien Que les Heures* (1926) was concerned with the passage of a single day in Paris. Extending the method of *Fait-Divers,* more impersonal and comprehensive in approach, it was the first film to explore fully the uses of rhythmical editing in this kind of documentary. Like most of Cavalcanti's work, *Rien Que les Heures* is uneven and rather lacking in warmth, and in spite of its fine compositions and its fluency, stops short of being a masterpiece; but its influence has been considerable. Later, of course, this type of film was so frequently imitated that the whole approach has become a cliché—but that, with a fresh imagination, it still need not be, was recently demonstrated by the Swedish director Sucksdorff in his *People in the City.*

A quality which has always characterized Grémillon's work is his highly developed sense of the dramatically expressive material in natural backgrounds, particularly of the sea, and in *Tour au Large* (1926), his extraordinarily beautiful film about the tunny fishing fleets, this sensibility is strikingly present. It is a film full of the surge of the waves and the sparkle of sunlight on the waters, in Grémillon's own words: "a film of impressions, a marriage of music and images." The music was written by Grémillon himself. In one sequence, the manner in which the fish loom up into focus from the depths of submarine mists is remarkably similar to a later work by Cricrson, *Drifters*.

Others directors, influenced probably by the experiments of Grémillon and Cavalcanti, made realistic studies; two of the most charming were *Paris-Port*, by André Sauvage and Jean Tedesco, director of the Vieux Colombier, about shipping on the Seine, and Georges Lacombe's film of a Paris market, *La Zone* (1928). Marc Allegret and André Gide produced a record of their African travels in *Voyage au Congo*, and Grémillon made another film of the sea, *Les Gardiens du Phare* (1928), a story of two lighthouse keepers from the book by Nicole Vedrés; it was again remarkable for the poetry of its seascapes, and also the robust treatment of simple characters which foreshadows his later *Remorques*.

It is strange that Cavalcanti's talent, after the promise of *Rien Que les Heures*, failed on the whole to develop. *La Petite Lilie* (1927) was a charming but very slight little burlesque film with Catherine Hessling, based on a popular traditional song, and done artificially with stylized sets and "gauze" shots; but in *En Rade* he had a subject of far greater scope. In a harbor-town a washcrwoman's son dreams of traveling, of far-away islands and landscapes. He plans to elope with a waitress (Catherine Hessling) but is prevented by his possessive mother and the unwitting intervention of a local idiot, strikingly played by Philippe Hériat, who wrote the scenario. The town backgrounds are studied in detail, with some really impressive compositions, but once again these cannot prevent a deficiency of feeling from showing through.

An important departure both from the films that found their means of expression in reality and in abstract images, Germaine Dulac's *La Coquille et le Clergyman* attempted to depict inward states of mind by visual symbols. A young priest, nerve-racked by the conflict between his compulsion of celibacy and his frustrated sexual desires, pursues a white-robed woman in dreamlike circumstances and surroundings—on all fours along a street, through a bare hall being swept by maids, on the edge of a lake and a cliff—and is constantly thwarted by a burly, muscled rival in uniform. The author, Antonin Artaud, conceived it as a surrealist film, for he wrote: "The visual action should operate on the mind as an immediate intuition." He added: "The scenario is not the story of a dream, and does not profess to be such," but the film's framework, with its bewildering changes of background, disappearing and reappearing figures, suggests a dream atmosphere. But to regard it, as some critics have done, as a psychologist's case-book consciously worked out beforehand in Freudian symbols, is misleading; the illuminating point, rather, of *La Coquille et le Clergyman* is how an artist, working intuitively and unconsciously, may achieve a symbolic picture of mental conflicts—that some of the symbols may also be found in Freud, not through design but as a result of the unconscious process, serves to emphasize validity. It does seem, however, that the director Germaine Dulac—keeping too rigidly, perhaps, to her conceptions of *"cinéma-pur"*—at times obscured Artaud's intentions by camera-angles too arbitrarily unorthodox and contrived. But the film, though uneven, is impressive and bears the impact of an original mind. A few months later Artaud himself played the young priest in Dreyer's *La Passion de Jeanne d'Arc*; and not long after this he became insane, and spent twenty years in an asylum before dying there this year.

Influenced partly by earlier German expressionist films, Jean Epstein's *La Chute de la Maison Usher* (1928), based on two stories by Poe, relies almost entirely on camera devices —low-key photography, slow motion, effective use of drapes, curtains, candles—to create drama and atmosphere. The camerawork is extremely fine, the compositions striking, but the narrative, unfortunately, is submerged by so much stylistic detail. But the treatment of Kirsanov's fourth film, *Brumes d'Automne*, transforms an unpromising subject. An old woman (Nadia Sibirskaya) recalls the past, and as she burns letters it is re-enacted on the screen; outside, rain is falling, there are reflecting pools of water in the streets, leaves drop from the trees; the symbolism is commonplace, but the photography, by Gouan, remarkably delicate and beautiful, an essay in subtle atmospherics.

Autant-Lara's *Pour Construire Un Feu* (1929) is a film of great experimental interest. Based on a story by Jack London —which describes in detail how a man, cut off in the northern snows, tries to light a fire to warm himself, wonders how he will survive—it was photographed and projected so that the screen shape and size might be continuously varied throughout the film, and so that subsidiary, parallel action could take place all around the main picture area. The same idea was suggested by Eisenstein to the Technical Branch of the Academy of Motion Picture Arts and Sciences in Hollywood a year later.

In 1929, also, the last year of the silent period, Luis Buñuel and Salvador Dali made *Le Chien Andalou.* This has become one of the most discussed of the surrealist films, the stock example, almost, of its type—and one with which the initiated are prone to tantalize the uninitiated and the young. Whatever its importance in the development of the *avant-garde* (which is primarily, perhaps, one of prestige), it wears badly. Though it starts with the promising title: "Nothing in this film symbolizes Anything," and is said to have been made with no conscious idea-pattern or dream symbolism, it consists of short sequences which can only be described as narrative in style. The room and the street where much of the action takes place are naturalistically shown, unchanging, the time sequence is specific enough to allow for a flashback. Compared with *La Coquille et le Clergyman,* it uses far fewer camera devices destructive of reality, and its effects, as well as settings and lighting, look amateur in the bad sense by comparison. Nor has it the earlier film's unity, either in narrative or the use of symbols. The shock tactics for which it is famous are no longer really striking, partly because one has read about them, more because of the absence of sound and effective presentation; the eye-slitting, the ants crawling over a hand, seem patently faked, and the clergymen and donkey-laden pianos suggest more a Marx Brothers joke gone wrong. (Though a modern equivalent could be imagined which would make audiences swoon as these once did.) *Un Chien Andalou* is most successful when it tries least—the episode of the mysterious girl in the street, which communicates a sensation that rightly defies analysis without appearing forced, and the moment of poetry when the heroine comes out of the house, previously established as in the center of the town, to find it facing immediately on to a deserted sea-shore.

The Passion of Jeanne D'Arc
by Harry Alan Potamkin

One of the first film critics of consequence in the United
States, Mr. Potamkin wrote frequently in the late Twenties
and Thirties for such publications as Close Up, Hound and
Horn, New Masses and Vanity Fair. This chapter appeared
originally in 1929 in the National Board of Review.

We are always waiting in the cinema for the eventual film
which will be the vindication of the major cinema devices. We
are always waiting for the film down to essentials and yet conveying a profound human experience. For the craft of the
movie, like the craft of any other art, is performance—of
camera, of film, of player, of screen. (Mr. Alexander Bakshy
has stated these four as the different cinema performances or
movements, a fundamental statement.) But as an art conclu-
sive the cinema must find its source in experience and its
final meaning in experience. Where is the motion picture—
we are always asking—profound in its exploitation of performance, and profound in its transmission of experience?
This query is the key to the importance of plot in the movie,
not as detailed or episodic narrative but as subject-matter.
The consideration of plot as narrative has been the cause and
result of the movie's literalness (particularly in America) and
the inability to include in the formation of the moving picture
the inferences of the theme, much more important than the
narrative. This inability has prevented a film so dramatically
effective as Feyder's recent *Thérèse Raquin* (adapted from
Zola's novel) from being a film of permanent importance.

In brief, we are always waiting for a film reduced but
with passionate human content. The purity of passionate apprehension. A film mindful of the plot as the subject-matter
of life. A film using the legitimate emphasis of the camera
(or other kino instruments) and realizing an experience of
form and content completely fused and fluid. We are always
waiting for the expression of a perspicacious knowledge of the
medium, and of the matter it is to convert into and by means
of itself. The American film has realized in its literalness a
pleasant but shallow ease of sequence. The German has stressed,

118

in the main, the device as virtuosity rather than as an incorporate, revealing utility. The Swedish film, like the notable *Atonement of Gosta Berling*, is a rigorous life-exposition, but it has not fully grasped the principle of the conversion of the subject matter. The French movie on the whole is too banal or too pretty or too frivolous (without being lively) to merit our interest. Yet the film which in this instance satisfies our anticipation is a French film. Its achievement may be explained by the fact that its director is a Dane, Carl Th. Dreyer. The film is *The Passion of Jeanne d'Arc*.

This profound and truly passionate motion picture concerns itself with the last day of Jeanne, the day of excruciating torment. The scenario is the combined work of the director and Joseph Delteil, the dadaist who wrote the prize-winning book on The Maid. It is, I hope, no libel of M. Delteil to suspect that the disciplining will of the director (a prime essential in the cinema industry today) kept the narrative within the strenuous limits of reverence. Reverence is a portion of the intensity of this film, an intensity to which everything submits —the decor by Jean Victor-Hugo, the photography of Maté, with its superb statement of personalities by the skin-textures and moles. In total accord with this intense and intensive exploitation of the subject-matter (remember there is really no plot here, on the last moment—the queries, the betrayal, the final conflagration), is the use of the succession of individual cine-photos. These are not close-ups (there is no "closing up" in the bland movie way), not stills (for the angles and curves are lovely and illuminating), but the bold concentration of individual faces and figures in the active, critical, voracious eye of the camera. This would suggest a static series of pictures, not Mr. Bakshy's "dynamic sequence," rather the mere physical basis of filming than the esthetic aspiration of the cinema. But it attests to Carl Dreyer's genius that the sequence is eminently fluid, dramatic, rhythmic. The succession has a definite time-order, a definite plastic arrangement in the time-order of exquisite curves (the performers exploited by the camera) and bodily angles, a definite utilization of the screen as the receptive instrument (advocated long ago by Mr. Bakshy, but very seldom realized), and a gradual almost unsuspected rise to the final mob explosion. There are diagonal curves of the moving performers, vertical inclines, a forehead above the lower frame boldly duplicating the moderated masses of the background.

There is no extraneous detail in the film. Not once does a detail fail to directly relate and contribute to the subject-matter. At one point, Jeanne sees the grave-digger pull up a skull. Unnecessary? Obvious? There is a swift succession, almost staccato in its brevity, to a field of flowers. The previous detail becomes inevitable, poignant. In fact, the entire film has that virtue, that at any moment the detail on the screen validates what preceded it. This is rhythm, this is art. The beautiful flight of birds, as Jeanne is perishing, the mother suckling her child—the former might be a sentimentalism, the latter a surrealistic simplicism; but by the severe control of the director, they become terrible convictions of the world that would let one who loved free flight perish bound, and one who herself would suck life burn at the stake. Creation against desolation!

The torment of the young peasant girl, "called Jeannette at home," convinced in her childishness and mysticism of her divine mission, becomes the emotional experience of the spectator. Her fears, persistent under the insistent examination, become heavy with the burden of the torment, become luminous with the momentary glamor and memory stirred by the queries. The heavy tear imparts to the spectator the sense of the days and months of anguish the girl has endured in her steadfastness to her inspiration. The luminous tear elucidates the girl's origins, her free fields, her home, and the momentum of the inspiration that has urged her into this betrayal. The tears of Falconetti, the portrayer of Jeanne, are not the tears of a Clara Bow, insipid, irritating, fraudulent. Her eyes enamored of God borrow no stage-pantomime, but with the grained skin and parched lips, the clipped hair, and chained walk, reveal the entire enterprise of God and land within the girl's body. Falconetti faithfully submits to the intensity of the unit, enters into it, and expresses it while she expresses Jeanne. She is the conception. She is the film. An identical loyalty is manifested by each of the accurately chosen, thoroughly participating cast. No specious prettiness, but hardiness, man in his physical variousness, man in his spiritual diversity serving the same master—Interest. The Interest of State, the Interest of God. Jeanne, serving God, alone of all has served herself, her systemic soul-and-body. She as the servant of herself becomes the everlasting, the others are left to weep upon the torment they have connived. The State alone (Warwick) remains unperturbed, save to halt the conflagration of Jeanne which threatens to burn down the power of England in Rouen. As no prologue was needed, no epilogue is asked for and no commentary from the distance of several centuries. How superior to Shaw's Joan! The inference all embodied in the unit-structure, not tagging along like loose threads, nor stressed like a moral to a fable. One fault alone disturbs the perfection of this grand film, a fault easily eliminated: there are too many captions, well written though they are. Fewer captions jotted in the staccato brevity of many of the images that pass almost before one sees them—these would have better suited the film's attitude, and not served to weaken (even if in the minutest degree, as the captions do at present) the demanding simplicity and rigorousness of this beautiful work.

The Passion of Jeanne d'Arc is an historical film, but not a costume film; an historical film that is contemporaneous in its universal references. *The Passion of Jeanne d'Arc* is a religious film, but not a sanctimonious film. Life, it urges, is transcendent. It is a transcendent film.

Eisenstein, Pudovkin and Others
by Dwight Macdonald

Mr. Macdonald, one of the most prolific and vigorous of the current essayists, is a member of the staff of The New Yorker and political writer for Esquire, which he served previously as film critic. This chapter appeared originally in the March 1931 issue of the publication Miscellany.

Ever since Eisenstein's *Potemkin* and Pudovkin's *Mother* were produced in 1926, the Union of Soviet Socialist Republics has been showing the rest of the world what can be done with the movies. As Tolstoi and Dostoevsky took up the European novel and played upon it variations so fundamental that the instrument seemed to change its very nature in their hands, so Eisenstein and Pudovkin have taken up the cinema and developed it so far that it, too, seems almost a different vehicle from what existed before in this country and abroad. The rapidity of this development* is all the more remarkable when one considers the masterpieces that have already come out of Russia. In the following pages I have tried, first, to discuss the relationship of propaganda to the Soviet cinema, second, to describe (as much as possible in the words of its two great directors) the theories behind that cinema's characteristic technique, and, third, to comment upon the work of certain directors, Russian and American, who seem to me important.

"Among all your arts the most important is that of the cinema."—*Lenin.* "Molding the feeling and intelligence of the masses is one of our political problems and for this end we find the movies most effective."—*Eisenstein.* Here we have a statement and an explanation. The statement is that the

---

* The movies made in Russia before 1926 have almost no connection in technique and theory with those made afterwards. So embryonic was the Russian cinema in 1924 that an authority on it could write: "Some of its extreme supporters have a vision of a socialist mass film similar in construction to but different in meaning from *The Birth of a Nation* in which the people themselves could take a part." Needless to say, the "vision" of the "extreme supporters" was realized two years later in *Potemkin.* And the same writer dismisses the whole Russian cinema thusly: "Today it occupies a place in the universal film world best described as the lower depths. The Russian film industry needs technical experts, it needs photographers who can take a photo. . . ."

cinema is of the first importance to the Soviet. Explanation: because it is an incomparably "effective" means of influencing the masses and educating them in the doctrines of Communism. This social purpose has shaped, distorted perhaps, every movie that has been made in Russia. Therefore, whenever Russian movies are mentioned, someone is sure to cry "propaganda!" as if that settled the whole business. Presumably he would find the same taint in "Paradise Lost," whose announced aim is "to justify the ways of God to man." The fact is that art is often aimed at the glorification of some social class. That the artists of the renaissance glorified the aristocracy and that the Soviet artists glorify the proletariat is not a very important distinction. The artist does not worry about the precise color of his social, moral, and religious views. He accepts those of his age and nation—or, if it suits his temper better, he revolts against them. But his primary interest is his art. He will take orders as to his views on Communism, Mormonism, or free trade, but he will not take orders as to the way he is to express these things in his art. The Hollywood director is subjected to just that sort of dictation: he must not bewilder his audience by telling his story in a subtle or original way. Every picture must be capable of being grasped by the 120,000,000 Lords and Masters of America, which means that every picture must come as close to mediocrity as is humanly possible. The Russian director has his orders plainly enough about the political tone of his pictures, but he is free to express this just as he pleases. He can be as bold and subtle and experimental as he wants as far as his technique is concerned; and this is the kind of freedom the artist must have.

This freedom, as contrasted with the intolerable bondage under which Hollywood groans, is the condition that has allowed Russian directors to so far outstrip their Hollywood comrades in movie technique. That it exists in Russia and not over here is nothing to the credit of either Russian directors or Russian audiences. The average Russian audience is undoubtedly even less *intelligent* than the average American audience. If the Russians take a national interest in brilliantly (that is to say, boldly, subtly, and, to the average person, incomprehensibly) directed pictures, it is because of that very propaganda which bothers the esthetes so much. This propaganda is the sugar coating on the bitter pill of art. Since the

Russian proletariat cannot get its political glorification without at the same time swallowing a certain amount of good art, it takes heart and gulps down both at once. The point the esthetes overlook is that the Russian cinema is primarily a manifestation of a great social renewal. The stimulus of a national awakening makes possible not only the enthusiasm of the people for movies experimental (hence difficult) in technique and serious (hence unattractive) in treatment, but also the creation of such movies by the directors. "New ideas can come only from new social forms," declares Eisenstein. "Russia has them and so Russia leads the world today. The renaissance, for instance, could come about only when the old order was changed. So it is with film art, which comes about only after a big social change. At present America and Europe seem to be groping about for something they cannot find. That is why they are using our ideas." It might be maintained that no people has ever supported good art unless the entire nation was drunk. The merchants who paid for medieval cathedrals were drunk with what Lenin calls "the opium of the people." The Athenian citizenry who sat all day on stone benches to hear Aeschylus and Sophocles were obviously drunk—with national pride, most potent of liquors. The Russians of today are intoxicated with a great new social theory, whence their insane delight in good cinema. We Americans are only too sober.

Thus propaganda, instead of being the fatal weakness of the Soviet cinema, is, philosophically and historically considered, its greatest source of strength. Though it sometimes leads to inartistic exaggeration, it also provides that seriousness of purpose, that elevation in the treatment of a theme which is so marked in the movies of Russia and so lacking in those of this country. "Romantic entertainment does not enter our films," contemptuously declares Eisenstein. "We always have a message to bring out that will help build up our country under its new regime. . . . For a subject we always go to the heart of the masses, find out what they need, and then build a scenario around it." The Russian director has a message to give to the people, a message that they are eager to receive. He delivers it in his own way, dictates his own terms to his audience, which accepts his terms for the sake of his message. The teachings of Christ must have often been incomprehensible to the people; we know they were sometimes so to his disciples. But he continued to speak in parables, letting wisdom fall from his lips for the people to gather up as they might. "But without a parable spake he not unto them: and when they were alone, he expounded all things to his disciples." Prophets, artists, philosophers cannot afford to compromise or condescend in their relations with the people. When the artist has no message, as today in America, he can preserve his integrity by keeping aloof from the people. But this course is not open to the movie director, whose work must be for the people as a whole. Since he has nothing to tell them (Henry Ford and Thomas Edison are the message-bearers, not King Vidor, not Josef von Sternberg) he must entertain them. If his work rarely comes out full and strong and living it is because his master, the mob, prefers the easily shallow, the safely dead. It is otherwise with the Russian director. His message makes him the master, the only tolerable position for a man of talent.

There are several qualifications that must be noted here to the foregoing discussion. The distinction between the Russian and the American director cannot be wholly stated in terms of "master" and "servant" or of "bondage" and "freedom." It is true that the Russian director is not "free" so far as his social viewpoint goes, that he must express Communistic ideas in his pictures, but it is also true that he is eager to do so anyway. He is as much inspired by the vision of Communism as anyone. The American has greater freedom in that his pictures do not have to preach any particular doctrine, but this very freedom puts him at a disadvantage. Since the Communist ideology provides the Russian director with a point of view he knows his audience also holds, it makes communication between him and his audience much easier. The Christian religion has done the same thing for generations of artists. The American director, with no such definite system to show him the limits within which he must work, is as much at sea on this vital point as the other artists of this country. Nor are the shrewd pants-pressers who run our movies much better judges of what the public wants, as could be amply illustrated by box office records. Another qualification must be made as to the "mastery" of the Russian director over his audience. Though it is accurate to term the American director the servant of his public, the Russian is so much in sympathy with the viewpoint of the people that no sharp distinction can be made as to which of the two parties is dominant. The relationship is that of colleagues rather than of ruler and ruled. There is one point that needs more qualifying than any other, namely, the alleged "freedom" of the Russian director to mystify his audience with trick technique as contrasted to the compulsion put upon the American to keep his technique within the grasp of the crowd. The fact is that Russian movies are designed for the masses even more deliberately than our own. Their brilliant technique is simply what Eisenstein and the others have arrived at after a scientific study of audience reactions. From this aspect the technical superiority of Russian movies is due not to a disregard of the people but to a more intelligent and intensive study of them. Whereas Hollywood has merely tried to please the public's taste (a hopeless effort, for popular taste is notoriously unstable, and a useless one, for popular taste is always bad), the Russians have brushed this aside as unimportant, and have gone straight to the heart of the matter: not what *pleases* audiences, but what *affects* them, what moves and influences them whether they know it or not and whether they like it or not.

In considering the cinematic technique of the Russians the first thing that impresses the American observer is the artistic sophistication of the Russian directors. Most Hollywood directors are practical fellows who know pretty well how to knock together a movie but who are noticeably silent when it comes to esthetic theory. The Russians, however, evidently have thought long and deeply about the nature of the cinema. It is the directors themselves who analyze their art, and it is they who lead in any discussion of its esthetics. Over here the directors, perhaps wisely, leave theory to the intelligentsia. The causes of this striking difference are too complex to be analyzed here. One curious but possibly important factor may be mentioned: the shortage of camera film in Russia for many years after the Revolution. This forced the directors to do a great deal of abstract thinking about their art before they ventured to use up any of the precious film. Many a Hollywood director would benefit from a strict rationing of film— though the masterful Von Stroheim works on precisely the opposite principle. Whatever the cause, the two great Russian directors are remarkably articulate about the cinema, so much that it will be possible to describe their achievements in technique largely through their own words.

The backbone of Russian movie technique is "montage," i.e., the arranging of the individual "shots" (a "shot" is the picture that is etched on the film every time the camera shutter opens) in a desired order. More fully: after the reels of film have been run through the camera, the director "mounts" the resulting shots. That is, he cuts them apart and arranges them in the order in which he wants them to be thrown on the screen when the film is projected. In emphasizing montage the Russians in effect declare that the important motion is not that which goes on before the camera but that which is created by one shot moving onto the screen as another moves off. "Cinematography is, first and foremost, montage," writes Eisenstein. And Pudovkin is equally emphatic:

I claim that every object is a dead object even though it has moved before the camera. For movement before the camera is not movement before the screen. It is no more than raw material for the future building-up of the real movement, which is that obtained by the assemblage of the various strips of film. Only if the object be related to other objects, only if it be presented as part of a synthesis of different separate visual images, is it endowed with filmic life. . . . Every object must, by editing [*i.e., montage*], be brought upon the screen so that it shall have not *photographic* but *cinematographic* meaning. Editing is the basic creative force by power of which the soulless photographs are engineered into living, cinematographic form.

Though Pudovkin and Eisenstein are the two great Russian directors, apparently they did not originate the principle of montage. According to Pudovkin, this conception was first advanced by Lev Vladimirovitch Kuleshov, also a director.

It was from Kuleshov [*writes Pudovkin*] that I first learned the meaning of the word "montage," a word which played such an important part in the development of our film art. From our contemporary point of view Kuleshov's ideas were extremely simple. All he said was this: "In every art there must be firstly a material, and secondly a method of composing this material specially adapted to this art." The musician has sounds as material and composes them in rhythm. The painter's materials are color, and he combines them in space on the surface of the canvas. What, then, is the material which the film director possesses, and what are the methods of composition

127

of his material?

Kuleshov maintained that the material in film work consists of pieces of film, and that the composition method is their joining together in a particular, creatively discovered order. He maintained that film art does not begin when the artists act and the various scenes are shot—this is only the preparation of the material. Film art begins at the moment when the director begins to combine and join together the various pieces of film. By joining them in various combinations, in different orders, he obtains differing results.

This is a clear enough explanation of what montage means in theory. Pudovkin has also given us an example of what it means in practice:

In *Mother* I tried to affect the spectators not by the psychological performance of an actor but by plastic synthesis through editing. The son sits in prison. Suddenly, passed in to him surreptitiously, he receives a note that next day he is to be set free. The problem was the expression, filmically, of his joy. The photographing of a face lighted up with joy would have been flat and void of effect. I show, therefore, the nervous play of his hands, and a big close-up of the lower half of his face—the corners of a smile. These shots I cut in with other and more varied material: a brook swollen with the rapid flow of spring, the play of sunlight on water, birds splashing in the village pond, and, finally, a laughing child. By the junction of these components our expression of "prisoner's joy" takes shape. I do not know how the spectators reacted to my experiment; I myself have always been deeply convinced of its force.

This, then, is montage. Both Eisenstein and Pudovkin agree on its importance. There has been some difference of opinion, however, as to the interpretation of this concept. In the course of a brilliant article in the latest (and last) Transition Eisenstein indicates this rift and develops his own interpretation:

A shot. A single piece of celluloid.
A small rectangular frame with, somehow organized into it, a bit of an event.
Sticking to each other, these shots form montage. When they stick in appropriate rhythm, of course.
This, roughly, is the teaching of the old old school of cinematography.
Kuleshov, for example, writes: "Should there be for expression any fractional idea, any particle of the action, any link of the whole dramatic chain, then that idea must be expressed, built up out of shot-ciphers, as if out of bricks. . . ."
The shot—is an element of montage. Montage—is a 'junction of elements.'

A most pernicious method of analysis.

One in which the understanding of a process as a whole (linkage, shot-montage) is derived merely from the external characteristics of its flow (a piece is stuck to a piece).

The shot is in no wise an *element* of montage.

The shot is a montage *cell*.

Just as cells in their division form a phenomenon *of another order*, the organism or embryo. So, on the other side of the dialectical leap from the shot, there is montage.

By what, then, is characterized montage, and consequently its cell—the shot?

By collision. By conflict of two pieces standing in apposition to each other. By conflict. By collision.

In front of me lies a crumpled yellowed sheet of notepaper.

On it a mysterious note:

"Linkage—P." and "Shock—E."

This is the material trace of a hot engagement on the subject of montage between E—myself, and P—Pudovkin. (About a year ago.)

This is the established order. At regular intervals he comes to me late at night and we argue, behind closed doors, on subjects of principle.

Here as before. Hailing from the Kuleshov school he heatedly defended the conception of montage as a *linkage* of pieces. Into a chain. Bricks.

Bricks, by means of their rows *narrating* a concept.

I confronted him with my point of view of montage as *collision*. A viewpoint that from the collision of two given factors *arises* a concept.

Linkage is, in my interpretation, only a possible *special* case.

You remember what an infinite number of combinations is known in physics in the matter of the impact (collision) of balls.

According to whether they be resilient, or non-resilient, or mixed.

Amongst all these combinations there is one in which the impact is so weak that the collision degenerates into the even movement of both in one direction.

This case would correspond to the point of view of Pudovkin.

Not long ago I had another talk with him. Today he stands in agreement with my present point of view.

True, during the interval he has taken the opportunity to acquaint himself with the substance of the lectures I gave during that period at the Central Cinematograph College.

This conception of montage, if one will take the trouble (no small one) to understand it, is immensely fruitful. In place of Kuleshov's idea of montage as merely the sum of the shots, Eisenstein substitutes a sort of "fourth dimension" of an entirely different order that is *created* by the interaction

129

of the shots. His viewpoint seems to me organic where Kuleshov's is mechanical, dynamic where Kuleshov's is static. Eisenstein continues his essay by demonstrating that his principle of "conflict" may be taken as the Lowest Common Denominator of all branches of movie technique:

Thus, montage is conflict.

The basis of every art is always conflict. A peculiar "image" transubstantiation of the dialectic principle.

And the shot represents a montage *cell.*

So, consequently, it also must be considered from the point of view of conflict.

Intra-piece conflict: potential montage, in the development of its intensity shattering its quadrilateral cage and exploding its conflict into montage impulses between the montage pieces.

And if montage must be compared with something, then a phalanx of montage-pieces, "shots," should be compared to the series of explosions of an internal combustion engine, multiplying themselves into montage dynamics and thereby serving as "impulses" to drive along a tearing motor car or tractor.

Intra-piece conflict. It may be of very varied nature:

Conflict of scales.

Conflict of spaces.

Conflict of masses (spaces filled with various intensities of light).

Conflict of depths.

Close and long shots.

Dark pieces with light pieces, etc.

And, lastly, there are such unexpected conflicts as:

The conflict of an object with its normal dimension, and the conflict of an event with its normal temporal nature.

This may sound extraordinary, but both these cases are familiar.

The first: an optical distortion of the lens; the second: speeding-up or slow motion.

The assembling of all properties of cinematography into one formula of conflict, the grouping of all cinematographic characteristics into a dialectical series under a *single* head— is no empty rhetorical diversion.

We thus seek a unified systematization of the method of cinematographic expressiveness that shall hold good for all its elements.

The regarding of the frame as a particular "cellular" case of montage—the smashing of the dualism "shot-montage," makes possible the direct application of montage experience to the question of the theory of the shot.

The same with the question of lighting. The conception of this as a collision between a current of light and an obstacle, like the impact of a gush of water from a fire-hose striking an object, or of the wind buffeting against a person, must result in a usage of it which is entirely different from playing around with "gauzes" and "spots."

The one available such interpretative principle is the principle of conflict:

The principle of optical counterpoint.

And let us not now forget that shortly we shall have to solve another and less simple counterpoint, namely *the conflict of auditory and visual impulses in the sound cinema.*

This masterly analysis and even more masterly synthesis makes it clear that Eisenstein is not obsessed with montage to the exclusion of all else. He well knows that although cinematography is "first and foremost, montage," it is a great many other things as well. Neither he nor Pudovkin belongs to the extremist school of Vertov, which holds that a director who knows how to edit can make a movie out of any shots that happen to be lying around the laboratory. Even to gentlemen with a pet theory it should be evident that, as one cannot make bricks without straw, so it is unlikely one can make a good movie without good shots. Our quotations from Eisenstein's remarkable Transition essay (which, by the way, is primarily a discussion of the cinematographic elements in Japanese culture) may be concluded with his views on the composition of the individual shot:

At the moment, however, let us return to one of the most interesting of optical conflicts: the conflict between the limits of the frame and the object shot.

The shooting-angle as the materialization of conflict between the organizing logic of the director and the inert logic of the object, in collision giving the dialectic of cinema viewpoint.

In this respect we are still impressionistic and devoid of principle to a point of sickness.

But, in spite of this fact, a sharp degree of principle is proper to the technique of this also.

The dry quadrilateral, plunging into the haphazard of natural diffuseness. . . .

And once more we are back in Japan!

For, thus—the cinematographic is one of the methods of drawing instruction used in Japanese schools.

What is our method of drawing instruction?

We take an ordinary four-cornered piece of white paper. . . .

And we cram onto it, in most cases even without using the corners (the edges are usually grease-stained with long sweating over it), some tedious caryatid, some vain Corinthian capital, or a plaster Dante (not the juggler at the Moscow Hermitage, but the other one—Alighieri, the comedy writer).

The Japanese do the opposite.

Here's a branch of cherry-tree, or a landscape with a sailing boat.

And the pupil extracts from its whole, by means of a square, or a circle, or a rectangle, a composition unit.

He takes a frame!

And just by these two ways of teaching drawing are characterized the two basic tendencies struggling in the cinema of today.

The one: the expiring method of artificial spacial organization of the event in front of the lens.

From the "direction" of a sequence to the erection of a Tower of Babel in the literal sense, in front of the lens.

And the other: a "picking-out" by the camera, organization by its means. The hewing of a piece of actuality by means of the lens.

With this bit of analysis, as penetrating as it is dynamic, let us contrast, in accordance with the principle of conflict already enunciated, a cool and no less penetrating paragraph on the same subject by Pudovkin:

To distribute the material shot and its movements in the rectangle of the picture in such a way that everything is clearly and sharply apprehensible, to construct every composition in such a way that the right-angled boundaries of the screen do not disturb the composition found, but perfectly contain it—that is the achievement toward which film directors strive.

So much for the forms into which Russian cinematography casts its material: its methods of composition within the shot and of composition among the shots, or montage, have been expounded. But what of the material on which the Russians train their cameras? In this, too, they have worked a revolution. Eisenstein, as usual, expresses the heart of the matter when he speaks of "hewing a piece of actuality by means of the lens." (And, as usual, he exaggerates, for his own superbly composed shots must be to some extent "artificially organized" and not entirely "hewn" out of actuality.)

The movie camera feeds best on reality. The Russians have accepted this great truth as completely as the Germans have passed it by. "Away from realism to reality," cries Eisenstein. "From the studio setting and the professional actor to the original place and person. A thirty-year-old actor may be called upon to play an old man of sixty. He may have a few days' or a few hours' rehearsal. But an old man of sixty will have had sixty years' rehearsal." "I want to work only with real material—this is my principle," Pudovkin declares. "I maintain that to show, alongside real water and real trees and grass, a property beard pasted on the actor's face, wrinkles traced by means of paint, or stagey acting is impossible. It is opposed to the most elementary ideas of style." Where the Germans with infinite labor and cunning paint lines on their actors' faces that *almost* look real and build palaces of lath and plaster that *almost* pass for solid stone, the Russians lazily and naïvely take their cameras to old men and photograph *real* wrinkles, set them up before palaces and photograph *real* stone. They have grasped the fact that the camera and the film it makes are the instruments of artifice in the movies as the brush and paints are in painting, and that what is before the camera is not another artifice but the raw material of reality corresponding to the landscape that is before an artist. For an artist to view his landscape through colored glasses or for a director to work mostly inside the studio—this is, in Pudovkin's words, "opposed to the most elementary ideas of style."

It is understating it to call the Russians faithful to reality. They are intoxicated with it. Compared to the pictorial scope of the Russian cinema, our own movies are cramped and monotonous affairs. The Russians have let the camera loose into the open air world of clouds, sunlight, rippling waters, mountains, palaces, fortresses, city streets, prairies. They have demonstrated the *extensive* powers of the camera, which can range over the world of matter with the tireless freedom known only to the machine. And on the other hand they have even more clearly demonstrated that the camera can, by means of the close-up, *intensify* its vision down to the minutest detail. They express a peasant's mode of life, for instance, largely by glimpses of such minutiae as the clay vessels from which he eats, the barbaric necklace his wife wears on feast days, the worn handles of his plow, the fences that lean crazily about his fields. In more complex social strata the realistic detail is even more abundant. A general is meticulously presented button by button from his oiled-flat hair to his shiny boots. Banquets, with their china, crystal, silver, and wine, are a favorite theme among Soviet directors. The Germans, too, are good at suggesting local color with such realistic detail. But there is a much more vital use of detail at which the

Russians are unrivalled: the use of the close-up to emphasize the dramatic rhythm. A superb instance of this in *Ten Days that Shook the World* is the gigantic close-up of Kerensky's eye as he caps the decanter with the imperial crown. By bringing the camera lens within a few inches of the eye and the crown, the dramatic relationship of these two objects is powerfully expressed. "The detail will always be a synonym of intensification," Pudovkin writes. "The camera, as it were, forces itself, ever striving, into the profoundest depths of life; it strives thither to penetrate, whither the average spectator never reaches as he glances casually around him. In the discovered, deeply embedded detail there lies an element of perception, the creative element that characterizes as art the work of man. . . . In the disappearance of the general, obvious outline and the appearance on the screen of some deeply hidden detail, filmic representation attains the highest point of its power of external expression."

The two primary principles of montage and of actuality have radically affected the status of the actor in Russian films. Montage has obliterated the distinction between the performer and the setting in which he performs. Everything is reduced to camera fodder. "The man photographed," writes Pudovkin, "is only raw material for the future composition of his image in the film arranged in editing." And Eisenstein declares: "I do not believe in stars or the star system. My main characters (in *Old and New*) are a milkmaid, a bull, and a milk separator." This viewpoint is simply a recognition of the fact that film rhythms are created entirely by the director through montage, and that in montage animals, landscapes, even inanimate objects like separators are as much "actors" as are human beings. There is no reason why a director cannot, on occasion, get as striking cinematic effects from an alarm clock as he could from the most capable actor. If montage has lessened the importance of the actor, the doctrine of "actuality" has brought about an even more revolutionary change. This is the almost exclusive use, by Pudovkin and Eisenstein at least, of nonprofessional actors in their movies. The sailors in *Potemkin* are real sailors; the hero of *St. Petersburg* is an accountant in real life; the heroine of *Old and New* is really a milkmaid; and so on. Eisenstein is actually worried lest his actors will become "artists":

I am always afraid high salaries and their new métier will cause my players to turn "Bohemian" so I never let them live like stars or in any way change their mode of living. They are always peasants working part time in the films. I give them parts to correspond with whatever they do in real life and never let them feel that they are artists for fear of spoiling their type.

The use of amateur actors, while it adds immensely to the "actuality" of the film, also places the burden of getting adequate performances entirely on the director. Pudovkin states the problem and gives one solution:

But what should one do? It is very difficult to work with stage actors. People so exceptionally talented that they can live, and not act, are very seldom met with, while if you ask an ordinary actor merely to sit quietly and not to act, he will act for your benefit the type of a non-acting actor.

I have tried to work with people who have never seen either a play or a film, and I succeeded, with the help of montage, in achieving some result. It is true that in this method one must be very cunning: it is necessary to invent thousands of tricks to create the mood required in the person and to catch the right moment to photograph him.

For example, in the film *Storm Over Asia* I wanted to have a crowd of Mongols looking with rapture at a precious fox fur. I engaged a Chinese conjuror and photographed the faces of the Mongols watching him. When I joined this piece to a shot of the fur held in the hands of the seller, I got the result required.

I more and more often work with casual actors, and I am satisfied with the results. In my last film I met the Mongols, absolutely uncultured people who did not even understand my language, and, despite this, the Mongols in that film easily compete, as far as acting honors are concerned, with the best actors.

Though Pudovkin and Eisenstein work almost wholly with "casual actors," the other Russian directors use professionals a good deal, perhaps most of the time. These professionals, most of them trained in the Moscow Art Theatre and other groups of the like prestige, are by all odds the most consummately finished actors on the screen. They are as sophisticated in theatrical technique as Pudovkin's Mongols are naïve—and it would be hard to say which group takes the acting honors.

This discussion of the doctrine of actuality may be concluded with a quotation from Pudovkin which should make it clear that the Russians are by no means realists of the school of Zola, that they well know the difference between actuality and art:

The material of the film director consists not of real processes happening in real space and real time, but of those pieces of celluloid on which these processes have been recorded. Between the natural event and its appearance on the screen there is a marked difference. It is exactly this difference that makes the film an art.

S. M. Eisenstein and V. I. Pudovkin are generally recognized as the leaders of the Russian school and by far its greatest exponents. Each has made three important films. Eisenstein: *Potemkin, Ten Days that Shook the World,* and *Old and New;* Pudovkin: *Mother, The End of St. Petersburg,* and *Storm Over Asia.* In my opinion Eisenstein is the greater cinematic genius. He seems to be the creator, the innovator; Pudovkin, the intelligent adapter—whether of Eisenstein's or Kuleshov's ideas. When Eisenstein theorizes about the cinema he expresses highly original ideas in terse, dynamic words that strike to the heart of the matter with the lightning swiftness of intuition. Pudovkin, on the other hand, while his writings show the greatest intelligence and imagination, seems to be ordering and clarifying existing ideas rather than developing any new paths of his own. Their movies contrast along somewhat the same lines. An Eisenstein film is pure cinema. Its form is created entirely by the succession of visual images, i.e., by montage. Dramatic tensions are created not by giving a sense of the passage of events in time (as in a play) but by suggesting the "collision" of events with each other in space. Instead of stringing out the action over a number of time points, Eisenstein compresses it into a few episodes which have a spatial rather than a temporal relationship to each other. Even in *Ten Days that Shook the World,* which deals with historical events, one gets no sense of a time sequence.*

Where Eisenstein cinematizes, Pudovkin narrates. The

---

* Eisenstein's disregard for temporal sequence is strikingly illustrated by his device of shooting the same movement from various angles and arranging his shots in sequence so that each new angle goes back to the beginning of the movement (as, the lifting of the drawbridge in *Ten Days*). "Filmic time," as Pudovkin has pointed out, "is distinguished from actual time in that it is dependent only on the length of the separate pieces of celluloid joined together by the director."

"shock-linkage" contrast sketched by Eisenstein between his point of view and that of Pudovkin is remarkably accurate. Though Pudovkin builds his pictures around certain key scenes, he links these together in a time relationship instead of letting them conflict in space. His pictures are more literary, less cinematic in form. As the novelist tells a story in words, so Pudovkin tells a story in pictures. Eisenstein's approach is purer, more absolute: he *composes* with his shots as if he were a musician composing with notes. Thus his movies are cinematic expressions of an abstract theme before they are narratives—he thinks a fine film could be made from Marx's "On Capital." Though Pudovkin also works with abstract themes, he approaches them as a novelist does: by narrating the story of an individual. The theme of both *St. Petersburg* and *Storm Over Asia* is the slowly developing revolt of a symbolic individual against a social order. To be effective such a psychological change requires the suggestion of the passage of time —a suggestion that is precluded by Eisenstein's technique.*

That Pudovkin's scenario in the main follows the career of an individual and that Eisenstein's follows the struggles and conflicts of the mass—this distinction is so obvious that it need not be elaborated beyond a qualification. This is, first, that as compared to our own movies those of Pudovkin center little enough on the individual and, second, that in his latest film, *Old and New*, Eisenstein goes much farther towards using a heroine than ever before.

When it comes down to shot composition and lighting, the same differences hold good. Here again Eisenstein's approach is purely cinematic, so that his shots would be interesting even were they not connected together in a dramatic whole. For to him the shot is evidently not only a part of a whole. It is also, and often, I suspect, primarily, an opportunity to *realize* on the film (as Cézanne "realized" on canvas) various aspects of the physical: the glitter of a row of water glasses, a fortress' stark, solid lines, the hoggishness of a hog, the fleshiness of a fat man. The power of expressing, in terms of

* Most of the movies in which Jannings has recently played also center around such a psychological change in the hero. The process is reversed, however, and the disintegration, not the development of a psychological attitude is the theme. In this reversal is implied all the decadence of the German school.

light and shade, such phenomena is the bedrock on which cinematography rests. Whether a director is skilled in montage or not, whether he can get good performances from his actors or not, he must possess this power. All the important directors —Griffith, Von Sternberg, Von Stroheim, Lubitsch, Feyder, Pudovkin, Eisenstein, Protozanov, Trauberg, and the rest— are sensitive to camera values, composition angles, lighting effects, so that their pictures are usually at least delightful to the eye. In these matters the director exercises that sensuousness which underlies every form of art. Montage, on the other hand, is an intellectual process. Eisenstein, the all-around genius of the cinema, excels in shot-composition as well as in montage. One has only to recall such shots in *Ten Days that Shook the World* as: the girl's hair slipping down off the bridge, the ball and the tower, the crystal chandeliers swaying in the bombardment, the golden peacock, the scattering of the crowd before Kerensky's machine guns, the masses streaming across the courtyard of the Winter Palace. There are few such inspirations in Pudovkin's films. Though his shots are always well composed, sometimes exceptionally so, he subordinates them to the general structure. Thus, while superb shots are scattered all through an Eisenstein film, they come only in the climactic portions of Pudovkin's pictures—as in the execution of the Mongol in *Storm Over Asia*. Perhaps as a result of the "link" theory of montage, Pudovkin's shots do not stand out individually. They are content to carry on or intensify the action and do not aspire to be what Eisenstein's are: expressions of reality that are interesting apart from any story they tell.

Sergei M. Eisenstein was born in 1898. During the war he served in the Engineering Corps, where, being a man of active mind, he not only built bridges and latrines but also developed a great interest in the Japanese theatre. After the war he became a member of the Proletcult Workers Theatre and in a few years was its stage manager. But he was irked by the inadequacy of the stage to present real life, and after a final effort in which he staged a play in a factory with the workmen as actors, in 1924 he resigned from the Proletcult to enter the movies. For some time he has been the leading teacher at the State Technical Institute of the Cinema, whither go young Russians who would become actors, cameramen, or directors. He also rejoices in the title of *Director of the Cinema Division of the Psychophysical Laboratories Organized for the Study of the Spectator's Reactions*—a mouthful whose scientific flavor is characteristic of the Russian, and especially Eisenstein's, approach to cinematography. As is well known, Pavlov's theories about reflex actions have had much influence on Russian movie technique. Eisenstein makes it clear that he views the cinema as a scientific, mechanistic, non-"artistic" medium. "At present I am working on the psychology of audience reactions," he said some time ago, "trying to measure the effects of a film on the audience. These laws, I believe, can be found by pure physics, not intuition, and so I am working on the principles of Pavlov and Freud." More point-blank is his celebrated statement: "I approach the making of a film in much the same way that I would approach the equipment of a poultry farm or the installation of a water system."

With the production of *The Battleship Potemkin* in 1926, the Soviet cinema leapt full-armed from Eisenstein's capacious brow. Although this is his first picture of any pretensions, Eisenstein here lays down in masterful fashion the foundation of all that he or anyone else has yet done with cinematography. After five years *Potemkin* remains "up-to-date" in technique, a great deal more up to date, in fact, than most later movies. Its form is wholly determined by montage rhythms. As for its closeness to actuality, the other great Russian contribution to the cinema, its creator declares: "In *Potemkin* nothing was filmed in the studio. We went to the fleet and lived there. Thus we absorbed the life and social habits of the sailor, and even had the help of officers who had been in the fleet for twenty years."

By the very nature of the cinema, a movie is an *extensive* affair, sprawling out over so much space and encompassing so much matter that a certain amount of confusion, of weaker, less vital stuff can easily creep in. An extreme example of this is *The Birth of a Nation*, a vast mosaic of short sequences, some of them extremely good and some extremely bad. The Russians, however, try above all things to give their films, through montage, a rhythmic flow that will hold them together in unity. *Potemkin* is remarkably unified in structure and consistent tone. Its structure is simple: there are three distinct movements in each of which tension gathers momentum, bursts into action, and then subsides. The first movement begins with the sailors' protest over the bad meat, mounts through increasing tension between sailors and officers to the open revolt in which the sailors seize the ship, and then subsides through the burial service of the dead leader, a calm and peaceful episode. The second is short and violent, beginning with the crowd cheering the *Potemkin* from the harbor steps, and bursting into a powerful climax: the celebrated march of the Cossacks down the steps. This violent movement is followed by the long sequence showing the sleeping crew of the *Potemkin* slowly awakening. Tension begins once more with the preparations to fight the approaching fleet. As the fleet appears on the horizon, the preparations for battle become more and more active, so that when finally the fleet steams past flying peace signals, the audience is fully as relieved as the sailors of the *Potemkin*—which is exactly as it should be.*

This analysis shows unity not only of structure but also of time and space: the action is over within twenty-four hours and there are only two settings of importance, the ship and the steps. The unity of setting, especially unusual in a Soviet picture, may be a reflection of Eisenstein's experience with the Meyerhold and Proletcult theatres. Certainly he uses the framework of the cruiser as a mechanical setting for the action much as the Constructivist theatre would. And the march down the steps is an effect such as Meyerhold could easily reproduce on the stage. But the chief cause of *Potemkin's* remarkable unity is Eisenstein's conception of montage as a relationship in space and not in time. All his movies can be analyzed into a certain number of distinct episodes which collide in space

---

* The rhythms of most successful films are determined by the building up and releasing of successive states of tension. The technique of tension is important to the movies because it can so easily and effectively be applied. At crucial moments the action can be slowed down, for instance, by the recording of simultaneous actions in succession. Thus the execution scene in *Potemkin* is rendered almost unbearably tense by alternating shots of the officer screeching "FIRE!" and the marines hesitating to obey. Here, too, the close-up comes into play as an intensifying agent. Tension can also be obtained by stopping all motion, as in *Turksib* where the idly swinging jaws of a steam shovel accentuate the suspense before a blast is set off. Griffith's famous last-minute rescues, with the camera shuttling between the endangered and the rescuers, are examples of montage used to get tension.

with very little time between them to check the force of the clash. *Potemkin* is more unified than his other pictures, largely because it has only three episodes. One of these, the march down the steps, is obviously connected with the other two by only the slenderest thread of narrative. But it is welded indissolubly into the picture's rhythmic structure—one more evidence that Eisenstein is more interested in cinematography than in narration.

Although Eisenstein's next picture, *Ten Days that Shook the World,* is constructed on the same principle as *Potemkin,* it is extremely complex in form. Whereas three big tides of movement successively rise and fall in *Potemkin,* innumerable waves and cross-currents of incident break against each other in *Ten Days.* For here Eisenstein's subject matter is not a single episode limited in time and space, but an entire historical movement: the ten-day Petrograd revolution which overthrew Kerensky's bourgeois government. The obvious, easy, and ineffective way to have constructed *Ten Days* would have been to narrate the events in their proper temporal sequence and from the view point of a single individual, the hero. But Eisenstein in *Potemkin* developed a way of organizing a movie as a series of montage-conflicts whose rhythms admit neither time nor a single point of view. Applying this method to *Ten Days,* he arrives at a series of episodes (even the attack on the Winter Palace which takes up the last quarter of the film is broken up into a rhythmic pattern of incidents) not related to each other by their succession of time or by their congruency to the story of an individual, but none the less (all the more strongly, indeed), creating a whole by their cinematic interaction as they flash on and off the screen. If one follows the "story" in *Ten Days,* one gets a headache. If one follows the dramatic interplay of the various episodes, one begins to understand.

I have seen *Ten Days* three or four times, each time with more understanding. In my present state of enlightenment, I think that the inter-episode relationships are less satisfactory than the intra-episode relationships. Episodes like the Cossack dance, for instance, are better than anything in Eisenstein's other pictures. Nor has anything approached the sequence of the machine-gunner and the scattering crowd in the square. The attack on the Winter Palace, although the brilliant episodes which precede rob it of its due weight as the grand finale, is extremely impressive. Mob scenes have never been so convincingly done as here—so much so, indeed, that it is said the palace suffered more from the movie mob than from the real mob of 1918. "When we pictured the storming of the Winter Palace," says Eisenstein, "two or three thousand factory workers came every evening bringing their own orchestras and worked for us. Many who played in this mob scene had actually taken part and been wounded in the real revolution and so they helped with the details of fighting scenes."

In *Ten Days* Eisenstein surveys the October revolution from as lofty and omniscient a height as if he were the very muse of history. Here he creates in the grand manner if ever an artist did, on a scale which takes away one's breath with its amplitude and with a power which renders the most trivial elements dramatic. It is a large, noble, full-blooded creation, whose propagandist bias is unimportant alongside its fidelity to art and nature.

Eisenstein's latest film, *Old and New*, is a farm idyll with a purpose. It aims to persuade the peasants that old methods are inferior to new ones, horses to tractors, milk pans to separators. Although its episodes are handled with the usual mastery, they are not composed into a whole. And so the film's structure is less effective than is that of the two preceding pictures. Another big difference is that here for the first time Eisenstein employs an individual protagonist: the delightful Marfa Lapkina. Static, uninspiring a theme as the mechanization of the farm would seem to most directors, Eisenstein extracts from it an amazing amount of drama, as in the testing of the milk separator and the death of the bull. If he gets more drama out of a bull's death than Cecil B. DeMille gets from the World War, it is because, unlike Mr. DeMille and most other people, Eisenstein sees what he looks at, sees it in all its intimate, revealing detail, sees the actuality of it. A picture with so undramatic a theme as *Old and New* reveals this visual power with special force.

Vsevolod Illarionovitch Pudovkin was born in 1893 of mixed Tartar-Russian stock. "I began real work in the cinema quite accidentally," he says. "Up to 1920 I was a chemical engineer and, to tell you the truth, looked at films with contempt. . . . A chance meeting with a young painter and theoretician of the film, Kuleshov, gave me an opportunity to learn his ideas, making me change my views completely." Elsewhere he gives D. W. Griffith credit for his conversion: "About that time I happened to see Griffith's great picture, *Intolerance*. In that wonderful work I saw for the first time the possibilities of the epic picture. Yes, Griffith was really my teacher. Later on I saw *Broken Blossoms* and I fell more and more under the spell of Griffith. My first three pictures were influenced by this great American director." For three years he and Kuleshov worked out their ideas before they ventured to put them into practice. Then they began making small experimental films for which Pudovkin wrote scenarios, in which he acted, and which he directed—extremely valuable, all-round experience. In 1926 he put out his first big production, *Mother*, following it with *The End of St. Petersburg* in 1927 and *Storm Over Asia* in 1928. Of his next picture, as yet unreleased, he writes: "So far I am regarded as the director of epic pictures, since my first three pictures have been of that order, but I shall not make any more epics, at least not for a long time. My next picture is to be quite a different type. It will be a simple story called *Life is Good* and will tell the story of a crisis in the life of a married couple. There will be no great catastrophe, nothing terrible will happen. Only that their happiness is threatened by a sudden, senseless incident. It is like a dream." Pudovkin, like Eisenstein, is a fluent and dramatic talker about his art. He has written several lucid expositions of movie technique, which have been collected by Victor Gollancz, the English publisher, into a book called "On Film Technique." He resembles Griffith and Von Stroheim in that he is an actor as well as a director, his latest rôle being the hero of Ozep's *The Living Corpse*. His cameraman for his three big pictures has been A. N. Golovnia.

The two Pudovkin films I have seen, *The End of St. Petersburg* and *Storm Over Asia* parallel each other in theme and plot. A country youth (a Russian peasant, a Mongol hunter) goes into the city (St. Petersburg, an Asiatic trading-post), where he comes into conflict with the ruling powers (the Czarist régime, the British army of occupation), with the final result that he is "awakened" and becomes a leader, and, still more, a symbol of the people's uprising against their oppressors. These heroes dominate the two movies. They are great creations. I. Chuvelev, the hero of *St. Petersburg*, was an accountant before he became an actor. He is tall, clumsy, and in this picture he conveys with much power the emotional forces lying unawakened beneath the inexpressive exterior of the peasant. Awkward, slow-witted, puzzled, he rebels ineffectually against the system he feels to be wrong, only to be frustrated and submerged, until at the end he, and the masses for which he stands, burst into expression with irresistible force. Moving as this conception is, it has something of a literary tinge to it. The real leaders of the revolution, as of any such movement, were shrewd, wide-awake politicians like Lenin. But only a supreme genius like Eisenstein can dramatize such personalities. He does it in the masterly glimpses of Lenin in *Ten Days,* and, above all, in the bright-eyed, supple-minded heroine of *Old and New.* V. Inkizinov, assistant producer in Meyerhold's theatre, gives a superb performance as the Mongol hero of *Storm Over Asia.* Though Pudovkin presents him, too, as an inarticulate giant, the role is not open to the criticism made before. For when he finally sweeps into action at the climactical ending of the film, he is frankly treated as a symbol who can pull down houses about him, send husky soldiers flying, and otherwise transcend the laws of probability and even of nature. Much the same contrast exists between the structure of Pudovkin's two films as has already been noted between *Potemkin* and *Ten Days.* The action of *St. Petersburg* is complicated by the inevitable scope and detail of historical events in an advanced civilization, and is therefore broken up into shorter and more numerous episodes. Dealing with a simpler milieu, *Storm Over Asia* has fewer and longer movements and a simpler narrative. Its effect on spectators, therefore, is much the more unified and powerful. Both films have many of those flashes of human feeling which are characteristic of Pudovkin, who seems more interested in human beings than does Eisenstein. His approach is more sympathetic, if less dramatic.

Eisenstein and Pudovkin are not isolated giants in the Soviet cinema. Rather they are the ablest exponents of a flourishing school of cinematography. Unfortunately I have not the space to comment on such interesting films as Reisman's *In Old Siberia,* Ozep's *The Yellow Pass,* Trauberg's *The China Express,*

Stabavoi's *Two Days,* Turin's *Turksib,* and Taritsch's *Czar Ivan the Terrible*. There are, however, four films I want to consider briefly: one because it is generally considered important; and the rest because they are *not* generally considered important. . . . The former picture is *The New Babylon*, directed by Kozintsev and Trauberg, collaborators of long standing, who are ranked after Eisenstein and Pudovkin in the Left Wing of the Soviet cinema. Of late they have joined Vertov in a movement called The School of Eccentric Cinema, a revolt against Eisenstein's doctrine of actuality. Judging from *The New Babylon*, they are working toward a more stylized, abstract, and intellectualized cinema, something on the order of *Caligari*. The actors are posed in striking rather than natural positions, the lighting is frankly artificial, and the camera angles are extreme. And yet details of costume (the setting is the Paris of the commune) are rendered with meticulous realism. Intellectually the picture is powerful, but emotionally it is thin and hectic. The disgustingly exaggerated pathos of the ending is reminiscent of the Teutonic cinema rather than of the heroic finales of Eisenstein. There is, in fact, a distinctly Teutonic flavor about the whole thing. . . . Of the three unrecognized films, Protazanov's *The Lash of the Czar* (Russian title: *The White Eagle*) comes closest to greatness. Based on a story by Gorky (or perhaps it's Andreyev), it is unique among the successful Russian movies I have seen in that it is a psychological study of an individual (among *unsuccessful* studies of this sort I may mention Petrov-Bytov's *Cain and Artem* and Ozep's *The Living Corpse*). The individual is the governor of a province in the old Czarist days, an intelligent, honorable, high-spirited man. Instigated by the Court, he represses a strike in his capital with much bloodshed—an act which causes him the greatest remorse and eventually leads to his death. Protazanov's direction of this tragedy of conscience is intelligent rather than inspired, but he keeps it on an elevated plane throughout without lapsing into heaviness or dullness. And he wisely lets the actors carry the drama on their shoulders—wise, I say, considering that the cast is headed by Anna Sten, lovely and talented, I. Chuvelev, the hero of *St. Petersburg*, V. E. Meyerhold, as capable an actor as he is a producer, and V. I. Kachalov, one of Russia's best actors. Kachalov's performance as the governor is the high-water mark of movie acting, more im-

pressive than anything even the mighty Jannings has done.
. . . If *The Lash of the Czar* is a "Macbeth," Shengelaia's *Caucasian Love* is an "Iliad," an epic whose action is swift, simple, based entirely on elementary motives. It is the best of the many Russian pictures dealing with uncivilized *milieus*—best because of its simple, effective movement and because of its remarkably fine acting. The hero, heroine, and most of the other characters are Caucasian tribesmen, and their acting has a realistic force which amateurs often attain. The effect is greatly enriched by the beauty of these Caucasians, who must surely be one of the handsomest peoples in the world. . . . *The Bear's Wedding*, made before 1926, has the poor photography and jerky movement of those pre-natal days of the Russian cinema. Despite its innocence of cinematography, however, it is an excellent piece of work. It is a cinematization of one of Mérimée's wild country legends. Time: late eighteenth century. Place: a castle deep in the forests of Lithuania. The story centers around Count Shemet, who is subject to fits of madness in which he imagines himself to be a bear, and who attacks people under that delusion. K. Eggert, the director, treats this theme in a vigorously romantic manner. His attack is sometimes so direct as to be naïve, but when power rather than subtlety is needed, it gets magnificent results. Thus the catastrophe of the action, the marriage of the Count and his subsequent murder of his bride, is masterfully handled. After the wild wedding revels, the Count and his bride retire. The suspense at this point, in view of the Count's obsession, is immense. There are a few shots showing the revels dying down and quietness coming over the castle—to the audience a quietness charged with tension. Suddenly Shemet's face leaps on the screen, mouth distended in a shriek, eyes glaring downward. Keeping his eyes on the bed, he slowly steps backward, pulling the bedcovers after him. As they are drawn away, they uncover the face and bloodstained neck of the bride. All these shots are mere glimpses, presented with such force and directness that they build up a climax of the most powerful terror. Like *Caucasian Love* and *The Lash of the Czar*, this film owes as much to the acting as to the directing. The parts are taken by members of the Moscow Art Theatre.

The Composition of *Potemkin*
by Sergei Eisenstein

This chapter by the great Soviet director, theorist, and teacher appeared originally in "Notes of a Film Director," compiled and edited by R. Yurenev and published in 1958.

When *Potemkin* is discussed two of its features are commonly noted: the organic unity of its composition as a whole and the pathos of the film.

Taking these two most characteristic features of *Potemkin*, let us analyze by what means they were achieved, primarily in the field of composition. We shall study the first feature in the composition of the film as a whole. For the second, we shall take the episode of the Odessa steps, where the pathos of the film reaches its climax, and then we shall apply our conclusions to the whole.

We shall concern ourselves with the compositional means employed to ensure these qualities. In the same way we could study other factors; we could examine the contribution to organic unity and pathos made by the actors' performances, by the treatment of the story, by the light and color scale of the photography, by the natural backgrounds, by the mass scenes, etc. But here we shall confine ourselves to one particular problem, that of *structure*, and shall not attempt an exhaustive analysis of all the film's aspects.

And yet, in an organic work of art, elements that nourish the work as a whole pervade all the features composing this work. A unified canon pierces not only the whole and each of its parts, but also each element that is called to participate in the work of composition. One and the same principle will feed any element, appearing in each in a qualitatively different form. Only in this case are we justified in considering a work of art organic, the notion "organism" being used in the sense in which Engels spoke of it in his *Dialectics of Nature*: "The organism is certainly a *higher unity*."

This brings us to the first item of our analysis—the organic unity of the composition of *Potemkin*.

Let us approach this problem from the premise that the organic unity of a work of art and the sensation of unity can

147

be attained only if the law of building the work answers the law of structure in natural organic phenomena, of which Lenin said that "the particular does not exist outside that relationship which leads to the general. The general exists only in the particular, through the particular."

The first analysis will provide material for the study of laws governing unity in static conditions; the second will enable us to study the dynamic operation of these laws. Thus, in the first instance we shall deal with parts and *proportions* in the structure of the work. In the second—with the *movement* of the structure of the work.

Outwardly, *Potemkin* is a chronicle of events but it impresses the spectators as a drama.

The secret of this effect lies in the plot, built up in accordance with the laws of austere composition of tragedy in its traditional five-act form.

The events, first taken as unembellished facts, are divided into five tragic acts, the facts themselves so arranged as to form a consecutive whole, closely conforming to the requirements of classical tragedy: a third act distinct from the second, a fifth distinct from the first, and so on.

This age-honored structure of tragedy is further stressed by the subtitle each "act" is preceded by.

Here are the five acts:

I. *Men and Maggots*

Exposition of the action. The conditions aboard the battleship. Meat teeming with maggots. Unrest among the sailors.

II. *Drama on the Quarter-Deck*

"All hands on deck!" The sailors' refusal to eat the maggoty soup. The tarpaulin scene. "Brothers!" Refusal to fire. Mutiny. Revenge on the officers.

III. *The Dead Cries Out*

Mist. Vakulinchuk's body in the Odessa port. Mourning over the body. Meeting. Raising the red flag.

IV. *The Odessa Steps*

Fraternization of shore and battleship. Yawls with provisions. Shooting on the Odessa steps.

V. *Meeting the Squadron*

Night of expectation. Meeting the squadron. Engines. "Brothers!" The squadron refuses to fire.

The action in each part is different, but permeated and cemented, as it were, by the method of double repetition.

In "Drama on the Quarter-Deck" a handful of mutinous sailors, part of the battleship's crew, cry, "Brothers!" to the firing squad. The rifles are lowered. The whole crew joins the rebels.

In "Meeting the Squadron" the mutinous ship, part of the navy, cries "Brothers!" to the crews of the Admiral's squadron. And the guns trained on the *Potemkin* are lowered. The whole fleet is at one with the *Potemkin*.

From a particle of the battleship's organism to the organism as a whole; from a particle of the navy's organism, the battleship, to the navy's organism as a whole—this is how the feeling of revolutionary brotherhood develops thematically; and the composition of the work on the subject of the brotherhood of toilers and of revolution develops parallel with it.

Over the heads of censors the film spreads in bourgeois countries the idea of the brotherhood of toilers, carrying to them the brotherly "Hurrah!" just as in the film itself the idea of revolutionary brotherhood spreads from the rebellious ship to the shore.

As far as emotional impact and idea are concerned, that alone would be enough to make the film an organic whole, but we would like to test its structure from the standpoint of form.

In its five parts, tied with the general thematic line, there is otherwise little that is similar externally. Structurally, though, they are perfectly *identical* in that each act is clearly divided into two almost equal parts, this division becoming more pronounced in part II.

The tarpaulin scene—mutiny.

Mourning for Vakulinchuk—meeting of indignant protest.

Fraternizing—shooting.

Anxiously awaiting the squadron—triumph.

Moreover, every "transition" point is emphasized by a pause, a *caesura*.

In part III it is a few shots of clenched fists, showing the transition from grief for the slain comrade to infuriated protest.

In part IV it is the title "Suddenly," cutting short the fraternization scene and ushering in the shooting scene.

In part II it is the motionless rifle muzzles; in part V, the gaping mouths of the guns and the exclamation "Brothers!" breaking the dead silence of expectation and arousing an avalanche of fraternal feelings.

The remarkable thing about these dividing points is that they mark not merely a transition to a merely *different* mood, to a merely *different* rhythm, to a merely *different* event, but show each time that the transition is to a sharply opposite quality. To say that we have contrasts would not be enough: the image of the same theme is each time presented from the *opposite* point of view, although it *grows out of the theme itself*.

Thus, the rebellion breaks out after the unbearable strain of waiting under the rifles (part II).

The angry protest follows the mass mourning for the slain comrade (part III).

The shooting on the Odessa steps is a natural answer of the reactionaries to the fraternal embraces between the mutinous crew of the *Potemkin* and the population of Odessa (part IV).

The unity of such a canon, recurring in each act of the drama, is very significant.

This unity is characteristic of the *structure* of the *Potemkin* as a whole.

The film in its entirety is also divided near the middle by a dead halt, a *caesura*, when the tempestuous action of the first half is suspended, and the second half begins to gain impetus.

The episode with Vakulinchuk's body and the Odessa mist serves as a similar *caesura* for the film as a whole.

At that point the theme of revolution spreads from one mutinous battleship to Odessa, embracing the whole city topographically opposed to the ship but emotionally at one with it. But at the moment when the theme returns to the sea, the city is separated from it by soldiers (the episode on the steps).

We see that the development of the theme is organic and that the structure of the film born of this thematic development *is identical in the whole as it is in its parts, large and small*.

The law of unity has been observed throughout.

In terms of proportions, organic unity is expressed in what is known in esthetics as "golden section."

A work of art built on the principle of the golden section is usually most effective.

This principle has been exhaustively applied in the plastic arts.

It is applied less in such arts as music and poetry, although we may safely say that there is a vast field of application in these.

I don't think that a motion picture has ever been subjected to a test on the golden-section principle.

All the more interesting, therefore, is the fact that *Potemkin*, whose organic unity is well known, has been based on this principle.

In speaking about the division of each part of the film and of the film as a whole, we said "two *almost* equal parts." In fact, the proportion is closer to 2:3, which approximates the golden section.

The main *caesura* of the film, the *"zero" point* at which action is suspended, is between the end of part II and the beginning of part III—the 2:3 ratio.

To be more exact, it is *at the end of part II,* for it is there that the theme of dead Vakulinchuk is introduced, and the *caesurae* in the individual parts of the film are likewise shifted. The most astonishing thing about *Potemkin* is that the golden-section principle is observed, not only with regard to the *"zero" point,* but with regard to the culmination point as well. The latter point is the raising of the red flag on the battleship. This occurs also at a point of the golden section but in *reverse proportion* (3:2), that is, at the point dividing the first three parts from the last two—*at the end of part III.* And the flag still figures at the beginning of part IV.

Thus, we see that each individual part of the film, as well as the film on the whole, its culmination and "zero" points are built strictly in conformity with the principle of golden section, that is, proportionally.

Now let us consider the second distinctive characteristic of *Potemkin*—its pathos and the compositional means by which it is achieved.

We do not intend to define pathos as such. We shall confine ourselves to studying the effect a work marked with pathos produces on the spectator.

Pathos arouses deep emotions and enthusiasm.

To achieve this, such a work must be built throughout on strong explosive action and constant qualitative changes.

One and the same event may be incorporated in a work of art in different guises: in the form of a dispassionate statement or in that of a pathetic hymn. Here we are interested in the means of lifting an event to the heights of pathos.

There is no doubt that the treatment of an event is primarily determined by the author's attitude to the content. But composition, as we understand it, is the means of expressing the author's attitude and influencing the spectators.

That is why in this article we are less concerned with the nature of pathos of one or another event, because this depends on one's social viewpoint. Nor shall we touch upon the nature of *the author's attitude* to this event, for this, too, is determined by his social outlook. What we are interested in is the particular problem of what compositional means are employed to express this attitude within a work of pathos.

If we wish the spectator to experience a maximum emotional upsurge, to send him into ecstasy, we must offer him a suitable "formula" which will eventually excite the desirable emotions in him.

The simplest method is to present on the screen a human being in a state of ecstasy, that is, a character who is gripped by some emotion, who is "beside himself."

A more complicated and more effective method is the realization of the main condition of a work of pathos—constant qualitative changes in the action—not through the medium of one character, but through the entire environment. In other words, when everything around him is also "beside itself." A classical example of this method is the storm raging in the breast of King Lear and everywhere around him in nature.

To return to our example—the Odessa steps.

How are the events arranged and presented in this scene?

Leaving aside the frenzied state of the characters and masses in the scene, let us see how one of the structural and compositional means—*movement*—is used to express mounting emotional intensity.

First, there are *close-ups* of human figures rushing chaotically. Then, *long-shots* of the same scene. The *chaotic movement* is next superseded by shots showing the feet of soldiers as they march *rhythmically* down the steps.

Tempo increases. Rhythm accelerates.

And then, as the *downward* movement reaches its culmination, the movement is suddenly reversed: instead of the headlong rush of the *crowd* down the steps we see the *solitary* figure of a mother carrying her dead son, *slowly* and *solemnly* *going up* the steps.

Mass. Headlong rush. *Downward*. And all of a sudden—

A *solitary* figure. Slow and solemn. *Going up*. But only for a moment. Then again a *leap in the reverse direction. Downward* movement.

Rhythm accelerates. Tempo increases.

The shot of *the rushing crowd* is suddenly followed by one showing a perambulator hurtling down the steps. This is more than just different tempos. This is a *leap in the method of representation*—from the abstract to the physical. This gives one more aspect of downward movement.

Close-ups, accordingly, give place to *long shots*. The *chaotic* rush (of a mass) is succeeded by the *rhythmic* march of the soldiers. One aspect of movement (people running, falling, tumbling down the steps) gives way to another (rolling perambulator). *Descent* gives place to *ascent. Many* volleys of *many* rifles gives place to *one* shot from *one* of the battleship's guns.

At each step there is a leap from one dimension to another, from one quality to another, until, finally, the change affects not one individual episode (the perambulator) but the whole of the method: the risen lions mark the point where the *narrative* turns into a *presentation through images*.

The visible steps of the stairs marking the downward progress of action correspond to steps marking qualitative leaps but proceeding in the opposite direction of mounting intensity.

Thus, the dramatic theme, unfolding impetuously in the scene of shooting on the steps, is at the same time the structural leit-motif, determining the plastic and rhythmical arrangement of the events.

Does the episode on the steps fit into the organic whole? Does it disrupt the structural conception? No, it does not. The traits characteristic of a work of pathos are given here great prominence, and the episode is the tragic culmination of the entire film.

It would not be out of place to recall what I have said above about the two parts into which each of the five acts is divided in accordance with the golden-section principle. I have stressed repeatedly that action invariably leaps into a new quality at each *caesura*; now I should emphasize that the range of the new quality into which the leap is made is always the *greatest possible*: each time *the leap is into the opposite.*

We see, accordingly, that all the decisive elements of composition conform to the formula of the ecstatic: the action always makes a leap into a new quality, and this new leap is usually a leap into the opposite direction.

In this, as in the case discussed above regarding the principle of golden section and its role of determining proportions, lies the secret of organic unity as manifested in the *development* of the plot. Transition from one quality to another by means of leaps is not merely a formula of *growth* but one of *development*. We are drawn into this development not only as "vegetative" individuals subordinated to the *evolutionary laws of nature*, but as part of collective and social units consciously participating in its development, for we know that such leaps are characteristic of social life. They are the *revolutions* which stimulate social development and social movement.

We can safely say that there is a third aspect of the organic unity of *Potemkin*. The leap which characterizes the structure of each compositional element and the composition of the entire film is the compositional expression of the most important element of the theme—of the revolutionary outburst. And that is one in a series of leaps by means of which social development proceeds uninterrupted.

The structure of a many-sided work, like that of a work of pathos, can be defined in the following words: a pathetic structure makes us *relive acutely the moments of culmination and substantiation* that are in the canon of all dialectical processes.

Of all the living beings on earth we are alone privileged to experience and relive, one after another, the moments of the substantiation of the most important achievements in social development. More, we have the privilege of participating collectively in making a new human history.

Living through a historical moment is the culminating point of the pathos of feeling oneself part of the process, of feeling oneself part of the collective waging a fight or a bright future.

Such is pathos in life. And such is its reflection in pathetic works of art. Born of the pathos of the theme, the compositional structure echoes that basic and single law which governs the organic process, social and otherwise, involved in the making of the universe. Participation in this canon (the reflection of which is our consciousness, and its area of application—all our existence) cannot but fill us to the highest point with emotional sensation—pathos.

A question remains: How is the artist to achieve practically these formulas of composition? These compositional formulas are to be found in any fully pathetic work. But they are not achieved by any single compositional scheme determined *a priori*. Skill alone, craftsmanship alone, mastery alone, is not enough.

The work becomes organic and reaches the heights of genuine pathos only when the theme and content and idea of the work become an organic and continuous whole with the ideas, the feelings, and the very breath of the author.

Then and then only a genuine organic-ness of a work will occur, which enters the circle of natural and social phenomena as a fellow-member with equal rights, as an independent phenomenon.

Part Two

The
Sound
and Color
Film
(1930-1950)

THE
BICYCLE THIEF
(1949)
DIRECTED BY
VITTORIO DE SICA

Introduction
An Expanding Art

Motion picture progress shifted gears when the new inventions of sound and color forced the medium to a further expansion of creative expression in new, unanticipated directions.

When the first talking pictures appeared in 1929–30, havoc prevailed in the studios. The new challenge made movie makers forget everything they had learned about silent film expression as they focused all their attention on the problems of aural reproduction, in particular dialogue. Newspapers and magazines were filled with discussions about the comparative merits of sound and silent pictures. Judging the "new talkies" by silent film standards, without taking into account the mechanical changes and readjustments that had to be made, many critics could see little in the future of the sound film and indeed bemoaned it as a retrogression.

Much of the criticism of the first sound pictures was justified. Mechanical drawbacks and technical problems were enormous. The unfamiliar microphone was immobile, and unselective; it picked up all noises mercilessly. This meant that photographing a film had to be conducted in absolute silence, and the motion picture camera, which made a great deal of noise, had to be placed in a sound-proof booth. So imprisoned, the camera lost all of its recently acquired mobility. Pictorial composition had to be abandoned; sets had to be lighted not for mood or pictorial effect, but to allow several cameras in different positions to obtain a single vocal record. Cinematography was now conceived as an accompaniment to dialogue. The complete shifting of camera, microphone, recording and electrical apparatus—a time-taking procedure required for every "set-up" further limited the sound medium. Movies thus shrank to a minimum number of static "master" scenes, resembling a recorded stage play. Editing became rudimentary, motion picture technique lost its sophistication and screen expression reverted to its primitive beginnings.

At first, sound itself was crude and the principles of its application were unformulated. Recording was a new and highly specialized skill, with few experienced in its use. The

158

immobility of the sound apparatus required actors to remain comparatively still if their speech were to be recorded clearly. Hence the sound scenes had to be utilized as shot. They were inflexible, permitting little or no manipulation.

Despite the mechanical and technical limitations of sound, movie craft underwent modification. Directors had to learn to direct in silence and to perfect a scene in rehearsal before shooting. No longer could stage directions be shouted while the camera was turning, or incidental music be played to enhance the actors' moods. The actors could not be allowed to improvise as they went along. Special dialogue-directors were recruited from the theatre to supplement the movie director's work. Engineers became the overlords of production, subordinating the medium to the needs of the microphone and the bulky sound apparatus.

However, once sound was accepted, swift progress began to be made in perfecting its instruments and in learning its functions and principles. Every phase of production was rapidly adjusted to free the director and actor from mechanical restrictions. Films steadily improved as the dependence of the camera upon the microphone was reduced. Improvements and technological advances gave to the microphone selectivity and mobility, so that the creative possibilities of sound became fully apparent and the values of this additional resource were recognized.

One of the first films to demonstrate that the camera need not be inhibited by the microphone was *Applause* (1930). In this picture mobility was restored by putting the camera booth on wheels and demanding that the microphone follow so that the visual flow would be uninterrupted. Sound was thus given fluidity and perspective. About the same time, it became evident that the camera need not picture what was being heard; image and sound could be separated and yet be seen and heard simultaneously. In *Broadway Melody*, for example, a girl is seen on the screen, while from the sound track a car is heard driving off. Such separation of sound and image opened up rich opportunities for contrast, counterpoint, and various psychological effects. In *Strange Interlude* (1932), the sound track carried the subconscious thoughts of the characters; in both *Private Worlds* (1935) and *Stage Door* (1937), the audience identified with the heroine and experienced her emotional crisis by means of the sound track which revealed the anguish in the girl's mind.

One of the first films to bring out the dramatic values of natural sound was *Hallelujah* (1930). In a swamp sequence where one man is pursued by another, what is heard is the labored breathing of the fugitive, the swish of grass, the rustle of branches, noise of birds and insects and the lapping of water. These natural sounds heightened the terror and tension of the pursuit. A somewhat similar use of natural sounds became the stock-in-trade of gangster films, where the dialogue was often counterpointed by the sound of automobile sirens, gun shots, smashing glass or running feet—all aimed to heighten the dramatic impact on the senses of the viewer.

Musical accompaniment was explored by Lubitsch, René Clair and Walt Disney. All three directors showed that music need not be used only to enhance dialogue, but that it could be blended creatively with the pacing of the images, could intensify the visual rhythmic flow, illuminate character, point up a situation or add dramatically to the pictorial scene. Their imaginative exploitation of the sound medium led the way to a creative integration of music and image, and to a contrapuntal relationship in which both would function as natural and integral parts of the whole, enriching each other.

Many contributions in the development of the art of sound came from European film makers. In the early Thirties, the directors of English documentaries, such as *Night Mail, Song of Ceylon* and *We Live in Two Worlds*, combined narration, song and speech in a variety of ways that produced subtle, provocative, and moving effects. Alfred Hitchcock revealed an imaginative and dramatic flair in the way he used sound to create dramatic transitions, associations, and to build suspense in pictures like *Blackmail, Thirty-Nine Steps*, and *The Lady Vanishes*.

Russian film makers in this same period made effective use of the counterpointing of sounds with images. *The Deserter* showed how strips of sound could be cut and mounted like strips of film and how a sound track could be given a unity of form independent of the image, though for meaning it depended on its relationship to the image. *The Last Night* offered an impressive instance of how silence could be made tense, and how naturalistic sounds could be used symbolically.

By the late Thirties cinematic art had regained a great deal of its former power and artistry. The debate of silent versus sound pictures had lost its vehemence. Sound had become an integral part of the enriched medium which was now at the threshold of a new creative phase.

Significantly, it was from a young talent, fresh from radio and the theatre, that the most strikingly original American sound film came. In 1941 Orson Welles' first picture, *Citizen Kane*, burst dramatically onto the American screen and was hailed as the most brilliant and accomplished picture made since the "silent" days.

Inventive and witty, *Citizen Kane* displayed a maturity of technique and form, and a vitality in its cinematic style, that showed a director in command of all the devices which the medium had developed since its earliest days. His brilliant innovations in the use of sound linkage for structural movement and a new kind of aural "montage" for uniting scenes, brought a new eloquence to the film medium and added new concepts to the body of screen art.

Further developments in the artistic manipulation of sound for dramatic purposes, particularly through the use of special techniques in dubbing and mixing of sound, came in the immediate post-war years from a vigorous group of film makers in Italy—a group that later became known as the neo-realist movement. This school of film makers drew its material from life in war-ridden Italy, taking as subject matter dire social problems. Impelled by this sociological interest, their films were serious in content and passionate in tone. In their handling of the sound film, they sought subtlety and complexity, as well as expressive intensity. They developed a naturalism in their art such that speech and the very noises of nature were close to that of real life. In *Open City* (1944–45), *Paisan* (1946), *Shoeshine* (1945), *We Live in Peace* (1947), *Bicycle Thief* (1948), and *Tragic Hunt* (1947), the most eminent of these pictures, a high mark was set both for the rhythmic flow of images and for the reality, spontaneity, and intimacy of the dialogue. The camera was not stalled waiting for the sound, nor did the actors seem to have been aware of the microphone's presence. Natural pitch and tones devoid of "microphone consciousness" added to the terse, vernacular, understated style of these films.

This use of sound imparted an urgency, a directness not unlike the later *cinéma vérité* style of the Sixties, and provided the medium with a fresh dramatic impact, a flexibility and perspective that brought a high level of maturity to the expanded medium.

The problem of the addition of color was solved more slowly than that of sound. By 1930 color technique had hardly reached the same stage of development as sound technique, although it had been available for a longer time. Two reasons accounted for this lag: one was economic, the other artistic. In the urge to survive when sound came along and in the competition with rival firms, film companies cooperated to improve sound apparatus and technology. Scientists, technicans, and creative personnel were given every opportunity to refine the instruments and techniques of sound and to use this element as creatively as they could.

The conditions affecting the progress of color were different. Most of the movie companies had a financial interest in Technicolor, which owned the patent rights to the process, so there was little rivalry to spur color's development. Also about this time, older color processes were reactivated, and the production of color pictures was surrounded with an air of deep mystery. All research was done in complete secrecy. There was little cooperation or exchange among movie companies, laboratories, scientists. What knowledge existed was held by a few. Negative and prints of color pictures were processed behind guarded doors. As in pre-World War I days, when attempts were made to keep movie cameras and projectors in the hands of the few who belonged to The Motion Picture Patents Company Trust, color cameras could not be bought, but had to be rented with camera operator, color technicians and lighting crews. This and the additional fact that color added greatly to the cost of production discouraged many producers from venturing into color pictures at all.

The first all-talking color pictures were crude; their color appealed little to audiences and critics; and for a while it looked as if color might be abandoned. But then Walt Disney launched a new independent company specializing in animated sound cartoons and seized upon color, using it so adeptly that color at last gained a creative role in film.

Disney was the first to realize that color in motion pictures

162

need not bear any resemblance to color in real life, that objects on the screen could be endowed with any pigmentation dictated by the imagination. Furthermore, he recognized that color on the screen need not be static, but could move and that such mobility, affecting the emotions, produced new visual experiences. In *Flowers and Trees* (1932) and *The Three Little Pigs* (1933), color was not something added merely for the sake of novelty, but served a formal and humorous purpose. In these film cartoons, and later in the Silly Symphonies series, color was applied with fertile imagination, being given a mobility integral to the picture's structural flow and whimsical intentions. As the animated characters danced, ran, or evolved into other shapes, their color too became animated, changing hues to express emotional developments. When Pluto, lost and frozen blue in the Alps, was found by a St. Bernard who forced whiskey down Pluto's throat, a luminous warm color slowly seeped back into his body as he thawed out; when the wolf tried to blow down the house of the three pigs, he literally blew himself blue in the face; when the north wind swept through an autumn forest, the entire color scheme changed from golden red to icy blue. Color previously shown rigidly chromatic, had achieved in the animated world of the cartoon an elasticity, adaptability and serviceability for the creative mind. Color had become an integral element of film structure, as important as movement or sound.

In the next years the potentialities of color as an element in dramatic story films were explored. The celebrated stage designer Robert Edmund Jones was engaged to experiment with the Technicolor process in the hope of advancing the dramatic use of color and demonstrating its creative directions in feature length films with real people and settings.

Jones spent several months in the Hollywood studios watching everything that was being done in Technicolor. It soon became apparent to him, as it had to Disney, that if color was to become an important component of film art and not merely a superficial addition, there would have to be a complete change in motion picture technique as radical in its own way as that when sound was added to silent film. "Color," he said at that time, "must be handled by colorists, just as music must be handled by musicians." Jones insisted a color picture had to have a color script worked out as carefully as a musical score, planned and designed from the beginning in relation to the emotional values of the story. Every single scene, every change in grouping, every transition had to be designed before shooting.

To prove his theories, Jones designed two color films: *La Cucaracha* (1934), a two-reel musical about a Mexican impresario and a dancer—which was in the nature of a test film—and the full length feature *Becky Sharp* (1935), adapted from Thackeray's novel "Vanity Fair" and directed by Rouben Mamoulian. In both pictures, Jones, instead of playing down color, or using it for its reproductive capabilities as was the common custom, emphasized color and made it creatively expressive.

In *La Cucaracha* the color heightened reality at every point. Rich harmonies of blue-greens underwent subtle changes in tone from scene to scene, thus establishing a kind of chromatic sensuality that played upon the spectator's feelings and underscored both the hedonism of the plot and the titillating rhythms of the music. The strikingly original conception and the brilliant rendition of color—never thought obtainable before—proved an impressive demonstration to the industry of color's emotional power.

Jones' second color film, *Becky Sharp*, was the first feature length color film to excite the general public and to receive excessive praise in the press for its color achievements. "It produces in the spectator all the excitement of standing on a peak in Darien and glimpsing a strange, beautiful and unexpected world," wrote Andre Sennwald in his review of the picture in the New York Times.

Chromatically, *Becky Sharp* possessed an extraordinary variety of color patterns, ranging from icy grays to hues which were luxuriant with heat and dramatic passion. Every scene, every costume was given a color scheme to accentuate and enhance the mood and spirit of the subject matter. The opening scenes at the Academy, where Becky is introduced, were photographed in pale blues and lavenders to create an atmosphere of gentility and cool serenity in which, by contrast, Becky's coarse and over-colored costume as a governess established her at once as an impoverished and alien outsider. Later, in a scene in Pitt Crawley's library, where Becky had gone to

164

borrow money to pay off her husband's debts, the ice-cold tones of the room and its sparse furniture piercingly emphasized the barren hypocrisy of Crawley's self-professed altruism.

The high point of the film was the great ball on the night before the battle of Waterloo. Here color was used as a vivid dramatic device to heighten the emotional impact of the episode and to contribute actively to the climax of sound and photography. The sequence began with an artfully designed pastel serenity—the cool blues and greens of a dance scene. Then as the news of Napoleon's battle preparations is passed around the ballroom, the color deepens and builds in intensity. With the rumble of off-screen cannons, apprehension seizes the dancers and they hurry from the dance floor in a rising crescendo of warm colors—yellows, oranges and dull red. Finally, as the sounds of battle are heard coming closer, pandemonium breaks out. Scarlet becomes the dominant color motif as there is a sudden inundation of officers who dash across the screen to their posts, their red cloaks exposing vivid crimson linings, thus bringing to a prismatic climax the mounting panic of the scene.

Becky Sharp, at its best, carried with it the excitement of pioneering. It became a promise of the future of color on the screen and forced the industry to the conclusion that color had become an integral motion picture element.

By the Forties color techniques had been refined and great progress had been made in efficiency and technical smoothness. Color had been studied in many ways, scientifically, historically, psychologically, and for its artistic and dramatic effects in conjunction with action and dialogue. Film makers had learned how to express themselves in the language of color as they had previously learned to express themselves in the language of black and white.

Color was to assume an even greater importance when, in the Fifties, competition between movies and television became widespread. Challenged by the newer medium, movies resorted to wide screens and a greater dependence upon color. In the effort to win back audiences, color was propelled into subtle technical refinements. It acquired a new dimension of realism, gained greater luminosity and sharper definition; more vigorous tonal harmonies and contrasts became available; and a greater flexibility became possible in making controlled color changes within and between scenes. By the mid-Fifties, color, like sound, had become assimilated into the body of screen technique and had further enlarged the creative potentialities of the medium. An art of sound and color devices had been created that paralleled the art of camera devices, enabling the film to acquire a subtlety and richness of expression, once impossible. Now highly sophisticated in technique, artful in style, and significant in humanistic values, film art was about to enter a new phase in its artistic progress.—*L.J.*

1. TABU
   (1931)
   DIRECTED BY
   ROBERT FLAHERTY

2. MAN OF ARAN
   (1933)
   DIRECTED BY
   ROBERT FLAHERTY

3. OPEN CITY
   (1945)
   DIRECTED BY
   ROBERTO ROSSELLINI

4. TO LIVE IN PEACE
   (1946)
   DIRECTED BY
   LUIGI ZAMPA

5. TO LIVE IN PEACE
   (1946)
   DIRECTED BY
   LUIGI ZAMPA

6. PAISAN
   (1946)
   DIRECTED BY
   ROBERTO ROSSELLINI

6.

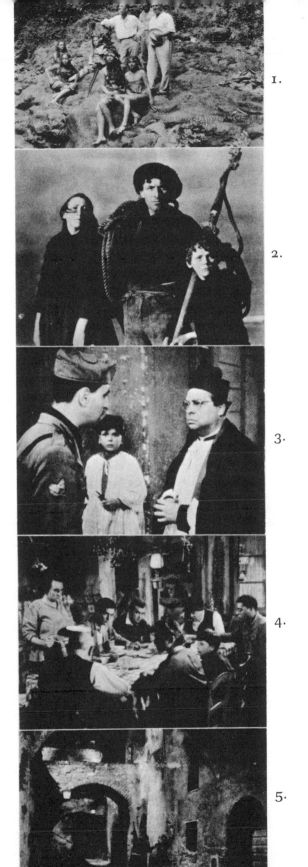

1.

2.

3.

4.

5.

7.

THE INFORMER 7.
(1935)
DIRECTED BY
JOHN FORD

THE GRAPES OF WRATH 8.
(1940)
DIRECTED BY
JOHN FORD

THE FUGITIVES 9.
(1947)
DIRECTED BY
JOHN FORD

CITIZEN KANE 10.
(1941)
DIRECTED BY
ORSON WELLES

CITIZEN KANE 11.
(1941)
DIRECTED BY
ORSON WELLES

CITIZEN KANE 12.
(1941)
DIRECTED BY
ORSON WELLES

8.

9.

10.

11.

12.

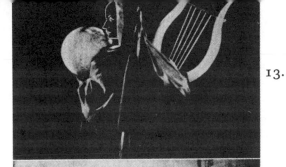

13.

13. BLOOD OF A POET
    (1931)
    DIRECTED BY
    JEAN COCTEAU

14. LE MILLION
    (1931)
    DIRECTED BY
    RENE CLAIR

14.

15. LE MILLION
    (1931)
    DIRECTED BY
    RENE CLAIR

16. BEGONE, DULL CARE
    (1949)
    DIRECTED BY
    NORMAN MCLAREN

17. GERALD MCBOING-BOING
    (1950)
    DIRECTED BY
    ROBERT CANNON

18. LOOPS
    (1949)
    DIRECTED BY
    NORMAN MCLAREN

15.

16.

18.

17.

The Sound Film

by Alberto Cavalcanti

Mr. Cavalcanti for more than three decades has been an active force in the development of experimental and documentary films in France and England. This chapter appeared originally in Cinema in 1938.

Extract from "Discoveries and Inventions of the Nineteenth Century," by Robert Routledge, B.Sc., F.C.S.: *The subjects reproducible in the kinetoscope include the most rapid movements, such as quick dancers, blacksmiths hammering on the anvil, etc., or incidents of ordinary life involving much gesture and change of facial expression, and nothing can be more amusing than to see all these shown to the life by the images on the screen, or by the pictures viewed through the lens, especially if, at the same time, the phonograph is made to emit the corresponding sounds.*

Mr. Routledge is writing somewhere around 1900.

If I am to give any reasonable account of sound in film, I must begin at the beginning. The story of sound in film begins not, as many historians have presumed, with the introduction of the sound film, but with the invention of film itself. At no period in the history of films has it been customary to show them publicly without some sort of sound accompaniment. In other words, the silent film never existed.

As soon as films were invented, and long before there were such things as picture palaces, film makers and showmen began to employ devices to provide a sound accompaniment and complete the illusion. First they used the phonograph, to which Mr. Routledge refers in the extract quoted above. But not for long. Phonograph records are fragile, and synchronization of records has always been a risky business. Furthermore, as films got longer and longer they needed more records than it was convenient to make and maintain.

The next device to which showmen turned was the "barker." In those early times, the bulk of film distribution was in the fair grounds, where barkers were easy to find. These early commentators had almost certainly many of the qualities of today's Pete Smith or Emmett. They went so far as to attempt synchronized speech: What he said to her, and what she said to him (the last in falsetto).

When the film started to move into special premises, called cinemas, the use of the barker in turn ceased to be a practical proposition. A man's voice could not be heard easily in a large hall. Besides, a running commentary was monotonous in a full length show.

Barkers did not disappear all at once. I heard one myself in a provincial British cinema as late as 1910 or 1912. Indeed, as is well known, the barker is still to be heard in the East, in places where the audiences are illiterate and cannot read subtitles, and where sound versions dubbed in the native language are not available. Moreover in certain Eastern countries, I understand, the barker has evolved a very high degree of technique, and individuals have become stars and box office attractions in their own right.

Let us leave these "atavisms" and get back to the main trend of cinema development.

As the barker went out, the subtitle came in to explain the action and comment upon it. I suppose that strictly speaking any discussion of subtitles is irrelevant in a disquisition upon sound in film, but I cannot resist digressing to give a brief resume of the progress made by this device.

Ambitious film makers raided novels and stage successes for film subjects, without giving any thought to real filmic possibilities, and indeed without any real conception of the essentially kinetic nature of film itself. Before long, films consisted of a long series of elaborate and lengthy titles linked together by scenes.

Continuous development along these lines had its effect upon the actual methods of production. The subtitles took care of the continuity. Actors at this period spent the morning on the sets, having their photographs taken in long and in mid shot, and the afternoon sitting by turn in front of an immobile camera, having their photographs taken in close-up with appropriate "expressions," or appropriate mountings of the lines quoted in the titles.

Subtitles, since they played such a large part in films, soon became arty. For some reason or other I have always remembered *Burning the Candle*, a story of moral degeneration and redemption, of which the subtitles all bore the picture of a candle behind the printed words. The length of the candle was the measure of the hero's moral status throughout the film. Perhaps I should not bore you with such a chance memory. No doubt you also have lively recollections of the lengths to which such symbolism was carried. Spiders' webs, books, lamps, and other bric-à-brac. A young friend of mine told me he always thought that the "art director" was so called because he drew the pictures which played such an important part in the film.

Moreover, title writing became quite a trade. Certain star title writers got a credit card all to themselves and became box office attractions. In certain countries, the title writers re-edited imported films to provide opportunities for cracks. I remember once seeing in a Belgian cinema a copy of Chaplin's *The Pilgrim* almost ruined by the insertion of hundreds of subtitles, mostly vulgar Flemish puns, each illustrated by cartoons which had nothing to do with the action.

So big a part did titles play in films, that when a German director, Lupu Pick, made a film without any subtitles at all, the film was regarded as a sort of curio, and had its publicity arranged accordingly.

Enough about subtitles. What was happening to the sound during the so-called silent period? Music came in. By acquiring a house of its own, the moving picture rose from the status of the peddler to a more bourgeois standard, to which the greater refinements of a musical accompaniment were appropriate.

At the beginning music was used for two very different purposes at once: (a) to drown the noise of the projectors; (b) to give emotional atmosphere.

As cinema developed commercially, the music became more elaborate and played a larger and larger part in the show as a whole. Cinema owners vied with each other to attract the public. The piano became a trio. The trio became a salon orchestra. The salon orchestra became a symphony orchestra.

Not only the composition of the orchestra but also the technique of musical accompaniment enjoyed, or suffered, continuous development. The system of leit-motifs was introduced. Certain themes were associated with certain characters, and played whenever they appeared on the screen. A cinema musician's desk contained a thick bundle of music of every possible kind—his music for the big picture. After every half dozen pieces, or so, there was a card inserted, bearing the legend Theme 1, Theme 4, Theme 3. Throughout the whole of the feature, the orchestra kept breaking into these themes, which the individual players kept open at the side of their desks, or on the floor, or "carried in their heads." (The largest film companies themselves prepared and published complete ready-made musical scores and "cue-sheets" for distribution with the films.) So it came about that the music kept hopping from Beethoven to Irish ballads, and back to Beethoven via Moussorgsky. One could quite often hear portions of Pique Dame, Londonderry Air, La Paloma, the Choral Symphony, Baby's Sweetheart, and the Mass in B Minor, all within a period of five minutes. And in the next five minutes the Death of Ase, Baby's Sweetheart again, L'Aube Radieuse, Kol Nidrei, Londonderry Air again, Symphony Pathetique. Such artistic purity consorted well with the architectural features of the cinemas, which often combined Moorish, Greek and Gothic elements in varied splendor. It is not unlikely that some future historian will call this the "surrealist" period in modern art.

Meanwhile the small harmonium used in the orchestra to make up for the lack of woodwinds had been supplanted by the cinema organ, equipped with every device for rendering "effects." As we all know to our cost, these organs survive, and in fact are used in most cinemas to provide what a friend of mine calls "the musical interruption." Take a look at the console of one of them next time you get the chance. In all probability (and with certainty if the organ was built in the so-called silent days) you will see a number of stops labelled train, chains, crockery, horse, siren, side drum, bass drum, cymbals, piano, airplane, child crying, and so on; this will give you some idea of the absurdity of referring to the "great days of the silent cinema."

In an incredible architectural setting, and in the midst of the most appalling noise, the so-called silent film expired.

The sound film came in. This was the time, this was the golden opportunity, for some brilliant analyst to come forward and work out then and there the principles which should govern the employment of the three sound elements: speech, music, and noise. For these elements, as we have seen, had been a part of cinema from the very beginning. Now the time had come when they could be organized properly within the fabric of the film itself, so that the creations of the director, in the domain of sound, could be made a permanent part of his film.

But alas, no analyst came forward. Film people, by and large, have never been given to constructive analysis, which is one reason why no proper "critique" of the film has ever been written. Film people, like the early scientists, prefer trial and error to any other method of investigation and construction.

The rest of my story, on the historical side, is thus a story of slow progress made with immense expenditure of time, money, and energy.

In the first place, many of the silent film directors, including some of the more intelligent of them, actually refused to believe that the sound film would ever establish itself at all. It would not last three months. (I notice that many film directors of the present day are making precisely the same mistake with regard to color.) Silence meant art. Sound was a new toy, of which the public would soon tire.

They were wrong about the public tiring. But they were right enough about the way in which sound was taken up. The public, and the producers alike, fastened upon the one thing which was apparently novel in the new invention—synchronized speech. The films went speech-mad.

While the recalcitrant silent film directors stood like Canute trying to stem the tide, a horde of theatrical people descended upon the studio in order to make films. Now that films can speak, they said, we are going to make them. They further confounded the situation, because they knew nothing about films, and started off with the absurd assumption that in order to make a sound film it is only necessary to photograph a play. Accordingly, as we shall see, the next few years saw millions of dollars poured into productions which were on the wrong lines, and which, after the first year or two, bored the public to such an extent that film producers were forced, in self defense, to adapt their methods.

Here someone might have seen the possibilities of the other form of speech—non-synchronized speech—commentary. But the naïveté of the public and producers alike was all against the exploitation and development of this excellent dramatic device. The people wanted to see the people speaking in sync. To my lasting regret, non-sync speech, i.e., commentary, was relegated to the comparatively minor role of providing continuity and "story" in travelogues, newsreels, and documentary. Yet even in this narrow field, on the rare occasions when commentary is used creatively, its value is at once apparent. Consider for instance the great effect produced by Pete Smith, or Emmett, wisecracking against the pictures. Consider more exalted uses of the device, in documentary. Think of Watt's *Night Mail*, Lorentz's *The River*, and Ivens' *Spanish Earth*, to take three recent examples. If you doubt that commentary, which the makers of dramatic theatrical films have thrown on one side, is a dramatic device of immense potentialities, think again about Ivens' *Spanish Earth*. The effect of this film, which no audience can resist, arises from the contrast between the cool, tragic dignity of Hemingway's prose on the one hand, and the terrors of the images on the other. One is reminded of Wordsworth's brilliant flash of insight expressed in his definition of poetry as "emotion recollected in tranquillity." In *Spanish Earth* as in *The River* and *Night Mail*, the direct emotional stimulus is in the images, while the commentary supplies in contrast the organized, universalized interpretation. The poetic effect is great. The emotion is on the screen, the tranquillity in the sound track. Out of the conflict between the objectiveness of the picture and the subjectiveness of the commentary comes a third thing, a dramatic feeling which is different in essentials from, and I think deeper in effect than, either of the two elements which are combined to create it.

But as I have said, the makers of dramatic films, at the beginning of the sound era, threw commentary on one side as being none of their business, and put all their energies into the production of photographed plays. Here the theatrical people felt that they were on ground they knew. They knew how to produce stage plays. But it never occurred to them that a film is not, and never can be, the same thing as a play. In order to reach this not very advanced conclusion they would have had to do some theoretical investigation, which as I said above was not their strong point.

They might have gone back twenty years, for instance, to the first dramatic silent films. If they had taken some of them out of the vaults and run them, they could have saved themselves a great deal of embarrassment. For the same mistake was being made in 1909 as they were proceeding to make over again in 1929. The early silent directors learned by a process of trial and error which lasted for many years that the technique of stage acting is not the same as the technique of film acting. The gestures and attitudes are far too striking. By a long process, a technique of film acting was built up, in which the skillful actor employed restrained gestures, attitudes, and expressions which, magnified and emphasized on the screen, got him the effects he wanted. At the beginning of the sound period, when the actors from the theatre poured into the studios, this lesson had to be learned all over again.

Further, a simple analogy might have been drawn which would have indicated at the outset that just as the screen required restraint in gesture, it also required restraint in delivery of speech. But this lesson had to be learned by trial and error. The microphone is a very searching instrument. The round-mouthed oratory of stage delivery becomes intolerable affectation when it is amplified by loudspeakers in the cinema (unless of course, as in some of the magnificent speeches of Paul Muni or Charles Laughton, the context justifies the use of rhetoric). A technique of voice delivery proper to the film was in the long run worked out, largely through the success of American Grade B pictures and the rise to fame of such actors as Spencer Tracy, James Cagney, and Gary Cooper. Film dialogue, it was discovered, was most effective and dramatic when it was uttered clearly, rapidly, and evenly, almost thrown away. Emphasis and emotional effect must of necessity be left to the care of the visuals.

But the difference between stage and screen goes far beyond such externals as the technique of miming and speaking. It is an organic difference. A play is all speech. Words, words, words. Now, when the early talkie directors put whole plays on the screen, they were forgetting the lesson the barker had taught them—that the continuous utterance of words in the cinema is monotonous. More important, the preponderance of the speech element in the resulting film crushed out the other elements—visual interest, noise, and music. In a stage play there is no room for any sound but the telephone bells and taxi hooters, which for a long time were the exclusive embellishment of the talkie sound tracks and thus in due course became excessively fatiguing and ridiculous.

Moreover, films must move or they become intolerable. Long stretches of dialogue inevitably cancel movement and visual variety, in spite of all that the most enlightened director can do. (You may remember how in the early "trial" films the camera used to be spun round in quick pans from one face to another in the court room, just because the director, stifled by words, words, words, felt that he had to get his visuals moving somehow.) In the years that have passed since the introduction of the sound film, film has fought for and won an ascendance over speech. In some of the most successful films, speech almost takes second place to visuals. In the trial scene of *Mr. Deeds Goes to Town*, for instance, the hero does not say a word during the first three-quarters of the scene. As a further example, consider the brilliant climax of *The Charge of the Light Brigade*, a film which in a sense represents the triumph of movie over stage.

So much for speech. Summing up, film producers have learned in the course of the last ten years that use of speech must be economical, and be balanced with the other elements in the film; that the style employed by the dialogue writers must be literal, conversational, non-literary; that the delivery must be light, rapid, and offhand, to match the quick movements of the action, and the cuts from speaker to speaker.

It must not be thought that all films adhere to these principles. Far from it. But nine times out of ten it will be found that where a film is ponderous and boring, it owes this defect to bad handling of the speech element in respect to some of the principles mentioned above (I am thinking, for instance, of *Winterset*).

Soon after the sound film was introduced, the "musical" film came into being. This was at first an exact analogy of the photographed stage play—only instead of a play, a big Broadway musical show was photographed. So great were the opportunities for spectacle and mass effects, that this kind of film had a big momentum at the beginning, and for some years such spectacles continued to be produced. But there was always something fundamentally wrong in them—something that the public gradually recognized and rejected. They were not films at all, in the pure sense of the word. Scenes stayed on the screen too long. "Numbers" dragged out their length on the track. The story was slight, and contained nothing exciting. The action did not advance—it flowed like an underground river to appear only between the "scenes" and disappear again. One of the last examples was *The Great Ziegfeld*—a huge, magnificent spectacle, but on the whole, a bore.

The "musical" film began to adapt itself.

Somehow or other, in the inter-reaction of public and producers, the musical melodrama was born. Sensing what was wanted, the producers called in the police. They built their film around a murder or a crime plot, and made the stage stuff a mere adjunct of the story. These backstage films had a great vogue.

Alongside the musical melodrama came the "hoofer" films —Astaire-Rogers, Eleanor Powell—the emphasis here was transferred to the personality of the stars. The story was strengthened, the films took shape, the stars and their adventures became more and more important, the spectacle less and less. "Film" was fighting back, against spectacle, in the "musical" film, just as it had fought back, and won, in the old "silent" days, during which the film people learned by trial and error that the public is interested in individuals and action, not masses and picture. Now they were learning that lesson all over again.

The prodigy performers, such as Shirley Temple, Judy Garland, Deanna Durbin, gave producers an excellent chance to put musical performance in its proper place in film. They combined in themselves performance-ability and a high degree of individual star-value. The public is far too interested in Shirley Temple's virtuosity in all departments to be content to watch a long series of songs sung by her in only one of her many capacities.

If you want to see *performed-music* used in films in a way that seems to me exactly right, consider the denouement of *Three Smart Girls Grow Up*. The technique here is amazing, and represents the musical film at its best. Deanna gets up on the dais to sing a song in honor of her sister, who is marrying the wrong man. The solution is to be a simple one—the substitution of bridegrooms, an old and respected device. Charles Winninger comes solemnly in with the bride on his arm, solemnly overshoots the parson, continues to the door, takes her out, comes back without her (but with his own hat, which her true lover offstage had appropriated early in the film) and as solemnly gives to the deserted bridegroom the girl he really wants. And all the while Deanna is singing. The continued song translates the whole thing to a realm in which all things are credible, because one is loth to disbelieve anything while Miss Durbin is singing. The song also gives feeling-tone (as the orchestra did in the best days of the "silent" cinema). The song also keeps Deanna the star, although the action concerns only her supporters. The song also makes the action "silent," while it is being sung, and gives the director a chance to use a technique of suggestion (such as the excellent hat gag) which sound-films had all but lost. It is a great piece of work—a triumph—for what? For silence? No. For music? No—for the creative combination of two elements, music and images. The unrelated song, the "silent" action—the fusion of these two creates a third element, a sort of dramatic excitement, in which both music and images are enhanced, and suspense, humor, sentiment, acquire almost sensational valency.

As it seems to me at present, that moment in Deanna Durbin's film (only the most obviously successful of many such moments) is the end of a period and the beginning of another. A musical performance is presumably worth *looking* at in a concert hall (because nearly everybody looks), but it is not worth looking at in a cinema. The screen is so selective and so emphatic and so commanding that things must happen on it—dramatic things—or the people get bored. Thus when musical performances came into the movies, they nearly wrecked them—but in the course of evolution, action has absorbed such music as it absorbed speech—conditioned it, employed it, subjugated it, transcended it. In the Durbin films, this process is all but complete.

So much for "performance" music. What about "incidental" music?—accompanying music in speech-films? Here there is no great progress to report. It is a sad story, but the sound film producers made the same mistake with music, when they got their hands on it, as the cinema-owners made in the past, when the responsibility was theirs. (Largely because the composers of the old ready-made scores became the musical directors of the sound studios.) Let me mention in turn the sins of commission and sins of omission.

They began with big orchestras playing big "symphonic"

orchestrations—they began where the "silent" film left off, as far as the size of the orchestra was concerned. And they have continued as they began. And as for the idiom employed in film music, it has varied little in the last ten years. It is an idiom suited to an atmosphere of pomp and display. In style, the music of the cinema, by and large, represents a fixation at a stage of development which the art itself left behind about thirty years ago. It is music of the late romantic period: Tschaikovsky, Rachmaninoff, Sibelius are the spiritual fathers of most cinema music.

Now there is nothing wrong with heavy romantic music (for those who like it) just as there is nothing wrong with suet-pudding or plum-duff. But I can scarcely suppress a smile when I hear the title music of a new film, because nine times out of ten it is the same as the title-music of the last film I saw, no matter what the subject of the film may be. It is a great swelling theme suggesting that the photo-play to be presented is the best, the weightiest, the most profound, that the world has ever seen. How pretentious and self-conscious this music is, the general public does not seem to notice, perhaps because they don't listen to it, and because it generally stops when the action begins. It did not always do so. In early talkies it ran under most of the action and even went so far as to point it with synchronized effects which were derived from the manner of the "silent" orchestra—and were just about the last word in outrageous absurdity. Happily that period is over. Nowadays music is used as an advertisement at the beginning and at the end of all films, and comes in during the film only at certain well defined places—a train journey, a pursuit, a transition.

It·is the omissions of the film producers that are most interesting. The main one is, as I have noted above, their omission to recognize that music is developing rapidly in modern times. The sonata was a structural formula invented in order to give internal relevance to musical compositions, so that they could be listened to as concerts in their own right, without a "programme" of events or a "story" in the form of a poem or a ballet. The trend of music, in the course of the last fifty years, has been away from the concert hall (sonatas and symphonies), towards the theatre (opera, ballet), and further out still into the world. You have only to think of Debussy's pictures, and Stravinsky's "Fire-bird," and such things as Alban

Berg's "Wozzek," and then to take some further examples, in order to realize that modern music is nearly all "descriptive," not "absolute." In any case, most "modern" music (Walton's "Façade," for instance) is written for a dramatic context and much of it sounds bad in a concert hall. Now does it not seem absurd that while music is clamoring for dramatic contexts as opportunities for expression, and the film is in great need of means of vital expression and suggestion, there is no marriage between film and modern music? Instead, the film makers on the whole insist on giving us music in a style which was stale in 1895. But what opportunities there are—if only they would take them! The modern composer specializes in all that is "counter, original, spare, strange" in suggestions and moods in terrors and nameless questionings, "fallings from us, vanishings"—excellent music for film. But most of the time we hear his music on the wireless, where it means nothing. In film, the modern music idiom, where it has been intelligently tried (as in France) is vital, immediate, and contributes much to the success of the production.

Consider in passing what happened to *Romeo and Juliet*. It is impossible to realize how bad this film was unless you reflect upon how good it might have been. The music—Tschaikovsky's—fitted the production perfectly. That is to say, it was music of the indoors, heavy with scent, unventilated, introverted, consorting well with the glorified seraglio that was the set-designer's picture of ancient Verona. Tschaikovsky's main musical theme has since come out in its true colors as a crooner's nostalgic drag called "Our Love." This is the musical accompaniment, if you please, of a play by Shakespeare which presents one of the purest love-stories of all time—full of stark, sharp, terrifying beauty. One can't represent such a love with Tschaikovsky's music. One might as well try to etch with a paintbrush. I would not have had any other music in that particular production, all the same. For that, it was perfect. But in another production, I should certainly like to entrust the music to a good modern composer. Shakespeare's strangely universal genius needs to be interpreted anew in every age—by the most modern means. The recent film *Romeo and Juliet* was thirty years out of date all the way through.

Not for the dignities of Shakespeare only, but also for all other dramatic presentations, I plead for modern music, mood-music, because I am sure that it has a great deal to contribute.

Finally, the third element, natural sound, or noise. Here it must be confessed that practically all natural sound used in films has been in synchronization: that is to say, the appropriate accompaniment of the thing seen. The door-bang, the telephone bell, the roar of the aero engine, the wheels of the train, the rushing of the waterfall. Such obvious sound images pass practically unnoticed. By now they are quite banal.

Yet there have been instances of the exceptionally skillful use of noise. To take a famous example. You remember in Fritz Lang's "M"—the murderer has the habit of whistling a few bars of Grieg's Troll Dance. Lang, with his usual brilliance, built this up to the climax of his film, at which the murderer was recognized by a blind man. Now, quite apart from the fact that Lang made the tune part of the plot, do you remember anything noteworthy about the effect of the sound on the dramatic intensity of the film? I do. I seem to recollect quite clearly that this harmless little tune became terrifying. It was the symbol of Peter Lorre's madness and blood-lust. Just a bar or two of music. And do you remember at what points (towards the end) the music was most baleful and threatening? I do. It was when you could hear the noise, but could not see the murderer. In other words, when the tune was used "non-sync," as film people say.

Now let us go further. Have you ever heard a noise in the night—non-sync—i.e., without having any notion of what caused it? Of course. And you left your bed and went down to find out what caused the bang, or the thump.

These two examples—Lang's whistle and the bump in the night which you got up to investigate—lead us to consider two ways of using sound for dramatic effect, both methods based on suggestion. Lang's way was to use a recognized and identified sound. He used it to suggest the menacing nearness of his character—without showing the character. Suggestion is always more effective in drama than statement. This particular trick is capable of great development. A black screen, feet crunching on gravel, and so on. A friend of mine, making a comedy, made an amusing effect out of the tick of a clock in a dentist's waiting room: he speeded up the tick when the nurse came to claim the victim. I have a bit of dog-barking in my sound library which I sometimes stick into the track when I wish to suggest the open air, and a pleasant, gay atmosphere. It is almost essential that there should be no dog on the screen, or the effect is lost, because then suggestion becomes statement. The crying of seagulls was a sound-suggestion-device which became so common with film experimenters that it was laughed out of court.

The other device is the use of unrecognized and unidentified sound. Now, let us go back to the noise that got you out of bed. Had it been a voice, you could have recognized it as your wife's or your son's or your neighbor's, or an unknown, and it would not have disturbed you. But noises have this quality—they do not inevitably suggest what made them. This means that certain types of noise can be used "incognito." An example: when we made *North Sea* we had to do a studio-crash, to represent a sudden catastrophe on board a ship. The sound staff approached the B.B.C. and everybody else, but they could not get a combination of sounds that would be sufficiently terrifying. They asked me. I told them at once that they would have to get a loud, unidentifiable sound to stick into the crash. They got it. A horrid metallic squeal which suggested that the vessel had been squeezed diagonally and had started all her seams. It was a wonderful noise—because it was unrecognizable. To take an example from the so-called "silent" days. An airplane was flying towards us. The music-director "cut" the orchestra, and a strange, frightsome sound began, and got louder and louder. It was nothing like an airplane, but very frightening. When I got home I was still wondering how this noise was done. Then I got it. It was a noise I had known all my life—an open cymbal beaten with two soft-headed drumsticks. How familiar! Yet it had lost its identity, and retained only its dramatic quality, used in conjunction with the picture. Pictures are clear and specific, noises are vague. The picture had changed a cymbal noise into an air-noise.

That is why noise is so useful. It speaks directly to the emotions. Babies are afraid of loud bangs, long before they can have learned that there is any connection between noise and danger—before they even know there's such a thing as danger. Many dogs can be made to run away by beating a tin tray. Pictures speak to the intelligence. Noise seems to by-pass the intelligence and speak to something very deep and inborn—as the instance of the baby seems to show.

This last reflection leads to my conclusion.

The outstanding characteristic of the screen-image is its literalness. The cinema-picture is a medium of literal statement. I have not the space to prove my point, but I doubt that it will be disputed. If you have seen a scene being shot, you will know what I mean. The scene looks like a studio set to you, because your "wide-angle" eyes take in a range of objects which includes the roof and walls of the studio. In the morning when you see the rushes, you find that the funnel-like gaze of the camera has somehow made it all look literally true. (Strangely enough, that is why costume plays often fail to convince on the screen. The camera is so literal-minded that if you show it actors dressed up, it *sees* actors-dressed-up, not characters.)

Now for sound.

I think that we have enough material in this review of sound to conclude that, while the picture is the medium of statement, the sound is the medium of suggestion. This is not to say that the picture cannot make suggestions, or that the sound cannot make statements. But I think we can allow that the picture lends itself to clear statement, while the sound lends itself to suggestion.

During what is called the "great silent days of the German cinema," we saw a great attempt to use visuals for suggestion rather than statement. While it cannot be denied that many startling effects were obtained, I think it must at the same time be admitted that this genre went out of fashion because the directors were attempting to use the camera in a way which is not proper to it. At this time the pictures got farther and farther away from reality, until a stage was reached at which they became ridiculous, because the credulity of the audiences was finally overstrained.

And I think that we can add that the present trend of visual is towards a more and more faithful representation of reality. In my opinion this process is inevitable, because of the nature of the camera itself as an instrument (and perhaps also because of the nature of vision itself as a sense).

184

I now propose to run briefly over this ground we have covered and see if we cannot reach a further conclusion about the technique of sound. I may as well give my own conclusions. I believe in the first place that suggestion is such a powerful device in presentation that film cannot be fully expressive if it allows itself to become primarily a medium of statement, and I believe that whenever the device of suggestion is required for dramatic or poetic purposes, the line to follow is the exploitation of the sound elements. I also think that we have discovered a clue in our review of the history of sound in film. And I think this clue can be indicated simply, perhaps too simply, in the cryptic expression "non-sync."

It seems to me that all the most suggestive sound devices have been non-sync.

The commentator appeared on the scene in the Nineties. He spoke non-sync, with an effect which we can only guess at, but which, arguing from an early historical parallel (the Greek chorus), was probably highly dramatic.

He allowed himself to transgress into sync speech, and I cannot help thinking that his efforts became absurd.

Then music came into the picture theatres. At first it was non-sync, and I do not think any of us are too old to remember how effective non-sync musical accompaniment could be. But then music in turn succumbed to the attraction of attempting synchronization (much more dangerous in the case of music than speech), and perished, by disrupting itself with bangs and whistles. Then came the great era of sync speech—which the public has found to be a bore, but which still continues. On the other hand non-sync speech (commentary), although it has not been exploited in dramatic films, is showing excellent dramatic results in the best short films and documentaries. I believe it is only a question of time until commentary comes into the dramatic films, at least in an experimental way. Indeed in *Confessions of a Nazi Spy*, the process may be said to have begun.

Finally, music and noise. I think I have indicated in my analysis of successful modern practice that the most suggestive way of employing these elements is to use them non-sync.

With noise, we must include silence. Even in the so-called silent days, a clever musical director would sometimes cut the orchestra dead at a big dramatic moment on the screen (producing an effect similar to Handel's general pause just before the end of the Halleluia Chorus). Yet sound-film directors do not appear to be aware of the possibilities of the use of silence. One brilliant early example, however, will remain always in my memory. It is in Walter Ruttmann's *Melody of the World*. He built up a big climax of guns in a war sequence, worked it up to a close-up of a woman emitting a piercing shriek, and cut at once to rows of white crosses—in silence.

In the hands of an artist of Ruttmann's calibre silence can be the loudest of noises, just as black, in a brilliant design, can be the brightest of colors.

Camera and Microphone
by John Howard Lawson

Mr. Lawson, playwright and film writer, is the author of such notable books as "Theory and Technique of Playwriting and Screenwriting," "Film in the Battle of Ideas," and "Film: the Creative Process." This chapter appeared originally in the May 1948 issue of Masses and Mainstream.

It is not surprising that the motion picture relies to a considerable extent on devices borrowed from the theatre. There are many superficial points of resemblance between the two arts. Films are shown in auditoriums which do not differ in any marked degree from other playhouses. Stage actors perform in films. Stage training is still regarded as a fairly satisfactory prerequisite for appearance before the camera. Actors, directors, and writers move from stage to screen with comparative ease and with what seem to be minor adjustments of their techniques and methods. It is often customary to draw a stage curtain back and forth to mark the beginning and end of the drama projected on the screen within the proscenium arch.

If we go behind the screen and examine the resources and techniques which enter into the making of a motion picture, it becomes apparent that the similarity in audience presentation conceals essential differences in the creative process. The performance within the proscenium arch is actually the way in which the play is made. The playwright can use only the means of production that are available in the stage-space bounded by the footlights and the walls of the playhouse. The convention of the theatre assumes that the audience observes the events on the stage through a transparent fourth wall. Thus the angle of vision from which the audience views the scene is constant.

The motion picture is not created within the limits of the proscenium arch, and it is not dependent on the technical resources which are there available. The angle of vision from which the audience views the picture is not determined solely by the relationship between the auditorium and the stage. The angle of vision is constantly changing, and it is determined by the camera.

The basic quality of the camera as a story-telling instrument is its mobility, its ability to search out and record the most diverse phenomena. The camera's facility in portraying movement and contrast is augmented by a quality that is not inherent in the camera, but is supplied by the cutting and arrangement of the strips of film. The process of cutting is properly described by the European term montage.*

Mobility and montage as the physical conditions that determine the film structure were discovered at a very early period of motion picture history. As long as they were used chiefly for trickery and illusion, shocks or surprises, they had no specific artistic meaning or emotional validity. Griffith and Chaplin undertook to explore the psychological and social potentialities that were inherent in the camera's movement and the interrelationship of scenes. They found, almost simultaneously, that the camera was especially effective in achieving psychological intimacy and in portraying panoramic movements of people and events, and that the dramatic essence of montage lay in the distinctive interrelationship between the intimate detail and the large movement.

The fact that the motion picture has a far greater sweep and more varied contact with reality than is possible on the stage may lead enthusiasts to conclude somewhat prematurely that the film is, at least potentially, a "greater art" than the theatre. The assumption can only be attributed to a misunderstanding of the relationship between a work of art and the reality that it mirrors. A work of art is an organized and unified interpretation of reality. The physical conditions of performance by living actors on a stage determine the dramatic structure, but the conditions do not place any limitations on the playwright's interpretation of life. The poetic splendor of Shakespeare's plays grew out of the system of production in the Elizabethan theatre, but it was not the open roof that permitted the lines to soar to heaven. The power of the plays lay in the creator's ability to see life in its wholeness and beauty, and his development of an organic structure that was whole and beautiful.

* The American industry uses the word montage to describe a jumble of shots superimposed or simultaneously shown on the screen to convey a mood or cover a time-lapse. Since almost all serious studies of the motion picture accept the European usage of the term as a description of cutting or editing, it seems wise to follow the general example.

The extraordinary scope of the action that the camera can portray has both advantages and disadvantages. It makes structural unity difficult, and encourages the irresponsible wandering in search of elusive drama that characterizes so many films. Many motion pictures seem to disintegrate before our eyes. We can say that the story is disorganized, but the weakness of the story is related to ignorance or willful perversion of the principles that govern the use of the camera and the arrangement of the visual image.

The camera's facility in recording diverse phenomena may seem to be too obvious to require extended comment. It can follow the criminal in his flight. It can pause to show ants making an ant hill or observe the slow setting of the sun, the rising of the evening star.

The camera's movement, however startling or rapid it may be, is not an end in itself. It has no dramatic value unless it reveals drama, a conflict of wills developing to a climax. Thus the chase, the struggle between the pursuer and the pursued, emerged as the first crude form of conflict in motion. The principle that the camera's movement must be related to a conflict in motion governs such diverse events as the men struggling on the train in *The Great Train Robbery*, the armies marching through the Alps in *Suvarov*, the lovers quarreling on the bus in *It Happened One Night*, the dilapidated truck moving along Highway 66 in *The Grapes of Wrath*.

There is nothing in the theatre that has a similar value. An effect of conflict in motion is occasionally achieved through mechanical means—for example, the tableau of Eliza crossing the ice in *Uncle Tom's Cabin*. But it would be difficult to argue that these mechanical effects, which were common in nineteenth century plays, altered basic concepts of dramatic art.

Action taking place within the limits of the proscenium arch has a creative life and vigor that is natural to the stage. These limits are unnatural for the camera, and when they are imposed upon it the action becomes stilted. It seems as if the conscious will and emotional drive of the characters are straitjacketed by the unnecessarily restricted environment. Directors who present action in purely theatrical terms frequently try to impose cinematic vitality on the scene by moving the camera and by rapid cutting. When the introduction of sound restricted the activity of the characters and temporarily immobilized the camera, muffled in a sound-proof booth, directors looked desperately for some trick to give the illusion of movement. Rouben Mamoulian wrote of the film, *Applause*, which he directed in 1929: "I lifted the sound-proofed camera off its feet and set it in motion on pneumatic tires. Scenes moved out of one room and into others without halt. The camera flew, jerked, floated, and rolled, discarding its stubborn tripod-legs for a set of wired wheels that raced over the studio floors."

The camera's feverish activity could not solve Mamoulian's problem. He had not discovered the secret of adapting sound to the principle of conflict in motion. The people talking in theatrical settings could not be brought to life by the camera racing on its wire wheels.

Let us now turn to the use of montage, which is another aspect of the presentation of conflict in motion.

Eisenstein observed that "there was a period in Soviet cinema when montage was proclaimed 'everything.'" The error, according to Eisenstein, arose from a one-sided and exaggerated recognition of the peculiar dramatic value of montage. The value "consisted in the fact *that two film pieces of any kind, placed together, inevitably combined into a new concept, a new quality, arising out of that juxtaposition.*"

Montage is an extension of the camera's mobility. The camera can go wherever human beings can carry and operate it. But film that has been taken by any number of cameras in any number of places can be put together so as to establish unpredictable relationships and varieties of experience. Here again we have a principle that is foreign to the stage. A play may have a great many changes of scene, but the driving force of the play is found in the inner content of the scenes and only to a minor degree in the contrast and linkage between them.

In the motion picture, the inner content of the scenes is continually transformed, given new meaning, driven forward by the movement between the scenes. In a sense, the movement is hidden; there is nothing between the scenes that we can actually see or get our hands on. But the transition is dynamic and meaningful because it possesses the quality of action. It conforms to our description of action as a *process of becoming,* a change of equilibrium involving prior and forthcoming changes of equilibrium.

Montage is as much an accepted convention of the film as the imaginary fourth wall in the theatre. The audience is not disturbed by the discontinuity of time and space which is one of the characteristics of montage. In general, time and space function normally within the limits of a scene. But the scene may be cut at any point, to carry us half way across the world, or back or forward through time. In *Intolerance*, the great city of Babylon falls, the Huguenots are massacred in seventeenth century France—and simultaneously, the boy in the modern story walks to the scaffold and mounts the steps to die.

Throughout this film, one feels that Griffith is searching for unity, for a meaning which he himself understands but which he cannot fully translate into the language of film. He partially succeeds in certain close-ups which bring the action into focus and define the relationship between human beings and the sweep of events. In these close-ups, Griffith intuitively approaches the principle for which he is seeking. The close-up is the key to the film structure. It provides the emotional insight, the pattern of will and purpose that bind the action together in a rational design. There are many flashes of this insight in *Intolerance*, but they are not sufficient to unify the vast historical pageant. Griffith's instinct was correct. Even his rather abstract image of the woman rocking the cradle is an instinctive attempt to use the close-up for emotional and psychological integration. The scene is a close-up of a person performing a humble and familiar act. But we do not actually get close to the woman. We do not see her face or know what she is feeling or suffering. We cannot do so because she is only an artifice, an idea which has no human function in the story.

In order to understand the use of the close-up in the motion picture, it may be of value to consider the development of a somewhat similar device in the drama. The Elizabethan soliloquy serves an analogous purpose. It defines the conscious will in relation to the whole scope of the action. Many of Shakespeare's soliloquies and long speeches are examples of the remarkable compression and extension that can be achieved through the *close-up* of the individual's mind, the intimate analysis of his conscious will.

The same effect is accomplished, without poetic elaboration and with greater dependence on visual communication, in Ibsen's plays. The second act of "Hedda Gabler" opens with Hedda alone loading a pistol. The scene suggests a close-up of the gun. Then, as Hedda looks off into the garden, we can imagine the camera panning to her face. Certainly a close-up is indicated as she raises the gun, points it off scene and says: "Now I'll shoot you, Judge Brack!"

At the end of "A Doll's House," when Nora stands at the door ready to leave, we want to see her face, her eyes and the movement of her lips as she speaks of "a real wedlock." Ibsen's stage directions after her departure describe Helmer's reactions with painstaking intimacy. "He sinks down on a chair at the door and buries his face in his hands. . . . Looks around and rises. . . . A hope flashes across his mind . . . he hears the door slamming below."

The introduction of electric lighting, illuminating the actor's face and enabling the audience to see changes in facial expression or pantomime with physical objects, was responsible in part for Ibsen's method of detailed characterization and his use of things as symbols. The possibility of studying the actor at close range, which inspired Ibsen's technical innovations, was fully realized a half century later, when the camera approached the performer's face to record every nuance of feeling, to move from a man's or woman's eyes to the thing that is being watched, to follow the hands as they reach out to touch or caress or reject.

It may be said that in practice the film uses the close-up in an empty and repetitious manner. The intimate contact with the audience is more likely to be slightly obscene than seriously psychological. Kisses, parted lips, and heaving bosoms are more common than the study of less obvious reactions. Nevertheless, the intimacy is there. Its misuse does not detract from its importance. Where it is misused, the structure is weakened, and psychological values are distorted.

While some film makers, especially in the formative period of the Soviet film, have tended to over-emphasize montage as the sole creative element in the motion picture, others have placed a one-sided emphasis on the close-up. Recognition of the importance of the close-up leads Dudley Nichols to the conclusion that it is a mistake to speak of the motion picture as the medium of "action." Nichols has this to say:

The truth is that the stage is the medium of action while the screen is the medium of reaction. It is through identification with the person *acted upon* on the screen, and not with the person acting, that the film builds up its oscillating power with an audience. . . . At any emotional crisis of a film, when a character is saying something which profoundly affects another, it is to this second character that the camera instinctively roves, perhaps in a close-up; and it is then that the hearts of the audience quiver and open in release, or rock with laughter or shrink with pain.

Nichols is right in suggesting the function of the close-up as the key to the human root and meaning of the action. But he misinterprets the relationship between the close-up and the action that precedes and follows it, and thus adopts an erroneous premise concerning the nature of the film story. The theory has broader philosophic implications that deserve attention. It may seem like a long jump from the cinema close-up to the cult of Nihilism that permeates so much of the intellectual life of our time. Yet if the close-up is used in the manner suggested—and there is a marked tendency to so use it in the contemporary film—the individual is depicted as the passive and tortured observer of a world in which his conscious will is inoperative, and moments of greatest tension arise from suffering or exaltation which lead to no decision and have no effect on the chaotic reality in which the individual moves. Many people take this despairing view of the postwar environment: We can imagine a close-up of the average "man of good will," confused by newspaper hysteria and frightened by war propaganda, hypnotized by chaos, *acted upon* and unable to act.

However, if we think a little about this close-up, we must come to the conclusion that its meaning and dramatic impact do not lie in the individual's passivity, but in his failure to act when action is necessary. If we are sure that he will continue to be acted upon and do nothing, the close-up lacks tension; it involves no struggle and no progression. Tension arises only when the individual seen in close-up is a participant in the events which he observes; what he sees is to some extent the result of what he has willed. It may be different from anything that he had intended or hoped, but the unexpected result brings him face to face with new and more portentous decisions. He must go on willing or die.

The law of life demands that man use his conscious will and exacts terrible penalties for his failure to do so. The same law determines the function of the close-up in the structure of the motion picture. It presents an intimate study of decision, of the will in motion, of man's recognition of what he has done and his search for remedies or solutions. Vacillation heightens tension only when it is related, as in Hamlet's soliloquies, to the necessity of action.

The motion picture is unlike the stage, in that it can jump without any break in continuity from the individual debating a course of action to the whole range of events on which his will is concentrated. It can move from the most intimate detail to the clash of historical forces, from the private decision to the unexpected public result. The close-up fuses the elements that are driving toward the climax. But the action must have the extension and magnitude that are characteristic of the film structure. The camera is not content to dwell upon intimate detail alone, and it is artificially restricted when it is forced to do so. It seeks space and movement, crowds and horizons. The motion picture tends to create a new kind of story, a mass-story, in which the lives of individuals are interwoven with the life of society and the fate of the individual is inextricably bound up in the fate of the crowd.

But the development of the film has shown that mass movement tends to be abstract and fragmentary when it is unrelated to the dramatic purpose of the individuals who compose the mass. Scenes depicting crowds are artistically complete only when we see enough faces to catch the mood of the group and give the flavor of its collective purpose. Similarly the structure is complete only when the pattern of relationships between individuals and the forces that constitute their environment are sufficiently defined to give form and meaning to the whole action.

The most creative artists of the cinema have shown a preference for historical subjects. History is people in motion. It offers material that is more closely related to the requirements of mobility and montage than stories that have been molded by the necessities of another art form in novels or plays. The limitations imposed on the American screen are especially indicated in its failure to grapple with the massive, vivid, dynamic stuff of American history and tradition.

The screen story is not told solely by the camera. In giving less attention to the microphone, we are merely accepting the realities of the contemporary system of production. The sound-track follows its pedestrian course; the skill of expert technicians is wasted on unimaginative dialogue, "descriptive" and intrusive music, and dutifully "realistic" effects of trains, bells, footsteps, thunderstorms.

The sound-track is strait-jacketed by the tradition of the theatre, where sound comes only from the voices of actors, or the efforts of stagehands manipulating crude machines. There has been so little experimentation with sound as an active dramatic agent that any assertions regarding its use must be tentative and based more upon speculation than upon experience.

A rare instance of the creative use of music, which suggests the interrelationship of music to dialogue and other sounds that are interwoven on the sound-track may be found in Pare Lorentz' musical instructions for *The Fight for Life,* a documentary film dealing with childbirth in a city hospital. Lorentz is insistent on tempo, and the precise synchronization of sound and action:

Every scene was directed to a metronome, and for dramatic effect the music must start exactly with the film—from the moment we see "City Hospital" until the baby is born, the beat of the music must not vary, and there must be no change in instrumentation sufficient enough to be noticeable—the conception in direction was that we would have the mother's heart beat—two beats in one, with the accent on the first one; with the echo exactly 1½ times as fast, and without an accent; factually, a beat of 100 a minute as against the fetal heart beat of 150 a minute.

When the story changes its scene and tempo, Lorentz suggests that "the music must always precede the picture." When the intern is leaving the delivery room, the music begins to suggest the raucous life of streets and saloons: "I feel, then, that we start one piano under the intern; that we start another piano as he walks out of the hospital; that the minute he hits the street, we suddenly hit the audience in the face with gin, women, despair, cruelty, and life, as crude as it is."

195

During this walk through the streets, we hear the intern's voice; he is talking to himself about the woman who has just died: "And now she is dead. . . . Now her striving body, that brought a life into the world, is cold and empty. . . ." He walks past lighted shop windows. He continues to speak, and the two pianos play blues. But "the words themselves carry the meaning and the tempo. . . . If the music attempts to narrate the city, to interpret it, then the music and the picture will overwhelm my dialogue. My man is all-important; he doesn't know where he is."

The distinctive values provided by the microphone are similar to the values offered by the camera in the visual field. There is a mechanical similarity: the microphone has the mobility of the camera, and the sound-track is like the strips of film—it is the record of segments of reality that can be arranged in any sequence or juxtaposition, without regard for space or time.

These physical characteristics provide the basis for a sound structure that resembles the visual structure in combining psychological intimacy with sweeping movement. The brief excerpts quoted from Lorentz' plan for *The Fight for Life* illustrate the basic factors in the use of sound. The microphone's mobility is evident; it keeps pace with the intern as he walks along the street. The scene involves a complex montage of sounds: the voice, the blues music, the sounds of the street. Lorentz recognizes that the primary dramatic factor is the close-up, portraying the man's feeling and purpose: "My man is all-important." The sound that corresponds to the visual close-up, the inner voice, must also be primary.

The history of the motion picture as an art and a business explains the partial neglect of the camera's potentialities and the far more complete neglect of the microphone. Commercial dependence on cheap situations and theatrical effects has led many serious photographic artists to assume that the use of the camera to tell a story is in direct opposition to its esthetic value in creating a visual image. They have disregarded, and often despised, the story-telling function as a degradation of an essentially pictorial art. The development of the cinema as a graphic art had reached a relative maturity, and had begun to exert some influence on commercial production, when the talking picture introduced a new element. Bringing a larger investment and a further concentration of monopoly control, sound tended to impose greater dependence on the theatre and further limitations on visual experimentation. To the artist intent on composition and the movement of light and shadow, sound was merely noise, an unwarranted intrusion on the legitimate art of the camera, justified only by its popularity as a crude story-telling device.

Thus the esthetics of sound received far less attention than the esthetics of the visual image, which had achieved some recognition as a valid, although subordinate, contribution to the story. Photography is treated with some respect in commercial production. But all that is demanded of the sound-man is technical proficiency in making the sound real and reasonably attractive to the ear.

Contemporary studio methods disregard the structural unity of the film. The story is supposed to have a form. It must have a beginning and an ending. It must hold attention and reach some sort of climax. But there is no fusing of the elements that compose the structure. In most cases the screenwriter has no knowledge of the camera. The cameraman knows nothing about story values, except what he has picked up in the course of his work on the set. The editor is given strips of film without any previous consultation concerning the script or the problems that it involves. The composer is given his assignment belatedly after most of the photographic work has been completed. The director, who in many cases does not participate in the preparation of the script and who may or may not know anything about the camera, is given the impossible task of unifying these separate and discordant elements.

The structural unity of the film must originate in the screenplay. There can be no unity unless the screenplay is actually a screen invention, fully realized in film terms, with genuine understanding of the function of the camera and the microphone and free creative use of these marvelous instruments.

The Composer and the Motion Picture
by Hanns Eisler

Mr. Eisler, the distinguished composer, first came into prominence
with his scores for the early Bertolt Brecht plays in Germany.
His career was also marked by his experimental work in correlating
music and cinema under the auspices of the Rockefeller
Foundation here in the United States. This chapter appeared
originally in his book "Composing for the Films," published in 1947.

The motion picture requires, at first glance, no specific technique of composing. The fact that both motion picture and music are temporal arts does not imply the need for a unique musical technique, and despite all talk about such a technique, the motion picture has not given a genuine new impulse to music. Motion picture music has merely adapted certain procedures employed in autonomous music.

Nevertheless certain principles are beginning to take shape. One is the need for short musical forms, corresponding to the short picture sequences. Such sketchy, rhapsodical, or aphoristic forms are characteristic of the motion picture in their irregularity, fluidity, and absence of repetitions. The traditional tripartite song form—*a-b-a*—with the last part repeating the first, is less suitable than continuous forms, such as preludes, inventions, or toccatas. The method of exposition and connection of several themes and their developments seems foreign to the motion picture because such complex musical forms require too much attention to be used in combination with complex visual forms. But even this is not an absolute rule. Large musical forms related, not to picture sequences, but to continuities of meaning are not inconceivable.

In short musical forms, each element must be self-sufficient or capable of rapid expansion. Motion picture music cannot "wait." Moreover, the composer must differentiate among the short forms themselves. For instance, a two-minute sequence is more suitable for developing a short motif than for a complete melody, and a thirty-second theme would be out of place here. But this does not mean that in a thirty-second *piece* the theme must be still shorter; on the contrary, it may very well consist of one long melody that covers the whole sequence.

The specific musical logic that assigns each of these elements a definite place and connects them must also be adequate to the requirements of the motion picture. Quickly changing musical characterizations, sudden transitions and reversals, improvisatory and "fantasia" elements should be predominant. To achieve this without sacrificing musical continuity one must resort to a highly evolved variation technique. Each small musical form accompanying a motion picture is a kind of variation, even though it has not been preceded by a manifest theme. The dramatic function is the real theme.

As has already been pointed out, the composer cannot disregard the planning that is demanded by the dramatic concern for the whole of the motion picture and its relation to the details. But while thus far planning has been bureaucratic and artistically barren, he must attempt to make it fruitful. He must consciously use the simple and the complex, the continuous and the discontinuous, the inconspicuous and the striking, the passionate and the cold elements of music. The free and conscious utilization of the potentialities created by the intrinsic evolution of music will make motion picture music fertile, if a specific motion picture music ever comes into being at all. Planning must be transformed to such an extent that it will amount to a new spontaneity. The negation of naïve "inventing" and inspiration in motion picture music should lead to their re-emergence on a higher level.

We shall mention at least the simplest consequences of the type of composing advocated here. With regard to the logic and the genesis of the work, there are, grossly speaking, two types of composition. In the first, the whole is derived from the details, conceived as musical germs, and developed blindly under the compulsion of their inherent drive. The works of Schubert and Schumann belong to this type, and originally also those of Schönberg, who said that when composing a song he allowed himself to be impelled by the initial words without taking the whole poem into consideration. In the second type, which is the inverse of the first, all the details are derived from the whole. The works of Beethoven belong to the second type. The greatness of a composer is essentially defined by the extent to which both types are integrated in his work—Bach, Mozart, Beethoven, and Schönberg are exemplary in this respect. If the composer clings undialectically to the first type of composing, as did Dvořák for instance, he produces a potpourri of "ideas" connected arbitrarily or schematically. The other extreme is represented by Handel, and leads to a sweeping though somewhat abstract conception of the whole, with sketchy, incomplete, and often superficial details.

Composers of cinema music are driven to adopt the second type of composing, as is, incidentally, the case for most works made to order. In motion picture music, the idea of the whole and its articulation holds absolute primacy, sometimes in the form of an abstract pattern that conjures up rhythms, tone sequences, and figures at a given place without the composer's specific knowledge of them in advance. The composer must invent forms and formal relations, not "ideas," if he is to write meaningfully. He can master the resulting difficulties only by realizing them clearly and translating them into well-defined technical problems, by dividing his procedure rationally into different steps and ultimately achieving "invention." He must have a kind of blueprint in mind, a framework which he must fill in at each given place and only then see to it that the fillings are vivid and striking. In a sense, he must have full control over elements that in traditional composing are, often wrongly, considered to be involuntary and purely intuitive.

This filling in, this consummation of the concrete, is the Achilles' heel of composing for motion pictures. Since the filling in is planned, by its nature it threatens at every step to degenerate into mere padding, which will appear dry, synthetic, and mechanical if the composer fails to bring in sufficient spontaneity to counter the impact of his own plan. The result is then one of those peculiar compositions, which despite their mediocre musical substance have a certain effectiveness that derives from a felicitous idea of the whole. The current demand for showmanship on the part of the composer refers to this specific musical ability, the flair for the function, without demanding an equivalent sense of the material by which it is being fulfilled. Once the composer has reached the level of planned composing, he must focus his whole energy and critical judgment on the problem of filling in.

Regarding the thesis of the primacy of the whole, or form in a broad sense, in motion picture music, it must be emphasized that the galaxy of forms evolved by traditional music and expounded in academic theories is largely useless. Many traditional forms must be discarded; others must be completely modified. To realize the primacy of the whole in motion picture music thus does not mean to take over the forms of absolute music and to adapt them by hook or crook to the film strips —by analogy with certain tendencies of contemporary opera, for instance those of Berg and Hindemith—but the very opposite. It means building complete form structures according to the specific requirements of the given film sequence, and then "filling in." Good motion picture music is fundamentally anti-formalistic. The inadequacy of traditional forms and the possibility of replacing them with advanced music has been discussed in other places, and the prosaic character of motion pictures and their general incompatibility with repetitions and musical symmetries have been defined as the most important factors in that inadequacy. We shall now discuss a number of other formal problems from the point of view of motion picture requirements, disregarding the specific musical resources.

The prose quality of motion pictures cannot be taken into account by the mere omission of repetitions in their various forms, such as the "a" part of the three-part song form, while in all other respects the composition follows the traditional pattern, for instance, that of the sonata exposition, which has been the prototype of all musical form for more than 150 years. In autonomous music there are a number of elements that have meaning only within the given formal set-up, in "looking forward" or "looking back" to some purely musical content. The recapitulation in the classical sonata, with its structural change of the modulation scheme that closes the circle of the form movement, is only the most tangible instance of this fact. But such elements are found even in the traditional exposition. The whole classical sonata form rests on the premise that not all musical moments are equally relevant as such—indeed, that not all of them are present to the same extent—but that the presence of musical events is more intense with entrance and re-entrance of the themes, and is meaningfully less intense in other passages. The very essence of the traditional sonata form is defined by the variable degree of presence of musical events, that is, their differentiation according to whether they are perceived "themselves," as anticipated or remembered, or only prepare for or lead away from such anticipations or recollections. Their articulation is equivalent to their different density or presence at different moments. Not the symphonic movement in which everything is equally present, or, to use technical terms, in which everything is equally thematic, is the best, but the symphonic movement in which the present and nonpresent moment are related in the deepest and most comprehensive manner.

Only in the latest stages of autonomous music, in such works as Schönberg's "Erwartung," are all the musical elements equally near the center. And even Schönberg, since he introduced the twelve-tone technique, seems to have been striving for differentiation according to the different degree of presence. Transitional parts, fields of tension, and fields of release of tension are some of the resources of this differentiation. It was just these elements of form, which, in contrast to the "inventions" or the actual themes, were most exposed to bad schematic treatment, but it was also through these same elements that the principle of the dynamic construction of the whole triumphantly asserted itself in great works, such as the "Eroica." These elements, whose meaning consists in the unfolding of an autonomous musical continuity, are denied to the motion picture, which requires a thoroughly and completely present music, a music .that is not self-contemplative, self-reflective, that does not harbor anticipations in itself. When transitions or fields of tension are needed, they come from the sequence of the picture, not from the inner movement of the music. This circumstance alone sets very narrow limits to the adoption of traditional patterns.

On the other hand, the composer is confronted with problems of form that hardly ever occurred in traditional music. For instance, a sequence can require the "exposition" of an event, but it must be done with a concentrated brevity that was completely alien to the sonata exposition before the disintegration of tonality. Thus the composer must be able to write music of a preparatory character that is also entirely present and does not utilize the stale means for creating moods, such as the repulsive tremolo crescendi or other devices of the same kind. He must be able to compose concluding passages, which round up a preceding dramatic development of the picture or dialogue, without a preceding purely musical and closed development—something like a *stretta* without a preceding *più moderato*. The concluding character must be found in the structure of the music itself, in the drastic characterization of its smallest components, not in their relation to preceding components, which do not exist in this case. Climaxes must sometimes be brought about directly, without crescendos, or only with a minimum of preparation.

This presents a considerable difficulty, for musically there is the greatest difference between a simple forte or fortissimo passage and one that has the effect of a climax. But while formerly a climax resulted from the whole development, here it must be achieved, so to speak, separately, "in itself." There is no general rule for such a procedure, but the composer must be aware of the problem. It may be said that such an "absolute" climax without preceding intensification can be achieved through the nature and emphasis of the musical profiles themselves, not through the mere impact of noise. Every musican knows that there are themes with an inherent "concluding" character, which is difficult to describe in words, but is accessible to careful analysis. The closing section of the exposition of the first movement of the Pastoral Symphony, the brief closing theme in the first movement of piano sonata op. 101, or bars 82 and following in the larghetto of the Second Symphony are instances of such themes in Beethoven. Likewise there are "primary" and "auxiliary" characterizations as such. The composer of motion picture music must be aware of such qualities in his material and attempt to produce them directly, without the detour of preparation and resolution. The effects in question require nothing that is alien to music. They have largely crystallized inside the shell of the traditional form language. But the point is to give them new validity by conceiving them as an independent result of that form language. It is necessary to emancipate them from their usual formal presuppositions that are incompatible with the cinema, to make them fluid, as it were.

Non-schematic forms are also known in traditional music under the name of fantasies and rhapsodies. While the latter often approximate the potpourri or, like Brahms' opus 79 and, to some extent, Schubert's "Wanderer Fantasy," are disguised song forms or sonatas, there is such a thing as a specific fantasy form, such as Mozart's famous piano fantasies in C-minor and D-minor. Official musical theory has kept aloof from such works and contented itself with declaring that they had no definite form. Yet Mozart's two fantasies mentioned above are no less carefully organized than the sonatas, indeed, perhaps even more carefully, because they are not subjected to a heteronomous order. Their formal principle might be termed that of the segment, or the "intonation." They consist of a number of parts, each of them unified, relatively complete, each following a single thematic pattern, in different tempos and keys. The art of the fantasy consists not so much in elaboration and development of a uniformly flowing totality as in balancing the various segments through similarity and contrast, careful proportions,* modulated characterizations, and a certain looseness of structure. The segments may often be suddenly interrupted. The less definite their form, the more easily can they be joined to others and continued by them. All this is similar to the requirements of motion picture music. Its composer will often be compelled to think in terms of segments rather than of developments, and what is accomplished elsewhere by the form resulting from the thematic development, he will have to achieve by relating one segment to another. This is a direct consequence of the postulate of "presence" in motion-picture music, and refers to relatively large pieces, which for the time being are infrequent.

The interrelation of several forms also raises questions that cannot be solved by means of traditional resources alone. Contrast through tempo is insufficient. From a dramatic point of view it may be deemed necessary that several movements in the same tempo should follow one another, and that, as in the older suite, they should differ sharply, but only in character. For instance, a slow tempo was out of place in the newly composed music to Joris Ivens' *Rain*, not because it was necessary to illustrate the falling of the rain, but because the music's task was to push forward this plotless and therefore static motion picture. The composer was forced to adopt means of contrast more subtle than the allegro followed by an adagio. Thus motion picture music does not necessarily lead to the use of coarser means; on the contrary, if it is emancipated, it will be a stimulus for new differentiations.

It must be kept in mind that the planning of the music

* Cf. the "closing" almost coda-like modification of the introductory adagio in the C-minor fantasy in its reprise. It differs from its first form more than does any sonata recapitulation of Mozart.

can be effective only if it is not separated from the planning of the picture; the two aspects must be in productive inter-relation. If the composer is faced with given sequences and told to contribute thirty seconds of music at one place and two minutes at another place, his planning is confined to the very bureaucratic function from which he should be freed. Such a planning is founded on the mechanical and administrative division of competence, not on the inherent conditions of the work. Free planning signifies combined planning, which could often lead to fitting the picture to the music, instead of the usual inverse procedure. This would of course presuppose genuine collective work in the motion picture industry. Eisenstein seems to be working in this direction.

The Problem of Color

by Robert Edmond Jones

Mr. Jones was one of America's foremost stage designers in the Twenties and Thirties. In the late Thirties he went to Hollywood to help develop Technicolor productions. He was co-author (with Kenneth MacGowan) of "Continental Stagecraft." This chapter appeared originally on February 27, 1938, in The New York Times.

Samuel Goldwyn's announced decision to make pictures exclusively in color has set a final seal upon Hollywood's acceptance of the newly perfected Technicolor process. Color, we are told, is about to take possession of the screen. Vast preparations are being made. Enormous sums of money are being expended. The entire industry is to be reoriented to the change.

A similar readjustment of values took place in the industry when sound was brought to the screen. Only the other day, it seems, we were marveling at the sounds of the first Vitaphone pictures. Today sound is a commonplace of motion pictures. Tomorrow color will have become a commonplace in its turn.

Unfortunately, however, color and Hollywood's idea of color are two different things. The fact is that Hollywood has not yet begun to think in terms of color. The color pictures now being made in the studios are not color pictures at all, in any real sense, but colored pictures. Their tones are agreeably subdued in order that they may not clash with one another and the individual "shots" often contain delightful pastel harmonies. But there is very little real color in these films and almost no color composition as artists know it. Black-and-white thinking still dominates the screen.

Current color films are successful, it seems to me, for two reasons. The color gratifies our desire for novelty—anything for a new sensation in the movies!—and it appeals to our sense of recognition. We take pleasure in seeing on the screen the actual tones of the flesh, eyes, hair, et cetera, of our beloved stars. Seeing Marlene Dietrich, Fredric March, Janet Gaynor in color is one step nearer to seeing them in person. But we should not allow this feeling of delighted recognition to blind us to the fact that up to the present time we have never seen a motion picture in which color exercises its true function.

It is only fair to state that this opinion is not shared by the makers of color pictures. The public is led to believe that every possible problem that can arise from the use of color has been met and mastered. Statements given out by the studios indicate that the making of color films no longer presents any real difficulty. It is now, we are told, a matter of routine. From a purely technical point of view these statements are correct. Each successive color film is a mechanical triumph. The real problem, however, is not a technical one, but an artistic one, and it is being evaded in a rather extraordinary fashion.

"The Technicolor people," according to a late release, "realized that their efforts would be useless unless they could make a picture which they, and hence the audience, would forget was colored. They have succeeded."

Here is a novel interpretation of the word success. The public is not expected to forget that there is music in a musical picture or that there is talk in a talking picture. But the public is definitely expected to forget that there is color in a color picture!

To do them justice, one imagines the makers of the present color films saying, "Why shouldn't we handle color as we handle sound? We are trying to make pictures of living people, just as they are in life. The closer we can come to actual life the better. We have learned to reproduce the sounds of everyday life on the screen. We don't bother about 'organizing' or 'composing' them. Let's not fuss about color. Let's get it on the screen as best we can. Let's photograph people and things in the natural colors of life, and we shall automatically have a good picture."

These ideas seem sound enough. But in following them, the essential point is disregarded. Color on the screen is unlike any other kind of color we have ever seen before. It does not belong to the categories of color in Nature or in painting and it does not obey the rules of black-and-white picture-making.

A new element is added—the color movies.

Here lies the key to all discussions of color in motion pictures. We are dealing, not with color that is motionless, static, but with color that moves and changes before our eyes. Color on the screen interests us, not by its harmony but by its progression from harmony to harmony. This movement, this progression of color on the screen is in itself an utterly new visual experience, full of wonder. The color flows from sequence to sequence like a kind of visual music and it affects our emotions precisely as music affects them.

The truth is that a new form of art is about to be born into the world, an art for which there is as yet no name but which holds an extraordinary and thrilling promise. Shall we call it visual opera? Color music-drama? No matter. It is enough to say that this new mobile color may quite conceivably turn out to be the art form of tomorrow.

The emotional quality of music is inherent in all moving color. When producers have grasped this idea they will have taken the first step toward the creation of true color films. We are sensitive to moving color as we are to music. The color in a film is like a musical accompaniment to the story, appealing to our eyes instead of to our ears. And here, precisely, is the difficulty the producers are facing, more difficult because they refuse to recognize it. Their problem is one not only of harnessing color on the screen but of harnessing a kind of color the world has never seen before. No wonder they pretend the problem doesn't exist!

But the problem does exist and until it is faced and solved, motion picture audiences will continue to feel the incessant slight irritation that goes on through the sequences of every color film. In every color film we are seeing something that is fundamentally false and wrong. We may not understand why the color is wrong. But it is not necessary for us to be trained musicians to feel a discord when we hear one. Nor is it necessary for us to be trained colorists to feel a color discord when we see one.

The color sequences in the first feature pictures to be made in the new three-color process were blatant and violent. The public realized this almost at once. What the public did not realize was that these early pictures were hastily planned, that they were directed without any conception of a color technique, and that they were so stupidly put together that the color sequences exploded against one another on the screen like bombs. The clash of color in these films rapidly assumed the proportions of an international scandal and the producers and the critics united their efforts to hush up the scandal at once.

Down with color! they cried. Take the color out of color! Get color out of the way at any cost! Accordingly, just as color was about to become a dramatic agent of real value to the screen, Hollywood took hold of it, subdued it, "rarefied" it (a new catchword of the studios), thwarted it, stunted it, and is now trying to ignore it.

But color will not be ignored. Underneath the subdued, controlled, rarefied color of the newest films the subtle discord still persists, and its curiously disturbing influence is being felt more and more powerfully every day. The conflict between color and drama is being carried on in whispers instead of being shouted out from the screen. But the conflict is still there.

The Man Who Was Colorblind
by Len Lye

*Mr. Lye was a pioneer in making motion pictures without a camera.
His films for the British Government in the mid-Thirties—
Color Box, Rainbow Dance, Trade Tattoo—influenced an entire
school of film makers. This chapter appeared originally in
Sight and Sound, Spring 1940.*

To consider color in film superfluous is tantamount to considering color in paintings superfluous. Of course if the tradition of painting had developed through the use of black and white pigments only, then, no doubt, the public would go to the National Galleries and be content with masterpieces in black and white paint. But now, if suddenly all paintings were deprived of color, most of their appeal would be lost.

Although color in films is no longer a novelty, it seems that its use has been entirely misunderstood. These notes attempt to point out how color could be a great asset to dramatic films if they were really scripted for production in color. An example is given of a particular story, with suggestions for a particular color treatment for it. Upon this suggested color treatment the final color continuity would be based. For in a color film the color continuity should be as integral a part of the production as the action and the dialogue.

By a color continuity I mean a strict selective color discrimination applied to the visual clues of a given story so that those clues seen in continuity are part of a recognizable color composition which clearly assists the telling of the story.

In a static color scene, color composition is obtained by contrasts and harmonies of tones and hues. But film is not static, and color composition should be obtained through the harmonies and contrasts of the progressive color scenes. The action of scenes must also be planned to include a control of the movement of colors within each scene.

If film is visual movement and progression of scene, then color, the external aspect of scene, must be considered in terms of progression and movement too. For instance, if in the progression of a color composition the action has been in predominant hues of red followed by predominant hues of blue, then the blues would of course seem more vivid than they really were, owing to their contrast with the memory of the reds previously seen.

Similarly, a knowledgeable and creative use of the whole chromatic range of colors in continuity would create an esthetic quality according to the nicety of their relationship with the outline of the story and with one another. The accenting and pianissimo of hues could assist emphasis of over- and understatement as desired in defining the dramatic nuances of the story.

Strictly speaking there has never been in all film history an attempt to script a film for a continuity to apply the great emotional value of color in heightening a story's dramatic outline. To do so a story would have to be broken down for scripting much further than is usual in terms of normal black and white film production. The color script would have to be the final preparatory phase guiding the production of the story in every shot.

As it is, popular films in color have not advanced much beyond the scripting methods employed for the production of normal black and white films, with the result that color is felt to be an adjunct which merely makes the film more costly to produce, and its entertainment value, as a color film, a superficial one. Certainly little sense of added artistic creation has been achieved by the use of color in films up to now.

A color script should be a guiding factor in the presentation of the story. For instance, if the black were a necessary link in continuity of color, then a black form such as a black teapot, head of hair or pair of shoes, might be included in the script according to the logic and literary license of the story at the point where the movement of black was required. If by any chance no object or form could be devised to carry black at that point of the story line, then the color continuity and action of the previous scenes would have to be adjusted so that black became necessary and the logical color of the scene in question became the right one for the color continuity.

Indeed it is because the scenes of present-day color films are still scripted in much the same terms as the black and white story-telling formula that often the color itself detracts from the clarity of the story. There occurs an uncontrolled galaxy of colors in scene upon scene which distracts the eye away from a scene's main visual story clue, and provides a hodgepodge of discordant color continuity.

It is for this reason that many people unconsciously prefer to see an honest-to-goodness black and white film without the trimmings and paddings of color. Yet any art follower knows that harmonies and contrasts of colors are of great value in a painting to direct and hold the eye to the important shapes of a composition, as well as to convey the "feeling" or "mood" of the whole.

People go to the cinema to "see" a story. If it is in color, they should "see" the story in color. Therefore the story script of a film should be fully adapted for presentation in colors leading the eye to the main story clues in each scene bound up within a carefully annotated color continuity.

These notes so far have been theoretical because there are no known examples of a sustained constructive use of color in films. It would be interesting to take a short story and see how it could be adapted for color treatment. For even in a short film it would be possible to show several definite advantages of "telling" a story in color.

A short dramatic fiction film should have a compact and easily defined plot, preferably with a "twist" in it. It would be ideal for our purpose of illustration if the color treatment for the plot could also be given a "twist." A suitable plot can be found in Peter Fleming's "The Face," published by Penguin Books, No. 170, Selected Modern Short Stories. The film synopsis might be as follows:

A man regains consciousness on a railway track but has lost his memory. He looks at the objects in his pockets to find out who he is. From a newspaper he finds in his coat he could be either one of two men. One, with a small dark moustache, has inherited a fortune. The other, with red hair, has killed his wife. He feels his upper lip and finds it clean shaved. But he "feels rich" and is sure he has recently shaved his moustache off. Yet his mind is torn in doubt. Is he a murderer? Plodding along the railway track he rationalizes his recent life as being that of a rich man. He arrives at a small country railway station and goes inside. He approaches the mirror of a slot-machine to look at his face. With a shock his memory returns. His hair is red.

Sequences of dramatic color scenes would define the "flash-back" element of the man's thoughts when he is trying to establish his identity in his mind. These sequences would gradually depart from realistic color. The man's hair would be of a mouse color until the final theatrically colored scene in which the operative color is entirely red.

On the other hand, the realistic scenes showing the man actually suffering from loss of memory would be shown in a special tone of black and white, representing the man's loss of memory—the inference being that as he does not know the color of his hair, neither should the audience, who are experiencing his emotions through *his* mind's eye.

The final scene in black and white, in which he is still suffering from loss of memory—the one in which he looks at his face in the mirror—could indicate to the audience the return of his memory by the color treatment itself; e.g., as he looks at his face in the mirror, in black and white photography, *he* sees the color of his hair although the audience cannot. The shock of what he sees makes his memory return. *Then* the scene changes to natural color photography, and the audience, too, sees that the man's hair is red. Here the climax of the color red is held. And in a sequence comprised of theatrical hues of red and chrome only, the quarrel, and accidental killing of his wife, is portrayed. The final scene shows the man voluntarily walking into a police station.

The technical treatment for the black and white scenes would assure good color treatment, inasmuch as they would be printed in the real black of Technicolor dyes as opposed to the false black of normal films. The Technicolor black is made up of dyes printed on film from printing matrices. The false black of the ordinary black and white film is produced by developing black grains of silver in a gelatine layer.

The advantage of portraying the realistic "loss of memory" scenes in black and white would be twofold. Namely, a black and white of true color hue would blend readily with scenes of three-color hues. So the absolute incongruity of mixing three-color sequences with the ordinary silver nitrate "black" of normal films would be avoided. (An instance of this incongruity could be seen in MGM's *The Women*, when a Technicolor sequence abruptly changes to the ordinary black and white of silver nitrate emulsion. The audience gasps at the "bleached out" appearance of the tones of the scene.) The contrast of the lacquer tones of the black and white scenes with the dramatic colors of the flash-back scenes would be a literary convention by which the audience could understand what the color was "getting at."

The film could be of either two or four reels, depending on the ability of a writer to build up cameo plots in the flash-back sequences and write in characterizations of interest.

A short color prologue of a train journey—boardings, station names, wheels, railway tracks, tickets, signals, roofs, trees, fences, telegraph poles and wires, green hills and clouds, would prepare an audience for the subsequent dramatic color sequences and would merge effectively with the opening scene of the story, namely, that of a man lying inert alongside a railway line. The climax of the prologue would also be made to indicate that someone had fallen from a train.

The beauty of the train effects in Renoir's *La Bête Humaine*, and in Ruttman's *Berlin*, are an indication of what could be achieved in a train theme prologue planned for color effects.

The opening scene of the story is in realistic three color. The man's shoulders are hunched, his arms protect his head, his feet are away from the camera. The white smoke of a train is seen in the distance. A cow grazes nearby. The man is sitting up holding his head. As he stares in front of him, the natural three-color rendering of the scene slowly changes to tones of black and white. He is looking at personal objects taken from his pocket.

He cannot recognize any of them. He tries to reconstruct his previous life from them. The first rendering of theatrical color treatment occurs in a flash-back from this sequence. It is a dramatic episode associated with a photograph in a newspaper which the man finds in his possession.

It would be pointless to further sketch in the story outline so far as these notes on color continuity are concerned. Subtleties of color on the screen can rarely be conveyed and visualized by written examples, no more, say, than music can.

As for the story, it could be made quite rich in dramatic detail. There are many case histories of loss of memory which would afford a writer inspiration for fine fiction material, as well as affording a good part for an actor.

214

Nanook
by Robert Flaherty

This chapter appeared originally in 1951 in a commemorative issue of the Screen Director, edited by Jack Glenn, in February 1951. Mr. Flaherty, who had died that year, was one of the outstanding figures in the development of the documentary film.

Film is the great pencil of the modern world, and it is unfortunate that men do not use it to full advantage. In communicating his ideas man started with pictures, and in the twentieth century he has discovered that pictures—motion pictures—provide a more graphic and cosmopolitan method of communication than the printed word. Film has given mankind its first universal language.

The future of the film could be so much greater if the men who are at the head of great affairs could realize what a powerful medium the motion picture is, to what lengths it can go in revelation, the strength of the emotional impact it has, and what a force a great dramatic film with access to theatres can be. Hitler knew the power of the motion picture. He spared no effort to make films and use them to get himself in power. The effect of a film on public opinion can often be incalculable. Up until the release of *Desert Victory*, an epic which portrayed the fight of the British against the Germans in North Africa, the prestige of the British soldier in the minds of thoughtless Americans was zero. *Desert Victory* rehabilitated the British in America and quickened the country's interest and participation in the war.

Although I have firm convictions today about the importance of films, my early interest in them was purely a by-product of a first love—exploration. People ask me how I came to use movies at all. Well, I first used it on one of my expeditions in the North, the purpose of which was exploration—mining exploration. It was suggested by my principal that I take with me a motion picture camera. I was eager to do this, but the only thought I had in connection with the use of the motion picture camera was to compile visual notes of the exploration, that is, notes about the people—who happened to be Eskimos—their life and habits as I saw them, and also scenes of the country and of the kind of territory we were exploring.

Some time after this expedition returned to civilization— we were away for a year and a half—I took up the matter of the film I had shot. I was getting it together in Toronto to ship to New York when carelessly, amateur that I was, I dropped a cigarette off the table in the little room where the film happened to be. It caught fire and some 70,000 feet of negative went up in a flash of flame.

However, there was an edited print of the negative that escaped the fire. I took this to New York in the forlorn hope that we might be able to dupe it, but in those days duping was almost impossible. I showed it to the American Geographical Society and then realized just how bad it was. It was utterly inept, simply a scene of this and a scene of that, no relation, no thread of a story or continuity whatever, and it must have bored the audience to distraction. Certainly it bored me.

My wife and I thought it over for a long time. At last we realized why the film was bad, and we began to get a glimmer that perhaps if I went back North, where I had lived for ten years and knew the people intimately, I could make a film that this time would go. Why not take, we said to each other, a typical Eskimo and his family and make a biography of their lives through the year. What biography of any man could be more interesting? Here is a man who has less re-sources than any other man in the world. He lives in a desola-tion that no other race could possibly survive. His life is a constant fight against starvation. Nothing grows. He must depend utterly on what he can kill. And all this against the most terrifying of tyrants—the bitter climate of the North, the bitterest climate in the world. Surely this story could be interesting.

It took several years before I could persuade anyone to finance such a film, for none of the picture people would listen to our idea. Who wanted to see a picture of people so utterly crude as the Eskimo? But finally Revillon Frères, the great fur company of Paris, who then were extending their trade in the far north, said they would finance it. I could go up to one of their posts on the eastern coast of Hudson Bay, take a camera with me, live there for a year and make the film.

It took two months by canoe and schooner to get to my

destination, Revillon Frères' little post called Port Harrison, on north-east Hudson Bay. I took with me two Akeley motion picture cameras. The Akeley then was the best camera to operate in extreme cold, since it required the minimum of grease and oil for lubrication. These cameras fascinated me because they were the first cameras ever made to have a gyro movement in the tripod head whereby one could pan and tilt the camera without the slightest distracting jar or jerk or vibration. I have used this gyro type of tripod ever since in all my pictures. I think I was, perhaps, the pioneer in its use. I know that if at that time in Hollywood the cameraman panned his camera the studio would more often than not throw out the scene, because the pans, being jerky, would be too distracting on the screen.

I also took with me the materials and chemicals to develop the film, and equipment to print and project it. My lighting equipment had to be extremely light because I had to go by canoe nearly two hundred miles down river before I got to Hudson Bay. This meant portages, and portages meant packing the equipment on my back and on those of the Indians I took along for the river trip. And God knows there were some long portages on that route—one of them took us two days to pack across.

The Eastman Kodak Company arranged my developing equipment for me and, in fact, showed me how to develop film. I spent some several weeks with them for that purpose and they spared no effort to start me off in the right way.

My printing machine was an old English Williamson Printer that screwed to the wall. I soon found when printing the film by the printer that the light from my little electric plant fluctuated too much; so I abandoned electric light and used daylight instead by letting in an inlet of light just the size of a motion picture frame through the window, and I controlled this daylight by adding or taking away pieces of muslin from in front of the printing aperture of the printer.

The greatest problem was not, however, printing the film or developing it, but washing it and drying it. I had to build an annex to the hut in which I wintered to make a drying room, and the only heating I could secure for this drying room was a stove that burned soft coal! Not only that, but I found that I ran short of lumber and didn't have enough to complete the drying reel that I set up in the room. So my Eskimos had to scour the sea-coast and finally pick up enough driftwood to complete its construction.

The washing of the film was the worst of all. My Eskimos had to keep a hole chiselled through six feet of ice all through the winter and then haul the water in barrels on a sledge with . an Eskimo dog-team up to my hut, and there we all cleared out the ice from the water with our hands and poured it for the necessary washes over the film. I remember the deer hair falling off the Eskimos' clothing bothered me almost as much as the ice did.

It has always been most important for me to see my rushes —it is the only way I can make a film. But another reason for developing the film in the North was to project it to the Eskimos so that they would accept and understand what I was doing and work together with me as partners.

They were amazed when I first came with all this equipment, and they would ask me what I was going to do. When I told them that I had come to spend a year among them to make a film of them—pictures in which they moved—they roared with laughter. To begin with, some of my Eskimos could not even read a still photograph. I made stills of several of them as preliminary tests. When I showed them the photograph as often as not they would look at it upside down. I'd have to take the photograph out of their hands and lead them to the mirror in my hut, then have them look at themselves and the photograph beside their heads. Then, with a smile that spread from ear to ear, they would understand.

Nanook was constantly thinking up new hunting scenes for the film. There was one scene in particular that became an obsession with him. There was a place far in the north that he knew about, he said, where the she-bear dens in the winter while she gives birth to her cubs. "That would make a picture," said he. "You know it is not hard to find the den of a she-bear although it is deep under big drifts of snow. There is always a vent from which a little steam which is the body heat of the bear rises out into the cold air. The dogs will smell this, and while you are getting your camera ready I'll crawl up to it on hands and knees with my harpoon, and with my snow knife I will begin to cut the snow away. Of course when I have made a hole big enough the she-bear will rush out, and she will be very angry when I do this. But then one of my men will have unleashed the dogs and they will make a circle around her, and then when you signal, I will launch my harpoon. There will be lots of fighting between the dogs and the she-bear as they run in on her. Sometimes she will throw the dogs high up in the air. Now do you think that will make a good scene?" Well, to make a long story short, that bear hunt took fifty-five days of traveling in the dead of winter and we covered 600 miles over the sea-ice, going and coming. And not an inch of film! For the conditions of the ice were so bad that Nanook couldn't kill seal. After losing two dogs by starvation we did finally get back, but we were lucky to get back alive.

When I got back to New York it took the better part of a winter to edit the film. When it was ready to be shown I started to make the rounds of the distributors in New York with the hope that one of them would be kind and give it distribution. Naturally, I took it to the biggest of the distributors first. This was Paramount. The projection room was filled with their staff and it was blue with smoke before the film was over. When the film ended they all pulled themselves together and got up in a rather dull way, I thought, and silently left the room. The manager came up to me and very kindly put his arm around my shoulders and told me that he was terribly sorry, but it was a film that just couldn't be shown to the public. He said he had tried to do such things before and they had always ended in failure. He was very sorry indeed that I had gone through all that hardship in the North only to come to such an end, but that he felt he had to tell me, and that was that.

So then I went to the next biggest company, and after seeing the film, they didn't even answer the phone when I called. I had to go humbly to the projection room and ask to be allowed to take the film away.

One day I showed it to Pathé Frères, who were then much larger distributors of film than they are today. Like Revillon Frères, Pathé was a French firm, and blood being thicker than water, thought I, here might be a chance to do something. Pathé looked at the film; they thought it was interesting but that it could never run as a feature—it should be broken up into a series of educational shorts. But a few days later I had occasion to run the film again at the Pathé projection rooms.

Mme. Brunet, the wife of the president of the company, was there, and also an old friend of mine, a journalist, who was with the company. Well, they caught fire! And gradually the enthusiasm of the Pathé people built up until finally they decided to take the film on and do their best to distribute it as a feature.

The problem then was to get one of the big theatres to show it. Now, the biggest theatre in New York was the Capitol, run by a great film exhibitor, Roxy. But we knew very well that to show it to Roxy cold was to invite failure. Said Pathé, "We'll have to 'salt' it." The sister of the publicity head of Pathé was a great friend of Roxy's. So it was arranged to show it first to her and some of her friends and tell them where to applaud through the picture, and then they would come along for the showing to Roxy in his very elaborate projection room at the Capitol. We also told them never to talk directly to Roxy about the film but to talk to each other across him as if he were not in the room. Well, by the time the film was over, Roxy was tearing his hair. He used such words as "epic," "masterpiece," and the like. He booked it. But even then Pathé was not too trusting, and they decided to tin-can it, that is, to tie it to *Grandma's Boy*, Harold Lloyd's first big feature film which every theatre in New York was scrambling for. Roxy could have *Grandma's Boy*, but he'd have to take *Nanook* too!

A few days later when Major Bowes, the managing director of the Capitol, saw the film he threatened to throw Roxy out. His rage knew no bounds. Desperately, poor Roxy tried to get out of the contract, but no—no *Nanook*, no *Grandma's Boy!*

So *Nanook* came out at the Capitol Theatre. The notices were mixed. One critic damned it with faint praise, but then wrote a better review a few weeks later. It wasn't until the film appeared in London and ran for six months at the New Gallery, and for six months at the Gaumont in Paris, and then ran even more sensationally in Berlin and Rome, that the repercussions came back to America and it was really accepted in America. This has been true of all our films, by the way; they have all done better in Europe, and particularly on the Continent.

People ask me what I think the film can do to make large audiences feel intimate with these distant peoples. Well, *Nanook* is an instance of this. People who read books on the

North are, after all, not many, but millions of people all over the world have seen this film in the last twenty-six years. And what they have seen is not a freak, but a real person after all, facing the perils of a desperate life and yet always happy. When Nanook died, of starvation, two years later, the news of his death came out in the press all over the world—even as far away as China.

The urge that I had to make *Nanook* came from the way I felt about these people, my admiration for them; I wanted to tell others about them. This was my whole reason for making the film. In so many travelogs the film maker looks down on and never up to his subject. He is always the big man from New York or from London. But I had been dependent on these people, alone with them for months at a time, traveling with them and living with them. They had warmed my feet when they were cold, lit my cigarette when my hands were too numb to do it myself; they had taken care of me on three or four different expeditions over a period of ten years. My work had been built up along with them; I couldn't have done anything without them. In the end it is all a question of human relationships.

The Films of René Clair
by Maurice Bardeche and Robert Brasillach

*This chapter appeared originally in "The History of Motion
Pictures," published in 1938, by the Frenchmen Robert Brasillach
and Maurice Bardeche and translated by Iris Barry, founder
of the Museum of Modern Art film library.*

It may be admitted that the first French talkie of any real importance, *Sous les Toits de Paris,* displayed faults inevitable at
that period, for it made use of music and also of silence in
rather haphazard fashion. The introduction of the street singer,
who keeps the film perfectly static while he sings his lines, was
almost obligatory at the time. Clair, however, through the expression on Préjean's face (and he never gave a better performance), contrived to keep the action going to a degree even
through the singing. These faults are so slight and so unimportant that even today we can look at *Les Toits* with the same
pleasure we took in it in 1930. Préjean, accompanied by a
blind accordion player, sings a delightful popular song which
René Clair must have had the greatest fun in composing.
Neither the general public nor the librettists suspected how
ironical it was. Around Préjean our old friends group themselves—the fat lady sings out of tune, the policeman in plain
clothes looks on, the old woman and the lovers gaze at each
other. When evening comes, the thin clerk takes a foot bath
in his Henri II dining room just as the deceived husband had
done in *Chapeau de Paille.* Later on during the night we see
the immense concierge, buried beneath a comforter, automatically turning over to pull the cord. Every detail is based
on real life, the most vulgar incidents of real life. But if we
compare this realism with that of the settings in German pictures, we see that in them the realism was dignified by a loving
care for lighting and by a prodigious use of the pictorial medium. Theirs was the realism of a painter; but René Clair's
realism is, as before, that of the ballet. He puts his characters
in fancy dress and provides them with the appropriate acces-
sories, but at the same time he stylizes them, simplifies their
outline, and leads them into that world which is peculiarly
his. At times, when we see a procession of clerks, or a too
typical baker's wife, we almost feel that it is life itself which

has copied René Clair, for here we come up against a real artist with a quite special manner of perceiving the universe. That is the real value of this truly creative worker. No matter how great their ability, neither Pabst nor King Vidor nor Eisenstein has created a world of his own. If there is a Chaplin world, it is the actor who created it. Independent of the actors there is a quite definite René Clair world.

Had Clair really been trying simply to tell us a story we should not come upon those sequences that drag, those moments when the plot refuses to develop. We are given a series of pictures rather than a true narrative, for just as in *Les Deux Timides*, where its technical discoveries were more important than the whole, so *Sous les Toits* introduces the ingenious *tours de force* to which Clair was to devote himself right up to the time of *Quatorze Juillet*. The quarrel between Albert and Pola in pitch darkness was a genuine invention in those early days: images and words no longer ran side by side but intersected one another in a sort of pattern. The magnificent fight with knives at night near the railway embankment, with the slow noises of freight trains and mist rising the length of the fence, owes its existence to a love of the medium alone; the main story is forgotten. In none of René Clair's films has the lighting been so perfect, and this extraordinary episode is therefore justified. He was much more concerned with beauty than with reality here. The tendency indicated in *Les Deux Timides* is continued, for the ballet no longer takes first place—it becomes an accompaniment as in Greek tragedy, where one by one the principal characters detach themselves from the group and the chorus is reduced to the role of commentator. It remains, however, as witness to the drama; and René Clair was never to abandon these onlookers, among whom his films had found their original inspiration.

Le Million affords striking proof of this. In turning again to an adaptation of a play, Clair created the most successful, if not the richest, of all his pictures. It derives from a whole succession of operettas which had followed Thiele's delightful *Drei von der Tankstelle,* though Clair was to perfect the formula, whereas Thiele relapsed into machine-made and valueless spectacles. The original model, however, provided an opportunity for all the indications in *Entr'acte* and *Chapeau de Paille* to be developed fully: the ballet troupe now takes possession of the entire stage in joyous tumult. The tale of Michel and Beatrice's love blends into the general movement, the lovers are now members of the ensemble—along with the grocer, the dairywoman, the policemen, the lunatic in running pants, the drunkard, the tenor, the lady singer—who run after each other in and out of the wings calling, "He went that way," and, "We can catch him as he comes back along here." It is the gayest of Clair's pictures, rich in minor characters conceived without a trace of exaggeration and seeming, against those luminous backgrounds, as fresh and unruffled as dolls in a shop window. As in *Le Chapeau de Paille*, the whole composition moves forward with appropriate animation, and there is also a similar technical experimentation and a similar tendency to chop the thing up into distinct sequences. Here creative invention has functioned completely, and we are as infinitely far away from everyday life as *Entr'acte* was. This world of police stations and of the Opera and its backstage life is an exquisite but purely imaginary realm. Even the characters have little real connection with the story; their movements inscribe a sort of cryptogram whose real meaning can be guessed if we hold the key to the cipher. Those characters in *Le Million* who are fighting over a coat suddenly take on the appearance of a football team whose play is accompanied by whistles, scrimmages, passing the ball, and so forth, as the tubes in *Entr'acte* gently rise up to assume the form of the most celebrated Doric columns in antiquity. The madman in pants belongs to either film indifferently, and *Entr'acte* is clearly the key to all Clair's work.

Or rather it is the key to his technique, for the lovers from *Les Deux Timides* from now on will be constantly with us. In *Sous les Toits* a third one appears: Pola hesitates between Albert and Louis as Michel hesitates between Wanda and Beatrice, or as Jean hesitates between Anna and Pola. Delicious emotions now suffuse the marionettes. Who could ever forget that first glimpse of Annabella, or the lovers' duet in that stage landscape under the cardboard arbors as stagehands fill the air with a rain of artificial rose petals? Clair has abandoned the open air of *Les Deux Timides* and has returned to the artifice of *Le Voyage Imaginaire,* inventing freely and creating a new form of poetry such as others of his generation and the generation previous, Max Jacob and Jean Cocteau,

224

had foreshadowed. The huge opera singer and the absurd tenor sing out of sight while the wooing of Michel and Beatrice lends reality to the factitious passions which they are screaming at the public. Beatrice can no longer resist, for the picture postcard décor itself becomes Michel's accomplice and even the spectator falls victim to the atmosphere of make-believe and garlands, utilized with unfaltering good taste and underlined with the most gracious and smiling irony.

The same gracious good nature suffuses the best part of *A Nous la Liberté,* unquestionably the most complete expression of Clair's genius and which a number of cinema theaters consequently suppressed. Here the subterfuges of the stage have vanished: we see, though only vaguely, the Luna Park where the workers from the factory are strolling. This setting, where Rolla France takes her sweetheart and where Henri Marchand will follow them, is clearly an unreal and enchanted place, a playground for birds that have flown out of picture postcards and figures from a merry-go-round. One is reminded of "Alice in Wonderland," in which pretense and absurdity are presented with such naturalness, for this is the world on the other side of the mirror. Birds speak, flowers sing—but they are stuffed birds and celluloid flowers. Nowhere has the cinema brought us so perfectly created a world as in this imaginative and innocent dream inspired by some tune from a hand organ. The very thought of irony is barely possible, unless as the excuse for introducing us to this universe, vaguely ninetyish with its bridges of artificial wood like those in the Parc Montsouris and the Buttes-Chaumont, its artificial forests and artificial waterfalls. Henri Marchand, subtlest of Clair's lovers, looks around, smiling like a child in ecstasy. He seems a little clumsier than the others, for Clair knows very well how to interrupt a dream when necessary, and the disillusionment of the unfortunate fellow in this landscape of romance is one of the most delicately bitter moments imaginable. The traditional cruelty of the artist, who suffers with his characters yet enjoys making them suffer, which renders Clair akin to Racine and to Marivaux, is underlined by the mockery of the setting, by all this pasteboard world of simple happiness. When Henri, standing in the shadow, thinks that the girl is smiling at him though in reality she is smiling at someone else, it is an old trick borrowed from Chaplin. But it affects us just as deeply as it did in the most famous scenes of *The Gold Rush* or *City Lights*.

A Nous la Liberté is rather imperfectly constructed, and it overstresses both the similarity between the factory and the prison as well as the numerous chases, but it is undoubtedly the film in which René Clair put most of himself. Memories of many celebrated pictures, such as *The Pilgrim, The Gold Rush,* and *City Lights,* are added to the creative qualities of *Le Million,* to themes repeated from *Entr'acte,* to atmosphere borrowed from *Les Deux Timides* or *Chapeau de Paille.* Yet Clair had never before penetrated so far into the world of pure imagination. By the time we reach the magnificent confusion of the end, he seems actually to have risen above his subject, his characters, his personal experiences, and even life itself. It would be an error to consider that extraordinary scene in which the breeze scatters a bagful of bank notes over the heads of the crowd as a mere piece of fertile invention, like that which suddenly suggested the football match in *Le Million.* If the members of the crowd at the inauguration were simply running after the bank notes, that would be the end of them: they would vanish along with their booty. As it is, they reappear, running here and there all over the factory without apparent aim but not without order, for they form skillful dance designs as they thread in and out; and in fact they *are* dancing. It is good, after the grief of Henri Marchand and the imaginary voyage to the land of tinted postcards, to be back again in a realm where pastime is your only king. With this penultimate scene in *A Nous la Liberté* Clair renews his youth and sings a hymn in praise of pure movement, just as he had in *Entr'acte.*

It is impossible not to like this ambitious and perhaps badly constructed film in which, twice over, Clair so fully expressed himself, both in delineating the sorrows of love amid the beauties of the make-believe landscapes, and in this game which has no other motive than play. He utilized everything, even his early novel "Adams," in this satire on Americanism. Two or three minor characters escaped from other films to link everything together, and the clear, lively music of Georges Auric preserves the unity which seems so often in danger of being broken.

What was left for Clair to tackle after this, unless he completely changed the very form and basis he had hitherto selected, and where would the ballet of dancing shapes lead him in the future? There have been those who said that *Quatorze Juillet* was a sort of turning back or period of repose in his work. His admirers and friends thought so. I do not feel that they were right. *Quatorze Juillet* is probably the most ambitious of any of Clair's ventures, only in this case instead of concerning himself with outward appearances he was concerned with inner content. "Nothing could be simpler at first sight," Alexandre Arnoux said, "than perfection such as this; it is as simple as writing a fable by La Fontaine." (It is extraordinarily difficult not to think of the classical writers when considering the work of Clair, for he is a member of their family, and makes it easier for us to understand them.) His avoidance of exterior shots, his wish never to surprise or astonish us (and he has traveled far since *Entr'acte*) enabled him now to make his best-constructed picture. There are richer things he has done, but none having greater internal unity. Even *Le Million* was a summing up of one particular cinematic method only; *Quatorze Juillet* sums up all the René Clair films.

It may well be that Clair will be compelled later on to abandon his most noticeable traits and much that lay at the roots both of his popularity and of his charm. But in this film it seems that he wanted to perfect a formula, to clear it of extraneous matter, to transmute it into classicism, and to avoid all else. With a severity which must surely have cost him a good deal, he avoided all obvious technical tricks and set himself none of those problems which formerly interested us so greatly. There is not one single scene which stands out particularly; the quadrille in *Chapeau de Paille,* or the fight in *Les Toits,* or the football match in *Le Million,* or the lovers' stroll in *A Nous* all stood out. This film is simple, almost unadorned, like certain German films and especially *Maedchen in Uniform.* The fete here is almost disappointingly brief, for we expected all sorts of delightful touches which his love of garlands and picture postcards might have suggested, as in the former films. But this fete is merely indicated, with a few charming and brief details. It was the first time he had not permitted details to overburden the main body of the film. The simple, beautiful story develops quietly, smoothly, with infinite discretion, and the end comes without our having been particularly struck by anything, unless it is perhaps the few moments when the lunar M. Imaque cleans his revolvers in the dance hall, or the even briefer moments when Annabella weeps while wiping away the tears of the little boy who had fallen down, or the death of the mother. Nothing stands out, the film drags a little, all the gestures in it are a trifle over-refined and emphasized. Yet at the same time we are enveloped in a sort of harmony which carries us back to the joys and griefs of adolescence.

From the dance of inanimate objects to *Quatorze Juillet* is a long way, yet this development is a natural one. We have still not left the world of the dance. The love troubles of the earlier films are essentially choreographic, like those in so many folk dances. Watch M. Imaque as he goes by: he isn't walking, he is dancing. Paul Ollivier moves constantly to the rhythm of some unheard music, just as he did in *Le Million* and *A Nous la Liberté*. René Clair does not need music. His characters are ever ready to take their places in the dance, the prodigious concierge and the members of the provincial-Parisian family as well as the bistro owner, the taxi driver, the dance-hall managers, and cloakroom attendants. It almost gives one the impression that he is holding them back, forbidding them to dance in order not to break the spell of this pitiful tale where Annabella laughs through her tears.

After *Quatorze Juillet*, René Clair abandons Paris—Paris, the only thing in which he really believes. *Le Dernier Milliardaire* was quite a disappointment to his admirers, and with some reason. Just as after *Les Toits*, *Le Million* and *A Nous la Liberté* took refuge in an imaginary world, so after *Quatorze Juillet*, *Le Dernier Milliardaire* abandoned Paris for burlesque and satire. Unfortunately, principally because the actors are mediocre and theatrical, this ambitious farce hardly succeeds in making one laugh. The best things in it are again the dance figures and the two or three comedy inventions. Everybody was struck by the scene where, in this land without money where barter is the rule, a customer in a restaurant pays for his drink with a duck and gets back, as change, two little chickens and an egg, which he leaves as a tip; while the man who lets his gun fall onto the roulette table wins thirty-six revolvers. Nevertheless, even those who do not admire the Marx Brothers must admit that their films are much fuller of movement than René Clair's. What is more, it seems to me that in *Le Dernier Milliardaire* there is a dryness and overintellectualization which

228

already threatened the earlier films and *A Nous la Liberté*. There is nothing here about love, unless it is something ridiculous; nothing of that poignancy which formerly gave so much value to backgrounds and to ballets alike. Clair this time offered us a feast of nothing but intelligence and irony; his touch is recognizable but it sometimes grates a little. If the future brings him back to imaginary worlds and music, bittersweet romance, ballets of lovemaking, and anxious lovers we shall forgive him. It would be foolish to try to put limits on what he may do.

He was the only film man in France whose work displayed both purpose and progress. There is no other such group of films as these, apart from the work of Chaplin, Eisenstein, and Pabst. His delicately shaded style, with its thin but strong line, suggests far more than it actually shows. Clair is one of the very rare directors of whom it can be said that their films gain by being seen twice and cannot be understood until that second time, like certain music and poetry.

The Method of John Ford

by Lindsay Anderson

Lindsay Anderson is a former editor of Sequence magazine, in whose Summer 1950 issue this chapter originally appeared. He has written film criticism for Sight and Sound, The New Statesman and other periodicals. He was the director of the film This Sporting Life.

To his admirers, as to his critics, John Ford has always presented something of an enigma. Unquestionably enshrined among the great, it has often seemed that he owes his celebrity rather to his association with a random group of distinguished films than to any consistent personal quality as an artist. Certain French critics, indeed, with their meaningless battle-cry of "A bas Ford, vive Wyler!" have crystallized this misapprehension into a heresy—coupling these two directors as impersonal master-craftsmen, neither of whom seeks any form of individual expression in his art. If one had taken this seriously, one would perhaps have been more surprised on seeking out one of Ford's lesser-known pictures (very few critics appear to have seen it) to find it a work of outstanding quality, one of the few great films to come out of the recent war, and especially remarkable for its combination of the broadest sweep of action with the most delicate strokes of imagination and feeling.

They Were Expendable is the story of a defeat—the rout of the American Forces in the Pacific in the first stage of the war against Japan. Above all, it is a personal film, with the sincerity and purpose of a dedicated work. This, at least, is how one feels it was regarded by its director. The credits carry not merely his name, but also his rank: Captain, U.S.N.R. Similarly, with its author (Cmdr. Frank Wead, who based his script on W. L. White's factual account of the campaign), cameraman (Lt. Cmdr. Joseph August), second unit director (Capt. James Havens) and leading actor (Cmdr. Robert Montgomery), all of whom had served with the Navy during the war. The impression of dedication is reinforced by two opening titles, both phrased with some solemnity. The first, from a speech by MacArthur, runs: "Today the guns are silent. A great tragedy has ended. A great victory has been won. . . . I speak for the thousands of silent lips, forever stilled among the jungles and in the deep waters of the Pacific, which marked the way." The second sets the time and the place: "Manila Bay. In the Year of Our Lord Nineteen Hundred and Forty-One."

The film starts with a sort of prologue, an introduction to the story's protagonist: Motor Torpedo Boat Squadron Three of the U.S. Navy. Led by its Commander, Lieutenant Brickley (Montgomery), the Squadron is showing its paces in Manila Bay before the appraising eye of its Admiral; after the exercise the Admiral makes a perfunctory inspection, and leaves with a few politely disparaging remarks. The sequence closes with Brickley alone on the quay, eyeing his boat with speculation. With a minimum of words the main threads of the story have been drawn: its element, the sea; the P.T. boats, graceful and dangerous weapons of war; official doubts of their worth (they are "expendable"); Brickley's quality as an officer, his faith in his boats, his deep and undemonstrative feeling for the Squadron—contrasted with the careless impetuosity of Ryan (John Wayne), his friend and second-in-command. That evening the news comes through of the Japanese attack on Pearl Harbor. Later the Admiral announces to his staff that war has been declared.

The war is soon a reality. Next day, enemy bombers attack in force and reduce the Squadron's base to a shambles. But in spite of rumors that a Japanese task force is in the vicinity, Brickley is ordered to stand by for messenger trips. It is not till after the fall of Manila that the Squadron's first real opportunity comes—an attack on a Japanese cruiser, sunk with the loss of one boat. Further actions follow, and further losses. Ryan is injured and sent, protesting, to sick-bay, where he meets an Army nurse. With charmingly humorous formality she is entertained at dinner by the officers of the Squadron. The Commander of one of the boats is wounded and dies in the hospital. All the time the enemy presses nearer. At last, the Admiral sends for Brickley and orders him to stand by: his boats are to carry "certain key personnel" south to Mindanao, *en route* for Australia. His spare crews must dwindle into soldiers, reinforcing the Army on Bataan. So, with the first of a series of farewells, the break-up of the Squadron begins. Carrying the Admiral and his staff, the Commander-in-Chief (MacArthur) and his family, the boats make off for Mindanao, while the two redundant crews stand watching them leave, then silently form up and march forlornly away to Bataan.

Losing one boat on the way, Brickley arrives at Mindanao with only three. He is refused permission to return to Bataan for his men, and is surrendered by his Admiral to the Army. An accident cripples two further boats, which have to be towed to a shipyard on the coast, still working under the tough old trader who has spent his life building it up. One of these is ready in time for Brickley and Ryan to go out on a last attack against a Japanese cruiser. On their return, the boats are separated. Ryan's is attacked from the air and blows up; two of his crew die with it. As he and his men sit silently in a bar, after burying their dead, they hear a radio announcement of the fall of Bataan. This presages the ultimate defeat. Making contact again with Brickley, Ryan finds the last boat being hauled away on a truck, turned over to run errands for the Army. Directionless and exhausted, what remains of the Squadron marches off, to lose itself in the confusion of defeat. Brickley, Ryan, and two junior officers are ordered back to Australia in the one plane that remains. As night falls, the remnants of the Squadron straggle away down the deserted beach, while over their heads the plane soars out to Australia, and Mac-Arthur's words come up to fill the screen: "We shall return."

The sweep is epic, its rhythm cumulative. The three fine battle-scenes are vigorously cut, but otherwise the story unfolds at an even, leisurely pace. Ford has shown no great concern for clarity of development; maps are used only once, to cover the flight south to Mindanao, and the continuity of action is not beyond reproach. Yet the occasional obscurity hardly matters at all. The essential continuity, of approach, is preserved without a lapse. It is based on a uniform authenticity of atmosphere and behavior. There is no trace of what the Services know as "bull." When war is announced, the news is taken gravely, but without surprise; there are no propagandist allusions to its causes, its purpose, or its consequences. The Japanese are neither discussed nor execrated; they are simply the enemy, anonymous and invisible. Tensions and relationships within the American forces are similarly convincing—between officers and men, between the Navy and the Army.

"Authenticity" should not be taken to imply a ruthless and objective realism. *They Were Expendable* is a film with a viewpoint, a purpose. It sets out not merely to relate, but to pay tribute to the courage and tradition of service in one section of the American Navy. Its theme is put into words by the Admiral when he explains to Brickley the reasons for their inactivity at the beginning of the campaign: "Listen, son. You and I are professionals. If the manager says 'sacrifice,' we lay down a bunt and let somebody else hit the home runs. . . . Our job is to lay down that sacrifice. That's what we were trained for, and that's what we'll do." Its characters are shown in the light of their sacrifice, ennobled by it—not through words, but through image after image of conscious dignity: Sandy, the Army nurse, assisting at an endless series of operations as casualties pour into the hospital on Corregidor; the men of the Squadron watching with amazement and pride as their Commander-in-Chief boards the leading P.T. boat.

In spite of its emotional unity, the mood of the film is by no means monotonous. It is frequently varied with humor, of a fond, colloquial kind: the young ensign who finds himself continually carried away by the dignity of his position; the officer who offends every canon of discipline by asking for MacArthur's autograph (one may even sense a further humor in the readiness with which the General grants it); the submarine captain who is blackmailed into surrendering half his torpedoes by an allusion to his performance, in former years, as Tess of the d'Urbevilles at the Academy ("And does your crew know?"). Equally true are the moments of serious emotion: Brickley, for instance, saying good-bye to the men who have to go to Bataan, and leaving his speech incomplete, unable to bring himself to utter hopes he knows cannot be fulfilled; or the visit of the officers of the Squadron to a friend they know is dying, each side rising to the occasion with pathetic, transparently false jocularity. The film is full of such moments of emotion, expressed in a word or two, an inflection, a silent pause.

This under-emphasis is saved from any taint of theatricality by the consistent sincerity and power of the feeling which inspires the film. Supported by acting of complete integrity, and by the magisterial technique of realization, this enables Ford to proceed with absolute freedom. Close-ups, noble or affectionate, are held at leisure; long-shots are sustained long after their narrative function is performed; a marginal figure is suddenly dwelt on, lovingly enlarged to fill the center of the screen. Informed with this heightened emotion, a single shot, abruptly interposed—a ragged line of men marching into nowhere, one of them playing a jaunty bugle-call on his harmonica—assumes a deeper significance than is given it by its position in the story. This is one of the properties of poetry; *They Were Expendable* is a heroic poem.

A pure example of an artist's style, if ever there was one, *They Were Expendable* demands, perhaps, for its full appreciation, a previous acquaintance and sympathy with the work of its director. (This, at any rate, would account for its general neglect by the critics.) Conversely, it has that compensating power of any very personal work, to illuminate films which come before it and reveal qualities in them which may up to now have gone unremarked. In its light, recognizable patterns emerge from the rather baffling diversity of Ford's films, so that, even at this late stage, a new attempt to set his career in perspective and his achievement at its proper worth, may not be valueless.

Sean O'Fienne arrived in Hollywood in July, 1914, at the age of nineteen. The second son of Irish parents—his father was from Galway, his mother from Aran—he came fresh from Maine University, which he had entered after failing for Annapolis, the Naval training college. Under the name of Francis Ford, his elder brother had established himself as a director and actor in serials, and it was for his company that Sean first worked, as property man, stunt man and actor. Within a year (now Jack Ford) he had graduated to the post of assistant director; in 1917 he directed his first film, *Cactus, My Pal,* a two-reeler Western for Bison-Universal, starring Harry Carey.

By 1920 Jack Ford had directed thirty Westerns, hearty adventure stories with titles like *The Range War, Thieves' Gold, A Fight for Love.* Harry Carey starred in all of these except the eighth, *The Scrapper,* in which Ford himself played the battling hero, Buck the Scrapper. With his thirty-first subject he broke new ground: *The Prince of Avenue A* featured the boxer, Gentleman Jim Corbett, in a comedy of Irish life in New York. There followed a random assortment of thrillers, romances, comedies, and Westerns, until in 1923 Ford (now working for Fox) was assigned his first "A" feature, *Cameo Kirby,* a romance of the South, starring John Gilbert, for which

234

he assumed the new dignity of John Ford. Three pictures later, he celebrated his half-century by directing his first great popular success, *The Iron Horse* (1924), an ambitious super-Western, Fox's reply to James Cruze's *The Covered Wagon,* produced by Paramount the year before.

"*The Iron Horse,*" writes Paul Rotha in "The Film Till Now," "was vast in conception, and John Ford, despite the hindrances of a story interest, handled it with a great degree of talent." No copies of the film appear to have survived in Britain; and this also, unhappily, applies to Ford's two other outstanding silent pictures, *Three Bad Men* (1926) and *Four Sons* (1928). This means that it is impossible today to estimate his achievements in the silent cinema. By the coming of sound he had directed over sixty films, and had gained experience in every variety of popular entertainment. How far the best of these would stand on their own merits today one cannot tell. It is obvious from their synopses that the majority would prove too naïve to be of much interest except as period pieces. It is evident, however, from repeated commendations in the trade press that they showed a progressively maturing craftsmanship, with repeated emphasis on their high visual qualities.

It was with his third sound film that Ford entered into a partnership which was to prove of the greatest importance in his career. His *Men Without Women* (1930) was written (from a story on which he had collaborated himself) by Dudley Nichols, one of the many talented journalists who had been drawn to Hollywood by the advent of the talkies. The story of fourteen men trapped in a crippled submarine, *Men Without Women* became one of Ford's favorite films. As a result the collaboration was continued intermittently until, in 1934, it achieved its first *succès d'estime* with *The Lost Patrol.* The favorable reception of this tragic melodrama (the story of a British patrol wiped out in the Mesopotamian desert) induced Ford and Nichols to persuade its producers, RKO, to let them undertake the subject they had planned for several years—an adaptation by Nichols of Liam O'Flaherty's novel, "The Informer."

A flop in New York, *The Informer* (1935) was transformed into an outstanding success by its reception in the provinces and among the critics. In this respect the *Crossfire* of its day, it was a cheap picture, made with great speed, which brought immense prestige to its maker. By it Ford and Nichols were established as two rebels against the Hollywood system, successful protestants against the domination of the American cinema by speculators and businessmen. For the next six years Ford divided his time between deliberately "artistic" ventures with Nichols—including adaptations from Maxwell Anderson (*Mary of Scotland*), O'Casey again (*The Plough and the Stars*), and O'Neill (*The Long Voyage Home*)—and his routine commercial chores for Fox, out of which grew a series of more ambitious pictures, firmly rooted in the American scene. This period of activity reached its climax with Ford's *annus mirabilis* —the span from March 1939 to January 1940, which saw the successive releases of *Stagecoach, Young Mr. Lincoln, Drums Along the Mohawk,* and *The Grapes of Wrath.* Three pictures later came the war, and Ford left Hollywood to help supervise the making of films for the Navy. Returning in 1945, he made *They Were Expendable,* which he followed a year later with *My Darling Clementine,* his hundredth film. Then, in 1947, Ford ventured into independent production. For his own company, Argosy Pictures, he went to Mexico and made *The Fugitive,* from a script by Dudley Nichols, based on Graham Greene's novel, "The Power and the Glory."

Nichols has written fourteen pictures for Ford. It is unfortunate that of the nine which are relatively unassuming, most are now inaccessible—an early assortment of adventure stories and comedies which includes two attractive-sounding regional pictures with Will Rogers, *Judge Priest* and *Steamboat Round the Bend* (both written in collaboration with Lamar Trotti). Of this group there now survive only three celebrated melodramas, *The Lost Patrol, The Hurricane,* and *Stagecoach.* The last alone can claim the label "classic." *The Lost Patrol* has dated badly, craftsmanlike in direction but embarrassingly theatrical in writing and performance. *The Hurricane,* remarkable chiefly for its final cataclysm (astonishingly staged by Basevi), is otherwise very patchy. *Stagecoach,* though, very nearly pulls it off. The first four-fifths, economically scripted and propelled along with irresistible urgency and drive, constitute perhaps the best chase film ever made—certainly the climactic pursuit of the stage across the salt flats by a party of whooping Apaches, the last-minute rescue by the cavalry, bugles sounding and pennants flying, could not be done better. One regrets only the faulty constructon which tacks on a two-reel anti-climax after the film has reached its natural end, and a certain banality of characterization, not wholly compensated by the sympathy and tact of the handling.

But it is on his more pretentious scripts that Nichols' reputation has been chiefly based. And it is on these, too, that critics have tended to concentrate in their estimations of Ford (*The Grapes of Wrath* is usually set apart, as though a miraculous and inexplicable sport). The most renowned is *The Informer*, almost invariably classed among the "great" American films. Others that may be grouped with it are *The Long Voyage Home* and *The Fugitive*. They are all adaptations. *The Informer* is from Liam O'Flaherty's terse, objective account of an Irish hood-lum, giant in size and strength but infantile in brain, who be-trays his Communist friend to the authorities and is hounded down and shot by the party. *The Long Voyage Home* is out of a collection of playlets by Eugene O'Neill set in the fo'c'sle of a British merchantman in time of war. *The Fugitive* is based on Greene's realist, tendentious study of the last priest to survive in the atheist, totalitarian state of Mexico. Widely different though these originals are, Nichols has managed to imbue them all with characteristics of his own: a sentimental simpli-fication of issues and characters, a highly self-conscious striv-ing for significance, and a fundamental unreality.

In degree of failure they are unequal. *The Long Voyage Home,* for instance, is an uneven work with whole stretches (particularly in the first half) of great power and success. As long, in fact, as the literary content is kept to a minimum, as long as the sailors are allowed to be themselves and the camera to speak for them, the film realizes its poetic intention. In the last half, however, it falls victim to O'Neill's sentimentality (in the mawkish episode of the English gent turned alcoholic), and to Nichols' eternal pursuit of the universal. Once off the ship, we are plunged into a symbolic no-man's-land, the sailors dogged by a bowler-hatted Cockney—an unhappy cross be-tween a pimp and a fate-symbol—through the incredible Wap-ping mists. Nothing points Nichols' wrong-headedness more clearly than the ease and beauty with which, in the last, silent sequence of the men's slow return to their ship, Ford and Toland convey the sad sense of impermanence, which the script, with its literary symbolism, has strained after so hard and missed so completely.

With *The Informer* and *The Fugitive* Nichols has lighted on excellent material (greatly superior to O'Neill) which he has cheapened and debased. He has his apologists. Thus Theodore Huff (of the New York University Motion Picture Dept.) on *The Informer:* "Nichols took a rather second-rate novel and by removing the extreme sectionalism and more unsavory elements, transmuted the story into a psychological study of Man's Conscience, giving the film a larger and more dramatic conflict with universal meaning." This means that the organization which Gypo betrays is no longer the Communist but the Irish Nationalist Party; this less sectional and more savory change enables Nichols to substitute for the ruthless, twisted leader of the book, a featureless, sympathetic Nationalist (Preston Foster) whose conversations with the betrayed man's sister are conducted with such lines as: "I love you, Dan; I'll always love you. No matter what happens, there'll never be anyone else." So that Gypo may adequately represent Man's Conscience, he is given an appreciable motive for his crime; but since he is played and presented throughout as the brutish creature of O'Flaherty's imagination, incapable of reasoned thought or planned action, no psychological conflict can emerge. The only successful sections of the film are those which remain true to the original.

The same would no doubt be true of *The Fugitive,* had not Nichols in this case jettisoned his original completely. Universality (that quality best left to develop by itself) is again the object of urgent seeking. Gone is Greene's "whisky priest," and in his place an indeterminate wraith, wandering uneasily through a maze of religious symbols. He makes his first appearance riding on an ass, and is harried constantly by a Judas-figure, and a Holy Mother-figure. Wholly without vitality, Nichols' conception is remarkable for a sickly dishonesty, which finds its typical expression in the sign of the cross which the principal and most determined enemy of God is shown to make as he hears the shot which signifies the death of the priest.

The tragedy of these films is less Nichols' than Ford's—that he should have devoted his great talent to material often meretricious, and foreign to the true source of his inspiration. He is, perhaps, an artist who has never realized where his real strength lies. It is characteristic that he should have disowned the films he made for Fox before 1940. Yet it is these which point on to his later poetic masterpieces.

It is no easier to define poetry in the cinema than in literature, if only because—granted the common factor of intensity—it can be so various in style and method. The artist's way of reaching, or suggesting, truths behind appearances, it may apprehend these realities through fantasy or myth, derive from inventions peculiar to his own temperament, or from the common inheritance of feeling and tradition. Ford has always found his true image of reality in this world, not in the deliberately fashioned symbolism of a literary invention. His symbols arise naturally out of the ordinary, the everyday; it is by familiar places, traditions and themes that his imagination is most happily stimulated. There is a sort of strain, apt to evidence itself in pretentiousness of style, about his attempts with material outside his personal experience or sympathy. It is significant that, in contrast to his success with American actors, he rarely succeeds in getting a good performance from a foreigner. *How Green Was My Valley,* in which the only satisfactory acting came from an Irishwoman, Sara Algood, is a case in point. One remembers also the stagey Britishers in *The Lost Patrol* (a true Irishman, Ford has no time for the English), Wallace Ford and Heather Angel in *The Informer,* Ian Hunter in *The Long Voyage Home,* and the startling crudity of the British Admiralty official in the same film.

The films which, of those that can still be seen, one would select as Ford's most completely successful are all distinctively American in theme; and the majority are set in periods other than our own. *Drums Along the Mohawk* takes us back to the days of the War of Independence, in a series of scenes from frontier life affectionately and excitingly sketched. *Young Mr. Lincoln* is a story of Abraham Lincoln as a young hick lawyer, how his common sense and sheer moral power saved two innocent boys from a lynching and a trumped-up charge of murder. *The Prisoner of Shark Island* is Dr. Mudd, one of several innocent people accused of complicity in the murder of Lincoln. *My Darling Clementine,* a history of murder and retribution in the primitive West, is more essentially a gentle and loving exploration of a pioneering township.

All these manage with remarkable success to revive the manners and appearances of past times. Designed with obvious care, they show a keen pleasure in their period appurtenances, in dresses and uniforms, furniture and decoration. Delighting in dances and communal celebrations of a long-forgotten style, there is a sense about them of regret for ways of living at once simpler and more colorful than those of today. This implied lack of concern with contemporary issues is evident also in Ford's present-day films. *They Were Expendable* is hardly, in the modern sense, a film about war, but rather a film about a species now almost extinct—the professional, dedicated warrior. In *Tobacco Road*, that strange mixture of the grotesquely humorous and the nostalgically sentimental, the emphasis is less social than human; the derelict sharecroppers, withering away on the burnt-out tobacco lands of the South, are presented for themselves rather than for the economic moral their predicament might suggest. Even of *The Grapes of Wrath*, justly described by Roger Manvell as "the most courageous social film Hollywood has ever produced," it may be observed that its greatness comes less from its significance as propaganda, than from its profound, uncircumstantial humanity.

The films all start with the advantage of a good story. Further, they are the work of expert writers—Nunnally Johnson (*Shark Island, Tobacco Road, The Grapes of Wrath*), Lamar Trotti (*Lincoln, Drums Along the Mohawk*), Samuel G. Engel and Winston Miller (*My Darling Clementine*)—experienced storytellers with no pretentious ambitions to transcend the natural bounds of their subjects. As a result their scripts leave Ford free to tell the stories at his leisure, to enrich and enliven them through his own humane inspiration. This is everywhere apparent. Sometimes it is explicit: the indignant trial scene in *Shark Island*, where the bewildered victims of expediency are herded into court to hear with terror and incomprehension the fantastic charges levelled against them; Abe Lincoln's sad rebuke to the lynch-mob in *Young Mr. Lincoln*; Tom Joad's fumbling intuitions of human solidarity and social justice in *The Grapes of Wrath*. More often—continually, rather—it is evident in the whole approach, the texture of the films: in odd, unscripted actions and gestures; in the robust humor which runs through them all, simple and genial, of character rather than incident; in the consistent dignity (rising

240

at times to grandeur) with which the human figure is presented.

This has resulted in a gallery of memorable portraits—not, of course, confined to these particular films: Jane Darwell and John Carradine as Ma Joad and Casey in *The Grapes of Wrath*; Carradine again as the Southern gambler in *Stagecoach*; Claire Trevor as the prostitute in the same film; a procession of loveable wrecks in the person of Francis Ford; Ward Bond as Chief Bosun's Mate Mulcahy in *They Were Expendable* or as Yank in *The Long Voyage Home*; Ernest Whitman as Mudd's faithful Negro servant (*Shark Island*); the self-possessed simplicity of Cathy Downs' Clementine. The response to life which finds its expression in these films is crystallized in the composite figure of their hero—the character who appears, with variations, in them all except *Tobacco Road*. (Even Tom Joad comes to approximate it through his playing by Henry Fonda.) Lieut. Brickley, who ruthlessly subordinates his personal feelings to the job in hand; Dr. Mudd, who stands by his duty to heal and minister in spite of the wrongs he has suffered; the young Lincoln who undertakes what seems a hopeless case and sees it through to the end; Wyatt Earp, the mild-mannered avenger of his brother, in *My Darling Clementine*—all are men of purpose, of principles unostentatiously but firmly held. Skillful and courageous in action, they combine their hardihood with a personal gentleness and moral grace; hesitant and tender in love, resolute against injustice. Owing the traditional reverences to God and to his fellow men, the Ford hero— particularly as personified by Fonda—is the cinema's most convincing representation of the righteous man.

The control of the medium which is evident in these films bears witness to the value of those long unpublicized years of Ford's apprenticeship in the silent cinema. It is a technique which has gained in expressiveness as it has gained in assurance—utterly distinct from the soulless craftsmanship of a Curtiz, or from the virtuosity of a Wyler, to whom the visual image is a means to an end, rarely the end in itself. Its basis is a firm and comprehensive photographic skill. Though he has worked with many different cameramen, Ford's films are remarkable for their consistent pictorial flair—most obviously, of course, in the spacious landscapes of his open-air pictures.

A rare adjunct to this is his effective manipulation of artificial light. A typical example is the fade-out of *The Long Voyage Home*, in which a lonely figure on the deck of the S.S. Glencairn is brought up into silhouette by a slow darkening of the foreground which powerfully accentuates its bowed and silent isolation. Similarly, in *Young Mr. Lincoln*, one of the film's most striking intimations is effected silently by a shift in lighting between long- and mid-shot. With its emphasis on the noble structure of the face, the piercing eyes gleaming from under the suddenly prominent stovepipe hat, the nearer shot brings an unexpected awareness of the formidable qualities implicit in the awkward, drily humorous young lawyer.

Closely allied to this skillful use of light is Ford's gift for composition. It is by a combination of the two that he achieves those close-ups which, in their power to confer dignity without diminution of humanity, have become almost the hallmark of his style. Varying in key from the bold chiaroscuro effects of *Young Mr. Lincoln* to the common-daylight tones of *The Grapes of Wrath*, the heroic portraits of *They Were Expendable*, they are the poetic (and philosophic) complement to those solemn long-shots which set man in his mortal perspective, lonely in silhouette against an early morning skyline, dwarfed by the vast panoramas of the natural scene.

His fine plastic sense enables Ford to develop his stories in a continuous succession of telling compositions. (It is worth noting that when Welles and Toland caused such stir with their use of ceilings in *Citizen Kane*, Ford and Glennon had been using them without ostentation for years—in *Stagecoach*, *Lincoln* and *Drums Along the Mohawk*.) His camera moves comparatively rarely, but so strong is his sense of the essential dynamism of the film that, even where movement *within* the frame is at a minimum, his films are never static. Ford's action sequences are justly famous for their vigor and grasp, their unrivaled ability to build and sustain tension.

Less often remarked, but perhaps even more to be admired, is his power to slow the pace almost to a standstill, to elaborate (and intensify) apparently insignificant moments of pause and silence—young Abraham Lincoln standing in reverie by the river bank, the youngest Earp boy (in *My Darling Clementine*) watching his brothers ride off into Tombstone, the hoary old trader in *They Were Expendable* sitting alone on the steps of his shack, a jug of whisky beside him and his shot-

242

gun across his knees, waiting for the arrival of the enemy.

In part this command of sustained movement in the slowest of rhythms results from Ford's ability to draw from his performers acting of extraordinary naturalism and relaxation. The same familiar faces appear again and again in his pictures, actors of tried worth both in leading parts and marginal characterizations. But fundamentally this power to sustain is the result of absolute integrity of feeling. It is not only on faces and discernible expressions that the camera lingers, but on long-shots also, on arrivals from a distance, departures, deliberate and prolonged.

Where such integrity is not preserved, where Ford's true sympathy is not with his material, or the material itself is counterfeit, this visual opulence can become overblown. This objection may be made to *The Informer*—a brilliant but sometimes showy exercise in the sort of expressionism one has come to associate rather with the German cinema, with its use of heavy-contrast lighting, studied grouping, and deliberate non-realism. Equally it is possible to criticize the last section of *The Long Voyage Home,* where the visual pretentiousness stems directly from the script; portions of *Tobacco Road,* in which Ford's tendency to idealize is not really in tune with the writing; or all of *The Fugitive,* where Figueroa has been given unfortunate license to reinforce Nichols' vulgarity with his own. But when the material is genuine, and Ford's response to it a spontaneous one, his technique is characterized by its extreme simplicity. Seldom indulging in the sophistications of camera movement, his films proceed in a series of visual statements—as sparing in their use of natural sound as of dialogue. Rich in phrasing, simple in structure, it is a style which expresses a sure, affirmative response to life—the equivalent to that Biblical prose which, today, it takes greatness of spirit to sustain.

Choosing for his theme "traditional sanctity and loveliness," Ford is, by Yeats' definition, also one of the last Romantics. Nothing is more typical of his films than the traditional songs, the popular tunes and marches which accompany them: "Red River Valley," "Rally Round the Flag," "The Battle Hymn of the Republic"; revivalist hymns like "Shall We Gather at the River?" and "Bringing in the Sheaves"; the Naval marches and bugle calls which echo through *They Were Expendable*—all in significant contrast to the pretentious symphonic scores by Steiner and Hageman for *The Informer* and *The Fugitive*. Heavily charged with emotion and nostalgic associations, this music carries us back to another, simpler world, of clear-cut judgments, of established and unquestioned values.

With the collapse of its popular traditions, Western art has become increasingly sophisticated and eclectic. The popular themes are in general left to be exploited, and degraded, by the opportunists. Ford's films, in this context, seem hardly to belong to our time at all. His art is not intellectual; his impulse is intuitive, not analytical. Unsophisticated and direct, his work can be enjoyed by anyone, regardless of cultural level, who has retained his sensitivity and subscribes to values primarily humane. He applies himself to traditional themes, and is happiest when his story is set in the settled society of another era. Typically, Ford's is a man's world, one in which woman's function is largely domestic, to build the home and bear children, to sympathize and support. Relationships in these films are never complex (which does not mean that they are not subtle). Ford's heroes do not analyze themselves into negation. Uncomplicated and instinctive they realize themselves in action; and they win. Even the defeated heroes of *They Were Expendable* are indomitable in disaster, and Ford ends his film with a positive symbol, a presage of the ultimate victory.

Whether the word "romantic," unqualified, adequately defines this attitude is questionable. It is typical of our sloppy habits of criticism that we tend to use "romantic" to express "poetic." "Romanticized" usually means little more than a view or a style not strictly realistic. Certainly Ford's art is inspired by an optimistic faith in man's nature, a reverence for the human creature which is evident always in choice of subject and manner of treatment. But this is combined with a firm emphasis on discipline, an implicit stress on moral and social duties which may properly be described as classical, and which are matched by a sympathetic decorum of style. The poetry which, at their most intense, the films attain, approximates more closely to the Johnsonian "grandeur of generality" than to the romantic's glorification of the particular.

But whatever the label, it is obvious that films of this kind are unlikely to be received with great favor by a public, the

244

majority of which has had its taste debased by years of commercialized cinema, while the minority finds its state of mind most satisfyingly mirrored in the elegant despair of *The Third Man,* or in the compassionate defeatism of *The Bicycle Thief. They Were Expendable,* which represents an extraordinary revitalizing of a tradition one might have thought dead, runs the risk of being unpopular with the many, for not being like *To the Shores of Tripoli,* and dismissed by the few, for being like *To the Shores of Tripoli* (and *not* like "The Naked and the Dead"). More serious is the possible effect of such isolation on the artist. It is possible, no doubt, to overestimate the importance of being fashionable, but an artist who cuts himself off —or finds himself cut off—from the thought and feeling of the world he lives in, is in danger of emasculating, even finally denying, his talent.

From his record over the past five years one fears that this may indeed be the case with Ford. Since the disappointment of *The Fugitive*—received well neither by the critics nor the public—he has devoted himself to a series of potboilers, varying in quality (the best, *She Wore a Yellow Ribbon,* has much of the old sweep and strength of sentiment), but realized generally with sadly wasteful impatience and lack of care. But whatever the cause of this decline—and the temptation to speculate and hope is irresistible—it cannot affect the validity of the contribution he has already made. How we regard his films, as manifestations of a still valid faith or merely as nostalgic reminders of a lost state of grace, will depend on the state of mind and heart in which we approach them. It is not in either case to be denied that they stand among the few truly noble works of art of our time.

The Animated Cartoon and Walt Disney
by William Kozlenko

*Mr. Kozlenko is a Broadway playwright as well as a Hollywood
screenwriter and story editor. This chapter appeared
originally in the August 1936 issue of The New Theatre.*

The animated cartoon, as exemplified by Walt Disney's successful film creations, occupies a singular place in the affections
of movie-goers today. It would seem necessary, therefore, to
determine the reason for its appeal, and especially for its appeal to adults, since most of its story plots are based on fairy
tales, fables, myths, and similar extravagant narrative. The
psychologist will undoubtedly tell us that this interest in make-
believe reveals a desire to revert to an adolescent state; an
inclination to escape from the rigors of a disordered existence.
From another point of view, this interest may be traced to a
latent desire on the part of adults to re-live the imaginative
experiences of their childhood. In either case, however, the
element of escape is perhaps the touchstone of the whole matter. The uniqueness of the animated cartoon lies in the fact
that, of all film forms, it is the only one that has freed itself
almost entirely from the restrictions of an oppressive reality.
Its whole conception of life and of movement is based on fantasy. When the audience accepts the logic of fantasy, it also
accepts its conclusions, and though the resultant situations may
be unlike those of reality, it does not question them.

It is true that though the characters of the animated cartoons are mainly zoological (as in Disney's films), they reflect
in many ways the behavior-patterns of human beings. But, in
action, they continue where we leave off. The characters walk
on air, fly over rooftops, swim under water, ride on clouds, and
carry on other extravagant maneuvers which transcend the
limitations of earthly life. The artist crosses the bridge from
a world of limited movement to one of unlimited movement,
which is, of course, *the dream.* Like in a dream, our actions are
unrestricted and free: we do what we wish and how we wish
it. And what is a frustration in real life is a consummation in
a dream. All our biological and material difficulties are solved:
we win the girl, we suddenly find ourselves wealthy, we over-

246

come obstacles that would be almost impossible to surmount in conscious life, we vanquish the "villain" (in whatever guise he may assume, such as our boss, or our neighbor, or our family, or even our environment). Like in a fantasy situation, our movements during the process of a dream are determined, as it were, by miracles. We get to places, not by walking or riding, but by flying; we find ourselves in situations that have neither antecedents nor causes. But, whereas there is a story plot in fantasy which holds its situations coherently together, this coherence or logic is absent in a dream. Things happen because we wish them to happen. In such a way do the incidents in an animated cartoon fulfill, in some measure, many of our unrealized objectives. What takes place before our eyes on the screen, takes place similarly in our dreams, and the pleasure we get from witnessing how easily Mickey Mouse, for instance, solves the most difficult problems in an almost haphazard and miraculous way, is a pleasure transferrable to ourselves.

In order to achieve a free interpretation of life, the method of fantasy must consequently be free. It cannot be tied down to laws that would tend to hamper its exploitation of fancy. To realize this exploitation to the fullest extent, fantasy must necessarily employ the techniques of metamorphosis. Thus, in an animated cartoon, a tree comes to life and starts running; a flower begins to dance; the wind, in the shape of an old man, is seen chasing a rabbit; a cloud is suddenly converted into an umbrella; a fish appears from the water and begins to strut. Metamorphosis is indeed the perfect instrument of fantasy; and fantasy is the romantic realization of our dreams and wish-fulfillments.

Though the content of the animated cartoon is based on fantasy, as we have just said, its situations and incidents are interpreted more or less in the light of contemporary events. The setting, manners, architecture, and costumes of the fantasy narrative are altered to bring them up-to-date. This transition from a mythical place to a real one, this change from a hypothetical situation to an actual one, helps explain why so many of Disney's cartoons attain a certain contemporary significance. The unusual success of *Three Little Pigs*, for example, is a good case in point.

The story, though based on fable, was at once associated

247

with the economic situation. Its lesson—if one wants to call it that—stressed the necessity of "sticking together," and suggested that only by building an "impregnable house" can the "big, bad wolf" be beaten. The wolf—long a symbol of hunger and privation—was accepted by all as representing the prevalent economic distress. This interpretation took on additional emphasis since it came at a time when President Roosevelt was asking for almost dictatorial powers; when bank failures and bankruptcies were rife; and when the President issued his famous appeal to the public to "stick together" (that is, with him), and "not give up hope." The verse—"Who's afraid of the big, bad wolf?"—became a national hit. The public apprehended the subtle argument of the film, and the cartoon, which originally started out to delineate in color and animation a popular children's tale, was seized upon by the canny politicians and used to disseminate a heartening message (so called) to the people. And here fantasy succeeded where realism no doubt would have failed, especially the kind of trumped-up realism which emanates from Hollywood. And why would realism have failed? Obviously because on the plane of reality audiences would have refused to accept the conclusion that they weren't afraid of "the big, bad wolf."

Since Disney's animated cartoons are not the only ones being shown today, it would be well to scrutinize the content of another type of animated cartoon, one almost as popular and representing a different aspect of psychological portraiture. I refer to the Popeye film. These films translate wish-fulfillment into terms of pure physical force: they are glorification of strength and violence. Popeye evinces no niceties of character. He is a tough, though apparently kind-hearted, pug. The salient features of his personality are illiteracy, stupidity, gruffness, and a pair of powerful muscles. (How versatile and refined, by comparison, is such a subject as Mickey Mouse, who can play the piano, ride a horse, conduct a band, fly an airplane, build a house, and do other constructive things with equal proficiency.) In fact, every cartoon character of Disney's is distinguished by some personal trait. We identify little Donald Duck, who gets under everybody's feet, with a helpless irascibility; Pluto, the dog, is a good-natured, though clumsy, bumpkin; and the wolf is a sly and incorrigible character. In short, each of Disney's animal subjects is an intelligent being, reflecting the essential characteristics of his own species. What, conversely, does Popeye represent in human nature? Here is a man who, after swallowing the contents of a can of spinach (a remarkable symbol, incidentally, of metamorphosis), goes completely berserk, and with a series of powerful punches destroys buildings, knocks down trees, and annihilates men normally stronger than himself. His philosophy of action is the doctrine that with physical strength man can overcome every obstacle; and his justification for this display of unbridled power usually takes the form of saving his girl from the unsavory clutches of the gargantuan villain. We are speedily convinced by all this that if a man cannot get satisfaction by persuasion, he can certainly get it by a knockout blow.

In this connection we must deplore the recent tendency of Disney to glorify violence for its own sake, as exemplified by such cartoons as *Mickey's Polo Game* and others. Not·only do *Mickey's Polo Game* and *Who Killed Cock Robin?* (in the latter we have in mind the treatment accorded Jim Crow) revel in unmotivated fury, but they depart entirely from their true character as fantasy by introducing screen personalities—Mae West, Bing Crosby, Laurel and Hardy, *et al.*

During the course of this article, I have at times touched on the odious word "escape." It is necessary at this stage to distinguish between the escape that represents a sickly perversion of reality as projected by numerous Hollywood movies and the Disney variety.

When an artist of the calibre of Disney can successfully remove himself to another world, and take us along with him, we do not have to give up anything of our organic world in order to share with him the pleasures and realizations of his world of fantasy. In short, he creates for us a world of image and fiction, which is related to some extent to our own dream world and which entails no unhealthy distortion of the world of fact. And, in this regard, we can say with Constant Lambert, the eminent British music critic, that: "There must be few artists of any kind who do not feel abashed when faced with the phenomenal inventive genius of Walt Disney, the only artist of today who exists triumphantly in a world of his own creation, unhampered by the overshadowing of ancient tradition or the undercutting of contemporary snobbism."

Since we have attempted an interpretation of the animated

cartoon, as exemplified particularly by Disney's work, it would be interesting at this time to write about his technical methods. Such fine examples, as he gives us, of cartoon animation must have a carefully evolved formula.

Disney's art is determined by many factors, as regards its processes of creation and production, but the most significant, in my opinion, is the fact that, though he is the governing spirit of his organization, the final creation of every cartoon is the result, not of one man—Walt Disney—but of the collective efforts of more than a hundred men who work with him. Yet the finished product reflects the tone and unique personality of that one man. Each cartoon, whether a Silly Symphony or a Mickey Mouse adventure, possesses those distinct qualities which distinguish Disney's work from any other in the same genre.

He is the director only in that he is the organizer and supervisor, but he believes with Cavalcanti that "no director can make a film by himself. He is dependent at every step upon skilled and specialized technicians. The best directors are those who can draw the individual ability from each member of their staff and direct the sum total towards the subject in hand."

Disney allows his fellow-workers complete freedom in their creative tasks. He attempts neither to hamper them in the projection of their own ideas nor does he seek to force upon them his own conceptions and treatment thereof. They are at liberty to work out their own creative impressions, develop them as best they can, and when ready, to submit them to the entire studio for approval. In short, it is the group as a whole, with all its departments—separate yet vitally interrelated—which decides on the merits of the stories submitted. Disney himself, though the "boss" of the organization, willingly submits to the opinions of his fellow-workers. If his idea is rejected in favor of another, he either discards it or changes it according to their specifications. For instance, *Three Little Pigs* was submitted by Disney to the members of his studio for a year before they finally approved it. And when we recall the extraordinary success of this film we realize the marvelous creative values engendered by collective collaboration.

A cartoon, from its inception as an incomplete story idea to the final process of filming, involves about four or five months of actual work. About half that time is devoted to the preparation of a carefully detailed scenario. For this specific function there is a story department, which consists of about a dozen writers. It is their job to conceive new ideas, rewrite old stories—such as fables, fairy tales, myths, romances—and work on material already accepted. It is here, in this department, that Disney's influence is most pronounced. Undoubtedly, the outstanding feature of a Disney film—apart from its remarkable craftsmanship, its schematic integration, its story coherence—is the extraordinary confluence of plot detail, treatment, music, and animation. It is Disney, by his acute suggestions, who helps effect this final integration, for his suggestions, gags, and hints are most frequently accepted.

When a story has been found satisfactory for picture purposes, Disney and members of his story department get together, study all the possibilities for pictorial and musical exploitation, and, after thoroughly going over all the details, the story is then assigned to one of the dozen scribes to rewrite in the form of a page synopsis. This synopsis, when finished, is distributed to several score members of the studio: animators, the musical director, and all other persons connected with the production of this particular cartoon. Each member studies the draft, concentrating on his particular angle of the story, although everyone is at liberty to contribute gags, work out new little actions, and suggest new embellishments of the plot.

After about a fortnight, all the workers involved in the production of the cartoon get together and go over the pile of suggestions which each has brought with him. These suggestions, mostly in the form of rough drawings with written annotations, are presented, criticized, and discussed by Disney, a few associates of the story department, the director in charge of the cartoon (a sort of coordinating foreman), the lay-out man, the musical director, and several animators. Hurried sketches are made and passed around for criticism during this conference. A composer, trying to correlate a particular rhythm or melody to a specific action sequence, rattles off a musical idea while another member rhythmically enacts an animal episode.

As soon as all the various phases of the work have been organized into a working conspectus—including a rough design of the action, a skeletal plan of the musical score, etc.—the actual work of assembling all this begins. A writer, having worked out a plan of the story, submits a detailed scenario which is illustrated by approximately fifty sketches of the main incidents in the action. The scenario is then turned over to the director of the production, who, with the aid of Disney and his associates, formulates a detailed time-sheet of every single movement. The time-sheet is developed further on the basis of beats in synchronization with the music, which is composed simultaneously with the script. In this manner, each movement has been synchronized with the music before either the music is recorded or the action animated. This simultaneous creation of music and action, this conjunction of sound and pantomime, is one of Disney's most valuable contributions to the development of the sound film. With the completion of all the details of the time sheet, the director distributes sections of the action to about thirty animators.

Now begins the process of animation. Inasmuch as an animator cannot make more than several drawings a day—equal to about six feet of film—it therefore requires about a month to complete the animation alone. The animation is divided in several ways. The backgrounds, for instance, are made by regular scenic artists, and only the moving figures are animated. Each animator is assigned to that phase of the animation for which he is best fitted.

Now, what essentially distinguishes an animator from an artist? There are, of course, many subtle and indivisible differences, but the one most prominent is that the animator, besides being something of an imaginative artist himself, must be able to inject a spirit of life in the characters and their movements which he draws. These characters must be able not only to lend themselves to movement, but their movement must have the semblance of real life. It is not enough to animate them; their animations must reflect the viability of men or animals. So, in order to portray this verity of movement, the animators frequently resort to various devices for their portrayals. They may watch their own mirrored reflections as they imitate the movements of their subjects, they may study similar motions simulated by other persons, and, when the subjects are animal, in order to endow them with real zoological characteristics as well as human traits, they frequently observe animals go through their antics in the zoo or on the screen. With all this experience garnered at first hand, they thus are able to reflect in their cartoons many elements of real life.

After a section is sketchily animated, it is photographed and studied by Disney and his aides as to its verity or authenticity. If it is satisfactory, then girls copy the drawings (of which there may be thousands) on celluloid with black paint, or if it is a colored cartoon then it is done in color.

The shooting takes about four or five days, and it is done by a mechanically complex stop-motion camera. The final endorsement of approval, as in the larger studios, is made at a preview at some local movie house. If a particular sequence fails to evoke a favorable response from the audience, the film is taken back to the studio and that sequence changed; although this happens very rarely. Because of the carefully planned and synchronized scenario, there is little that requires changing after the consequent filming of the cartoon.

And so, after about four months of labor, involving the efforts of hundreds of persons, the animated cartoon is ready for its few minutes of life on the screen.

Cartoons as Art
by Aline Saarinen

Aline Saarinen's urbane and incisive commentaries on America's cultural life have been conveyed in the prints and on television. This chapter appeared on August 23, 1953, in The New York Times.

Out in Burbank, in the shadow of the giant movie studios, is a low, unpretentious building with a ring of offices opening onto a patio. There are no red-headed stars, no platinumed starlets, no façades of Western ghost towns nor tanks for storms at sea, no monster-like camera or microphones moving on the ends of giant antennae, no enormous crew of cameramen, property girls, wardrobe mistresses, extras, and directors in canvas-backed chairs.

Instead there is a group of men, most of whom are busy drawing and painting and two cameras whose eyes point down to a flat surface. The walls of the offices are covered with a series of four-by-five-inch pencil drawings thumb-tacked to large boards, and here and there, above a desk, are reproductions of modern art—a Modigliani portrait or a Preston Dickinson landscape.

The stars in this studio are a motley lot. Among them are a round-eyed little boy who can speak only in sound effects; a near-sighted, mettlesome, somewhat irascible but completely endearing old gentleman whose optic affliction leads him into humorously confusing situations; a little girl who "on her stomach has a scar" and an unruly youngster who turns into a chicken when he cannot get his way.

Their names are Gerald McBoing-Boing, Mr. Magoo and Madeline, and Christopher Crumpet. They are very popular stars, but their footprints do not appear in concrete at Grauman's Chinese Theatre. They have no footprints. These vivid personalities exist only as drawings—the creations of United Productions of America (UPA), a company which makes admirable animated cartoons.

In the past, among such many roles as those of decorator, portraitist, and "design consultant," the major artist also had a necessary function as a story-teller. Sometimes he told a commentative story, like the sculptured newsreel that unwinds around Trajan's column, sometimes a sacred story, like the frescoes by Giotto that line the walls of the Arena Chapel.

Today there are other media which tell stories visually. There are, for instance, comic strips, series of photographs, films, and animated cartoons. Freed of the job of visual narration, along with most other functional activities, the fine artist has concentrated on a personal, subjective, and often abstract expression. When he is a great artist—a Picasso or a Matisse or a Miró—his personal expression is a "primary statement" and it has within it rich and generative visual material. This is used in lifeless, superficial clichés by artists who are making only "restatements," but in imaginatively transformed and original ways by those who are making what might be called "secondary statements."

The directors, artists, animators and others at UPA might be thought of in this latter relation to the pioneering, personal artists of our time. But the significant fact is that these cartoon makers have used the visual raw material (or "art language" of our time) in new and germane ways. They have completely adapted this language to their own purposes and, importantly, have developed an idiom which is so integral a part of their medium, so uniquely suited to it and so apposite for their storytelling intention, that they are creators in their own right. Their "secondary statement" is a creative act, secondary only in terms of the profundity of its emotional impact, and surely of more value and vitality than the more pretentious "restatements" which are called "fine art."

UPA of course, has produced among a vast number of cartoons those concerned with the "stars" mentioned above: *Willy the Kid, The Unicorn in the Garden, Rooty Toot-Toot, Brotherhood of Man*, training films for the armed services, promotional films for CBS radio, and *Tell-Tale Heart*. Almost all show unswerving respect for the potentials and limitations of the medium.

Unlike most animated cartoons, UPA ones never try to imitate a photographic or "artistically" realistic, three-dimensional setting. Space is treated as abstractly as desirable. Emptiness becomes a positive value against which are drawn a few architectural motifs or a single, telling prop.

Nor do they try to animate or activate realistic figures. All the best films capitalize on line, which is, mathematically speaking, basically the trace of a moving point and thus an element implicitly concerned with motion. For instance, when Christopher Crumpet does his quick-change act into a chicken the lines of his body swirl into an animated Jackson Pollock. In *Family Budget*, the Fudgets live their lives against graph paper and dissolve back and forth into line.

But even in the more conventional figures, the emphasis is on line rather than modeling, line used for stringently expressive drawing. There is the distillate of an image (and here one recognizes the debt to such fine artists as Picasso, Matisse, Steinberg, and above all, to Modigliani).

Color, too, is used expressively rather than realistically or illusionistically. It is bright, flat, clear, unmodulated. It can flood an entire scene to communicate mood as in *Rooty Toot-Toot*, the stylized satire on "Frankie and Johnny." Or it can be an expressive accent, as in *Crumpet*, where the story is told in black and white except for the vermillion of Christopher's six-pronged cowlick and his chicken's caruncle.

Animation, the technique of "designing movement in space," is also used expressively. Budget considerations become the challenging therapeutic limitations they often are in the arts. For example, in a scene of chatter, only the lips will move, a device which allows for simplest animation work yet makes the sense of talk paramount.

If you ask Robert Cannon, one of UPA's most imaginative directors, where a UPA cartoon begins, he will tell you "first, you have to get hold of an idea." Actually, the ideas are part of these cartoons' distinctions. They are significant on two levels: first, they are ideas suitable to the medium and those which allow for the greatest creativity in their execution—fantasy satire, the unreal, the real carried to so logical a point it becomes fantasy —and second, they are ideas which for all their humor and entertainment value have serious implications, such as McBoing-Boing which tells of society's callousness to an individual's idiosyncrasy—a lesson in tolerance.

UPA's special skill in making abstract ideas and statistical information visually graphic is especially apparent in the cartoons made for CBS radio. Sound becomes a visual image; facts become striking and easily assimilable. One wonders why educators have not worked with this group to make teaching films —from math to music.

The one cartoon in which, to our knowledge, UPA has abandoned its characteristic techniques in favor of more pictorial and "fine artsy" ones is *Tell-Tale Heart*. For all the creative approach of the tale told through the madman's eyes, for all its use of graphic symbols (the staring eye to suggest the paranoiac's sense of being watched, the black and red abstract shapes to indicate the heartbeats, the transformations as of table to tombstone, etc.) and for all its use of the subconsciously revelatory devices of Dali and de Chirico to force emotional response, the film seems to this reviewer to lack the marvelously simple, unique animation and the succinct, excellent drawing of the others.

In this period of the individual artist's isolation, it is refreshing to see here teamwork, collaboration, and mutual respect. Though most of the men also studied fine arts and paint and exhibit "easel paintings," one feels their most living and progressive contribution—their real "statement"—lies in the UPA cartoons. These prove that "art" can also be entertainment and story-telling can be "art."

UPA has even extended into another field—that of television commercials—and these visual delights are among the best "art" programs so far to be seen on TV.

Movies Without a Camera
by Harold Benson

Mr. Benson is a film maker whose comments on films and film making have appeared in a number of publications. This chapter appeared originally in the January 1955 issue of the American Cinematographer.

One might think that no story, no script, no conferences, no camera, no shooting and no processing could only mean *no film*. Yet Norman McLaren, "the only name now connected with motion pictures in Canada that means anything outside of the country," to quote a Toronto critic, owes his reputation to movies made with just these limitations.

Of course, he does use a camera for occasional films, though never quite like anyone else. His pixillated production, *Neighbours,* is one example. But usually McLaren prefers to dispense with the processes which he feels tend to restrict a film maker's efforts at getting really personal work onto the screen.

His technique was born twenty years ago when, as an eighteen-year-old student at Glasgow School of Art, he soaked the emulsion off a worn-out 35mm print and hand-painted a 300 ft. abstract film with color dyes. Later *Color Cocktail,* a 200 ft. 16mm production made in a similar way, won an award at the Scottish Amateur Film Festival, and so excited John Grierson, the British documentary pioneer, that he took McLaren to London and set him to work at the G.P.O. Unit, where the most advanced experimental work in Europe was being done.

McLaren responded well to the congenial environment. Among the shorts he produced in this period was *Love on the Wing,* which made further use of the hand-drawn cameraless technique.

In 1939 McLaren emigrated to America with only a hundred dollars in his pocket. Luckily he was introduced by an NBC television engineer to a few wealthy folk who paid him to decorate their homes with murals. Meanwhile he made several more abstract films, including *Allegro, Scherzo, Dots, Loope, Stars and Stripes,* and *Boogie Doodle,* and sold a few to the Guggenheim Museum of Non-Objective Art.

During a brief spell as script and lyric writer with Caravel

Films, Inc., New York, McLaren was again contacted by Grierson, who put him in charge of animation at the National Film Board of Canada. The five wartime propaganda films which McLaren produced for the N.F.B.—*Mail Early, V for Victory, Five for Four, Hen Hop,* and *Dollar Dance*—were all made without a camera. So were three of McLaren's best-known postwar productions, *Hoppity Pop, Fiddle-De-Dee,* and *Begone Dull Care.*

There are two principal techniques employed by McLaren in making his cameraless films. The first is used for the productions which he says are simply designed "to give the intellect a rest," and have evolved from his earliest experiments with color dyes. This kind of film presents a non-stop series of vigorously changing patterns accompanying equally vigorous music.

In *Fiddle-De-Dee,* the track was of "Listen to the Mocking Bird" played by an old-time fiddler. *Begone Dull Care* was made to music played by the Oscar Peterson jazz trio. Dazzling colors dart about the screen at a breathtaking pace, yet still convey innumerable subtle hints and asides about the music they illustrate. No one is more thrifty with footage than McLaren. At the end of *Begone Dull Care* his own name is scratched on a single frame followed by ten or twelve frames of black leader. Persistence of vision does the trick.

The tremendous pace of these abstract films is hardly surprising; McLaren explains that the technique he uses largely ignores individual frame divisions. In other words, the film is hand-painted two or three feet at a time. There is no attempt at creating an image by image effect.

In making *Fiddle-De-Dee,* McLaren used celluloid dyes, inks and transparent paints, and frequently painted on both sides of the clear 35mm film. He achieved his textures by brush stroke effects, scratching off the paint, spraying, stippling and mixing different types of dyes on the film to provoke a kind of "oil-and-water" reaction.

The sound track had been measured before painting began, of course, and the lengths in which the film was painted were metrically organized to fit the music. The painted film acted as a master positive for all subsequent color release prints.

In *Begone Dull Care,* McLaren and his assistant, Evelyn Lambart, went one stage further and made a considerable part of the film on a running moviola. For some sequences a sponge was used to apply a quick-drying paint having a cellulose base ("Craftint") to the film as it ran through the machine. By moving the sponge from side to side stripes were made to sway across the film. Another sequence involved scratching lines on running black leader with a pin.

A tooth comb, ball bearings, lace, hair nets, and gear wheels also were used in applying the paint. An ordinary fly spray gun shot the stuff onto the film through everything from dishcloths to chicken wire to give different textures. Some of the film was sandpapered before the paint was applied to give a smoky result. Doodling with a pointed knife on a layer of paint was tried, and found successful. Both acetate and nitrate stock were used, and every surface reacted differently to the paints.

But *Fiddle-De-Dee* and *Begone Dull Care* were simple to produce compared with such films as *Hen Hop, Dollar Dance,* and *Boogie Doodle,* which used McLaren's second principal animation technique. In these cases individual frames *are* respected, and the subject, be it chicken, dollar, or doodle, is actually drawn direct onto each frame in turn. This means over 7,000 drawings for a five-minute film.

Obviously characters have to be reduced to a minimum for work of such immensity. Fortunately McLaren has a genius for expressing emotion through the simple movements of matchstick figures. This is the system he uses in producing a film of this nature.

After the music has been recorded, each note, phrase, and sentence is marked on the track with a grease pencil. The notes are measured cumulatively from zero as the track is run on a frame counter, and measurements are put against the notes on a dope sheet, usually a simplified musical score. The length of each note in frames is calculated, and the grease-pencilled sound track is run through a two-way winder together with a roll of clear leader, known as the "dummy." The notes are copied and identified with India ink on the dummy.

The actual drawing is done with the aid of an apparatus adapted by McLaren himself from a camera gate. The claw mechanism is used to hold the film in place and advance it one frame at a time. An ingenious optical system reflects the image of the frame just drawn onto the new frame about to be drawn.

The clear machine leader to be drawn on is threaded into this apparatus with the dummy below it. The drawing is done with

260

pen and ink from the first frame to the last in natural sequence. Finally the drawn film goes into the lab for two prints—one for checking sync and one as a master for release printing. When color releases are needed, various kinds of dupes are made from the master and are assembled in parallel to act as separation negatives for the color process used.

Only McLaren could have thought of using his cameraless technique for one of the first 3-D films ever publicly shown. *Now Is the Time* was made in 1950 for the ultra-modern Telecinema at the Festival of Britain, held in the following year, and McLaren's matchstick men stepped out from the screen to chase each other among the enthusiastic audience.

But the most intriguing of the stereoscopic films shown was *Around Is Around*, another McLaren experiment, this time made *with* a camera. But as I said earlier, he never uses a camera like anyone else.

Editor's note: The inventor of the technique of cameraless movies was Len Lye, a native of New Zealand who worked in Australia and England from the late Twenties to the end of World War II, when he came to the United States. While in England he produced a series of abstract movies distinguished for their design, color and rhythmic tensions. An essay on color by Mr. Lye, now an American citizen living in New York, appears in this book.

The Study of a Colossus: *Citizen Kane*

by Peter Cowie

*Mr. Cowie is the editor of "The International Film Guide"
and author of "Antonioni-Bergman-Resnais" and "Swedish Cinema."
In 1963 he published "The Cinema of Orson Welles," in which
this chapter originally appeared.*

PLOT OUTLINE—Charles Foster Kane dies at the age of 76 in his immense castle, Xanadu; his dying word is "Rosebud." In the projection room of a newsreel firm, a group of reporters note that Kane's public life—wealth, political and social events —does not contain the answer to the enigmatic "Rosebud." A reporter sets out to find the solution and, after reading the details of Kane's ruptured childhood, interviews four leading figures in the magnate's life: Bernstein, Leland (both associates of Kane at the height of his fame); his second wife, Susan Alexander, who Kane had forced to become an opera singer against her will and who is now drunk in a dingy night-club; and Raymond, Kane's butler in the concluding stages of his life at Xanadu. All these are most forthcoming, some even give different versions of the same events, but none can explain the word "Rosebud" to Thompson, the reporter. The answer is given to the audience at the end. As Kane's belongings are packed up and removed from Xanadu, a workman tosses an old sled into a fire. Painted on it is the word "Rosebud." It is the dim memory of his childhood toy that has haunted Kane throughout his life and on his deathbed.

Citizen Kane is above all the study of a personality. It is not, as critics have often been led to assert, a frontal attack on the monopolies of American big business and politics (as is, say, Robert Rossen's *All the King's Men* or Elia Kazan's *A Face in the Crowd*). Nor is it the study of a man's mind and private preoccupations (as is, say, Ingmar Bergman's *Wild Strawberries*). Kane remains a personality whose eminence and publicity depend solely on his ability to project his own magniloquent image; he becomes a symbol ("few private lives were more public" booms the newsreel). The fact that he is a press magnate helps to counterpoint the excessive publicity he achieves, but is no more vital to the theme than "Rosebud" itself. His life and influence are seen not through his own eyes, but through those of other people. The entire film is a major reportage (without using the term in its pejorative sense), an enlargement and extension of the newsreel at the beginning. Thus the flashback method employed by Welles and Mankiewicz is vital to the success of the film. Mankiewicz's previous work had demonstrated his interest in biography, and in a narrative style that aimed at objectivity by accounting for several, often quite disparate, viewpoints.

Kane is all things to all men. To Welles himself, "Kane is a man who abuses the power of the popular press and also sets himself up against the law, against the entire tradition of liberal civilization . . . at once egotistical and disinterested . . . at once an idealist and a swindler, a very great man and a mediocre individual." To Thatcher, his erstwhile guardian, he is "nothing more or less—a communist" and a ruthless egotist who does not know how to handle money; rather more than a spoilt child. To the newsreel compilers and to "44,000,000 news readers," he is a colossal, larger-than-life tycoon who dominated four decades of American life. To Susan, his mistress and subsequent wife, he appears as an awesome monster who launched her on her disastrous career as a singer without even asking her permission—mean, materialistic, and incapable of loving anyone. To Leland, his college friend, he is cynical and faintly malevolent ("he never gave you anything, he just left you a tip"), and "always trying to prove something." To Bernstein, his general manager, he was perhaps most congenial, "a man who lost nearly everything he had," a man to be pitied and revered.

(It is interesting to note, by the way, that Welles' own mentor in youth was a certain Doctor Bernstein who presented him, among other things, with a puppet theatre when he was in his infancy.)

To Raymond, his calculating *major domo* at Xanadu, Kane is a pathetic old fool. To himself, Kane is quite simply a wholly *autonomous* man. "There's only one person in this world who decides what I'm going to do, and that's me" he tells Emily in the scene with Gettys in Susan's rooms. When his newspapers are hit by the 1929 depression he says to Thatcher and Bernstein, "If I hadn't been very rich, I might have been a great man." Yet with the years this honesty of appraisal gradually vanishes. Kane weaves about himself a myth that ultimately even he acknowledges to be the truth. His fleeting references to "Rosebud" always emanate from his subconscious and so he can never quite grasp the exact nature of the lacuna that has

263

prevented him from plotting an entirely satisfactory life. As André Bazin observed in this context, it is worth nothing to conquer the world if one has lost one's childhood.

As if to make up for the loss of his beloved sled, Kane devotes a major part of his life to the collection of material objects. He garners them omnivorously, from the world's biggest diamond ("I didn't know he was collecting diamonds," says Leland. "He's collecting someone who collects diamonds," replies Bernstein) to "the biggest private zoo since Noah." And all that he achieves through these acquisitions are manifold reflections of his own ego, symbolized in the mirror Kane limps past at Xanadu near the end. The statues and other artistic bric-à-brac of Xanadu suggest Kane's futile inability to *create*. Nothing remains after his death, except the black smoke that wells into the air from the chimneys of his palace, as his "junk," the sled amongst it, is consigned to the flames. Of the people who linger within his power, Bernstein alone remains a faithful apostle. Leland denies him, as Peter denied Christ. Bazin maintains that Kane is at last revenged on his parents and on Thatcher "by playing with his social power like a huge toboggan, so as to thrill himself with the dizziness of fortune, or by hitting those who dare to cast aspersion on the moral basis of his actions and his pleasure." His obsessions are hinted at in the final lines of *The Lady from Shanghai*—"She was dead and now I had to try and forget her . . . innocent or guilty, that means nothing, the main thing is to know how to grow up."

The problem of "Rosebud" deserves some attention. Welles himself is the first to admit that "it's a gimmick, really, and rather dollar-book Freud." And as Thompson says resignedly at the end of the film, "I don't think the word 'Rosebud' could explain any man's life. I guess 'Rosebud' is just a piece in the jigsaw puzzle." The sled is not so precious in itself to Kane (one never sees him look at it, even though it lies amid his belongings at Xanadu) but it conjures up for him memories of a childhood innocence far removed from the "Chicago, New York, and Washington" to which he was so brusquely introduced by Thatcher. The scene in the paperweight that he finds in Susan's room in Xanadu and keeps close to him until his death is of a cottage in a snowstorm, strikingly similar to the lodging house of Mrs. Kane. "The three clues to 'Rosebud' appear at times when Kane is being treated most remotely—in the cryptic death scene in the beginning, in the unfriendly memoirs of his banker guardian, and in the final flashback narration of a cynical butler. The narrations of his closest acquaintances yield no clues to the symbolic truth of his life." Welles' most overt emphasis on the sentimental importance of "Rosebud" is in his three lap-dissolves, showing the abandoned sled being gradually covered by a snowfall after the young Kane has left with Mr. Thatcher. Just how the sled eventually reached Xanadu is not explained, although one may conjecture from Kane's first conversation with Susan Alexander, that he rescued it with his mother's belongings "in a warehouse out West."

Negatively, because Rosebud does *not,* as one would expect (and as even Bernstein expects) turn out to be the name of a girl, it stands as a token of Kane's unhappy relations with people in general. He has no friends, only acquaintances, because he insists on setting himself on a pedestal above those who seek to know him. Arrogance and lack of moral respect are the vices that lead to his isolation. Thompson, in his second interview with Susan at El Rancho, observes: "All the same, you know, I can't help being a little sorry for Mr. Kane." To which Susan replies without a moment's hesitation, "Don't you think I am?" It is of course partly due to Welles' own rather sympathetic performance that one feels a measure of pity for this magnate who strives so hard to overcome his fundamental lack of spiritual fibre. Is there, in effect, a sound case to be argued for Kane? Susan's charge—that he made her into an opera singer against her will—is quite patently unfair, especially as in her first meeting with him she admitted that she had always longed to be a singer (although, of course, this is recalled by Leland, and is therefore suspect because presumably Leland heard only Kane's version of the encounter). Leland himself, though outwardly an endearing personality, is surely ungrateful to Kane when one considers Bernstein's remark that he was the son of a man whose debts at his death were immense. Raymond, with his transparent lust for money (he asks Thompson for a thousand dollars in exchange for information about "Rosebud") is quickly revealed as no more than a parasite on the aging Kane. And Thatcher's testament is of purely biographical interest, its irascible attacks on his *protégé* consisting of part jealousy, part disgust, and part hypocrisy. When all is considered, the two unforgivable sins (in the eyes of the world) committed by Charles Foster Kane are his neglect of the perfectly harmless Emily, his first wife, and his overriding egotism, which ruins the lives of so many, even if some of them almost ask to be maneuvered by his fancy. His insatiable desire for material wealth also condemns him in the opinion of society; but the point to be stressed here is surely that Kane at least *spent* his money, spent it moreover on works of art that endure in fossilized solitude rather than on sensuous pleasures. Indeed, the actual comforts of Xanadu seem Spartan in the extreme, and the massive picnic at the end seems rather inappropriate as a result. In the final analysis, no one can deny that Kane earned every ounce of his fortune through his own labor and enthusiasm. He was never one to live on his interest.

Citizen Kane was made in the early autumn of 1940, and it took Welles nine months, working six days a week, to edit. Earlier, he had studied the more important films in cinema history at the Museum of Modern Art. "John Ford was my teacher. My own style has nothing to do with his, but *Stagecoach* was my movie text-book. I ran it over forty times." Then, just prior to shooting the film, he spent several weeks on the sets, making himself familiar with the routine and the equipment. He refused to listen to technicians who told him that what he wanted to do was impossible.

Almost more space has been devoted by critics to the outcry caused by *Citizen Kane* at the time of its opening than to its cinematic merits. However, a short account of events may help to place the film in its historical context. The trouble began when word reached William Randolph Hearst that Welles' film was a caricature of his life. Hearst was a newspaper tycoon like Kane, and the resemblance between the two men appeared to extend even to small details. Susan Alexander was immediately said to correspond to Marion Davies, a starlet with whom Hearst had fallen in love in 1918, only two years after Kane had supposedly met Susan. Hearst offered RKO the $800,000 the film had cost to make if only they would burn it before it was released. When this move failed, he threatened to attack the entire American film industry in his press. RKO encountered difficulty in obtaining circuit bookings for the film as Warners, Loews, and Paramount all relied heavily on the Hearst papers for advertising outlets. Eventually RKO exhibited *Citizen Kane* solely in its own cinemas, and in New York and Los Angeles independent halls had to be hired. Hearst banned his papers from mentioning any RKO films as a result. The scheduled opening was originally February 14, 1941, but the violent clash between Hearst and the production company delayed the first public screening until April 9, 1941 (although the press saw the film privately during March). To this day Welles studiously denies that he modeled Kane on Hearst ("Kane would have liked to see a film of his life, but not Hearst—he didn't have quite enough style"). The film could equally have been based on the life of Jules Brulatour, the owner of Kodak, who wanted to make his wife an important singer.

Citizen Kane is of primary importance in the history of the cinema because of the audacity and virtuosity of Welles' technique, and because of the influence that the style was to exert on films in all parts of the world for the next two decades. It can now be regarded as a clear fifteen years ahead of its time, and even then does not fit into any pattern of esthetic progress. It remains, like some of Welles' other work, a creation fantastic and unique, a breathtaking reflection of the genius of its inventor. Critics have tried to pin down its significance by drawing literary and dramatic parallels: "For the first time on the screen we have seen the equivalent of a novel by Dos Passos" and "Apart from its cinematic importance, *Citizen Kane* constitutes, from the point of view of construction, a revolution such as dramatic art has scarcely undergone since Aeschylus." And, more lucid, Dilys Powell's review when the film first came to England in 1941: "There is no question here of experiment for experiment's sake; it is a question of a man with a problem of narrative to solve, using lighting, setting, sound, camera angles and movement much as a genuine writer uses words, phrases, cadences, rhythms—using them with the ease and boldness and resource of one who controls and is not controlled by his medium."

Yet many of the technical devices used so successfully by Welles had been introduced prior to 1940. His brilliance stems from his ability to synthesize and harmonize all possible stylistic methods into a coherent instrument for telling his story.

267

Only Gregg Toland, the lighting cameraman, agreed with Welles in adopting deep-focus photography and covered sets, and was rewarded with a credit equal in size to that of the director himself on the finished film. Toland was born in Illinois in 1904, worked a great deal with Wyler and, on his death in 1948, was the highest-paid cameraman in Hollywood. "There's never been anyone else in his class," says Welles today. Each scene in *Citizen Kane* was provided with a ceiling, not partial but complete. "I suppose that closing the top of the set was the real revolution we caused . . . It's disastrous to let a cameraman light a set without a ceiling—it's artificial." Toland was able to use the "pan-focus" process he had developed for two years. It allowed the camera to record objects at a range of twenty inches or several hundred feet with equal clarity. The lens aperture never opened more than f. 5.6, and the lens itself was specially coated and this, together with the use of very fast film stock, enabled Welles to shoot scenes that were very brightly lit.

Deep-focus had been exercised, rather haphazardly, at earlier stages in the history of the cinema. An example is to be found in Griffith's *Musketeers of Pig Alley* where the characters advance towards the camera until those in close-up are in as sharp focus as those still following in the background. But after 1925 the use of panchromatic film stock obliged cameramen to abandon deep-focus lenses in favor of "brighter" lenses; and these, when recording close-ups, tended to make everything in the background misty and out of focus. When the sensitivity of film stock improved during the Thirties, Renoir was one of the first directors to see the advantages of deep-focus. Several shots in *Boudu sauvé des Eaux* (1932) and *La Règle du Jeu* (1939) demonstrate this. But Welles, assuming that deep-focus presented no technical problems to a lively camera crew, systematically employed the lens with the result that his film achieves very much the field of vision encompassed by the human eye, even to the gigantic closeups (e.g., the lips of the dying Kane as he mumbles "Rosebud"). In later films, particularly *Touch of Evil* and *The Trial*, he was to use this 18.5 mm focal length increasingly.

The deep-focus photography throughout *Citizen Kane* is apt to echelon the characters, as it were, showing several actions—several points of interest—simultaneously. I will note

268

five out of several examples of Welles's enrichment of the film in this way. First, when Mrs. Kane is signing the form whereby Thatcher is to be the guardian of the young Kane, Welles places the father at the left of the frame, the mother at the right (in close-up), with Thatcher leaning over her, and, in the background, beyond the window, the boy playing in the snow. This shot is not merely economical, but it also keeps one constantly aware of the person whose future is being discussed and decided. Second, the celebration scene at the offices of The Inquirer. Leland and Bernstein are seated at the end of a long table with other members of the newspaper staff ranged along each side. In the background Kane is dancing with a troupe of showgirls. Suddenly he strips off his jacket and tosses it towards the camera into the arms of Leland, who is in close-up at the left of the frame. The flying jacket demonstrates the three-dimensional quality that the deep-focus lens creates, and provides just as much of a visual shock as the objects flung "out of the screen" in the much publicized 3-D films thirteen years later. Third, when Kane finds that the besotted Leland has begun an unfavorable review of Susan's operatic *début*, he types out the remainder of the notice himself. Welles shows Kane at his typewriter in close-up at the left of the frame, and one sees Leland stagger down the length of The Inquirer news-room (in sharp focus) towards his boss. By avoiding a series of direct cuts here, Welles counterpoints and visually extends the lull before the quarrel that seems inevitable between the two men. The sharp, deliberate tapping of Kane's machine on the "foreground" soundtrack, as it were, contrasts appropriately with Leland's voice in the background, and accentuates the spatial relationship.

Fourth, when Susan drugs herself in misery after her disastrous performance at the opera house, Welles conveys the implications and urgency of the situation in one remarkable shot, on three levels: in close-up are the glass and the phial of poison resorted to by Susan; in mid-shot the head of Susan, lying in shadow on the pillow; and in the background the door, beneath which appears a strip of light. All this is given dramatic intensity by the soundtrack, with the labored breathing of Susan, and the thunderous knocking of Kane on the locked door. And lastly, when Susan is practicing her singing with Matisti, Welles places the piano in the foreground, with Matisti gesticulating on the left, and Susan singing pathetically on the right. Unseen by them both, Kane enters the vast room by a door in the far background. Caught in clear focus, he watches the abortive lesson. This dramatic irony again arouses a feeling of realistic suspense, for the spectator knows that Kane is about to intervene in his usual domineering manner. He is kept in sharp focus all the time as he advances towards the piano.

André Bazin, who has investigated this aspect of Welles' early work so thoroughly, sees in deep-focus a greater freedom for the spectator, who can choose at any one instant in the same shot the elements that interest him, and he underlines how much events and characters can gain in ambiguity, because the significance of each moment of the action is not arbitrarily stressed. This use of deep-focus is closely allied to Welles's keenness to show how his characters can be influenced by their surroundings. For instance, Kane as a man is dwarfed by the lofty, public hall in which he gives his election speech, but his voice and his promises are magnified and boom out over the soundtrack, creating a sense of bombast and inflated power. Similarly Kane is often viewed from a camera setup at floor level. The tilt, and the corresponding exaggeration of the human figure, display Kane's dominance over the people in his life. When Leland meets him one night in The Inquirer offices, only Kane's trouser leg is seen in close-up at the left of the frame while Leland sways on his feet in the background. And when Kane and Susan have one of their final quarrels, in a tent during the picnic near Xanadu, the camera views him alternately from below (as he listens to Susan's harangue, with the screaming of some outraged woman guest outside the tent providing a subtle aural aside) and from above (as he towers over Susan and tells her that he has only helped her out of love). His shadow obscures her and seemingly overawes her. This preponderance is symbolized most unostensibly of all in Susan's bedroom immediately before she leaves her husband. As she stands talking to Kane in mid-shot, a stuffed doll sits near the camera, in parallel profile to Susan, suggesting the true nature of her position in the eyes of Kane—that of a marionette.

Welles also used two other common cinematic devices, creatively and incisively. The wipe, which is usually so artificial, is ironically suitable for bridging the six episodes in which Welles shows the deterioration of the marriage between Kane and Emily at the breakfast table (Kane becomes gradually more and more morose, and Emily ends by reading The Chronicle, arch-rival of Kane's own newspaper, The Inquirer). Then there is one startlingly successful vertical traveling shot, in the opera scene. The camera rests on the figure of Susan, singing in rehearsal on the stage; then it moves slowly upwards and at last reaches the topmost catwalk above the curtains. Two technicians look at each other, and one expresses his disapproval. Thus the fact that Susan has a feeble voice and generates only boredom and disgust in her audience is brought home.

Citizen Kane is also rich in "shock images," none of which are so gratuitous as those sprinkled across Buñuel's work. The opening of the film has a sombre tone as Kane's death is revealed in expressionistic terms, but the fade-out on the lighted window in Xanadu is succeeded abruptly by the strident music of the "News on the March" credit card. Thus, within a few minutes of the start of the film, Welles has shown both the distorted, brooding image of Kane's existence, and the brash, realistic version known to the public. Another jolting cut is from Raymond's saying "Like the time his wife left him . . ." to a close-up of a screeching white parakeet behind which, on the veranda of Xanadu, Susan walks away in high dudgeon. This visual shock represents the mental shock sustained by Kane when he realizes Susan has gone, and explains his violent wrecking of her room. It is as though he has suffered a heart attack.

The technical grammar of the film is so richly condensed that a complete exegesis would take up more space than is possible here. No study of *Citizen Kane* would, however, be complete, without mention of Welles' fondness for dissolves and "lightning mixes" (scenes linked by the soundtrack but not by the images). The dissolves are immediately in evidence when at the start of the film the camera crawls up from the "No Trespassing" sign and the wire fences dissolve into heavy gates, then into a series of views, in closer and closer proximity to the palace, with—successively—a cage of monkeys, gondolas, a ghostly, oriental pavilion, an abandoned golf course marker, and an open-air swimming pool in the foreground.

These quick shots, merging one with another, convey the remote, portentous power with which Kane has hedged himself in during his life at Xanadu. The "lightning mixes" are more plentiful and rather more difficult to catalog. Two of the most striking instances are (1) when, during Thatcher's recollections, the shot changes from his wishing the young Kane "a merry Christmas—" to the same man, somewhat older, continuing the sentence "—and a prosperous New Year" just before his *protégé's* twenty-fifth birthday; and (2) when Kane's clapping at Susan Alexander's piano recital in her own parlor is dovetailed with the applause from a small crowd as Leland campaigns for Kane to be Governor in the 1916 elections, and then almost, immediately afterwards, Leland's sentence "—who entered upon this campaign . . ." is replaced by that of Kane himself (a second later) in the huge assembly hall, ". . . with one purpose only." This dramatic continuity illustrates Kane's frightening rise to power.

But *Citizen Kane* is important for its basic construction as well as for the myriad details that form its style. Flashbacks were used often before 1940—perhaps Carné's *Le Jour se Lève* explored their advantages most thoroughly—but Welles was the first director to use them not merely at random but so as to present five biased views of one person. The memories of Thatcher, Bernstein, Leland, Susan, and Raymond, while carefully arranged in chronological order, are all slightly prejudiced. "Each major flashback begins at a later point in time than its predecessor, but each flashback overlaps with at least one of the others, so that the same event or period is seen from two or three points of view." For instance, Susan's *début* in "Salammbo" at the Chicago Opera House is seen three times altogether in the film—in the newsreel, in Leland's flashback when it is seen at rehearsal through his bored eyes in the dress-circle, and in Susan's own memories when the audience is seen as a black, hostile void beyond the glaring footlights. This gives the episode an additional narrative dimension, which is reflected spatially in the lighting and camerawork.

Moreover, these recollections are not marred by the customary aura of age and remoteness, because Welles has so cunningly summarized the key facts of Kane's life in the newsreel. Several of the incidents covered by the "News on the March" bulletin are made to look grainy and shaky, as though

272

drawn from some archive, and yet later in the film the *same* shots appear in the course of the flashbacks in crystal *clear* vision. Thus Welles causes events literally to come to life in the flashbacks (the shot of Susan and Kane climbing into a carriage after their wedding, for example). Welles himself recalls that when the film opened in Italy just after the war, a lot of people booed and hissed and even shook their fists at the projection box because they thought the newsreel material was sheer bad photography. The newsreel has a further significance in that it provides a salient outline of Kane's life and enables Welles to dispense with a strictly logical narrative style.

The form of *Citizen Kane*, superficially so diffuse, is in reality highly disciplined. Practically every movement has its complement at another point in the film. Apart from the opening and closing scenes, when the camera begins and ends by focusing in close-up on the "No Trespassing" sign outside Xanadu, one can cite the crane shot that climbs up, over the roof, and down through the skylight of the El Rancho nightclub in Atlantic City. When Thompson first arrives, the neon sign "Susan Alexander-Cabaret" is flashing; when he returns much later in the film and much later in time, the sign is out, signifying the decline of Susan's fortunes since Kane's death. A French critic has noted that the shot is also "the physical image of that violation of consciences and intimacy that the press has perpetrated and that *Citizen Kane* seeks both to represent and to attack."

Nearly all the players in *Citizen Kane* were unknown when the film appeared. Oddly, few of them have established a major reputation over the years. Joseph Cotten still plays the occasional role (most recently in Robert Aldrich's *The Last Sunset*); Agnes Moorehead and Everett Sloane also appear in minor parts, though always with distinction, and Erskine Sanford (Carter in this film) was seen to rather better effect as the judge in *The Lady from Shanghai*. Nearly all these actors and actresses had worked with Welles in his Mercury Theatre group, and the performances in *Citizen Kane* are as near perfect as can be. Welles himself has never had a role since that suits his capacity as well as Kane. His first appearance, brash in braces and open-necked shirt, and swinging on his chair as he simultaneously lights his pipe and rebuffs the

273

protests of Walter Thatcher, oozes the almost pardonable arrogance that is the making of Kane's career. Never once does Welles dispel the magnetic aura that Kane seems to carry about with him, even in old age (the make-up staff of RKO succeeded remarkably in making the 25-year-old Welles look at least sixty in some sequences). He has that supremely self-confident air of one who knows in advance precisely what his detractors will say and disarms them with a single witticism or command.

Citizen Kane remains Welles' finest film, a treasury of cinematic metaphors and devices, and a portrait of an incredibly powerful personality. The theme of the life of a grandiose figure ending in tragedy is the blueprint for nearly all Welles's subsequent work *(The Stranger, The Lady from Shanghai, Macbeth, Othello, Confidential Report, Touch of Evil)*. Irrespective of the fluctuations of critical opinion (and in the 1962 Sight and Sound poll it emerged as the film cited most by critics asked to list the ten best films ever made), it will remain one of the few films of which the long-term influence on the history of the cinema was as remarkable as its initial impact.

The Course of Italian Neorealism
by Arthur Knight

*Film critic and historian of the first rank, Mr. Knight
is best known for his reviews in Saturday Review
and his historical survey of the movies, "The Liveliest Art,"
published in 1957. This chapter is from that book.*

In Italy during the pre-sound period the Fascist government at
first took little interest in the motion-picture field. There was,
of course, official encouragement for historical films celebrat-
ing the rise of the Fascist party or re-creating the life and
times of such popular heroes as Garibaldi, Ettore Fieramosca,
and Salvator Rosa, but nothing more tangible. Fascist interests
were, at that time, satisfactorily served by the flow of propaganda shorts and newsreels turned out by the government-
owned LUCE. When the talkies arrived in 1930 this company
promptly added three sound trucks to its equipment, with the
result that impassioned harangues by Mussolini became part
of all their newsreels. These, together with any other shorts
turned out by LUCE, were shown by government decree in
every motion-picture house throughout Italy. But aside from
such minor inconveniences, Italian producers, distributors, and
exhibitors were left pretty much to their own devices until
1935. Between 1935 and 1940, however, things began to
change. Mussolini was launching those wars and campaigns
through which he hoped to extend the Italian empire and
increase his own stature. National feeling, national pride had
to be whipped up to a fever pitch. It was during this period
that the government gradually gained control of the motion-
picture industry, achieving this not by outright ownership but
by a weird and complicated form of patronage that the State
held out to the eighteen accredited producing studios. Producers now could easily borrow up to sixty per cent of the
cost of a picture from the State-controlled banks; if they were
able to show that their film was either popular, artistic, or
propagandistically useful, they had only to repay a small portion of the loan. Under such conditions, it became virtually
impossible for a studio to lose money no matter how unsuccessful its pictures might be. Before long the studios were
offering top jobs to political favorites because of their ability

to wangle even more profitable concessions from the venal officials directing the banks and the State credit agencies. When Mussolini's son Vittorio entered the industry as head of Europa Films, Italy's largest studio, the pattern of nepotism and patronage was complete.

The government further increased its influence over the industry when it decreed that all foreign films shown in Italy had to be dubbed, and that the dubbing had to be done by Italians. This not only created more film jobs, it also made it simple to eliminate from foreign imports any sentiments that were not fully in accord with Fascist ideology—a neat, unobtrusive form of censorship. At the same time, the State awarded the valuable licenses for dubbing and distributing these films to those studios that produced the most or the most expensive pictures each year—a form of patronage that proved completely demoralizing. Indeed, no system could have been more ideally designed to encourage wastefulness and to discourage creativity.

Considering the amount of control the government actually held over the film industry both economically and by the appointment of political favorites to key positions, it is surprising how few of the pictures were made as outright Fascist propaganda. The Italians were satisfied, it would seem, with a primarily negative propaganda. They were content if their film simply ignored all ideas of democracy, civil rights, civil liberties or similarly "decadent" notions. Ettore Margadonna, one of the leading historians of the Italian film, has estimated that "out of more than five hundred feature films [produced between 1930 and 1942], those which were one hundred per cent Fascist in content may be counted on the fingers of one hand." These exceptions would include *Black Shirt* (1933), Blasetti's *Old Guard* (1935), *The Siege of the Alcázar* (1940), proudly revealing Italy's part in the Spanish Civil War, and Carmine Gallone's soporific extravaganza *Scipio Africanus* (1937). Rumored to have been written by Benito Mussolini himself, it presumed to see in the ancient Italian victory in Africa the heroic counterpart of Mussolini's own campaign in Ethiopia. Filmed in Africa and on the giant stages of the new, State-financed Cinecittà, it was one of the most costly, most opulent productions of all time—and also one of the most overblown. Critics delighted in pointing to the telephone poles that sprouted from the hilltops of Imperial Rome, the wrist watches on the Roman legionnaires, and to the stupefying emptiness of the vast spectacle. Nevertheless, because it was an official film, the government made special efforts to have it shown abroad. Its reception did little to enhance the reputation of the Italian film makers. A few of the Italian opera films were also exported, notably Gallone's *The Dream of Butterfly* (1939), featuring long passages from Puccini's opera beautifully performed by Maria Cebotari, and a tear-stained story of a diva who, like Butterfly herself, loved not wisely but well. Aside from these—nothing.

But if the corrupt and corrupting Italian studios were unable to produce a masterpiece, at least they enabled talented people to gain a mastery of their art. Clearly, the neorealist movement that burst forth with such vitality after the war could only have come from men whose artistic impulses had long been bottled up, from men who knew the techniques of film making but lacked the opportunity to use them significantly. Many had been trained at the government-operated Centro Sperimentale, the official film school in Rome. Many had worked under the dispiriting studio conditions that marked the final years of Fascism. Vittorio De Sica, for example, had alternated between stage and screen as a matinee idol throughout the Thirties. He turned to directing in 1940, specializing in sentimental comedies which he handled with a good deal of superficial charm and, on occasion, sharp insights into the behavior of children. Roberto Rossellini worked on a number of documentaries before being assigned as assistant director on *The White Ship* (1941), a wartime propaganda film almost totally lacking in human feeling. Two more features, *The Return of the Pilot* (1942) and *The Man of the Cross* (1943), seem to have been equally devoid of any hint of his postwar style. Of the old guard, only Alessandro Blasetti gave any suggestion of the new themes and new techniques that lay ahead. His *Four Steps in the Clouds* (1943) for a moment took the Italian film out of the world of "white telephones" and official attitudes. It was a touching, warm-hearted comedy in which a kindly man from the city finds himself pretending to be the husband of a country girl he has met by chance—and the father of her unborn child. Though far from political, its picture of peasant life, its Italian peasant types and natural settings strongly foreshadowed the neorealist films of the post-war era. Indeed, when *Four Steps* was first shown in New York, undated, critics assumed it had been made *after* the war, as part of the movement touched off by *Open City*.

For all its excellences, *Four Steps in the Clouds* remains a modest work, a harbinger. But late in 1942, when Mussolini's hold on his people was fast disintegrating, there appeared Luchino Visconti's *Ossessione*, a true masterpiece that contained all the seeds of the postwar neorealist movement—the concern for people, the use of natural settings and types, the overwhelming sense of looking at life as it really is. An adaptation (although uncredited) of James M. Cain's "The Postman Always Rings Twice," its sordid theme was played against the background of a small *trattoria* on the marshes of the Po and a fair at Ancona. And though Visconti used such familiar Italian actors as Massimo Girotti, Clara Calamai and Elio Marcuzzo, under his direction they performed with a naturalism that blended with the sweaty peasants who crowded the bar at the shabby inn and thronged the amusement booths of the *festa*. The camera work was always arresting, using long traveling shots to keep the principals in screen center as they moved through the crowds, using concealed cameras for sequences in public parks and streets, mounting the camera on a crane to rise from a close-up of an actor to panoramas of an entire landscape within a single shot. Here were the faces of real Italians, the sights and sounds of everyday Italy mobilized upon the screen to tell a powerful and affecting story. It was a revelation, a film so far beyond anything produced in the twenty years of Fascism that its impression upon other Italian film makers could only have been profound. Unfortunately, it is a revelation that few Americans seem destined to share. Not only was Visconti's film a fairly flagrant violation of copyright, but the film rights to Cain's novel already belonged to MGM, which produced its own version of the story in 1946. MGM has been adamant in refusing to permit prints of *Ossessione* to enter the United States.

As the war progressed, film making in Italy became increasingly chaotic (as did life itself). Loyalties were divided. Some favored the Allies—or thought the Axis a losing cause; some clung to their Fascist beliefs. After the fall of Mussolini, with war still ravaging the south and the Nazis occupying the remainder of the peninsula, film making came to a virtual standstill. In 1944 only sixteen pictures were produced in Italy, most of them coming from Scalera's studio in Venice, the last stronghold of the Fascist elements in the industry. Meanwhile, anti-Fascists went into hiding, awaiting the liberation of the Allied forces, awaiting the withdrawal of the Nazi army of occupation. Late in 1944, even before the Germans had completed their evacuation of Rome, Roberto Rossellini was already at work on *Open City*, the key film in the entire neorealist Italian revival. In it he sought to re-create, as accurately as possible, the tensions, the trials, and the heroic resistance of the common people of Rome during the years of the Nazi occupation. Aside from the principals, few in the cast were professional actors. Many, indeed, were simply citizens—or Nazi soldiers—photographed on the fly by cameras concealed on rooftops or hidden in cars. Little of the film was shot in a studio, partly for financial reasons, partly because Rossellini (and Cesare Zavattini, who wrote the script) sensed that the documentary value of actual streets, apartments, and courtyards would heighten the authenticity of their story.

What emerged was a film strikingly unlike anything that had been seen before. Technically, it was far from flawless. Rossellini had been forced to use whatever scraps of film stock he could lay his hands on, while the lighting—particularly in those interiors not taken in a studio—was often too weak for dramatic effects or even adequate modeling. Indeed, shooting had to be abandoned entirely several times while the director set about raising the necessary funds to continue. But the very passion that had inspired the production of *Open City* seemed to create the centrifugal force that held it all together. Its roughness, its lack of finish became a virtue. And the cumulative power of Rossellini's feeling for his subject was translated into a visual intensity that made the picture sometimes almost unbearable to watch. Here was true realism—the raw life of a tragic era. "This is the way things are," said Rossellini in presenting his film. It became the credo of the entire neorealist movement.

Within the next five years there appeared in Italy a cycle of films in every way as remarkable and exciting as the great Russian pictures of the late Twenties—and inspired, like them, by the sudden discovery of a national identity and the simultaneous liberation of creative talents. The complete breakdown of the Fascist régime removed all previous restraints. The years of repression under the Nazi occupation forces, the disenchantment under the Allies produced a social awareness that found its fullest expression in the neorealist movement. At the outset, the mere ability to treat dispassionately the daily life of the ordinary Italian was inspiration enough for directors like Rossellini and De Sica. Rossellini's *Paisan* (1946) was an epic study of the last months of war in Italy. De Sica, the former matinee idol, revealed again his concern for children in *Shoeshine* (1946), but with a depth and passion unsuspected from his earlier films. It is a poignant, muted tale of an appealing group of Roman street urchins caught up in the black market that swept through Italy during the war years. The boys are jailed, then friend is set against friend so that their captors may gain a little more information on the gangsters who have been using them. De Sica makes it amply clear that the authorities are neither brutal nor stupid, merely hard pressed. But because they take the easy, obvious course, friends become enemies and murder is the final outcome. All of this is offered without either bitterness or cynicism as a dramatization of actual conditions. And if his revelations disturbed his audience it was, after all, up to them as citizens to do something about it. In such films can be detected the emergence of a truly democratic spirit—the objective presentation of social fact, with social action left to the conscience and the intelligence of the viewer.

With Rossellini and De Sica as its leaders, the neorealist movement quickly gathered momentum and was confirmed in the work of a dozen or more directors in the period immediately after the war. Drawn irresistibly to social themes, they were united by a common philosophy that was perhaps most clearly expressed in Luigi Zampa's *To Live in Peace* (1946). Zampa selected an incident from the very end of the war to suggest that all men—even Nazis—could live together in friendship if they followed their instincts instead of their ideologies. An Italian farmer has given shelter to two American soldiers caught behind the German lines, one white and one colored. During the night the German sentry from the village comes to the farm. In order to cover up the noises of the Negro drinking in the cellar, the farmer gets the German drunk. Suddenly the American bursts out of his hiding place, and there is a suspenseful moment as Nazi and Negro face each other. But all hate, all conflicting ideology has been drowned in the wine. The two wrap their arms around each other and go roaring through the village, "The war is over—Der Krieg ist kaput." In *Angelina* (1947), Zampa reiterated the same theme, that man's better instincts are subverted by his blind obedience to orders. In the title role, Anna Magnani gave a wonderfully funny and sympathetic performance as a working-class housewife who becomes the leader of all the women in her neighborhood against the local politicians and landlords.

Other directors took actual incidents from the postwar scene to create images of shocking or pitiable truth. In the first half of *Tragic Chase* (1947), Giuseppe De Santis drew a remarkable picture of the chaos, the lawlessness that followed the end of hostilities in northern Italy, and although a taste for melodrama marred its second part, his scenes of peasants organizing and fighting for the right to return to their land were both moving and convincing. Also quite melodramatic (almost inevitably) was Alberto Lattuada's *Without Pity* (1947), centered on another serious postwar problem in Italy, the Negro G.I.'s who had deserted the Army and were living lawlessly in the Tombolo, north of Leghorn. There was sensitivity in this story of a Negro and his love for a white prostitute, but sensationalism as well. (The film was cut drastically for exhibition in the United States.) From Visconti, the director of *Ossessione*, came a ponderous but searching and indubitably sincere study of the lives of impoverished Sicilian fishermen, *The Earth Trembles* (1948), made documentary-fashion without actors or studio settings—and in a dialect so special that not even all Italians could follow it. Again it was a film that said, with sympathy: "This is the way things are. What are we going to do about it?"

Out of all these films—and many more—there emerged the image of the ordinary Italian. With a vividness and humanity unequaled by any other nation, the drama of commonplace joys and sorrows was projected from the screen. Curiously enough, such pictures were not at first too well received in Italy itself. Perhaps they reflected the ordinary too accurately. What the Italians wanted was the glitter, the glamor, the romance of the Hollywood movies after their years of misery and privation. In any case, it was the critical reception abroad of such pictures as *Open City, Shoeshine, Bicycle Thief,* and *To Live in Peace* that opened the eyes of most Italians to what they really had. All of them proved far more successful on their sub sequent runs in their native land than when first released.

As economic stability began to return to Italy, the Italian producers began to consolidate their gains. In Cinecittà, just outside Rome, they had not only the largest and best equipped studios in all Europe but also, at the film school there, a well-trained corps of artists and technicians to draw upon. Furthermore, the new government took a healthy interest in film production, recognizing its value as a source both of good-will and of revenue for the country. Outstanding pictures were rewarded with special tax rebates. As an additional aid to the home industry, acting on a plan put forward by the Italian producers themselves, the government permitted the American studios to take out of the country a portion of their war-frozen dollars provided that some of this money were allocated to the development of a market in the United States for Italian pictures. In 1950 the American producers agreed—and found themselves in the unprecedented position of actively encouraging the growth of a rival industry in their own country. Except for the British, no nation has ever before made such a concerted effort to break into the American market. To overcome the resistance of the average moviegoer to subtitled foreign films, they even set up their own dubbing studios in New York, matching the voices of Broadway actors to the lips of the Italian performers. Today, Italian pictures travel far beyond the art-house circuit, with frequent bookings in the profitable drive-ins and neighborhood theaters.

Indeed, the Italians have become so terribly anxious for wide box-office approval that, within the past few years, the original tenets of neorealism have been increasingly distorted. *Bitter Rice* (1949), for example, begins as a tale of migratory rice workers in northern Italy, but soon degenerates into a sordid melodrama of rape and violence. Both *Rome, 11 o'Clock* (1952) and *Three Forbidden Stories* (1953) tastelessly exploit an actual tragedy that shocked all Italy. Over two hundred girls had turned up at an office in response to an ad for a single position, thronging the stairs to await their turn. When the stairs gave way, scores were killed or injured. In *Rome, 11 o'Clock*, this incident is recreated and then, flash-back fashion, the film goes into the lives of several of the victims—a girl who had left home to live with an artist, a prostitute who wants to go straight, a girl disillusioned about finding a glamor job in radio, a shy girl in search of her first position. In *Three Forbidden Stories* the treatment is even more frankly sensational. One of its heroines is a lesbian, another a dope addict.

Most of the recent "realistic" films from Italy have had their origin in similar incidents, in real-life stories gleaned from the newspapers. All too often, however, the stories built out from these backgrounds have been an exploitation rather than a revelation of their themes. True, reality has not been prettied up in these films, as is so often the case with our own American pictures. On the contrary, there seems to be a concentrated effort to make everything as grim as possible—"this is the way things are"—but with increasing emphasis on such marketable aspects of reality as sex and sadism. And in place of the earthy, hearty Anna Magnani, the Italian screen now abounds in cover girls like Gina Lollobrigida, Silvana Mangano, Silvana Pampanini, Sophia Loren, and Eleanora Rossi-Drago—sleek, well-developed creatures, delightful to look at, but scarcely ideal as the heroines of neorealistic dramas. In fact, as so often happens, the word itself has become little more than a catch-phrase today. The Italian cinema may continue to advertise its neorealism, but what we have been seeing of late is largely a series of melodramatic shockers photographed against natural exteriors.

In the meantime, several neo-neorealisms have emerged that hold new promise for the Italian screen—if the producers have the courage to follow them up. All of them are based firmly in the everyday life of ordinary Italians and motivated by a sympathy and affection for the common man. But a new dimension has been added, a new element of comedy, fantasy, even poetry. We can see now that De Sica's strange, fanciful *Miracle in Milan* (1951), with its hoboes soaring on broomsticks high above Milan's cathedral, was in fact the point of departure for this whole new genre. Renato Castellani's *Two Cents' Worth of Hope* (1952) and Luigi Comencini's *Bread, Love and Dreams* (1953), for example, created a fine sense of the reality of small-town life in the Italian hills, then used this as the background for broad comedy that also veered off into fantasy. Federico Fellini's *La Strada* (1954), a somber, tragic study of an itinerant sideshow strong man and a simple-minded girl clown, explored a new blending of realism and poetry, a heightening of emotion through skillfully stylized performances juxtaposed against natural backgrounds. *Love in the City* (1954), a project conceived and organized by Cesare Zavattini and directed by half a dozen youthful enthusiasts, also seems to mark a new direction. Here the emphasis is returned again to documentary realism, with people re-enacting their own tragedies or speaking urgently of their lives and problems directly in front of the cameras and microphones. But by skillful use of the camera, by dubbing and editing, Zavattini has transformed simple documentation into genuinely artistic creation.

Here is fresh ore for the Italian film, new directions to be explored and developed with all the passion and enthusiasm that marked the renaissance of the Italian film industry ten years ago. It is evident that the directors still have abundant vitality to tackle new themes and to work in new styles. The question now seems to be, will the Italian producers, obsessed with dreams of conquering the international market, permit them to do so? Will they be allowed to follow the lines sketched in by De Sica, Fellini, Castellani, Comencini, Antonioni, and Zavattini? Or must they dissipate their talents on sordid studies of passionate drug addicts and frustrated telephone girls? Such pictures, sold not on their artistry but on their sensationalism, can only result in the eventual suffocation of first the art, and then the industry itself. For it is the artists in film—the directors and the writers—who tap the new and occasionally profitable veins of cinematic ore. The odd thing about movies is that once the industrial side moves in and begins to commercialize the operation, the outcome is frequently disappointing to the audiences, to the artists, and ultimately to the producers themselves.

284

Part Three

The
Creative
Present
(1950
to present)

LAST YEAR AT
MARIENBAD
(1961)
DIRECTED BY
ALAIN RESNAIS

Introduction

New Realities, New Visions

Beginning in the early Fifties and continuing to the present, the art of the movies experienced a creative upsurge on an international scale that has resulted in some of the finest films in screen history. Only once before, in the years 1920 to 1930, has there been an artistic rise of such magnitude. The dazzling productions from Germany, France, and Russia during the close of the silent film era are being paralleled today—some fifty years later—in the creative dynamism of a new post-World War II generation of film makers, again centered in Europe, with smaller outposts of creativity in the Far East and the United States. Like the earlier artistic movement, the present one has captured the attention of the world by the production of movies of distinctive originality with fresh viewpoints and significant themes. The resulting creative ferment has propelled the motion picture into the forefront of international art, elevating it to a central and dominant position in contemporary culture.

This new artistic thrust is distinguished by the work of discerning, uniquely gifted directors, men who have a great awareness of human complexity as well as great intensity and feeling for their medium. Their work moves us through the refined dynamics of an art whose criteria of excellence have been gained from a study of the classics of cinema and of the giants of the past. Akira Kurosawa, Ingmar Bergman, Michelangelo Antonioni, Alain Resnais, Federico Fellini, Jean-Luc Godard, Roman Polanski, and François Truffaut in the fifties and sixties, and Luis Buñuel, Robert Bresson, Yasujiro Ozu, Miklós Jancsó, Dušan Makavejev and Rainer Werner Fassbinder in the sixties and seventies, share, in varying degrees, the distinctive characteristics of directors who impose themselves strongly on their material and make a statement that is both personal and universal.

These directors I have mentioned are obsessed with movies and regard film making not as a corporate process, but as an individual creative act, an artistic engagement between man and medium. They demand from movies the same intellectual and esthetic level which is expected from artists in other media. And like those other craftsmen, these movie makers are passionately self-conscious, their work the embodied idea of one individual who coordinates, controls, and shapes the film from its very conception. Their greater autonomy and creative control manifests itself in an intransigent individualism and in the ability to put a distinctive signature on whatever pictures they make. Their art is not the work of a single school, but rather that of a broadly-based movement. A wide range of styles is caused by the play of very different minds, engaged in the medium at its deepest and richest level.

For this group of film makers, there are no "forbidden" subjects and no proscribed themes. Part of the broad cultural upheaval of an era that has recognized the changed condition of man in contemporary society, these men are exploring arresting new areas of subject matter. The celebration of man as the idealized hero-figure of an earlier, more stable society has been swept away and replaced by an image of man as the anxiety-ridden victim, confronting a life that seems to have lost its coherence in a world both confusing and uncertain. The assumptions and conventions of codified dramatic problems, and the surface exploration of political and social issues, with their clear-cut answers, no longer seem valid in a world threatened by the big bomb, the cold war, and other factors which help break down humanistic values and impose a sense of crisis in modern life.

The delineation of this human predicament is the dominant interest of Bergman, Antonioni, Resnais, Fellini, Buñuel and Fassbinder, all more or less united in their insistence on dramatizing the individual's alienation from society and retreat into self. The focus of such films as *Wild Strawberries, Silence, Persona, L'Avventura, La Notte, Hiroshima Mon Amour, Last Year at Marienbad, 8½, Juliet of the Spirits, Viridiana, Tristana, Ali: Fear Eats the Soul,* and *The Merchant of Four Seasons* is not on neat problem situations, codes of conduct, or social evils, but on individuals as prisoners of their own private consciousness attempting to live on an immense emotional plane, detached from significant social activity.

This cinematic depiction of consciousness represents a fundamental break with traditional subject matter. The new material, not necessarily better, is more complex, is new, and lends itself to an abundant and vibrant dramatic reality. In the attempt to bring out in sharp relief the soul of man as distinct from the physical part, in the effort to strip away the layers of man's metaphysical nature, plot and action are reduced to a minimum, feelings and fancies, desires, frustrations, intimations, visions, and insights are intensively scrutinized. The outward behavior of characters is deliberately minimized in order to probe the emotional currents and psychic flow. The interplay of mind, memory and emotions is emphasized to make visible the unconscious, the half-conscious, underlying the conscious. To clarify the inchoate and reveal aspects of non-verbalized reflections, the minutiae of man's fragmented thoughts are re-integrated. To objectify suppressed desires and wish fulfillments, use is made of symbols, of inner monologue, of details linked by free association. Memories start up, evoked in contexts that join the past and present, either through contrast or similarity. Things unsaid, expressed in evasion or the attempt to keep the secrets of self private are made evident in meaningful silences and unspoken exchanges between lovers, friends and even strangers.

In breaking with the old subject matter, the new directors also departed radically from the familiar story patterns and techniques of the past. The order of the narrative film of dramatic events, with its formal clash, climax and resolution, celebrated since *The Great Train Robbery*, was replaced by a freer form that achieved effects of unpredictability and improvisation in its use of symbols, ideas, and associations. In these films the interest and suspense are aroused and maintained not through the construction of a dramatic plot, but through a strict control and arrangement of images expressing the discontinuity of the psychic processes. Startling effects, associations, juxtapositions, the interior monologue and effective silences are all used to establish objective correlates for the emotions of characters and to dramatize something beyond the stated and defined.

Antonioni and Ozu, in films that at first glance appear to be naturalistic, probe the barrenness of human relations and family life. While showing their characters discovering, or failing to discover, their alienation or loneliness, they create scenes out of essentially sensory images of filial love and solitude. Antonioni, using the industrial environment and the ritual objects of modern society, builds his scenes into cinematic

288

patterns that resemble prose poems in their concentrated ambiguity. On the other hand, Ozu, concerned with family experience, saturates his films with a heightened sense of objective reality and precise character delineation. With no interest in plot or dramatic emphasis, Ozu brings together the humiliations, frustrations, and guilt of parent-child relationships with fastidious nuances of sensibility. Using a narrow range of technical resources in a way that seems almost an absence of style, he employs subtly controlled compositions, habitually shot from the low angle of a person sitting. His meticulous selection of details to comment on the personality of his characters, his static camera holding the leisurely spacing of movements and silences, mark an exquisite restraint of personality reflecting his own deep feelings about the steady fragmentation of Japanese homelife.

Ingmar Bergman, in a highly stylized and different way, is passionately preoccupied with the deeply personal and meta physical problems of people who find it difficult to meet the rigid conditions of life. Depicting lives charged with frustrations and obsessions, using techniques of confession and memory, he has created a highly symbolic vocabulary. The charged intensity and rhythmic continuum of his imagery admits a formal complexity similar to that found in certain "confessional" poets.

Alain Resnais' major thesis is the necessity and impossibility of terminating a past marked by traumatic memories in order to establish a meaningful rapport with the world outside self. He uses a kind of stream of consciousness technique such as figured actively in the work of James Joyce, Virginia Woolf and William Faulkner. Though the technique is different (more grandiloquently evident), a similar approach can be found in the later films of Federico Fellini, who seeks to present the pathos of erotic frustration and the longing for identity in people afraid to face the consequences of a true emotional relationship.

For Luis Buñuel most films "glory in an intellectual vacuum." A nonconformist who has never abandoned his surrealist vision for mocking humor, he uses his works to rail against the moral, judicial, religious and political values of a middle-class world. While there is no particular technique in his films that can be described as "directorial touches" or principles of cinematic style that can be called "esthetic," the real fascination of the work of this social rebel are revelations of social attitudes and political nuances that fall into place as if instinctive.

Miklós Jancsó, the most celebrated of Hungarian directors, is also one of the most original stylists in contemporary film. His films, which concern themselves with conflicts of Hungarian political affairs after World War II, eschew the traditional naturalistic approach and narrative techniques of film construction, utilizing instead a method that is highly choreographic in design and ritualistic in structure. Foregoing the conventional shot-scene-sequence method of shooting and editing, his camera is in continuous motion—flowing, rising, falling, turning—in precise, balletlike patterns of immensely long "takes" (sometimes as long as ten minutes), which are interwoven with the patterned mise-en-scène of the performers. The effect is that of an elegant ritualized spectacle.

The most striking director to emerge in recent years is the West German, Rainer Werner Fassbinder. Still in his early thirties, he has already made more films than many directors do in a lifetime. Taken together, his pictures are among the most exciting made by any contemporary filmmaker. Focusing on themes that reveal the dark side of postwar Germany, his movies depict alienated characters mainly from the lower levels of society. Because his people are morally weak or otherwise incapable of dealing with the day-to-day realities of living, and because of society's prejudices, relationships between characters in the films inevitably fall apart. Fassbinder's urge to strip away pretension and his uncommon insights into motives and behavior generate observations that are knife-edged, bitter, remorseless. The result is a penetrating criticism of bourgeois society, undeniably irritating but completely alive, embodied in an idiosyncratic ambience that is both brilliant and powerful.

Each of these directors has sought a unique form and style in which to objectify the complexity of his ideas, feelings and impressions. Their films present individual minds wracked by modern life, a life characterized by instability and by the breakdown of human communication.

There are, of course, other vital forces at work in the films of these men. In their drive for sharply fresh and organically alive motion pictures, this new breed of film makers, genuinely concerned with, and even oppressed by, the moral values of their age, objectifies the consciousness of men and women today with a frankness, candor and artistic distinction seldom attempted or achieved before in motion pictures. Their challenges, liberations and insights have extended the range and boundaries of movie art and transformed chaos into something comprehensible and deeply revealing.

With the thrust of present creative energies still on the rise, with genuine film artists of every variety receiving ever-widening recognition, and at a time when experimentation in technique and subject matter seems more rampant than ever before in screen history, film art displays extraordinary presence and has great contemporary significance.—*L.J.*

1. JULES AND JIM
   (1961)
   DIRECTED BY
   FRANCOIS TRUFFAUT

2. RASHOMON
   (1950)
   DIRECTED BY
   AKIRA KUROSAWA

3. HIROSHIMA, MON AMOUR
   (1959)
   DIRECTED BY
   ALAIN RESNAIS

4. L'AVVENTURA
   (1959)
   DIRECTED BY
   MICHELANGELO
   ANTONIONI

5. 8½
   (1963)
   DIRECTED BY
   FEDERICO FELLINI

6. BEFORE THE REVOLUTION
   (1964)
   DIRECTED BY
   B. BERTOLUCCI

1.

2.

3.

4.

6.

5.

7.

8.

9.

10.

11.

12.

LA NOTTE 7.
(1960)
DIRECTED BY
MICHELANGELO
ANTONIONI

WILD STRAWBERRIES 8.
(1957)
DIRECTED BY
INGMAR BERGMAN

THE SILENCE 9.
(1962)
DIRECTED BY
INGMAR BERGMAN

ALPHAVILLE 10.
(1965)
DIRECTED BY
JEAN-LUC GODARD

GOODBYE IN THE 11.
MIRROR
(1964)
DIRECTED BY
STORM DE HIRSCH

JULIET OF THE SPIRITS 12.
(1964)
DIRECTED BY
FEDERICO FELLINI

13. HEAVEN AND
    EARTH MAGIC
    (1962)
    DIRECTED BY
    HARRY SMITH

14. GUNS OF THE TREES
    (1963)
    DIRECTED BY
    JONAS MEKAS

15. THE CHAIR
    (1963)
    DIRECTED BY
    RICHARD LEACOCK

16. SINS OF
    THE FLESHAPOIDS
    (1965)
    DIRECTED BY
    MIKE KUCHAR

17. CHELSEA GIRLS
    (1966)
    DIRECTED BY
    ANDY WARHOL

18. ANATOMY OF A MURDER
    (1959)
    TITLES BY
    SAUL BASS

13.

14.

15.

16.

17.

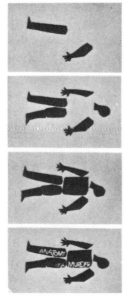

18.

19.

20.

21.

22.

23.

24.

AN AUTUMN AFTERNOON 19.
(1962)
DIRECTED BY
YASUJIRO OZU

RETURN OF 20.
THE PRODIGAL SON
(1966)
DIRECTED BY
JÁN KADÁR

WR: MYSTERIES OF 21.
THE ORGANISM
(1971)
DIRECTED BY
DUŠAN MAKAVEJEV

FOUR NIGHTS 22.
OF A DREAMER
(1971)
DIRECTED BY
ROBERT BRESSON

CHINESE ROULETTE 23.
(1976)
DIRECTED BY
RAINER WERNER
FASSBINDER
(NEW YORKER FILMS)

THAT OBSCURE OBJECT 24.
OF DESIRE
(1977)
DIRECTED BY
LUIS BUÑUEL

THE RED AND THE WHITE 25.
(1969)
DIRECTED BY
MIKLÓS JANCSÓ

25.

Why I Make Movies
by Ingmar Bergman

This chapter by the distinguished Swedish director appeared originally in the September 1960 issue of Horizon.

During the shooting of *The Virgin Spring,* we were up in the northern province of Dalarna in May and it was early one morning, about half past seven. The landscape there is rugged, and our company was working beside a little lake in the forest. It was very cold, about 30 degrees, and from time to time a few snowflakes fell through the gray, rain-dimmed sky. The company was dressed in a strange variety of clothing—raincoats, oil slickers, Icelandic sweaters, leather jackets, old blankets, coachmen's coats, medieval robes. Our men had laid some ninety feet of rusty buckling rail over the difficult terrain, to dolly the camera on. We were all helping with the equipment— actors, electricians, make-up men, script girl, sound crew— mainly to keep warm. Suddenly someone shouted and pointed toward the sky. Then we saw a crane high above the fir trees, and then another, and then several cranes, floating majestically in a circle above us. We all dropped what we were doing and ran to the top of a nearby hill to see the cranes better. We stood there for a long time, until they turned westward and disappeared over the forest. And suddenly I thought: this is what it means to make a movie in Sweden. This is what can happen, this is how we work together with our old equipment and little money, and this is how we can suddenly drop everything for the love of four cranes floating above the treetops.

My association with film goes back to the world of childhood. My grandmother had a very large old apartment in Uppsala. I used to sit under the dining-room table there, "listening" to the sunshine that came in through the gigantic window. The bells of the cathedral went ding-dong, and the sunlight moved about and "sounded" in a special way. One day, when winter was giving way to spring and I was five years old, a piano was being played in the next apartment. It played waltzes, nothing but waltzes. On the wall hung a large picture of Venice. As the sunlight moved across the picture, the water in the canal began to flow, the pigeons flew up from the square, gesticulating people were engaged in inaudible conversation. Bells sounded, not from Uppsala Cathedral, but from the picture itself. And the piano music also came from that remarkable picture of Venice.

A child who is born and brought up in a vicarage acquires an early familiarity with life and death behind the scenes. Father performed funerals, marriages, baptisms; he gave advice and prepared sermons. The Devil was an early acquaintance, and in the child's mind there was a need to personify him. This is where my magic lantern came in. It consisted of a small metal box with a carbide lamp—I can still remember the smell of the hot metal—and colored glass slides: Red Riding Hood and the Wolf, and all the others. The Wolf was the Devil, without horns but with a tail and a red mouth, strangely real yet incomprehensible, a picture of wickedness and temptation on the flowered wall of the nursery.

When I was ten years old I received my first, rattling film projector, with its chimney and lamp. I found it both mystifying and fascinating. The first film I had was nine feet long and brown in color. It showed a girl, lying asleep in a meadow, who woke up and stretched out her arms, then disappeared to the right. That was all there was to it. The film was a great success and was projected every night until it broke and could not be mended any more.

This little rickety machine was my first conjuring set. And even today I remind myself with childish excitement that, since cinematography is based on deception of the human eye, I really am a conjurer. I have worked it out that if I see a film with a running-time of one hour, I sit through twenty-seven minutes of complete darkness—the blankness between frames. When I show a film, I am guilty of deceit. I use an apparatus which is constructed to take advantage of a certain human weakness, an apparatus with which I can sway my audience in a highly emotional manner—make them laugh, scream with fright, smile, believe in fairy stories, become indignant, feel shocked, charmed, deeply moved, or perhaps yawn with boredom. Thus I am either an impostor or, where the audience is willing to be taken in, a conjurer. I perform conjuring tricks with apparatus so expensive and so wonderful that any performer in history would have given anything to own or to make use of it.

A film for me begins with something very vague—a chance

remark or a bit of conversation, a hazy but agreeable event unrelated to any particular situation. It can be a few bars of music, a shaft of light across the street. Sometimes in my work at the theater I have envisioned actors made up for yet unplayed roles.

These are split-second impressions that disappear as quickly as they come, yet leave behind a mood—like pleasant dreams. It is a mental state, not an actual story, but one abounding in fertile associations and images. Most of all, it is a brightly colored thread sticking out of the dark sack of the unconscious. If I begin to wind up this thread, and do so carefully, a complete film will emerge.

This primitive nucleus strives to achieve definite form, moving in a way that may be lazy and half-asleep at first. Its stirring is accompanied by vibrations and rhythms that are very special, and unique to each film. The picture sequences then assume a pattern in accordance with these rhythms, obeying laws born out of and conditioned by my original stimulus.

If that embryonic substance seems to have enough strength to be made into a film, I decide to materialize it. Then comes something very complicated and difficult: the transformation of rhythms, moods, atmosphere, tensions, sequences, tones, and scents into words and sentences, into an understandable screenplay.

This is an almost impossible task.

The only thing that can be satisfactorily transferred from that original complex of rhythms and moods is the dialogue, and even dialogue is a sensitive substance which may offer resistance. Written dialogue is like a musical score, almost incomprehensible to the average person. Its interpretation demands a technical knack plus a certain kind of imagination and feeling—qualities which are often lacking even among actors. One can write dialogue, but how it should be delivered, its rhythm and tempo, what is to take place between the lines— all this must be omitted for practical reasons. A script with that much detail would be unreadable. I try to squeeze instructions as to location, characterization, and atmosphere into my screenplays in understandable terms, but the success of this depends on my writing ability and the perceptiveness of the reader, which are not predictable.

Now we come to essentials, by which I mean montage,

rhythm, and the relation of one picture to another: the vital third dimension without which the film is merely a dead product from a factory. Here I cannot clearly give a key, as in a musical score, or a specific idea of the tempo which determines the relationship of the elements involved. It is quite impossible for me to indicate the way in which the film "breathes" and pulsates.

I have often wished for a kind of notation which would enable me to put on paper all the shades and tones of my vision, to record distinctly the inner structure of a film. For when I stand in the artistically devastating atmosphere of the studio, my hands and head full of all the trivial and irritating details that go with motion-picture production, it often takes a tremendous effort to remember how I originally saw and thought out this or that sequence, or what the relation was between the scene of four weeks ago and that of today. If I could express myself clearly, in explicit symbols, then the irrational factors in my work would be almost eliminated, and I could work with absolute confidence that whenever I liked I could prove the relationship between the part and the whole and put my finger on the rhythm, the continuity of the film.

Thus the script is a very imperfect *technical* basis for a film. And there is another important point which I should like to mention in this connection. Film has nothing to do with literature; the character and substance of the two art forms are usually in conflict. This probably has something to do with the receptive process of the mind. The written word is read and assimilated by a conscious act of the will in alliance with the intellect; little by little it affects the imagination and the emotions. The process is different with a motion picture. When we experience a film, we consciously prime ourselves for illusion: putting aside will and intellect, we make way for it in our imagination. The sequence of images plays directly on our feelings without touching on the intellect.

Music works in the same fashion; I would say that there is no art form that has as much in common with film as music. Both affect our emotions directly, not by way of the intellect. And film is mainly rhythm; it is inhalation and exhalation in continuous sequence. Ever since childhood, music has been my greatest source of recreation and stimulation, and I often experience a film or play musically.

It is mainly because of this difference between film and literature that we should avoid making films out of books. The irrational dimension of a literary work, the germ of its existence, is often untranslatable into visual terms—and it, in turn, destroys the special, irrational dimension of the film. If, despite this, we wish to translate something literary into film terms, we must make an infinite number of complicated adjustments which often bear little or no fruit in proportion to the effort expended.

I myself have never had any ambition to be an author. I do not want to write novels, short stories, essays, biographies, or even plays for the theater. I only want to make films—films about conditions, tensions, pictures, rhythms, and characters that are in one way or another important to me. The motion picture and its complicated process of birth are my methods of saying what I want to my fellow men. I am a film maker, not an author.

Thus the writing of the script is a difficult period but a useful one, for it compels me to prove logically the validity of my ideas. In doing this, I am caught in a conflict—a conflict between my need to transmit a complicated situation through visual images and my desire for absolute clarity. I do not intend my work to be solely for the benefit of myself or the few but for the entertainment of the general public. The wishes of the public are imperative. But sometimes I risk following my own impulse, and it has been shown that the public can respond with surprising sensitivity to the most unconventional line of development.

When shooting begins, the most important thing is that those who work with me feel a definite contact, that all of us somehow cancel out our conflicts through working together. We must pull in one direction for the sake of the work at hand. Sometimes this leads to dispute, but the more definite and clear the "marching orders," the easier it is to reach the goal which has been set. This is the basis of my conduct as director, and perhaps the explanation for much of the nonsense that has been written about me.

While I cannot let myself be concerned with what people think and say about me personally, I believe that reviewers and critics have every right to interpret my films as they like. I refuse to interpret my work to others, and I cannot tell the critic what to think; each person has the right to understand a film as he sees it. Either he is attracted or repelled. A film is made to create reaction. If the audience does not react one way or another, it is an indifferent work and worthless.

I do not mean by this that I believe in being "different" at any price. A lot has been said about the value of originality, and I find it foolish; either you are original or you are not. It is completely natural for artists to take from and give to each other, to borrow from and experience one another. In my own life, my great literary experience was Strindberg. There are works of his which can still make my hair stand on end—"The People of Hemsö," for example. And it is my dream to produce his "Dream Play" someday. Olof Molander's production of it in 1934 was for me a fundamental dramatic experience.

On a personal level, there are many people who have meant a great deal to me. My father and mother were certainly of vital importance, not only in themselves but because they created a world for me to revolt against. In my family there was an atmosphere of hearty wholesomeness which I, a sensitive young plant, scorned and rebelled against. But that strict middle-class home gave me a wall to pound on, something to sharpen myself against. At the same time my family taught me a number of values—efficiency, punctuality, a sense of financial responsibility—which may be "bourgeois" but are nevertheless important to the artist. They are part of the process of setting oneself severe standards. Today as a film maker I am conscientious, hard-working, and extremely careful; my films involve good craftsmanship, and my pride is the pride of a good craftsman.

Among the people who have meant something in my professional development is Torsten Hammaren of Göteborg. I came there from Hälsingborg, where I had been head of the municipal theater for two years. I had no conception of what theater was; Hammaren taught me during the four years I stayed in Göteborg. Then, when I wrote my first screenplay, *Torment*, Alf Sjöberg, who directed it, taught me a great deal, as did Lorens Marmstedt after I had directed my first (unsuccessful) movie. Among other things, I learned from Marmstedt the one unbreakable rule: you must look at your own work very coldly and clearly; you must be a devil to yourself in the screening room when watching the day's rushes. Then there is Herbert Grevenius, one of the few who believed in me as a writer. I had trouble with script writing and was reaching out more and more to the drama, to dialogue, as a means of expression. He gave me great encouragement.

Finally, there is Carl Anders Dymling, my producer. He is crazy enough to place more faith in the creative artist's sense of responsibility than in calculations of profit and loss. I am thus able to work with an integrity that has become the very air I breathe—one of the main reasons I do not want to work outside of Sweden. The moment I lose this freedom I will cease to be a film maker, because I have no skill in the art of compromise. My only significance in the world of film lies in the freedom of my creativity.

Today, the ambitious film maker is obliged to walk a tightrope without a net. He may be a conjurer, but no one conjures the producer, the bank director, or the theater owners when the public refuses to go to see a film and lay down the money by which producer, bank director, theater owner, and conjurer live. The conjurer may then be deprived of his magic wand. I would like to be able to measure the amount of talent, initiative, and creative ability that has been destroyed by the film industry in its ruthlessly efficient sausage-machine. What was play to me once has now become a struggle. Failure, criticism, public indifference all hurt more today than yesterday. The brutality of the industry is unmasked—yet that can be an advantage.

So much for people and the film business. I have been asked, as a clergyman's son, about the role of religion in my thinking and film making. To me, religious problems are continuously alive. I never cease to concern myself with them, and my concern goes on every hour of every day. Yet it does not take place on the emotional level but on an intellectual one. Religious emotion, religious sentimentality, is something I got rid of long ago—I hope. The religious problem is an intellectual one to me: the problem of my mind in relation to my intuition. The result is usually some kind of tower of Babel.

Philosophically, there is a book which was a tremendous experience for me: Eino Kaila's "Psychology of the Personality." His thesis that man lives strictly according to his needs —negative and positive—was shattering to me, but terribly true. And I built on this ground.

People ask what are my intentions with my films—my aims. It is a difficult and dangerous question, and I usually give an evasive answer: I try to tell the truth about the human condition, the truth as I see it. This answer seems to satisfy everyone, but it is not quite correct. I prefer to describe what I would *like* my aim to be.

There is an old story of how the Cathedral of Chartres was struck by lightning and burned to the ground. Then thousands of people came from all points of the compass, like a giant procession of ants, and together they began to rebuild the cathedral on its old site. They worked until the building was completed—master builders, artists, laborers, clowns, noblemen, priests, burghers. But they all remained anonymous, and no one knows to this day who rebuilt the Cathedral of Chartres.

Regardless of my own beliefs and my own doubts, which are unimportant in this connection, it is my opinion that art lost its basic creative drive the moment it was separated from worship. It severed an umbilical cord and now lives its own sterile life, generating and degenerating itself. In former days the artist remained unknown and his work was to the glory of God. He lived and died without being more or less important than other artisans; "eternal values," "immortality," and "masterpiece" were terms not applicable to his case. The ability to create was a gift. In such a world flourished invulnerable assurance and natural humility.

Today the individual has become the highest form, and the greatest bane, of artistic creation. The smallest wound or pain of the ego is examined under a microscope as if it were of eternal importance. The artist considers his isolation, his subjectivity, his individualism almost holy. Thus we finally gather in one large pen, where we stand and bleat about our loneliness without listening to each other and without realizing that we are smothering each other to death. The individualists stare into each other's eyes and yet deny each other's existence. We walk in circles, so limited by our own anxieties that we can no longer distinguish between true and false, between the gangster's whim and the purest ideal.

Thus if I am asked what I would *like* the general purpose of my films to be, I would reply that I want to be one of the artists in the cathedral on the great plain. I want to make a dragon's head, an angel, a devil—or perhaps a saint—out of stone. It does not matter which; it is the sense of satisfaction that counts. Regardless of whether I believe or not, whether I am a Christian or not, I would play my part in the collective building of the cathedral.

The Literary Sophistication
of Francois Truffaut
by Michael Klein

*Mr. Klein is a young film maker from the University of
California at Berkeley. This chapter appeared
originally in the Summer 1965 issue of Film Comment.*

Truffaut is not literate merely because his films contain allusions to Renoir, Walsh, Vigo, and Hitchcock, although they are the sources of the film conventions he manipulates, nor because *Jules and Jim* contains references to Shakespeare, Goethe, "Don Quixote," Mozart, Picasso, and Baudelaire. Truffaut's literary sophistication is a matter of technique and sensibility.

Because most films deal with people and situations and tell some sort of story, directors cope with problems that dramatists and novelists face; often they solve them in a way akin to that of their literary counterparts. Resnais in *Last Year at Marienbad* and Dreyer in *Vampyr*, for example, maintain a unity of tone that would have pleased Poe. Antonioni probes small incidents and paces his exploration like Henry James.

I would like to focus upon two techniques, interesting in themselves, which help us to grasp the meanings of Truffaut's *Shoot the Piano Player* and *Jules and Jim*. The first technique, used in the modern novel and in continental drama, is the technique of dislocation. The second technique, irony, is basic to all forms of literature. Because I am using these terms in a special sense, especially "dislocation," I will discuss them before illustrating how they work in Truffaut's films.

Dislocation, like Brecht's alienation, is an effect; it is experienced by the audience or reader because it is potential in the art object. When the spectator is alienated, he is distanced from a play or film or story, so that he may respond with the creative intellect. The artist, in employing the technique of dislocation, attempts to prevent this, because he fears his audience will think in conventional patterns. He may fragment the narrative, use an unreliable narrator, distort space, alter the temporal sequence, etc., to this rhetorical end. The dislocated reader or viewer, confused by distortions in the narrative, has to accept the author's view to make sense out of the material.

Truffaut expresses concern, in his interviews, about audience reaction to his films. Like him, playwrights as diverse as Brecht, Genet, and Pirandello have devised new techniques to overcome the difficult problem of communication with an audience. An *avant-garde* dramatist often assumes that audiences come to a play with a set of commonplace expectations and prejudices that block their relating to the work of art. The artist intends to put his audience in touch with themselves and with the world; that is to say, he wishes to prod and to stimulate by imposing his vision of the world upon their minds and sensibilities. Unfortunately, traditional means of presentation often do not suffice, and the audience has to be lured, tricked, and seduced.

Often this involving of an audience consists of careful manipulation of literary conventions, which are traditional ways of looking at life. This occurs whenever a new literary genre is being created. For example, an eighteenth century reader of Defoe's "Robinson Crusoe," as Virginia Woolf has pointed out, expected an exotic romance and instead was baffled into accepting an island on which life is a series of tasks. On the other hand, film makers like Hawks, Truffaut, and Godard, instead of beginning with a new stylization of life, use old conventions and manipulate the audience's stock responses to achieve their ends. In this their films share a characteristic of twentieth century literature.

For example, seeing Brecht's "The Good Woman of Setzuan," we quickly identify with Shen Te. Like us, she is altruistic and generous; like us, she has a fatalistic attitude toward the privations and social injustices of life. She is good and so, like us, believes that individual acts of charity will remedy social problems. Therefore, when she becomes a shop owner, she devotes herself to helping others. Then, after we are trapped, after we have identified smugly with Shen Te, Brecht has her step in front of the curtain and sing revolutionary anti-capitalist songs.

In modern fiction—for example, in Conrad's "Heart of Darkness"—dislocation is achieved in a more formalist way, through time shifts, changes in the narrative point of view, and by the use of the literary equivalent of montage—paratactic syntax. I can illustrate dislocation, and thus define the tradition in which Truffaut is working, by briefly looking at a shorter work by Joyce, who imposes his vision also by dislocating us in time and space. "Eveline" begins in the evening; the heroine is seated at her apartment window, in Dublin, waiting for her fiancé and thinking about her past. The narrative consists of memories and her judgment of past events. Toward the end, she thinks "Frank would take her in his arms, fold her in his arms. He would save her." And then, the following paragraph: "She stood among the swaying crowd in the station at the north wall. He held her hand. . . ." This seems to be a continuation of her reverie—she is thinking of how it will be when he comes for her. Only when events take a turn for the worse—the point of view (Joyce's) suddenly becomes distanced and objective—do we realize that this is an account of her failure to elope—she is now at the station, not dreaming but unable to act. She is paralyzed.

He rushed beyond the barrier and called to her to follow. He was shouted at to go on but he still called to her. She set her white face to him, passive, like a helpless animal. Her eyes gave him no sign of love or farewell or recognition.

The conclusion shocks us into a multiple recognition: of Joyce's trick; that Dubliners live in a dream when awake; of Eveline's awful failure; and of the sterility in Dublin life that has made her what she is.

Because reading is a temporal experience, our perception of a story can be viewed as a process. Prior to our recognition, we were confused by Joyce's shift of time and place. At some point between the paragraph that begins "she stood among the swaying crowd" and the concluding paragraph, we, the audience, are uncertain whether the events are taking place in the girl's mind or at the station. Baffled, dislocated, we are receptive to the particular solution that Joyce wishes to give us.

Another example of dislocation. Seeing Renoir's *Rules of the Game*, we relax and enjoy a good comedy. Renoir tells us in the credits that the film will be fun. We may sense implications, but they are not disturbing. We accept the film. The maid's husband is chasing her would-be lover with a gun, upsetting the crowded household. It is very funny. Suddenly, after the *dance macabre*, the gun is fired—a lamp is shattered in the foreground and the main characters become frightened. For a second it seems as if the host is shot. The film becomes serious.

But it is unexpected. We're stunned, and the film continues to develop before we can build up our conventional defenses against Renoir's vision.

This last example is similar to Truffaut's use of guns and knives in *Shoot the Piano Player*. But before illustrating this technique in relation to his films, I must briefly discuss irony.

In literature, irony may be achieved by subtle manipulation of language. Shakespeare's "Troilus and Cressida" begins with a speech by a Prologue who, in epic tones, fills in the background of the Trojan War. He speaks a highly formal latinate language; it is like Chapman's "Homer," which praised the war as a moral struggle. "In Troy there lies the scene. And the deep, drawing barks do there disgorge/their warlike fraughtage." However, if we examine the language carefully we discover that it undercuts itself. It is anti-heroic and critical of the war. "Disgorge" suggests vomit; later in the play the Greeks are often associated with disease. "Fraughtage" refers to cargo; later the Greeks are linked with commercial terms. They are not noble warriors. They are merchants out to ransack Troy for plunder and profit.

In the early books of "Paradise Lost" Milton uses a similar technique to ridicule Satan. Like Milton, many authors manipulate their audience in order to make a limited and specific critical statement. At worst, these techniques may serve authoritarian or propagandistic ends. However, they also can function to enlarge the audience's vision of life. In literary terms this is called creating ambiguity. Techniques are used to make the audience accept several meanings of an incident instead of to simplify experience; this is the spirit of plentitude, and is basic to Truffaut.

Perhaps one final example from the drama will be useful. Ionesco's "The Lesson" concludes with a "murder." The Professor stabs the Pupil with an invisible knife because she has a toothache. Up to then the situation has seemed comic. Now the violence of the act impels us to view it as a killing. "Aaah! That'll teach you!" (Striking the Pupil with a very spectacular blow of the knife.) But as the girl falls "her legs spread wide." "A noticeable convulsion shakes" the Professor and he says: "Bitch . . . Oh, that's good, that does me good." It is, as well, a rape.

Truffaut also uses techniques of dislocation and irony, often in the spirit of plenitude. In *Shoot the Piano Player* they tend to be ends in themselves. In *Jules and Jim* they are used to make us recognize the richness and complexity of the characters' lives and to view their experiences with tolerance.

Throughout *Shoot the Piano Player* Truffaut juxtaposes different conventions or genres in order to dislocate the audience. The film begins with a conventional gangster chase that quickly becomes slapstick. Yet at times it seems to be a serious psychological study of Charlie And during the flashback scene, it appears to be a conventional success-and-fall-of-the-performer film (complete with a shot of the concert pianist from in front of the footlights). At other times it seems to be a story about an honest, tough waitress's attempt to help a laconic, broken piano player. The film concludes in a slapstick gun battle, with a breathtaking Hitchcock form falling down a white hill, and with the killing of the waitress and with Charlie benumbed.

All of this makes us unable to decide what kind of a film *Shoot the Piano Player* is. We cease forcing it into our narrow system of classification and instead have to take it on its own terms. Truffaut's use of irony within conventions that are so radically juxtaposed also contributes to this end. Often irony makes us uncertain of how to react to even an isolated section of the film. However, it also guides us to respond in a sensitive way.

For example, consider the flashback scenes. It is a wonderful parody of the Horatio Alger success myth, plus Antonioni. A young boy, whose brothers are hoods, is sent to study with a famous pianist, is discovered by chance in a restaurant, and enjoys a spectacular rise to fame—concerts, interviews, more and more expensive cars. But he and his wife are bored and increasingly estranged. His wife confesses that she slept with the producer to get him discovered. The piano player makes a dramatic exit. She jumps out a window, and we see her corpse on the street.

It is an excellent parody of something that, with variations, has been done so many times. However, ironically, it isn't what we expected. The suicide gives us a jolt and we view the problems raised as serious. In short, Truffaut has rendered a cliché by parodying it. He has made us respond to a situation that, portrayed in a straightforward consistent manner, would have been dismissed easily.

The conclusion of the film works in a similar way. By ironically undercutting the gun battle and making it slapstick, Truffaut is able as well to render it as serious. The bad guys sniff their gun barrels and twirl the guns. They are perturbed and ridiculous. Lena is running. They shoot. Lena is dead. We see Charlie and her corpse in a brutal closeup.

The techniques work to make the film both extremely funny and extremely serious. Parody operates upon a dislocated audience to render meaningful a cinematic cliché. Charlie is not just the conventional Alger hero or the conventional laconic loner made funny. He is also a person to whom we respond with sympathy and horror. *Shoot the Piano Player* is both a gangster comedy and a study of a disillusioned man in a pre-schizoid state of withdrawal.

Truffaut's use of clichés is best studied in *Shoot the Piano Player*. A cliché is an overused convention. It is a symbol that no longer evokes powerful responses in audiences but still stands for something basic. Instead of creating new symbols for universal experiences, Truffaut works to resuscitate traditional signs.

However, the film ultimately is a magnificent exercise in technique, an astounding formalist *tour-de-force*, rather than a dramatic success. The techniques are used better, in a more integrated way, in *Jules and Jim*.

Techniques of dislocation are less obvious but equally effective in *Jules and Jim*. Consider, for example, Dwight Macdonald's response: "I was constantly being buffeted, shocked, puzzled and put off by what seemed to me perverse changes of mood." At times the film seems charming and idyllic. Other sections seem a probing study of love and friendship. Sometimes it appears to be sentimental. But then it becomes sharply satirical. The cremation scene is graphic and brutal. But the car plunge into the river is visual slapstick. Parts of the film are slowly paced and the frames look static. But in the early part of the film the characters are in motion and Truffaut's audacious cutting is sufficient itself to make the audience breathless—to disarm the audience.

While Truffaut buffets and dislocates the audience, he asserts that all these ways of looking at the story of Jules and Jim and Katherine are valid, that life is more complex than the categories with which we attempt to understand it. The form or technique of the film expresses the theme.

Let's see how this works at the conclusion of the film. Most of the scenes in the German chalet are directed in a straightforward manner. Suddenly the cutting becomes more erratic and genres are again mixed. Katherine brandishes a gun and Jim disarms her in detective film style. Albert re-appears—a whacky coincidence, too whacky for a "serious film." Katherine's and Jim's death is slapstick, but their cremation (hot bones and ashes) is sickeningly real. Jules, numb and grief-stricken, is leaving the cemetery. The narrator tells us that Jules feels relieved. The music is gay—a cliché Hollywood crescendo. These shifts in style and tone exhaust the audience's conventional responses.

Our view of Jules at the conclusion is most important because this is the focal point for our response to the whole film. Is Jules relieved or is he sad? Is he relieved *and* in grief? Our answer depends upon whether we are relieved or grieved or both, and this determines our view of Katherine. By making Jim's and Katherine's death slapstick, Truffaut prevents us from responding in a conventional, sentimental way (cry, don't think, quickly forget), which would have been a monstrous oversimplification. Because it is unexpected, the cremation scene makes an impact. We are shocked by "life," not by a serious film. But this is a visceral response. The gay music is then first heard as irritating and puzzling. The music is trite and inappropriate and we attempt to deny it. (It is like jumping on stage and interfering with the action, preventing a murder.) We became involved and respond from within the film. We experience grief and empathy. However, the music and the narrator cannot be completely ignored. As Jules begins to become distanced from his past experience, we also begin to become distanced from the film.

The beginning of the film is as crucial as the conclusion. In the opening scenes Truffaut uses irony to undercut, and it functions to enlarge our conception of life, not to make a specific statement of ridicule. The film is paced fast. The music is gay. Jules and Jim begin an idyllic friendship. Jules meets Katherine. She gets into a tramp outfit and all three go out for a romp. They race across a bridge. Katherine starts early and wins. Jules and Jim are laughing. At first we are charmed by the scenes, but we begin to feel that the music overstates a bit; it is slightly too gay for the action. The cutting is too abandoned, slightly hysteric. We become suspicious—it is a bit forced and overdone. Therefore we take a close look at the bridge scene. It seems significant that Katherine jumps the gun in order to win. We watch her face contort while she is running and mark her ecstatic cry of victory. Katherine must defeat Jules and Jim—she must exert power. She must cheat, and then run hard to beat them. And she knows they are unsuspecting. We are horrified; our expectation of innocence is destroyed. And yet the race isn't just a parable. The music is gay. Jules and Jim are happy. All three are having a good time. They look beautiful. And silly. The scene, then, is *both* an idyll and an ironic rendering of a cold psychological truth. It is *both* innocent and diabolic. Because we *suspect* the idyll, it becomes more important. We are charmed *and* we are horrified. In the same way—Katherine's leap into the river, a mad youthful funny impulse after a dull night at the theater, yet threatening.

The result is ambiguity and plenitude—maturity. We respond to life in the film in a complete way. First of all, we do not judge the characters as we would in life or in a conventional film. We do not wish to punish them. Truffaut admired Renoir's *Rules of the Game* because it was "the first psychological film in which the notion of a good and bad personage had been entirely eliminated." He has qualified his admiration for the gangster film by disliking its simple good/bad dichotomy and its cruel code of justice. His *The 400 Blows* is a protest against our concepts of crime and punishment. Truffaut uses all the techniques at his command to get us to see life as complete, to regard life with tolerance.

Katherine, then, is not just a demonic *uber-fraulein* (the term is Truffaut's)—a self-absorbed, insecure monster who forces people to serve her will. Nor is she merely a paragon of moral courage and a person of great charm who brings happiness and catalyzes a "beautiful relationship" (Truffaut again). She embodies *both* polar concepts, and all that is in between. Jules and Jim are not only silly romantics who overvalue Katherine, silly and repulsive herself, questing for a childhood idyll. They are not just mature, intelligent, sensitive men courageously acknowledging the problems of life and attempting to cope with them. They are both "types" and more.

312

Jules emerges as the most interesting character because of the role he plays in relation to the theme of tolerance. Slightly withdrawn, he is compassionate and accepts life as complex and responds to it on its own terms. Jules seldom judges Katherine but instead attempts to make the best of their lives. He is not vindictive; he instead attempts to arrange for Katherine's and Jim's happiness and to salvage a bit for himself.

Katherine, on the other hand, has a vindictive sense of justice. She keeps a bottle of vitriol for "lying eyes." She sleeps with a former lover to punish Jules, whose mother was rude to her, and to punish Jim for tarrying with Gilberte. She demands justice, simplicity, and a clean slate. But she believes that the ultimate judge is compassionate toward her. "She thinks that whatever she does, God will forgive her in advance."

Society, pre-1930, is viewed as tolerant. It nurtured Jules, Jim and Katherine and the "free life" before the war. In Germany, in the 1920's, people have a similar spirit of tolerance. The village people were startled by the *ménage à trois* and by their antics. "The village called them the three lunatics, *but* respected them." After Hitler, things change and significantly Truffaut shows us film clips of Nazi book burnings when Jules, Jim, and Katherine meet in a movie house after long separation.

In the novel Jules was Jewish. This would have complicated the movie. Truffaut's literary sophistication is evident in the way he adapted the social and political elements of Henri Pierre Roche's novel. Our stock responses to Jews and Naziism would have galloped roughshod over the delicate psychological balance of the film. Truffaut retained a sense of history but made it function within the film in relation to the tolerance theme and subordinate to the *ménage à trois* situation.

The progress of the characters' lives reflects the history of the times during the twenty-plus years of the film. Life is simple before the war, more complicated after the book-burnings. As we approach the time of the book burnings the *uber-fraulein* aspect of Katherine becomes stressed. Katherine brandishes a gun at Jim. She wears steel-rimmed glasses and begins to look "Germanic," especially when we see her immediately after the film-clips. Then follow suicide, immolation, cremation, and the graveyard scene. The cremation might suggest Nazi death-camps—willful Katherine is linked with fascism.

The symbols in *Jules and Jim* are handled with skill and subtlety; for example, Jules' and Katherine's child (Sabine) plays a game at the chalet. It is, first of all, a charming dance and romp. Soon Jim and Katherine appear—more antics. But the game is Sabine (a reflection of Katherine) whipping Jules and making him skip to her lash. It is a concise symbol of Jules' and Katherine's idyllic-demonic relationship.

Truffaut's symbols seldom force themselves upon the viewer. Katherine, who loves power, may be characterized as "Napoleonic." She briefly mentions Napoleon and in Katherine's room there was a photograph of Napoleon on the wall, out of focus and scarcely noticeable. In the chalet Katherine sings a little pop-song about love and missed kisses. It is a light moment. But the song—together we are caught up in life's whirlpool—sums up life in *Jules and Jim*.

And automobiles are obvious symbols of the new technology: a car first appears in *la guerre sociale* scene, while last is Jim's and Katherine's death car. Bicycles represent the old life. But cars are first of all cars, and Katherine's car functions as a device of characterization; it is an extension of one aspect of her personality. Curiously, it resembles a hearse, particularly when she drives it silently, ominously, around and around the little corner square in front of Jim's house.

Aside from the literary aspects of Truffaut's films, other factors are equally important: Truffaut's joy in the process of film making (the home movie spirit of his films); Coutard's photography (horizontal motion—the camera, dance rhythms within the frame). I have focused upon Truffaut's literary sophistication because, in addition to his good heart and a good eye, few film makers have his quality of mind.

In this article I have attempted to work from a critical approach that applies both to film and to the literary arts, and which may also be a guide to film makers. For insofar as an artist is able to structure and to manipulate, he succeeds in creating a work of art that will haunt his audience. That is the ultimate test of a film, play or novel.

A Movie Is a Movie Is a Movie Is a
by Andrew Sarris

Mr. Sarris is film critic for The Village Voice and editor-in-chief of the English edition of Cahiers du Cinema. He wrote "The Films of Josef von Sternberg" and edited the recently published "Interviews With Film Directors." This chapter appeared originally in The New York Film Bulletin, No. 46, 1964.

According to the latest unconfirmed reports, Jean-Luc Godard's latest film, *La Femme Mariée,* already entered in this year's Venice Film Festival, has been completely suppressed by the French Government. The problem is not so much the artful nudity, but the director's allegedly subversive attitude toward the modern French married woman. This is not Godard's first brush with the censors. In his first feature film, *Breathless,* Godard displeased Generalissimo De Gaulle by linking a shot of De Gaulle following Eisenhower on the streets of the Champs-Elysées to a shot of Jean-Paul Belmondo chasing Jean Seberg along the sidewalk. This mocking linkage was never seen by American audiences, but technically it was worthy of the Eisenstein of *October.* Only just try to imagine Eisenstein mocking Stalin instead of Kerensky, and you get some idea of Godard's audacity.

Godard's second film, *The Little Soldier,* described some of the intrigues of the Algerian War without resolving the issues. The story is told from the point of view of an uncommitted intellectual, who, in many ways, resembles Godard. The film was completely suppressed for two years. When you add provincial and international inhibitions over Godard's penchant for nudity, recurring controversies with other critics and film makers, and wildly varying reactions from audiences, Godard would seem to be eternally embattled, trapped between the steady cross-fire of his defenders and his detractors.

It is strange, however, that film makers who consider themselves far more *engagé* or committed than Godard never seem to have as much trouble with the authorities. The explanation is simple. Most left-wing directors, despite an occasional exception like Francesco Rosi, prefer to deal in universals rather than specifics. Their concern is Man in general, not men in particular. *The Bicycle Thief* is their model, and who would

315

dare call such an abstractly humanistic tract Communist or even Marxist in orientation. After all, we are all brothers, and every man should have his own bicycle. It would be difficult even for Franco to argue the contrary. The fact remains that Jean-Luc Godard is the only French director who has ever indicated on the screen that "Humanité" is a Communist paper read and published in Paris. Not only that, but Godard's male protagonist in *Une Femme est une Femme* reads it casually while he is listening to the soccer match. Two policemen invade his apartment to investigate a bomb incident, snoop around a bit, and then sarcastically congratulate him for reading "Humanité" and advise him to continue. *Une Femme est une Femme* is ostensibly a frivolous musical comedy, but I cannot recall when an Italian film has shown me anyone reading a Communist paper on the screen. Nor have any left-wing French directors bothered to indicate that there is any such thing as a Communist party in France. Even Jean-Paul Sartre's *Dirty Hands* is set in an imaginary Iron Curtain country.

This is one of the many fascinating paradoxes in the cinema of Jean-Luc Godard. Although Godard is the most self-conscious film maker in the world, the most addicted to inside jokes for the initiates and to internal esthetic judgments for himself, he is also in many ways the most realistic director of all time. Obviously, however, to call Godard realistic is to re-examine what we mean by realism, a term which has acquired a pejorative connotation over the years because of its association with too many dull movies. We are all familiar with some of the mannerisms of realism. No background music. Unprofessional actors. Bad sound recording. An emphasis on exteriors. A concern with the social problems of the lower classes. Black and white, small screen, and oodles of montage. Above all, realistic movies must pretend not to be movies at all, but impersonal documents of reality. Godard has broken most of these rules at one time or another. His characters are liable to look at the audience (and the camera) from time to time just to remind us that we are watching a staged illusion. Godard's Galatea, Anna Karina, is most guilty of this mannerism, and we are thus unable to avoid the conclusion that Godard is making love with his camera. Yet, as Godard would argue, what could be more realistic than the visual assertion that a movie is a movie? And more modern as well. After all, why should Godard be condemned for allowing Karina to look confidentially at the audience when Tony Richardson is praised for doing the same thing with Albert Finney and Joyce Redmon in *Tom Jones*, not to mention Jules Dassin's indulgence of Melina Mercouri in *Topkapi*. The irony is that Godard did it first and took the blame only to see imitators Richardson and Dassin take all the credit.

However, looking at the camera is not the sole index of Godard's realism. What Godard acknowledges in every foot of film he shows is his own point of view and moral responsibility. Look, he says. This film did not just happen. I made it happen, and I made it happen here and now. Each of my films is an entry in my diary, the diary of an artist, a critic and a journalist. Each film, no matter how fictional and far-fetched the plot, is a documentary on my state of mind at the time I made the film. In a sense, this has always been true, but it is Godard's contention that film making is now entering a new era of self-awareness. For the first time, there are film makers with a sense of film history, and as audiences shrink, they become more specialized and sophisticated. Godard, unlike Truffaut, is not hedging his bets with anything resembling the conventionally well-made film. His films are searching for a new audience, an audience willing to break with the comfortably illusionist past.

Although Godard has always admired American movies, he has never imitated their pragmatic virtues. He has always been much closer to Rossellini, for example, than to Hitchcock. Like Renoir, Godard will always sacrifice form to truth. He admires the classical confidence of the American movie storytellers, but he is too racked by intellectual self-questioning to follow in their footsteps. This is what makes his films so modern, and I insist, so realistic. He is speaking to a new generation of moviegoers, and it is significant that most of his admirers grew up in the Fifties when the idealistic momentum of the Depression and World War II had largely spent its force. The American and European critical establishment still believes in the moral conventions and clichés of the Thirties and Forties, and, quite logically, has singled out Godard as its most dangerous antagonist. The cinema, allegedly the most modern of the arts, has lagged far behind the other arts in its naïve conceptions of form, content, and the social benefits of mass communication. Consequently, Godard's allegedly revolutionary position is comparable to the positions of Stravinsky, Picasso, Joyce, and Eliot. It is not that Godard is superior to classical masters like Renoir and Dreyer any more than Stravinsky is superior to Mozart or Picasso to Rembrandt or Becket to Shakespeare, but that Godard is more symptomatic and representative of our time than his would-be neo-classical colleagues.

Godard's career has undeniably been shaped to some extent by necessity. If he had had the chance, he would have preferred to make lavish technicolor films with Kim Novak and Tony Curtis, but dire economies have driven him to the very edge of the 16 millimeter abyss. He has made do, however, with eight features and four shorts in less than five years. He has even managed to work twice with wide-screen and color (*A Woman Is a Woman* and *Contempt*). He has rendered the reality not only of Paris (*Breathless, A Woman Is a Woman, My Life to Live, Band of Outsiders, La Femme Mariée*), but of Switzerland (*The Little Soldier*) and Italy (*Contempt*). The photography of Coutard and the musical scores of Legrand and Delerue have contributed to the stylistic consistency of Godard's career, and the faces of Jean Seberg, Anna Karina, Brigitte Bardot, and Macha Meril constitute a uniquely Godardian gallery. Nevertheless, Godard's cinema is defined mainly by the extraordinary treatment of reality as a volatile mixture of the subjective and the objective, fact and fiction, logic and improbability, plausibility and actuality. Godard's characters often read the newspapers aloud on the screen, and what they read from the authentic journalism of our time is infinitely more bizarre than anything Godard could invent. Truth is stranger than fiction, and history is hysterical. This is Godard's narrative esthetic, and he accepts full responsibility for it. He is not saying that this is life, but that it is life as it is filtered through the camera. To accept one's responsibility as a director is to deny an impersonal objectivity to the camera. Every nuance of technique is a personal expression since it is Godard himself who once said that tracking was a moral statement. This acceptance of responsibility is the ultimate source of Godard's personal brand of realism. By standing between us and his characters, Godard forces us once and for all to accept the director as a creative force. For those of us who realize that films do not materialize miraculously on the screen, Godard becomes the foremost realist of the modern cinema.

Some confusion has been caused by erroneous assumptions about Godard's attachment to the ethos of Hollywood. Godard is a hopelessly European director who admires American movies, but can only comment on them without ever capturing the directness of Hollywood découpage. *Breathless* renders the gestures of the gangster movie without providing the gestation of motivations. Belmondo is not Bogart, but a stylistic elaboration of Bogart, replacing American necessity with French nihilism. The hero of *The Little Soldier* is too esthetically political to suggest any transposition to the American landscape. The clumsiness with which the rival agents of the Arab FLN and the ultra-French OAS dispose of each other reflects the chasm Godard senses between the theoretical and the practical. On the physical level, Godard seems to assert, European reflection is no substitute for American reflexes, but Godard himself is irrevocably a European, and like all Swiss intellectuals, an instinctive Bohemian.

A Woman Is a Woman pays its homage to the American musical, but Godard's token choreography is about as graceful as Donald Duck attempting "Swan Lake." Out of the six left feet of Karina, Belmondo, and Brialy, Godard almost achieves a charming effect of anti-rhythm. *A Woman Is a Woman* reflects the admiration of a director who can't dance for those elfin sprites who can. It is the director's admiration reflected in spasmodic twitches of melodiousness which makes *A Woman Is a Woman* such a beautiful movie. With *My Life to Live*, Godard passes irrevocably into that European cinema which can never return to the classical past. He is now not commenting on the Monogram quickie or the Metro musical, but on the sublime art of Carl Dreyer. In a series of twelve tableaux, Godard dissects a human soul in terms of the full range of cinematic vocabulary. Godard alienates once and for all those of his American admirers who misinterpreted *Breathless* as a serious tract on juvenile delinquency.

The Rifleman is too rigorously intellectual in its conception even for Europeans, and too historically erudite even for the most fanatical film buffs. Godard moves here into the cinema of the absurd with a form of storytelling, cluttered frame by cluttered frame, which seems unconscionably primitive. He ridicules both war and the glossy illusionism of anti-war movies. There is one brilliantly comic moment when a soldier sees his first movie, and keeps trying to invade the screen where a nude girl is bathing. First, he keeps shifting from one side of the auditorium to the other to get a better camera viewpoint. (The impiety of innocence.) Finally, he rushes up to the screen to assault it only to find that the illusion has vanished.

No other film has so aptly rendered the banality of war, and yet *The Rifleman* seems willfully inaccessible to audiences. Godard has labored mightily to truncate the emotions of both war and pacifism so that the entire spectacle will be devoid of facile moralizing. This degree of intellectual integrity could be commercially fatal.

Contempt may go down in history as the classical contretemps of international co-production. Delerue's curious score reflects the peculiar tension in the film between an intellectual austerity in the midst of scenic luxuriance. Delerue's score resembles a Bach melody orchestrated by Stokowsky, and Coutard's color photography intoxicates a spare scenario in which human emotions break under the weight of the words needed to express them. Brigitte Bardot, Fritz Lang, Jack Palance, and Michel Piccoli float through a deterministic dream in which the unity of the world of Homer, like that of Lang, disintegrates before our eyes. The marriage of Bardot and Piccoli dissolves in a climactic tracking scene of classical interiors and robes reducing the resiliency of living flesh. By merely expressing the idea of contempt, Bardot comes to feel the emotion. Modern relationships, Godard argues, are destroyed by the words we use to define them. The act of definition becomes the act of dissolution. By contrast, the art of a Homer or a Lang consists of a faith in the world as it appears. Godard appears in the film as Lang's assistant, but it is clear nevertheless that Godard agrees with Moravia on the dissolution of modern personality through excessive analysis. It is to Godard's credit in *Contempt* that he realizes he would like to be an integral artist like Lang, but that he cannot be anything but what he is, the analytical conscience of the modern cinema.

Movie Brutalists
by Pauline Kael

Miss Kael, whose movie reviews have appeared in Life, Holiday, Vogue and many other publications, is film critic for The New Yorker. She is the author of "I Lost It at the Movies" and the recent "Kiss Kiss Bang Bang." This chapter originally appeared in the September 24, 1966 issue of The New Republic.

The basic ideas among young American film makers are simple: the big movies we grew up on are either corrupt, obsolete, or dead, or are beyond our reach (we can't get a chance to make Hollywood films)—so we'll make films of our own, cheap films that we can make in our own way. For some, this is an attempt to break into the "industry"; for others it is a different approach to movies, a view of movies not as a popular art or a mass medium but as an art form to be explored.

Much of the movie style of young American film makers may be explained as a reaction against the banality and luxuriant wastefulness which are so often called the superior "craftsmanship" of Hollywood. In reaction, the young become movie brutalists.

They, and many in their audiences, may prefer the rough messiness—the uneven lighting, awkward editing, flat camera work, the undramatic succession of scenes, unexplained actions, and confusion about what, if anything, is going on—because it makes their movies seem so different from Hollywood movies. This inexpensive, inexperienced, untrained look serves as a kind of testimonial to sincerity, poverty, even purity of intentions. It is like the sackcloth of true believers which they wear in moral revulsion against the rich in their fancy garments. The look of poverty is not necessarily a necessity. I once had the experience, as chairman of the jury at an experimental film festival, of getting on the stage in the black silk dress I had carefully mended and ironed for the occasion, to present the check to the prizewinner who came forward in patched, faded dungarees. He got an ovation, of course. I had seen him the night before in a good dark suit, but now he had dressed for his role (deserving artist) as I had dressed for mine (distinguished critic).

Although many of the American experimentalists have developed extraordinary kinds of technique, it is no accident that the virtuoso technicians who can apparently do almost anything with drawing board or camera are not taken up as the heroes of youth in the way that brutalists are. Little is heard about Bruce Baillie or Carroll Ballard, whose camera skills expose how inept, inefficient, and unimaginative much of Hollywood's self-praised work is, or about the elegance and grandeur of Jordan Belson's short abstract films, like *Allures,* that demonstrate that one man working in a basement can make Hollywood's vaunted special effects departments look archaic. Craftsmanship and skill don't, in themselves, have much appeal to youth. Rough work looks in rebellion and sometimes it is: there's anger and frustration and passion, too, in those scratches and stains and multiple super-impositions that make our eyes swim. The movie brutalists, it's all too apparent, are hurting our eyes to save our souls.

They are basically right, of course, in what they're *against.* Esthetically and morally, disgust with Hollywood's fabled craftsmanship is long overdue. I say fabled because the "craft" claims of Hollywood, and the notion that the expensiveness of studio-produced movies is necessary for some sort of technical perfection or "finish," are just hucksterism. The reverse is closer to the truth: it's becoming almost impossible to produce a decent looking movie in a Hollywood studio. In addition to the corpses of old dramatic ideas (touched up here and there to look cute as if they were alive), big movies carry the dead weight of immobile cameras, all-purpose light, whorehouse decor. The production values are often ludicrously inappropriate to the subject matter, but studio executives, who charge off roughly thirty percent of a film's budget to studio overhead, are very keen on these production values which they frequently remind us are the hallmark of American movies.

In many foreign countries, it is this very luxuriousness that is most envied and admired in American movies: the big cars, the fancy food, the opulent bachelor lairs, the gadget-packed family homes, even the loaded freeways and the noisy big cities. What is not so generally understood is the studio executives' implicit assumption that this is also what American audiences like. The story may not involve more than a few spies and counterspies, but the wide screen will be filled. The set decorator will pack the sides of the image with fruit and flowers and furniture.

When Hollywood cameramen and editors want to show their expertise they imitate the effects of Japanese or European craftsmen and then the result is pointed to with cries of "See, we can do anything in Hollywood." The principal demonstration of art and ingenuity among these "craftsmen" is likely to be in getting their sons and nephews into the unions and in resisting any attempt to make Hollywood movie-making flexible enough for artists to work there. If there are no cinematographers in modern Hollywood who can be discussed in the same terms as Henri Decae or Raoul Coutard or the late Gianni di Venanzo it's because the studio methods and the union restrictions and regulations don't make it possible for talent to function. The talent is strangled in the business bureaucracy, and the best of our cinematographers perform safe, sane academic exercises. If the most that a gifted colorist like Lucien Ballard can hope for is to beautify a John Michael Hayes screenplay—giving an old tart a fresh complexion—why not scratch up the image?

The younger generation doesn't seem much interested in the obstacles to art in Hollywood, however. They don't much care about why the older directors do what they do or whether some of the most talented young directors in Hollywood like Sam Peckinpah (*Ride the High Country, Major Dundee*) or Irvin Kershner (*The Hoodlum Priest, The Luck of Ginger Coffey, A Fine Madness*) will break through and do the work they should be doing. There is little interest in the work of gifted, intelligent men outside the industry like James Blue (*The Olive Trees of Justice*) or John Korty (*The Crazy Quilt*) who are attempting to make inexpensive feature films as honestly and independently as they can. These men (and their films) are not flamboyant; they don't issue manifestos, and they don't catch the imagination of youth. Probably, like the students in film courses who often do fresh and lively work, they're not surprising enough, not different enough. The new film enthusiasts are, when it comes down to it, not any more interested in simple, small, inexpensive pictures than Hollywood is. The workmen's clothes and crude movie techniques may cry out, "We're poor and honest. They're rich and rotten." But, of course, you can be poor and not so very honest and, although it's harder to believe, you can even be rich and not so very rotten. What the young seem to be interested in is brutalism. In certain groups, automatic writing with a camera has come to be considered the most creative kind of film making.

Their hero, Jean-Luc Godard—one of the most original talents ever to work in film and one of the most uneven—is not a brutalist at so simple a level, yet he comprises the attitudes of a new generation. Godard is what is meant by a "film maker." He works with a small crew and shifts ideas and attitudes from movie to movie and even within movies. While Hollywood producers straddle huge fences trying to figure out where the action is supposed to be—and never find out—Godard is in himself where the action is.

There is a disturbing quality in Godard's work that perhaps helps to explain why the young are drawn to his films and identify with them, and why so many older people call him a "coterie" artist and don't think his films are important. *His characters don't seem to have any future.* They are most alive (and most appealing) just because they don't conceive of the day after tomorrow; they have no careers, no plans, only fantasies of roles they could play, of careers, thefts, romance, politics, adventure, pleasure, a life like in the movies. Even his world of the future, *Alphaville*, is, photographically, a documentary of Paris in the present. (All of his films are in that sense documentaries—as were also, and also by necessity, the grade B American gangster films that influence him.) And even before *Alphaville,* the people in *The Married Woman* were already science fiction—so blank and affectless no mad scientist was required to destroy their souls.

His characters are young; unrelated to families and background. Whether deliberately or unconsciously, he makes his characters orphans who, like the students in the theatres, feel only attachments to friends, to lovers—attachments that will end with a chance word or the close of the semester. They're orphans, by extension, in a larger sense, too, unconnected with the world, feeling out of relationship to it. They're a generation of familiar strangers.

An elderly gentleman recently wrote me, "Oh, they're such a bore, bore, bore, modern youth!! All attitudes and nothing behind the attitudes. When I was in my twenties, I didn't just loaf around, being a rebel, I went places and did things. The reason they all hate the squares is because the squares remind them of the one thing they are trying to forget: there *is* a Future and you must build for it."

He's wrong, I think. The young are not "trying to forget"; they just don't think in those terms. Godard's power—and possibly his limitation—as an artist is that he so intensely expresses how they do feel and think. His characters don't plan or worry about careers or responsibilities; they just live. Youth makes them natural aristocrats in their indifference to sustenance, security, hard work; and prosperity has turned a whole generation—or at least the middle-class part of it—into aristocrats. And it's astonishing how many places they do go to and how many things they can do. The difference is in how easily they do it at all. Even their notion of creativity—as what comes naturally—is surprisingly similar to the aristocratic artist's condescension toward those middle-class plodders who have to labor for a living, for an education, for "culture."

Here, too, Godard is the symbol, exemplar, and proof. He makes it all seem so effortless, so personal—just one movie after another. Because he is skillful enough (and so incredibly disciplined) that he can make his pictures for under $100,000, and because there is enough of a youthful audience in France to support these pictures, he can do almost anything he wants within those budgetary limits. In this achievement of independence, he is almost alone among movie directors; it is a truly heroic achievement. For a younger generation he is the proof that it is possible to make and go on making films your own way. And yet they don't seem aware of how rare he is or how hard it is to get in that position. Even if colleges and foundations make it easier than it has ever been, they will need not only talent but toughness to be independent.

As Godard has been able to solve the problems of economic freedom, his work now poses the problems of artistic freedom —problems that few artists in the history of movies have been fortunate enough to face. The history of great film directors is a history of economic and political obstacles—of compromises, defeats, despair, even disgrace. Griffith, Eisenstein, Von Stroheim, Von Sternberg, Cocteau, Renoir, Max Ophuls, Orson Welles—they were defeated because they weren't in a position to do what they wanted to do. If Godard fails, it will be because what he wants to do—which is what he *does*—isn't good enough.

Maybe he is attempting to escape from freedom when he makes a beautiful work and then, to all appearances, just throws it away. There is a self-destructive urgency in his treatment of themes, a drive toward a quick finish. Even if it's suicidal for the hero or the work, Godard is impatient for the ending; the mood of his films is that there's no way for things to work out anyway, something must be done even if it's disastrous, no action is intolerable.

It seems likely that many of the young who don't wait for others to call them artists but simply announce that they are, don't have the patience to make art. A student's idea of a film maker isn't someone who has to sit home and study and think and work—as in most of the arts—but go out with friends and shoot. It is a social activity, an extroverted and egotistic image of the genius-creator. It is the Fellini-Guido figure of *8½*, the movie director as star. Few seem to have noticed that by the time of *Juliet of the Spirits* he had turned into a professional party-giver. Film making, carried out the way a lot of kids do it, is like having a party. And their movie "ideas" are frequently staging and shooting a wild, weird party.

"Creativity" is a quick route to power and celebrity. The pop singer or composer, the mod designer says of his work, "It's a creative way to make a living"—meaning it didn't take a dull lot of study and planning, that he was able to use his own inventiveness or ingenuity or talent to get to the top without much sweat. I heard a young film maker put it this way to a teen-age art student: "What do you go to life-class for? Either you can draw or you can't. What you should do is have a show. It's important to get exposure." One can imagine their faces if they had to listen to those teachers who used to tell us that you had to be able to do things the traditional ways before you earned the right to break loose and do it your way. They simply take short cuts into other art forms or into pop arts where they can "express themselves" now. Like cool Peter Pans, they just take off and fly.

Godard's conception of technique can be taken as a highly intellectualized rational for these attitudes. "The ideal for me," he says, "is to obtain right away what will work—and without retakes. If they are necessary, it falls short of the mark. The immediate is chance. At the same time it is definitive. What I want is the definitive by chance." Sometimes, almost magically, he seems to get it—as in many scenes of *Breathless* and *Band of Outsiders*—but often, as in *The Married Woman,* he seems to settle for arbitrary effects.

And a caricature of this way of talking is common among young American film makers. Some of them believe that everything they catch on film is definitive, so they do not edit at all. As proof that they do not mar their instinct with pedantry or judgment, they may retain the blank leader to the roll of film. As proof of their creative sincerity they may leave in the blurred shots.

Preposterous as much of this seems, it is theoretically not so far from Godard's way of working. Although his technical control is superb, so complete that one cannot tell improvisation from planning, the ideas and bits of business are often so arbitrary that they appear to be (and probably are) just things that he chanced to think of that day, or that he came across in a book he happened to be reading. At times there is a disarming, an almost ecstatic, innocence about the way he uses quotes as if he had just heard of these beautiful ideas and wanted to share his enthusiasm with the world. After smiling with pleasure as we do when a child discovers the beauty of a leaf or a poem, enabling us to re-experience the wonder of responsiveness, we may sink in spirit right down to incredulity. For this is the rapture with "thoughts" of those whose minds aren't much sullied by thought. These are "thoughts" without thought; they don't come out of a line of thought or a process of thinking, they don't arise from the situation. They're "inspirations"—bright illuminations from nowhere—and this is what kids who think of themselves as poetic or artistic or creative think ideas are: noble sentiments. They decorate a movie and it is easy for viewers to feel that they give it depth, that if followed, these clues lead to understanding of the work. But if those who follow the clues come out with odd and disjunctive interpretations, this is because the "clues" are *not* integral to the movie but are clues to what else the artist was involved in while he was making the movie.

Putting into the work whatever just occurred to the artist is its own rationale and needs no justification for young Americans encouraged from childhood to express themselves creatively and to speak out whatever came into their heads. Good, liberal parents didn't want to push their kids in academic subjects but oohed and aahed with false delight when their children presented them with a baked ashtray or a woven doily. Did anyone guess or foresee what narcissistic confidence this generation would develop in its banal "creativity"? Now we're surrounded, inundated, by artists. And a staggering number of them wish to be or already call themselves "film makers."

A few years ago a young man informed me that he was going to "give up" poetry and avant-garde film (which couldn't have been much of a sacrifice as he hadn't done anything more than talk about them) and devote himself to writing "art-songs." I remember asking, "Do you read music?" and not being especially surprised to hear that he didn't. I knew from other young men that the term "art" used as an adjective meant that they were by-passing even the most rudimentary knowledge in the field. Those who said they were going to make art movies not only didn't consider it worth their while to go to see ordinary commercial movies, but usually didn't even know anything much about avant-garde film. I did not pursue the subject of "art-songs" with this young man because it was perfectly clear that he wasn't going to do anything. But some of the young who say they're going to make "art movies" are actually beginning to make movies. Kids who can't write, who have never developed any competence in photography, who have never acted in nor directed a play, see no deterrent to making movies. And although most of the results are bad beyond our wildest fears, as if to destroy all our powers of prediction, a few, even of the most ignorant, pretentious young men and women, are doing some interesting things.

Yet why are the Hollywood movies, even the worst over-stuffed ones, often easier to sit through than the short experimental ones? Because they have actors and a story. Through what is almost a technological fluke, 16 mm movie cameras give the experimental film maker greater flexibility than the "professional" 35 mm camera user, but he cannot get adequate synchronous sound. And so the experimentalists, as if to convert this liability into an advantage, have asserted that their partial use of the capabilities of the medium is the true art of the cinema, which is said to be purely visual. But their vis-

328

ual explorations of their states of consciousness (with the usual implicit social protest) get boring, the mind begins to wander, and though this lapse in attention can be explained to us as a new kind of experience, as even the purpose of cinema, our desire to see a movie hasn't been satisfied. (There are, of course, some young film makers who are not interested in movies as we ordinarily think of them, but in film as an art-medium like painting or music, and this kind of work must be looked at a different way—without the expectation of story content or meaning.) They probably won't be able to make satisfying *movies* until the problems of sound are solved not only technically but in terms of drama, structure, meaning, relevance.

It is not an answer to toss on a spoofing semi-synchronous sound track as a number of young film makers do. It can be funny in a cheap sort of way—as in Robert Downey's *Chafed Elbows* where the images and sound are, at least, in the same style; but this isn't fundamentally different from the way George Axelrod works in *Lord Love a Duck* or Blake Edwards *What Did You Do in the War, Daddy?* and there's no special reason to congratulate people for doing underground what is driving us down there. Total satire is opportunistic and easy; what's difficult is to make a movie about something—without making a fool of yourself. Kenneth Anger did it with *Scorpio Rising.* Yet few others have taken that wonderful basic precaution of having a subject or of attempting to explore the world.

Is Hollywood interested in the young movement? If it attracts customers, Hollywood will eat it up, the way *The Wild Angels* has already fed upon *Scorpio Rising.* At a party combining the commercial and non-commercial worlds of film, a Hollywood screen writer watched as an underground film maker and his wife entered. The wife was wearing one of those classic film makers' wives' outfits: a simple sack of burlap in natural brown, with scarecrow sleeves. The screen writer greeted her enthusiastically, "I really dig your dress, honey," he said, "I used to have a dress like that once."

Dostoevsky with a Japanese Camera
by Donald Richie

Mr. Richie is best known as co-author, with Joseph Anderson, of "The Japanese Film," the definitive book on Japanese cinema. His most recent book is "The Films of Kurosawa." This chapter appeared originally in the July 1962 issue of Horizon.

Akira Kurosawa was once described as "the most complicated man in films: completely Japanese and, so far as the West is concerned, almost completely Western." Since his debut as a motion-picture director in 1943, he has been called an idealist and a realist, a typical Japanese intellectual and an American-type fact-finder. He has been defended as a humanist and attacked as a despot. In 1951, when a producer demanded that Kurosawa cut his three-hour-and-ten-minute film *The Idiot,* the director snapped back, "If you want to cut it in half, you had better cut it lengthwise." His penchant for making such retorts has earned him the derisive sobriquet of Kurosawa-*Tenno,* "The Emperor Kurosawa."

In spite of the difficulty critics have in placing Kurosawa in the East or the West (and perhaps partially because of that difficulty) his ferociously guarded independence, his spirited experimentation, and his vigorous break from traditional Japanese film standards have won him an esteem about which there is little argument: he is considered one of the best directors Japan has produced; indeed, in the opinion of many critics he is one of the world's foremost. Public recognition first came to him in 1948 with the appearance of *Drunken Angel,* and by 1951 his *Rashomon* won the Venice Film Festival Grand Prix, the Academy Award for Best Foreign Film, and prizes from the National Board of Review and the New York Film Critics Group.

Born in Tokyo in 1910, Kurosawa developed an early interest in painting—a taste that is reflected in the emphasis on pictorial beauty in his films—and while still in his teens he attended a private Western-style art school. However, when he found he could not make a living by painting, he began to look for a job. In 1936, with a minimum of enthusiasm, he responded to a newspaper advertisement for an assistant director at Photo-Chemical Laboratory, one of Japan's first movie-producing companies (now called Toho). He got the job, largely owing to an essay he was required to write. With characteristic rebelliousness he chose as his subject: "What Is Wrong with Japanese Movies."

For the next seven years Kurosawa worked as an assistant on several films and spent most of his spare time writing scenarios (none of which was then produced); finally, in 1943, he directed his first film, *Sanshiro Sugata*. It dealt with a young judo champion who pursues the Buddhist ideal, and strives for enlightenment—the perfection of his spirit—through a rigorous physical discipline. The most notable aspect of the film, however, was the early indication it gave of the style that characterizes much of Kurosawa's work: the scenes follow one another relentlessly, switching abruptly from "stillness" to action and back again.

This tightly-woven style, more fully developed, is used to good effect in *Rashomon*, Kurosawa's most widely known film. The plot of *Rashomon* is simple. A samurai and his bride meet a bandit in the woods. The samurai is murdered, the girl is raped, and the events are witnessed by a woodcutter. The film consists of four separate versions of the story, each depending on the viewpoint of the person telling it. According to the girl, she was raped against her will; according to the bandit, he was lured by her and persuaded to kill her husband. As the personal motives are unmasked, it becomes apparent that there is no "true" version; truth, like beauty, lies in the eye of the beholder. Yet Kurosawa was not content to end with unresolved despair (he finds distasteful the ordinary Japanese film with its "almost obligatory unhappy ending")—and so he added an epilogue in which the woodcutter adopted an abandoned child.

In *Rashomon*, Kurosawa shows his characteristic interest in violence, action of the most heightened order, and the use of the camera itself to achieve dramatic effects. In the opening forest sequence the moving camera looks straight through leaves into the sun to make palpable the glare and shade on the samurai and his lady. Such effects are achieved by painstaking work and the director's absolute control over all phases of a production. Ten feet of film are shot for every one that finds its way onto the screen, and Kurosawa uses two or three cameras to photograph the same scene from different angles.

He carefully plots each perspective, and he is one of the few directors who insists upon the right to "frame" his own scenes. Unlike many directors, he cuts and edits the footage himself.

To insure unity of mood in his adaptation of Gorky's "The Lower Depths" (*Donzoko*, 1957, released in America in February of this year)—a difficult feat when transferring a play to a different country and a different era—Kurosawa ordered a forty-day rehearsal period with full costumes in use from the first day. It was an unusual demand from a film maker, but it produced an admirable, consistent, ensemble effect.

One of Kurosawa's most arresting displays of technical virtuosity was *Throne of Blood* (*Kumonosu-jo*, 1957, shown in America in 1961), in which he transplanted Shakespeare's "Macbeth" to medieval Japan. In Kurosawa's version of the story, Lady Macbeth's influence is only incidental; Macbeth is given full responsibility for his actions. In technique, too, there are numerous inventions, one of the most striking being the director's experiment with the sound track. Kurosawa turned off all the "highs" so that the voices would be masculine and gruff. Indeed, they often sound more animal than human. There is a stunning scene in which hundreds of birds, disturbed by the destruction of their forest, fly into the banquet hall, considerably unnerving the hero. Then, when the couple speaks of the murder and of sleeplessness, the sound of a horse in the courtyard, galloping endlessly round and round in a circle, heightens the dialogue. The march of the forest on the castle is photographed in slow motion, distorted by the use of a telescopic lens, with trees swaying like gigantic seaweed and descending wave after wave upon the castle. The conclusion is an almost ritualistic murder of Macbeth when, arrow by arrow (and there are hundreds of them), he is immolated.

The technical effects Kurosawa employed in *The Record of a Living Being* (*Ikimono-no Kiroku,* 1955) were also startlingly appropriate. In this film Kurosawa tells the story of a man obsessed with the fear of atomic extinction. The man attempts to move his family to Brazil, where he believes they will find safety, but the family, complacent and cynical, succeeds in having him judged insane. Eventually he does become insane, and we see him in the asylum, looking at the sun and believing the earth is finally on fire.

Set in the hottest days of August, the atmosphere of a

332

brutal summer permeates *Record of a Living Being.* Clothes stick to the flesh, characters fan themselves incessantly, and in the corner of most interior shots there is an electric fan stirring the heavy air, providing more noise and irritation than relief. A flickering, disquieting motion is present in every scene. During one of the climactic moments, Kurosawa places the camera so that the pages of a magazine, blown by an electric fan, confuse and fatigue the spectator with their incessant and meaningless motion. The camera, like the hero, peers myopically at the objects like telephones and typewriters until they become huge and menacing.

In the final scene, in the asylum, the camera sets itself between floors, one flight of stairs leading up, the other down. The doctor, an old man who has been sympathetic toward the mad hero, goes down the stairs, passing but not recognizing the young man's mistress, who is carrying a baby upstairs—possibly the hero's child—for a visit. This concluding comment of rebirth has been a persistent theme in Kurosawa's films; and it suggests, along with less tangible influences, the contribution of the director's early interest in Dostoevsky.

Kurosawa read "The Idiot" and "Crime and Punishment" over and over again as a youngster, and Dostoevsky's imprint was unmistakable in even the first of his major films, *Drunken Angel (Yoidore Tenshi,* 1948, shown in America in 1959). The film tells the story of an alcoholic doctor who finds a tubercular young hoodlum and attempts to nurse him back to health. The gangster is almost as afraid of the doctor as he is of the disease. The doctor, already a failure, insists on saving this apparently worthless young man. The young man, also a failure in his own world, feels that salvation at the hands of someone who so attracts and repels him would represent defeat. Their mutual antagonism, a parable on the responsibilities of compassion, is set in the ruins of postwar Japan, where social and ethical norms have been completely destroyed, and where an entire society lies helpless and festering. Kurosawa once said of Dostoevsky, "I know of no one so compassionate . . . Ordinary people turn their eyes away from tragedy; he looks straight into it."

Intended as a comment on postwar Japan, an effort to revive the spirit of that decimated country, *Drunken Angel* received the "Best One" award from the Japanese film maga-

333

zine "Kinema Jumpo," and Kurosawa followed it with a similar comment in *Stray Dog* (*Nora Inu*, 1949, not commercially shown in America). In this film a detective pursues a seasoned criminal who has stolen a pistol and committed a number of murders. When the cop finally catches the robber (and there is a "cops and robbers" feeling about this film, a detective story of the classic genre), they fight among the flowering weeds of early spring. Completely covered with mud, finally exhausted by their fight, the two lie side by side. Then the camera, for the first time dropping its aloof and dispassionate documentary attitude, peers curiously at them through the blossoms and finds them identical. Muddy and unrecognizable, lying side by side, cop and robber are one and the same: neither hero, nor villain. But, once again, expressing a desire for postwar resurrection, the camera looks up and sees in the distance a group of school children on a hike, singing in the sun for the first time after a long winter.

Ikiru (*To Live*, 1952, shown in America in 1960) is a further variation on Kurosawa's theme of compassion and hope. A petty government official learns he is dying of cancer and, for the first time in his life, realizes that he has accomplished nothing. His reaction is to have a good time. He takes all his savings and spends them in a long, wild evening. But this proves disappointing. In one scene, drunk to the world and cold sober within, he sings, tears running down his cheeks, a faded little song he remembers from childhood. Before he dies, the clerk uses all his strength to implement a petition that has been lying for months on his desk and on the desks of others—a request for a park. In the teeth of official indifference and antagonism, he pushes his project through. Finally it is complete and that night, sitting on a swing in the park, with the snow falling around him, he dies. *Ikiru*, as sweeping an indictment of bureaucracy as has ever been filmed, is not an angry motion picture. Kurosawa is not concerned with a bad society so much as with a good man—a flawed, less-than-ideal, but good human being.

Of all the films Kurosawa has made, *Seven Samurai*, or *The Magnificent Seven* (*Shichinin-no Samurai*, 1954, shown in a cut version in America in 1956), is generally considered his masterpiece. Bandits are about to attack a small village. The villagers seek the aid of a group of masterless samurai, men as outside society as the robbers they are asked to fight. The samurai agree, they win, and a number of them die. The villagers are grateful, but it is spring planting season, and they have work to do. The remaining samurai leave the village they have defended.

It is only toward the end of the film that the two sides, samurai and bandits, engage in combat. And then, where most films would have ended—a battle and the victory for the right side being judged enough—Kurosawa begins. The screen darkens, as though a chapter had ended, and in a lyrical sequence the villagers emerge for the first time as the figures of importance. It becomes apparent then that the samurai were fighting only for themselves, fighting for an ideal that those of them who survive come to understand as hollow. In the final scene the camera raises to the burial mounds, and the leader of the samurai says, "We have lost . . ." (there are no victors in war). Samurai and bandits are one, equally defeated; but the villagers, the enduring people of the world, oblivious of the "brave" deeds, will go on planting new rice. *The Magnificent Seven* cost more money than any previous Toho movie, took more than a year to complete, and had (in the uncut version) a running time of just under three hours. The film remains Kurosawa's strongest statement of the moral theme common to all his films: that human frailty must be accepted, but not passively, for man may overcome adversity and achieve his own salvation. All the contradictions embedded in Kurosawa's cinematic philosophy are brought together here, and the very tensions between them give the film its great strength.

There has been a looping back to earlier themes in Kurosawa's more recent films, *Yojimbo* and *Sanjuro Tsubake*, which revert to the satire of, for example, his *Those Who Tread on the Tiger's Tail*, made in 1945. *Yojimbo* won a Venice Festival prize in 1961.

In this hilarious lampoon of empty heroics, Toshiro Mifune (an actor who appears in many of Kurosawa's films) comes to town in time to stop a war between rival families. The families have disguised all their ruling passions—greed, hate, malice—as "noble determination" and "pride." Only Mifune, like the little boy who sees that the emperor has no clothes, realizes the truth and succeeds in exposing the sham heroism at the end. More incisive, and even funnier, is *Sanjuro Tsu-*

bake (made in 1962), which might be considered a sequel to
Yojimbo. Nine young samurai are on a mission of revenge.
They are filled with the usual intensity of spirit, self-impor-
tance, involvement, and dedication—until they meet a masterless samurai (again played by Mifune) who takes them
thoroughly apart. At the same time, the samurai helps the
young men and teaches them. At the start, when the grateful
youngsters all bow low and say they do not know how they
can ever repay him, his casual suggestion that they try money
is totally disillusioning to them. Here Kurosawa is firmly explaining that the real samurai is someone who, no less human
than others, simply tries harder.

These recent films show Kurosawa at his best, his style
and statement complementing and reinforcing each other to
produce a genuine work of cinematic art. He is not, of course,
infallible. The most frequently repeated criticism of his work
is that it is marred by an "infatuation with the look of his own
image," and thus suffers from "dragginess." He has also been
criticized for achieving "triteness" instead of the profound
compassion that he admires in Dostoevsky; for excessive introspection, even narcissism; for permitting his style to obscure
his statement, producing elaborate works of photographic
beauty that amount to so much stylistic gymnasticism. And
one critic found, even in his first film, "too many hidden implications."

This sort of criticism derives not so much from Kurosawa's
concern for technique as from his philosophy, and from a
failure on the part of his critics to understand it. Far from
having broken with Japanese tradition, he has made its
uniquely Japanese quality understandable and meaningful.
His formality—in film structure, in acting style—is the formality of Japanese art, as in the *haiku* or in the classical theatre.
His preoccupation with technique is completely Japanese; it
is what one sees in the potter or carpenter, those other Japanese professions in which simple craftsmen may achieve a
style. His obscurities are also those implicit in Japanese
thought, in the classical Japanese conflict between duty and
inclination. Kurosawa is at the same time so individualistic
that many Japanese critics find him "Western." He does not
subscribe to the Japanese myth of human (which is to say,
Japanese) infallibility, the preference for demigods over men.

336

For Kurosawa the "merely human" is quite enough, even if it leads him into his not-quite-convincing reliance on the message of hope. Action may define and save a man (in Japan as elsewhere), but if truth is merely relative, mere hope is not enough. It is perhaps this dilemma in Kurosawa, precisely this tension, that makes his films meaningful and provocative in both his world and ours.

Director of Enigmas: Alain Resnais
by Eugene Archer

Mr. Archer, formerly with The New York Times movie department, for the past several years has been in Europe observing and writing about film makers there. This chapter by Mr. Archer originally appeared in The Times on March 18, 1962.

Brigitte Bardot notwithstanding, the most expressive French words in the intellectual movie-goer's current vocabulary are Alain Resnais. Mention of the name evokes a pair of films as brilliant as they are difficult—the two-year-old prize-winner, *Hiroshima, Mon Amour,* and the latest cocktail-party conversation piece around New York, *Last Year at Marienbad.* It also identifies a cinematic style so original that it has made Resnais, at 39, one of the most idolized young directors in the world.

Reviewing *Marienbad,* fascinated New York critics echoed the Parisians who described Resnais as "a revolutionary artist" and "a genius who has achieved a fusion between the visual imagery of the cinema and the psychological explorations of the new novel." But a few viewers, baffled by *Marienbad's* incomprehensible mélange of past, present, and future with no attention to characterization, chronology, or plot, have openly wondered what it is all about.

To the movie industry's surprise, the public, its appetite perhaps whetted by the intellectual exercises of Ingmar Bergman, seems determined to see for itself. While Hollywood extravaganzas are playing to empty theatres a few blocks away, Manhattan's tiny Carnegie Hall Cinema has posted its "standing room only" sign regularly since *Marienbad* arrived. Coffeehouse habitués have temporarily abandoned their usual charades to play the Marienbad game, a Chinese matchstick puzzle introduced by actors in the film. The object of the game is to lose the matches, since the loser wins.

This sort of contradiction delights Resnais, a tall, elusive, stubbornly enigmatic Breton who insists on guarding his privacy in one of the least private of the world's professions. Since *Hiroshima* brought him, somewhat reluctantly, into the international spotlight after an unobtrusive decade directing fine but little-known short subjects, Resnais' personality has proved almost as mysterious as his films.

"How can anyone ever really understand anyone else?" he is apt to demand fretfully. "Other people supply the scripts for my films, and I merely photograph them—I never change a word; I wouldn't dare. And still, when I see my films on the screen, I feel completely exposed. My only protection is that most people see only themselves in *Hiroshima* and *Marienbad,* instead of looking for me."

Accepting the challenge, the critics who have sought clues to Resnais' character in his work have unveiled a curious mixture of social awareness and "art for art's sake" esotericism. Observers who interpreted the anti-nuclear *Hiroshima* as a work of social protest could point for confirmation to Resnais' left-wing political background. Resnais emphatically denies Communist affiliations, but the attitude of the rebel is mirrored in some of his early short films.

Night and Fog, a devastating documentary of Nazi concentration camps, intercut actual newsreel footage of the atrocities at Dachau and Auschwitz with beautiful color photography of the camps today, overgrown with flowers and foliage. By emphasizing the inherent animalism of human nature, the film stunned observers with the suggestion that they, not the Nazis, were actually responsible for the horrors.

Similarly, *Guernica,* a study of Pablo Picasso's painting, concentrated on the ravages of the Spanish Civil War. *The Statues Also Die,* which showed African art corrupted by European influences, indicted colonialism so pointedly that French Government censors banned it from exhibition anywhere in the world.

Yet here, too, the contradiction persists. Although Resnais' signature on last year's *Free Algeria* manifesto caused *Marienbad* to be excluded from competition at Cannes (shown at the Venice Film Festival instead, it won the grand prize), his producer, Raymond Froment, scoffs at the idea of Resnais as a political figure. "The trouble with Alain," he said, "is that he's *not* political, and is ashamed of it. All of his friends are so concerned with world issues that he hates to admit his only commitment is to art."

Froment's view is partially confirmed by Resnais. "I don't like to talk about World War II, because I wasn't in the underground," he revealed, explaining with considerable embarrassment his asthma-induced absence from the Army. "During the occupation, I was studying in the theatre, and I was so immersed in it that I didn't even know there was an organized resistance. But I don't think that's a good excuse."

Those who regarded Resnais as a socially committed film maker were disillusioned by *Last Year at Marienbad*. Except for its underlying theme of revolt against convention, the new film has no pretensions to social significance or to reality of any kind. A mystifying story about a stranger's successful attempt to persuade a married woman that their imaginery love affair had actually taken place, it wanders back and forth through time, space, and illusion. It is sheer art.

Resnais is a poised, handsome, inordinately timid individual whose passion for movies is equaled only by his love for comic strips. He started reading comics as a boy in his chemist-father's comfortable home in the provincial city of Vannes, and began adapting their story-telling principles to his own home movies at the prodigious age of ten. Resnais still insists his films are modeled after comic strips, and has a New York correspondent mail him the daily adventures of his favorite, "Dick Tracy."

"Everyone wants to think of me as a dedicated intellectual," he complained, "but, truthfully, I don't really like making films. If I didn't have to earn a living, I wouldn't work at all."

In a different mood, he readily admits that he is only happy behind the camera. The truth is that Resnais has seldom strayed far from his chosen métier. After an adolescence plagued by asthma and the German occupation, he moved his collection of cameras and comics to Paris' Latin Quarter, briefly tried stage acting and film editing, and soon found a job directing commercials. In 1949 his first professional short, an impressionistic study of the painter Vincent Van Gogh, brought him an Academy Award.

For the past decade Resnais has maintained bachelor quarters in a ground-floor apartment in the semi-fashionable Rue des Plantes in Paris. His friends, for the most part little-known actors and technicians from the theater, find him the most considerate of companions, when they can find him at all. Resnais seldom answers his telephone, and frequently disappears from his apartment for weeks at a time. When he reappears, he blithely explains that he has been to Switzerland or Cambodia or the United States.

These incognito visits to New York—he has been here three times since *Hiroshima* attracted public interest—have distressed his American distributors and outraged their harried press agents, but Resnais is a man who prefers a solitary hamburger in Greenwich Village to lunch at Sardi's.

Hiroshima, Mon Amour came about when a Japanese company signed a co-production contract with a French firm for a film to be made in both countries, involving one Japanese and one French star. Resnais, who had repeatedly refused offers to direct commercial scripts, accepted only when guaranteed complete freedom. When Françoise Sagan refused an offer to write the script, he turned to the symbolic novelist Marguerite Duras, with firm orders to be "literary."

Mme. Duras recalls the writing period with nostalgia, as a collaboration unmarked by harsh words or temperament. (Although Resnais denies ever setting pen to paper on a film script, his influence upon his scenarists, through long consultations during the writing period, is considerable.) When the film was finished, she was astonished to hear Resnais disown the heroine ("I don't particularly like the woman") and tell interviewers that the French woman remains with the Japanese at the end of the film, after Mme. Duras had said the opposite. Alain Robbe-Grillet, who wrote *Marienbad,* had a similar experience recently when, in a joint interview, he found Resnais blithely contradicting everything he said.

The "new wave" director, François Truffaut, who is both a personal friend and a perceptive critic, has his own explanation for the enigma of Resnais.

"With *Marienbad,*" he said, "Resnais carried the cinema further than it had ever gone before without worrying about whether or not audiences would follow. If he were a novelist or a poet, this wouldn't matter—but in the cinema you're supposed to worry about your audience. Alain knows this, and that's why he seems so contradictory and mysterious. He's trying to hide his obsession with his art."

Despite his flair for dissimulation, Resnais' peculiar obsession is apparent to everyone he meets. When he is in the mood, he is apt to compare film making to musical orchestration, to sculpture or to a novel. Like modern novelists, he is concerned with communication, or the lack of it; with time, both actual and imaginary; and with the difference between illusion and reality.

To bring the art of film making to this abstract plane, he has eliminated the "non-essentials"—plot, action, and rational explanations. "My films," he maintains, "are an attempt, still very crude and very tentative, to visualize the complexity of the mechanism of thought."

Fellini's Double City
by Eric Rhode

Mr. Rhode has written extensively on contemporary film directors. A selection of his essays was recently published in the book "Tower of Babel." This chapter appeared originally in the June 1964 issue of Encounter.

"If I were to make a film about the life of a sole," said Federico Fellini, "it would end up by being about me. . . ." One would like to call his bluff; but one sees what he means. No other director has an ego so inflated, no other director's work is so directly autobiographical. The *oeuvre* is like a poet's diary, continually in search of something, immensely consistent in its development of themes.

The nature of this search is made clear in his latest film, 8½. Guido Anselmi, the film director, is depressed and confined to a spa; he is unable to work on his most recent project, and he is surrounded by a group of seemingly hostile figures. But fortunately his surroundings evoke memories of the past —he is haunted by suggestions of some half-forgotten beauty —and his companions cannot trouble him too deeply. When his scriptwriter objects to the scenario of the coming film, Guido has the presence of mind to realize that his kind of film cannot be created through the dictates of theory. "Do you support the Catholics or the Communists?" asks a critic. But of course the question is far too simple. Like a man trapped in a car, Guido must try to free himself, especially from mere doctrine. His art, he realizes, must include all his past obsessions, all that makes up his present self. The irrational must enter so that the web of false symbolism, of false meanings, may be destroyed and the true candid images emerge. "Are all lies and truth the same to you?" cries his wife. To which Guido might answer that lies and evasions are part of his search for the authentic self.

And so, though Fellini/Anselmi fears his critics—and in fantasy imagines them as driving him to suicide—he does finally manage to reject their taunts and exhortations. "I am what I am and not what I want to be. . . ." Much as Proust was unable to explain why the *petite madeleine* brought him such ecstasy (and took an unconscionable time in doing so);

343

Fellini/Anselmi likewise is unable to discover why his images bring him such happiness. A magician summons up those inexplicably fascinating, personal images of people he can only love when they become part of himself, and these people join him in the glittering circus of childhood memory. Only then, as the circle is completed, can Fellini/Anselmi see how these images shore him against his ruin, and save him and his boyhood self—a child who plays the piccolo against the encroaching darkness.

Fellini likes greatly to use Roman Catholic ritual to suit his own ends; and 8½, perhaps purposely, takes the form of a confession. In this Fellini reminds us of another lapsed Roman Catholic. "Wilde," writes W. H. Auden, "is the classic case of a man who wants to be loved for himself alone. . . . Nothing is clearer in the history of the three trials than his unconscious desire that the truth should come out." Fellini also assumes that to know all is to forgive all; there is nothing like a good confession for washing our dirty linen whiter than white. What is so cavalier about such magic—as used in a work of art anyway—is that Fellini/Anselmi expects us to condone everything. He tries to give the impression that he is the only real, lovable human being; because of which he feels free, like Madame Ranevsky, to let everyone down. Fellini/Anselmi in short is unable to make the distinction between the truths of the mind, in which lies and evasions are part of the totality, and the clearly knowable truths of behavior.

One would be unfair, though, to doubt the courage of Fellini's confession. Quite justly his persona in 8½ feels persecuted by the critics. Most critics have been grudging in their praise of Fellini, and quite a number of them—those at any rate who are Marxist nannies—have taken a great pleasure in giving him a regular thwacking. "He has," said one of them, making him sound like a lunatic, "a sickening lack of mental firmness, of fundamental moral aliveness and of taste." "Out of this charivari of cruelty and gloom, of subtle malice and sentimentality, of introspection and of half-baked mysticism," said another, "emerges a persistent note of squalor."

The Italian tongue lends itself to superb invective, and Fellini's critics haven't spared themselves in exploiting this bias. But why are they so antagonistic towards him? Could it be that the world doesn't love a self-lover? In part maybe; but the truth of the matter, I would say, is that these critics see Fellini as "a traitor to neorealism."

It is difficult to see on what grounds they can so describe him. Neorealism was more a state of mind than a worked out theory; "a sense of expectation" said Fellini, and that is as good a definition as any. In 1943 Umberto Barbaro, a professor at the Centro Sperimentale Film School in Rome, made a highly rhetorical attack on Fascist rhetoric. He wanted, he claimed, a new kind of film that would rid itself of "those grotesque fabrications which exclude human problems and the human point of view." Neorealism was to be an attempt to show things *as they were,* and not as the religious or the secular authorities wanted them to be. The call was liberal, and it was a call to individual responsibility. "The reality buried under myths slowly reflowered. Here was a tree; here a house; here a man eating, a man sleeping, a man crying," wrote De Sica's scriptwriter, Cesare Zavattini.

Zavattini realized, one assumes, that this urge to escape artifice was as old as art—and that in the cinema it goes back as far as Lumière's brief sequence of a train steaming into a station. The exuberance with which the Italian film makers surveyed, as though for the first time, the cold, wet, luminous world of the post-war years was new however. There was a sense of rebirth; like the prisoners in *Fidelio,* these directors had come up into the light: partisans sink noiselessly beneath the bland waters of the Po, a father watches his hungry son devour a plate of spaghetti. . . . "What De Sica can do, I can't do," boomed Orson Welles. "I ran his *Shoeshine* over recently and the camera disappeared, the screen disappeared; it was just life. . . ."

But alas life, pure life, when found unadulterated in a work of art becomes something of a bore; and neorealism, though its originators didn't seem to realize it, was no more than that dullest form of art, naturalism. "The first concern of the naturalistic writer," said Zola, "will be to collect his material and to find out what he can about the world he wants to describe. . . . When all the material has been gathered, the novel will take place of its own accord."

"Of its own accord"—with this simple phrase Zola manages to slip round the central problem of form. Such a leger-

345

demain applies also to the neorealists. None of them ever approached Zavattini's ideal of filming ninety consecutive minutes in a man's life; artistically speaking, the project was far from feasible. They merely poured new insights into old forms; *Bicycle Thief*, for instance, has the form of a well-made play, while *La Terra Trema* has the form of a socialist realist novel. Moreover, though De Sica and Zavattini make humanist claims, they regress into child-cult and into an Augustinian despair at man's inability to solve his own problems. Visconti also lapses—in his case into the dialectic of history. The authority of Fascism gives way to the authority of the Vatican and the Kremlin. If anyone was treacherous, it was these directors surely. They lacked the technique—and possibly the will—to confront, as individuals, the problems of the post-war world.

Rossellini, who was probably the most liberal of these directors, shares their failure. In *Roma, Città Aperta* "everything," asserts Franco Valorba, "was raised to an abstract ideal of liberty versus tyranny. But liberty from what and for what? And tyranny from what and for what?" Not only is the German intention left unexplored but, more seriously, "both priest and communist use the same concepts of liberty, patriotism, and justice; each of them uses these concepts in a different way, yet each of them is unaware of the difference."

Neorealism was based on the assumption that I-am-a-camera, and that the camera never lies—well, not so long as *I* handle it. This epistemological naïveté is endearing and somehow suits the excitement of a new age. But it could not last. There was a financial crisis; bliss faded as the dawn gave way to the complexities of day. The neorealists fumbled, and some of the old guard were unable to cope with the challenge. Those who did however had to learn that the eye is more than a camera, and that our perceptions involve the need for discrimination; only then was the movement able to flower for a second, and perhaps more magnificent time.

Because of this, Fellini's search for the authentic self through fantasy takes on a historical significance. It may be no more than a coincidence that he directed his first feature in 1952, the year of the financial and ideological crisis; but I doubt it. If there had been no Fellini, we would have had to invent him. All the same, Fellini's interest for us doesn't lie alone in his concern for the inner world of fantasy which becomes tedious when divorced from the outer world; nor does it lie in his ability to "analyze sentiments"; Antonioni was already doing that in 1951, with *Cronaca di un Amore,* and with considerably more precision.

Antonioni and Fellini: a little like Tolstoy and Dostoevsky, Henry James and Dickens, they represent those polarities of experience which often seem to arise when an art form is at its peak. Ardent admirers of one are seldom ardent admirers of both. One remembers the bickering over *L'Avventura* and *La Dolce Vita*: Antonioni was "the more mature" said some, Fellini was "the more exuberant," said others. Certainly Fellini cannot match Antonioni's insight into the sex-war. He is too much in love with himself for his lovers (well, his women anyway) to be more than stereotypes. There is something sick about his idea of love too, which is completely sexless. The recurring situation in an Antonioni film is of a man trying to resolve a love-battle by what Wyndham Lewis calls "amorous treatment, vigorously administered"; with Fellini however we have the eunuch, be it clown or half-wit, at the center of the scene. This anti-eroticism disinfects everything. Sexual disorder was a central theme in *La Dolce Vita*—and although the eunuch has an assured place in tragedy ("an achieved calm"), his role in such a study, surely, should have been peripheral. The result was bizarre, to say the least; one felt that Aunt Edna was working out a blueprint for an orgy in Highgate.

Fellini is very much an intuitive director, improvising on the floor, making up his mind at the last moment. ("To trap fleeting reality, one must avoid any suspicion of cold technique.") This spontaneity, egotism, and clearly neurotic reluctance to handle adult themes tempts one to describe his work in psychoanalytic terms—and no doubt such an approach would tell us a great deal about the structure of his mind. But it would fail to tell us much, if anything, about the quality of his intelligence—his talent, if you will—and it is this singular quality which gives his films their importance and justifies our interest in them.

We are in the presence of an archaic mind, which is, perhaps, unconscious of its singularity. Like a long-legged fly upon the stream, this mind moves over landscape and seashore, town and city, attuned to local texture and mood, remarkably sensible to each difference. Localities stimulate it more than anything else, yet the stimulus is more than one of atmosphere; many of these localities arouse an awe and a sense of communion which are best described as mystical. In *La Strada*, Gelsomina, the half-crazed traveling player, communes with trees and telegraph poles; the world is sacred to her though she doesn't understand why. She meets an acrobat who is as blessed as herself, an angelic fool with whom she falls in love; and during their one moment of confrontation he tells her, echoing Hamlet, that everything in the world, even the smallest pebble, has a meaning. Shortly before her death Gelsomina is found clinging to a pebble as though it were an emblem of her faith.

Like D. H. Lawrence, Fellini has a feeling for the genius of a place—for those gods and demons who inhabit a specific locality. These gods are older and wilder than the Christian God; they are pagan gods, often nameless, often the dark gods celebrated by Lawrence. But unlike Lawrence, Fellini never uses these gods as a major theme; it is as though he lacked the courage of his intuition. In *La Dolce Vita* a wild woman, possibly a medium, says that "Italy is a land full of ancient cults." She is one of a crowd of spectators waiting in a field for two children to carry out a faith-healing performance— the children claim to have had a vision of the Virgin Mary on this spot. But rain falls; the spectators flee, and the sick and lame are drenched. For Fellini the genius of a place can be illusive, can fail us, can be sometimes no more than a conceit.

Yet everything—his visual brilliance, his flair for atmosphere and mood—stems from locality. The castle at Bassano di Sutri, shrouded by night, with its Roman busts and its hollow stone rooms, is the scene for a cult of the dead. A party is in progress. Aristocrats, some of them slumbering, some of them dancing as though drugged, rise up before us like totems —enchanted, burdened by some abstracted despair for which their ancestors alone know the reason. A great door wheels open, and we see round a table princelings and sycophants gathered in the eerie rituals of a seance, seeking from the past some understanding of the present. At the end of a hall is a whispering well; voices carry from room to room a disembodied, false declaration of love. A masque of death: at dawn the guests proceed across a lawn and up a Palladian staircase, the women's gowns as elaborate as those worn at the court of Henri VI. Then the dead awaken: the family priest appears at the end of the garden, and the noble family, as though drawn by a thread, follow him to celebrate mass. Ruefully the other guests depart.

Some localities recur and obsess; one feels that Fellini has often journeyed through them, if not physically, at least in mind. If we were to draw a map of these localities we would find that they made a consistent world of the imagination. We would find, too, that this world had one broad division: between the provinces and the city.

Fellini was born and brought up in Rimini, and the provinces of his imagination have the bleakness of the Adriatic coast. (Though one should add perhaps that his most complete study of provincial life, *I Vitelloni,* was filmed at Viareggio, probably to release his powers of invention.) These provinces sub-divide into various regions, the most primitive of which is a rocky mountainside, studded with desolate crofts. Peasants, as flinty as their surroundings, inhabit these crofts. They are remote, dehumanized and speak an alien tongue; yet they are not without kindness. Zampanò, the Caliban of *La Strada,* perpetually returns to this mountainside, as though it were the one place he might call home.

Fellini appears to associate this place with memories of earliest childhood; the ages of man become a microcosm of the world's history, and we are here at the beginning of creation. The ASA NISI MASA sequence in *8½* gave us the most complete picture of this place: a primeval crone, her head concealed in a balaclava, sleeps in a high chair; sustained chords of music in a minor key shift and change; and there is a terrible sense of desolation and of loss. Playing children are the one sign of life, yet their games are no more than glimpsed at, and remain as enigmatic as their laughter. The whole region presents us with a mystery; here the gangster Augusto in *Il Bidone* is left to die beside a mountain path and dying is redeemed as he sees peasants toil up this path; here, too, Gelsomina finds redemption. Yet the climate has nothing exotic about it; the air is fresh, clumps of snow melt between the rocks, and from a nearby monastery a bell sounds clearly. Many of the regions Fellini describes are familiar to us; none is so unusual as this mountainside with its aura of mystery and its deep sense of peace; none so extends our sensibility.

A similar mystery, perhaps a more theatrical one, bathes the provincial town at night: newspapers swirl round the piazza and lights sway in turbulent alleys. In *I Vitelloni* especially, where the five layabouts represent (we assume) various aspects of the youthful Fellini—though some of them are aged close on thirty—the provincial town is viewed through the eyes of adolescents. At night there is promise of exciting encounters or, less idealistically, of pick-ups in cinemas. But at dawn, after the carnival, this promise proves to be deceptive: the thought of love turns bitter when Alberto's sister runs away with a crook; ambitions sink back into torpor. By light of day the provincial town shows itself as oppressive.

Yet the town is not without its gods, and these are often admirable. Fellini idealizes the provincial father, showing him as an honest, straightforward, *good* man who worships the gods of morality. But such a life is too dour for Fellini's layabouts; they crave for an easy life, for gods more exotic and more central to their needs. Bored, they stand on a jetty and contemplate the sea.

This seascape is familiar to us; it recurs more than any other Fellini locality—and it is the one locality that cries out for a symbolic interpretation. In this case it represents both the inner turbulence of the *vitelloni*—it spews up strange fish—and also, more importantly, it represents reality itself—all that baffles the understanding and chills the imagination.

The layabouts want to escape; yet at the film's end only one of them does so, the sensitive, ingenuous Moraldo. As his train pulls out of the station, an elegant series of traveling shots show us his friends asleep in bed. Perhaps these friends are sensible in not trying to realize their dreams; for though Moraldo may throw off the torpor of provincial life, his awakening will lead to disillusionment. The sequel to *I Vitelloni* was to have been *Moraldo in Città*, in which Moraldo was supposed to have fallen amongst con-men and tricksters. In time this sequel became the less dramatic but no less disillusioned *La Dolce Vita*.

The city, of course, is Rome; and the warring gods of this city preoccupy Fellini more than any other. Who are they, these gods? In *8½* Fellini/Anselmi asks a cardinal how he can find happiness, and is answered by a quotation from the eunuch Origen—only through the church can truth be found. He is then offered the uncompromising choice: *civitas dei* or *civitas diaboli*. We cut at once to a fashionable street and to the glamor of Cianciano. Guido has chosen damnation; but rightly so, perhaps, for he does find a temporary happiness in his images, in his dream of an innocent girl—a girl called, almost inevitably, Cardinale.

"For Freud, as for everyone else in the world, Rome means two things," Ernest Jones writes in his biography. "There is ancient Rome whose culture gave birth to European civilization. Then there is Christian Rome that destroyed and supplanted the older one. This could only be an enemy to him . . . but then an enemy always comes between oneself and the loved object."

For Fellini also, Rome is a double city whose allegiances cannot be reconciled. If we exclude the mediocre *Luci di Varietà*, which he co-directed with Alberto Lattuada, we find this conflict plays a major part in his first feature, *Lo Sciecco Bianco (The White Sheik)*. Two provincials, Oscar and Wanda Cavalli, come to Rome on a honeymoon, on the last day of which they hope to attend a Papal audience. Wanda is a secret reader of *fumetti*, those Italian serials told in photographs, and is infatuated with the hero of one of these serials, The White Sheik. Very much wanting to meet her idol, she slips off to the *fumetti* office on her first morning in Rome. By chance she passes a staircase down which actors in costume are descending. She is enchanted—to her the actors appear to be fabulous Bedouins and houris—and when some of them invite her to join them on a trip to the seaside where they are shooting the latest episode, she willingly agrees. And there, by the pitiless sea, she meets her white sheik and is disillusioned—the sheik turns out to be a philanderer. The girl runs away from the troupe and eventually returns to her husband. In the final scene she and her husband are reconciled, and hand in hand wend their way, not out of Eden, but across St. Peter's Square and towards the Pope, beneath the benediction of stone angels.

This final scene, though moving, is unsatisfactory. The couple may be reconciled, but their reconciliation is childlike and seems an unlikely basis for a happy marriage. Nor can one believe that Fellini wants the Pope to win over the White

Sheik—the enemy has come between him and the loved object. He is uneasy; he too is attracted to an apparently indefensible glamor. And because he is unable to defend this impulse he is forced to take refuge with the stone angels and the morality of the provincial fathers. His uneasiness shows itself in malice: he ridicules the *Bersaglieri* as they trot past in all their finery, and he exposes almost masochistically the shabbiness of the *fumetti* actors. One critic (John Coleman) has justly claimed that Fellini is obsessed with the mediocre and the second-rate. Taking this a step further one could say that Fellini needs to destroy the metropolitan, to turn it into the provincial; if he cannot belong to the glamorous city, he must rob it of its glamor.

Though *civitas diaboli* may win out in his later films, Fellini continues to feel uneasy about it. Many people saw *La Dolce Vita* as a pæan to the pleasures of an orgy, and ignored the irony of the title. Certainly there were "pornographic moments," as regular as those in an Olympia Press novel and just as often fluffed, but the *tone* of the film was one of condemnation; one was reminded of the William Hickey column with its hypocritical prudery. The astounding success of *La Dolce Vita* can be put down, I think, to this effete dallying with *civitas diaboli.* Much of the action was incredible, yet many people swallowed it whole. One wonders why. Could it be that urban man has begun to accept the values of the popular press as a norm? Could it be that its eroticism and violence, its glitter and spangles, have become for him a kind of Nature?

However, Fellini's passion for unusual faces and for first-night crowds has another dimension. In *8½* someone says that "it all stems from Scott Fitzgerald." But even this is true only in part. Fitzgerald was attracted by the golden dream—by "the extraordinary gift for hope, the romantic readiness" that lay beneath the dusty exterior of the Jazz Age. Fellini's obsession with glamor is far more primitive than Fitzgerald's, and is close to the *grammar* of witchcraft.

The "smart" people and the film stars who make Roman society have the power of pagan gods; when the prostitute Cabiria is picked up by her favorite star she is unable to touch him. Indeed these people *are* pagan gods. When some of them first appear they are seen in mid-air, like icons of Christ in ascension: the White Sheik is on a swing, Gelsomina's acrobat is on a tightrope, and the legendary Anita Ekberg descends from an aeroplane like a *diva ex machina*. Anita, of course, is Aphrodite or Venus, and quite the best thing in *La Dolce Vita*. She transforms *civitas dei* into her own kingdom as she paddles in the Fontana dei Trevi or walks down alleys with a kitten on her head. Through her the conflict between the two aspects of the city takes on visual complexity. Dressed as a cardinal she climbs to the top of the trembling dome of St. Peter's and is goddess of all she surveys until her cardinal's hat is blown away—and rising up before the camera, blots out the city. *Civitas dei* remains omnipotent, though its inner sanctuary may be penetrated.

This omnipotence is rapidly diminished in "The Temptation of Dr. Antonio," Fellini's episode in *Boccaccio '70*. Here Anita is without doubt a goddess whose glamour is witchcraft. She appears as a thirty-foot advertisement for milk, posted before the window of the prim and pious doctor. He is shocked by this exhibitionism and throws ink at the giantess. Enraged, she comes to life and teases him into submission by wreathing him in tulle and by dangling him over her capacious bosom. *Civitas diaboli* wins the day; but as one might infer from this grotesque situation, the victory is hardly one to be gloated over.

Does Fellini describe *civitas dei*, or is its presence merely felt by absence? One example suggests an answer. Fellini, we know, likes to secularize church ritual, especially processions. In *La Strada*, Gelsomina watches four happy clowns dance along by a ditch playing fantastic musical instruments (similar figures appear at the end of 8½). By contrast, we cut to a religious procession: trumpets bray, the crowd bows before holy images, and the earth trembles. Our sense of *terribilità* is only diminished a little by the brief shot of a pig, crucified in a butcher's window.

The reason for this fear and disrespect of the Church is given in 8½, where priests are shown as tormenting the child Anselmi into impotence. This is a fairly weak argument, and no doubt Fellini is being unjust to the Church. Still, no one would ever claim that Fellini's view of things was a balanced one. His is a religious mind, alienated from any particular religion, unable to conceive of a liberal, secular city (cf. his one agnostic intellectual, introduced by the characteristic line,

"Thanks to Father Franz I've at last found this ancient Sanskrit grammar. I've been looking for it everywhere"). All the same, we would be wrong to think there was only one choice: between the terror of the Church and the hell of the *beau monde*; though this primitivism—fulfilled in the baroque style, the vividly etched images, the thunder and lightning—is powerful certainly, and reminds us of the Polish Marxist, Andrej Wajda, who is also ensnared in a Roman Catholic past. (It reminds us too of Verdi, on whom Fellini, with his absurd anachronistic hat, has obviously modelled himself.)

Nonetheless, Fellini would probably agree with St. Augustine that *civitas dei* is not to be found in the Church alone, if at all. In so far as it does manifest itself on earth, *civitas dei* is to be found in the lives of holy innocents—holy because they are in touch with the gods of the ancient Italian countryside. Some of them are religious: monks and nuns living in isolated communities, even the awesome cardinal who reads legends into a bird's song. Some of them are innocents in spite of themselves: the "Umbrian angel," the station master's boy. But unfortunately this concept of innocence doesn't bear much close attention. We cannot believe in Gelsomina's madness nor in Cabiria's purity; we are conscious merely of the actress trying to sustain both character and symbol, and failing in both.

"When Pastoral fails," William Empson wrote, "it takes refuge in child-cult." The neorealists often fail in this way. The De Sica-Zavattini combine, for instance, uses child-cult to escape from dealing with social problems on an adult level. The same is true of Fellini. If we understand by innocence an idealized state of mind where guilt and anxiety have no place, then we must see Fellini's dream of innocence as escapist. Too often he tries to flee from the pressure of experience, nowhere more obviously than at the end of *La Dolce Vita*, where he retreats into a mawkish symbolism. Still, one has difficulty in dismissing this scene—as one has difficulty in dismissing anything of Fellini's. Though the characters may appear as false, the locality in which they breathe is so deeply realized that it takes on the clarity of vision—as figures move like dryads between the pine trees or wave to each other before a mysterious prospect of the sea.

The Event and the Image
by Michelangelo Antonioni

These comments by the distinguished Italian director appeared first in Cinema Nuovo, No. 164. The English translation was printed in the Winter 1963–64 issue of Sight and Sound.

A film maker is a man like any other; and yet his life is not the same. *Seeing* is for us a necessity. For a painter too the problem is one of seeing; but while for the painter it is a matter of uncovering a static reality, or at most a rhythm that can be held in a single image, for a director the problem is to catch a reality which is never static, is always moving towards or away from a moment of crystallization, and to present this movement, this arriving and moving on, as a new perception. It is not sound—words, noises, music. Nor is it a picture— landscape, attitudes, gestures. Rather it is an indivisible whole that extends over a duration of its own which determines its very being. At this point the dimension of time comes into play, in its most modern conception. It is in this order of intuition that the cinema can acquire a new character, no longer merely figurative. The people around us, the places we visit, the events we witness—it is the spatial and temporal relations these have with each other that have a meaning for us today, and the tension that is formed between them.

This is, I think, a special way of being in contact with reality. And it is also a special reality. To lose this contact, in the sense of losing this *way* of being in contact, can mean sterility. That is why it is important, for a director even more than for other artists, precisely because of the complexity of the material he has between his hands, to be committed morally in some way. It is almost superfluous to point out that our effort as directors must be just that of bringing the data of our personal experience into accord with that of a more general experience, in the same way as individual time accords mysteriously with that of the cosmos. But even this effort will be sterile if we do not succeed in giving, by this means, a sincere justification of the choices which life has obliged us to make.

The sky is white; the sea-front deserted; the sea cold and empty; the hotels white and half-shuttered. On one of the white seats of the Promenade des Anglais the bathing attendant is seated, a Negro in a white singlet. It is early. The sun labors to emerge through a fine layer of mist, the same as every day. There is nobody on the beach except a single bather floating inert a few yards from the shore. There is nothing to be heard except the sound of the sea, nothing to observe except the rocking of that body. The attendant goes down to the beach and into the bathing station. A girl comes out and walks toward the sea. She is wearing a flesh-colored costume.

The cry is short, sharp, and piercing. A glance is enough to tell that the bather is dead. The pallor of his face, the mouth full of saliva, the jaws stiff as in the act of biting, the few hairs glued to the forehead, the eyes staring, not with the fixity of death but with a troubled memory of life. The body is stretched out on the sand with the stomach in the air, the feet apart and pointing outwards. In a few moments, while the attendant attempts artificial respiration, the beach fills up with people.

A boy of ten, pushing forward a little girl of about eight, shoves his way through to watch. "Look," he says to the girl, "can you see?" "Yes" she says, very quietly. "Can you see the spit on his mouth?" "Yes." "And the swollen stomach? Do you see? It's full of water." The little girl watches as though fascinated, in silence. The boy goes on, with a kind of sadistic joy. "Now he's still white, but in a few moments he'll go blue. Look under his eyes; look, it's starting." The girl nods in assent, but remains silent; her face shows clearly that she is beginning to feel sick. The boy notices this and looks gloating. "You scared?" "No," the little girl replies in a thin voice. "Yes you are," he insists, and goes on almost chanting, "You're scared . . . you're scared . . ." After ten minutes or so the police arrive, and the beach is cleared. The attendant is the only one who remains with the policeman. Then he too goes off, summoned by a lady with violet hair for her usual lesson of gymnastics.

It was wartime. I was at Nice, waiting for a visa to go to Paris to join Marcel Carné, with whom I was going to work as an assistant. They were days full of impatience and boredom, and of news about a war which stood still on an absurd thing called the Maginot Line. Suppose one had to construct a bit of film, based on this event and on this state of mind. I would try first to remove the actual event from the scene, and leave only the image described in the first four lines. In that white sea-front, that lonely figure, that silence, there seems to me to be an extraordinary strength of impact. The event here adds nothing; it is superfluous. I remember very well that I was interested, when it happened. The dead man acted as a distraction to a state of tension.

But the true emptiness, the *malaise*, the anxiety, the nausea, the atrophy of all normal feelings and desires, the fear, the anger—all these I felt when, coming out of the Negresco, I found myself in that whiteness, in that nothingness, which took shape around a black point.

Shape Around a Black Point

by Geoffrey Nowell-Smith

Mr. Nowell-Smith is a British journalist who writes frequently on motion picture personalities. This chapter appeared originally in the Winter 1963–64 issue of Sight and Sound.

There is one brief scene in *L'Avventura,* not on the face of it a very important one, which seems to me to epitomize perfectly everything that is most valid and original about Antonioni's form of cinema. It is the scene where Sandro and Claudia arrive by chance at a small village somewhere in the interior of Sicily. The village is strangely quiet. They walk around for a bit, call out. No reply, nothing. Gradually it dawns on them that the village is utterly deserted, uninhabited, perhaps never was inhabited. There is no one in the whole village but themselves, together and alone. Disturbed, they start to move away. For a moment the film hovers: the world is, so to speak, suspended for two seconds, perhaps more. Then suddenly the film plunges, and we cut to a close-up of Sandro and Claudia making love in a field—one of the most ecstatic moments in the history of the cinema, and one for which there has been apparently no formal preparation whatever. What exactly has happened?

It is not the case that Sandro and Claudia have suddenly fallen in love, or suddenly discovered at that moment that they have been in love all along. Nor, at the other extreme, is theirs a panic reaction to a sudden fear of desolation and loneliness. Nor again is it a question of the man profiting from a moment of helplessness on the part of the woman in order to seduce her. Each of these explanations contains an aspect of the truth, but the whole truth is more complicated and ultimately escapes analysis. What precisely happened in that moment the spectator will never know, and it is doubtful if the characters really know for themselves. Claudia knows that Sandro is interested in her. By coming with him to the village she has already more or less committed herself, but the actual fatal decision is neither hers nor his. It comes, when it comes, impulsively; and its immediate cause, the stimulus which provokes the response, is the feeling of emptiness and need created by the sight of the deserted village. Just as her feelings (and his too for that

358

matter) are neither purely romantic nor purely physical, so her choice, Antonioni is saying, is neither purely determined nor purely free. She chooses, certainly, but the significance of her choice escapes her, and in a sense also she could hardly have acted otherwise.

The technical means by which all this is conveyed are no less interesting, and give further clues about Antonioni's general attitude to life and to the cinema as a means of expression. When the first shot of the village comes up, one expects it to be what is generally known as an establishing shot—that is to say something to set the scene, to establish the location and atmosphere in which the scene will develop. In fact, however, the shot *is* the scene, not an introduction to it, and the location is not just somewhere for the event to take place, but synonymous with the event itself (equally the event is the location and not just something that happens there). Antonioni does not cut away from the background to concentrate on the characters, at least not immediately. He holds his shot, all his shots, just that bit longer than would be strictly necessary for them to make their point, if there were a point to be made. He holds them in this case for as long as it takes for the spectator to become aware not only of the background, but of the characters themselves becoming aware of the background. There are no ellipses; screen time and real time virtually correspond. But although the camera is subjective in matter of time, in that the audience's sense of time follows that of the characters, the general impression is of extreme objectivity. The spectator is never put in the character's place and encouraged to feel what the character is supposed to be feeling. On this occasion he will no doubt react in much the same way to the sense of absurdity and desolation put across by the landscape; but the important thing is not this, but rather that he should watch, with the camera, dispassionately and almost scientifically, the reactions of the characters themselves.

He has no certain guide to what they are feeling or thinking except their purely exterior reactions, fragments of behavior; and in Antonioni films this behavior will often seem at any given moment arbitrary and unmotivated. As a result the meaning of the film is forever in a state of flux. The behavioristic form of observation suggests an initial determinism; somewhere in the background there is a basic pattern of cause and effect. But in practice everything is disconnected. There is something almost capricious in the way people behave; directions are always uncertain until it is too late; and the sense of an event is never clear until after it has happened, and something else has occurred to define the significance of what went before.

A world in which everything is surrounded by a faint halo of indeterminacy is going to be insecure in other ways as well. Empiricism has always been the agnostic's epistemology, and Antonioni is a radical agnostic. In his films there is never any certainty, any definite or absolute truth. The meaning of single events is often ambiguous, and cumulatively these events add up to a picture of a world from which order, value, and logic have disappeared. This should not be taken in too metaphysical a sense. The characters in Antonioni films do not go around, like the followers of Sartre or Merleau-Ponty, earnestly trying to put back the essences into existence. They are simply faced with the business of living in a world which offers of itself no certainty and no security, at least not in the immediate present. And when a character does seem to have assured himself somehow, through his job or through his relationship with another person, his security is probably (though not necessarily: again Antonioni is not Sartre) an illusion, for which he will have to pay before long.

This sense of fundamental insecurity which affects the more lucid of Antonioni's characters (the stupid ones are generally more or less immune, and probably happier as a result) is no doubt largely subjective. Their particular existentialist inferno is very much of their own making. But in a less acute form the same general malaise can be seen to affect the whole of society, and to be reflected in the physical environment which modern man has created for himself and in which he has chosen to live. The deserted village in *L'Avventura* is a perfect example. Visually it recalls instantly the vacant surfaces and deranged perspectives of Chirico's *pittura metafisica*, and it means much the same thing. This civic townscape, devoid of citizens, dehumanized and absurd, in which two people come together and make love, acts in a sense as a symbol, or a parable, for the whole of modern life. Man, it seems to say, has built himself his own world, but he is incapable of living in it. He is excluded from his own creation, and his only refuge lies in fortuitous encounters with another being in the same predicament. In a word, he is "alienated."

Like *L'Avventura, The Eclipse* too sets out to expand and develop its author's ideas about the modern world, about the difficulties of living and loving in a world that has grown incomprehensible even to itself. It is therefore, like *L'Avventura*, as the critics were not slow to point out, a film about "alienation"; but it is so indirectly, and almost incidentally. Antonioni himself is categorical about this. As he sees it, the nucleus of his film is not, and could not be, a concept, particularly one so vague and indeterminate as alienation. The nucleus of *The Eclipse*, as of all his films, is a story, however slight and undramatic (and the story of *The Eclipse* is so slight as to make that of *L'Avventura* seem almost melodramatic by comparison).

The question is primarily one of emphasis. By insisting that each of his films begins with a story, particular people in a particular situation, Antonioni is asking the critic to look more at the particulars and less at the sublime but depressing generalities they supposedly reflect. The point is well taken. Except for *La Notte*, which still seems to me a deeply pessimistic film, and rather dogmatic in its pessimism into the bargain, none of Antonioni's work is ever so arid, or so alienating, as a conventional analysis of his ideas might suggest. In each of his films there is a positive pole and a negative, and a tension between them. The abstraction, the "ideology," lies mostly at the negative pole. The concrete and actual evidence, the life of the film, is more often positive—and more often neglected by criticism.

As with all Antonioni's later films, the story of *The Eclipse* is cast in the form of a sort of spiritual journey towards, ideally, self-discovery and the discovery of the world. The discovery may not be consummated; indeed the journey may end, as with *Il Grido*, and perhaps *La Notte*, only in destruction. But it remains the ideal goal to which the central character is always being carried forward. Clelia in *Le Amiche*, Aldo in *Il Grido*, Claudia in *L'Avventura*, Lidia in *La Notte*, and Vittoria in *The Eclipse* are all variations on a single theme, always on the move, searching, questioning, however inarticulately, until they arrive at some sort of conclusion. In *The Eclipse* Vittoria starts by renouncing a stable relationship which she feels obscurely to be somehow unsatisfactory to both sides. She then wanders, half purposefully, more often drifting, through the void left by the break-up, until she hitches up tentatively, almost experimentally, with another man. The film ends with the future of the new affair still in suspense, but with the odds heavily against it continuing. Journeys traditionally end with lovers meeting; this one ends on a question mark, with a missed rendezvous. And what the question seems to ask is, "Was it worth it? Was your journey really necessary?"

Abstractly, on the face of it, one can only answer, no. Like the other Antonioni heroines (and they are mostly heroines, not heroes, in Antonioni films), Vittoria has only come up against a wall of incompatibility, non-communication, failure; and beyond the failure, once acknowledged, no further prospect of success. But I cannot help feeling that concretely, as it is given from moment to moment in the unfolding of the story, the message of the film is very different. In this perspective what matters is not the result, which remains in any case uncertain, but the journey itself, the search, and the way it is lived out by Vittoria, the heroine. It is Vittoria who is there, in situation; and as I suggested in analyzing the village sequence from *L'Avventura,* we are not being asked to respond directly to the situation, but only through our observation of Vittoria, the observer observed. In Antonioni's intention *The Eclipse* is a positive film, and if this comes across in effect it is because Vittoria herself is so positive. She is bright, she is honest, she is ravishingly beautiful, she is unquenchably alive, she is even (shock to the critics) happy, or capable of being so. She is also, sometimes, rather tiresome, but that is by the way. The important thing is that in a situation where at times everything seems to conspire to destroy her and all that she stands for, she survives—at least until the next round. The search will go on, and it will have been worth while.

To say that *The Eclipse* is a film about alienation, therefore, is largely to miss the point. The film is not about alienation, it is about Vittoria. If in the course of the film the spectator is moved to feel, or rather to think, that Vittoria is in fact alienated, that she has an alienated relationship with an alienated world, this is a different matter entirely. But even on this relatively concrete level the word remains a blanket concept, and a wide one, in danger of stifling whatever lies

362

underneath. Throughout the trilogy, and even in the earlier films, there are sequences and shots which reflect a consistent view of the world and of the human situation from which alienation, or some related concept, could be isolated as a key factor. Such, for example, is the Stock Exchange sequence in *The Eclipse*. Vittoria here is seen as an outsider, a looker-in on a world which has a dynamism of its own, which she cannot share in or even understand. Watching the curious spectacle of finance in action she is both alienated from it and conscious of her alienation. But is it Vittoria here who is alienated, or is it not rather the Exchange and the whole financial game itself—alienated in that its players live in a neurotic world in which scraps of paper have taken the place of the solid material values they are supposed to represent? Either way there is a lack of essential *rapport*. As in the deserted village sequence, there is something about this world that refuses to make sense. Both sequences function artistically by generating an impression of strangeness, lack of connection, and out of the strangeness comes the idea that the world is more than strange: estranged in fact—for which alienated is a synonym.

From the earlier films one might cite Aldo's estrangement from his village environment, best characterized in the final sequence when, as his former comrades run away from the village, away from the refinery, to take part in a protest meeting against the building of an airfield, Aldo himself is shown moving against the stream, back to the village, to Irma and to the refinery, to his death. But on the whole the alienation depicted by Antonioni is psychological rather than social, and takes various forms. At one point in *The Eclipse* Vittoria and Piero mimic the love play, observed, of other couples, and then suddenly the mime turns into an imitation of themselves, a playback of their own recorded experience. This also could be called alienation, but at a different, perhaps deeper level. It suggests that Vittoria at least is no more at home in herself than she is in society, or at any rate that she has what is in context an alarming capacity for standing outside herself. This particular kind of detachment, shared in less degree by the other Monica Vitti characters, by Claudia in *L'Avventura* and Valentina in *La Notte*, indicates in general an exacerbated self-consciousness and an inability to play things straight without turning in on the self to observe and to question. This contrasts sharply with the character of the men in Antonioni films, who have neither the intelligent self-awareness nor the morbidity of the women characters, and therefore fail to understand them when understanding should have been possible. Again the theme is lack of *rapport*, but here it is not really alienation for all that.

Nor is Antonioni's way of showing his characters as outsiders, non-participants, symptomatic of quite the same thing, though it is related. When Lidia, in *La Notte*, watches the two men fighting on the wasteland in the Milan *periferia*, she is in a position of uncomprehending outsider like that of Vittoria at the Exchange. But what makes the scene powerful is not the banal observation that she and the men are worlds apart, but what happens afterwards. She seems powerless and cut off, as if hypnotized by the performance, unable to intervene, horrified and yet equally unable to move away. Then, suddenly, she shouts out "Stop!" and, incredibly, they do stop. The spell is broken, but the atmosphere remains heavily charged. One of the men gets up and follows Lidia, and one senses between him and the composed, rather frigid, middle-class woman, before she finally turns away and runs, a sort of instinctive animal *rapport* which is a direct and dramatic reversal of the original situation. Very quickly Lidia reverts, and rejects the scabrous implications of the situation; civilization gets the better of a dubious instinct, and if a clear meaning can be extracted from this episode, it is surely that for better or worse civilized and distinctively human values demand that she should be in a position to reject, and by implication that self-awareness should win through. Alienation, if that is what it is, becomes part of the necessary fabric of civilized life.

As should be clear from his films, Antonioni's main concern as an artist is with things and with people, with shapes, light and shade, social facts and human thoughts and emotions. He is not concerned, as far as I can see, with any apparatus of concepts and symbols. His films cannot be fitted easily into any pre-cast conceptual mould, and his way of expressing his ideas is generally speaking direct and literal, and does not require symbols or symbolic interpretations to achieve significance. Each action, each visual detail, has its place in a particular plot. The recurrence of some of these details and of

364

certain themes may suggest that they are meant to have a general as well as a particular validity. This is only reasonable: Antonioni is a very consistent and consistently thoughtful director. But it is not possible to isolate details from their immediate context and attribute to them the value of universal symbols.

Contrary to what is often thought, Antonioni has a horror of obvious symbolic correspondences. It did not take him long to realize that his starting point for *L'Eclipse,* the actual solar eclipse, would provide in the finished film only a tedious and unnecessary metaphor—"the eclipse of the sentiments"—for what he really had to say. So he cut it out, and it survives only as an allusion in the title. Speculating here, I should also say that if it had been pointed out to him that the shots of the emptying water butt and the water running to drain in the final sequence of the same film would be taken conceptually as a straightforward symbol of Vittoria and Piero's affair running out, then he would probably have cut them out or altered them so as to minimize, if not eliminate, the association. The meaning of this final seqence, even in the cut version shown in London, is extraordinarily rich and complex, and is diminished rather than enhanced by this sort of interpretation. It depends, like much of the best lyric poetry, on a subtle interplay of subjective and objective, of fact and feeling; but it derives most of its imagery from the narrative structure of the earlier part of the film.

Piero and Vittoria have agreed on a rendezvous, "same place, same time." The camera turns up to keep the appointment, but neither of the protagonists. The rendezvous was for late afternoon; night falls, and they still don't come. Presumably neither of them will come that evening. There are plenty of reasons why either or both might have failed to come, but none is given. Nor is it certain that this is their last and only chance, that the affair is definitely over. One presumes that it is, but the only convincing reason for believing this is the atmosphere of finality that broods over the scene as afternoon yields to evening, to twilight, and then to darkness.

For ten minutes of film the camera offers a montage of mainly fixed-angle shots that record the passage of time in the movement of buses, in the switching on and off during the last hours of daylight of the hoses watering the grass, in the ebbing of the sunlight and lighting-up of the street lamps. The process is utterly impersonal and mechanical. It happens, and every day it happens the same way. As it gets darker, so the people in the streets get fewer, and those that remain seem not to have any human identity. In three successive shots, closing in, we see a man getting off a bus; the newspaper he is reading with a headline about the bomb; and his face, the utterly blank intensity of his eyes distorted by the lenses of his spectacles. Each of these images has a story of its own to tell, but all are subordinated to the main story. We are only here because we are waiting for Piero and Vittoria, who do not come; and the camera only looks in the directions it does because here are the points where Piero and Vittoria have been before, and where we are expecting to see them again. If these locations are dehumanized it is only because the lovers are no longer there to people them; and the sense is not only that they have been caught up in the wheel of time and that their affair has run its course, but also that everything that is sinister in the process of night falling on the city is due to a human failure, in particular to the failure of Piero and Vittoria to keep an appointment.

Yet while both these things are true, or at any rate asserted by the film, there are further overtones which serve to counter-balance the portentous aspects of the scene. Most important, despite the air of finality given to the images, we don't really know that this is the end at all. It may not even be the end for Piero and Vittoria as a couple; it is certainly not the end of the world. As Antonioni himself has put it (I quote from memory), this is an eclipse not the millenium, and "up to now no eclipse has yet been definitive." One should not forget either that a highly selective and elliptical montage such as Antonioni uses in this sequence is one of the most subjective of all cinema techniques. Uniquely in this sequence he is offering a purely lyrical (and for that reason not literal, but not symbolic either) interpretation of the events shown. His camera here is the voice of a lyric poet who draws on real material but fuses it together in a purely imaginative way in order to envisage sub-jectively a purely imaginative possibility—that the light should have gone out on the love between Piero and Vittoria. The idea of indeterminacy, axiomatic in Antonioni's work, insists that we admit theoretically an alternative possibility, and that further events may yet falsify the picture we have built up of what is happening. At any instant we have only the moment to go on in provisionally interpreting the events, and at this moment it seems to be the end. It feels like the end, and that is what Antonioni is really trying to say.

This final sequence of *The Eclipse* is unique in Antonioni's work in that it does to a certain limited extent rely on symbols for effect, and in that he does seem for the first time to want to break away from the Flaubertian realism which is his normal vein into a more imaginative and lyrical style. This breakaway is in fact foreshadowed in parts of *La Notte*, in particular in the long, disturbing sequence of Lidia's solitary walk around Milan. But even in *The Eclipse,* except at the end, what I would call the Flaubertian note remains dominant—the note of the painstaking and accurate stylist, the careful investigator of behavior and environment, the ruthless analyst of sentimental and intellectual failure, the essential realist. Antonioni's realism is not naturalism or *verismo*. It is too finely wrought, pared down too sharply to the essentials of what has to be said. It is also too interior, as much concerned to chart the movements of the mind, however objectively regarded, as it is to observe physical emotions and things. But—and this is why Antonioni, like Flaubert, remains basically a realist—movements below the surface are generally left to be deduced from surface reactions. They are not artificially exteriorized in terms of convenient symbols, as in expressionism, nor are they supposed to inhabit a metaphysical world of their own.

Like the sea bottom, the mind remains part of the natural physical world, but one which does not happen to be visible, and is therefore mysterious. The analogy is imperfect, because it implies 'a more radical form of determinism than is in fact the case with Antonioni. The apparent indeterminacy of the movements of consciousness is not just the product of our ignorance of the causes; it is real. But its sphere of action is limited, and above all (and this is a basic difference between Antonioni and directors like Bresson, Rossellini and Godard) it implies no spiritual metaphysics. Antonioni's films show him, as near as makes no odds, a resolute materialist.

It is tempting, none the less, to try to discern bits of expressionist symbolism dotted around Antonioni's work, and I admit that if such could be found, they would make things easier for critics. But the temptation must be resisted. Such symbols as can be found are more often figments of the critic's imagination, or at best jetsam of the director's unconscious, than significant elements of the artistic structure. In all Antonioni's films together (except perhaps *Cronaca di un Amore*) the expressionist details could probably be counted on the fingers of one hand, and even those few dismissed as irrelevant. There may be something in the idea that in *Il Grido* the refinery tower is Aldo's positive symbol, while the river is a symbol of Irma and his love for her. Such a symbolism is both sexually and dramatically appropriate (Aldo's failure to break away from dependence on the woman is, as it were, symbolized by his inability to go far from the river, or to leave the valley entirely). But even here, where the symbolism, if such it is, is built into the structure of the film, it is clearly not intended to be expressive as symbolism. If it is important, which it is not, it can only be because Aldo himself is obscurely aware of what the tower and the river mean *for him*. It is not a bit of expressive shorthand in the style, aimed at underlining heavily what should, after all, be already obvious from the plot.

An Italian critic has remarked, very suggestively, that one of the salient features of Antonioni's style is that it makes no bid to communicate in the mass. It is essentially untheatrical. It does not project itself at an audience, but demands that each individual spectator should involve himself privately with what is going on. There is nothing hectoring or demagogic about it; it calls for intelligent observation, not participation. It is also very much a pictorial style, which communicates through the image and uses the sound track as a complement to the image, and rarely as an independent vehicle for the ideas. As a result it makes rather special demands on the sensibility of the spectator *moyen intellectuel,* who is the only type who normally gets round to seeing the films. Apart from that it is not really a difficult style to come to terms with. Much of what is apparently outrageous is so as the result of being extremely compressed, as if every shot were trying to extract the maximum significance from every detail of the material. The form of observation may seem abnormal, but it is nearly always apposite—suited to the location, the time of day, the state of mind of the characters, the general situation.

When, for example, one has been up all night and is very tired, one's mode of perception (mine at least) is subtly altered; one is more susceptible to resonances in the physical properties of objects than under more normal conditions. It is this feeling that is communicated, very sharply, by the opening sequence of *The Eclipse*, not only in the tense exhaustion of the characters but in the oppressive presence of objects, in the buzzing of an electric fan that grates persistently on an already exposed aural nerve. The effect is both irritating and, to a spectator not yet attuned, unnatural; but perhaps for that very reason, all the more authentic and true.

Where in this oppressive physical and social environment do the characters find any escape? How can they break out of the labyrinth which nature and other men and their own sensibilities have built up around them? Properly speaking there is no escape, nor should there be. Man is doomed to living in the world—this is to say no more than that he is doomed to exist. But the situation is not hopeless. There are moments of happiness in the films, which come, when they come, from being at peace with the physical environment, or with others, not in withdrawing from them. Claudia in *L'Avventura*, on the yacht and then on the island, is cut off, mentally, from the other people there, and gives herself over to undiluted enjoyment of her physical surroundings, until with Anna's disappearance even these surroundings seem to turn against her and aggravate rather than alleviate her pain. In *The Eclipse* Vittoria's happiest moment is during that miraculous scene at Verona when her sudden contentment seems to be distilled out of the simple sights and sounds of the airport: sun, the wind in the grass, the drone of an aeroplane, a juke-box. At such moments other people are only a drag—and yet the need for them exists. The desire to get away from oneself, away from other people, and the satisfaction this gives, arise only from the practical necessity for most of the time of being aware of oneself and of forming casual or durable relationships with other people. And the relationships too can be a source of fulfillment. No single trite or abstract formulation can catch the living essence of Antonioni's version of the human comedy.

Richard Lester
by Philip French

*Mr French, for a number of years a producer for the BBC Third
Programme, is now drama critic for The New Statesman
and film critic for The London Magazine. This chapter appeared
originally in the Autumn 1965 issue of the British publication Movie.*

The bed-moving sequence in *The Knack* is perhaps Richard
Lester's best sustained piece of cinema to date, and towards the
end of it there's a moment that might be interpreted as the key
to his work. Tom, Nancy and Colin have brought their vehicle
to rest beside a parking meter in St. George Street. They sit
down on it, eating their sandwiches, free from interference by
the officious traffic warden; for a brief while they have a right
to this minute space in the center of London. Around the corner
in Hanover Square is the gleaming London office of ABC Television; down the street we can see the venerable portico of
the fashionable St. George's church, Hanover Square, and beside it the Hanover Gallery, London dealers of pioneer Op
artist Victor Vasarely and several major surrealists including
Max Ernst and René Magritte. Disgruntled, envious, puzzled
passers-by contribute another series of verbal clichés which
punctuate the film like a sort of walking commentary.

One of these comments is a line that screenwriter Charles
Wood also places in the mouth of the prurient protector of
public morality in his play "Meals on Wheels": "I come from
Hampton Wick myself so I'm no stranger to innuendo." Among
the rapid shots of spectators, as this and other lines fly out, the
sharp observer will have noted the quizzical presence of the
man behind it all, the balding yet long-haired Richard Lester.
Lester does not come from Hampton Wick—he was born in
Philadelphia thirty-three years ago—but he is no stranger to
innuendo.

I have, of course, deliberately read into this scene more
than could possibly have been intended; nevertheless it does
seem to present in their clearest form the technique and
themes of Lester, to demonstrate the difference between his
film and Anne Jellicoe's play, and symbolically to define Lester's
esthetic and his cultural situation. The rest of what I have to
say will be merely an elaboration of this. The critic can com-

pete in seriousness with a "serious" film maker, but he is ill advised to compete in the same sense with a comic director. Some reviewers of *A Hard Day's Night* and *Help!* have tried, only to finish up as sheep in Tom Wolfe's clothing. So if I write anything which would appear to impute too great a seriousness or deliberation to Lester, I'm conscious of doing it over the live body of his work.

Lester was suddenly "discovered" last year with *A Hard Day's Night* and at the time no one seemed capable of distinguishing his contribution from that of the Beatles, Alun Owen, and Gilbert Taylor. This was however his third feature film, being preceded by *It's Trad Dad!* (1962) and *Mouse on the Moon* (1963). There had also been the celebrated short *The Running, Jumping and Standing Still Film*, not to mention his considerable experience (and professional reputation) as a director of TV shows and commercials.

The eleven minutes of *The Running, Jumping and Standing Still Film* immediately established his rapport with Goonery. With it Lester found a visual style that was absent from earlier Goon films (such as *Down Among the Z Men*) and present only intermittently in the television Goon programs which he directed. (It must be recognized, however, that the Goons—the comedy team comprising Peter Sellers, Spike Milligan, Michael Bentine, and Harry Secombe have never subsequently reached the inspired comic heights that their radio programs of the 1950's so consistently attained. Their partnership was the last great creative blast of radio comedy in Britain and their achievement stands comparison with the best of the Marx Brothers.) There is the use of silent film techniques, the camera trickery, the Sisyphian surrealism of scrubbing the grass, the brutal slapstick of the hand luring the simpleton across the field only to sock him for his pains, the comic chauvinism of the Union Jack-bedecked kite being prepared for spaceflight, and the nostalgic sepia tone print of the film itself. All these elements together with the mood of tough yet relaxed inconsequentiality, the pursuit of logic beyond the bounds of sanity, the rather disturbing national ambivalence (of the kind reflected in the title of Michael Bentine's stage show "Don't Shoot, We're English!"), were to reappear later. Indeed, they were to appear in part almost immediately in *It's Trad Dad!*

On the face of it *It's Trad Dad!* must have seemed an unattractive assignment—a musical with a threadbare story of two teenagers (the unpromising combination of Helen Shapiro and Craig Douglas) enlisting the assistance of a trio of disc jockeys to attract some Dixieland bands to their New Town. The object of the exercise was to persuade the local mayor and civic functionaries to tolerate their sort of music. This teen-agers-versus-the-older-generation situation has been a stock formula for B-feature musicals since the Forties, if not earlier, and has been revived for Rock and Twist quickies. Lester, how-ever, seized the opportunity to make one of the most extraor-dinarily inventive movies of the last ten years which is not only highly amusing but gently satirized its own convention as well. Using a *Hellzapoppin*-type narrator who talks to the actors and assists in furthering the action, the film opens with the statement that the place in which the story is set must remain nameless—and there, sure enough, is the "You are now entering" sign on the outskirts of the town with the name miss-ing. Watching the picture is like going around the exhibition of "Ten Years of Graphic Design by Former Students at the Royal College of Art" which was put on the following year at the lively institution where Lester had a considerable cult reputation before he came to national prominence. This is par-ticularly noticeable in the presentation of numbers in TV shows. The Acker Bilk band is shot through a grille to resemble blown-up news photos (or Lichtenstein paintings), a few frames are shown in negative; the screen is blacked out and the Terry Lightfoot jazzmen introduced one by one in cut out sections until the screen is filled; the Kenny Ball outfit is shown in interlocked vertical strips; the film cuts between identical positionings of the Brooks Brothers, each beside a blown-up photograph of himself. The best and least modish of these scenes is perhaps that displaying the Temperance Seven, a group specializing in Twenties-style pastiche, itself incidentally a product of the Royal College of Art. Their groupings change entirely with almost every shot, French subtitles accompany a song in French, a horn player suddenly has a dog beside him like an HMV trademark, the camera shoots through vocalist Paul Macdowell's megaphone etc. Later on at the big band rally in the town square, a flash-bulb pops and is followed for the next few bars by still-photographs of the musicians. No doubt deliberately, this scene of teenage "defiance" begins with

Lightfoot's band playing "Maryland" (i.e., The Red Flag with a Dixieland beat), and concludes, after the narrator has picked out the mayor, the boy, and the girl with arrows and titles, with the comment: "So the boy, the girl, and the mayor lived happily ever after—at least until after the finale."

It's Trad Dad! is a slight film, basically dead at the center. Yet looking back on it, one is astonished that the almost prodigal comic and visual imagination behind its direction should have gone largely unnoticed. One can see in it and its brief predecessor the seeds of everything that was shortly to be admired in *A Hard Day's Night, The Knack,* and *Help!*

Before the first Beatles' picture, however, there came *Mouse on the Moon,* a not unamusing though almost totally unmemorable sequel to *The Mouse that Roared.* It was funnier and faster than *The Mouse that Roared* and more interesting in its use of color, as I rather vaguely recall. But although Lester turned in a competent job one could sense that he was little engaged by the standard British comedy leads at his service, or the whimsical celebration of pseudo-Ealing tweeness that the tedious script made inescapable. Then suddenly, as if breaking free from this straitjacket, Lester came up with his next three films in the space of little more than a year—a creative burst that established him immediately as one of the three or four most accomplished directors in Britain today.

Of course he got the *Hard Day's Night* assignment partly because he had done *Mouse on the Moon* for Walter Shenson and it is greatly to Shenson's credit that he gave Lester a wide measure of freedom for the picture. Commercial prudence might well have suggested the choice of some safe man-of-all-works to pilot a depersonalized vehicle like those shaped for Presley, Richard, or Steele. Lester was certainly fortunate in his collaborators. The Beatles were as a group and individually more interesting than any other pop idols on the current scene (though this had not yet got through to the public at large) and *The Running, Jumping and Standing Still Film* was one of their favorite movies. The screenwriter Alun Owen had worked with Lester on television and is one of the outstanding playwrights to have been produced by British television; he specialized initially in plays set in his native Liverpool and his best work has always come when he's returned to Merseyside for inspiration. Lester was also fortunate to have Gilbert Taylor as cameraman; they'd collaborated before on *It's Trad Dad!* and Taylor had received excellent notices for his contribution to *Dr. Strangelove*. (Excellent as Taylor's work is, the distinguished photography in contrasting modes of the less experienced David Watkin for *The Knack* and *Help!* has done something to restore the credit balance.)

Though his presentation of straight music numbers in *It's Trad Dad!* is more interesting than in *A Hard Day's Night*, Lester found in the Beatles a harder core around which to build his picture. And anyway, the straighter treatment of the set numbers is in line with the documentary form. Strangely enough it is the experienced professionals introduced to strengthen the movie, to shore up the Beatles, that most weaken it. Norman Rossington, John Junkin, and, particularly, Wilfred Bramble (as the fictional manager, assistant and grandfather), damage almost every sequence in which they appear; this failure might suggest that Lester is not yet a particularly accomplished director of actors (*The Knack* bears this out) and furthermore does not find it easy to handle comedians whose talent has been developed in a more traditional context. Equally some of the supposedly satirical encounters, such as the one between George Harrison and the with-it TV producer (Kenneth Haigh), border on the embarrassing. The picture is at its best in episodes like Ringo's walk around London (with its sympathetically observed conversation with the young truants) and the game in the field outside the TV theatre. Here Lester is at his unforced best, and not only at his best but even closer to documentary than in his more obviously hand-held *vérité* moments. These scenes are almost "documentary" in the sense implied by Alexandre Astruc when he said a couple of years back that "all great films are documentaries, but they are documentaries of a little moment of the soul, of the heart of man in 1963." And Astruc also remarked that a film maker must let things express themselves directly: "When you photograph something you also photograph the soul . . . you must never pressure the reality; if you pressure it it dies."

Naturally, Lester's cinema is some way from Astruc's but the point is well taken. He is trying to reveal, to present, not to state, though in the process he doesn't so much pressure reality as kick it around. In a recent radio interview (from which all later quotes are drawn), Lester said: "In making

374

films, the Eisenstein syndrome isn't in it. It's just a matter of communication. If you want to show exuberance or show emotions in a raw state to an audience just go out and do it, and use any device that you know—whether it be borrowed or new. I mean we're all terribly eclectic anyway in film making because there are all those films that one has seen and loved and you must profit by these and use them to create your own vocabulary."

This attitude derives in part from Lester's experience in TV, and he has made it clear that he is not working for posterity: "I don't really have any desire for any of my films to go into time capsules. And I expect *Hard Day's Night*, which I haven't seen for a year, to be absolutely dreadful now. Because it was of that period, of the pop explosion."

The extreme opposite of this position is, say, George Stevens' intention of making *The Greatest Story Ever Told* "a valid and lasting picture, one that will lose no part of its validity even four decades from now when the second millenium of the birth of Jesus Christ will be celebrated." There is no knowing what people will think of Stevens' picture then, but it scarcely managed to last out at London's Casino Cinerama Theatre from Easter until Whitsuntide.

Lester's pictures are of their moment—as it says on the wall outside Tolen's bedroom in *The Knack*, "There is no tomorrow. Then how about this afternoon?" His style is not consciously elaborated. His films are made with a free-wheeling exuberance; always a good deal of room is left for improvisation, though rarely in the dialogue. Which is to say that the improvisation tends in the direction of communication between the performers (or director) and the audience through action, rather than between characters themselves in terms of deepening understanding. Indeed, one feels that Lester has a fear of anything that might slow down the impetus of his action. There is a risk here that all comedy directors should be aware of and that Lester has yet properly to face. There are just too many jokes in his pictures. He doesn't seem to know how *not* to get a laugh or even to appreciate that it might sometimes be a good thing not to. Eric Bentley (in "The Life of the Drama") describes Sir John Gielgud's technique of suppressing the value of certain lines in "The Importance of Being Ernest" in order to get the best out of the others, and he goes on: "If a laugh meter could measure the merit of a show then the ideal show would be one that elicited a single uninterrupted peal of laughter which lasted from eight-thirty till eleven o'clock. It would therefore consist of a play which not only would not proceed but could not begin. Actually there is no ratio between enjoyment and the duration of audible laughter. But too little laughter is better than too much. If no comedy, however great, could make people laugh all the time, there could be a great comedy that never made them laugh at all."

The influences and traditions from which Lester's work derives and from which he has formed his vocabulary are many and, in some cases, obvious. In films: Mack Sennett, Chaplin, and Keaton; early Buñuel (he dislikes *Viridiana* but admires *L'Age d'Or*); he has a high regard for Jean-Pierre Mocky's *The Snobs,* a film I personally dislike though I can see what attracts Lester ("I like surrealism to be amusing because I think it has its biggest value when it's being funny"); W. C. Fields, *cinéma-vérité*, Godard, Tashlin. He has clearly been influenced by the Goons, and directly or through them, by Lear, Carroll, and Joyce. In the visual arts: Pop, Op, the surrealists (particularly, one would think, Magritte), Jasper Johns. Commercial design, deriving as it does from the modern movement, obviously intrigues him, and in *Help!* one of the most striking influences is the graphic technique of the strip cartoon.

Many of these influences occur simultaneously, and the way in which Lester can combine and control them is the essence of his style. Take, for instance, the sequence where Colin nails up the door in *The Knack* which lasts at the most a couple of minutes. Firstly, there is the image, originally shot at 120 frames a second and four out of five frames removed to give it the slightly jerky effect of silent movie activity, a technique much more interesting than merely speeding up the film. Then on the soundtrack there is both music and the comments of the crowd, though this time unseen, with the remarks growing increasingly abstract. And to top it off, as Colin proceeds about his task in an orderly fashion, there are titles superimposed— beginning with "The Uses of the Saw" and then identifying each tool. The type used for these titles is stencilling—the form of lettering employed by Jasper Johns, and also by Larry Rivers in his painting "The Vocabulary Lesson," which Lester has surely seen in the Tate Gallery. The type, therefore, extends the reference beyond the immediate one of a joke about "do it yourself" to the appearance-and-reality, names-and-objects concerns of Jasper Johns and, before him, Marcel Duchamp.

If I have said that Lester seems insufficiently sure of himself to slow down the pace, that he always feels it's necessary to keep piling on the gags, there is at least one quite conscious motivation behind the complexity of his technique. "Audiences," he says apropos of the door-battering sequence, "seem to be able to grasp such an extraordinary amount in any given frame of a film, that I'm sort of trying to find the upper limit of it."

As his principal aim is to make people laugh he has run into less trouble than those whose overt objective is what Alan Solomon calls "the manipulation of rational attitudes in search of more complex experience." And Solomon (in his introduction of Johns' retrospective at the Whitechapel Gallery), after discussing the unease that some people have with art that directly confronts them with problems of perception, remarks that: "it scarcely appears to be an accident that this tendency has often been exercised more freely in less self-conscious situations, where the issue has not been central, but where the creative necessity has been just as great, as in the comic films of Chaplin and the Marx Brothers; the audience, which might in other circumstances respond antagonistically, accepts their manipulation of reality unselfconsciously and sympathetically."

It is however a mark of Lester's approach that these preoccupations do from time to time become more central than in the work of other commercial directors—as they do for instance in the sequence just described.

Curiously enough, *Help!* has been subjected to unfavorable comparison with the Marx Brothers. "The gags," one typical criticism goes, "despite their Marxian craziness, lack the build-up, the comic momentum, the sustained invention of a Marx Brothers film." Now granted that Lester has been influenced by the Marx Brothers, we are here faced with the recurrent comparison with the only generally accepted sacred cows in the history of post-silent Hollywood.

Admittedly the Marx Brothers were extremely funny—but they were funny only sporadically and in a string of bad films, at least three of which were well-nigh total disasters. Much of their material was feeble beyond belief. But more to the point, very few of their gags were conceived in exclusively cinematic terms (as the fact that their more elaborate routines were polished by pre-film trials before live audiences indicates), and their so-called anarchism is scarcely to be recognized now either on the screen or in their biographies. Virtually every film is hobbled by appallingly staged musical numbers, provided by the studios or by the Brothers themselves, and never once did they work with a director who made any contribution himself. One wonders what the result would have been had Lester worked with them, for there is in any one of the best five minute sequences of *Help!* more inventive use of the cinema than in any five Marx Brothers pictures.

But back to *Help!* and *The Knack.* Lester's increasing technical mastery aside, the two new films take him on from *A Hard Day's Night* along parallel tracks. Thematically all three are related; they are about the revolution of youth against crusty middle-age and they are a celebration of this revolt. Lester explains that these attitudes spring from the material rather than being the expression of a personal program: "I prefer the social attitudes of the young people to the disapproval of their parents . . . If you deal with a subject, you have to take sides somewhere so I've chosen the side which I have most sympathy for and therefore I suppose it could be called anarchy because it's a youth revolution. But it isn't a conscious attitude—it's not anarchy in its political sense."

This is a central issue in *A Hard Day's Night* inasmuch as it is about the Beatles themselves as a social phenomenon. Its expression is direct, and generally amiable, though sometimes it can be brutally crude as in the confrontation with the military gentleman in the railway carriage. In *Help!* it is largely peripheral (though it is reflected in the Beatles' own speech) for essentially *Help!* is a formal exercise.

The Knack is immediately concerned with this revolution as was the original play, but there's no reason to believe that Lester has any serious ideas about society or any compelling interest in social problems. Indicative of Lester's own thinking, however, is the way in which he and Charles Wood have worked on Anne Jellicoe's text. The play appears to have been completely re-written; in fact it has only been rearranged, but in such a way as to alter its meaning. Most of Miss Jellicoe's

378

dialogue remains, but scattered throughout the film. The only scenes left intact are the lion-taming game and, in part, the "rape" sequence. Tolen, the man with "the knack," was originally represented as a proto-fascist—on the basis of some pseudo-Reichian psychologizing about power and sexual inadequacy; in the films he emerges as a figure of fun rather than a social portent. The play draws some of its theatrical viability from taking place in a social vacuum and I greatly enjoyed it on the stage. Had Lester, in adding a necessary social dimension, followed Miss Jellicoe's thinking he might have finished with something resembling a heterosexual version of Kenneth Anger's *Scorpio Rising*, which explicitly connects sadistic, narcissistic motor-cyclists in California with Hitler and the Nazi movement. Instead of having Tolen propelling Colin towards the goose-step and disappearing through the window gently laughing as he does at the end of the play, the film has Tolen experience a fantasy rejection at the Albert Hall rally (in itself perhaps a joke on this "fascist" aspect of the character) shot in the same white-on-white manner as the credit sequence in which Colin is unsettled by Tolen's amorous success. What Tolen is identified with, right from the beginning of the picture, is the signs and symbols of a consumer society—the uniform dress of his girls (as later contrasted with Nancy), the graphic style of advertising and fashion photography, and so on. One of the girls actually comes out of Tolen's room licking a sheet of Green Shield stamps. His speech is the confident, even, husky whisper of the commercial, his pat advice, the jargon of the contemporary success manual. When finally Colin and Nancy stroll at ease along the Thames embankment watching the traditional symbolic firework display (here ironically reduced to a couple of feeble rockets), Tolen joins the chorus of gossiping, disapproving spectators. More than anything else, Tolen emerges as the enemy of youthful solidarity.

In effecting this change of tone, this complete transformation of the play, the role of Tom has been weakened, though Donal Donnelly's performance prevents one from becoming aware of it while one is seeing the film.

The charge made against a good deal of *The Knack* is that it is gratuitous; and one must concede that there is some truth in this argument. Nevertheless it is possible to relate most of what happens thematically to a total concept and an overall spirit. As a continuous exercise in a type of surreal logic it holds together very well—from the monks in the bus through the egg breaking like a bomb and returning into its shell to the Albert Hall Reunion. These fragments and incidents are part of an experience of a city at the time the picture was made, part of a film which sets out to present the relationship of these four people within their rapidly changing environment: *Londres nous appartient,* or does it?

The Knack's superficial resemblance to *Help!* arises from the fact that it is the work of the same production team. But *Help!,* it seems to me, is an enterprise of a wholly different character. I could scarcely disagree less with the remarks of one critic that: "Had the film not been completed before *The Knack* got the Grand Prix at Cannes I would have said that success had gone to his head. As it is, the frenetic style must be attributed to lack of confidence—not in his players, surely, but in his script."

To see nothing but frenzy in *Help!* is to miss the point entirely, and to misunderstand the nature of a film which, though slighter than *The Knack* in the sense of "content," is Lester's most ambitious undertaking. In fact to see frenzy as the picture's principal note, is to misread an extremely cool, self-conscious movie. Its flaws, such as they are, are largely attributable to the height of the ambition rather than to any inherent weakness in the conception.

Lester himself, in a characteristically self-mocking way, has provided the best description of *Help!:* "I said in a more fatuous moment recently that it's Wilkie Collins' *The Moonstone* drawn by Jasper Johns."

It is a paradoxical movie—its innovatory character lies precisely in its apparent lack of originality, its depth in the consistency of its two-dimensionality, its informality in its deliberately mannered style.

Let me try to distinguish the various strands. The principal influence, the controlling idea, is the adventure strip cartoon of the Superman-Batman genre, some examples of which are arranged on the music rest of the organ in the Beatles' apartment, the suggestion being that they are to be played as music. This conditions the narrative style: the pace, the range of color, the dialogue and the use of captions which are often placed in the corner of the screen as in a comic square. This is the chosen film-form and adhered to throughout, not used merely as a point of departure. One example of its use is in the hollowed-out numbers which introduce the five rapid assaults on Ringo in the early part of the film.

Subsidiary visual techniques include the devices of color and design of Sunday supplement photographers and commercial artists; Lester employs these openly and ironically. And, of course, and inevitably, surrealism.

From the cinema comes the idea of the total chase picture, both serious and slapstick, of which this is the extreme form. The allusions to other pictures are endless and, such being the way of Lester, immensely affectionate. Some are gentle parodies of genre conventions, e.g., John Lennon as the wounded war hero on Salisbury Plain. Some are specific parodies, such as the Indian throwing his limply unwinding turban in the manner of Odd-job's lethal bowler in *Goldfinger*. Some of the allusions are reaction or echoes of well-known situations—ranging from the table split by a sword, which is vintage Sennett, to the rubber tubing in Buckingham Palace which invokes Jacques Tati's *Mon Oncle*. They are conceived of as acts of homage rather than as self-contained jokes.

Thirdly, there is an exploitation of the role that Indians play and have played in British culture. The classic expression of the traditional form of this role is found in "The Moonstone," "The Sign of Four," Lord Dunsany's "A Night at an Inn"—stories of villainous oriental pursuers whose long arm inexorably reaches into the remotest corner of the English countryside. This once totally serious attraction-repulsion relationship with the exotic, terrifying East is now bound up with two modern factors: "the comic oriental" and end-of-Empire nostalgia, both staple features of Goonery. The ambivalence of this nexus of attitudes is compounded by a touching recognition that some Indians are more English than the English themselves, that in certain areas of life on the Indian sub-continent (e.g., the army, the universities) are to be found the last repository of the old English spirit.

Finally there is the contemporary British scene—the Beatles themselves, older, more individualized now, more assured, *sui generis* yet representative of a new and puzzling generation; the Establishment, symbolized by Scotland Yard, Buckingham

Palace, the West End jeweler, the army, fundamentally un-
changed but attempting to use the Beatles, simultaneously
patronizing and identifying with them; the New Men—the
scientists bitterly reconciled to the superiority of foreign resources, swimming against the current on the rim of the brain
drain. (These last named are the weakest link in the picture;
too much emphasis in the writing perhaps.) It is the highly
stylized treatment of all these figures that gives them a validity and vitality lacking in their more realistic counterparts in
A Hard Day's Night.

As I say, none of this is new; what is extraordinary is the
logic with which Lester weaves these various strands together.
Take the point of departure—a sacrificial ring stolen from an
oriental temple and sent to Ringo by an Indian admirer: a
perfect combination of two iconographies (as well as a recognition of the fact that Ringo is the quartet's most gifted
comedian). Then see the role of the High Priest Clang (Leo
McKern). He begins by conducting a temple ritual in a Church
of England intonation, and proceeds to adopt a series of disguises, none of which is arbitrary once the initial premise is
appreciated: driving around London in a Harrods electric van,
attending an ecumenical conference with his fellow Common-
wealth churchmen, accompanying his army on Salisbury Plain
correctly attired as a Great War padre, traveling over the Bahamas in an airship, leading an Indian takeover of a British-
staffed Indian restaurant, receiving a winter sports prize while
his own flag is hoisted and anthem played, and finally preparing for the sacrifice of Ringo with a sympathetic Anglican
minister beside him.

The colored darts thrown by Clang at the black and white
film of the opening song imposes the Indian theme (literally
and figuratively) on the surface of the Beatles' world. The title
number itself has an uncustomary nostalgic tinge: "When I
was young, and so much, much, younger than before," "and
now my life has changed in oh so many ways." It is immediately followed by the sharply satirical post-credit sequence
presenting the Beatles' current situation as an established part
of the social landscape. The simple row of houses is the
group's façade of unaffected normality: "They're so natural.
Success hasn't changed them a bit," says one of the middle-
aged women in the street. Lester then cuts to the open-plan

interior of the four houses: this is the world in which they live, a world of "contemporary" gracious living as exemplified by the taste of the Sunday supplements and the glossy magazines, the economic freedom to indulge in fantasies of sunken beds, shiny vending machines against the wall, a servant to cut the grass carpet with false teeth. (The "lawnmower" is played by Bruce Lacey, who also appeared in *It's Trad Dad!* and *The Knack* and with whose humor and comic mechanical constructions Lester's work has strong affinities. Here, too, we have the surreal reverse of the grass scrubbing in *The Running, Jumping and Standing Still Film.*) But no longing for the simple life is remotely implied; what is seen is the contradictory demands that are made on public figures. There is however more than a hint of nostalgia for a time when comics could be taken seriously (which is to say on their own terms) just as the whole film recognizes the passing of a simple age in which one could get an unaffected frisson from stories of oriental menace.

Lester rarely milks a single gag. His technique in *Help!* is more the building of a comic house of cards concluding with the addition of a perilous joker, which he leaves miraculously tottering as he passes on to the next exercise. This is how he develops the sequences of the assault on the Beatles' London apartment and the lion-taming in the pub cellar which precede the quartet's departure for respectively the Alps and the Bahamas. Granted it is an overworked image but *Help!* also suggests a rotating kaleidoscope—a constant change of symmetrical figures produced by a realignment of the same disparate elements, with a few new ones thrown in. It is Lester's own feeling for the material and his sense of cinematic rhythm that produce the symmetry.

For what Lester seems able to do is to bring together diverse strands of contemporary life, of the very moment he makes his picture, transmute (but not dilute) them, and present them in such a way that the result is immediately acceptable to a wide-ranging international public. What in effect he has is the genius of the greatest popular entertainers. He involves his audience, often without them knowing it, in the consideration of problems and the acceptance of experiences that in other circumstances they might well reject.

Saul Bass
by Raymond Gid

Mr. Gid writes on graphic artists for the Swiss magazine Graphis.
This chapter appeared originally in Graphis 89.

The graphic design and layout of the present day are obsessed
with rhythm; generous use is made of the picture's third dimension, which is time. Rhythm of composition, of typography,
of the sequence of pages, link modern design to the idiom of
the film. Saul Bass, whose graphic work is integrated with
cinematographic vision, remains the champion of the movement. He gives an exemplary lead, and an examination of his
work is always rewarding.

Traditional opera employed an overture to lift the spectator
above the preoccupations of everyday life before plunging him
into the magic of the stage. In the days when book clubs were
at their height, book advertising made almost excessive use of
unfolding sequences. The screen has found in Saul Bass the
creative artist capable of distracting the spectator from his
own immediate experience. His references to the rhythm of
the canvases of Rubens or to Eisenstein's notes on the *mise en
scène* of Leonardo da Vinci's paintings introduce us into this
world of the immobile-mobile and mobile-immobile to which
he has specially dedicated himself. It is entertaining to note
in passing that the three thousand-year-old Japanese writing
also referred to by Eisenstein directly supplied for wall and
screen, the sign of *Bonjour Tristesse* (water + eye = sadness),
while in the magic of Bass the seedlings of glinting flowers
turned to tears in their petals.

A few fortunate members of the Lurs group one day had
the opportunity to see in succession the titlings of *Bonjour
Tristesse, The Man with the Golden Arm, Anatomy of a Murder,* and the overwhelming opening of *Around the World in
Eighty Days,* and were thus able to enjoy to the full the various
facets of an essentially nimble and versatile talent that uses
benevolent humor (I am thinking of the race against the clock
in *Around the World*) with the same ease as the more serious
idioms: one remembers St. Joan, her sword broken before the
Satanic graphic formulation of her own name.

There can be few who have seen *West Side Story* who do not remember the network of Mondrianesque lines, isolated on the screen, transporting us to New York by the spell of their obsessing and motionless presence, who cannot call vividly to mind the epilogue that juggles, through the changing scenes, with the inscription on a piece of furniture, a design on a wall or a placard seen in passing, in an unbroken traveling sequence that reaffirms the principle of the credits epilogue on condition that it is really worth watching and does not empty the rows. This is the most recent Bass, restored in motionless sequences. Yet can a sequence by Bass possibly remain motionless in the imagination as in the memory? Here we see *Spartacus*, where the hand of the *Man with the Golden Arm* becomes a fist to brandish the lightning as it brandished the rifle, in the advertisements, to dominate the flames of *Exodus*. In each of these films, it is Bass himself who leads the adventure, living it fully and prefacing it with his graphic weapon: his own hand. And every one of these adventures is carried to its graphic extreme: the *auto-da-fé* of *Storm Center* brought Bass face to face with the flame. He was to have no respite till he had found the synthesis that presides over the destinies of *Exodus*.

In all these film titlings, through all their virtuosities, those who know him see Bass constantly in love with the well-presented image, marvelously modulating each emotion, and with a sensibility perfectly balanced by a sense of humor. A goldsmith in the world of typography, making use of the letter to be read, the letter to be looked at, the letter that spells suspense, or the letter that is an object in itself, he also takes pleasure in the refinements of the different vibrations of screens, as in *Nine Hours to Rama*. He uses all registers, and nobody is better qualified than the "inventor of graphic film titling" to put over to us in a minimum of time the complete message he has to convey. This is what makes his work so effective in the publicity field, where the intensity of communication must be at its highest. All in all, this is the work of a complete man.

Cinema of Common Sense:
A View of Cinéma-Vérité
by Colin Young

Mr. Young is chairman of the Theatre Arts Department at the University of California at Los Angeles and a member of the motion picture faculty. This chapter appeared originally in the Summer 1964 issue of Film Quarterly.

The term *cinéma-vérité* has been used, loosely, by critics to label documentary films which employ the technical advantages of the new light cameras and sound recorders, and which usually do not begin with a script but with an actual on-going event which they try to record, or a situation which they attempt to describe, always, allegedly at least, with the minimum of interpretation. In attempting to get at the *truth* of a situation, the preconceived script is disallowed, the film maker does not *direct* (in the sense of controlling what is in front of the camera), and the editing process is faithful to the actual event —its continuity, its relationships, its entire character. No one, I maintain, really expects to find such a thing as the "objective statement," although some of the new documentary film makers sometimes permit themselves to talk as if that's what their films were concerned with. In less polemic moments they will admit to the "subjectivity" of their cameras and their editing, but will insist that they are trying, to the limit of their own discretion, to represent the events or situations as they found them—not as they expected to find them, not as they wish you to believe they found them, but as they saw them through the camera.

This, then, could more accurately be called the cinema of common sense, the naturalist cinema—Louis Marcorelles prefers "direct cinema," Drew Associates have dubbed their program "The Living Camera." It can readily be distinguished from the conventional cinema which deals, and revels, in contrivance—the immaculate control which a film maker can exercise on his material so as to present to an audience his very personal vision of it. In its traditional forms this has led the director on to the sound stage where by set design, costuming, lighting, and casting he can place in front of his cameras the precise image he seeks to represent, and for the editing he supplies himself with those shots which he can then redirect into the controlled interpretation of the image which will be shown to an audience. Generally speaking, most such controls are abandoned by the *cinéma-vérité* director; and he tries, during editing, to be dictated to by his subject, rather than conversely.

This seems familiar—it fits with one possible interpretation of what Robert Flaherty was about (what Frances Flaherty calls nonpreconception). It is also very unfamiliar because it has resulted in some rather startling films—films which do not seem to follow at all the traditional lines of the story film.

In this space I had meant to write a full-scale polemic on behalf of *cinéma-vérité*, but circumstances prevented me from undertaking it. The polemic is needed, it seems to me, because the new styles in documentary are either being attacked (at least in part through misunderstanding) or ignored (by timorous exhibitors and television bookers). Henry Breitrose asks what is meant by calling a "Living Camera" film *interesting* (Leacock and the others at Drew Associates used to say they were merely trying to get on to subjects which were "interesting" and present them as faithfully as possible to an audience). He says that the films are usually as good as their subjects are interesting, but that the most successful ones work because their subjects have a structure which permits the "story" to unfold "naturally." He concludes that whenever the meaning of the event is externally evident, and when the event's structure is sufficiently similar to the traditional structure of dramatic conflict, there is a good chance of the film's working.

This seems to me to beg the question—just as Peter Graham does when he implies that all cinema must be judged by the same set of standards—*Potemkin* and *Le Chemin de la Mauvaise Route* equally, even though these standards were arrived at and set down before Herman made a film, before Rouch or Leacock or the Maysles ever held a camera. There was the day when a documentary film maker argued, at the first Flaherty Seminar in 1954, that a documentary film maker, if he could not have a set script in his hand, should at least have a strong outline in mind and should see to it that all material shot would relate to that outline and would contribute to the argument of the film. Who said that? Leacock. Seven years later he was saying something else. The cinema had moved forward. The critics want to hold it back.

Nevertheless, Breitrose is justified in keeping some kind of score. Among the Drew Associates films some are vastly more successful than others. *On the Pole* (the story of Eddie Sachs' 1962 race at Indianapolis) is a fascinating document of a man chasing a lunatic ambition. Undoubtedly, this is the most articulate film made by the group. They chose Sachs, firstly because he had the favored position (earned by the driver with the fastest qualifying heat), and secondly because he was a talkative, outgoing man. But the film succeeds because of the film makers' skill in putting the audience in a position to judge what is being said. Knowing that they could not predict the outcome, they took us inside Sachs' ambition to win and then stayed with him when he lost, forced out of the race by car trouble. It is here, in this early example of "Living Camera," that one myth is quickly destroyed—namely that the presence of the camera interferes with the audience's chances of seeing a person behave naturally. We see Sachs standing disconsolately by the track, with the race still in progress, a race no longer his. He becomes aware of the camera, tries to pretend he has not seen it, but we become aware of his bluff—we see him putting on an act, we see him gradually becoming resentful of the camera he had earlier accepted and welcomed; and because of this we see more clearly below the surface of a man who lived to win and who lost—precisely because, when Sachs was no longer lost in his own task, the camera became an intrusive element.

It was perhaps remembering this that led Leacock and Gregory Shuker to make a fatal mistake in *Nehru*. At the outset they had undertaken not to interfere or intrude in any way —except by being there. In return for permission to follow Nehru, they promised to ask no questions and make no demands of any kind. But in editing the film, Leacock has said, they found themselves without any dramatic material, without the usual elements of narrative conflict. They had just faithfully followed and recorded the work of an extraordinary man over a short period. But in looking for some threat to tie together the various parts they concluded that the key was in the promise they had made to Nehru—a promise they had, in the end, broken. Thus, in the film (broadcast May 31 on KHJ-

388

TV, Los Angeles, and like the other "Living Camera" films available for other TV bookings) they keep pointing to this sequence, building it up, and then finishing the film with it. Unfortunately it is a complete fizzle. Shuker asks Nehru a question or two, Nehru answers them, in a perfectly straight conversational tone. Nothing much is said—we learn little new. It is as bad a gimmick as in Gitlin's *The Comedian* in which a perfectly straightforward account of Shelley Berman opening a show in Florida is tricked up by promises of fireworks in the last act—when Berman's act is "ruined" by an off-stage telephone ringing. What, left to itself, could have been a savage little moment, is dressed up as melodrama and then flops.

These errors of judgment are a hold-over from the conservative classical drama. They ought to be totally unnecessary. It ought to be enough to spend fifteen days with Nehru (or, more questionably, three or four with Berman), so long as the film maker is telling us something we did not know before, and probably could not know very readily by any other means. Thus both *Primary* (1960) and *Crisis* (1963) by the "Living Camera" teams did show us a part of politics that went beyond simple screen journalism. In *Primary* we are following the Humphrey-Kennedy battle in Wisconsin. In *Crisis* the subject is the Kennedy-Governor Wallace battle over the token integration of higher education in Alabama. The New York Times editorialized against the latter film on the grounds of improper interference with the due processes of government. Crucial to their argument was the contention that Leacock *et al.* could not witness the President, the Attorney-General, and others without materially affecting their work and decisions. Again, on the screen, we can tell when Robert Kennedy is putting on an act. It is hard to believe that the act substantially alters what he would have done in the same situation if the cameras had been absent. The great service of the film is that it successfully captures a few moments in the problems of government. By having one crew with the Attorney-General in Washington and another in Alabama the film makers were able to cover the conflict with a thoroughness which was not really matched at the time by any of the participants. We see Kennedy hesitating over a decision, needing information from Alabama which the cameras have already (in the edited film) shown to us in the audience. The result is to dramatize the complexity of the situation, and to clarify the nature of the crisis and the difficulty in arriving at a correct and tactically appropriate decision. This was editing of a more traditional sort—juxtaposition to force a certain interpretation—but it was arrived at by the simple device of extending the reportage situation from one location to two.

After *On the Pole,* I find *Football* and *Petey and Johnny* the most interesting of the Drew Associates' films. (I belong to the minority not liking *The Chair.*) *Football* exploits a situation of straightforward conflict. Given extroverts in front of the camera a skilled crew cannot miss. But *Petey and Johnny* is a failure—defeated by the dilemma which all *cinéma vérité* must face up to in the end: how to be faithful to a subject which does *not* fit neatly into the structural patterns of conventional drama, without betraying the audience. Drew chose what he considered the best of two betrayals. He slicked up the situation, concentrated on a gang member's marriage to provide a focus point, wrote narration for the social worker (the film was shot in Harlem), and threw away hours of taped conversation recorded wild on the streets.

The French, and French-Canadians, have different problems. Michel Brault (and Pierre Perrault) walked into a small Quebec fishing village and documented the villagers' decision to take up again the hunt for the white whale that had formerly provided them with their principal source of income. It so happened they caught a whale, and that these men, and their families, had a natural grace and wit which Brault and his recordist Carrière could catch. But there is also a strong "traditional" element to *Pour la Suite du Monde*—the scenes, though not directed, are set and the camera always tries to place the people in their landscape. The film ends up by being as close to Zavattini as to Flaherty and, with a minimum of narration, is a victory for the naturalist cinema. The Brault-Jutra-Carrière film *La Lutte* (on professional wrestling in Montreal) and Wolf Koenig's *Lonely Boy* manage at the same time to be accurate documents of their subjects and (without narration) scathing commentaries on the society which nurtures them. By comparison, the Ballentine-Shepherd production *The Most* is contrived and rigged, although also enjoyable. It is only if you insist, with Graham, that all films must meet the same standards that we have to choose between *The Most* and *Lonely Boy*. To say you like both is not to admit to a collapse of critical judgment, but to suggest that critical ideas may need broadening.

Rouch began as an ethnographer and fell into the cinema. He has always had to contend with the effect that his shooting is having on his subjects—in *Moi, Un Noir* "Edward G. Robinson" went into prison, in *Chronique d'un Eté* the Renault worker *does* lose his job. But if this is irresponsibility, as Graham suggests, it is irresponsibility of a very special kind. Rouch is not a callous observer. He is no more indifferent than he is detached. It is possibly his lack of detachment that flaws his films, but it also gives them much of their excitement. I think Graham completely misreads his intentions in *Chronique* and is deaf to Rouch's own protestations of failure. All *cinéma-vérité* worth the name reveals its conventions to its audience. Thus it is in character for Leacock and Shuker to introduce *Nehru* with an explanation of their methods—what they shouldn't do is reprint shots (*Nehru* climbing onto a platform; Paul Crump's warden walking down the prison corridor to test the electrocution equipment—although this last was Drew's doing). Rouch may not be making a "film" in *Chronique*, but definitions never stopped something as dynamic as the cinema from moving on. Rouch makes his methods elaborately clear, and puts us in a perfect position to judge. So also, I would have thought, does Ruspoli in *Regards sur la Folie*. Graham suggested in correspondence that I must have had definite views about madness before seeing Ruspoli's film and that this is why I find the film richly informative and suggestive. I do not think the weeks spent as a nurse in a Glasgow asylum told me very much but in any case Ruspoli does *not* leave us totally at sea. First with one style (interview) then another (reportage, witness) we get a picture of the life the inmates of the hospital lead. The experience for an audience is emotional rather than intellectual, but it is certainly not totally vague and indeterminate. In *Les Inconnus de la Terre* (a better film), Ruspoli talks with farmers who don't want to move off the land and go into the city—and from time to time moves his camera far enough away so that we see the recordist sitting with his gear across from the men in the fields. There is no reason for this, except to remind us that we are, in part, watching a record—that Ruspoli's film, interpretative in part, is also rooted in the fact of these people's lives.

But where Graham is totally unsympathetic to a new mood in the cinema is with Jean Herman's brilliant *Chemin de la Mauvaise Route* (formerly called *Bon Pour La Vie Civile*). Here the film maker is found guilty of mixing his styles—of recording lengthy interviews and then presenting them out of continuity, of interpreting his interviews with iconographic material and reportage; he also stages some scenes with his two principals and re-enacts others. This might be called "using the resources of the cinema"—it is also very easy to follow (apart from the alarming rapidity of some of the cutting) because it declares itself as it goes along—nothing is hidden, or faked. In the end, I suppose, we must count heads—Graham's sympathy is smothered, mine is not. What I see as a series of devices to render coherent something which came out in a garbled, inarticulate way, Graham sees as marionetting. For in fact the more the young gypsy and his mistress appear like the figures they emulate the more I sympathize with them —because Herman has also taken the precaution to make us like them, not in the first place, but gradually as the film progresses. It is so obviously a document about these two people that this fact holds together the other threads Herman develops. Marker does it brilliantly in *Le Joli Mai* too, but Herman's film stands as a fascinating prototype for a possible series of films which an American film maker might do well to consider, if, and this is an important reservation, he can ever hope to get the confidence of his subjects as Herman clearly did here.

The Maysles brothers, Albert and David, are a special case. They consider themselves the purists of the movement—in *Showman* (about distributor-producer Joe Levine) and *The Beatles* they attempt to present their subjects completely without bias. As for the first, I have been told (in Hollywood) that the film is too critical of the "industry" and of Levine, and (in New York) that the film is a whitewash of the industry *and* Levine. I suppose, then, that the Maysles succeeded. Those who don't like *Showman* say they learn no more when it is over than after ten minutes—that it stays on the surface. The same would be said of *The Beatles*. The Maysles think that they should not interfere in shooting, that they should never set things up—the sequence in *Showman* with Susskind arguing at Levine in a Boston radio station just happened—for to do so would break the deal with their subject and, equally important, upset their own equilibrium as observers.

None of the film makers discussed above would agree that he has been making superficial films. I am not even convinced this is the crucial point. An American philosopher called Mrs. Ladd Franklin once said she was surprised she rarely met another solipsist. The idealist critics should not run away when they meet an empirical film maker. He is neither obscene nor dangerous. He is merely exploring a part of the cinema—the part Kracauer claimed (falsely) is the whole.

The Auteur Theory Re-examined

by Donald E. Staples

Mr. Staples, who is teaching and making motion pictures at Ohio State University, is a familiar contributor to trade and technical publications. This chapter appeared originally in the 1967 issue of the Journal of the Society of Cinematologists.

All of us have read about the *Auteur* theory and some of us have written about it. Most of us have talked about it and each and every one of us seems to know what it is or purports to be. But, do we really have a complete picture of the *Politique des Auteurs*?

For my own edification I have attempted to draw together some of the more basic writing about the theory, much of it from original French sources in the hope of gaining a better understanding of what the theory was intended to be and do and what it might mean to serious students of film today.

I wrote this paper for the first time two years ago when the controversy was hot and heavy. During the interim period I have been whittling away at it, trying to cut away the personal arguments in an attempt to get at the bare bones of the theory. Therefore, in cutting it in half, I have left out some of the most verbally exciting material but I have tried to retain the essentials of the theory, which are intellectually exciting. Although André Bazin harshly criticized the *Auteur* theory and pointed up its many faults, it was one sentence of his that kept me going—"The *Politique des Auteurs* appears to me to harbor and protect an essential critical truth which the cinema needs more than all the other arts. . . ."

The development of the *Auteur* theory and the subsequent controversy over it can be traced both chronologically and geographically. It can be followed from its start in 1954 and brought up to the present; and similarly it can be considered as a flow from France to England and on to the United States.

It started in Paris in 1954 (this has been erroneously reported as 1957 in some film journals) with the publication of an article by François Truffaut in the monthly periodical Cahiers du Cinéma. Jacques Doniol-Valcroze who was an editor of Cahiers du Cinéma at that time has said:

. . . that the publication of that article marked the point of real departure of what represents today, wrongly or rightly, *Cahiers du Cinéma*. A leap was made, a process was initiated for which we were mutually responsible, something gathered us together. Henceforth, it was known that we were *for* [certain directors] and against [other directors]. Henceforth there was a doctrine, the "Politique des auteurs" . . .

It is interesting that Truffaut's article founding the *Auteur* theory was not a piece of writing which was intended to establish a framework of criticism, nor was it strictly an appeal to directors to become *Auteurs*. It was more of an anti-screenwriters article, against the traditional and commercial French writers for film.

Truffaut pointed out that the French cinema was suffering from a "tradition of quality"—making films for film festivals rather than exercising artistic integrity—and he stated that something should be done to remedy the situation. He noted that French film making had shifted from a "poetic realism" which had existed before World War II to a "psychological realism" during the post-war period, and that the writers of this "psychological realism" were completely underestimating the capacity of film by attempting in each film to continue the "tradition of quality." In this attempt, they would always choose subjects which contained the habitual dose of nonconformist elements and gloom combined with an easy daring, and create characters typifying the lowest, the basest, the most abject in human nature.

Truffaut went on to complain that films of this type were writers' films, and that the film was truly completed when the writer finished writing it; that the director was only a craftsman who went out to get it on film.

That school [psychological realism] which aims at realism always destroys it at the same time of finally capturing it, the more careful it is to enclose beings in a closed world, barricaded by formulas, plays on words, maxims instead of letting us see them for ourselves with our own eyes. The artist cannot always dominate his work.

This domination of the work by the *Auteur* is of foremost importance in the eyes of the Cahiers critics, and Truffaut noted that "the directors are, and wish to be, responsible for the scenarios and dialogues that they illustrate."

After condemning the "abject characters" who pronounce

"abject phrases" in films of "psychological realism" he concluded:

I know a handful of men in France who would be incapable of conceiving them, [and Truffaut names several French directors—then goes on to say] these are, however, French *cinéastes*, and it happens—curious coincidence—that these are *Auteurs* who often write their dialogue and some of them invent themselves the stories that they direct.

Thus François Truffaut was ready for a break from the old and was unknowingly establishing some groundwork for the new in saying that "I cannot believe in the peaceful coexistence of the *tradition of quality* and *a cinema of auteurs.*"

In December 1955, Cahiers du Cinéma published a list of sixty top contemporary American directors, and since that time the list has been taken much too seriously. An introduction to the list points out that there are approximately 380 directors working in Hollywood and that Cahiers had picked sixty of the most important and the most promising directors —leaving out especially the older ones, whose inspiration, they felt, had vacillated. They were interested in citing relatively young talent and merely list the 320 others at the end.

Instead of taking issue with the list, it is more significant to look at it in context with other lists of this nature which have appeared in Cahiers du Cinéma. The May 1957 issue contains a similar list citing sixty French directors and, in April 1961, a dictionary of French television directors appeared. In May 1962, fifty-four Italian *cinéastes* were recognized, and in December of that year a list was published which noted the appearance of 162 new French *cinéastes*. This compulsion for listing tends to make certain individual lists much less important.

An article entitled "De La Politique des Auteurs" by André Bazin appeared in Cahiers in the April 1957 issue, and it was here that the *Auteur* theory was first discussed in great detail with its strengths and weaknesses pointed out.

It is important to notice that Bazin mentioned that the *Politique des Auteurs* had never been formally written down, and that it was a theory that had evolved from a body of criticism and from a multitude of film reviews which had been written by the contributors to Cahiers du Cinéma.

According to Bazin, one of the main desires of this group

is to find the Shakespeares and the Rembrandts of film.

It is evident that the "Politique des Auteurs" is only an application to cinema of a notion generally admitted in the individual arts.

And even though Mr. Bazin did not mention it, this "policy" of considering authors or artists in terms of their total output and considering a work in terms of the artist, is an accepted pattern for studying as well as criticizing works in all of the performing arts, visual arts and literature.

This procedure has also frequently been used for film study and the organization of film writing; however, it has not obtained a place of importance in the field of criticism. Until this policy is understood, analyzed, revised and put to use, the Shakespeares and Rembrandts of film will never be found. However, proponents of the *Auteur* theory usually carry this practice to extreme. Bazin says:

Of the equation *Auteur* + *Subject* = *Work* they wish to retain only the *Auteur*, the *Subject* being reduced to zero. Certain ones will pretend to agree with me that, the strength of the *Auteur* being equal to others, a good subject is obviously worth more than a bad one; but the most frank or the most insolent will swear to me that it is just as if their preference ran on the contrary to little B films, where the banality of the scenario leaves more room for the personal contribution of the *Auteur*.

And Bazin goes on later:

The "politique des auteurs" consists in sum, in choosing in the artistic creation the personal factor as a criterion of reference, then in postulating its permanence and even its progress from one work to the following. It is well recognized that there exist "important" or "quality" films which escape that frame of reference, but justly, one will systematically prefer to them those where one can read in filigree the imprint of the *Auteur*, were it on the worst scenario possible.

This progress of the *Auteur's* talent from one work to the next is an important tenet of the *Auteur* theory, and Bazin and others have questioned whether this can be applied as strictly to films as it can be in the more traditional arts. In music, painting, or literature it is easy to find a one-to-one ratio between artist and work. One artist: one work. In film, however, the artistic variables are so numerous and so constantly changing from one production to the other that it is difficult to establish a one-to-one ratio and discover who the *Auteur* of any film really is. Thus the thread of artistic advancement by an *Auteur* is tenuous in considering most works.

There are two symmetrical heresies inherent in criticism generally, according to André Bazin. They are: 1) the objective application of a critical grid or overlay, a master frame of reference to the work, and 2) considering sufficient the critic's affirmation of his pleasure or distaste with the work. "The first denies the role of taste, while the second sets forth *a priori* the superiority of the taste of the critic over that of the *Auteur*."

Mr. Bazin went on to point out that the system of values proposed by the *Auteur* theory commits the first heresy by departing from any system where taste and sensitivity play a foremost part. It is more a question of being able to discern the contribution of the artist as such—beyond the elements of subject and technique—finding the man behind the style. Thus, for the *Auteur* theorist, analysis of a film begins with the principle that if the film is by an *Auteur*, it is good, and the framework that this imposes on the work is therefore an esthetic portrait of the director which has been drawn from his previous works.

On the other hand, the *Politique des Auteurs* is the most perilous for its criteria are very difficult to formulate. It is significant that, practiced for three or four years by our finest writers, it is still waiting for a great part of its theory.

Instead of developing a real theory, its proponents have limited themselves to dogmatic and, it must be added, somewhat subjective assertions as to who the real *Auteurs* are. "One sees the danger of an esthetic cult of personality."

Mr. Bazin felt, however, that if the *Auteur* theory were practiced by people of taste who remained vigilant, the cult of personality would not be the principal aspect. What bothered him about the *Auteur* theorists more than their negative approach to good films made by non-*Auteurs* was their conferring of praise upon films which did not merit the praise, but were works of directors whom they had labelled *Auteurs*.

Mr. Bazin's article did much to clarify many points concerning the *Auteur* theory, and his death the following year dashed hopes of any follow-up articles.

His April 1957 article concluded thus:

The *Politique des Auteurs* appears to me to harbor and protect an essential critical truth which the cinema needs more than all the other arts, exactly to the extent that the act of true artistic creation is more uncertain and menaced in it than elsewhere. But its exclusive practice would lead to another peril: the negation of the work to the benefit of the exaltation of its *Auteur*. . . .

Useful and fruitful, it seems to me thus, independently of its polemic value, that [the politique des auteurs] should be completed by other approaches to the cinematographic fact which would restore to the film its value as a work. This is not to deny the role of the *Auteur*, but to restore to him the preposition [of] without which the noun *Auteur* is only a lame concept. "*Auteur*," without doubt, but of what?

Unfortunately, some of the later articles which have attempted to criticize the *Auteur* theory have been done with a tongue slightly in the cheek, and they rarely propose the idea that it is not the *Auteur* theory which gives cause for argument, but only the application of it, particularly as it involves labelling directors.

It is also necessary to point out that the *Auteur* critics are performing a particular service to the overall field of film criticism in their efforts to originate and utilize a vocabulary for film criticism that can express the ideas to be conveyed very simply. They are taking existing phrases or coining new ones to try to establish words and phrases that are peculiar to film and very exact in their usage. At present, however, we are still in that period in which some of these new words, or new uses of words and phrases, are not clearly defined, or at least the definitions are not completely agreed upon by all critics—especially when they have had to hurdle the language barrier. Quite probably this problem will gradually work itself out.

Having seriously considered the *Auteur* theory, it is difficult to balance the advantages and disadvantages of this theory against each other, much less compare them to any other such set of principles for film, since few seem to exist. Most other forms of film critical theory have been peculiarly individual and have used as a base an understanding of older forms of criticism founded in philosophy and the arts. This is not necessarily wrong; however, these forms of criticism are so dissimilarly based that common grounds for comparison are elusive. Earlier film critics and most of the leading ones today have adapted the body of criticism from their favorite adjacent subject (philosophy, painting, music, drama, ballet, sculpture, poetry, prose, etc.). After cannibalizing the most useful parts of a discipline's critical principles, they have colored it with their personal preferences, thrown in a dash of popular culture or box office appeal, and added a flavoring style of acid sarcasm, ludicrous assertion, wordy trickery, or pedantic lesson. A few have been thoughtful, serious, and un-prolific. None of these have added up to a critical theory of film which could be applied, adjusted and evaluated. Thus the advent of a principle of cinematic criticism is to be praised simply for its being, and for any other advantages that might be found. Even if one feels that the disadvantages outweigh the advantages to the extent that the entire theory should be discarded, the fact of the existence of the *Politique des Auteurs* is still significant.

Just as each individual member of an audience sees a particular film slightly differently from his neighbor, it follows that individual film critics will see films and film history from slighty different points of view. And, if they think deeply about film and attempt to analyze their thoughts and ideas they may come up with other theories of film.

Although it is easy to criticize and find fault with almost all theories, it is necessary to have theories against which films can be tested and examined. They are necessary for the beginner as guidelines and hypotheses which he can side with, rebel against or revise. It may be that Richard Dyer MacCann's book "Film: A Montage of Theories" will be an accumulation and evaluation which the beginner can use as a sounding board for his own theories.

This paper has been a call to the origin—a call to go back to the original version of *La Politique des Auteurs* and to examine it closely.

It's always convenient to choose a theory of film that embraces our favorites as examples. Each theoretician has done it. It is much more difficult to grant a theory which does not let in all of our personal preferences. Although as critics we should be flexible in order to bend with the time and the place, the criteria upon which various theories are based should be inflexible—not adaptable to every situation.

Let's admit the realistic tendency to sometimes like bad

films and sometimes dislike good films. Let's not change the criteria to accommodate our temporary tastes.

There will never be a "perfect" theory of film, but let's have more theories and let's make the theories we have basic, and available in their theoretical form.

Free Cinema and the New Wave
by Jonas Mekas

Mr. Mekas, film maker and poet, is the guiding spirit behind the underground film movement in New York. He is also the editor of Film Culture, and it was in the Summer 1960 issue of that publication that this chapter originally appeared.

Not since the early postwar years, when the Italian neorealist films *Open City* and *Paisan* suddenly revealed to America a completely new school of film making, has any group of film makers attracted as much attention as the so-called Nouvelle Vague. Coming, or, more accurately, skyrocketing into public attention during the last Cannes film festival, this "wave"— including François Truffaut, Claude Chabrol, Alain Resnais, Marcel Camus, Jean Rouch, Louis Malle, among others— suddenly became public property. And whereas it usually was three to four years before an "art" film got to the States, it took no longer than two months for the films of the New Wave to reach the American shore.

What are the reasons for this extreme interest in the Nouvelle Vague, and its sudden coming into existence? When we begin to look closer, one of the first things we discover is that the symptoms leading up to it were noticeable for quite some time. Further we discover that there is a very close affinity between the Nouvelle Vague and the modern film movements in other countries, particularly those of England and the United States. For a considerable period of time now the more perceptive film critics writing for Cahiers du Cinéma in France, Sight and Sound in England and Film Culture in the States, were proclaiming the death of the contemporary commercial cinema. Over the last several years we have been made aware of the magnitude of the transition our world is going through, with its technological, economic, and psychological changes affecting the actions, emotions, and dreams of the people. An entire new generation has come into being, with completely different needs and surroundings that influence their very physical movements, their speech habits, their dressing habits and, naturally, their love habits. Therefore, to keep in step with the changing times and to be seen and liked by this generation, the film had to change also, or else face half-empty theatres, or theatres full of old people.

Thus the need became not only one that called for new directors but one that demanded a contemporary, modern cinema, modern in its subject matter, modern in its style and in its temperament. The newly acclaimed directors coming out of American or European "Hollywoods" were not fulfilling this need at all. They were simply extending and perpetuating long-dead styles and approaches, making more and more films which did not speak to the sensibilities of the new generation. After dragging on this way for another few years, the cinema finally entered a stage which became intolerable. Thus the first fresh fruits began to explode in various corners of the budding underground.

The first sign of an openly recognized and effective movement was seen to appear in London some four years ago, almost simultaneously with the emergence of the so-called Angry Young Man. No doubt the date of Osborne's stage production of "Look Back in Anger" will not only become part of the history of the theatre but will also enter into the history of the social life of the mid-century, as one of the most significant dates heralding the very beginning of the beginning.

In the spring of 1956 the National Film Theatre in London presented a series of independently made films under the name Free Cinema. The program consisted of a series of short films —*Nice Time*, by Claude Goretta and Alain Tanner; *Every Day Except Christmas*, by Lindsay Anderson; *O Dreamland,* also by Lindsay Anderson; and *Momma Don't Allow,* by Tony Richardson—which immediately became a *cause célèbre* in London. Soon the news was spread throughout the rest of Europe and the States that the young cinema had come into existence.

The films of Free Cinema no longer had anything to do with polite slick old plots. In their harsh, black and white colors and direct documentary approach, they brought to the screen images of contemporary London, with its dance halls, its night streets, its playgrounds, its warehouses. The people in these films were real, not actors. They looked and acted and spoke and behaved and moved as their contemporaries did. And there was no phony glamorizing, no artificial tragedies. *Every Day Except Christmas, Momma Don't Allow, O Dreamland* were films without plots; they were collections of actions, moods, scenes, observations. They were real, dynamic, and modern—modern to the point that Rudolf Arnheim was prompted to exclaim (Film Culture, N.17): "It never occurred to me before how closely the style of some documentaries is related to characteristic tendencies of modern abstract art. Was there in the earlier documentaries the same fatiguing endlessness, the same noises and milling of the crowds, the rapid turnover of innumerable objects and passers-by, adding up to an even texture of unceasing disorder, cut from the loom of time more or less at random, and thus directly related to the abstract paintings of the Jackson Pollock school?"

It was these films that led to the rejuvenation of the commercial British film, to Jack Clayton's *Room at the Top* and Tony Richardson's *Look Back in Anger*, two of Britain's most successful contemporary films. They are not completely free from cliché, and they lean heavily on the theatre, but they have broken a wide gap between the old and new.

The coming of the New Wave in France was still more sudden and even more spectacular. Overnight the Cannes film festival became a camp of insurgents. Not only did they take over the prizes and the publicity, they also gathered together—some twenty of them—and attempted to arrive at a manifesto. However, there happened to be present as many different personalities, styles and directions as there were heads, and no common agreement was reached. They stressed insistently that they were not a movement but, using Truffaut's words, rather an eruption—an eruption of new film makers whose first and fundamental characteristic, and the only one on which they all agreed, was to have complete control over their own productions. In Venice, two months later, with Rossellini himself presiding, there was another attempt made to get out a common statement—but again it failed. In the true French spirit, they insisted on their independent individualities.

We have had the opportunity to see in New York a good number of the films made by these young directors: Louis Malle's *The Lovers*, François Truffaut's *The 400 Blows*, Marcel Camus' *The Black Orpheus*, Jean Rouch's *I Am a Negro*, Claude Chabrol's *Le Beau Serge* and *The Cousins*. With three of the most important works still missing—Resnais' *Hiroshima, Mon Amour*, Hanoun's *Le Huitième Jour* and Godard's *A bout de souffle*—we cannot pass judgment on the true achievements of the movement; nevertheless, it is already possible to indicate some of its moods, aims and tendencies.

It would be wrong to think that Free Cinema had any great direct influence upon the new French directors. Its influence was more an indirect one, a strengthening of their determination to make their own films as free as those of their British colleagues. A more direct influence—and this is acknowledged by the young directors themselves—has been exerted by some of the leading figures of the older generation, particularly by Rossellini, Renoir, and the American directors Howard Hawks and Alfred Hitchcock.

In their best work, all four directors admired by the Cahiers du Cinéma group, have one thing in common: in their films the consciously imposed form seems to give place to a spontaneous, even hazardous flow—a style full of bits of slightly indirect details that do not always progress the plot but add to it indirectly, as moods, atmospheres, observations. And it is particularly these asides, these between-the-action remarks, that helped these directors to develop their very distinct personal styles and to inject their films with a live, natural, and fluent quality. It is similar to the way we sometimes get to know people better by their side remarks and their little everyday actions than from their big official lives. Thus, in these films, life seems to happen without much forcing—without any obvious premeditation. This is further strengthened by advanced techniques of film cutting and camera work: the increasing predominance of the long shot and the disappearance of montage cutting, leaving most of the cutting to the *mise-en-scène* and camera. And this becomes one of the most important characteristics of the new French directors too: cinema in which the conscious plan is no longer visible, cinema as a fluid personal expression, a fluidity punctuated only by the temperament of the film maker himself. So *The* 400 *Blows* becomes a perfect manifesto of this direction, with a simplicity that is enthralling and a subjectivity that reminds us of Vigo and Buñuel—cinema of the author *par excellence. The Cousins,* although it has more of a direct plot, attracts us first by its style, too, a style through which we can feel the impatient intellect of its maker. It is not the plot (which is the weakest part of the film), not what the film says that is of primary importance in these films, but *how* it is said and by *whom.*

It is the style, the temperament through which the modernity, the contemporaneity of their films manifest themselves, differentiating them radically from those of the older generation.

Jean Rouch's *I Am a Negro* illustrates another very important aim of the Nouvelle Vague, which, again, corresponds with the aims of their colleagues in England and the States: their constant attempt to free cinema from the stage, to develop a spontaneous dialogue and a spontaneous action. Whereas Malle or Chabrol, being more commercial, fail in these aims, Rouch, completely independent, and less "professional," achieves them admirably. The film, made in Africa with non-professionals, was shot without rehearsing, with local people enacting themselves, improvising their actions and dialogues before the camera. Truck drivers, prostitutes, idlers become alive, real, with their own imperfections of speech (*argot*) and behavior. The spontaneous and un-lied quality of their dialogues and actions is without comparison in modern European cinema, and it makes us forgive many of the film's imperfections.

However, not only the stylistic and formal aspects separate or bind the Nouvelle Vague from/to their predecessors. There are other equally important differences. The most obvious of all is the very fact that these films are made by a *new* generation, and thus, very naturally, they reflect *new* temperaments and *new* ideas: those of the cold-war generation. These ideological and temperamental beginnings go deeper than the Cannes film festival. In fact, the real birth of the Nouvelle Vague should be dated with the appearance of Françoise Sagan, Roger Vadim, and Brigitte Bardot. Sagan and Vadim were the first ones to sum up the mores and dreams of their contemporaries, and, by pushing them into an irrational emotional extreme—the same way Elvis Presley pushed the lust for materiality to the extreme by purchasing four cars—made their contemporaries see the absurdity and decadence of those mores and those dreams. Their more sensitive contemporaries are becoming conscious of the pretension, falseness, and bad faith pervading their lives. This awareness gives birth to doubt and anxiety which eventually leads to chaos in which one can search anew for a true basis of one's life. In France this transitional, cold-war generation is often being called "les tricheurs," the cheaters—an unjust name, because these young people cheat less than those who, out of stupidity or laziness, passively accept values they do not believe in. The "cheaters" live their lives—recreated so well in Chabrol's *The Cousins*—for the experience of the moment, like their American counterparts, the beats. But though they try to grasp the very essence of life and liberty through pleasure, they are neither hedonists nor are they depraved. They pose their honesty and their adolescent genuineness against the falsity of their surroundings. Simone de Beauvoir summed it up well when, writing in Esquire on Bardot, she said: "BB does not try to scandalize. She has no demands to make; she is no more conscious of her rights than she is of her duties. She follows her inclinations. She eats when she is hungry and makes love with the same unceremonious simplicity. Desire and pleasure seem to her more convincing than precepts and conventions. She does not criticize others. She does not ask questions, but she brings answers whose frankness may be contagious. Moral lapses can be corrected, but how could BB be cured of that dazzling virtue —genuineness. It is her very substance."

All this is reflected more and more in the young French cinema. If the "beat" rebellion against the mechanization of life and art in America is expressed through a spontaneity and emotionalism bordering on irrationality, their French counterparts, although in a more restrained emotional manner, begin by debunking the same "bourgeois" conventions: parenthood, marriage, family, love—searching at the same time for the origins and meaning of them. They take for granted, and rightly so, that man doesn't know anymore what these conventions are or what they mean. Everything has to be found and cleaned anew. In *The Lovers*, the young wife, bored with the monotony of her domestic life, falls in love with a passing young stranger. They forget the reality of their situation, since they do not much care for it, nor for the husband, friends, or even the child, who, anyway, will grow up to be just another copy of everything they dislike. So they create their own free, pure romantic world in the midst of this bourgeois home, and enjoy one night of the most basic love, stripped of all pretension.

And this has to be admitted: whatever the esthetic contributions of the Nouvelle Vague will be, their very attitude of search and doubt, their sincere attunement to their times, is a positive act. They are bringing French cinema up-to-date. It is enough to see Chabrol's *The Cousins* to realize the difference between the generation of Renoir and that of Chabrol. Chabrol's generation not only has different problems facing them but the very physical movements of their bodies, their voices, their reactions, their turning around, their standing, their walk—everything is different. And we have to admit that only the directors of the Nouvelle Vague were able to feel this and register it so perceptibly. It is their generation.

If nothing else, the Nouvelle Vague has done one thing in America: it has prompted America to search for its own new generation of movie makers.

As always, there are new films being made by new and often young men, both in and outside of Hollywood. A recent issue of Variety listed about 25 low-budget (under $100,000) movies being made in New York alone. Since these movies are made with the intention to sell them later on to bigger companies—thematically, formally, and visually they stay on familiar and safe grounds. Nevertheless, some of them succeed in revealing more of the true face of their makers. We could use as examples *Stakeout on Dope Street*, by Irvin Kershner; *Crime and Punishment, U.S.A.*, by the brothers Sanders; *The Proper Time*, by Tom Laughlin; *Private Property*, by Leslie Stevens. None of great individuality, they nevertheless introduce new fresh faces, new locations and have an eye for more contemporary settings and dialogue, with new sensibilities and the attitudes clearly noticeable. Sooner or later all these directors will graduate to Hollywood, working professionally beside their older masters, without any great revolutions stirred. It was this way that half a decade earlier an entire school of young able directors graduated to Hollywood with nothing in particular happening. I mean directors like Sidney Lumet, Martin Ritt, Delbert Mann, Arthur Penn, Robert Aldrich, Stanley Kubrick, Jack Garfein, etc.—the entire school of the Fifties. All they did was to bring American cinema a little bit closer to earth, or perhaps I should say, closer to the Bronx—a cinema of the middle class, as best illustrated by *Marty* and *12 Angry Men*. A more drastic change, the change which the new generation of French film makers is attempting and which the Free Cinema group in England is striving for, a cinema of the author, this was left for the next decade. And it is this coming generation—a generation in the bud—that I want to talk about here, since it is this generation that will create an author's cinema in America—a generation that grew up with the new, changing America. Still weak, still often frail, manifesting itself only through a few works and commercially not recognized, this New American Cinema is not only coming but may, eventually, influence and change the attitudes and aims of even the preceding generation of the Fifties.

To see what is really happening, one has to leave the official palaces of the commercial cinema and descend into another, younger level, into that young underground where the ideas and dreams germinate, where the new climate is being formed before it reaches the larger public and official recognition.

Before discussing concrete examples of the New American Cinema, a few other important factors should be brought to attention for a better understanding of the circumstances in which the New American Cinema is growing:

1. The increasing role of New York. New York has always been in opposition to Hollywood, not only geographically but ideologically as well. It is here that the most perceptive American film critics and film historians live and work—Lewis Jacobs, Parker Tyler, the late James Agee, Herman G. Weinberg, Richard Griffith, Gilbert Seldes, the "Film Culture" group, and the entire experimental film movement. The late Robert Flaherty preached from New York; and then there is Sidney Meyers of *Quiet One*; Kazan of *Boomerang*; and Morris Engel, and Chayefsky. American recognition of the Nouvelle Vague and Bergman was brought about by New York critics. No wonder then that the most advanced and original ideas and work of the New American Cinema, the entire reaction against Hollywood, is to be found on the East Coast.

2. It has to be stated here that the role of the Hollywood independents has been greatly exaggerated. The best Hollywood tradition movies (*Anatomy of a Murder, Giant, Ben Hur*) still come from the larger Hollywood producers. The best anti-Hollywood movies, however, have little to do with Independents. They come from individual East Coast film makers, from those film makers who came under the direct influence of the East Coast cinematic climate (*Shadows; Weddings and Babies; On the Bowery*).

3. Bergman and the Nouvelle Vague have stirred American critics and the American public out of a long lethargy. And now the search and campaigning for a more contemporary cinema begins. Growing public enthusiasm further provokes and inspires the New Film Maker. He knows that in this changing climate he has a better chance to get the sponsorship and the distribution for his low-budget movie. He has more courage to dare, to break into fresher grounds. He doesn't always know the direction he should take, but he knows that the old directions are no good for him. More than that: the film makers, tired of begging the distributors and theatre owners to take their films, begin to open their own theatres. Lionel Rogosin did so (The Bleecker Street Cinema) after nobody wanted to show his *Come Back, Africa.* Another theatre, The New Yorker, was opened by the film critic Daniel Talbot, with a premiere of *Pull My Daisy.* Both theatres may become the tribunes of the New American Cinema. Both theatres have openly declared that they want to show primarily works of the new film makers. The underground is beginning to boil, to open up, to shoot out.

4. A considerable influence could be traced to the postwar experimental cinema, which, through the works shown at the film societies, and through its main apostles, Cinema 16, Film Culture magazine and the film critic Parker Tyler, has succeeded in putting across the idea that the film maker, in order to express himself freely, to make his art a personal art, has to abandon his dream of receiving help from the commercial theatres or the blessing of the industry—an abandonment and disillusion which becomes the first condition of cinematic freedom. On the other hand, this attitude is fortified by the spirit and the tendencies governing the new America in general—even among those who are no longer a part of the young generation but, rather, live on the margins of it. Since the older generation could not develop an attitude to life of their own, we might say they are now borrowing it from their children.

Before I go into more detail on what the New American Cinema is, I will list here a few films that, more or less successfully, manifest the new tendencies, and thus, represent the avant-garde of modern American cinema:

410

John Cassavetes' *Shadows* (first version);
Robert Frank's—Alfred Leslie's *Pull My Daisy*;
Morris Engel's *Lovers and Lollipops* and *Weddings and Babies*;
Bert Stern's *Jazz on a Summer's Day*;
Brothers Sanders' *Crime and Punishment, U.S.A.*;
Stanley Brakhage's *Desistfilm*;
Lionel Rogosin's *On the Bowery* and *Come Back, Africa.**

The change of climate, and the historical date of the new American film making, occurred in autumn, 1958. The film was John Cassavetes' *Shadows*.

The screening of *Shadows*—shot on 16mm for some $15,000 and then blown up to 35mm—not only indicated clearly the tendencies of the new American cinema, but also destroyed the myth of the $1,000,000 production. At that time Film Culture in its editorial "A Call for a New Generation of Film Makers" wrote: '*Shadows* proves that a feature film can be made with only $15,000. And a film that doesn't betray life or cinema. What does it prove? It proves that we can make our films *now* and by *ourselves*. Hollywood and the miniature Hollywoods of our 'independents' will never make *our* films."

The movement of the underground was on the march.

The film itself, *Shadows*, is a plotless, episodic film, shot without a script. Primarily, it is a series of improvisations describing a few incidents in the life of a Negro family, two brothers and a sister. Since most of the film takes place at night, it has a texture of lonely dark streets, bars, and neon lights. Through improvisations and outbursts of feeling, the film slowly builds up and grows, without any evidence of imposed force, and simultaneously an image of the city emerges,

* Among the films in production that will definitely explore and develop further the New American Cinema could be mentioned: Shirley Clarke's *The Connection* (from Jack Gelber's play); Robert Cordier's—Edward Hochman's *Stoning Machine* (James Baldwin's original script); H. L. Humes' *Men Die* (based on his own novel); Robert Frank's *The Sin of Jesus* (based on a short story by Isaac Babel); Gregory Markopoulos' *Serenity* (based on a novel by Venezis); Adolfas Mekas' *Hallelujah the Woods* (from his own original script); Jonas Mekas' *Guns of the Trees* (from his own original script); Sheldon Rochlin's *Night Thoughts* (his own original script); Edward Bland's—Mark Kennedy's film, untitled yet, based on their own script. All these films should be finished before the Spring of 1961, which may become the Spring of the New American Cinema.

with its night streets and its night people. The mood of the city, the relationships of its people, the tender love and family quarrels, are all forcefully revealed to us. The film begins and ends in the middle; nothing much is changed or resolved. But this casual, fragmentary quality is precisely why it is so convincing, so spontaneous, and so truthful.

The success of this film is partly due to the sensitivity of Ben Curruthers who plays the lonely youth—a character that grew out of a short paragraph, all that there was of a written script concerning his part:

> BENNY. He is driven by the uncertainty of his color to beg acceptance in this white man's world. Unlike his brother Hugh, or Janet, he has no outlet for his emotions. He has been spending his life trying to decide what color he is. Now that he has chosen the white race as his people, his problem remains acceptance. This is difficult, knowing that he is in a sense betraying his own. His life is an aimless struggle to prove something abstract, his every day living has no outlet, and so he moves . . . (Here the script ends.)

Here I have to make a digression, which really isn't a digression at all. There exist two versions of *Shadows*. After the screening of the first version the reaction from the younger generation was ecstatic. Distributors, however, were shocked. They succeeded in persuading Cassavetes to re-shoot and re-edit the film, to make it more suitable for the commercial theatres. The result was a bastardized, hybrid movie which had neither the spontaneity of the first version, nor the innocence, nor the freshness. It is this second version that the producers are now sending to festivals and trying to sell. And since many will see it, I don't want to be misunderstood. All the virtues which I am bestowing upon *Shadows* concern only the first version of the film and *only* this version (which begins with Ben walking the streets, meeting his friends, the titles coming much later. The second, bastardized version, begins with a rock-and-roll session and the titles come immediately, similar to *Look Back in Anger*).

What *Shadows* (first version) did was to use, often to perfection, many elements which are among the essential characteristics of the New American Cinema and which, very often, correspond to the characteristics of the Nouvelle Vague film makers, particularly when one compares *Shadows* with the work of Truffaut and Jean-Luc Godard. Louis Malle, even after seeing the mutilated version of *Shadows*, could not but admire its qualities of spontaneity. *Moi, Un Noir* comes closest to it, with the difference that Cassavetes used "real" actors instead of "real" people.

Since there was no written script, the actors had to improvise most of their lines on the spot. The language, the situations, and the incidents have all the freshness of such an improvisation. Since the director was only the moderator, a mid-wife (we remember here the freedom which Renoir gives to his actors), there is no imposed one-point view, no imposed morality. The episodes were objectively improvised situations, happenings which left the formulation of the moral to the viewer, just as Truffaut did in *The 400 Blows*. The photography itself enhanced this quality of witnessing life in action. Sharp black & white, rough, with no Hollywood schmaltz & polish; no beautification, no John Alton & Co., no make-up, no arty conscious angles. Only occasionally some old-fashioned close-ups, remnants of the old school, showed up.

The weaknesses of *Shadows* are those of any new beginning, any groping for the new in a fresh and unfamiliar landscape. Cassavetes was not clear about his aims, not conscious of his real artistic intentions. What Cassavetes achieved was more a result of "not-knowing" than of his "knowing." (We remember Orson Welles' remark about *Citizen Kane*: "I didn't deliberately set out to invent anything. It just seemed to me: Why not? There is a great gift that ignorance has to bring to anything, you know. That was the gift I brought to *Kane*—ignorance.") The very imperfections, the "unprofessionalism" of his techniques became an integral part of the film, its very style, giving it a certain roughness, a certain impurity that made it more authentic, less official. Cassavetes, without knowing it, came upon the same sense of roughness and impurity which is a fundamental part of all modern American art; the music of Allan Kaprow, the theatre of Julian Beck and Judith Malina, the paintings of Alfred Leslie, the sculptures of Richard Stankiewicz, the writings of Kerouac or Ginsberg—everywhere you'll find these touches of visual or aural "slang" and "impurity" which in an instant destroy any feeling of respectable classicism. In painting, for instance, Alfred Leslie's final touches on the work consist of splashes and drippings of paint with which he intentionally destroys the illusion of Art, reminding one of the studio and brushes—a touch of actuality and action which has a strong quality or lyricism, and which we find in all modern American art and life. It is this quality of spontaneous action that marks *Shadows*, and it is the same quality which Alfred Leslie himself later brought to cinema with *Pull My Daisy*. As if they were saying: to live, to have a contact with life, is more important than to create Art.

Pull My Daisy (directed by Robert Frank and Alfred Leslie) is a free improvisation on a scene from an unproduced play by Jack Kerouac. It is about an evening at the place of a young Villager, a "railway worker" who is being visited by some poet friends, and by a young "Bishop" of some unidentifiable church. There are the poets themselves, Gregory Corso, Allen Ginsberg, Peter Orlowski, talking and gesticulating and going through a series of improvisations; the Bishop's mother playing the organ and his sister blowing the bellows. They talk, drink beer, discuss God, play trumpet, talk again. Nothing much happens. . . . The camera harshly and pitilessly reveals the bedroom, the sink, the table, the cockroaches . . .

One of the most exciting features of *Pull My Daisy* is its sound track. The picture was shot silent and Jack Kerouac speaks for all the characters, also commenting freely on their actions. During the recording of the commentary, Kerouac spoke the lines of each character without any preparation or previous study of the film—in a sort of intoxicated trance. His commentary has immediacy, poetry and magic that is without a precedent in American cinema. As *Hiroshima, Mon Amour*, or *Moi, Un Noir* will lose much of their aural beauty to English speaking audiences, so *Pull My Daisy* will lose much of its sound track in non-English countries.

The following is a statement on the film by Robert Frank and Alfred Leslie:

The intention of the makers of this film was to create a situation whereby one might comply with James Agee's tender request:

"The films I most eagerly look forward to will not be documentaries but works of pure fiction, played against and into, and in collaboration with unrehearsed and uninvented reality."

Pull My Daisy is a tragi-comedy about an ex-junkie (drug addict) named Milo and his wife. Hoping to convert her husband to middle-classism through spiritual salvation she invites a young self-ordained "Bishop" and his family to meet and talk with him. Milo has also invited his poet friends.

414

The conflict of identities is inevitable and here it is sharpened. Exactly . . . who is who . . . what is what . . . why is why . . . how is how . . .

It is a mad evening, an insane visit, a heroic and bedraggled circle. (End of statement.)

Pull My Daisy is not a film of plot, action, or logical statements. It is, rather, a portrait of the inner condition of an entire generation. It could even be called a "beat" film—and the only truly "beat" film if there is one—in the sense that beat is an expression of the new generation's unconscious and spontaneous rejection of the middle-class way, the business men's way. And it is a thoroughly truthful film despite its apparent robe of nonsense—as a matter of fact, the most truthful American film in I don't know how long a time. There is no lie, no pretension, no moralizing in it.

We know that Richter and Cocteau have used friends—painters and poets—in their films. However, they used them in symbolic situations, movements. *Pull My Daisy* has nothing to do with any such literary symbols. The situations are everyday situations, with no other intentions. Still, the total impact of the film is a strange world of inconsequentialities which has its own logic and sense. At the same time, it strikes us as unmistakably our own, as the essence of our own world, or, more truly, that of the young, beat generation. The photography again, in black and white, is completely subjugated to the creation of this climate. Lyrically drab, never arty or obtrusive, humble, it continuously concentrates on the details and actions which, although seemingly inconsequential, contain the most essential qualities of contemporary American realities. Robert Frank, the cameraman (whose book, "Les Américains," came out in Paris last year, and just recently in New York) succeeded in destroying the static, pictorial, arty frame, of which the advocates of the silent cinema are so fond and which still mars most of the modern cinema. It is enough to look at Frank's still photographs to realize that even his still photographs are actually never still or static. They are framed, cutout in such a way that the balance of the image is constantly destroyed—it always swings and moves towards the borders of the frame, towards something bigger, towards the totality of life in action. When the "professionalists" of the official cinema shout that Frank doesn't know how to frame, that he cuts the heads off—etc., they miss the entire point of true cinemadynamics. What Frank really says is: Down with the vignettes; down with beautifully, statically composed collections of moving stills; down with Alton & Co.'s flat schmaltzy lighting; away and down with the frame! The dethroning of Hollywood, or so-called "official" cinematography, is one of the fundamental contributions of the New American Cinema. The work of Morris Engel, Rogosin, and Robert Frank in black and white, and the work of Bert Stern in color (for *Jazz on a Summer's Day*) has pushed American cinematography at least one decade forward—more or less, they have caught up with the cinematographic esthetic where G. R. Aldo left it five years ago, when he died.

Here we should note another important preoccupation of the new American film maker; namely, the freeing of the camera itself. This until now was best achieved—and almost to perfection—by Stanley Brakhage in a short film called *Desistfilm*.

Desistfilm employs all the techniques of a spontaneous cinema. It describes a wild party held by a young group of youths, with all their youthful exhibitionisms, adolescent games, and adolescent love images, and was shot in one evening at a real improvised party with a 16mm camera, most of the time hand-held, following every movement wildly, without any premeditated plan. This technique of the freed camera enabled him to recreate the mood and tempo of the party, with all its little details of foolish, silly, marginal actions, its outbursts of adolescent emotions. The camera, freed from its tripod, gets everywhere, never intruding, never interfering; it moves into close-ups, or follows the restless youths in fast, jerky tilts and pans. There seems to be a perfect unity here of subject matter, camera movement, and the temperament of the film maker himself. The free flight of life has been caught, and the film has vitality, rhythm, and also the temperament of a poem by Rimbaud, of a naked confession—all improvisation, with no artist's hand visible, though at the same time the distance between reality and art is established; the dynamic of *Desistfilm* is not one of reality but one of a work of art. (This point is more important than one would like to think. The work of Morris Engel, and a great number of neo-realist films, for instance, fail only because this distance between reality and art is not sufficiently established.)

Any of the new directors—Rogosin, Cassavetes, Frank, Engel, Leslie—are better film authors than the preceding generation, meaning that we see in their films more personal style. On the other hand, none of them are very familiar with film theory or film history. Neither are they intellectuals. They are, rather, emotional, unpredictable men who follow their own intuitions and visions, with little respect for any accepted conventions. And we know that the best of American cinema has been created by such emotional "ignorants," Griffith not excluded. The new American film maker seems to have an inborn immunity against the clichés of the official cinema. By sheer intuition he is navigating American cinema into fresher, unexplored grounds. It is sincerity that matters more to him than technique or theories.

The author's sincerity, the innocence of his attitude in modern American art very often plays a greater role than the perfection of the work. The denouncing of Hollywood itself is very often based not on the bad quality of the film making, but, more often, on the insincerity, the pose and the business way of life that seeps through Hollywood films, be it *Defiant Ones, The Nun's Story, Middle of the Night, The Diary of Anne Frank, Anatomy of a Murder*—there is always something pretentious and phony about them. If the ideals and way of life of the older generation—the generation of Eisenhower and Nixon—were to be crystallized, they would undoubtedly and always wind up in a Hell of Immorality. On the other hand, if you take the perspective lines of the beat generation and extend them to infinity, they would probably end somewhere at the feet of St. Francis. Any pretension is immediately noticed. Innocence, sincerity, and openness has become the main quest of all modern American art. The new American film maker prefers some of the technically and esthetically inferior juvenile melodramas and science fiction films, if they are honest (and many of them are), to the more perfect but insincere and pompous works of Film Art.

For very similar reasons, the new generation of film makers is against even such an uncommercial film maker as Sidney Meyers. He is being attacked on purely moral grounds: in *The Savage Eye* the human tragedy is being used for purely visual effect, for visual shock and not for the sake of truth or love. When shown out of context, a religious passion, a striptease, a lonely face, a homosexual in a woman's dress—everything becomes ridiculous and "inhuman," whereas we know that all these acts are "human" and often sad and tragic. Neither Rogosin nor Frank nor Cassavetes would laugh about it as cynically as Sidney Meyers does. His laugh is savage but without a heart.

Even the work of Morris Engel, when compared to *Shadows* or *Pull My Daisy*, looks formalistically pretentious, arty, with exaggerated and obvious intentions. Although Morris Engel is an undeniable influence on the New American Cinema, he has never succeeded in handling actors and mastering the timing of his improvised scenes or in masking his intentions as well as Cassavetes or Frank. Engel's use of spontaneity and improvisation seems to be formalistic, for its own sake, which is just the opposite of what the new American film maker seeks. For him, neither spontaneity nor improvisation are aims in themselves. Neither are they means to esthetic goals. For the new American generation spontaneity serves an ethical purpose. Spontaneity as liberation, as bliss, as a means of freeing one's self from the moral, social clichés, out-dated mores, the business way of life. It is an outgrowth of the same ethical preoccupations, of a desire to be close to earth, of believing only in an immediate experience, in an action, which, in a different way, could also be found in Robbe-Grillet's demystification of man, a coming down to facts. Thus, it is the sincerity, almost humility with which the makers of *Shadows*, *Pull My Daisy* or *Come Back, Africa* approach reality that is the key to their originality and their modernity.

I have stated earlier that the center of the New American Cinema is undoubtedly New York. However, there are signs of a changing climate on the West Coast too. *Private Property* is one of the first West Coast productions in which a more drastic break with the Hollywood line can be perceived—in its low budget ($60,000), in its use of unknown, new actors, in its more contemporary settings, and, above all, in its temperament. And it seems to me that *Private Property* may also prove to be a very typical example of what the West Coast contribution to the New American Cinema will be.

Although spiced with some modern psychological motiva-

418

tions and symbolism, *Private Property* is in no sense a modern film. Nor is it a serious film. It is a Hollywood melodrama to please a middle-class high brow. Perhaps the shadow-killing and all-leveling California sun affects one differently (which may also be the reason for what Hollywood really is)—basically, the West Coast film makers seem to take life as a plain, one-level phenomenon, without any shadows or nooks and corners. In this shadow-less sun all the proportions of life seem to have been bleached out. Death, Birth, Sickness, Sex—everything acquires the color of a wax-museum. Even Sidney Meyers' *The Savage Eye*, as it is, with its cynical detachment, can be explained only by the fact that it was shot in California. In New York the same scenes would have acquired a certain sadness, a certain humaneness.

And if the Hollywood productions, as well as most of the independent productions coming from the West Coast, could be compared with newsstand literature, then the aims of Frank, Engel, or Rogosin correspond to those of the serious writers. These East Coast productions represent something that the American dramatic feature film needs most: the filmic equivalent of the serious novel. The depiction of Negro family relationships in *Shadows,* and particularly the long scene towards the end (which, fortunately, was included in the second version of the film), where Janet, while preparing herself to go out, lets the young man who came to take her out to a dance wait for two hours while everybody makes a joke of it —is one of the most truthful, most humorously descriptional, almost ethnographical, scenes in contemporary American cinema. The tension and interest is sustained not by twists of plot, but by the subtle twists of daily actions and daily behavior moods. It is not the continuous action but the almost continuous non-action that sustains this sequence as well as the whole of *Shadows, Pull My Daisy,* or *Weddings and Babies*—something that until now only the best of novels were able to do. But the ice is broken: the cinema has matured enough to dare venture into areas of serious description and narrative, without any feeling of inferiority, without the fear that it is becoming "literature" or "uncinematic." Who was it, was it Pierre Kast who, apropos *Le Bel Age,* said that his images are only a commentary to the text, and not the opposite. And so, when Robert Frank declares, without making any fuss about it, that in *Pull My Daisy* sometimes it is the camera that illustrates Kerouac's text, sometimes it is Kerouac who comments on the images—we have the same complete freedom of cinema, for the first time in film history.

To sum up:

It should be clear by now that the new American arts, and, therefore, the New American Cinema, is not an esthetic but primarily an ethical movement. Before any esthetic can be built there are other, more important things to build: the New Man himself. And I would call a fool anybody who would demand of this generation works of art that contain clear and positive philosophies and esthetics. There will be nothing of that! This generation is too young, too alive for that. This decade will be marked by an intensified search and by the further loosening of sensibilities for the purpose of reaching still deeper into less contaminated depths of man's soul, trying desperately to escape the clichés of art and life.

The New American film maker seeks to free himself from the over-professionalism and over-technicality that usually handicaps the inspiration and spontaneity of contemporary cinema, guiding himself more by intuition and improvisation than by discipline; he aims desperately, as his colleague action painter, or poet and dancer, at art in its very flight, at a free, a spontaneous inspiration: art as an action and not as a status quo; art as various states of feeling and not as a series of facts, nature-morts, or pastiches. And since the main tendency of a modern American film maker becomes "to grasp life from within and not from without" (Suzuki) by loosening the sensibilities, these films could be described as a spontaneous cinema. ("With the conscious mind we are able, at most, to get within reach of the unconscious process, and must then wait and see what will happen next,"—C. G. Jung).

Further—summing up—the spontaneity of the new American artist is not a conscious or an intellectual process; it is rather his way of life, his whole being; he comes to it rather intuitively, directly.

The new artist neither chooses this spontaneous route himself nor does he do so consciously: it is imposed upon him by his time, as the only possible route.

Being constantly exposed to the reality which Allen Ginsberg summed up like this: ". . . a vast national subconscious

420

netherworld filled with nerve gases, universal death bombs, malevolent bureaucracies, secret police systems, drugs that open the door to God, ships leaving Earth, unknown chemical terrors, evil dreams at hand,"—the artist, somehow intuitively, out of his own desperation, in his quest for an un-corrupt basis for his life, descends deeper and deeper into that valley of irrationality where—as all modern and ancient thinkers and religions seem to agree—all our past and the core of our lives rests. This being the most characteristic expression (and task) of the new generation—and the New Man in general—it is therefore the only route that doesn't betray him. As for the audience, since it no longer knows what truth or beauty is, all it can do is to trust its artists, its deep divers into the subconscious of man.

Film Happenings
by Jonas Mekas

This chapter was printed originally in the December 2, 1965, issue of The Village Voice, where Mr. Mekas' fresh and illuminating observations appear weekly.

The unusual festival of film happenings at the Cinematheque is continuing. When they are bad, they are very bad; when they are good, they are almost great. Last week, Ken Dewey, Dick Higgins, Ed Emshwiller, Gerd Stern, Ken Jacobs, and, less intensely, Jackie Cassen, Aldo Tambellini, Elaine Summers, Ray Wisniewski continued the series of new visual discoveries.

Ed Emshwiller remains the craftsman and the scientist of the avant-garde cinema. His piece *Body Works* may be not only the best piece he has ever done, but also the first successful attempt at cinema ballet. Whereas most of the other film makers who use multiple projections leave much to chance, Emshwiller presented a completely controlled and almost scientifically planned work dazzling in its visual effects. He played tricks with our eyes, with our vision, with the depth of field, with the long shots and close-ups; right there before our eyes he snapped his fingers and the dancer changed into a skeleton or became a huge hand or became two dancers.

Gerd Stern's evening was less dazzling but it was more beautiful for the eye. Here again was a planned presentation of multiple imagery (defraction boxes, strobes, carousel projectors, live action) but with enough holes for chance so that the effect wasn't as scientifically abstract as that of Emshwiller. Gerd Stern is more attracted by the soft and pictorial conglomerations of light, color, motion. He admits a great influence of Marshall McLuhan. Their complete trust in McLuhan permitted them (Gerd Stern and his collaborators, Michael Callahan, Brian Peterson, Jud Yalkut) to abandon themselves completely, not to bother about what art or cinema is and work on this sensuous sea of color, motion, and light that seems to surround us completely and we swim in it almost bodily and it is like going through the most fantastic dream.

I state here openly, I admit that I have experienced subtle esthetic illuminations during Dick Higgins, Gerd Stern, Ken

422

Dewey, Ed Emshwiller shows, and my esthetic senses are not easy to please. I have spent thirty years of my life doing nothing but perfecting these senses. I realize perfectly that there are many questions to ask here concerning this festival, and I will be asking them later, at the end of this, by now, revolutionary festival—questions that will begin with What Is Art, What Should Art Do, etc. etc.—but at this time I would like to remain a chronicler, albeit an emotional one.

Ken Jacobs—who, with his ten unfinished (money, money, money) films, is probably the least known, although one of the most productive (creative), beautiful, and influential of modern film makers—gave us a strange piece, as part of the festival, a political romance performed as a shadow and light play (and some color prisms).

Ken Dewey's piece wasn't a shadow play, but it was shadowy from somewhere deep, or far, repeating repeating, and over-lapping themselves, and there was light going on and off, and when it was on, you could see four or five women standing on the white stage, all white like milk, five women in milk and in wedding gowns, like in a store window on a misty morning, with streets still empty, in Williamsburgh, Brooklyn; and it was a sad piece. The voice said, and repeated in one thousand different ways and shades the phrases: "I," "That's not you," "It's me." ("I have great respect for an artist who is as nervous as he is," said David Brooks, and he has studied more Freud and psychology than I.) And the movies were running along the ceiling, a most perfect use of the inside of the theater I have ever seen—Dewey used the ceiling beams as screens, breaking the image into four or five depth levels. He also defracted light through the carefully placed and angled mirrors on the sides and the back of the theatre and they caught, at certain moments, glimpses of light and image creating almost ecstatically beautiful pure crystal light experience that sounded like Mozart; I almost could write down the notes.

But the thing I wanted to say at this point is really this: Ken Jacobs, by making his show into a shadow play, pointed out, intentionally or not—and he has been always right—the direction most of the artists at this strange festival have been going to, from many different directions and through many different and complicated side routes: the art of the Shadow Play.

423

Permit my insane head a few heresies: Isn't it possible that CINEMA is really nothing new? Isn't it possible that the art which we thought was Our Art, the twentieth century art, isn't our art at all? Isn't it possible that the Shadow and Light artists of Persia, of China, of India were the real masters, the real magicians of the art of Light, Motion, Image? How little we know about it. Aren't we coming back to it, though, closer and closer to it, as the least naturalistic, as the most stylized, most controlled art of telling the stories and creating magic through light, motion, images?

When I watched the shows of Ken Jacobs, Gerd Stern, Don Snyder, Stan Vanderbeek, Jack Smith, Emshwiller, Tambellini, or Jackie Cassen, I suddenly saw them as the new Shadow Play magicians. I felt that there was practically nothing that couldn't be done by a shadow artist. Motion picture camera can be eliminated from most of these shows with new gains for the creative imagination. I am exaggerating now, no doubt, for making my point, but what I saw with my dazed head was the rebirth of this forgotten art of the past, the art of Shadow Play that will become, during these few coming years, the controversial challenger of cinema as we know it today, and a new source of inspiration. Not that it will push out the cinema as we know it today—but it will make it look only one, and, perhaps not the largest, part of the motion, light, image art. The ground is shaking and the cinema we knew is collapsing, the screen, the projector, the camera and all. Suddenly, and without any bang (I am the only bang) the entire so-called Underground, avant-garde cinema has shifted in time and space and has become part of the Classical Cinema, for our own and children's enjoyment. The new avant-garde of cinema (light play) has moved ten years forward, into new explorations, and, if you'll permit me to contradict Marshall McLuhan, what the artists are doing, their dreams are so much further advanced than the rest of the human activities that it will take at least another ten years, maybe, to catch up with the artist and to create proper tools to enable him to put those dreams into reality.

The Film Generation
by Stanley Kauffmann

Mr. Kauffmann, film critic for The New Republic, has been at various times a novelist, actor, director, TV interviewer, and drama critic of The New York Times. He is the author of "A World on Film," published in 1966, from which this chapter is taken.

Some of the following remarks were included, in differing forms, in talks delivered recently at several universities, colleges, and seminars. In one of the audiences were a distinguished poet and a critic of the graphic arts. Afterward, the critic came up to me and said, "You destroyed us. You wiped out our professions. You rendered my friend and me obsolete." I said that I neither believed nor intended that. Then he said wryly, stroking his chin, "On the other hand, if I were twenty years younger, I know I'd go into films."

His dismal reaction had been prompted by my assertion that film is the art for which there is the greatest spontaneous appetite in America at present, and by my reasons for thinking so. I must be clear that this is not to say that it is the art practiced at the highest level in this country; the film public depends more on imports today than does any other art public. But observation and experience, and the experience of others, make me believe that this uniquely responsive audience exists.

Or, in another phrase, there exists a Film Generation: the first generation that has matured in a culture in which the film has been of accepted serious relevance, however that seriousness is defined. Before 1935 films were proportionately more popular than they are now, but for the huge majority of film-goers they represented a regular weekly or semiweekly bath of escapism. Such an escapist audience still exists in large number, but another audience, most of them born since 1935, exists along with it. This group, this Film Generation, is certainly not exclusively grim, but it is essentially serious. Even its appreciations of sheer entertainment films reflect an overall serious view.

There are a number of reasons, old and new, intrinsic and extrinsic, why this generation has come into being. Here are some of the older, intrinsic reasons.

1. In an age imbued with technological interest, the film art flowers out of technology. Excepting architecture, film is the one art that can capitalize directly and extensively on this century's luxuriance in applied science. Graphic artists have used mechanical and electronic elements, poets and painters have used computers, composers have used electronic tapes. These are matters of choice. The film maker has no choice: he must use complicated electronic and mechanical equipment. This fact helps to create a strong sense of junction with his society, of membership in the present. American artists have often been ashamed of—sometimes have dreaded—a feeling of difference from the busy "real" American world around them. For the film maker the very instruments of his art provide communion with the spirit of his age. I think that the audience shares his feeling of union, sometimes consciously (especially when stereophonic sound, special optical effects, or color processes are used). The scientific skills employed are thus in themselves a link between the artist and the audience, and are a further link between them all and the unseen, unheard but apprehended society bustling outside the film theater.

There is a pleasant paradoxical corollary. In an era that is much concerned with the survival of the human being as such, in an increasingly mechanized age, here a complicated technology is used to celebrate the human being.

2. The world of surfaces and physical details has again become material for art. Just as the naturalistic novel seems to be sputtering to a halt, overdescribed down to the last vest button, the film gives some of its virtues new artistic life. A novelist who employs the slow steam-roller apparatus of intense naturalism these days is asking for an extra vote of confidence from the reader, because the method and effects are so familiar that the reader can anticipate by pages. Even when there is the interest of an unusual setting, the reader is conscious that different nouns have been slipped into a worn pattern. The "new" French novel of Robbe-Grillet, Duras, Sarraute attempts to counteract this condition by intensifying it, using surfaces as the last realities, the only dependable objective correlatives. Sometimes, for some readers, this works. But both the old and the latter-day naturalisms must strain in order to connect. Rolf Hochhuth, the author of "The Deputy," has said:

426

When I recently saw Ingmar Bergman's *The Silence,* I left that Hamburg movie house with the question, "What is there left for the novelist today?" Think of what Bergman can do with a single shot of his camera, up a street, down a corridor, into a woman's armpit. Of all he can say with this without saying a word.

Despite Hochhuth's understandable thrill-despair, there is plenty left for the novelist to say, even of armpits, but the essence of his remark rightly strips from fiction the primary function of creating material reality. The film has not only taken over this function but exalted it: it manages to make poetry out of doorknobs, breakfasts, furniture. Trivial details, of which everyone's universe is made, can once again be transmuted into metaphor, contributing to imaginative art.

A complementary, powerful fact is that this principle operates whether the film maker is concerned with it or not. In any film except those with fantastic settings, whether the director's aim is naturalistic or romantic or symbolic or anything else, the streets and stairways and cigarette lighters are present, the girl's room is at least as real as the girl —often it bolsters her defective reality. Emphasized or not, invited or not, the physical world through the intensifications of photography never stops insisting on its presence and relevance.

This new life of surfaces gives a discrete verity to many mediocre films and gives great vitality to a film by a good artist. Consciously or not, this vitality reassures the audience, tangentially certifying and commenting on its habitat. Indeed, out of this phenomenon, it can be argued that the film discovered pop art years ago, digested this minor achievement, then continued on its way.

3. The film form seems particularly apt for the treatment of many of the pressing questions of our time: inner states of tension or of doubt or apathy—even (as we shall see) doubts about art itself. The film can externalize some psychical matters that, for example, the theater cannot easily deal with; and it can relate them to physical environment in a manner that the theater cannot contain nor the novel quite duplicate. The film can dramatize post-Freudian man, and his habitat—and the relation between the two. One does not need to believe in the death of the theater or the novel—as I do not—in order to see these special graces in the film.

427

4. Film is the only art besides music that is available to the whole world at once, exactly as it was first made. With subtitles, it is the only art involving language that can be enjoyed in a language of which one is ignorant. (I except opera, where the language rarely needs to be understood precisely.)

The point is not the spreading of information or amity, as in USIA or UNESCO films, useful though they may be. The point is emotional relationship and debt. If one has been moved by, for instance, Japanese actors in Japanese settings, in actions of Japanese life that have resonated against one's own experience, there is a connection with Japan that is deeper than the benefits of propaganda or travelogue. No one who has been moved by *Ikiru* can think of Japan and the Japanese exactly as he thought before.

Obviously similar experience—emotional and spiritual—is available through other arts, but rarely with the imperial ease of the film. As against foreign literature, foreign films have an advantage besides accessibility in the original language. The Japanese novelist invites us to recreate the scene in imagination. The Japanese film maker provides the scene for us, with a vividness that our minds cannot equal in a foreign setting. Thus our responses can begin at a more advanced point and can more easily (although not more strongly) be stimulated and heightened.

This universality and this relative simultaneity of artistic experience have made us all members of a much larger empathetic community than has been immediately possible before in history.

5. Film has one great benefit by accident: its youth, which means not only vigor but the reach of possibility. The novel, still very much alive, is conscious of having to remain alive. One of its chief handicaps is its history; the novelist is burdened with the achievements of the past. This is also true of poetry. It flourishes certainly; as with fiction, the state of poetry is far better than is often assumed. But poetry, too, is conscious of a struggle for pertinent survival. In painting and sculpture, the desperation is readily apparent; the new fashion in each new season makes it clear. But the film is an infant, only begun. It has already accomplished miracles. Consider that it was only fifty years from Edison's camera to *Citizen Kane*, which is rather as if Stravinsky had written "Petrouchka"

fifty years after Guido d'Arezzo developed musical notation. Nevertheless the film continent has only just been discovered, the boundaries are not remotely in sight. It is this freshness that gives the young generation—what I have called the Film Generation—not only the excitement of its potential but a strong proprietary feeling. The film belongs to them.

These, I think, are some of the reasons for the growth of that new film audience. But they raise a question. As noted, these reasons have been valid to some degree for a long time, yet it is only in about the last twenty years that the Film Generation has emerged. Why didn't this happen sooner? Why have these reasons begun to be strongly operative only since the Second World War?

In that period other elements have risen to galvanize them. Some of these later elements come from outside the film world: the spurt in college education; political and social abrasions and changes; moral, ethical, religious dissolutions and resolutions. All these have made this generation more impatient and more hungry. But, since the Second War, there have also been some important developments within the film world itself.* These developments have been in content, not in form. Three elements are especially evident: increased sexuality, an increase in national flavor, and an increased stress on the individual. The latter two are linked.

As for the first, sex has been important currency in the theater since "The Agamemnon", and with the first films came the first film idols. In fact there are scenes in many silent films that would have censor trouble today. But apart from sexual display or the sex appeal of any actor or actress, there is now—in many foreign films and some American ones—

* These do not include linguistic developments. Nothing has changed the language of film as, for example, electronics has changed music or abstract expressionism has altered the vision of painting. There have been many technical film developments—wide screens, stereophonic sound, color refinements—but so far they have largely been peripheral to the art itself. They, and the improved hand-held camera and recorder, may affect the basic language of film in future; they have not yet markedly done so. This fact can be taken as an implied strength. Experiments in artistic technique are usually a sign that a boundary has been reached with old techniques. In film there is no hint of exhaustion in the techniques that were known to Griffith and Eisenstein forty years ago.

a sexual attitude that can be respected: an attitude closer to the realities of sexual life than the mythology that is preached by clergy of every faith, by mass media, by parents. This relative sexual freedom, long established in fiction and the theater, has been slower to arrive in films because of their wider availability to all ages and mentalities, and the consequent brooding of censors. Now, in a more liberal time, this freedom makes films even more pertinent to this generation. The mythology that still passes for sexual morality is prescriptive, these films are descriptive; but there is more to their merit than verisimilitude. Not by nudity nor bedroom calisthenics nor frank language but by fidelity to the complexities of sexual behavior, these films provide more than recognition. By accepting and exploring complexities, they provide confidence in the fundamental beauty of those complexities, in the desirability of being human, even with all the trouble it involves.

The second element, national flavor, has been described by the English critic Penelope Houston in The Contemporary Cinema (1963):

However partial or distorted an image one gets of a society through its cinema, it is still possible to discern the national face behind the screen. It is difficult to conceive of a neorealist idealism [in Italy] without the jubilant preface of the liberation of Rome; or to look at Britain's films of the past few years without reference to our redbrick radicalism; or to ignore the effect of the political climate on a French cinema which declares its awareness of strain in the very insistence with which it puts private before public life and creation for creation's sake before either.

It would be easy to add a similar sentence for almost every major film-producing country. Japanese films are concerned with contemporary unrest, directly and indirectly. Many of their costume pictures about samurai swordsmen are set in the 1860's when the feudal system was crumbling and immense social metamorphosis was taking place. The Soviet film has deepened in lethargy as revolutionary fervor wore off, as Stalinist despotism made it nervous, as some subsequent economic and scientific successes made it smug. It has become, with a few exceptions, either war glory or the ideologic equivalent of the petty bourgeois confection. As for America, the poor boy and rich girl story (or rich boy and poor girl) which was the staple of the popular film before the Second War has

disappeared. Money as romance, the Gatsby dream, has re-
ceded, not because everyone is now rich but because the
middle-class image has replaced both the poor image and the
rich image. What American would now relish the ancient compliment "poor but honest"? And what is the difference *in appearance* between the clerk's car and the boss'? The much-
mooted ascendancy of the middle class has reached the point
where it is strong enough to control cultural forms, to magnify
its own image in art.

With this ascendancy we have seen the emergence of a
new romantic hero, posed against this bourgeois background,
since all such heroes must contrast with their societies. The
new romantic is the liberated prole, with a motorcycle or a
Texas Cadillac, seeking his life by assaulting convention and
morality, rather than by striving for success in accepted modes,
either with money or with women. This hero scoffs at ideals
of excellence and aspiration at the same time that he wants
to dominate. There are signs that this hero may have run his
course, but in the last twenty years or so he was pre-eminent.

A lesser companion of his still continues: the Frank
Sinatra-Dean Martin figure, the smart, cool operator just inside
the law, a philanderer righteously resentful of any claims on
him by women. His casual *persona* derives in part from the
night-club microphone, which was first a necessity, then became a prop, then a source of power and ease for those who
had little power and could achieve nothing but ease. The invisible hand-held microphone accompanies the crooner-as-hero
wherever he goes. His oblique, slithering solipsism seems likely
to persist after the Brando figure, more directly descended
from the proletarian rebel and Byronic individualist, has passed.
Mere "coolness" persists; purposeful rebellion fades.

All the national colors described above apply both to popular and serious films. If we concentrate on serious film—film
made primarily as personal expression, not as contractual job
or money-spinner—then we often find, besides intensified national color, an intensified introspection. This is the third of
our elements: a concern with the exploration of the individual
as a universe. It is not a novelty in films. No more introspec-
tive films have ever been made than Wiene's *The Cabinet of
Dr. Caligari* (1919) or Pabst's *Secrets of the Soul* (1926). But
merely to mention such names as Bergman, Antonioni, Fellini,

Ozu, Torre Nilsson, Olmi, Truffaut is to see that, for many outstanding directors, there has lately been more reliance on inner conflict than on classic confrontation of antagonists. These men and others, including some Americans, have been extending the film into the vast areas of innermost privacy, even of the unconscious, that have been the province of the novel and of metaphysical poetry. Saul Bellow has complained that the modern novelist doesn't tell us what a human being *is* today. Bellow is a notable exception to his own complaint; but whether we agree or not, we can see that many contemporary film makers have tried to answer that question, with a more consistent application than ever before in the history of the art.

These two elements—national color and the exploration of the individual—are obviously inseparable. Society and the man affect each other, even if it is in the man's withdrawal. These elements are further linked in a curious contradictory motion against our time. In an age when internationalism is promulgated as a solution to political difficulties, national colors have become more evident in films. In an age when social philosophers have begun to question the durability of individualism—which is, after all, a fairly recent concept in history and almost exclusive to the West—the film is tending to cherish the individual. Does this indicate a time lag between the film and the advances of political and social philosophy? On the contrary, I believe it indicates a perverse penetration to truth. The truth of art sometimes runs counter to what seems politically and intellectually desirable; that is always a risk of art. I think the film is showing us that nationalism, in the purely cultural sense, is becoming more necessary to us as jet planes and Telstar threaten to make us one world. I think that just at the time when technological and power structures challenge individualism, our own minds and souls have become more interesting to us. Up to now, technology has outraced self-discovery. Only now—in this postreligious, self-dependent age—are we beginning to appreciate how rich and dangerous each one of us is.

These elements have led, directly and by implication, to the phenomenon we are examining; the historical moment for the rise of the Film Generation, a surge of somewhat nostalgic revolution; a reluctance to lose what seems to be disappearing, accompanied by an impulse to disaffection, an insistence on an amorphous cosmos. ("Stay loose." "Swing.") Doubtless that nostalgia is sentimental, an unwillingness to be banned from an Eden of individualism that in fact never existed. But much of the revolution is clearheaded; not so much an attempt to halt change as to influence it; a natural and valuable impulse to scratch on the chromium fronts of the advancing tanks of factory-society "Kilroy was here."

The divided attitude toward social change leads to another, crucial polarity. This generation has an ambivalent view of cultural tradition. On the one hand there is a great desire for such tradition, admitted or not. Everyone wants to know that he came from somewhere; it's less lonely. But this desire is often accompanied by a mirror attitude that looks on the past as failure and betrayal. It is of course a familiar indictment, the young accusing the old of having made a mess, but now the accusation is more stringent and more general because of the acceleration of change and the diminutions of choice.

This ambivalence toward tradition—this polarity that both wants and rejects it—has created a hunger for art as assurance of origins together with a preference for art forms that are relatively free of the past. Outstanding among these is film. Even though it has been on hand for sixty-five years or so, the film seems much more of the present and future than other forms. It has its roots—of content and method—in older arts: drama, literature, dance, painting; yet it is very much less entailed by the past than these arts. It satisfies this generation's ambivalent need in tradition.

So far, this inquiry has been almost all celebration; now a concern must be raised. So far, we have discussed certain phenomena as cultural dynamics and social facts: now a word must be said in value judgment of the revolutionary standards involved. Not all the films that the Film Generation venerates seem worth its energy and devotion. It is not my purpose to lay down an artistic credo: I could always think of too many exceptions. Taste is a matter of instances, not precepts. One forms an idea of another's taste—or of one's own—from the perspective of many instances of judgment and preference, and even then, general deductions must be drawn delicately. But, drawing them as delicately as I am able, I am left with a concern to posit against the foregoing celebration.

There are enthusiasms of this Film Generation that I do not share, there are many enthusiasms of mine that they seem not to share. For the most part this is nobody's fault and probably nobody's virtue. But there is one enthusiasm in particular that has taken many members of this generation—not all, but a large proportion—that seems potentially deleterious and therefore to need discussion.

On college campuses around the country, in some film societies and small theaters (there are at least three in New York at this writing), much is being made of certain experimental films. The passion for experiment, as such, is eternal and necessary, but out of disgust with much commercial and fake-serious fare, there is a strong tendency to value experiment for its own sake, to regard it as a value instead of a means to value. And since, at this period in social and political affairs, a passion for these films has been taken to have other significances as well, the phenomenon is especially important.

The films to which I refer are often called underground films. In America a large proportion of them come from a group centered in New York but not confined there, variously called New American Films or the Film-maker's Cooperative. It is an association of dedicated film makers and dedicated apostles. (The apostles carry the word widely. Two minutes after I met Federico Fellini in Rome, he asked me whether I had seen Jack Smith's *Flaming Creatures*.) The group also has a circle of apostolic critics.

Predictably, this group considers itself the element of poetry in an otherwise prosaic film situation in this country and the world. Also predictably, its works are difficult to describe because it is not a school like neorealism or surrealism It includes these and many more styles. It welcomes anyone who uses film as a form of personal expression. The most lucid general statement about this group that I know was written by Ken Kelman (The Nation, May 11, 1964). He divides their works into three main categories. First, "outright social criticism and protest" (Dan Drasin's *Sunday*, Stan Vanderbeek's *Skullduggery*). Second, "films which suggest, mainly through anarchic fantasy, the possibilities of the human spirit in its socially uncorrupted state" (Jack Smith's *Flaming Creatures* and *Normal Love*). The third group "creates, out of a need to fill our rationalistic void, those actual inner worlds which fall within the realm of myth" (Kenneth Anger's *Scorpio Rising,* Stan Brakhage's *Anticipation of the Night* and *Window Water Baby Moving*).

Kelman's article, like others on the subject, is a ringing statement written with inner consistency and a fire that outstrips mere sincerity. The difficulty is that, when one sees these films (I have seen all those cited and numerous others), one finds small consonance between the descriptions and the works. Not to belabor individual films, one can say that most of them represent the attitudes and intents that Kelman describes but that their acceptance as accomplishment reflects a deliberate disconnection from cultural and social history. For me, most of the "new" techniques are dated, most of the social criticism is facile or vacuous, the mythic content undernourishing, the general quality of inspiration tenuous, strained, trite. Much of the work seems made for a young audience that insists on having its *own* films, at any critical or cultural price.

One of the grave liabilities in the situation is that writing like Kelman's and the attitudes it promotes tend to encourage the symbiotic state that exists today in the graphic arts. There is not much direct relation between film and audience, nothing so simple as the audience coming to the theater and being affected, or not, by what it sees. The audience exists jointly with these films in a highly verbalized critical environment; its preformed attitudes are eager dramatizations of credos and exegeses. Much of modern painting—op, pop, collage, latter-day abstraction—seems to have its life almost as much in what is written about it as on canvas. Indeed many of the paintings seem to have been made to evoke esthetic disquisition, to exist verbally and in viewers' attitudes. The underground film has entered this territory—of art as "position"—a position sustained as much by the polemic-conscious audience as by the material on the screen. It has long been an indictment of Broadway and Hollywood hits that the audience is preconditioned, whipped into line by newspaper raves. Here is very much the same situation at a higher intellectual altitude.

Another grave liability is the pressure brought to bear by the underground movement for disconnection from cultural history. Generally, as has been noted, the Film Generation has at least an ambivalent attitude toward tradition: this underground movement pushes—by implication and otherwise—for complete rejection of the standards that have been continuingly evolved through some centuries of Western art. They are not to be evolved further, they are to be discarded. It is easy to chuckle patronizingly at this belief as one more instance of the perennial artistic rebellion of the young, but current social upheavals give it a momentum that takes it out of the sphere of mere youthful high spirits—or low spirits. And the morning or the year or the decade after the excitements of rebellion have passed, it may be discovered that a valuable continuum in culture has been seriously injured—to the detriment of the very aims for which the action was taken.

I do not argue against change, including radical change. I do argue against nihilism as a necessary first step for progress. Besides, this film nihilism contains a bitter contradiction. It is often a manifestation in art of discontents elsewhere, of anger at older generations' betrayal of certain ideals. But the best art of the past—in all fields—is expression of those ideals, often despite society's apathy toward them. In discarding that inheritance of art, the rebels discard much of the best work that the human race has done for the very ideals that galvanize this new rebellion.

There is a parallel between this devotion to the underground film in many of the Film Generation and an element in the "new left," the new political radicalism. Some of radical youth are engaged in genuinely creative action: antimilitarism, antidiscrimination, support of various economic programs. But many of them equate radicalism with personal gesture and style—revolt consummated by bizarre hair and dress, unconventional sexual behavior, flirtations with drugs. One who is aware of the valid basis for disaffection can still regret the introversions and futilities of these gestures. Likewise, one hopeful for the invigoration of the American film can doubt the pertinence of comparable gestures in this field: the exaltation of meaninglessness in film as a statement of meaninglessness in the world: the praise of juvenile irreverence—perennial in art—as a new formulation of myth; the approval of a social criticism that is devoid of intellectual foundation and political belief.

I dwell on the partiality to these experimental films not to counterbalance the happy fact of the Film Generation's existence but precisely because of its existence. Art has never been well created for long independently of an audience; in fact, history shows that audience response feeds great eras of art (painting in Renaissance Italy, the drama in Elizabethan England and neoclassic France, the sudden, ravenous world-wide appetite for silent-film comedy).

Speaking in the large, I believe that the Film Generation has the power to evoke the films that it wants, even though that generation is a minority and despite the harsh conditions of production and exhibition around the world. *All* films will not alter, nor should they, but if the dynamics of cultural history still obtains, an insistent group of art takers can—sooner or later, one way or another—have an effect on art makers. The effect is circular. The audience obviously cannot do it alone; there have to be talented artists. But talent is a relative constant in the human race; it is sparked by response and, even at its best, can be dampened by neglect. (Think of Herman Melville's twenty years in the Customs House.)

Thus, by a logical progression, we can see that the Film Generation has extraordinary powers. If it is true (as I have claimed) that film is the most pertinent art at present; if it is true that the young generation is closer to the film than to other arts; if it is also true that audience appetite can evoke art; then, it follows that the Film Generation has the opportunity to help bring forth the best and most relevant art of our age. And it is the possible impediment to this opportunity that makes a devotion to culturally baseless, essentially sterile films seem wasteful.

I am aware that the above puts an almost ludicrously large burden on this Film Generation. In effect, it is almost to ask them to solve the problems of cultural transition, to define what culture will become. The problem is not to be solved in any one locus, even when the locus—film and its audience—has come into being quite naturally. It is never to be solved; it is only to be confronted continually, particularly in an age that is *not* an age, that is a rapid series of continually shifting points. But the size of the conclusion does not diminish the opportunity.

There is not much question among the thoughtful that we live in a time of the most profound cultural change, when the very purposes of art, as well as its content, are being trans-

437

formed. The New American Cinema is one manifestation of that upheaval. In my view, most of its films that I have seen are of minuscule importance, but the implication in most of them is important: the implication that what's past is quite dead. The art of the future may be divorced from present concepts of humanism; it may find its pertinences in modes that, to most eyes, now look cold or abstract or even antihuman. But they will have been made by men who would not be what they are, whatever that may be, without the precedents of culture, and if that new art, whatever it may be, is to be held to its highest standards, the best of the past needs to be brought forward with us. The real *use* of our inheritance in the contemporary situation would throw a good deal of illumination on much of the new that is now adulated. The Kelmans tell us that an Antonioni is only seemingly free, that he is trapped by attempting to renovate the past. But, to take Antonioni as an example, it is precisely the effort to alter in an altered cosmos without returning Western culture to Year One that may keep a cultural future possible; may sustain us as we travel from a terrain that once was fruitful to one that has not yet been sighted. We don't want to starve en route.

As an important part of this process—this rescue operation, if you like—the Film Generation can demand a new film from the serious film maker that is more than a gesture of denial. Such a generation, joined with the past and therefore truly equipped to outgrow it, may eventually get in its films what the Kelmans have prematurely claimed: a new social cohesion, a new fertile and reassuring mythos. If these come, they will manifest their presence, not so much by the blown prose of rhapsodists as by an irony: middle-of-the-road art will imitate the new film. That film will certainly not be ignored, as the majority now ignore underground efforts. When the imitation begins, then authentically progressive artists and audiences will know that they have thus far succeeded, and will know it is again time to move forward.

So the Film Generation, flaws and all, represents both a circumstance and an opportunity. On the whole it is, I believe, the most cheering circumstance in contemporary American art. That generation can be a vital force, or it can twiddle its strength and chances away in irrelevant artistic nihilism, in engorged social petulance. One does not ask them to "save"

438

film forever. In the long run, the history of the film will be the same as that of all arts: a few peaks, some plateaus, many chasms; but the present chance—a rare one—could save much time in the development of this young medium. The foreseeable future is all that, reasonably, we can have hopes or anxieties about in art. The Film Generation can help to make the foreseeable future of film interesting and important. Let us see.

A Minor Masterpiece—
Dušan Makavejev's
WR: *Mysteries of the Organism*
by Lawrence Becker

*This selection is reprinted from
the September 1972 issue of Film Journal.*

Political films (as opposed to films with political significance)
tend to be heavy-handed. Sex films (as opposed to films with
sex in them) tend to be contrived. Most films of both genres
are alternately embarrassing for their clumsiness and disappointing for their predictability. Thus it has become customary
to regard both types with *a priori* suspicion, and to comment,
with respect to each disappointing example, how sad it is that
the filmmaker felt he had to club people with a blunt instrument.

WR: Mysteries of the Organism is both a political film and
a sex film—and it explodes any contention that the blunt
approach to either topic is necessarily disappointing. Dušan
Makavejev's film is a minor masterpiece. Minor because
it doesn't say anything we don't already know, nor even use
any illuminatingly new images. But a masterpiece nonetheless
because it lays out some important commonplaces in a fascinating way.

Its contentions are that trying to force people into line—
politically, sexually, or intellectually—is stupid and cruel, that
such repression simply leaves the world littered with heart-
breaking casualties, that it is joyously exciting and funny to
be randy, and that although freedom (sexual or otherwise)
often has ludicrous or even pathetic results, the real perversions come from making our whole beings into fists for hammering away at each other—whether in pursuit of personal
power or social justice. What we need to do is unclench—to
relax enough to breathe, to let the air (rather than other
people) absorb our miseries and hatred. Hands are better than
fists.

Those are the film's political commonplaces, and the images too are not extraordinary, but they are unfailingly right,

ingenious, and moving: the socialist anthem over the shot of a couple making love in a meadow has just the right feel; the yippie in tattered battle dress patrolling Lincoln Center is very funny; and some (but not all) of the scenes of Reichian therapy are inexplicably moving.

The eroticism in *WR* is heavy—too heavy to be regarded as a subsidiary element or a device—but it is not oppressive. From the straight, very explicit lovemaking scene near the beginning (shown with obvious approval, multi-image, softly tinted and textured, rather than "slick") through the burlesques of both hetero and homosexuality, the heavily sensual scenes of (individual) Reichian therapy, to the apotheosis of the penis (the plaster casting of Jim Buckley's equipment), Makavejev's choices avoid all of the familiar pitfalls. He does not tease, cutting conveniently to faces or trees or sky when things get interesting, or dashing the viewer with cold water (e.g., in *La Dolce Vita* when the owner of the villa storms in switching on lights at the crucial moment of the striptease sequence). Nor is he merely a voyeur: there are some witty complications which—far from distracting—give a sense of humanity to the sexual scenes. The music often does this: the anthem mentioned above, and the very funny break into Smetana's *Moldau* which rises, with parts of Mr. Buckley, from Nancy Godrey's casting couch.

The business about Reich (to whom the film is dedicated) is superbly handled. Reich was a martyr to intellectual and moral repression, and his disciples clearly believed he cared deeply about "whole" people—cared about them as inviolable, almost holy, integrities, and cared about making them whole again when they were broken from beatings taken in the name of civilization. But that does not mean that Reich's theories and therapies were sound, or that Reich himself didn't have a bit of the charlatan in him. In fact, the tension created by those two possibilities is precisely the point: Reich claimed the right to be outlandish without being declared an outlaw by his social order. How such claims are handled is a crucial test of justice for any society. Makavejev says we bungled it in Reich's case, just as communism has bungled related tests of justice: specifically, in its attempt to conflate personal and collective satisfactions.

Reich apparently thought that, instead of forcing people to sublimate their sexual energy, only to have it crop up in the grossest and most destructive perversions of power, we should get people to sublimate their destructive energies in sex. (The film comments on this with shots of Stalin, Hitler, Mao, and, a bit less directly, images of military fetishism and the insane scramble for "the good life.") But the workability of that is not really the point. The point is that whenever we try to smooth out all the "imperfections" (however defined), whenever we attempt a ruthlessly efficient moral or social order with a constant rate of progress and unanimity of values, aspirations, and behavior, we create an intolerable list of human casualties. And so as the noble ideologies are recited, it is good to see, on the screen, what we are forced to do to and for those casualties —the force-feeding, electroshock therapy, and the rest.

There are flaws in the film: the lighting in some shots appears to have been in the process of being adjusted when the camera was started, for example. But they are minor, and rarely interfere. The film as a whole is what is important. And it is too good to be bothered by a few technicalities. To the rhetorical questions of its opening sequence (Who will police the police . . .) the answer must be Makavejev and people like him. The film itself, along with the moving ballad sung at the end of the film, is the sort of song to sing when your hands feel bloody, and when the victims of virtue smile wryly and forgive. We are, all of us, without excuse. But that does not justify either nihilism or ruthlessness. It justifies, rather, that we treat ourselves and others with some gentleness for a change. And have a little joy, too.

The Zen Artistry of Yasujiro Ozu

by Marvin Zeman

*Currently a professor in the Department of
Mathematics at the University of Illinois,
Marvin Zeman has published articles on film
in several magazines. This selection, revised
by the author, originally appeared in Film Journal,
Fall/Winter 1972.*

> I know not what
> Is here enshrined
> Only the tears
> Well up from my heart
> Overflowing with reverence
> > Priest Saigyo

One of the primary reasons why most of Yasujiro Ozu's films were not available for viewing in the United States until the seventies was the attitude of the Japanese themselves toward Ozu. They considered him the most Japanese of all film directors and felt that his films were too esoteric for export to the West. In addition Ozu had a reputation for utilizing the most austere of all shooting styles, having renounced the pan, the zoom, the fade, almost everything but the simple cut. I must admit that I went to my first Ozu film with many apprehensions. I was therefore surprised to discover that Ozu's films were very enjoyable and not at all difficult to respond to. What was difficult though was understanding how Ozu managed to effect this with the severely limited techniques at his disposal.

My discussion of Ozu's oeuvre will be based on Japanese art because art is often the personal molding of tradition; an artist filters the human condition through his personal experience. In order to understand an artist's expression of the universally human, it is important to consider the cultural tradition which engendered that expression. One can, of course, discuss Ozu's films in the context of world cinema, but I believe this approach is unsatisfactory because any such discussion will be necessarily one-sided since the film is, in general, a Western art, and, at most, one will be able to dig up those characteristics of Ozu which are most accessible to the West, leaving out the Eastern side of Ozu—the essence of Ozu. Ozu

443

is a Japanese artist, using film as a tool in the way a philosopher uses pen and paper.

The basic idea behind Japanese art is Zen. Zen is the immediate and therefore inexpressible individual experience whose aim is inner enlightenment. D. T. Suzuki has stated that "Zen is not subject to logical analysis or to intellectual treatment. It must be directly and personally experienced by each of us in his inner spirit." Art is the form-language of the human soul. The soul tries to disclose through art beauty—the revealing principle of the cosmos. This beauty is found in the *mu* (roughly translated as nothingness). If one can penetrate the *mu*, then one can achieve inner enlightenment. However, there are few cultures which have acquired the power to set the inexpressible and deepest ground—the *mu*—at the central point of their artistic formation. Japanese culture has been able to do this due to a continuous tradition of transcendence.

Japanese art has certain qualities which help it reveal the *mu*. These qualities can be found in all of Japanese art whether it is Haiku poetry, flower arrangement, Sumiye ink drawing, or the tea ceremony. I will list some of these essential qualities and utilize them in my discussion of Ozu's art. According to Shinichi Hisamatsu, Zen has seven characteristics as seen in Japanese art (i.e., all of these characteristics must be present for the work of art to be called a Zen work). The characteristics are as follows. First, asymmetry—as R. H. Blyth chooses to call it: "unsaintly saints." Second, simplicity—the omission of all insignificant or irrelevant details. If the *mu* is to be penetrated, one must see through the many-colored world; everything inessential must be eliminated. Third, agedness—the calm outlook on life usually attained with age. This quality can be found in a young man's art as well. Claude Chabrol's *La Femme Infidèle,* for example, has it. Fourth, naturalness—innocence, no compulsion; things happen without tension. Fifth, latency—an infinite heaven in a puddle. Sixth, unconventionality—there is no "great subject." Toshimitsu Hasumi wrote that "art sees the features of the Absolute in ordinary life and gives them expression, direct, unmediated and formative." Seventh, quietness. As Hasumi states, "There is harmony of forms, colors, and materials, harmony of expres-

444

sion, harmony of order, harmony of place and time; harmony of heaven, earth, and man; harmony of harmonies."

One finds Zen embodied best in Ozu's later works, although his early films are remarkable in their own right. This is quite understandable because all Japanese art demands a complete mastery of technique, which can be attained only after years of practice. This mastery of technique is twofold. What matters first, in all fields of art, is to learn the "primary form" and to attain complete command of it. In the older arts the "primary form" is the original, generalized prototype which has been laid down and defined by several earlier masters. Ozu, however, working in so young an art, had to invent his own prototype.

Along with outward technique, Ozu had to develop an inward technique. Hasumi wrote that "outward technique by itself is not art. It is only through long training of the soul that the pupil is brought to the true inward technique. In art it is not merely a question of artistic dexterity, but of the artistic process within the artist. It is the 'art-less art,' and its meaning is 'art of the soul.' For us Japanese the arrangement of colors, composition and line forms means a step on the way to the absolute aesthetic world of the soul. That is 'Zen in art.' " Inward technique is what most distinguishes Ozu's early films from the later films; in the early films, Ozu was developing it, while in the later films, he was utilizing it.

In the early films Ozu exhibited his bitterness about the decrees of fate. In *A Story of Floating Weeds* (*Ukigusa Monogatari,* 1934) Otsune reacts very bitterly when Kihachi, the leader of the theatrical troupe and father of her son, decides to leave her again. This bitterness is not displayed in the remake of the film *Floating Weeds* (*Ukigusa,* 1959). In *I Was Born But* (*Umareta wa Mita Keredo,* 1932) the two young brothers, Ryoichi and Keiji, find out that although they are obviously better than the rest of the children they play with, they will have to kowtow to others when they grow up just as their father does to his boss. Throughout the film the two lord it over the rest of the children, particularly over Taro, the boss's son. Their illusions are shattered when they see a home-movie in which their father acts the clown in front of his boss. As the father later tells the mother: "It's a problem they'll have to live with the rest of their lives."

Ozu's youthfulness which led to this restlessness of both outward and inward techniques had its advantages. The comedy scenes in the early films are livelier than in the later ones. Many of these scenes deal with children, and Ozu is more sympathetic and closer to children in the early films than he is in the later films. In *What Did The Lady Forget?* (*Shukujo wa Nani o Wasuretaka*, 1937) Okada, assistant to a Tokyo professor, is given a job tutoring a boy. It turns out that the assistant knows less than the boy, and a friend of the boy takes on the job of instructing both the boy and the tutor. When an outsider walks into the room, however, the assistant takes over. The quick switch from pupil to instructor is hilarious. These scenes were done from the youngsters' point of view, something which Ozu did not repeat in his later films, not even in *Good Morning* (*Ohayo*, 1959), a loose remake of *I Was Born But*. This is not to say that Ozu's later films are devoid of humor; humor is one of the distinct elements of Zen. But the humor in the later films is more serene and deals predominantly with adults. It is also more illuminating, revealing the depth of the relationships of Ozu's characters.

The experimenting finally ended with the making of *There Was a Father* (*Chichi Ariki*) in 1942. All the elements which went into the later films are evident in *There Was a Father*. It is the first film of Ozu's that I've seen in which the remarkable and unique structure of the Ozu film manifests itself. For instance, the use of parallels—a very important component of the structure of Ozu's films—is evoked throughout the film: the train scenes near the beginning and the end, the two fishing scenes separated by fifteen years, the shot from behind of the son crying when leaving his father to go to school repeated upon the death of the father. Most important, however, are the parallels in the behavior of father and son. They pay reverence to the shrine of the dead wife and mother with the same emotion and sincerity which they express toward each other. The formal but gentle way in which the son, and then the father, kneel down and pray before the shrine causes the entire scene to approach a state of grace. This feeling of grace is felt in both of the trout-fishing scenes. There is a remarkable affinity between father and son which is achieved even while fishing. The actions of the two are identical; the way the two swing their poles in unison is beautifully choreographed and tells us more about their relationship than hours of dialogue.

In *There Was a Father* and the films which followed, Ozu was able to solidify his outward and inward techniques and to have them complement each other. As Hasumi wrote, "Japanese art is neither more nor less than an art of the soul: in it inward and outward art flow together." Although Ozu's outward technique is extremely formal—all the supports of his art are highly visible—his inward technique is immeasurable. Ozu is a magician: he shows you everything, and you still wonder how he does it.

What makes one component of Ozu's outer structure—the use of parallels—so important is that it points out two very important ideas of Japanese art—limitlessness and the quality of not being finished. The universe goes on, unlimited by the time length of the film. *Tokyo Story* (*Tokyo Monogatari*, 1953) begins with the elderly couple, Shukichi and Tomi Hirayama, preparing to visit their married children in Tokyo. A neighbor passes by and comments on their journey. At the end, the husband is alone—his wife is dead—and the neighbor again comes by. Hirayama will continue to live, and the neighbor will continue to pass by, even after the film is over, one feels.

Another way in which Ozu indicates the limitlessness of the universe is his use of the establishing shot before almost every scene. Ozu has dispensed with the fade-in and fade-out which are usually used to indicate a change of scene, and in their place he has substituted the establishing shot. When finished with one scene, Ozu cuts to a shot which, among other functions, tells us where we are and what time of the day it is. For example, after a bar scene taking place at night, he might cut to a shot of the exterior of an office building bathed in the glorious light of the sun. (And with Ozu, the light is indeed glorious.) Whenever Ozu returns us to a certain locale, he invariably uses almost the same establishing shot. Thus, in an Ozu film, we immediately know where we are. In *An Autumn Afternoon* (*Samma no Aji* which translates to *The Taste of Mackerel*, 1962) Ozu introduces scenes taking place in Hirayama's house with a shot of the corridor leading from the front door. In *The End of Summer* (*Kohayagawa-ke no Aki* which translates to *The Autumn of the Kohayagawa Fam-*

447

ily, 1961) he cuts to scenes taking place at the brewery with shots of barrels lying in the sun. The establishing shot impresses upon us the fact that a man's life is insignificant in the face of the total universe. The corridor, the barrels, and the office building will continue to stand regardless of the tribulations of any one man.

This concept of the insignificance of a man's life also has a complementary notion. Once we realize that life does not come in select and highly special moments which can change the universe, we can concentrate upon those "little" joys which are the truly essential components of life and which make life worth living. This is why Ozu's films have no plots. Ozu knows that plots are essentially artificial because they put limitations on universal life. As Ozu himself said: "Pictures with obvious plots bore me now. Naturally, a film must have some kind of structure, otherwise it is not a film, but I feel that a film isn't good if it has too much drama." He is, instead, content to point out the little things which occur in everyday life. The mother listening blissfully to the radio in *Equinox Flower* (*Higanbana,* 1958), the grandfather sneaking out of the house while ostensibly playing hide-and-seek in *The End of Summer*, the three actors seated around a table, wondering how to get up the money to buy more sake in *Floating Weeds*, these are what Ozu films are made of. Thus, although what happens in an Ozu film is rather ordinary, his themes are highly unconventional, especially when compared to the themes of the vast majority of Western cinema which tend to deal with the extraordinary.

One of the things that one notices in reading Haiku poetry is that there is almost always a word indicating the season. Until recently Haiku was, in fact, simply the poetry of the season. The season word in a Haiku poem is usually an indication of a whole world of emotions, of colors, sounds, scents. This helps us to understand why many of Ozu's later films have a seasonal title: *Late Spring* (*Banshun,* 1949), *Early Summer* (*Bakushu,* 1951), *Early Spring* (*Soshun,* 1956), *Late Autumn* (*Akibiyori,* 1961), *The End of Summer* (*Kohayagawa-ke no Aki,* 1961). These titles serve a function similar to that of the establishing shot. As the establishing shot prepares us for a new scene, informs us where we are and at what time, so the seasonal title prepares us emotionally. The seasons correspond to emotions usually connected with different ages. Spring is a time of optimism, of youth, a time we can look forward to the rest of the year. Summer is middle age, a time of laziness, spring behind us, but autumn and winter still ahead. Autumn is a time of melancholy. We will soon come face to face with winter, which is death.

The seasons can be associated with the four basic moods of *furyu*—moods of the general atmosphere of Zen "taste" in its perceptions of the aimless moments of life. These moments are the basis of all Zen art. The four moods are *sabi, wabi, mono-no-aware,* and *yugen.*

When the mood of the moment is solitary and quiet it is called *sabi. Sabi* is usually associated with summer. The mood is called *wabi* when a feeling of depression or sadness comes over a person and reveals the incredible "suchness" of something quite ordinary. As Buson wrote:

> Before the white chrysanthemum
> The scissors hesitate
> A moment

Autumn is very much around the corner. *Wabi* was generally the mood in which Haiku poets created. As Hasumi wrote: "Out of *wabi* developed harmony, respect, purity, poverty— harmony of color, form, light, touch, movement; respect for the guest, for oneself, for nature; purity of soul, purity of space, purity of the world; poverty of man, poverty of nature." *Mono-no-aware* evokes a more intense and lasting sadness than *wabi*. It is melancholic and nostalgic, very much connected with autumn and all that autumn implies.

> The light in the next room also
> Goes out;
> The night is chill
>
> Shiki

When a man suddenly perceives of a mysterious unknown never to be discovered, winter is already here, and the mood is called *yugen.*

These moods did not appear to any extent in the early Ozu films for a number of reasons. These moods are intimately

449

connected with agedness. Youth and spring do not allow one much time for reflection on what has passed; Ozu was too busy fighting fate in the early films. He was also utilizing the early films to construct the machinery capable of handling these moods.

The mood of *sabi* is especially felt in those moments when quiet and calmness reign. In *Tokyo Story* the old couple, sent to a resort by their children to get them out of the way, are sitting on a ledge in front of a lake in early morning. We see them from the back at first, and the shot is held. The way the two sit, as one, evokes a serenity, harmony and contentment with the world. Basho wrote:

> Summer in the world
> Floating on the waves
> Of the lake

Wabi can be felt in the scenes in *The End of Summer* in which the two unmarried sisters are alone together. In one scene the two sisters are kneeling in front of a lake and talking. They have both been "interviewed" for marriage, but are not sure what they should do. Akiko, the middle-aged widow of a professor, must decide whether to marry the steel mill owner introduced to her by her brother-in-law. Noriko, the younger sister, must choose between an acceptable young man who would help the family business and a poor skiing instructor with whom she is in love. We then see a long shot of the two getting up in unison, then turning, also as one. Every move is controlled by Ozu to evoke just the right mood.

Mono-no-aware is felt mostly in the last films, which invariably have the word autumn in their titles. It is also felt in the closing moments of *Equinox Flower*, which basically deals with a man who is dead set against his daughter marrying a young man who, although quite acceptable, is not of his choosing. The mood throughout the film is light, and it is filled with comedy. Certainly nothing in the film prepares us for the last shot. The girl finally does marry the young man, and the father is on a train, travelling to Hiroshima to make up with her. He looks out the window, and the look on his face conveys extraordinarily the mood of *mono-no-aware*. He realizes at this particular moment that old age has finally arrived—autumn is here.

The Autumn wind
Goes through into the very bones
Of the scarecrow

Choi

The mood of *yugen* is felt most strongly in the very last shot of *An Autumn Afternoon*, Ozu's last film. The film deals with Hirayama, a widower who is trying to marry off his twenty-four-year-old daughter. At first, the girl doesn't want to leave her father, and Hirayama, accustomed to having her take care of him and the home, is satisfied with things as they are. But when he meets the Gourd, a former teacher of his, and the Gourd's unmarried daughter, Hirayama's future is revealed to him, and he decides to get his own daughter married, even if it means remaining alone. At the end the girl is married, and Hirayama comes home. The last scene of the film shows him sitting alone in the kitchen. He then starts crying. Autumn afternoon has turned into an evening in early winter: Hirayama stands on the threshold of death.

Shake, O tomb!
My weeping voice
Is the wind of Autumn

Basho

The first thing one notices about Ozu's outward technique which evokes these moods is its utter simplicity. His camera technique is as spare as possible. There is very little camera movement in the later films. Ozu allows no zooms or pans. His camera tends to be stationary for so much of the time that when he does use an occasional dolly shot, the effect is jarring and makes one pay much closer attention to how the camera is used. In *Early Summer*, for instance, Ozu ends the film with a boom shot; in *Early Spring* he cuts twice to a tracking shot of an empty corridor which he uses to establish several scenes. His only camera position is that of a person seated on a *tatami*—a mat on which people sit when talking, listening and thinking. (It was also the favorite position of the Haiku masters.) Ozu would sit on the *tatami* cross-legged with his eyes three feet above the floor. In fact, he used the low camera angle as an excuse for his immobile camera. As Ozu said: "The reason is that we don't have a good camera installation. My camera angle is very low, and we don't have a camera which can move at such a low angle." But when pressed, Ozu admitted that even if he had a camera which could move at that angle, he would not use it for that purpose because "it is an artificial device, not an authentic one."

Similarly he didn't use the dissolve. "The only successful use of the dissolve is in Chaplin's *A Woman of Paris*. You won't see such a perfect use of technique more than once in twenty years. All the others are cheating."

Ozu allowed himself three shots: the long shot, the middle shot, and the semi-close-up. The long shot is used sparingly, only at special moments when Ozu wants to isolate and thus point out something which he feels requires emphasis. In *Tokyo Story*, for instance, he shows us the old woman talking with her grandson on a hill. She is asking the boy what he wants to be when he grows up. She then tells him that she might not be alive to see it happen. The boy is picking flowers, not paying attention to anything the woman is saying. The two are then shown in long shot, thus emphasizing the solitude of the old woman, even with the boy at her side. The middle shot is the standard shot used for all purposes. The close-up is used for intimate moments. But Ozu never allows his camera to come too close. One reason for this is that the low camera angle would never allow it. A more fundamental reason is that Ozu would not allow the camera to evoke emotion. All emotion in an Ozu film comes from the characters, and any feeling of emotion which might come by using a "big" close-up is as much cheating as any other artificial camera technique.

Another element of his outward technique which Ozu puts to outstanding use is editing. Ozu is always interested in reaction and not action because reaction is what best reveals character—one of the primary objects of the Ozu film. In *An Autumn Afternoon*, for instance, the girl is finally ready to marry, but the boy, with whom she is half in love, is unavailable, having married a different girl because he was told that Hirayama's daughter was not ready to marry. We get her reaction to this news very obliquely. She leaves the table and goes to her room. Instead of seeing her crying or hearing her sobbing voice coming from her room, we find out about her unhappiness when her brother walks in and asks, "Why is Sister crying?" Since the film is concerned primarily with Hirayama, his reaction is most important, and Ozu shows it to us first.

As I have mentioned earlier, Ozu has eliminated the fade-in and fade-out as editing techniques. However, he often uses music to connect one scene with the next: a theme is heard toward the end of a scene and is continued as Ozu cuts to the next scene. The theme alerts us to the coming of an establishing shot, and in addition helps to release us from the ending scene. Often we will hear this theme at the end of an interior scene and will be rewarded with a glorious shot of flags blowing in the wind, or a seashore or a mountain. We are released not only from the room but also from the drama we have just witnessed and we feel an exhilaration in being out-of-doors, free.

Another noticeable aspect of Ozu's outward technique is his composition. Everything that goes into the shot is manipulated so that the effect of the whole is right. This especially means the actors. As Chishu Ryu, who had appeared in all but two of the fifty-three films Ozu had made, wrote: "Ozu gives a lot of thought to the form and composition of a scene. The performance of his actors, therefore, must be harmonized with the composition. I remember one scene in *Record of a Tenement Gentleman* (*Nagaya Shinshi Roku*, 1948) in which the fortune teller or palm reader, which was my role, has to draw the lines of a palm with a calligraphy brush. When the brush touched the paper, I bent my head forward. But Ozu told me not to move my head, which was a very difficult thing to do. But I saw what Ozu was aiming at: if I had moved my head, it would have ruined the unity of the composition. This is why Ozu gives his actors such precise instructions."

The basic intent of Ozu's composition is harmony. The way the elements of a scene are set up can emphasize the harmony and, conversely, the lack of harmony between the characters. In *A Story of Floating Weeds* the two young lovers are standing together contemplating the girl's impending departure. As they stand, they are enclosed in the frame by telephone wires, which reinforce the unity felt between the two. In the remake, *Floating Weeds,* the leader of the troupe and his son are fishing. As Ozu uses a fishing scene in *There Was a Father* to emphasize the harmony between father and son, here he uses it to establish just the opposite. In *There Was a Father* the two stand almost motionless, only moving when swinging their poles in unison. In *Floating Weeds* the two fidget and talk as they fish. Ozu presents the scene with a large number of cuts, hardly ever including the two in a single frame. Included in the scene are telephone wires, as in *A Story of Floating Weeds*. However, one notices in the few shots of the father and son together that the wires on the father's side do not mesh with those on the side of the son. This discordance between the wires contributes to the total lack of harmony between them.

The most important element of Ozu's outward technique, however, is the actor. One of Ozu's main aims in a film is the revelation of character. Because acting means so much in his films, Ozu controls it as much as he does any other facet of his outward technique. As Ryu writes: "As to Mr. Ozu's way of direction, he had made up the complete picture in his head before he went on the set, so that all we actors had to do was to follow his direction, from the way we lifted and dropped our arms to the way we blinked our eyes. That is, we hadn't to worry about our acting at all. In a sense, we felt quite at home when we were playing in his picture. Even if I did not know what I was doing and how those shots would be connected in the end, when I looked at the first screening I was often surprised to find my performance far better than I had expected. He paid this minute attention not only to the actors' performances but also to stage settings and properties, and sometimes even painted appropriate pictures on the sliding doors used for the set. Therefore, what was called Mr. Ozu's production was, I think, the film produced by himself."

Of course, this complete control of the acting is not unique. Robert Bresson and Sergei Eisenstein of *Ivan the Terrible* come prominently to mind. But where Bresson demands non-acting from non-actors and Eisenstein demanded the most aching positions from his actors to achieve magnificent pictorial compositions, Ozu achieved a naturalness and serenity with his actors, consistent with the other elements of his technique. The subtlety of the acting demanded by Ozu rivals that of the acting in a Noh play. In a Noh play stillness does not represent immobility but a perfect balance of opposing forces. Passionate weeping and grief, for instance, are represented by raising very slowly one stiff hand to within some inches of the eyes, and as slowly lowering it.

Ozu used the same actors over and over. One can almost

call his group of actors a stock company. Among these, a number stand out. The most important is Chishu Ryu. As I have stated before, he appeared in all but two of Ozu's films. Their respective careers paralleled each other's, Ryu joining Shochiku Studios as an actor in 1925, and Ozu becoming a director at Shochiku in 1927. Ryu's first featured role came in *I Flunked But* (*Rakudai wa Shita Keredo,* 1930), an Ozu film, and his first big role was in *College Is a Nice Place* (*Daigaku Yoi Toko,* 1936), also an Ozu film. The two became close personal friends, and in the later films Ryu became the persona of the director. Out of himself Ozu created the character of the father, which he used in almost all of the later films, and Ryu portrayed the role in many of these films, most notably *There Was a Father, Late Spring, Tokyo Story,* and *An Autumn Afternoon.*

What makes Ozu's actors seem part of a stock company is the way an actor might star in one film and play almost an extra in the next. Ryu, for instance, who plays a big role as the father in *Good Morning,* plays only a bit role as the owner of the theater in *Floating Weeds.* On the other hand, he plays a very small role as a rag washer toward the end of *The End of Summer,* before playing perhaps his greatest role in *An Autumn Afternoon.* The use of the same actors in film after film extends even to the smallest roles. And Ozu uses this very advantageously. For instance, in *Equinox Flower* and *Late Autumn,* Ozu presents two very similar scenes of three friends seated in a restaurant. Not only are the three friends played by the same actors in both films, even the proprietress is played by the same woman.

Just as he used the same actors in different films, Ozu used the same people behind the screen in film after film. Ozu's collaborator on the screenplay was Koga Noda who helped Ozu with every script since 1949 (*Late Spring*). Similarly, Takanobu Saito composed the music for almost all of the later films. The photography for the Ozu films was handled almost exclusively by two men: Hideo Shigehara, the early films up to *The Only Son* (*Hitori Musuko,* 1936), and Yushun Atsuta, almost all the rest, starting with *The Brothers and Sisters of the Toda Family* (*Toda-ke no Kyodai,* 1941). Ozu felt that those who collaborate on a film should have an affinity between them, and that is why he used the same people over and over. This was especially true about the association between Ozu and Noda. As Ozu had stated: "When a director works with a scriptwriter they must have some characteristics and habits in common; otherwise they won't get along. My daily life—what time I get up, how much sake I drink and so on—is in almost complete agreement with that of both Noda and Saito. When I work with Noda, we collaborate even on short bits of dialogue. Although we never discuss the details of the sets or costumes, his mental image of these things is always in accord with mine: our ideas never crisscross or go awry. We even agree on whether a dialogue should end with *wa* or *yo*. Of course, sometimes we have a difference of opinion. And we don't compromise easily since we're both stubborn."

The close relationship between Noda and Ozu was necessary because there had to be an especially harmonious affinity between the screenplay and direction. Although exactly what is said is not important, the very presence of words in certain situations is because this is one way in which the exact relationship between people is manifested. As Suzuki wrote: "But, as we all know, we human beings cannot live without language, for we are so made that we can sustain our existence only in group life. Love is the essence of humanity, love needs something to bestow itself upon; human beings must live together in order to lead a life of mutual love. Love to be articulate requires a means of communication, which is language." (Language per se is the theme of *Good Morning*. The two brothers, Isami and Minoru, go on a silence strike because they feel that most language used by adults is unnecessary—phrases like "Good morning," "Nice weather we're having," etc.)

This is not to say that Noda's and Ozu's scripts are not literate; at times, the lines approach Haiku-like depth and brevity. One such instance occurs in *The End of Summer*. The family has gone to Arashiyama to visit the dead mother's grave for the first time in a long while. Consequently, the grave site is unkempt, and one of the relatives comments: "Moss grows unusually fast." The fact that the family has not been to the grave site often enough and the guilt felt by the family for not going are both revealed in one very short sentence.

Ozu's aim, throughout, is to reveal character and not to pass judgment on it. In *Equinox Flower*, although the father

456

is clearly wrong in opposing the marriage of his daughter, Ozu presents him very sympathetically. Ozu's characters are always human, possessing all the human frailties. In *The End of Summer*, after Manbei dies, his supposed illegitimate daughter goes on a date with one of her Americans (an action that Ozu seems to disapprove of), but before she leaves she displays one last gesture of respect. Both of the men played by Ganjiro Nakamura in *Floating Weeds* and *The End of Summer* have led fast lives, one having an illegitimate son and the other an illegitimate daughter (he thinks so, anyway), but Ozu presents them in such a way that we can't help but sympathize with them. They are the perfect embodiment of the phrase "unsaintly saints."

A complaint which has been leveled at Ozu is that his films are unrealistic: his sets are much too neat, his compositions much too pretty. For those who believe only in a kitchen-sink type of realism, this is quite true; one finds no slums and slumlords who push poor innocent people around in Ozu films. But Ozu achieves a different type of realism, one which I believe is much superior. First, Ozu conveys the impressions of the characters so well that many times we feel exactly what the character feels. As Donald Richie wrote: "We feel by objectively sharing the object of the emotion and not by subjectively observing the mere emotion upon the face of the character. This is a kind of impressionism in that Ozu brings us both the impressions and the things which created them, combining them in such a way that the impression upon us is the same as that upon the characters." Second, the impression that Ozu presents is so true: the people in Ozu films react the way people react in "real life." Ozu, who has spent his entire career examining and revealing people's reactions, is also the best one at it. The only director who comes close to Ozu is presenting people as they truly are is Chaplin. One aspect of Chaplin's realism is his so-called "vulgarity," something which some critics considered in bad taste. This aspect of realism also appears in Ozu films, but the East, unlike the West, does not frown upon it. As Issa wrote:

> Chrysanthemum flowers;
> And wafted along also,
> The smell of urine

457

Issa realized that the urine acts as a fertilizer, helping the chrysanthemum to grow.

Ozu imbues with grace even a "vulgar" scene centered on a man relieving himself. In *The End of Summer* Manbei recovers from a near fatal attack, and, as he waddles to the bathroom, all the grief-stricken relatives get up in wonder and follow him. He turns around, waves to the crowd and then goes in singing, while his nurse stands outside, resigned to waiting, with her hands and head down. Roger Greenspun wrote that the scene is "one of the oddest and most satisfying crises of joy I have ever seen in a movie." This natural approach to the natural functions is repeated in many of Ozu's other films. In *Floating Weeds* the actors are parading through the town, advertising their show. On the way the youngest member of the troupe detours to the side for a moment to urinate.

As I have tried to show, Ozu embodies Zen in his art to an extraordinary degree. But this leads to problems caused by the latency of Zen. Latency is the most subjective quality of any work of art. This is perhaps the most basic reason why the critics are so split on Ozu. Thomas Merton commented on this very appropriately: "Zen enriches no one. There is no body to be found. The birds may come and circle for a while in the place where it is thought to be. But they soon go elsewhere. When they are gone, the 'nothing,' the 'no-body' that was there, suddenly appears. That is Zen. It was there all the time but the scavengers missed it, because it was not their kind of prey." Some look at an Ozu film and see nothing, while others see *mu* which, although it can be translated as "nothing," is actually everything.

Jancsó

Plain

by Gideon Bachmann

**This selection appeared originally
in the Fall 1974 issue of Sight and Sound.**

Since material shapes the requirements for its representation, the methods of directors may change from film to film. Reports on a director at work are thus beset by the impossibility of generalizing, except in the case of directors who tend to make the same film over and over again. It is fortunate that some of the great masters fall into this group, and repetition may end up being a cause why Fellini and Bergman will end up in a pantheon not accessible to capable men like Bogdanovich or Coppola.

Certainly this is not to say that Miklós Jancsó is a great director just because one tends to be unable to distinguish among his films. But the fact that what distinguishes them from each other is largely an increasing intensification of stylistic abstraction helps one to remember their chronology; *The Round-Up* (1965), his fifth feature, held all the formal promise of the later work, but lining up the best of the films which followed it and analysing the degree to which each managed to perfect certain stylistic elements, even a layman observer will recognize that their sequence could be none but this: *The Red and the White* (1967), *Silence and Cry* (1968), *The Confrontation* (1968), *Agnus Dei* (1970) and *Red Psalm* (1971).*

These stylistic elements are: a reduction in the number of shots, a pre-montage in the camera, an increase in the number of possible levels of interpretation, elimination of the obvious, and calculated interaction of the following dialectic elements: foreground and background, sound and silences,

* This list does not include the two films Jancsó made in Italy in 1973/74, with the help of Italian television, *Technique and Rite* and *Rome Wants Caesar Back*, nor *Winter Wind* (*Sirocco,* 1969, a French co-production), which I have not seen, nor *La Pacifista* (1970), which I dislike. It thus contains all his totally Hungarian films and none of the ones made elsewhere.

prolongation and condensation of time, the logical and the illogical, the rational and the poetic. The visual cement is provided by Jancsó's extraordinary camera movements, by now his trademark, the refined orchestration of sensual impacts, causing a constant assault on our habitual lines of vision.

A particle of light travels reflected from an object to the lens in our eye, is caught as a lance on a pivot in the iris, its laser rigidity painting movement on the retina. Our mind is thus accustomed to assume that a movement on the retina corresponds to a movement "in reality." In film and photography the lines are broken, because we regard a secondary image, with its own movement in the case of film, without physical connection to the primary image it purports to reproduce. Try to move a lens of minus 4 or 5 dioptres, through which you see a reduced image of reality, up and down in front of your eye, and "reality" will move with it; that is the basic effect of the cinecamera, except that we have become accustomed to accepting its falsifications. The effect has often been analysed in moral terms, but rarely technically; we know that reality in the cinema is illusion, but we chalk this up to a mystic quality of the medium or the abstraction necessitated by the need to choose a viewpoint. Jancsó is the first who has not only perceived the technical root of the phenomenon but is using it creatively.

All this sounds considerably more complicated than it is, like all analysis after the fact. In practical, filmmaking terms, Jancsó is reducing traditional elements to a minimum and creating heightened motion consciousness; thus approaching, in cinema, a Hegelian definition, whereby each form of art has a single, central vehicle. For Jancsó, the definition of film is the art of movement. All else only serves its purpose: time manipulation, decor, color, story, sounds and drama. But shining with pristine presumptuousness, it is the movement of the camera that creates his style.

A few weeks ago, Jancsó, his girl friend and collaborator Giovanna Galleardo and myself were driving back in a small car from the Puszta to Budapest, after rain had washed out a day's shooting on his latest film, *My Love, Elektra,* and lightning had struck the decorations, burning the straw roofs. It was a

Sunday, and on the following Friday Jancsó was to leave for Rome to begin working for Carlo Ponti on his next film, *The Blood Countess*, to be shot in Italy near Parma. Half of *Elektra* (four shots) was in the can, leaving four more shots to go. The rain usually takes two days to dry. Jancsó had to finish the film before leaving. I was amazed at his calmness. He explained that he would finish the film on Tuesday and Wednesday, shooting two shots a day instead of one, and still make his plane. "Are you going to come back later for the montage, then?" I asked. "No," he answered, "I will do it on Thursday."

Considering that he overlaps action at the beginning and end of each shot, and that his main aim in cutting is to make even the seven cuts that this picture will require as invisible as possible, the feat seemed realistic. But the simplicity is misleading; this nonchalance (and the good story that it makes) is only possible because by the time he shoots, the work of making the film has already been practically finished. Putting it on film and sticking it together is only a requirement of the commercial need to get it seen. This shift to "pre-cameratic" creativity is another key to his style. *My Love, Elektra* (the translation is mine; the film may eventually be released under another title) is based on a play by Laszlo Gyurko that has been running continuously in repertory in Budapest for the past five years. The play is an adaptation of the Greek original, and Jancsó has again adapted the adaptation, resurrecting both Elektra and Orestes more than once in the course of the "action" and providing—in the script version, at least—a 20th century finish, where a red ("of course, red," he says) helicopter carries the pair off and returns them to a world where perhaps tolerance may become possible, after all. A hope upon which, mercifully without elaboration, the film is to end.

Jancsó is working as usual with Gyula Hernádi, his favorite scriptwriter, a noted figure on the Hungarian literary scene. The camerawork is by János Kende, who has shot all the recent Jancsó films, including the ones made in Italy, and who must be considered as the third foot of the creative triangle. It is, essentially, the friendly, run-in collaboration of these three, the smooth, by now often wordless understanding they have of each other as people and of the material Jancsó throws up, that is at the base of the uncanny, almost oily accuracy of the finished products. Every angle, every meaning, every movement is worked out in elaborate detail as the rehearsals advance. The finished *kép* (the pronunciation of which, a long, drawn out k-e-h-p, most suitably conjured up its meaning; it approximately translates "one-shot sequence," or, as Pasolini terms it, a *piano-sequenza*) is only the crystallization of innumerable eliminations. In *My Love, Elektra,* the eight *képs* run to an average length of between 10 and 12½ minutes.

There is a script; it runs to about fifty pages and is based on the play, thus consisting almost entirely of dialogue. Every ten pages or so Jancsó has marked the top of a sheet with a scribble in his strong, somewhat angular but quite fanciful handwriting: 1st *kép*, 2nd *kép*, and so on. The spoken lines are theatrical, stylized, meandering monologues, some running to three or four pages of typescript. There is a bare indication of action, but no camera movements, no indication of focal length, no lighting instructions. Obviously, since the whole film is shot in a daylight exterior.

The set is essentially the Puszta, the Hungarian plain. The word itself just means empty, or devoid of, the place where naught is. It is the Apai Puszta, the "small" *puszta* around the town of Kecskemét, more exactly the village of Kunszentmiklós, and *Agnus Dei* was shot here; the house which was the central element of decor in that film appears in the background of this one. I am being assured that the name of the village ("the place of Saint Miklós") predates Janscó's choice of it as a favorite site.

These plains are absolutely flat, grassy, clay alluvial deposits. Where a tree creates a perpendicular exception, you may be sure it has been planted by human hands. The rain doesn't make mud; it makes a slippery, grey mush, on which horses slip and fall, and which provides the raw material for the unfired clay-and-hay bricks of which Jancsó's decors are built. These are a bare minimum of structures: a gigantic hayloft open to the air on three sides, an open court which is basically just a thick mudwall enclosure, some clay brick columns topped by a thatched lean-to and, in the distance, some round, pointed *trulli*, resembling those of Puglia, indicating the location of a well. Most of the structures are white washed, resembling both the typical Puszta house and the Greek originals where *Elektra* might have been set.

In fact, the visual aspect of the place is indeterminate. This could be the Hungary of the Middle Ages or the Greece of antiquity. The culture of which we see manifestations is, as Hernédi pointed out to me, "vaguely nomad-agricultural mystic" and not historically defined. As such, *My Love, Elektra* fits in well with Jancsó's other Puszta films like *Agnus Dei* and *Red Psalm*, which, while defining their period, liberally transgressed both history and rationale.

The king is played by József Madarás, the perennial epileptic priest from other Jancsó films, and Elektra herself by Mari Töröcsik, who played the daughter in Károly Makk's *Love*. What Jancsó has woven into the story is his central concern for the violence that men do to each other and the futility of it, recreating in this legendary setting his relatively conventional anti-Stalinist theme. We see the familiar horders of peasants, chased by horsemen carrying torches emanating red smoke; the naked peasant girls (this time accompanied by naked men) going through elaborate, inconclusive rites, marching across the horizon in flashes of nude line-ups; an incongruous aside of a reflecting pool in which body paint has been applied hippie-fashion to the more attractive of the nude female backsides; and the ever-encroaching, circling whirlpools of bland-faced lackeys of dictatorship, just allowing the space for the straight lines of old women in white to march by, before unleashing their whips and cracking them ever closer to the group of the innocent, misled herd of the erstwhile faithful.

Essentially the work of putting all these by now familiar elements together is akin to that of an orchestra conductor, rehearsing one of his own compositions with his chamber group. Nobody seems much concerned with the content; it is all a matter of how the form chosen can best express it. There is no interference from the group in the message department; it is quite clear that Jancsó is the master provider and the apostle in one. As another Hungarian director, with a smile but not without envy, called him: the socialist prince.

The working day starts when the sun goes *down*. In the small houses of the village where the crew live, the members of the inner circle stir and move down towards the end of the lane where Jancsó and Giovanna share a house with Kende. There may or may not be dinner, depending on whether anybody has thought of shopping. The assistant director (one of three) usually cooks; sometimes Yvette Biro, former editor (recently removed from office by party decree) of *Film Kultura*, Hungary's intellectual film monthly, and Jancsó's old friend and collaborator, does the chores. Hernádi, Kende, Gyurko (who is there the whole time, hoping against hope to salvage some part of his play), some of the actors, the set nurse, a singer and his girl, Yvette, Giovanna, myself, and an occasional technician or grip, sit around the table idly sipping a variety of Tokay wines and other spirits. Somebody has actually popped some corn, the singer's guitar gives out a few hesitant chords. It is the start of the session from which tomorrow's shooting will eventually grow.

The cross-fertilization of historical epochs utilized in this film expresses Jancsó's view that the problems of mankind have not changed, and that despite the patent hopelessness of our social and political cul-de-sac, there is no reason to think that mankind will not again save itself by the thin strands of its perennial hope for a better tomorrow. In this *Elektra* he uses musical elements from westerns, and the theme song is actually a composition made up by a young Hungarian folk singer about the mythical hero that Lee Van Cleef has become for thousands of Hungarian moviegoers. Jancsó is not only using the music; the whole song is in the film, including the reference to the actor by name. The first evening I am there is spent in rehearsing the song, over and over again, with everyone finally joining in the singing, and in adjusting the rhythm and the words to the exact needs of the scene in the film where they will be used. It is tomorrow's scene, and it is a scene between Elektra and Orestes. As the wine and the music get to all of us, slowly and warmly the problems are solved. In the end, long after midnight, with the damned song engraved forever in everyone's head, but the film assured of another well-ordained *kép*, we trundle home, each to his own Puszta farmhouse.

If you want to follow the creation of a sequence from its inception, you have to get up early. By the time I disentangle myself from the well-meaning daughter of my landlord, with whom communication is by word-*kép*, or single-word sentences, and realise that the loo is in the yard and breakfast not on the program, the few cars that go to the set have long since left. I have to go with Giovanna, who speaks little Hungarian and thus is allowed latecomer's privileges, usually having a car sent back for her around 9:30. This means that Jancsó has been rehearsing for two-and-a-half hours by the time I arrive. It also means that the five hundred extras, who have come down from Budapest in a special train and a fleet of smoky buses, have been up since shortly after midnight. There is no overtime, but the day rate is still better than the factory, the school or the shops.

Of the thirteen girls and six men who will appear nude in the scene (apart from two of the main actors, who do the same), one is an amateur actress from a small street theatre group in Buda, a few are models, one is a striptease artist, and the rest are either from the school of actresses or have been picked at random from among Budapest shoppers. To appear in a Jancsó film is like a ticket to stardom; the aura that attaches to me just because I appear to be a friend of his is immense. Weeks later, when I call up the Hungarian embassy in London for help with the translation of a Hungarian word, the switchboard operator, remote from her homeland but evidently imbued with national spirit, recognises the word as being part of the title of a film, and proudly adds ". . . directed by Jancsó."

The actual preparations for the day's *kép* begin with the laying of the track. There is always a track, sometimes 60 or 70 feet long, curving in and out of the buildings, like a children's train set. But considering the complexities and acrobatics which the camera performs along its lines, these are remarkably simple, sometimes forming half an ellipse or the form of two J's, joined at the top and standing on each other, or just half or three-quarters of a slightly squashed circle. On these tracks the camera rides at the end of a counterweighted beam, extending some ten feet outwards, and itself balanced on a hydraulic telescoping lift which can raise it twelve or fifteen feet in the air. If you have ever dreamt of floating through the world free from restrictions of weight or space, this would be the vehicle you would have to use. As it is, it carries only your eyes.

As Kende, who operates his own camera, including the zooming, and only has an assistant to help pull focus, rides atop this contraption with his eyes glued to the finder, the rehearsal starts. It can take a whole morning, and sometimes a whole day, often leaving just enough time before the light goes to shoot the take. The best description I can think of that might resemble the movements being rehearsed is a fish tank full of water, enormously enlarged to include the entire set with actors, camera, tracks and crew, with the camera representing a delectable lady-fish aimlessly gliding about in her three-dimensional realm, pursued by every living thing in sight.

For despite the fact that ostensibly it is she, the camera, that observes what surrounds her and moves to do so, in reality every movement is being planned for her and every action exists only for her approval. Thus order is reversed: it is reality which is set in motion by deft manipulation in order to be at the right place at the right time. As soon as she has passed them, actors jump up, throw off a costume or don another, run ahead of her along her planned path, and crouch down again ready for another fleeting close-up. Whole herds of horses, over whom she has passed, gallop in a wide circle behind her back to catch up again with their own image where it has been planned on her itinerary. And central actors, courted by her concentric embrace, move against her in their own curves, creating that doubly broken line of vision which makes some viewers dizzy. That is why the line of the track can be relatively simple; the major part of the movement is orchestrated for the camera in a ballet of calculated fabrication.

Lines are spoken, but in whisper tones; they will be dubbed in later at the correct levels. The whole thing is a military operation of exacting accuracy. No deviations are permitted; a few inches off and a shot might have to be repeated. The same goes for the sun: a few degrees Kelvin off, and the colors of the shots won't match. I have spent entire days waiting for just that degree of cloudiness that the previous *kép* was shot in. On the day in question, the 500 extras had to return to Budapest without having worked, for just this reason. It may seem simple to say that everything is shot in one set in one light and in only eight shots with the whole montage created within the frame, but it isn't as simple to put this into operation.

The instructions to the actors are primarily choreographic. The main *personnages* are more often than not in the foreground, sometimes in full close-ups, while action of no less importance goes on at twenty yards distance behind and unsharp. There is a great deal of play with shifting focus, and a good deal of zooming, but the zoom is not used to approach or repulse an object or a face, but to change framing and to arrive at the next object in the camera's path with a shorter or longer focal length than the preceding one. The differing psychological effects created by different focal lengths of the camera lens are taken into consideration; unlike many directors, who use zooming in its banal, TV application of changing distance from the viewpoint to the object, Jancsó uses it to see a face in greater or lesser distortion, and with greater or lesser flattening (the first being caused by the short and the second by the long focal lengths). Thus, what the actors are told is only where to be at exactly what point, where to look and what to do, and how long to remain there. Since they have often participated in the previous evening's session, they know what is expected of them in terms of dramatic content without Jancsó having to insist unduly.

This spatial choreography, however, requires constant cues, and thus necessitates constant communication between crew and actors during the shooting. This is accomplished by a network of walkie-talkie systems, which activate loudspeakers hidden all over the set. Each crew member carries a broadcasting unit, some set for unison and some for diversity wavelengths. The air is filled with a constant crackle and electronic interference, and on the afternoon of the rainstorm a stranded loudspeaker in a lonely puddle in the middle of nowhere in the Puszta continued for an hour to broadcast happy weather reports being exchanged between ham radio sailors at sea off Sardinia. The wavelength had got tangled up in a resonance band. Needless to say, the Tyrrhenian sea was calm and the sun was shining. Fortunately, batteries manufactured in Hungary have a way of running down very quickly. After a while, only a sad occasional pip-squeak drifted in to us, huddled under makeshift straw roofing and freezing in clothes soaked by a cloudburst.

An uncanny *deus ex machina* atmosphere thus pervades the set. Everything is subjected to the tyranny of the camera path, and everyone who sees something about to go wrong begins to scream into his walkie-talkie, adding to the general din. Jancsó himself is more irascible than one would expect under the suave exterior of the socialist prince, who in his private life and interviews seems totally imperturbable. He is wont to scream at the top of his voice and let loose the worst of Hungarian curse words (also one of the commonest of that language of the steppes, and meaning the sexual organ of a horse). But he returns equally fast to total equilibrium when his outburst has done its work of pulling things back into shape.

While rehearsals can go on a whole day, shooting is short. Each *kép* is usually repeated only four or five times, rarely going to seven or eight takes. The same night the exposed film is developed, after having been rushed to the studio in Budapest, and after four days of shooting, I was able to view the first half of the film in rushes. It is, of course, unlike any screening of rushes I had ever attended: seeing the four shots, I had seen the first half of the finished film. The Hungarians use Kodak emulsions, but they develop it themselves, and they develop it excellently well. Within hours of its arrival, positive rushes are printed. Work-print seems as good in quality as a corrected one.

Although the cutting can be taken care of in a single day, that doesn't of course mean that the film will actually be ready to be projected as soon as it's been edited. In fact, the whole process of finishing it takes a lot of work, and it is only because over the years Jancsó has managed to develop a faithful and well-trained staff of collaborators that he can afford to be absent from Hungary while the film is being looped for synchronization, dialogues are being re-recorded, the sound tracks are mixed and finally a print is married. Clearly he will have to return to Hungary when some of this work has been done, and the film will not, in effect, be ready to be seen before the autumn or early winter.

But all these are technical necessities which Jancsó considers essential but extraneous to his creative work, and it is the warm and fertile moment of the evening discussions which precede the shooting and the detailed, critical preparation of the camera movements that make up the exciting moments of filmmaking for him. There is always singing and a bit of drinking, friends drive down from Budapest, it is a real festivity. In fact, when he is not shooting, the circle of his friends and collaborators in Budapest is a little less alive, a little less connected to the stream of life. He has the ability to make each and every person feel important, never contradicts anyone directly, and achieves his devotions obliquely; like a truly encompassing creator he is automatically at the center of all activities he shares. Even when he sings, as he often does, with a smile of ridicule but also an air of nostalgia, the old partisan songs from his youth, people join in without the comments which in today's Hungary normally greet expressions from the romantic days. In a country that has come a long way from one form of Stalinism and has still not accepted that it is heading for another, the leisurely disdain for the generation of the war is one of the few ways of manifesting a rebellious spirit.

In 1945 Miklós Jancsó was 23, and was active in the free university movement of those days; *Confrontation* is his real story. He was formed under Stalinism, and it has remained, in one form or another, a major influence. "I am an expert of Stalinism," he says, "but that no longer interests anybody today. I am no longer young. I have done many things in my life, all useless. I no longer believe in big causes. Now I want to do different things, cook, for example. And to discover physical relationships, direct relationships. In my films I want to show that humanity can't go on the way it's going. On the other hand, I have played Christ long enough. What's the point? We know how the end will come. In fact, sometimes I think we're a bit ahead of schedule."

Politics and Poetry
in *Two or Three Things*
I Know About Her
and *La Chinoise*
by James Roy MacBean

This selection on Jean-Luc Godard
is taken from MacBean's book,
"Film and Revolution," published
by the Indiana University Press.

"Words, words, words." Hamlet's reply to Polonius when questioned about his reading might well be the response one would make when questioned about these two films by Jean-Luc Godard, for never has the cinema been so wordy as in *Deux ou trois choses que je sais d'elle (Two or Three Things I Know About Her)* and *La Chinoise (The Chinese Girl)*. But with Godard, as with Hamlet, there's a method in the madness. And, in any case, rarely have words been held up to such painful scrutiny, to such a desperate search for *sense*, as in these two maddeningly provocative films.

Deux ou trois choses, however, is particularly maddening in that, first, the narration (by Godard himself, in a running commentary on the film and its making) is spoken in an often barely audible whisper. Second, all of the commentary and much of the dialogue are spoken off-camera or away from the camera, thus eliminating any real assistance from lipreading. And, third, both the commentary and the dialogue are systematically covered, and often smothered, by the noise of construction machinery, low-flying jets, pinball machines, electric appliances, huge tractor-trailer trucks, passing automobiles, etc. Consequently, the "viewer-listener" of *Deux ou trois choses* has to strain at every moment to pick up even two or three words, and to attempt to assimilate the words and reconstruct the *sense* of what has just been said, while all the time trying not to fall behind the torrent of words that continues to pour forth.

However, the strain of coping with such an overwhelming tidal wave of words and noise is really what *Deux ou trois choses que je sais d'elle* is all about. And one of the "two or three things" Godard knows about Paris (nominally, the "elle" of the title) is precisely the fact that within such an urban environment an individual is unable to find a moment's peace and quiet. Moreover, by letting the viewer-listener *experience* this alienation—through noise, among other things—which separates us from our own thoughts and from others, Godard succeeds in putting across a message in the way best calculated to leave its imprint on the audience, for it is the viewer-listener who realizes during the course of this film (in case he or she hasn't realized it before) just how intolerable is this constant roar of noise in which we live in the modern city.

It is worth pointing out, by the way, that Godard's manipulation of the sound track in *Deux ou trois choses* is by no means a radical new departure for him: while it is true that he has always (or at least from *Une Femme est une Femme* on) relied heavily on direct recording of natural sound, he has also experimented a great deal with various ways of arranging, or composing, the raw material into what we might call "sound-blocks" of alternating levels of intensity. *Une Femme est une Femme*, for example, juxtaposes sound-blocks of a tremendous variety of sound possibilities—dialogue recorded in studio, dialogue recorded over natural sound, fragments of music, entire songs, dialogue over music, silence, etc.—and in *Bande à part*, in particular, the sound track is no longer the harmonious counterpart of the visual image but is rather the audio counter*point* to the visual image.

This contrapuntal form of composition is developed most fully, however, in *Deux ou trois choses*, where Godard's insistent forcing of the spectator out of his normal passivity is carried out in a relentless flood of seemingly unrelated images and sounds—of *signs*, both audio and visual—which, in the words of the main character, "ultimately lead us to doubt language itself and which submerge us with significations while drowning that which is real instead of helping us to disengage the real from the imaginary." In short, Godard both tells us and shows us, in *Deux ou trois choses*, that we in western civilization are adrift on a sea of significations, victims of our own signs, the only escape being to sink or swim: to drown in *non-sense* or to struggle for *sense*.

One of the main problems, then, in the struggle for sense,

is the problem of endurance. At the beginning of the film, presumably, everyone (or at least everyone who knows some French) will be willing to *try* to hear the words and assimilate what is said, but over a period of more than an hour and a half, with only occasional and very brief "rest stops" (snatches of Beethoven's last string quartet and, once or twice, a few precious moments of sweet silence), it seems unfortunate but inevitable that sooner or later a certain portion of the audience is going to sink (or, as happens, simply walk out), exhausted and exasperated by the constant struggle to separate words from noise, sense from non-sense.

One might be tempted simply to ignore the often unintelligible dialogue and commentary, and to look for sense exclusively in the visual image; but perhaps it is not until and unless the spectator begins to understand how noise in the context of this film makes sense—how noise in this film does not impede sense but rather is a vehicle of sense—that the film as a whole can begin to emerge from the bewildering complexity that is at first glance deceptively similar to non-sense. The act of confronting the bewildering complexity of modern urban society and of learning two or three things about it is, after all, the not so easy task Godard himself has undertaken: is it then asking too much of us, as we confront the complexity of this film, that we, in turn, attempt to learn two or three things about cinema?

This double action of analyzing society and how it works, and at the same time analyzing art and how *it* works, is precisely the double action of *Deux ou trois choses*, a film in which Godard *qua* sociologist scrutinizes the "social pathology" of the modern city at the same time that Godard *qua* filmmaker scrutinizes the cinematic means of transposing the social analysis into art. Moreover, in the whispered commentaries in *Deux ou trois choses*, we overhear Godard questioning himself (as he does in *Far From Vietnam*), as both sociologist and filmmaker, as to whether these are the right images, the right words, and whether his perspective is from too close or from too far. In short, *all* is put in question in *Deux ou trois choses*: the impersonal cruelty of Gaullist neocapitalism; the prostitution, in one form or another, of the modern city-dweller; the American imperialist aggression in Vietnam; the fragmentary assimilation of culture in a society flooded with paperback

472

books; the thousand and one amenities of modern life (radios, beauty salons, super-sudsy detergents, the latest style in dresses, and the modern bathroom plumbing still unavailable to seventy percent of the French people): *all* is put in question, including, and perhaps especially, the notion of cinema.

Godard, it is clear, wants a revolution in both art and society; and he hopes to make his contribution to the revolution of society by accomplishing in film the revolution of art. It is this double action, in art and in society, that Godard advocates when he speaks of the need to "struggle on two fronts"—an idea he seems to develop more fully in his fourteenth film, *La Chinoise*.

Godard has very often acknowledged that in his view art is a very serious matter with a most important role to play in the social revolution he sees taking place today in western civilization. Moreover, Godard's art (like Gide's *Les Faux Monnayeurs* or the play-within-a-play that Hamlet stages for the king) is very calculatingly constructed of a most disquieting mixture of the fictional and the real; and one of the dominant refrains that haunt *La Chinoise* is the Hamlet-like assertion that "art is not the reflection of reality, but the reality of the reflection." There is, indeed, something very Hamlet-like in Godard's hyperlucid introspection, in his intense desire to understand a situation and at the same time to act upon it and influence it; in his genuine desire to commit himself to the social and political life around him and in his aesthetic inclination to maintain an ironic distance from that life, to play with words, to pun, to mimic, to jest. But where Hamlet found social commitment and aesthetic distance incompatible and the wavering between them inimical to an active life, Godard seeks to resolve the dilemma, not by eliminating one or the other of its horns but by jealously guarding them both in the creation of a work of art, like *La Chinoise*, that is at the same time sincerely and sympathetically committed to social revolution and yet ebulliently ironic in its insistence on delineating the sometimes infantile and dangerous excesses of the very heroes and political stands with which he, Godard, and we, the audience, may sympathize and perhaps identify. *La Chinoise*, like all of Godard's films, contains within itself its own self-critique: it is social thought and the critique of social thought, art and the critique of art. For an audience accus-

tomed to having their politics and their art be one thing only—
serious or funny, pro or con, tragedy or comedy—*La Chinoise*
must indeed be very perplexing; but it would be a grave mistake to reduce this film, as some viewers seem to do, to one
category or another—hilarious spoof or dead-serious militance,
insouciance or hardline propaganda, aesthetic dilettantism or
didactic non-art. Godard, one should have learned by now,
cannot be explained away so easily; and his well-known
taste for contradictions might better be understood as the
ability to achieve a dynamic balance amid seeming oppositions.

Godard is in many ways a Hamlet who has found his calling: he is Hamlet as playwright, Hamlet as artist. It is art
which enables Godard to achieve and maintain that dynamic
balance; and, conversely, it is his intense desire to achieve
such a harmony amid seeming discord which brings him inevitably to art. As Godard himself puts it in *Deux ou trois
choses*, the goal of achieving a new world in which both men
and things will know a harmonious rapport—a goal both political and poetic—explains, in any case, the rage for expression
of Godard the writer-painter, of Godard the artist. Hamlet, too,
knew that art and politics could serve each other, that art
could be the mousetrap for the conscious of society; but it is
significant that Hamlet staged only one play and from then on
attempted to deal with life "directly," without the mediation of
art, whereas Godard stages play after play after play, and
deals with life by dealing with art.

In *La Chinoise* this interplay between art and life, between
reality and the reflection of reality—and, most important, the
inevitable interdependence and overlapping of the two—are
expressed dramatically in the memorable sequence early in
the film when the young actor Guillaume (played by Jean-
Pierre Léaud) begins by reciting in very traditional style several lines from a text he is rehearsing, then stops short, grins,
and, in answer to a question unheard by the audience (again,
it is more or less whispered by Godard himself), acknowledges
that "Yes, I am an actor" and then launches into an im-
promptu monologue on the dilemma of an actor committed to
social revolution. At the close of this scene, however, Guillaume
protests vigorously that one must avoid the temptation not to
take his words seriously just because he is an actor performing
in front of a camera, and he insists that he is sincere. At this

474

moment we are suddenly shown a cameraman (Raoul Coutard) who has been filming Guillaume's speech and who is, in turn, now filmed himself in the act of filming the actor Jean-Pierre Léaud for the film we are presently watching. However, Godard's use of this complex procedure evokes little, if any, of the Pirandellian confusion of illusion and reality, but emphasizes rather the very Brechtian paradox that the film-within-a-film, like the film itself, must be seen not only as a work of art but, like all art, also as an activity engaged in by real people who may be sincerely committed to the ideas they are acting out in artistic form. As Godard explained when answering questions from the audience in Berkeley, Guillaume is an actor committed to the revolution who hopes to make his contribution to the revolution by *acting* in a revolutionary way in revolutionary films and theater. In this sense, Guillaume's revolutionary activity with the Marxist-Leninist cell is not so much a *secondary* activity as it is a *corollary* activity of the committed art he practices as an actor. In short, Guillaume is a revolutionary actor acting for the revolution; and this, too, seems to be what Godard is getting at when he advocates the "struggle on two fronts."

Godard recently indicated in a *Cahiers* interview that he was interested in the filmmaker's opportunity to create in his own modest way "two or three Vietnams in the heart of the immense empire of Hollywood-Cinecittà-Mosfilm-Pinewood, etc., and economically as well as aesthetically—that is to say, in struggling on two fronts—create national and free cinemas that are brothers, comrades and friends." From this statement and from others like it, we can see that Jean-Pierre Léaud's role in *La Chinoise* as a revolutionary actor acting for the revolution is, in a very real sense, the role which Godard believes is the most authentic role he himself can play as a committed artist.

This problem of the artist's particular kind of commitment arises again in *La Chinoise* as we witness the very intense dialogue in a train compartment between Véronique and Francis Jeanson, the deeply committed colleague of Jean-Paul Sartre at *Les Temps Modernes* and the man who was in the forefront of political agitation in opposition to French colonial rule in Algeria at the time of the Algerian uprising. Jeanson, in *La Chinoise*, willingly puts himself in what is for him the rather paradoxical position of seeking to oppose or at least restrain the revolutionary activities advocated by the young would-be terrorist played by Anne Wiazemsky. Jeanson senses very acutely and very visibly the uncomfortable paradox of his position vis-à-vis the younger generation of radicals, but he argues sincerely and penetratingly—and with a wonderful feeling of warmth and genuine personal concern for his youthful student—as he attempts to make her realize the need, first and foremost, of creating a solid base of mass popular support for social change. Without this popular support, he points out, his own revolutionary activity in the Algerian crisis would have been futile, if not impossible; and it is precisely this need to create popular support for social change which involves Jeanson at the moment in a project designed to bring revolutionary theater to the people in the provinces.

Once again, the notion of the revolutionary actor acting for the revolution seems to be the artist's way of carrying on the "struggle on two fronts." But even here, in presenting what is essentially his own view and what he believes to be the only authentic role for the artist in contemporary France, Godard's extreme honesty, sincerity, and lucidity force him to acknowledge, as we see in the scene with Francis Jeanson, that the artist's position will inevitably appear an equivocal one, for the militant activists will never consider the artist's contribution bold enough or even of any real significance in the revolutionary struggle; and the artist's particular way of committing himself will always contain at least a hint of self-interest, inasmuch as the artist continues to pursue his artistic career while at the same time claiming to align his art with the revolutionary cause. In both of these respects, then, it is understandable that in spite of Jeanson's obvious sincerity and the excellence of his arguments, we find it difficult to listen without slight annoyance, slight embarrassment, or both, when he speaks of the way his little theater troupe will enable him to engage in social action and at the same time enable him to get away from Paris, where he no longer finds himself able to concentrate on the books he is writing. "In going to the provinces," he explains with enthusiasm, "I'll be able to carry out this social action and, moreover, carry on my writing at the same time."

It is hardly surprising, however, that Jeanson's arguments, however right they may be, do not dissuade Véronique from

476

advocating, and then committing, acts of terrorism. The artist can speak of the "struggle on two fronts" precisely because for him there are the two fronts of art and society, but for the ordinary individual (like Véronique, Yvonne, or Henri, the young man expelled for "revisionism") there is only the single front of a world that is not right, of a world with something rotten at its core, of a world that must, in one way or another, be taken apart so that it can be reassembled in a better way. While the artist can create on paper, on canvas, or on film a new and "perfect" world (and perhaps encourage others to attempt to create a new world in real life), it seems that the dirty work of going out and attempting to create this new world in real life falls inevitably to the ordinary individual who deals directly with life without the mediation of art; and it is the ordinary individual who, no matter how much he may be encouraged by the example of "committed art," must bear the burden of the fact that a bullet fired in reality takes a man's life, whereas a bullet fired in a film is art.

Hamlet himself, one will recall, found great sport in creating a work of art (his play-within-a-play) in which the king was murdered; but the same Hamlet found it nearly impossible in spite of the best of reasons to kill the king in real life. Given this predicament, the ordinary individual can react in many ways, the two extremes being either to sit back, do nothing, and, like Hamlet, complain that "the time is out of joint. O cursèd spite that ever I was born to set it right" or, like Véronique in *La Chinoise*, to accept the consequences of setting it right and go out and shoot somebody. In Berkeley Godard admitted that while he himself would never take up a gun, he now felt that he had to support those (like the North Vietnamese, or Régis Debray, or Che Guevara, or the Black Panthers) who, in the name of positive social reform, were willing to pick up a gun and if need be, use it. Godard also expressed admiration for a society like China, which he sees with the advent of the Red Guard youth movement as virtually turned over to the young people between fifteen and twenty-five years of age. As Godard puts it, "there are lots of things in this world that would be better off if they were turned over to the young people who have the courage to start again from zero."

This notion of starting again from zero (which was Juliette's conclusion at the end of *Deux ou trois choses*) recurs repeatedly in *La Chinoise*: Véronique wants to close the French universities so that the entire notion of education can be rethought from zero; she would bomb the Louvre and the Comédie Française so that painting and drama can likewise be rethought from zero; and Guillaume pushes his own investigation of the nature of theater to a notion of "The Theater of the Year Zero"—which is visualized cinematically by a shot of two individuals (an older woman in a sort of bathing suit and a young girl nude) knocking on either side of a large panel of transparent plexiglass through which they can see each other but which separates them—an image, perhaps, of the first primitive nonverbal efforts to communicate between one human being and another. Moreover, this notion of starting again from zero is implicit in the fact that in both subject and form *La Chinoise* is a film of revolution, a film that traces the progress of movement around the circumference of a circle until one completes the circle and returns to the point of departure. There is a strict logical sequence (as an intertitle states in announcing the film's final shot) which demands that the film end with the same shot with which it began—the shot of the balcony of the activists' apartment.

In beginning and ending at the same point, the film itself can be said to undergo a complete revolution; but to say that the film ends at the point of departure is not to say that the action within the film accomplishes nothing. On the contrary, it is the action within the circle which permits the return to the point of departure and the opportunity to start again from zero. Although they contain the same shot of the balcony, the opening and closing shots of the film reveal very different actions and attitudes within the development of the film narrative. In the opening shot, we see the balcony with its bright red shutters opened, and we hear, and then see, a young man (Henri) reading aloud. Then, as the film unfolds, Henri is seen to be the character who develops the least, the one who adheres most rigidly to the French Communist Party line, the one whose attitude remains static (and it is significant that Henri is the one character—aside from Kirilov, who is also extremely rigid—who is always filmed in static shots without cuts).

In the closing shot of the film we see the same balcony, at

that very moment being reoccupied, so to speak, by the bourgeoisie—represented by the girl whose parents have let Véronique use the apartment during the summer vacation. The girl scolds Véronique for having made such a mess in the apartment and tells her it must be cleaned up before the return of her parents. Finally Véronique is left alone on the balcony with the parting advice to "think over carefully all that she has done." As Véronique leaves the balcony and closes the red shutters, we hear her unspoken thoughts explaining that she has already thought over her actions, that the end of the summer means the return to the university and the continuation of the struggle for her and for her comrades, and that she has now realized that the summer's activity with the Marxist-Leninist cell, which she originally thought represented a major breakthrough in revolutionary action, represents in reality only "the first tiny step in what would be a very long march"—words taken by Godard from a speech by Chou En-lai. Thus, the sequence of events that began on the balcony with Henri mechanically reading comes to an end on the same balcony with Véronique thinking out for herself the realization that what she has done is merely a beginning in an ongoing struggle ten thousand times longer. As Godard indicates in the final intertitle, the "end" of the sequence of events that comprises the film is only "the end of a beginning."

Godard himself gives the impression that the end of each new film is only "the end of a beginning"; and it is clear that as Godard develops as a filmmaker, more and more he is putting into question both the entire notion of western civilization and the entire notion of cinema. He has often remarked that when he made *A bout de souffle* (his first feature), he had lots of ideas about films, but that now, after making more than a dozen of his own, he no longer has any ideas about films. This confession, however, should not be taken as an indication of despair; rather it is for Godard a genuine liberation. He is clearly a man who has the courage, as well as the will, to start again from zero and to do it every time he makes a film. Even Hamlet, after all, despite his hesitations, managed at least, even if only inadvertently, to wipe the slate clean and enable Denmark to start again from zero. "Readiness is all," he proclaimed. Godard, at the end of *La Chinoise*, seems ready.

The Dark Night
of the Soul
# of Robert Bresson
by Colin L. Westerbeck, Jr.

*This article, which has been revised by
the author, appeared originally in the
November 1976 issue of Artforum under
the title "Robert Bresson's Austere Vision."
Westerbeck, who teaches at Fordham
University, was president of the National
Society of Film Critics at this writing.*

With Robert Bresson, the place to begin is a detail, one as small
and irreducible as possible. Near the end of *Diary of a Country
Priest* (1950), for instance, the priest enters a café in Lille.
He has come to this city from his poor village parish to have
the stomach pain that afflicts him diagnosed (the diagnosis is
cancer), and he has come into this café because he found himself unable to pray at the local church. As he sits alone in the
room, he writes in the diary that has, through his voice-over
recitations from it, served as the source for the film's story.
The woman who owns the café comes in to chat, mistaking
the diary for a sermon, and absently throws a crumpled piece
of paper into the stove. Although Bresson isolated it with a
close-up, the piece of paper thrown into the stove seems almost an incidental detail. The close-up does too, for that matter. Yet they give us a rare chance to look on Bresson himself.
They are a chink through which we glimpse Bresson's own
feelings directly. Through the impassive and cold style of the
film, we here see Bresson reacting for the moment to this
priest who is his hero.

The same discarding gesture, which is so casual here, is
the central event of two earlier scenes and, through them, of
the film as a whole. Both scenes involve the priest's relations
with the family of a count whose estate is in the priest's parish.
In the first scene the count's daughter uses the priest's confessional to proclaim her unrepented hatred of her father,
and in the midst of her outburst the priest suddenly guesses
blindly but rightly that she has a letter she plans to send her

480

father denouncing him. Abandoning the role of confessor, the priest demands the letter from her and soon burns it, unopened, in his stove. In the second scene the priest calls on the countess at home and, again without solicitude, becomes the audience for another outburst of bitterness and grief. The cause of the countess's despair is the death of her son, and at the height of her frenzy, she hurls a locket containing mementos of him into the fireplace. Where the priest earlier burns the letter wrested from this woman's daughter, he now plunges his arm into the fire to retrieve the locket the woman has thrown away.

Like these two scenes, the one near the film's end when the priest writes his diary in the café involves an act of confession. That is what a diary is, a confession. It is confession in the most private, personal, truthful form, and the priest's capacity for such relentlessly private experience as the diary represents is what Bresson admired in him. Moreover, like an ancient relic which turns to dust the moment it is exhumed, the sort of truth this diary tells always turns to something disreputable when the eyes of the world fall upon it. Made public, its private sacrament looks profane. Unable to pray in church, where a pious attitude would be apparent, the priest instead prays in a café by keeping his diary. This unread testament is the only prayer he has. But the café owner misconstrues it for a rather slovenly practice of writing sermons, public declarations of faith, while tippling. Like the crumpled paper when it hits the fire in the stove, the priest's holiness is instantly consumed by misinterpretation when it is exposed to the café owner's idle curiosity.

This is hardly the first time that the priest's goodness has been lost on the world. When he has that talk with the countess, for instance, her daughter eavesdrops and later reports the incident to his superiors in a way that results in his being charged with misconduct. Even the martyrdom of his cancer is mistaken for a sin—the sin of alcoholism—by his only friend, a vicar from a neighboring parish. Under these conditions, the only faith possible is less a matter of otherworldliness than of simply absenting oneself from this world. The good works that the priest does are all acts of prevention, refraining, or silence. He stops the countess's daughter from sending that letter to her father. He refuses to defend himself when he is charged with misconduct. Etc. To accept opprobrium thus is the priest's way of suubmitting to the will of God. His dying words are, "All is grace." They come, quite literally, as a revelation, since nothing *seems* grace and salvation is at best a hidden presence in the world—since the life the priest leads constantly shrivels and folds in upon itself in the heat of the world like the paper in the fire. To all appearances, "All" is not grace, but ashes.

All of this is to say that *Diary of a Country Priest* is an exceptional film, one that deals affectingly with something movies almost never seem able to touch upon: the soul of man, the movement of the spirit within the rock. And that shot of the crumpled paper thrown into the café stove is an extraordinary detail here because it is, not least of all in its inobtrusiveness and understatement, the perfect summary image in this context. It figures forth for us this priest whose life is so unapparent to the world. While it *is* only a detail, and I don't want to make it sound too crucial to the overall effect of the film, it is also remarkable in another way: because it and the close-up containing it are practically the only details of Bresson's film not taken right out of the Georges Bernanos novel on which the film is based. This is why the crumpled piece of paper becomes, as I said before, an unusual instance of self-disclosure on Bresson's part.

Every Bresson adaptation has been extraordinarily faithful to the book on which it was based, but *Diary* is the most literal translation of them all. In an essay included in the collection *What Is Cinema?*, the French critic André Bazin even went so far as to suggest that Bernanos would have taken more liberties with the novel than Bresson did. This is quite a claim, considering that Bernanos once rejected an adaptation written by the most renowned screen collaborators in France, Jean Aurenché and Pierre Bost, because it was not close enough to his novel. Certainly Bresson's script, which he wrote himself (as he has those for all nine films since *Diary*), is as close as conceivable to Bernanos's fiction. Bresson's film takes out some of Bernanos's material, condensing the action of the novel in ways that a film can scarcely avoid. But Bresson added virtually nothing, except the piece of paper tossed into the café stove.

This is not to say that Bresson's film is just a "faithful

adaptation" in the usual sense. Faithful adaptations are literal-minded. They take the plot and dialogue from a novel exactly as they find them. Bresson did that, of course, but in his scrupulous rekindling of the fires in the novel he took the imagery as well. What the fire he introduced into the café scene does is acknowledge that imagery in Bernanos's novel and enhance its significance by extending it in the film. It adopts Bernanos's values and intentions as well as adapting his story. More than mere adaptation, this is an act of submission to the imagination of another. It is for Bresson as an artist an act of self-effacement and self-abnegation comparable to the priest's own.

The imagination to which Bresson was submitting was, to put the matter more accurately, not Bernanos's so much as the priest's. The source of the novel's power over Bresson lay in its being a first-person narration. Through repeated shots of diary pages covered with the priest's handwriting, Bresson took great care to preserve our sense that this is the priest's own version of his life that we are seeing. The film becomes in effect not a fiction film, but a documentary on the priest's diary. The austere, montonous look of the film results from its documentarist's approach to the diary, which was for Bresson, as André Bazin put it, "a cold, hard fact, a reality to be accepted as it stands." Because the diary became for Bresson the word made manifest, *la parole originaire*, it permitted him to use the techniques of realism to film the life of the spirit.

The result of having given over his imagination to Bernanos this way was that Bresson emerged as an artist in his own right. Having lost himself in the spiritual life of the priest, he found his identity as a filmmaker in a way that he had not done before. This is clear from his films before and after *Diary,* and it really does seem a paradox in which film-making for Bresson approached, as it were, a religious experience. From immersing himself in the character of the priest, he acquired a new insight into cinematic style.

I do not mean to suggest that Bresson's style issues from *Diary* full-blown like Athena from the head of Zeus. Signs of it can be seen already in the preceding film, *Les Dames du Bois de Boulogne* (1944). That film, based on a tale by Diderot, concerns a woman who, jilted by her lover, gets revenge by flinging at his head a girl everyone except him knows to be a whore. At the church where her lover is marrying this whore, the woman tells him the truth about her; and as the woman arrives gloating at the reception afterwards, her former lover, too distraught now to face his guests, is driving off. At this point Bresson did something which is, in this film, peculiar. He cut to a point-of-view shot through the window of the car door so that the woman, standing beside the car smirking, is framed by the window. Then, as her ex-lover drives off, she passes out of the frame to one side, leaving it, for a final moment, empty.

In later films a scene which ends with the frame vacant like this becomes one of the most distinctive features of Bresson's style. But in this film it is still only a tentative and uncertain experiment. Bresson resorted to the car window as if he were uneasy that he needed some pretext for emptying the frame. In the films after *Diary*, he would let the camera stay where it was and simply have the characters leave the frame. He would no longer mask his perception in clumsy point-of-view shots as if it were the character's rather than his own. He would do such shots on his own authority, having realized in *Diary* why the impulse to empty the frame came to him in the first place.

In *Les Dames*, he did not yet realize this. Despite its promise of the work to come, it is essentially a film about alienation. The point-of-view shot at the end does repeat an image of empty picture frames seen on the walls of the whore's apartment earlier (the paintings having been hocked). But the real purpose of the shot through the car window is to fit into an imagery—a rather conventional one for the theme of alienation—in which characters are seen outside doorways, the windows of their rooms, etc. Although characters in *Diary* and subsequent films are often even more mean-spirited than in *Les Dames*, the theme is no longer alienation but its opposite. And in those later films, the evacuated frame comes to imply a fullness that we cannot see, rather than just the emptiness that we can.

As I said initially, the place to begin with Bresson is a detail. This is because the style that came out of Bresson's experience making *Diary* concentrates on detail as no other filmmaker's ever has. It is not that Bresson's style is attentive to detail, nor are his films rich in detail and fretwork. On the contrary, detail counts for much in Bresson's films because his style reduces human experience to nothing but a few details. Delimited more and more with each successive film, this style reached its most severe and rigorous form in Bresson's 1961 feature *Le Procès de Jeanne d'Arc*.

To some of Bresson's admirers this film goes too far. For example, at the end of an essay included in *Against Interpretation*—perhaps the best essay on Bresson besides Bazin's—Susan Sontag apologized for *Le Procès* on the grounds that "a conception as ambitious as [Bresson's] cannot help but have its extremism." What a conception as ambitious as Bresson's really cannot help, though, is needing time for us to get used to it. Like all truly original work, Bresson's makes us uncomfortable at first. Ms. Sontag formed her opinion in 1964, when *Le Procès* was still Bresson's most recent film. I wonder whether she would judge it so harshly now that she has lived with it longer. In Bresson's case especially, it seems to me that if you accept the premises of his art, then you cannot balk at its ultimate conclusions. The intention to press this art toward some ultimate conclusion is already implicit in the premise itself. If you yield to the power of *Diary*, then I cannot see how you draw the line short of *Le Procès*. Bresson himself certainly could not have.

Like *Diary*, *Le Procès* begins with the word. In a preface to the film Bresson said, "Joan had no burial, and we do not have any portrait of her. But there remains for us something better than a portrait: her words before the judges of Rouen." *Le Procès*, therefore, sets out from Joan's testimony at her trial much as *Diary* does from the testament of the priest. Like *Diary*, too, *Le Procès* forges its spirituality out of those circumstances in it which seem most inimical to the spirit. It transforms alienation into affirmation and sacrament. It finds the model for its own art in the very way that the church persecuted its heroine.

That way, as Bresson perceived it, was to trivialize her faith. The film's moments of greatest tension are those when the scratching of the clerks' quills is the only sound to be heard and the only movement to be seen. This is how the word becomes an image in this film. The Church's whole attack on Joan resolves itself into this eking out of a trial record against her. Thus does the film show Joan being driven to the stake by the subtlest increments of canon law imaginable. It is a process—due process—that receives its perfect summary image near the film's end when Joan is at last being driven to the stake physically. A foot comes out of the crowd to trip her up, just as her judges have tried to do. But what is more humiliating, the shift she is to be burned in hobbles her feet so that she can take only tiny, mincing steps. They make it appear as if she were rushing to the stake.

Bresson's entire film becomes the condensation of history into minutiae like those mincing footsteps. After Joan has told the judges at the beginning that she feels it her duty to try to escape, her cell door is sometimes left open just a crack, enough to be a provocation but not to let in any real hope. The judges repeatedly spy on Joan through a chink in her cell wall so small she does not realize it is there until a ray of light seeps through it one night. The sheer physical restraint her English jailers keep her under is simply noted in a shot where a heavy ankle chain she wears falls a few inches from a block of wood to her cell floor. Amidst this subtle violence, the only hand raised in her defense, literally, is the hand a young cleric sometimes moves to caution her against a devious question. But even the movement of that hand is only a febrile, fluttering gesture. The tracking of a quill, setting ajar of a door, covert gesturing of a hand, dropping down of a few links of chain—these are the events by which Joan's whole world is defined.

It is perhaps already apparent how the process of reduction extends from the content of the film into its form—how the judges' attempts to wear away Joan's resistance carry with them a wearing away of all that is extraneous in cinematic style. Stripped of the illusion that there are momentous events, human experience becomes only a series of details, and limited to the depiction of such details, the scenes in the film often become a single, elliptical shot. Several scenes in *Le Procès* are only one line long, and two have no lines of dialogue at all. One of them simply fades in on Joan as she cries quietly to herself in her cell, and then fades out. The other shows two men meeting at the top of a stair and exchanging glances before each passes on his way.

In a style as restrictive as this, there is obviously no room for histrionics. Short, uneventful scenes afford scant opportunity for acting anyway, and Bresson's direction reduces the opportunity further. His actors are made to deliver their lines as inexpressively as possible. Even their posture is rigidly determined, all characters walking with arms held down at their sides, backs stiff and torsos immobile. For the same reason that he does not permit acting, Bresson never employs stars. His whole effort is to do away with personality, both the sort an actor creates for a character and the sort a star creates for himself. In order to get at what is universal in human experience, Bresson eliminates everything that is individual or idiosyncratic in his characters.

Gradually in *Le Procès* we realize that what these stylistic restrictions and reductions are leading to is a total negation of Joan herself. Like the country priest, Joan is ultimately to be known to us by her absence. The whole purpose of the subtractive style Bresson evolved after *Diary* is to approach more nearly human spiritualization, and in Joan's martyrdom this style finds its perfect story. Bressonian style combines with historical fact literally to eradicate Joan from existence. The entire film becomes an analogue for that most typical of all Bresson's shots, where the camera lingers on empty space after the character has left the frame.

In this shot, especially as it is used whenever Joan leaves the courtroom in *Le Procès*, we see the character's back receding as the emptiness fills in behind her. But in this film we also have a whole scene that anticipates in the same way, by focusing on Joan's back, the emptiness that will occur in the film's ending. It is a scene following an attempt, permitted the English by the Church, to molest Joan sexually. As the chief trial judge enters her cell, Joan sits with her back to him, and we see her that way too. The anonymity of this view reflects the way the Church has seen her in allowing her to be abused physically. But as always in Bresson, deprivation and depravity become the very occasion for the human spirit to manifest itself. The same anonymity serves the inexpressiveness Bresson always tries to achieve in order to generalize and abstract a character's experience. As Joan sits with her back to the judge, she reviles him for what he has permitted; and when she at last turns to face him, and us, it is to retract dispassionately the confession she made to save herself from the stake.

Various other scenes prepare the way as well for the total voiding of Joan from our sight at the end. At one point, for example, the shift in which she is to be burned is brought in. Held stiff and erect before the camera, it looks, though empty, almost as if it were being filled by some human form that we cannot see, a human form divine, an invisible presence. In the end, when Joan has been burned at the stake, all these images of diminution and negation come together in a final shot of the stake itself. On it the chains that bound Joan now hang limp and empty, Joan herself having been consumed away as completely as those scraps of paper thrown into the stove 10 years earlier in *Diary*.

To see fully the unique achievement of Bresson's film, it might be worthwhile to compare its ending with that of Carl Dreyer's 1928 *The Passion of Joan of Arc*. Joan's story has been so attractive to filmmakers, being done in at least half a dozen versions, that it is practically a genre all its own. But Dreyer's is the only other version that is comparable to Bresson's. Dreyer was after the same spirituality in Joan's martyrdom that Bresson sought, and he worked from the same records of Joan's trial and rehabilitation. It is all the more remarkable, then, that Dreyer's film arrives at an ending almost the opposite in form from Bresson's. Bresson acknowledged Dreyer's film and its influence on him by opening his film with the same tracking shot of feet walking that *The Passion* begins with. But it is apparent almost from that moment on how different Bresson's approach was to be.

Both filmmakers, for example, wished to make us feel the extent to which the court was able to dominate Joan. Dreyer put this across by keeping the angle and position of the camera fixed when it is on Joan, but varying both wildly when the camera is on the judges, so they appear to tower over and surround her. Bresson achieved this disproportion between his antagonists by far more neutral means characteristic of his style. He often showed us a point-of-view shot of Joan through the chink in her cell wall which the judges used to spy on her, and occasionally he did a reverse shot back through the chink from the same distance inside the cell. In the latter shots, the ragged edges of the chink that framed Joan's whole figure a moment ago now framed only the eye of a judge or soldier. We begin to feel that their imprisonment has shrunk Joan's existence until she is like an insect being scrutinized in a bottle.

At the end of Dreyer's film, the gyrations of his camera become extreme. The alternation of high and low angles somersaults into an overhead shot that begins from dead vertical and tilts until the image is upside down. At several other points the camera is placed in a free-swinging harness like a pendulum, and at the moment Joan dies a riot breaks out. In Bresson's film, on the other hand, the ending attempts to approach what Dreyer's film has from the start: silence. This is not in Bresson's film just the silence of no sound, but the fuller silence of religious experience which lies beyond all language. Having worked its way through all the rhetoric of Joan's trial in the dialogue, the film does arrive at near soundlessness now. There has been no music since a drum beat at the beginning, so the only sound to be heard as she is burned is the crackling of the fire, which intensifies momentarily and then also fades away. After that there is only the cooing of a few doves that are, in Dreyer's film, a great swooping flight of birds.

But the silence in Bresson's film is, as it were, visual too. It is a stillness of action as well as of sound. At the moment Joan dies her judges stand fixed in their places, neither moving nor speaking as they watch. The chains hang limp and empty on the stake, and the cross which was held up to Joan as she burned intermittently emerges from and disappears in the swirling smoke. *Diary* ends with the same image of a cross. But the one held up to Joan differs from that to which Bresson cut in *Diary* by being made in an open-work design. That is, the cross itself is formed by an iron frame describing and enclosing empty space. It is an apt image for what *Le Procès* attempts more forcefully than any other work Bresson has done.

Bresson's style is at heart a form of epistemological humility. It approaches its truth by paring away all extrapolation and fancy. In *Le Procès* Bresson was dealing with the inaccessibility of history as well as the human spirit, which is perhaps why his style is even more severe and disciplined here than before. The remoteness Bresson felt from his characters' lives and the indirection with which he approached their feelings do not, however, make his film a mere intellectual exercise. The difference, as Susan Sontag explained it in her essay on Bresson, is that:

there is art that involves, that creates empathy. There is art that detaches, that provokes reflection.

Great reflective art is not frigid. It can exalt the spectator, it can present images that appall, it can make him weep. But its emotional power is mediated. The pull toward emotional involvement is counterbalanced by elements in the work that promote distance, disinterestedness, impartiality. . . .

In the film, the master of the reflective mode is Robert Bresson.

A moment ago I was comparing Bresson to Carl Dreyer, but stylistically a filmmaker to whom he might almost more readily be compared is John Ford. Ford's stationary camera, refusal to use editing in editorializing ways, and economical storytelling are all aspects of a film realism like Bresson's. But the purpose of such techniques in Ford's films is to allow us to identify with history and feel our kinship to the characters on the screen. To watch a Ford film is to belong to a community. It is a socializing experience. A Bresson film is the opposite. Watching it is a process that isolates and, as Sontag said, "detaches" us. Like our own experience of it, the experience we see in it is not communal and shared, but unique and utterly private. It is always to get at some otherness in human experience that Bresson makes a film. In fact, Bresson makes films the way he does—conservatively, by sticking to bare essentials and avoiding all excess—out of respect for such otherness.

Bresson's first color film, *Une Femme Douce* (1969), begins where *Le Procès* ends: with a total negation of the character. The woman to whom the title refers kills herself by jumping off a balcony, and like the death of Joan at the end of *Le Procès*, the woman's death dispossesses her completely from our sight. Someone who witnesses the event looks into the room beyond which the balcony lies. A table on the balcony tips over, toppling a potted flower, and a rocking chair rocks. A white shawl flutters earthward as cars below slam on their brakes. Thus does the woman kill herself without ever being present to us until after she is dead. At the end of the film we see this same sequence again, the events that lead up to her death having been narrated in the meantime by her husband as she is laid out in the bedroom from which she jumped. And in that interim, as in *Le Procès* (whose ending we also know, of course, when the film begins), Bresson prepared the way for the woman to die again at the end. Like Joan, this woman disappears from our view gradually in scene after scene until, at the end, we are ready for her assumption into the void of Bresson's style.

There are a couple of scenes early in the film, for instance, that are erotic. In the first the woman goes into the bathroom on her wedding night and, after running some water there, comes out clad only in a towel to push her husband over playfully on the bed. In the second, he goes into the bathroom on a subsequent night to retrieve a dropped bar of soap while she lounges nude in the tub. What these two scenes then lead to is a third that is a reprise of them both, except that the woman herself is not present this time. This scene occurs after her relationship with her husband has begun to disintegrate, and he has stormed out following a fight with her. When he returns home, he enters the bathroom to find the tub water running but his wife gone; and as he comes out of the bathroom he slumps on the bed from which she is now absent, but in which her sexual presence lingers suggestively because of some underwear discarded there. The garter belt and bra lying on the bed here look back on this woman's consummation of her marriage much as Joan's empty shift looks forward to her consummation, in another sense, at the stake.

For all its similarity to *Le Procès*, though, *Une Femme Douce* has in its ending something entirely different too— something foreign to the art of the earlier film. The toppled flower pot, the shawl floating to earth, and the sounds of automobiles may all come in the absence and aftermath of the woman when she dies. They may stand in her place and be a voiding of her herself from the film. But they are also a coming to fruition of certain imageries that Bresson imposed on her experience. An opposition between organism and mechanism has been elaborated throughout the film in a contrast between the sight of flowers and the sound of automobiles, or the living flight of birds, so like the graceful descent of the woman's shawl, and the machine flight of airplanes. These currents of images are intersected by others that distinguish different kinds of perception, the machine-made perceptions of photographs, phonographs, movies, or television and the man-made perceptions of painting and theater of the immediate perceptions of experience itself.

In part this unaccustomed wealth of imagery may result from Bresson's having been working for the first time in color, which is by nature a more florid medium than black and white and encourages a more ornamental style. More important, no doubt, was the fact that for once Bresson was not giving himself up wholly to his narrator's view. On the contrary, the effect of the film depends largely on our perceiving a discrepancy between events and the husband's view of them. In order to offer a counter view, Bresson had to assert rather than efface himself. Instead of serving as what Keats once called "the chameleon poet," Bresson needed to impose imageries of his own on the husband's story. In the first paragraph of the Dostoyevsky novella on which the film is based, the husband confides to us, "That's the horrible part of it—I understand everything!" But in truth the horrible part is that he understands nothing. Bresson now found himself dealing in a film with a first-person narration that does not redeem, but deceives.

It may even be that Bresson was attracted to Dostoyevsky's story precisely because it offered an opportunity to dissociate his art from the act of suicide. Suicide is of course the ultimate act of self-effacement, self-abnegation, and maybe it is the form of spiritualization for which Bresson's art was always striving. (Certainly there always seemed to be in Bresson's Catholicism a disconcerting undertone that was stoical.) Bresson's next film after *Le Procès* is *Au Hasard Balthazar* (1965). In it, while continuing to eschew symbolism in any conventional sense, Bresson attempted to find in the suffering of a donkey an adequate vessel for the arbitrary and unredeemed suffering of humanity. In the film after that, Mouchette (1966), which is the one before *Une Femme Douce*, such suffering is no longer deflected. It is endured by a 13-year-old girl and drives her to kill herself. This is a death that Bresson seems to have accepted, or perhaps even embraced. Like all the other deaths before it in Bresson's work, this one is unmediated by interpretation and unrelieved by his art. Mouchette is Joan stripped of her holiness and sainthood. It is as if the ineluctable process of reduction in Bresson's style had deprived Joan of all her resources, and then abandoned her to a world so indifferent, so godless, she had to martyr herself.

The line that Susan Sontag drew at *Le Procès* I would draw here, at *Mouchette*. *Une Femme Douce* suggests Bresson also drew the line here. In the greatest art, content proposes form. The two achieve a unity. Bresson's work is unarguably great in this way, yet in *Mouchette* the union of form and content seems to become almost a conspiracy against life itself. In *Une Femme Douce*, Bresson's work retreats from, or else passes beyond, the absolute null point to which his art had brought him. Because the strictures of his style are loosened in *Une Femme Douce*, Bresson's filmmaking becomes, though more conventional perhaps, also more playful and various. Maybe this easing was necessary. The dark night of the soul holds terrors from which one must finally awaken to daylight. If the dark night does have its terrors, however, it also has its beauties that are rarer than anything the light of day can reveal. Whatever films Bresson is yet to make—and they may be very great films indeed—*Le Procès de Jeanne d'Arc* will remain the perfection of his art.

The Ideological Foundations
of the Czech New Wave
by Robin Bates

*This selection is from the Summer 1977
issue of the Journal of the University
Film Association. The author is in the
English Department at Emory University.*

The use by the American Press of the word "miracle" to describe Czechoslovakia's cinematic output during the 1960s
was not simply an instance of empty journalese. It was rather
the predictable response of a culture attracted by but unwill-
ing to come to terms with socialist art. Critics attempting to
account for the Czech New Wave usually singled out three external factors: the nationalization of the film industry in 1945,
which provided the economic base; the establishment of a film
school (FAMU) in 1947, which provided the technical training; and the de-Stalinization policies of the Czech government in the early 1960s, which provided the necessary artistic
freedom. While the New Wave could not have come into being without these developments, such an explanation fails to
account for its vital and unified artistic consciousness. Greater
political freedom does not in itself provide substance for an
aesthetic movement. The impulse behind the New Wave is to
be found instead in the ideological foundations of Czech society.

The same socialism which bears the responsibility for stifling its artists' creative efforts in the 1950s must also be cred-
ited with shaping their artistic vision in the 1960s. From 1962
to 1968 a basic goal of the Czech filmmakers was to liberate
the ideals of socialism from the reified state in which those
ideals had been trapped.

While this vision necessitated social criticism, it did not involve rejection of the socialist system. For the New Wave filmmakers, most of whom were born in the 1930s, socialism was
not an issue but an assumed tenet. As director Miloš Forman
noted in 1967:

Reality has become the main focus of attention, and the ideals
are considered merely a part of that reality. The practical

494

meaning of this is that our films no longer show unreserved but cheap enthusiasm over every success, so characteristic of an earlier era; nor do we condemn every erring sinner to hell and damnation; and we value a sense of humor. I can understand why our attitude is sometimes regretted by those who, in a whole lifetime, have experienced nothing but a struggle for the realization of their ideals. We never saw our fathers struggling. We grew up in a world which they had prepared for us.[1]

Acceptance of the totalistic socialist vision gave the film-makers a concrete idealistic base which American artists do not have (unless the artist can find his value base in capitalism, he must opt for mystical "humanitarian values") and allowed a touch of optimism in even the darkest of their works. It is significant that director Evald Schorm concludes *Every Day Courage* (1964), a film about the betrayal of revolutionary ideals, with Kafka's assertion, "The man who, in the midst of his doubts, perceives a ray of hope, will not say, 'I have lost.'"[2]

De-Stalinization in Czechoslovakia was set in motion by the Twenty-Second CPSU Congress in 1961 and the Twelfth Congress of the Czechoslovak Communist Party in December 1962.[3] Although Czech president Antonín Novotný resisted the trend, the artistic council, responsible for all administrative decisions concerning film, began to adopt a more flexible policy. During the 1950s the council, which consisted of the country's cultural elite until its dissolution in the mid-1960s, had been forced to apply rigid formulae to all production, the result being static films and loss of audience interest. But, although the council realized that a loosening of the controls was a prerequisite for artistic achievement in such an expensive and highly technical medium, it also realized that it would be inviting criticism of the government. Its course of action was one which George Steiner has described with regard to the Soviet Union:

In an intricate cat-and-mouse game . . . the Kremlin allows the creation, and even the diffusion, of literary works whose fundamentally rebellious character it clearly realizes. With the

1. Miloš Forman, "Chill Wind on a New Wave," *Saturday Review,* 23 December 1967, p. 11.

2. Claire Clouzot, "Sons of Kafka," *Sight and Sound* 36 (Winter 1966/67):35–36.

3. The de-Stalinization process is described in Galia Golan's *The Czechoslovak Reform Movement* (Cambridge Univ. Press, 1971), especially pp. 124–126.

passage of generations, such works . . . become national classics. . . . The hounding of individual writers, their incarceration, their banishment, is part of the bargain.[4]

Jiří Trnka, the great puppet filmmaker, essentially describes this relationship in *The Hand*, the story of an artist (a potter) battling against a giant hand which tries to persuade him to sculpt hands instead of flower pots. The artist resists promises and threats, is imprisoned, and finally dies as an indirect result of the harassment. The final scene shows the hand giving him full burial honors.

Harassment of the Czech New Wave involved alteration and rejection of scripts, reprimands and threats, and delay or suppression of films. Despite the harassment, some very controversial films were released. Jan Němec's *Report on the Party and the Guests* (1966), a film about a guest at a banquet who refuses to be happy or to adapt his opinions to those of the host and who eventually leaves, only to be hunted down with dogs, is obviously a parable about "the adoption of a dominant ideology—and about the destruction of those who do not adopt it." [5] As a further red flag to the authoritarian government (although this touch was apparently accidental), the host, who kidnaps his guests and then persuades them that they came of their own free will, is a "carbon copy" of Lenin. President Novotný, who screened many of the New Wave films, is said to have "hit the ceiling, and stayed there throughout the screening." Nevertheless, the film was eventually released after a year's delay, a practice which exiled Czech writer Josef Škvorecký notes, "had become almost customary with the films of the New Wave."

Since 1968, a number of films have been banned and confiscated, but none has been destroyed. The Communists believe that, despite the simplifications of the great revolutions, reality is ultimately complex and art cannot simply be dismissed for its resistance to formula.

This attitude differs considerably from that of the Nazis,

4. "Under Eastern Eyes," *New Yorker*, 11 October 1976, p. 159.

5. Němec's difficulties with the government are described in Josef Škvorecký's *All the Bright Young Men and Women*, trans. Michael Schonberg (Toronto: Peter Martin Associates Lmtd., 1971), pp. 121–61. Škvorecký's mostly anecdotal history is essential to anyone studying the Czech New Wave, and I have relied upon it heavily here.

who gratuitously destroyed works of art, and the capitalist West, which defuses works of art by abstracting them from their social context and ignoring their political implications. Steiner asserts that, in contrast, the whole of Russian consciousness may seem to turn on a poem,[6] and Škvorecký points out that "in Czechoslovakia, films and literature are not just entertainment on different levels of sophistication, nor are they the subject of snobbish conversation, as is all too frequently the case in the West. They play an important part in the lives of wide masses."[7] That Novotný privately screened many productions of the New Wave indicates that he shared Lenin's regard for the art form, and the artistic council, for all its petty haggling, clearly saw art as an effective social and political force. Škvorecký, a scriptwriter who saw many of his scripts rejected or altered, nevertheless admits this atmosphere:

Even the tedious arguments between the directors of the New Wave and Novotný's bureaucracy were in a sense more dignified than the quarrels of the same directors with some of their Western profit-oriented patrons. They argued aesthetico-political approaches, and nobody was terribly concerned about the box-office profit; at most some bureaucrat despaired about the safety of his position.[8]

The struggles were usually over departures from the formulae laid down by the official aesthetic of socialist realism. The filmmakers' rejection of socialist realism, however, should not be interpreted as a rejection of socialism in general. The rejection was artistically necessary because the aesthetic had become a handmaiden of the state rather than of history and had consequently lost all integrity. While maintaining the basic philosophical assumptions of socialist realism, the Czech New Wave sought to couch revolutionary ideals in a new form.

To understand the Czech rejection, we must first examine the aesthetic itself. As Russian critic Semyon Freilikh points out, socialist realism has been misunderstood by the West, which sees it as "Something that exists outside the practice of art, independently of it, . . . and grafted on to the practice

6. "Under Eastern Eyes," p. 159.
7. Škvorecký, pp. 248–49.
8. Ibid., p. 249.

and dictated by orders and decrees."[9] The reaction is understandable coming from a culture which does not accept socialism's totalistic vision, believing it instead to be an arbitrary system imposed on society by dictatorship. The socialist realists, on the other hand, see art as growing organically out of history as the articulation of that history. (Freilikh writes, "art does not illustrate a tendency or an idea; it is a form in which they exist."[10]) Since a perfect communist state has not yet been attained, the age will contain contradictions, and a work of art, insofar as it reflects its age, will embody those contradictions. For instance, Freilikh praises Grigory Chukhrai's 1956 film *Forty-First* for refusing to oversimplify the revolutionary struggle:

> The makers of the film do not deprive Govorukha-Otrok [the negative hero] of culture, bravery and sense of duty. At the same time, we are shown the weakness and certain limitations of Maryutha, who personifies the positive ideal. The director elevates Maryutha as action develops, he does not intend to anticipate history but tries to catch its direction. The world is not schematised in this film, but revealed in its tragic conflict.[11]

The socialist realism aesthetic has certain affinities with André Bazin's belief that film should force reality (by which Bazin means present reality) to "reveal its structural depth, to bring out the pre-existing relations which become constitutive of the drama."[12] In a work of art, therefore, the ultimate reality (pure communism) should clash with the present reality. The artist, sensing the trends in history, juxtaposes appearances with the ultimate reality, exposing the first and giving the second, insofar as he articulates it, a more concrete existence.

The danger that socialist realism encounters, however, is the reification of the state, which counters the revolution, sometimes in the name of consolidating it. The state, as a solid form, becomes divorced from the flux of history. As a result, its own existence becomes a matter of concern, and the tendency of history seen by the artist becomes a threat. The state now sees the function of art as perpetuating the status quo

9. *Socialist Realism in Literature and Art,* trans. C.V. James (USSR, 1971), p. 196.

10. Ibid., p. 201.

11. Ibid., p. 204.

12. André Bazin, *What Is Cinema?*, translated by Hugh Gray (University of California Press, 1967), p. 27.

(which can include a schematised notion of "progress"). It dislikes exploration because exploration can expose the discrepancy between appearance and reality; instead it encourages the artist to adopt its own reified version of reality.

This is in effect what hampered the Czech cinema of the 1950s. As Škvorecký notes:

The real dramas of a truly dramatic period were reduced by the socialist-realists to a crude puppet show. Its characters were squeezed into stereotypes with unchangeable attributes: class-conscious workers, understanding Party officials, wavering small peasants, intellectuals who started out as reactionaries but soon unerringly recognized the truth, villainous kulaks and factory owners—the real incarnations of Satan.[13]

By simply mouthing the official interpretation of reality, the Czech films of this period abdicated their artistic responsibility. If they did not actually bore their audiences, they were still little more than consumable entertainment prompting no introspection.

To revitalize the dynamic elements of socialist realism, the Czech New Wave could either attack its formulae or dispense with it altogether. In fact, although it is difficult to find patterns within so limited a period as five years, it might be possible to argue that the first course of action was necessary to prepare the way for the second. Once the filmmakers could assume that their viewers saw the discrepancies between appearances and reality, they could pursue more subjective visions.

Penelope Gilliatt made the insightful observation after seeing a number of mid-Wave films (Jiří Menzel's *Closely Watched Trains*, 1966; Věra Chytilová's *The Daisies*, 1966; *Every Day Courage*; Zbyněk Brynych's *The Fifth Horseman Is Fear*, 1964) that they "seem to start from the assumption that everyone in the audience notices everything, that everyone is sick to death of public utterance that nibbles round the edges of things as they are, and that there is not a man left in the country who could honestly be deceived. It is a powerful context for filmmaking." [14]

Jan Zalman describes a movement from *cinéma vérité* in the early New Wave to "strong stylization and extreme meta-

13. Škvorecký, p. 34.
14. "Current Cinema," *New Yorker*, 1 July 1967, p. 54.

phorical character" in the late New Wave,[15] and it may be possible to explain this development in light of the demythologizing and bureaucratic rubbish-clearing undertaken by directors like Forman and Schorm. Typical of Forman's art is a scene in a 1967 film, *The Fireman's Ball*, in which a speaker finds himself at a loss for a word and refuses to continue until he thinks of it. The word, it so happens, is "solidarity," the point being that the revolutionary ideals have been abandoned. Less humorous in Schorm's *Every Day Courage* in which an enthusiastic shock-worker of the 1950s becomes a remnant of the past and finally a pathetic figure as he harangues his fellow workers for their bourgeois consumerism and for replacing their old slogans with a new one: "Who doesn't steal from the state, steals from his family."

The movement toward increasing subjectivism has been noted by Andrew Sarris in reviewing Ivan Passer's *Intimate Lighting* (1965):

If Passer's films . . . now seem somewhat richer and mellower than Forman's, it is because Forman remains a miniaturist, a director who reduces his subjects in his lens to the proper scale for satiric inquiry and symbolic evocation. Forman himself remains outside the spectacle so as to function with scrupulously scientific detachment. Passer, by contrast, passes through the lens into the landscape of his characters. The comic confrontations, so grotesquely plotted in Forman's films, taper off in Passer's films into gentle incomprehension, ambiguous smiles, and generous silences.[16]

If Forman analyzes society from without (although this does not do him complete justice) and Passer mingles sympathetic identification with his objectivity, then Němec takes the process one step further. While acknowledging the importance of external reality, he sees it as only a stage:

I believe that a movement striving to achieve the most accurate externals of life . . . is only one of the developmental stages. It will certainly enrich the film language; but I maintain that the trend should be towards stylization. It is necessary for the author to create in a film his own world, which is totally independent of reality as it at that particular moment appears. . . . If I were to aim my films predominantly at an

15. "Question Marks on the New Czechoslovak Cinema," *Film Quarterly* 21 (Winter 1967/68):19–20.

16. "Intimate Lighting," *Film 1969/70*, ed. Joseph Morgenstern and Stefan Kanfer (New York: Simon and Schuster, 1968), pp. 119–120.

external similarity with the world, I would waste a lot of energy and divert the viewer's attention from the crux of the matter with which I am dealing.[17]

Jaromil Jireš, in his post-invasion *And My Love to the Swallows* (1971), fragments time and space to delve beneath the official version of reality. The film is about a female prisoner in a Nazi camp, and Jireš, according to Peter Hanes, "succeeds in making the necessary connections in a film that looks simple but is, in fact, both structurally and technologically complex. It achieves psychological truth through its ability to follow the movements of the heroine's mind—pursuing a story constructed from fragments and continually intertwined with elements of past and future." [18] The film takes a standard socialist realism genre, the resistance film, and gives it a twist: where the socialist realist portrayed Nazism as a political manifestation of the counterrevolution occurring at a specific place and time, Jireš shows it to be also a state of mind threatening individuals and maybe unconsciously existing within them. As Hanes notes, "This kind of subject matter could . . . have given rise to a Socialist propaganda film of the old school, but Jireš avoids the trap, achieving an emotional purity and overall effect that can only be described as one of spiritual intensity." [19]

In another anti-Nazi resistance film, *Closely Watched Trains*, the hero blows up a train carrying munitions, but director Menzel seems more concerned with his growing to manhood than with his political act. The Soviet socialist realists, judging the film by their standard formulae, saw the film as "an insult to the anti-Nazi resistance movement." [20] But Menzel's purpose in having Miloš grow to sexual maturity before engaging in political action is to show, as Jireš shows, that Nazism is in part a state of mind which can only be fought effectively by mature individuals. Therefore, midway in the film, Miloš is dismissed as harmless by his German captors when they see the suicide slashes on his wrists; and Miloš's grandfather, a humorous example of immaturity, tries to hypnotize the invading German tanks to a standstill and is run over for his pains. Despite these excursions into individual

17. Quoted by Škvorecký, p. 120.
18. "Czech Mates," *Films and Filming* 20 (April 1974):54.
19. Ibid., p. 54.
20. Škvorecký, p. 170.

minds, however, the Czech directors never lost sight of the social vision. As Jireš says:

We live in a period when man's intimate experiences are connected with the main currents of world events. Each of us bears within him a piece of the collective human conscience without being able to help it. For the first time in history, the responsibility of the individual has assumed the character of social feeling.[12]

Along with the increasing stylization and subjectivism appeared an increasing emphasis on fantasy. This fantasy is extremely subtle in Passer's *Intimate Lighting*, a seemingly moral tale about a city dweller visiting his friend in the country and the two discovering how they have wasted their lives. But as Claire Clouzot observes, "Passer does not let *Intimate Lighting* fly low for very long in its moralizing world of 'intimacy.' Suddenly he propels it into a new dimension by introducing at unexpected moments something slightly unusual, a little too prolonged or too insistent, just enough to disturb us and make us aware of a palpable crack in the solid wall of ordinary reality." [22]

The fantasy becomes more pronounced in Němec's Kafkaesque nightmare, *Report on the Party and the Guests*, and in Jireš's lyrical exploration of a young girl's mind, *Valerie and her Week of Wonders* (1969). In the work of Ján Kadár and Elmar Klos, meanwhile, one sees a dramatic shift from *Shop on Main Street* (1965), a somewhat sentimental treatment of Slovakian Jews during World War II, to *Adrift* (1969), a stunningly beautiful portrayal of a man's inner struggle in which there are imperceptible shifts between the subjective and objective worlds.

The danger of extreme stylization, of course, is that the work of art can lose all contact with the world and become empty illusion. Extreme subjectivism, meanwhile, can become self-indulgent and may slip into solipsism. (These dangers, more than a fear of hidden criticism, are the reason that socialist authorities distrust works they cannot understand.)

21. Andrew Sarris, "Movers," *Saturday Review*, 23 December 1967, p. 38.
22. *Film Quarterly* 20 (Spring 1967):40. *Loneliness of the Long Distance Runner* uses a similar strategy. In the car theft, for instance, the camera is speeded up, giving the incident a silent film look and recalling the joyful rebellion of the silent comedians.

Both trends have appeared in Hollywood in recent years, the first in its empty parodies of its own now-empty genres (*Murder by Death*, the Mel Brooks films), the second in the emergence of the ideologically isolated hero whose social pessimism makes all commitment absurd. With regard to the latter trend, the total relativism of all ideologies often culminates either in a fatalistic aimlessness (*The Graduate* and its successors) or in the animal instinct for survival, with its corresponding value system (the Charles Bronson movies).

It is instructive to examine the kind of changes that occur when a Czech makes a film in America. In *One Flew Over the Cuckoo's Nest*, with its metaphor of society as insane asylum, Forman turns Nurse Ratched into an almost allegorical figure embodying all the evils of the institution. To do otherwise, to suggest that she too is a victim of the system, would tarnish McMurphy's rebellion because he would appear to be insensitive to her humanity. Compromise is not possible if the heroic act is to have any validity because, lacking any specific ideology, McMurphy derives his entire identity from his resistance to the system. Because the system defines the rebellion, that rebellion paradoxically confirms rather than refutes the system. Forman tries to give a positive meaning to McMurphy's sacrifice by showing its impact on Chief (and by extension on the movie viewer); but McMurphy's exact accomplishment can only be described in mystical terms. What, after all, is Chief going to do? take American back to its roots (whatever that means)? establish an alternative society in the wilderness (which solves none of society's problems)? reject outer reality for inner fulfillment (also escapist)?

Contrast the ending of *Cuckoo's Nest* with that of *Fireman's Ball* in which a fireman, a petty bureaucratic functionary, shares a bed with a victim of a fire and of society's insensitivity. This symbol of their common humanity, despite their differences, expresses an ultimate faith in the communist ideal of community. Forman's socialist vision gives him a concrete idealism in his Czech film which is lacking in his American film. Škvorecký notes that the directors of the Czech New Wave, while not Party members (the Communist Party in Czechoslovakia being stagnant), nevertheless were all socialists.[23] And it is not surprising that there is not the same em-

23. Škvorecký, p. 63.

phasis on revolt in Czech film that there is in American. It is almost impossible to imagine the early Forman (or even late Forman), who describes himself fascinated by the child-parent relationship, producing a film like *Joe* or *Wild in the Streets*. Forman contends that "what is interesting and true in a personal relationship . . . is not the head-on collision of people who cannot communicate and totally misunderstand each other but the little conflicts of people who basically understand each other very well, who like or even love each other, but nevertheless go on acting according to their own different ideas of what is best for everybody." [24] He departs slightly from this view in his American film *Taking Off* (1970), in which there is genuine misunderstanding between two middle class parents and their counter-culture daughter. But in the final scene of *Loves of a Blonde* (1965), Forman crowds a piano player into a bed with his parents and has them discuss what they should do about his girl friend, who has been led to believe that their relationship is more serious than it actually is and has unexpectedly shown up. For the Czech New Wave, one is tempted to say, disagreement can take place in the same bed.

Individuals are generally treated sympathetically in a cinema which seeks communality despite difference. (Even the collaborators in *Closely Watched Trains*, while satirized, are not treated harshly.) What has been said of Forman applies to many members of the New Wave: "Forman believes, not sentimentally but as an observable truth, in the general goodness of human beings." [25]

Since hard times and false doctrines (such as fascism) may corrupt people, the Czech filmmakers concentrated on people themselves rather than the circumstances which separate them. This may explain popularity in Czechoslovakia of the sketch form (in literature as well as in film) which finds a unity underlying diverse elements.

In Němec's *Martyrs of Love* (1967), three dissimilar sketches are subtly united, according to Škvorecký, by the common theme of shy lovers.[26] In *Something Different* (1963),

24. Arkadin (*pseud.*), "Film Clips," *Sight and Sound* 35 (Winter 1965/66):46.
25. Ibid., p. 46.
26. Škvorecký, p. 129.

meanwhile, Chytilová treats in parallel the lives of two women: an Olympic gymnast who sacrifices everything including her family for a gold medal, and a housewife whose sacrifices for her family are taken for granted by her husband. The women never meet, but their lives, which seem so different, are fundamentally similar in that both women seek to abstract something from life and do not try to live it as a totality.

But perhaps the film which best captures the spirit of the New Wave is *Little Pearls from the Bottom* (1965). Six directors, Menzel, Němec, Schorm, Chytilová, Passer, and Jireš, shot six sketches by Czech writer Bohumel Hrabal, with each being careful not to watch what the others were doing. According to Jireš, "We take the risk of disparity rather than impose a predetermined unity which would lead to compromise." Clouzot comments, "He did not need to worry, for the unity summed up in *Little Pearls* has probably no equivalent elsewhere." [27] The unified vision of the Czech New Wave was one of the main reasons for its success. Film production, which Bergman has compared to medieval cathedral building, is the result of a communal effort, and a truly unified work can best be obtained when all individuals involved share the same vision.

In Czechoslovakia in the 1960s, the de-Stalinization process activated examination of the revolutionary ideals inherent in the socialist society and prompted attempts to revitalize those ideals. The result was the Czech "miracle." The totalistic vision of the films and their concretely based optimism is what made them so attractive to the relativistic and cynical West. With the tightening of governmental controls, unfortunately, few genuine explorations are still being made, or at least released, and the current trends appear to be toward consumable entertainment. [28]

27. "Sons of Kafka," p. 35.
28. Derek Elley sees Czech films becoming Disney-like in "Ripples from a Dying Wave," *Films and Filming* 20 (July 1974):32–36.

Luis Buñuel: An Integral Vision of Reality

by Randall Conrad

Randall Conrad is a filmmaker in Boston and a contributing editor of Cineaste and Film Quarterly. This chapter, abridged and revised by the author, appeared originally in Cineaste, VII,4,1977 under the title "A Magnificent and Dangerous Weapon."

Two of Luis Buñuel's films are explicitly about a crisis of class allegiance in urban working-class individuals (*The Brute* [1953] and *Illusion Travels by Streetcar* [1954]—minor works in Buñuel's opinion, it is true), and the director's work as a whole is imbued with a strong polemic coming specifically from the left. At the same time, a "correct" reading of the class struggle is perfectly tangential to Buñuel's representation of reality. If Buñuel is interested in labor and artifact, he sees them chiefly as signs of the repressed and sublimated drives he finds at the origin of civilization. Explosions, erection of buildings, and digging the earth for treasure are important as collective projections of the sexual impulse. Civilization viewed as the product of instinct has no more manifest purpose than the idealess societies of ants and termites, Buñuel implies. The dam site workers in *This Strange Passion* (1953) are filmed as tiny figures moving in organized teams, mastering the terrain through an efficient division of labor.

Undermining this efficiency, however, are counterproductive instincts as well as progressive ideals. Humans on the one hand evolve ethical schemes, rationalizing and improving their societies; on the other hand they can scarcely contain antisocial impulses which threaten to undo the work of civilization. Rebellion, the revolutionary motive in Buñuel, belongs sometimes to the first category, sometimes to a superimposition of both. Buñuel apportions the ideals to his bourgeois professionals and the destructive impulses to his bourgeois madmen. In *This Strange Passion*, the first category is typified by Francisco's rival in love, a reasonable engineer. The second is embodied in the insane Francisco himself, who looks down at the crowd from his tower (a perspective upon the insect colony) and cries, "Worms I could crush in an instant!" Even an irrational reaction is socially conditioned, and Buñuel ironically identifies Francisco's position as the expression of a

506

class ideology (the bourgeoisie having usurped the nobility). "Egotism," Francisco explains after his outburst, "is the essence of a noble soul."

It is Buñuel's goal to achieve a perfectly ambivalent representation of human reality. Unreason and reason, the private world of the individual and the public world furnished by society, inner and outer realities, psychology and politics, cease to be the polarities they are in normal usage. "An integral vision of reality" (as Buñuel once called it) is the intent behind not only the director's masterpieces but also the humblest studio pictures of his commercial career.

For example, what animates the class conflict in *The Brute* is Buñuel's implied parallel between Pedro's dawning class consciousness and his archetypal progression from brutality to humanity by means of his discovery of love and tenderness. With this parallel, Buñuel is able to say two things at once. First, the capitalist form of society is not civilization at all, but a brutal state preceding it; it is Pedro's awakening sense of class responsibility that promises civilization. Second, however, Buñuel implies through the archetypal theme of father-killing that Pedro's violence, while potentially revolutionary, inescapably revives the Oedipal murder. (*The Brute* further contains this crucial paradox: remorse of conscience, the Christian use of guilt feelings, is both the source of Pedro's capacity for love and the reason for Pedro's undoing at the hands of a society that denies love.) Revolution itself, without necessarily losing its positive value, is thus assimilated to the irrational rebellion which, for Buñuel, underlies civilization permanently and generates its conflicts.

Similarly, Buñuel is exploring two things at the same time in *Robinson Crusoe* (1954). On the one hand, Friday stands for taboos which Crusoe must overcome anew in re-establishing civilization. At the same time Buñuel is out to expose the racism with which Crusoe's imperialist civilization arbitrarily asserts its superiority over that of Friday. The character of Friday must thus do double duty, symbolizing both a primitive life which must be domesticated anyhow *and* a civilization which just happens to be alien to the white man and so reveals Crusoe's unconscious norms.

If Buñuel's irony in *Robinson Crusoe* is not always adequate to the task of superimposing these two perspectives perfectly, it only proves the difficulty of Buñuel's ambition. The archetypal and the political views are not immediately reconcilable even if they somehow ought to be; quite the contrary, they represent opposing doctrines (bourgeois determinism versus revolutionary optimism) in the usual controversies over art and ideology.

From the beginning of his commercial career nevertheless —when he was making a comeback from obscurity with *The Young and the Damned* (1950)—Buñuel set himself the goal of achieving this contradictory synthesis. Rereading *Cahiers du cinéma* at the time of this film's French premiere, one is unexpectedly struck by the urgent, polemical spirit in which Buñuel's supporters readied a defense against political objections to it. The anticipated controversy seems to have materialized only as far as the following conversation, however:

When Luis came to the opening of his film in Paris in the spring of 1951, I personally had disliked *The Young and the Damned*. For the wrong reasons (in which I had an iron belief). I told myself: this is a pessimistic film, people will be disgusted with their own humanity, they'll see atomic annihilation as a blessing. I was so deeply persuaded of this that I couldn't conceal it from my very dear friend. Embarrassed and sad, I resolved to tell him shortly before he left Paris. He replied that I was wrong, that one must show life in all its facets, and that the atrocious poverty of children in Latin America is one of those aspects. And he said if I was right, if it could be proved to him, he'd cut off his—what separates a bull from an ox.

The writer is George Sadoul, Buñuel's ex-surrealist friend whose film criticism reflects the line (later the revisionism) of the French communists. Sadoul adds that he later changed his mind. One would conclude that Buñuel got the better of the exchange. Actually Buñuel was cautiously missing the point; his communist friend, I think, was objecting not to the showing of poverty but to the perverse psychological determinism and the lack of positive solutions in *The Young and the Damned*. The poor are amoral and vicious, and every character is motivated by destructive forces as inescapable as destiny in ancient tragedy. In this ultimate realism (perhaps the true test of our compassion, since for Buñuel the children are to be cherished in all their cruelty and violence, not just partially), or is it pessimism as Sadoul means it, a capitulation to bourgeois defeatism?

508

Although Buñuel rejected positive realism, he was not unmoved by political criticism like Sadoul's. *Men Call It Dawn* (1955) expresses the drama of class consciousness through the dilemma of a petty bourgeois character obliged to decide between a life of compromise and a moral stand which in this case is not strictly political but entails a shift of class sympathy nevertheless. In spite of some deliberate complications the class spectrum in this film is a simple one; the oppressed are sympathetic and the oppressors are not; it is Buñuel's nearest approach to an optimist rhetoric and it stands at the opposite pole from *The Young and the Damned,* in which the unredeemable rebel Jaibo has no civilized qualities and never acquires any.

Here and there in Buñuel's work one finds a pair of pendants, as if it was easier to tell the same story twice over— once in the archetypal vein and once in the political—rather than superimposing the two perspectives. Two humorous entertainments by Buñuel, *Mexican Bus Ride* (1952) and *Illusion Travels by Streetcar,* are identical cousins in this way. Bus and streetcar symbolize social routine and at the same time the possibility of escaping it; both stories are predicated on the idea that the hero's courtship must be interrupted by his initiation into certain mysteries of life before it can be consummated. In *Mexican Bus Ride,* however, the archetypal mysteries are largely moral (at the end the innocent hero has experienced the gamut of life's injustices and learned that conventions are relative; society being what it is, he may practice deceit if it is to accomplish good); in *Illusion Travels by Streetcar,* the adventures add up to a demystifying knowledge of the political realities of the class-divided, capitalist society which stands in the way of utopian togetherness.

Buñuel is intrigued by idealists who stubbornly believe they have the explanation, if not the solution, for human suffering. The innocent practitioners of Christ's charity in *Nazarin* (1959), *Viridiana* (1961), and *Simon of the Desert* (1965) unwittingly sow violence in their own path. In *Viridiana* the religious illusion is confronted by a modern society characterized by a division into antagonistic classes. The balance of power, moreover, shifts from the landowner to the bourgeois; certainly a political interpretation is indicated. Viridiana's failure, rape, and capitulation could symbolize the role of religion in abetting Spanish politics. One can detect an echo of the Civil War and its resolution beginning with the Last Supper scene: the anarchistic beggars enjoy their moment of freedom before they are dispersed by the new householder and the police. Nevertheless, *Viridiana's* archetypes are psychological as well. One can view the violent, motley bunch of beggars as a symbol of the psyche in its contorted effort to free itself from the demands of conformity. While the forces of the libido (symbolized by the sightless "traitor" and the lusty "leper") lash out with exhilarating fury, the superego (a little old sage) is too drunk to keep order and receives a custard pie in the face. Buñuel's critique, though it affects religion and politics and reflects a general schema of psychology, nevertheless remains internal to the drama itself, which associates Viridiana's unnaturally prolonged innocence and its consequences with the search for her own repressed humanity.

As with *Viridiana*, the initial episode of the pilgrimage in *Nazarin* appears to confront Nazarin's Christian values with those of organized capitalist society. Nazarin offers to work on a rail crew for food, unaware that he is taking leverage away from laborers who need a job that pays money. His brief presence on the crew precipitates murderous violence between the angered workers and their gun-toting boss. But we never see the outcome of the brawl; we only hear a shot as Nazarin proceeds toward some new tribulation. What this beginning scene has illustrated is actually Nazarin's inconsequence. Although it gives some political cast to the rest of the story— enough to identify the critique as coming from the left—Nazarin's test will not take place on political grounds. The rest of the story takes place in a virtually timeless landscape of misery, with no further allusion to the specific social relations of capitalism as symbolized by the work crew.

For in *Nazarin* Buñuel criticizes idealism from within. He gives his hero every break. Acting to relieve injustice and suffering, Nazarin always does the right thing from the viewpoint of common sense as well as that of Christian love. Yet he cannot budge the real world's reactionary inertia, and finally he has added to superstition and discord in the very act of combatting them.

If *Nazarin* depicts the impossibility of Christian practice,

The Milky Way (1969) dramatizes impossible Christian theory itself—the doctrine which the church has elaborated and which rests upon irrational, irreconcilable mysteries. Buñuel obtains paradoxes by taking literally all efforts to *explain* the mysteries, which historically have resulted in a succession of heretical dogmas. The humor of *The Milky Way* thus arises from taking logic from an absurd premise to absurd extremes, and from giving unexpected concreteness to objects of veneration. "But Christ could laugh, sweat and cough, couldn't he?" asks a character. "They always picture him walking so solemnly with his hands in the air. But he must have walked like everybody else." Cut to Jesus in person, late for the feast at Cana and running to catch up with his disciples. "What time is it?" he asks breathlessly.

What emerges vividly from Buñuel's picaresque representation of Christian belief is the spectacle of humanity at war with its own contradictory nature and with its mortality; what the Christians constantly deny (in an astounding variety of ways) is the body and its obedience to nature, life and desire—and to death. Not only does a Jansenist order herself to be crucified ("My daughter, Jesus does not require this much of you"), but (in a different period of history) even those who gather to enjoy the pleasures of the flesh in a moonlit grove assert before God that by thus humiliating their contemptible bodies they are liberating the soul by degrees.

Christian history brings no progress or liberation; Buñuel represents it as a process of revolt and repression, each endlessly renewed in the constant fear of death. Symbolic of this process is a medieval exhumation: a bishop in splendid regalia looks upon the rotten earthly remains of his predecessor, denounces the insensate skeleton as a dangerous heretic, and then orders the capture of two heckling heretics—who for their part radiate the confidence and energy of young revolutionaries as they scandalize the auto-da-fé by shouting *their* slogans (about the unity of the Trinity). The lack of true history is most obviously represented in *The Milky Way* by the absence of chronology; the episodes occur in no chronological order (and in no one form: some are discussions in the present about the past, some are actions taking place in centuries past, one or two are flashes of fantasy). Most (but not all) of the episodes are witnessed by a pair of tramps who take no particular interest in the miraculous goings-on around them, and who are, along with Jesus and perhaps Sade (notwithstanding their being despised by the police and prosperous classes throughout their voyage), the only free characters in *The Milky Way*, because they are free from Christian conditioning. (Freedom is understood idealistically: standing outside a closed history.)

The seminal film of Buñuel's late period is *Diary of a Chambermaid* (1964). Celestine, rightly suspecting that Joseph is the man who raped and killed a little girl, compromises her own integrity voluntarily in attempting to bring him to justice in a devious way of her own. Ironically her false evidence does not hold up in court, and Joseph is free to prosper as a shady café owner aggressively boosting the rising fascist movement.

Knowing Joseph is guilty, we gladly see him arrested; we overlook Celestine's immorality since it serves a greater justice. But Joseph is freed by a judical system which is biased anyhow. Celestine's effort to nudge the wheels of justice is doomed to fail, Buñuel suggests, because individual morality is powerless against the organized immorality of the state; on the contrary, morality is contaminated and reversed by the social order. Buñuel draws no tight connection between Celestine's private drama and the political developments; in a sense, the disproportion between the private and public dramas is his theme as much as the relationship between the two.

Perhaps *Diary of a Chambermaid* best represents the political cinema Buñuel has sought. The parallel resolutions in Buñuel's dovetail ending abruptly force the individual drama outward into politics. The film can be taken as a perfectly class conscious demonstration of the proposition that individual freedom is a bourgeois illusion and worse, an illusion that conceals and perpetuates oppression.

It can just as readily be taken as bourgeois pessimism, the representation of a closed universe. Not only because fascism encounters no effective opponents as it flexes its muscle, or because Celestine's individual effort (moral or immoral) has come to naught—but because there is an unconscious kinship, a smoldering love, between Celestine and her antagonist which Buñuel suggests amounts to a complicity. "You and I are alike in our souls," Joseph tells Celestine. In manipulating justice, Celestine is exorcising (finally, failing to exorcise) a dark side of herself she cannot face.

Buñuel forces the political dimension upon the story in a similar way in *Tristana* (1970). Although the entire film is taken up with the relationship between Lope and Tristana, in one quick scene a small demonstration of workers is charged by mounted police and chased past Lope's house. This mysterious flash—ironically, the sole witness is a deaf and mute boy who cannot utter what he has seen—forces us into some realization of the wider social context without especially opening up the isolated world in which Tristana and Lope live out their private conflict.

In contrast to the political ambivalence of *Diary of a Chambermaid*, Buñuel charges *The Discreet Charm of the Bourgeoisie* (1972) with an accessible polemic from the left. (In spite of the sinister-sounding content, however, the weapon of choice is humor.) The chief character is an ambassador from a Latin American "republic" who smuggles heroin. Politically-pointed barbs season the polite cocktail conversations. At one gathering, the guests discuss the war in Vietnam with surreal logic: "If the Americans bomb their own troops, they must have their reasons." At another, they pester the ambassador with sly questions about his country's extraordinary homicide rate, its repression of leftist students ("like swatting flies"), etc. Death and torture are normal not only in the police stations but also in quiet bourgeois streets and restaurants.

At the same time, both the partying and the torturing in *The Discreet Charm of the Bourgeoisie* prove to be the fantasy of one character or another. Finally the narrative consists of dreams within dreams. Buñuel's integral vision of bourgeois society—with its warfare on the one hand and its fixation on the poetry of the inner life on the other—is summarized in one long shot: the bourgeois are seated at one of their perpetual dinner parties, with a colonel and his entire battalion installed as guests at side tables; everyone listens appreciatively to a dream (about death) told by one of the enlisted men.

The ambassador gets away with murder in seeming immunity until finally he is arrested in a surprise raid by a dutiful police inspector and his efficient men. However, no sooner are the ambassador and his friends languishing behind bars than the unfortunate inspector receives orders from high places (a call from the minister of the interior) to let them go immediately. Buñuel's polemic against the charade of bourgeois justice is plain; this is the same archetype as when Joseph is freed though guilty in *Diary of a Chambermaid*.

At the same time (and without detracting from the political content) the archetype also refers to a psychology of repression and conflict. The corrupt ambassador stands for a component of the psyche which pursues pleasure aggressively but cunningly (diplomatically). The police curb the pleasure-seeking instincts through guilt, in the name of conscience. However, conscience (the minister of the interior) is unreliable; in reality it does not wish to suppress the quest for pleasure, and so the minister hypocritically authorizes the diplomats to remain at large, thus prolonging the conflict indefinitely.

Even a conservative psychological determinism is conceivable, given the relations Buñuel establishes among sexual frustration, sadism, and political reaction in this film. Perhaps the conflicts in society are entirely secondary to those of the psyche, which they simply mirror. However, Buñuel subjects even this pessimism to political caricature, when the ambassador permits himself the luxury of intellectual disputation —"Mao didn't understand Freud"—with the woman he will shortly cause to be done away with (since she failed to kill him first).

In making shaggy dog stories of the violence and obsession with death which underlie the charm of the bourgeoisie, Buñuel caricatures the ruling class's collective dread of its own eventual violent end, inviting a political interpretation above all even if a psychological interpretation is also appropriate. *The Phantom of Liberty* (1974) on the other hand treats violence and obsession with death as something fundamental—society's paradoxical reason for existing. The class aspect of contemporary society is identified but not emphasized.

Each scene is originally some commonplace of melodrama, some aspect of bourgeois society's sentimental image of itself. But some discordant element enters the picture, makes nonsense of the conventional content, and discloses the archetypal meaning of the common place, which always has to do with the latent fear of death. For example, a mass murderer is brought to justice and sentenced to die, then is uncuffed, congratulated, and freed from custody on the spot. The archetype and its ambivalent meanings are familiar. The craving for instant justice which we conventionally project into a courtroom melodrama—and which Buñuel thwarts—is no doubt a collective form of our private wish to arrest death's inexorable progress. Finally, all of civilization in *The Phantom of Liberty* appears as no more than a frantic concerted effort to deny death, which appears—unexpected and disturbing—in everything.

Deceptively, *The Phantom of Liberty* begins with historical episodes—first the execution of Spaniards by Napoleon's occupying militia (an actual incident in 1808), then a French captain's desecration of Queen Elvira's tomb. The whole edifice of history crumbles to the ground, however, as Buñuel cuts unexpectedly to present-day France, where the remainder of the film takes place. A nursemaid in Paris has been reading the foregoing episodes from a book, none to comprehensibly at that. History vanishes like a disturbing dream in daylight. The murky tale of death and lust presides obscurely over the whole film—a complex of archetypes, not an interpreted reality (not least is the archetypal contrast which Buñuel later elaborates in *That Obscure Object of Desire:* France the superego, a conquering civilization, a false freedom; Spain a dark irrational underworld where the sexual instinct and death instinct engage in conflicts). A Marxist might interpret this as meaning that bourgeois society does not produce real history, only necrophiliac fables for the nursemaids of the bourgeoisie. Yet the historical incident itself is deprived of transcendence. The Spanish partisans' perverse cry of *Vivan las cadenas* ("Long live chains," or "Down with freedom") before they are shot leaves no room for a positive form of freedom. The only form in which we glimpse the phantom of freedom is death, as it flits among the unconnected lives in Buñuel's film.

Beneath the surface of his dramas Buñuel allows us to watch the unspoken dynamics that really move things. We feel—and it is an important clue to the exact nature of Buñuel's pessimism—that the characters *must* play out their

515

destructive games before we can grasp the possibility of genuine relationships. This is particularly true in the films in which castaways must reinvent the social contract or else perish: *Robinson Crusoe, The River and Death* (1954), *Death in This Garden* (1956), *The Young One* (1960). The obligatory process is "demonstrated" in *The Exterminating Angel* (1962), which contains a variation on the theme of the imprisonment of the criminal bourgeoisie. Inexplicably free from their incarceration, the characters find themselves trapped all over again, in their church; the implication is that to be free in the end they would have to kill God, no less. (The political correlative is given by a corresponding expansion of the outside context. The police cordon in earlier scenes, which quite normally keeps curiosity-seekers at a distance from the place of imprisonment, has escalated in the final sequence into officers on horseback firing into a screaming crowd in a public square, a metaphor for fascism.)

Then again, genuine relationships may never be *more* than a possibility in the closed worlds of most Buñuel films. The family in particular represents in the inescapable opposite of freedom for Buñuel. In *Tristana* the quasi-incestuous wedlock which Lope creates for his personal convenience is a false sexual freedom that oppresses Tristana and finally Lope too. Lope is both guardian and jealous lover; Buñuel superimposes the protective and the possessive, the parental and the marital relation together as a single domination (and a defiance of taboo). This travesty of a family is Buñuel's symbol for the false consciousness which confines both Tristana and Lope (who calls himself a socialist, yet despises work and equality) in oppressive sexual and class relations while allowing them to believe they are free individuals.

In *That Obscure Object of Desire* (1977), Buñuel also represents a sexual partnership that is sadomasochistic beneath its guise of free play. The oppressor Mathieu becomes the victim; the pursuer becomes haunted, possessed by the "object" Conchita, who now dominates him. Mathieu has a friend, a magistrate. The judge may be powerless against terrorists (who perpetrate violence freely throughout the film) but he unfairly uses his influence to expel the innocent Conchita from France as a favor to Mathieu, who hopes thus to be relieved of his tormenting passion. (Mathieu's attempt to banish desire from his conscious life does not work, naturally.) The magistrate's role is one symbol of the interrelation of crime and respectability. The young robbers, for instance, are scrupulous in their fashion (they don't want Mathieu's whole wallet, just a specified amount); they may even be victims in turn, unless it's an excuse ("we were on tour but our agent left with the money").

The terrorists themselves are primarily the correlative of Mathieu's erotic obsession—mysterious, explosive, and threatening to Mathieu himself. At the end of this film nevertheless—and in the midst of its most enclosed, subjective, "psychological" sequence (the apparition of the lacemaker in a display window of an arcade)—Buñuel constructs a political polemic using the terrorism theme. A broadcast announces new violence wrought by a band of "extreme leftist" groups, followed by the formation of a counteralliance on the extreme right. Meanwhile (the broadcast specifies) the Curia Romana and the Communist Party have each denounced the attacks, which have paralyzed a prelate. Buñuel thus represents the whole of "Western civilization" mobilizing for a wave of destruction; jointly with the governing body of the church, the ex-party of revolution symbolizes the establishment now. The whole—establishment and guerrillas together—forecasts some nascent global totalitarianism, and in this regard the film's ending is comparable to that of *Diary of a Chambermaid* with the political terms modernized. At least as much as in that film, the essential theme of *That Obscure Object of Desire* (in spite of the *correlation* between Mathieu's desire and the terrorism) is the irreducible *separateness* of the private world and the public world, which is merely the incidental field through which the prisoners of desire wander distractedly.

Society in Buñuel's films has dispatched its criminal in two very different ways. The rebel Jaibo and the "brute" Pedro are shot down in the street by police (so is Severine's criminal lover in *Belle de Jour* [1967]). They threaten bourgeois order, which protects itself murderously. In recent films, however, far fewer human killers are captured, judged, and then set free.

One can argue that Buñuel is erasing the old lines of battle and redefining the political enemy in our own time. Society today tolerates and even condones the killer-poet, the ambassador-smuggler, or Joseph the fascist childkiller. Still, the ambivalence in the recent films belongs as much to psychology as to politics, perhaps more so. On this level, victory belongs neither to the superego (as with the death of Jaibo or Pedro) nor to the rebels (Buñuel's surrealist films *An Andalusian Dog* [1928] and *The Golden Age* [1930] are not considered in this article). Rebellion is a permanent convulsion animating the whole.

With its unusual effort to treat political and psychological realities as an indissoluble unity, Buñuel's work consciously reflects the struggle between idealism and materialism that has characterized its era. Hence the paradoxes which keep Buñuel's art alive and make it politically provocative, not least to the left it presumably serves. Buñuel rejected the label "pessimist" at the time of *The Young and the Damned* yet volunteered it at the time of *The Discreet Charm of the Bourgeoisie:* "I'm pessimistic; but I hope to be a good pessimist. In any society, the artist has a responsibility." Ultimately for this good pessimist, society is founded on a basis so conflicted that its essential injustice cannot perhaps be eradicated; yet it is nothing other than the constant effort to eradicate it which defines humanity.

Merchant of Four Seasons:

Structures of Alienation

by Barbara Leaming

This selection appeared originally in Jump Cut, #10/11, 1977.

Rainer Werner Fassbinder is certainly the most prolific, and perhaps the most significant, filmmaker to emerge from that diverse group now known as "The Young German Cinama." Fassbinder's films are the product of the second wave of directors working in West Germany, a group whose cinema is bringing to fruition some of the aspirations expressed by the original signers of the now famous 1962 Oberhausen Manifesto. This manifesto proclaimed the death of the already moribund postwar German film and called for the birth of a new state-subsidized, nonprofit-dominated cinema. It eventually animated a striking western experiment in the possibilities for a cinema largely freed from the ruthless demands of the market. State subsidies were set up according to a system in which a portion of any profits were then appropriated for new productions. Today, the original law has been severely modified with the addition of a proviso requiring that a filmmaker, to qualify for a subsidy, must present a previous film which has earned a certain percentage of profit. This proviso, of course, has the effect of curbing the more extreme filmic experiments. And, together with other revisions of the terms of the state subsidies, this proviso has largely undermined the most positive aspects of the original plan. However, during the years when the subsidized cinema was operating effectively, the West German cinema was regenerated and the new filmmakers became firmly enough established that, now, the West German cinema is among the most interesting in Europe.

At the age of thirty, Fassbinder is one of a widely diversified range of directors who developed within this context. With a startling number of feature films already to his credit, Fassbinder has continued at the same time to work in the theater. Very often he moves back and forth between the two media with a single work and identical cast. The results of this astonishing productivity have been remarkably and consistently significant.

In a filmic oeuvre as diverse and complex as that of Fassbinder's, it is difficult to select a single film as representative. One might look closely at the reflexivity of his supremely elegant *Beware the Holy Whore*—a film which explores the semantic limits of the use of camera movement; or one could deconstruct the apparently seamless "objectivity" of his *Fear Eats the Soul*—a film which in fact is perhaps one of Fassbinder's most highly stylized works to date.

Yet, if one chooses to look closely at a single film of Fassbinder's his 1971 *Merchant of Four Seasons* seems particularly characteristic of the director's concerns thus far in a still emerging career. *Merchant of Four Seasons* stands as a remarkable articulation of the structures of alienation. Rife with structures of disjuncture, the coherence of their articulation enables Fassbinder's film to function as a reflection of the alienated subjectivity of the central character, Hans the fruit peddler.

Hans's story is quite simple: he is excessively mediocre, rather short, fat and quite unattractive. Through the use of flashbacks, we see that his life has been a series of confrontations with pressures imposed on him by various women, each of whom seems to be either taller, more beautiful, or more powerful than Hans. The women in turn see Hans as an embarrassment of one sort of another. His marriage—to the much taller Irmgaard—is a complex of mutually inflicted injuries. After a particularly savage drunken assault by Hans, Irmgaard takes the couple's young daughter and flees to her in-laws, thus precipitating the central actions of the film. Hans pursues her there, only to have the heart attack which necessitates his metamorphosis into an employer and, ultimately, his retreat, first into silence, and finally, into death. After his heart attack, unable to continue his heavy work of pushing a fruit cart himself, Hans is forced to hire a man to do the work for him. Prior to this metamorphosis into employer, Hans's alienation has been largely felt as a purely philosophical or psychological condition; after his transformation into one who purchases the labor of another, Hans's alienation becomes a felt political and social condition.

Unknown to Hans, his first employee has had a brief

and abortive sexual encounter with Irmgaard. Humiliated and dehumanized, Irmgaard instigates a scheme whereby the man will cheat Hans out of a share of his profits and share them with her. Actually, she is acting in revenge, for she is aware that Hans is covertly observing each of the hawker's transactions. The man is quickly discovered and fired.

A chance meeting with an old pal from his days in the Foreign Legion, results in Hans's hiring of Harry, his second helper. Harry works so well that he gradually subsumes Hans's role at home as well, as Hans sinks deeper and deeper into a silent retreat. As the film ends, Hans has killed himself with whiskey (forbidden after his heart attack)—while his wife and friends, passive and isolated by their alienation, watch him without stirring. Irmgaard then begins the whole cycle anew by proposing to—and being accepted by—Harry.

In its inability to make cause and effect connections, Hans's consciousness may be read as an illustration of alienation. Like the worker on the assembly line who cannot see beyond the part to the whole, Hans is unable to perceive the connection between the small bit of control he exercises directly and the finished product, which is no longer comprehensible —either psychologically or in actual fact—as the product of *his* labor. Thus Hans perceives his life as a series of discrete and disconnected events. Unable to perceive any cause and effect relationships, he is thus unable to assert the possibility of control over his own life. Hans, quite simply, is not capable of seeing how *he* can change the things which seem to "happen" to him. His condition seems "natural" to him—as if it is not subject to alteration. Unable to comprehend history—even his personal history—as something made by people, Hans is doomed by his subjective vision of disjuncture which limits his capacity for efficacious analysis and action.

It is this alienated subjectivity, then, which is reflected— or more significantly, revealed—in the structures of Fassbinder's film. It is principally a structure marked by a sense of isolations, of connections cut off, of fragments. Stylistically and structurally, Fassbinder refuses wholeness—and the illusion of the natural as well. There is nothing beyond the dislocated fragments which sucessively occupy his screen: Fassbinder does not allow for connections between the successive views of Hans's world.

521

The film is marked by an extremely significant and specific use of the close-up. In *Merchant of Four Seasons* the close-up shots, in which the part is viewed in isolation from the whole, are done in such a way as to underline the isolation of the fragment. For example, when Hans and Irmgaard are seen in bed together after his return from the hospital, there is no real sense in which the giant close-up of her nipple can be said to exist in any meaningful connection to a whole and human person. Rather, the nipple, which fills the frame, serves explicitly to undercut the surface impression of genuine eroticism which we might have expected from such a scene. Examined under the relentless microscope of the camera eye, Fassbinder has given us a formal equivalent for the reified eroticism all too typical of our experience. He has replicated the experience of the close-up we have all heard spoken of in film histories in which the naive film audience, unaccustomed to the conventions of the close-up, unable to "read" them, is terrified—here "distanced" is the operative terminology—by the dismembered body it sees on the screen. Fassbinder's effect, not only with his fragmented close-ups of the human body but from the episodic fragmented structure of the narrative itself, is also terrifying—but terrifying in terms of the critique of alienation which is implicit in the very structure of the film itself.

The microscopic blowups of details characterizing the close-ups are echoed in the overblown gestures of the actors in the film. *Merchant of Four Seasons* is characterized by an insistence on posing, on hollowing of familiar gestures which by being exaggerated are emptied of any genuine meaning. Many are gestures of kitsch and pornography—the woman adjusting her garter beneath the upraised skirt of her dress; the fantastic protective gesture of the brother-in-law who sweeps all of the women behind him to shelter them from the brutish menace of Hans—but most striking of all are the repeated postures of the odalisque. In the desperate scene when Hans makes a last visit to "The Love of His Life," we see her strip and recline tensely posed on the bed, her hip arched so sharply that the gesture rivets our attention. It moves instantly beyond eroticism, baring itself rather as a subject for our analysis: "The Love of His Life's" odalisque pose is never a naturalistic gesture, as the hip remains frozen in a gesture of provocation long after Hans has closed the door and left the room. It is a gesture which expects no response—a gesture which never calls out for completion in the way the uncompleted gestures in John Ford often do, for example. Fassbinder's filmic gestures remain deliberate and brutal disruptions, underlining the absence of connections between characters and events—the ambience of alienation—in much the same manner as his dialogue does.

The cliches, which constitute the only language available to the characters who people the world of Fassbinder's cinema, force us to recognize the impossibility of communication between these characters. They cannot talk to each other, for they speak only in a language which has been systematically emptied of meaning. They speak words which are never their own—once again there is mediation at every level, even that of words. They cannot name their thoughts, for to name them would be perhaps to begin to act. Instead, the dialogue, which we and the characters themselves expect to serve as a means of breaking out of the terrifying isolation from which they suffer, only effects a further intensification of the barriers which separate them one from another. They remain cut off, trapped —and brutally exposed at the same time to the merciless eye of the close-up shot and to the brutally unyielding flatness of the very color of the film itself.

Merchant of Four Seasons is shot in brilliant primary colors of an extraordinary flatness, perhaps most similar to the kind of color used by Alfred Hitchcock in *Marnie*. Unlike a rich, dense color film which provides a sensuous background which surround the figures of the characters themselves, the flatness of the impenetrable brightness of Fassbinder's backdrops seems to force the figures out into our vision. It provides no shadow, no measure of escape from our scrutiny and analysis. It is as closed as is the extraordinary spatial construction of the film.

Fassbinder's characters live in confining fortresses or traplike spaces. You cannot navigate the geography of Hans's apartment. It is a series of boxlike rooms without connecting passages between them. It is an apartment, particularly in the montage of interviews when Hans hires an assistant after his illness, from which people depart or enter only by magic—the magic of editing—and never by ordinary means. It is a filmic

523

space which insists on asserting its theatricality by the refusal to utilize the existing off-screen space. The release which the continuous space might have provided, the sense of continuity, is entirely unsuited to Fassbinder's world view here, and thus it is denied. There is never any place else to go. Even the dream sequences, the flashbacks, are clearly disjunct from the trap of the everyday reality because of the utilization of blue tinting which makes them "different"—unconnected—and hence unable to function as alternative worlds which might relieve the claustrophobic reality Hans exists in. The other major spaces of the film, in addition to the confines of the apartment, are the courtyards where Hans and his assistant hawk the produce. The courtyards are also mazelike closed spaces, made more oppressive by the circular pans of the camera which pick up the turns and upwards stares of the peddlers. As the camera points up and turns round and round, it seems to try to climb over the walls of the trap—and almost succeeds. Here again then Fassbinder is deliberately creating an overtly theatrical anti-illusionistic space, going even further, in fact, by actually creating a kind of wing structure as Hans seems to go and come from the wings to spy on his worker.

The closed courtyards echo Fassbinder's much-favored shots through doorways or windows, forcing us repeatedly not simply to share Hans's mediated subjectivity but finally to analyze it. By refusing to allow us simply to "identify," by his structures of alienation, Fassbinder establishes us the audience as critical observers of what traditionally would be expected to be the most fitting subject matter for the style of naturalism. For here the stylized acting, gestures, space, and overall structure of the film remain in basic tension with the superficial subject matter of the film. A closer reading of this tension reveals that in fact the banality is no more than superficial and that the actual subject matter of *Merchant of Four Seasons* is a highly complex investigation of the structures of alienation in modern industrial societies. As we have seen, the formal disjunctures we have located in the film cinematically illustrate that social alienation. Cinematic devices assume the task of social critique.

Acknowledgments

The author wishes to thank the following for permission to reprint copyrighted material:

Lindsay Anderson, "The Method of John Ford," reprinted from *Sequence,* Summer 1950, by permission of the author; Michelangelo Antonioni, "The Event and the Image," reprinted from the English translation in *Sight and Sound,* Winter 1963–64, by permission of Guidio Aristarco and Penelope Houston; Eugene Archer, "Director of Enigmas: Alain Resnais," © March 18, 1962, by The New York Times Company, reprinted by permission of the author; Gideon Bachmann, "Jancsó Plain," reprinted from *Sight and Sound,* Fall 1974, by permission of *Sight and Sound* and the author; Maurice Bardeche and Robert Brasillach, "The Films of René Clair," from *The History of Motion Pictures,* translated by Iris Barry, 1938, reprinted by permission of W. W. Norton & Company, Inc.; Robin Bates, "The Ideological Foundations of the Czech New Wave," reprinted from the *Journal of the University Film Association,* Summer 1977, by permission of the author; Lawrence Becker, "A Minor Masterpiece: Dušan Makavejev's WR: Mysteries of the Organism," reprinted from *Film Journal,* September 1972, by permission of *Film Journal* and the author; Harold Benson, "Movies Without a Camera," reprinted from *The American Cinematographer,* January 1955, by permission of the editor; Ingmar Bergman, "Why I Make Movies," reprinted from *Horizon,* September 1960, by permission of the author; Alberto Cavalcanti, "The Sound Film," reprinted from *Cinema,* 1938, by permission of the author; Randall Conrad, "Luis Buñuel: An Integral Vision of Reality." Revised by the author. Originally published in *Cineaste,* Vol. 7, No. 4, 1977 as "A Magnificent and Dangerous Weapon: The Politics of Luis Buñuel's Later Films." Reprinted by permission of *Cineaste* and the author; Peter Cowie, "The Study of a Colossus: Citizen Kane," from *The Cinema of Orson Welles,* copyright 1963 by A. S. Barnes & Company, Inc., reprinted by permission of the author; Sergei Eisenstein, "The Composition of Potemkin," from his *Notes of a Film Director,* 1958, compiled and edited by R. Yurenev, translated from the Russian by X. Danko, by permission of the Foreign Languages Publishing House, Moscow, USSR; Hanns Eisler, "The Composer and the Motion Picture," from *Composing for the Films,* copyright 1947 by Oxford University Press, Inc., reprinted by permission of the Hanns Eisler estate; Robert Flaherty, "Film: Language of the Eye (Nanook)," from *The Screen Director,* February 1951, a special issue dedicated to Robert Flaherty and edited by Jack Glenn, reprinted by permission of the editor; Philip French, "Richard Lester," *Movie* No. 4, Autumn 1965, reprinted by permission of the author; Raymond Gid, "Saul Bass," *Graphis* 89, reprinted by permission of Saul Bass; Lewis Jacobs, "George Melies: 'Artificially Arranged Scenes,'" "Edwin S. Porter and the Editing Principle" and "D. W. Griffith: New Discoveries," from *The Rise of the American Film,* 1940, reprinted by permission of the

Griffith: Social Crusader," from *The New Theatre*, November 1936, reprinted by permission of the author; Colin L. Westerbeck, Jr., "The Dark Night of the Soul of Robert Bresson." Revised by the author. Originally published in *Artform* as "Robert Bresson's Austere Vision," copyright © California Artform, Inc., 1976, reprinted by permission of the author and *Artform*; Colin Young, "Cinema of Common Sense," *Film Quarterly*, Summer 1964, copyright 1964 by the Regents of the University of California, reprinted by permission of the author and the Regents; Marvin Zeman, "The Zen Artistry of Yasujiro Ozu," reprinted as revised by the author from *Film Journal*, Fall/Winter 1972, by permission of *Film Journal* and the author.

Photos courtesy Museum of Modern Art Film Library, Filmmakers Distribution Center, David Grossman Collection, New Yorker Films, John Springer Associates, and Lewis Jacobs Collection.

Index of Names and Titles

Abel, Alfred, 88

A bout de souffle (Godard), 479. See also *Breathless.*

Abraham Lincoln (Griffith), 84

Adrift (Kadár, Klos), 502

Adventures of Dolly, The (Griffith), 39, 40, 41

After Many Years (Griffith), 44, 45, 46. See also *Enoch Arden.*

After the Verdict (Galeen), 108

Agee, James, 409, 414

Agnus Dei (Jancsó), 459

Aldo, G. R., 416

Aldrich, Robert, 273, 408

Aldrich, Thomas Bailey, 56

Alexander Nevsky (Eisenstein), 59, 68, 71, 72, 78

Algood, Sara, 239

Allegret, Marc, 115

Allegro (McLaren), 258

Allgeier, Sepp, 98

All the King's Men (Rossen), 262

Allures (Belson), 322

Alphaville (Godard), 324

Alten, Ferdinand von, 105

America (Griffith), 38, 58, 59, 61, 77, 84

Anaemic Cinema (Duchamp), 114

Anatomy of a Murder, 384, 409, 417

Andalusian Dog, An (Buñuel), 518. See also *Le Chien Andalou.*

Anderson, Lindsay, 403

And My Love to the Swallows (Jireš), 501

André, Victor, 16

Angel, Heather, 239

Angelina (Zampa), 281

Anger, Kenneth, 329, 379, 435

Anne Boleyn, 109

A Nous la Liberté (Clair), 225–226, 227, 228, 229

Anticipation of the Night (Brakhage), 433

Antonioni, Michelangelo, 284, 286, 287, 288, 290, 305, 309, 347, 358–369, 431, 438

Applause (Mamoulian), 159, 190

Arabella (Grune), 106

Arnheim, Rudolf, 404

Arno, Siegfried, 105

Arnoux, Alexandre, 227

Around Is Around (McLaren), 261

Arsenal, 62

Artaud, Antonin, 112, 114, 115, 116

Arvidson, Linda, 40. See also Mrs. David Wark Griffith.

As It Is in Life (Griffith), 51

Asphalt (Pommer), 86

Astaire, Fred, 178

Astruc, Alexandre, 374

Atonement of Gosta Berling, 119

At the Crossroads of Life (Griffith), 39

At the Edge of the World (Grune), 88, 96, 106

Au Hasard Balthazar (Bresson), 492

Auric, Georges, 226

Autant-Lara, 111, 112, 116

Autumn Afternoon, An (Ozu), 447, 451, 452, 455

Axelrod, George, 329

Baillie, Bruce, 322

Bakshy, Alexander, 118, 119

Ball, Kenny, 372

Ballard, Carroll, 322

Ballard, Lucien, 323

Ballentine, 390

Bamberger, Rudolph, 88, 103–104

Bande à part (Godard), 471

Bandit's Waterloo, The (Griffith), 41

Band of Outsiders (Godard), 318, 327

Barbarian, The (Griffith), 43

Barbaro, Umberto, 345

Bardot, Brigitte, 318, 320, 338, 406, 407

Barrymore, John, 34

Baruch (Dupont), 110

Bass, Saul, 384–385

Battle of Elderberry Gulch, The (Griffith), 52

Battleship Potemkin (Eisenstein), 59, 86, 95, 122, 134, 136, 139,

Battleship Potemkin (*continued*) 140–141, 144, 147–155, 387. See also *Potemkin.*
Bazin, André, 264, 270, 394, 396–399
Bear's Wedding, The (Eggert), 146
Beatles, The, 371, 373, 374, 378, 380, 381, 382, 383
Beatles, The, 392
Beck, Julian, 413
Becky Sharp (Mamoulian), 164–165
Beelzebub's Daughters (Méliès), 17
Begone Dull Care (McLaren), 259, 260
Behrendt, Hans, 110
Belle du Jour (Buñuel), 517
Belmondo, Jean-Paul, 315, 319
Belson, Jordan, 322
Ben Hur, 409
Bentine, Michael, 371
Bentley, Eric, 375
Beranger, André, 66
Berger, Ludwig, 88, 91, 103–104
Bergman, Ingmar, 1, 262, 286, 287, 289, 290, 296–304, 336, 407, 410, 427, 431
Bergner, Elizabeth, 90
Berlin (Ruttmann), 90, 214
Bernhardt, Kurt, 91, 110
Bernhardt, Sarah, 54
Bettauer, Hugo, 94
Beware the Holy Whore (Fassbinder), 520
Bewitched Inn, The (Méliès), 11
Bicycle Thief, The, 161, 245, 282, 315, 346
Big Parade, The (Vidor), 59, 70, 71
Big Trail, The (Walsh), 59
Biograph Company, 16, 39, 40, 41, 43, 44, 45, 46, 47, 49, 51, 52, 53, 54, 55, 56, 57, 61
Birth of a Nation, The (Griffith), 4, 37, 54, 58–79, 81, 83, 139
Bitter Rice, 282
Bitzer, Billy, 16, 41, 44, 47, 48, 62, 70
Blackmail (Hitchcock), 160
Black Orpheus, The (Camus), 404
Black Shirt, 276
Blackton, Stuart, 16
Blasetti, Alessandro, 276, 277

Blood Countess, The (Jancsó), 461
Blue, James, 323
Bluebeard (Méliès), 14
Boccaccio '70 (Fellini), 353
Body Works (Emshwiller), 422
Bogdanovich, Peter, 459
Bold Seal Rover, The, 91. See also *Hurrah, I'm Alive.*
Bonjour Tristesse, 384
Boogie Doodle (McLaren), 258, 260
Boomerang (Kazan), 409
Borlin, Jean, 113
Boudu sauvé des Eaux (Renoir), 268
Bowes, Major, 220
Brakhage, Stanley, 411, 416, 435
Bramble, Wilfred, 374
Brandes, Werner, 104
Brault, Michel, 388
Bread, Love and Dreams (Comencini), 283
Breathless (Godard), 315, 318, 319, 327, 404
Breitrose, Henry, 387, 388
Bresson, Robert, 286, 367, 454, 480–493
Broadway Melody, 159
Broken Blossoms (Griffith), 65, 83, 143
Brooks, David, 423
Brooks, Louise, 97
Brooks, Mel, 503
Brotherhood of Man, 255
Brothers and Sisters of the Lodo Family, The (Ozu), 455
Brulatour, Jules, 267
Brumes d'Automne (Kirsanov), 116
Brunet, Madame, 219–220
Brute, The (Buñuel), 506, 507
Brynych, Zbyněk, 499
Buñuel, Luis, 117, 271, 286, 287, 376, 405, 507–518
Burning Heart, The (Berger), 103, 104
Burning the Candle, 171
Bush, W. Stephen, 34

Cabinet of Doctor Caligari, The (Wiene), 85, 86, 87, 107, 109, 145, 431
Cactus, My Pal (Ford), 234

Cagliostro's Mirror (Méliès), 11

Cagney, James, 176

Cain and Artem (Petrov-Bytrov), 145

Call to Arms, The (Griffith), 51

Cameo Kirby (Ford), 234

Camille, 54

Camus, Marcel, 402, 404

Cannon, Robert, 256

Capture of the Yegg Bank Burglars (Porter), 35

Carey, Harry, 234

Carné, Marcel, 272, 356

Cassavetes, John, 411, 412, 413, 418

Cassen, Jackie, 422, 424

Castellani, Renato, 283, 284

Cat and the Canary, The (Leni), 108

Caucasian Love (Shengelaia), 146

Cavalcanti, Alberto, 111, 113, 114, 115, 250

Cebotari, Maria, 277

Chabrol, Claude, 402, 404, 406, 407, 408, 444

Chafed Elbows (Downey), 329

Chair, The, 390

Chapeau de Paille (Clair), 222, 223, 224, 226, 227

Chaplin, Charles, 70, 91, 172, 188, 223, 225, 229, 376, 377, 452

Charge of the Light Brigade, The, 177

Chayefsky, Paddy, 409

Child of the Ghetto, A (Griffith), 51

China Express, The (Trauberg), 144

Chinese Parrot, The (Leni), 108

Chomette, Henri, 112, 114

Christians, Mady, 90, 104, 107

Christmas Dream, The (Méliès), 14

Chronique d'un Eté (Rouch), 391

Chukhrai, Grigory, 498

Churchill, Winston, 73

Chuvelev, I., 144, 145

Chytilová, Věra, 499, 505

Cimarron (Ruggles), 59

Cinderella (Berger), 88, 103, 104

Cinderella (Méliès), 12, 13

Cinque Minutes de Cinéma Pur (Chomette), 114

Citizen Kane (Welles), 161, 242, 262–274, 413, 428

Clair, René, 91, 112–113

Clayton, Jack, 404

Cleopatra, 54

Clifton, Elmer, 66

Closely Watched Trains (Menzel), 499, 501, 504

Cocteau, Jean, 224, 325, 415

Coffin Maker, The (Kobe), 87. See also *Torgus.*

Coleman, John, 352

College Is a Nice Place (Ozu), 455

Color Cocktail (McLaren), 258

Columbia and Shamrock Yacht Races, The (Porter), 21

Come Back, Africa (Rogosin), 410, 411, 418

Comedian, The (Gitlin), 389

Comencini, Luigi, 283, 284

Confessions of a Nazi Spy, 185

Confidential Report (Welles), 274

Confrontation, The (Jancsó), 459, 469

Conjurer Making 10 Hats in 60 Seconds (Méliès), 11

Conquest of the Pole, The (Méliès), 18

Contempt (Godard), 318, 320

Converts, The (Griffith), 51

Cooper, Gary, 176

Coppola, Francis Ford, 459

Corbett, Gentleman Jim, 234

Corner in Wheat, A (Griffith), 61, 62

Count of Monte Cristo, The (Porter), 34

Cousins, The (Chabrol), 404, 405, 407, 408

Coutard, Raoul, 314, 318, 320, 323

Covered Wagon, The (Cruze), 59, 70, 235

Crazy Quilt, The (Korty), 323

Cricket on the Hearth, The (Griffith), 45

Crime and Punishment, U.S.A. (Sanders Brothers), 408, 411

Crisis (Pabst), 92, 94, 96, 389

Cronaca di un Amore (Antonioni), 347, 368

Crossing the American Prairies in the Early Fifties (Griffith), 52

531

Crusades, The (DeMille), 82
Cruze, James, 59, 70, 235
Curruthers, Ben, 412
Curtiz, Michael, 241
Czar Ivan the Terrible (Taritsch), 145
Czinner, Paul, 110

Dagover, Lil, 99, 102
Daisies, The (Chytilová), 499
Dali, Salvador, 117
Damnation of Faust (Méliès), 17
Dassin, Jules, 317
Daughter of Destiny, A (Galeen), 96, 108. See Mandrake.
Death in This Garden (Buñuel), 516
Decae, Henri, 323
Defiant Ones, 417
Delerue, 316, 318, 320
Delteil, Joseph, 119
De Mare, Rolf, 112
Demille, Cecil B., 56, 82, 142
De Santis, Giuseppe, 281
Deserter, The, 160
Desert Victory, 215
De Sica, Vittorio, 277, 280, 283, 284, 345, 346, 354
Desistfilm (Brakhage), 411, 416
Desperate Encounter (Porter), 35
Destiny (Lang), 88, 98, 99, 110
Devil in a Convent, The (Méliès), 11
Dewey, Ken, 422, 423
Diary of a Chambermaid (Buñuel), 512–513, 514, 517
Diary of a Country Priest (Bresson), 480–482, 483, 484, 485, 487, 488, 489
Diary of a Lost Girl, The (Pabst), 92, 98
Diary of Anne Frank, The, 417
Dictator, The (Porter), 34
Die Hose (Behrendt), 110
Discreet Charm of the Bourgeoisie, The (Buñuel), 513–514, 518
Disney, Walt, 160, 162–163, 246–253
Di Venanzo, Gianni, 323
Doctor Mabuse (Lang), 87, 99, 100
Dr. Strangelove (Kubrick), 374
Dollar Dance (McLaren), 259, 260
Doniol-Valcroze, Jacques, 394

Donna Juana (Bergner), 90
Donnelly, Donal, 379
Don't Play with Love (Pabst), 92
Donzoko (Kurosawa), 332
Dots (McLaren), 258
Douce (Autant-Lara), 112
Dovzhenko, Alexander, 62
Down Among the Z Men (Lester), 371
Downey, Robert, 329
Dracula (Murnau), 101, 107
Drasin, Dan, 434
Dream of a Rarebit Fiend (Porter), 21, 32, 33
Dream of Butterfly, The (Gallone), 277
Drei von der Tankstelle (Thiele), 223
Drew Associates, 386–390
Dreyer, Carl, 87, 91, 116, 119–120, 305, 318, 319, 488–489
Drifters (Grierson), 115
Drums Along the Mohawk (Ford), 236, 239, 240, 242
Drunkard's Reformation, The (Griffith), 44, 47
Drunken Angel (Kurosawa), 331, 333–334
Duchamp, Marcel, 113, 114
Dulac, Germaine, 115, 116
Dupont, E. A., 89, 90, 110
Duras, Marguerite, 341, 426
Durbin, Deanna, 178–179
Dymling, Carl Anders, 302
Dziga-Vertov, 87, 131, 145

Early Spring (Ozu), 448, 451
Early Summer (Ozu), 448, 451
Earth Trembles, The (Visconti), 281
Eclipse, The (Antonioni), 361–363, 365–367, 369
Edgar Allan Poe (Griffith), 45
Edwards, Blake, 329
Eggert, K., 146
Ehrenburg, Ilya, 94
8½ (Fellini), 287, 326, 343–344, 349, 350, 352, 353
Eisenstein, Sergei M., 1, 59, 62, 68, 71, 78, 95, 117, 122, 124, 126, 127, 128–132, 134–135, 136–142, 143, 144, 145, 190, 223, 229, 315, 325, 375, 384, 454

Ekberg, Anita, 353
Elvery, Maurice, 100
Emak Bakia (Man Ray), 114
Emshwiller, Ed, 422, 423, 424
End of St. Petersburg, The (Pudovkin), 134, 136, 137, 143, 144, 145. See also *St. Petersburg.*
End of Summer, The (Ozu), 447–448, 450, 455, 456, 457, 458
Engel, Morris, 409, 411, 416, 417, 418, 419
Engel, Samuel G., 240
Enoch Arden (Griffith), 37, 43, 53. See also *After Many Years.*
En Rade (Cavalcanti), 86, 115
Entr'acte (Clair), 112, 223, 224, 226, 227
Epstein, Jean, 116
Equinox Flower (Ozu), 448, 450, 456–457
Eternal City, The (Porter), 34
Every Day Courage (Schorm), 495, 499, 500
Every Day Except Christmas (Tanner), 403
Ex-Convict, The (Porter), 21, 31, 35
Exposition des Arts Decoratifs, 113
Exterminating Angel, The (Buñuel), 516

Face in the Crowd, A (Kazan), 262
Fairbanks, Douglas Sr., 59, 68
Fairyland or The Kingdom of the Fairies (Méliès), 17
Fait-Divers (Autant-Lara), 112, 113, 114
Falkenstein, Jules, 88, 103
Family Budget, 256
Fanck, Arnold, 98, 109
Far from Vietnam (Godard), 472
Fassbinder, Rainer Werner, 286, 287, 290, 519–524
Faust (Murnau), 88, 102, 103, 110
Fear Eats the Soul (Fassbinder), 287, 520
Fellini, Federico, 284, 286, 287, 289, 290, 326, 343–354, 431, 434
Feyder, Jacques, 118, 138
Fiddle-De-Dee (McLaren), 259, 260
Fields, W. C., 84, 376

Fifth Horseman Is Fear, The (Brynych), 499
Fight for Life, The (Lorentz), 195–196
Fight for Love, A (Ford), 234
Fine Madness, A (Kershner), 323
Finis Terrae (Epstein), 87
Fireman's Ball, The (Forman), 500, 503
Five for Four (McLaren), 259
Flaherty, Frances, 387, 390
Flaherty, Robert, 387, 409
Flaming Creatures (Smith), 434
Floating Weeds (Ozu), 445, 448, 453–454, 455, 457, 458
Flowers and Trees (Disney), 163
Fool and a Girl, A (Griffith), 38
Football, 390
Ford, Francis, 234, 241
Ford, Henry, 125
Ford, Jack, 234. See also Ford, John.
Ford, John, 230–245, 266, 490, 523
Ford, Wallace, 239
For Love of Gold (Griffith), 42
Forman, Miloš, 494–495, 500, 503–504
Forty-First (Chukhrai), 498
Four Devils, The (Murnau), 103
400 Blows, The (Truffaut), 312, 404, 405, 413
Four Sons (Ford), 235
Four Steps in the Clouds (Blasetti), 277, 278
Frank, Robert, 411, 414, 415, 416, 417, 418, 419
Free Algeria (Resnais), 339
Freund, Karl, 89, 98, 102, 103, 109
Fritsch, Willy, 90, 98, 104
Froment, Raymond, 339
"From the Earth to the Moon and Around the Moon," 14
Fugitive, The (Ford), 236, 237, 238, 243, 244, 245

Galeen, Hendrik, 107, 108
Gallone, Carmine, 276, 277
Galveston Cyclone, The (Porter), 21
Gambler, The (Lang), 99
Gance, Abel, 59, 113
Garbo, Greta, 93, 97

Gardner, Helen, 54
Garland, Judy, 178
Genuine, 109
Gerlach, von, 89
Giant (Stevens), 409
Gide, André, 115
Gielgud, Sir John, 375
Ginsberg, Allen, 413, 414, 418–421
Gish, Lillian, 37, 83
Gitlin, 389
Glass of Water, A (Berger), 103, 104
Glennon, Bert, 242
Godard, Jean-Luc, 286, 306, 315–320, 324–327, 367, 376, 404, 412, 470–479
Goetzke, Bernard, 88, 99
Golden Age, The (Buñuel), 518. See also *L'Age d'Or*.
Gold Is Not All (Griffith), 51
Gold Rush, The (Chaplin), 70, 226
Gold Seekers, The (Griffith), 51
Goldfinger, 381
Goldwyn, Samuel, 206
Golem, The (Wegener), 88, 107
Gollancz, Victor, 143
Golovnia, A. N., 143
Good Morning (Ozu), 446, 455, 456
Goretta, Claude, 403
Gouan, 116
Graduate, The (Nichols), 503
Graham, Peter, 387, 390, 391, 392
Granach, Alexander, 88, 105
Grandma and Grandpa series (Porter), 21
Grandma's Boy (Lloyd), 220
Grapes of Wrath, The (Ford), 189, 236, 237, 240, 241, 242
Greaser's Gauntlet, The (Griffith), 41
Greatest Question, The (Griffith), 61
Greatest Story Ever Told, The (Stevens), 375
Great Train Robbery, The (Porter), 18, 21, 26, 27–31, 33, 43, 80, 189, 288
Great Ziegfeld, The, 178
Greed (Von Stroheim), 93
Grémillon, Jean, 111, 113, 114–115
Grevenius, Herbert, 300
Grierson, John, 115, 258, 259

Griffith, David Wark, 1, 4, 21, 25, 27, 33, 34, 36–57, 58–79, 80–84, 138, 143, 188, 191, 268, 325, 417
Griffith, Mrs. David Wark, 47. See also Arvidson, Linda.
Griffith, Lawrence, 40, 49, 52. See also Griffith, David Wark.
Griffith, Richard, 409
Grune, Karl, 59, 87, 88, 89, 91, 106–107
Guernica (Resnais), 339
Guilbert, Yvette, 103
Gulliver's Travels (Méliès), 17
Gulstörss, Max, 103, 105
Gypsy Blood (Lubitsch), 54

Hallelujah (Vidor), 160
Hammaren, Torsten, 301
Hand, The (Trnka), 496
Hands and Feet (Nalpas), 113
Hands of Orlac, The (Wiene), 107
Hanoun, 404
Happy Hooligan series (Porter), 21
Harbou, Thea von, 99
Hard Day's Night, A (Lester), 371, 373, 374, 375, 378, 382
Haunted Castle, The (Méliès), 11
Hawks, Howard, 306, 405
Hearst, William Randolph, 266–267
Heart of Oyama, The (Griffith), 43
Hearts of the World (Griffith), 61, 81
Helm, Brigitte, 96, 97, 106
Help! (Lester), 371, 373, 374, 376, 377, 378, 380–383
Hen Hop (McLaren), 259, 260
Hériat, Philippe, 115
Herlth, Robert, 88, 102, 103, 106
Hessian Renegades (Griffith), 47
Higgins, Dick, 422
High Treason (Elvery), 100
Hiroshima, Mon Amour (Resnais), 287, 338, 339, 341, 404, 414
Hitchcock, Alfred, 160, 305, 309, 317, 405, 523
Hitler, Adolf, 215, 313, 379
Hochhuth, Rolf, 426–427
Hoffman, Karl, 98, 106
Homecoming (Pommer), 86, 91
Hoodlum Priest, The (Kershner), 323

534

Hoppity Pop (McLaren), 259
Horn, Camilla, 103
House with the Closed Shutters, The (Griffith), 51
Houston, Penelope, 430
How Green Was My Valley (Ford), 239
Huff, Theodore, 238
Humanity Through the Ages (Méliès), 18
Hunte, Otto, 88, 98
Hunter, Ian, 239
Hurrah, I'm Alive, 91. See also *The Bold Sea Rover.*
Hurricane, The (Ford), 236
Hypnotist at Work, A (Méliès), 11

I Am a Negro (Rouch), 404, 406
Idiot, The (Kurosawa), 330
Idol Dancer, The (Griffith), 61, 75
I Flunked But (Ozu), 455
Ikiru (Kurosawa), 334, 428. See also *To Live.*
Il Bidone (Fellini), 349
Il Grido (Antonioni), 361, 368
Illusion Travels by Streetcar (Buñuel), 506, 509
Impossible Voyage, The (Méliès), 17–18
Informer, The (Ford), 235–236, 238, 239, 243, 244
Informer, The (Robison), 105, 106
Ingram, Rex, 98
Inkizonov, V., 144
Inn Where No Man Rests, The (Méliès), 17
In Old California (Griffith), 51
In Old Siberia (Reisman), 144
In the Season of Buds (Griffith), 51
Intimate Lightning (Passer), 500
Intolerance (Griffith), 4, 56, 58, 59, 67, 70, 75, 76, 82, 83, 143, 191
Iron Horse, The (Ford), 235
Isn't Life Wonderful? (Griffith), 58, 84
It Happened One Night (Capra), 189
It's Trad Dad! (Lester), 371–373, 374, 383
Ivan the Terrible (Eisenstein), 454

Ivens, Joris, 175, 204
I Vitelloni (Fellini), 349, 350
I Was Born But (Ozu), 445, 446

Jacob, Max, 224
Jacobs, Ken, 422, 423, 424
Jacobs, Lewis, 407
Jancsó, Miklós, 286, 290, 459–469
Jannings, Emil, 88, 89, 90, 102, 103, 104, 108, 146
Janssen, Walther, 99
Jazz on a Summer's Day (Stern), 411, 416
Jealousy (Grune), 106
Jeanne Ney (Pabst), 87, 90, 91, 92, 94–96
Jeffries-Ruhblin Sparring Contest, The (Porter), 21
Jehanne, Edith, 97
Jellicoe, Anne, 370, 378, 379
Jeux des Reflets et de la Vitesse (Chomette), 112
Jireš, Jaromil, 501–502, 505
Joan of Arc (Méliès), 14
Joe, 504
Johnson, Arthur, 40
Johnson, Nunnally, 240
Jones, Robert Edmund, 163–165
Joyless Street, The (Pabst), 89, 91, 92, 93, 94, 96, 110, 113
Judge Priest (Ford), 236
Judith of Bethulia (Griffith), 34, 39, 55, 56, 57, 59
Jules and Jim (Truffaut), 305, 309, 310–314
Juliet of the Spirits (Fellini), 287, 326
Junkin, John, 374
Jutra, Claude, 390

Kachalov, V. I., 145
Kadár, Ján, 502
Kaila, Eino, 302
Kaprow, Allan, 413
Karina, Anna, 316, 317, 318
Kast, Pierre, 419
Kazan, Elia, 262, 409
Keaton, Buster, 376
Kelman, Ken, 434, 435, 438
Kennedy, Robert, 389
Kerouac, Jack, 413, 415, 420
Kershner, Irvin, 323, 408

Kettlehut, Erich, 88, 98
Kevensky, 134, 138, 141, 315
Kingdom of the Fairies, The (Méliès), 17. See also *Fairyland.*
Kirkwood, James, 45
Kirsanov, Dimitri, 116
Klein-Rogge, Rudolf, 100
Kleptomaniac, The (Porter), 21, 31, 35
Klöpfer, Eugen, 109
Klos, Elmar, 502
Knack, The (Lester), 370, 373, 374, 375, 376, 378–380
Knight in London, A (Pick), 109
Kobe, 87
Koenig, Wolf, 390
Körtner, Fritz, 105
Korty, John, 321
Kozintsev, Grigori, 145
Krampf, Gunther, 107
Krauss, Werner, 88, 93, 94, 102, 106, 108
Kubrick, Stanley, 408
Kuleshov, Lev Vladimirovitch, 1, 127, 128, 129, 130, 136, 143
Kumonosu-jo (Kurosawa), 332. See also *Throne of Blood.*
Kurosawa, Akira, 286, 330–337

La Bête Humaine (Renoir), 214
Laboratory of Mephistopheles, The (Méliès), 11
La Casemate Blindée (Pick), 109
La Chinoise (Godard), 470, 473–479
La Chute de la Maison Usher (Epstein), 116
Lacombe, Georges, 115
La Coquille et le Clergyman (Dulac), 111, 112, 115–116, 117
La Cucaracha, 164
La Dolce Vita (Fellini), 347, 348, 350, 352, 354, 441
Lady from Shanghai, The (Welles), 264, 273, 274
Lady Vanishes, The (Hitchcock), 160
La Femme Infidèle (Chabrol), 444
La Femme Mariée (Godard),
La Folie du Docteur Tube (Gance), 113
L'Age d'Or (Buñuel), 376
La Guerre est Finie (Resnais), 287

La Lutte, 390
Lambart, Evelyn, 259
Lambert, Constant, 249
Lang, Fritz, 88, 90, 91, 98–101, 110, 112, 182, 320
La Notte (Antonioni), 287, 361, 363, 364, 367
La Pacifista (Jancsó), 459
La Passion de Jeanne d'Arc (Dreyer), 87, 116, 119–121, 488–489
La Petite Lilie (Cavalcanti), 115
Lapkina, Marfa, 142
La Règle de Jeu (Renoir), 268, 307, 312. See also *Rules of the Game.*
La Roue (Gance), 113
Lash of the Czar, The (Protozanov), 145, 146. See also *The White Eagle.*
Last Cab, The (Pick), 109
Last Drop of Water, The (Griffith), 52
Last Laugh, The (Murnau), 85, 86, 87, 89, 101, 102, 110
Last Night, The, 160
La Strada (Fellini), 284, 348, 349, 352
Last Sunset, The (Aldrich), 273
Last Year at Marienbad (Resnais), 287, 305, 338, 339, 340, 341
Late Autumn (Ozu), 448
Late Spring (Ozu), 448, 455
La Terra Trema, 346
Lattuada, Alberto, 281, 351
Laughlin, Tom, 408
Laughton, Charles, 176
L'Avventura (Antonioni), 287, 347, 358–359, 360, 361, 362, 363, 369
Leacock, Richard, 387, 388, 389, 391
Le Amiche (Antonioni), 361
Leather Stockings (Griffith), 47
Le Ballet Méchanique, 112
Le Beau Serge (Chabrol), 404
Le Bel Age, 419
Le Chemin de la Mauvaise Route (Herman), 387, 392
Le Chien Andalou (Buñuel and Dali), 11, 117
Le Dernier Milliardaire (Claire), 228–229
Le Diable au Corps (Autant-Lara), 112

Léger, Fernand, 111
Legrand, 318
Le Huitième Jour (Hanoun), 404
Le Joli Mai (Marker), 392
Le Jour Se Lève (Carné), 272
Le Million (Clair), 223, 224, 226, 227, 228
Leni, Paul, 105, 107, 108
Lenin, V. I., 122, 124, 144, 148
Le Procès de Jeanne d'Arc (Bresson), 485–489, 490, 491, 492, 493
Le Quatorze Juillet (Clair), 113, 223, 227–228
Les Dames du Bois du Bologne (Bresson), 483–484
Les Deux Timides (Clair), 223, 224, 226
Les Gardiens du Phare (Grémillon), 115
Les Inconnus de la Terre (Ruspoli), 391
Leslie, Alfred, 411, 413, 414, 417
Lester, Richard, 370–383
L'Etoile de Mer (Man Ray), 114
Levine, Joseph E., 391
Le Voyage Imaginaire (Clair), 224
L'Herbier, Marcel, 111, 112
L'Horloge (Silver), 113
Life Is Good (Pudovkin), 143
Life of an American Fireman, The (Porter), 20, 22–26, 27, 31
Lindsay, Vachel, 53
L'Inhumaine, 111
Little Pearls from the Bottom (Menzel, Němec, Schorm, Chytilová, Passer, Jireš), 505
Little Soldier, The (Godard), 315, 318, 319
Living Corpse, The (Ozep), 143, 145
Lloyd, Harold, 220
Lonedale Operator, The (Griffith), 52
Loneliness of the Long Distance Runner (Richardson), 502
Lonely Boy (Koenig), 390, 391
Lonely Villa, The (Griffith), 45, 46, 52
Long Voyage Home, The (Ford), 236, 237, 239, 241, 242, 243
Look Back in Anger (Richardson), 404, 412

Loope (McLaren), 258
Looping the Loop (Robison), 105, 106
Lord Love a Duck (Axelrod), 329
Lorentz, Pare, 175, 195, 196
Lo Sciecco Bianco (Fellini), 351–352
Lost Patrol, The (Ford), 235, 236, 239
Love (Makk), 463
Love Among the Roses (Griffith), 51
Love in the City (Zavattini), 284
Love on the Wing (McLaren), 258
Lover's Tale, The (Griffith), 45
Lovers, The (Malle), 404, 407
Lovers and Lollipops (Engel), 411
Loves of a Blonde (Forman), 504
Love's Sacrifice, 91
Lubitsch, Ernst, 99, 138, 160
Luci di Varietà (Fellini and Lattuada), 351
Luck of Ginger Coffey, The (Kershner), 323
Lumet, Sidney, 408
Lusts of the Flesh (Pabst), 94. See also *Jeanne Ney*.

M (Lang), 182. See also *Metropolis*.
MacArthur, Douglas, 230, 231, 232, 233
Macbeth (Welles), 274
MacCann, Richard Dyer, 400
Macdonald, Dwight, 310
MacOrlan, Pierre, 111
McBoing-Boing, Gerald, 254, 256
McCutcheon, George, 16
McKinley's Funeral Cortege (Porter), 21
McLaren, Norman, 258–261
McLuhan, Marshall, 422, 424
Mme. Sans Gene, 54
Maedchen in Uniform, 227
Magnani, Anna, 281, 283
Magnificent Seven, The (Kurosawa), 334–335. See also *Shichinin-no Samurai*.
Maiden's Paradise, The (Méliès), 14
Mail Early (McLaren), 259
Major Dundee (Peckinpah), 323
Makavejev, Dušan, 286, 440–442

Makk, Károly, 463
Malina, Judith, 413
Malle, Louis, 402, 404, 406, 412
Mallet-Stevens, Robert, 111
Mamoulian, Rouben, 164
Man and the Woman, The (Griffith), 41
Mandrake (Galeen), 108. See also *A Daughter of Destiny.*
Mankiewicz, Herman, 263
Mann, Delbert, 408
Manolescu (Tourjanski), 91
Manon Lescaut (Robison), 105, 108
Man of the Cross, The (Rosellini), 277
Man Ray, 111, 112, 113, 114
Man's Genesis (Griffith), 53, 54
Manvell, Roger, 240
Man Who Laughs, The (Leni), 108
Man with the Golden Arm, The (Preminger), 384, 385
Marcorelles, Louis, 386
Marcuzzo, Elio, 278
Margadonna, Ettore, 276
Marker, Chris, 392
Marmstedt, Lorens, 301
Marnie (Hitchcock), 523
Marquis d'Eon (Grune), 91, 106
Married Woman, The (Godard), 324, 327. See also *La Femme Mariée.*
Martin Luther, 91
Marty (Ritt), 408
Martyrs of Love (Němec), 504
Marvin, Henry, 40, 44, 47, 48
Marx Brothers, 228, 371, 377–378
Mary of Scotland (Ford), 236
Massacre, The (Griffith), 54, 55
Master of Nürnburg, The (Berger), 103
Maté, Rudolf, 119
May, Joe, 90
Mayer, Carl, 89, 102
Maysles, Albert, 387
Maysles, David, 392
Mazzei, Andrew, 100
Meistersingers, The (Berger), 91
Méliès, Georges, 1, 10–19, 20, 21, 22, 23, 27, 30, 33, 36, 66
Melody of the World (Ruttmann), 186

Men Call It Dawn (Buñuel), 509
Men Without Women (Ford), 235
Menzel, Jiří, 499, 501, 505
Merchant of Four Seasons (Fassbinder), 287, 520–524
Merchant of Venice (Reinhardt), 109
Metropolis (Lang), 90, 96, 98, 100–101, 112, 182. See also *M.*
Metzner, Ernö, 98
Mexican Bus Ride (Buñuel), 509
Meyerhold, V. E., 140, 144, 145
Meyers, Sidney, 409, 417–418, 419
Mickey's Polo Game (Disney), 249
Middle of the Night (Mann), 415
Milky Way, The (Buñuel), 511–512
Miller, Winston, 240
Miller's Daughter, The (Porter), 21, 35
Miracle in Milan (De Sica), 283
Mr. Deeds Goes to Town (Capra), 177
Mockey, Jean-Pierre, 376
Moi, Un Noir, 391, 413, 414
Momma Don't Allow (Richardson), 403
Mon Oncle (Tati), 381
Money-Mad (Griffith), 43
Montgomery, Robert, 230, 231
Moraldo in Città (Fellini), 350
Most, The, 390, 391
Mother (Pudovkin), 122, 128, 136, 143
Mother Love (Griffith), 55
Mouchette (Bresson), 492–493
Mouse, Mickey, 247, 248, 250
Mouse on the Moon (Lester), 371, 373
Mouse That Roared, The (Lester), 373
Muni, Paul, 176
Murder by Death, 503
Murnau, Fred, 72, 88, 89, 101–103, 107, 110
Music Master, The (Griffith), 39
Muskateers of Pig Alley (Griffith), 268
Mussolini, Vittorio, 276
My Darling Clementine (Ford), 236, 239, 240, 242
My Life to Live (Godard), 318, 319
My Love, Elektra (Jancsó), 460–468

Mystères du Château de Dé (Man Ray), 114

Nalpas, Louis, 113
Napoleon (Gance), 59
Nazarin (Buñuel), 509, 510
Necklace, The (Griffith), 45
Nehru (Leacock and Shuker), 388, 391
Neighbours (McLaren), 258
Němec, Jan, 496, 500–501, 502, 504, 505
Neppach, A. D., 106
New Babylon, The (Kozintsev and Trauberg), 145
New Year's Eve (Pick), 89, 109, 110
Nibelungen Saga (Lang), 88
Nice Time (Goretta), 401
Nichols, Dudley, 192–193, 235, 236, 237, 238, 243
Nielsen, Asta, 54, 88, 89, 93, 97
Night and Fog (Resnais), 339
Night Mail (Watt), 160, 175
Nina Petrovna (Pommer), 86, 91
Nine Hours to Rama, 385
Nitzschmann, Erich, 107
Nju (Dupont), 110
Nora Inu (Kurosawa), 334. See also *Stray Dog*.
Normal Love (Smith), 434
North Sea (Cavalcanti), 183
Now Is the Time (McLaren), 261
Nun's Story, The (Zinnemann), 417

October (Eisenstein), 315
O Dreamland (Anderson), 403
Off to Bloomingdale Asylum (Méliès), 14
O'Fienne, Sean, 234. See also Ford, John.
O'Flaherty, Liam, 106, 235, 238
Old and New (Eisenstein), 62, 134, 136, 137, 142, 144
Old Guard (Blasetti), 276
Old Isaacs the Pawnbroker (Griffith), 39
Old Maid series (Porter), 21
Olive Trees of Justice, The (Blue), 323

Olmi, Ermanno, 432
One Flew Over the Cuckoo's Nest (Forman), 503
Only Son, The (Ozu), 455
On the Bowery (Rogosin), 409, 411
On the Pole, 388, 390
Open City (Rossellini), 161, 279, 282, 402
Ophuls, Max, 325
Orphans of the Storm (Griffith), 59, 84
Ossessione (Visconti), 278, 281
Ostler Joe (Griffith), 39
Othello (Reinhardt), 109
Othello (Welles), 274
Out of the Mist (Wendhausen), 90
Over Silent Paths (Griffith), 51
Owen, Alun, 371, 373
Ozep, 143, 144, 145
Ozu, Yasujiro, 286, 432, 443–458

Pabst, G. W., 85, 89, 90, 91–98, 109, 110, 113, 223, 229, 431
Paisan (Rossellini), 161, 280, 402
Pandora's Box (Pabst), 92, 97–98
Paris-Port (Sauvage and Tedesco), 115
Parrotville Fire Department, The, 71
Pasolini, Pier Paolo, 462
Passer, Ivan, 500, 505
Peckinpah, Sam, 321
Penn, Arthur, 408
People in the City (Sucksdorff), 114
Perrault, Pierre, 390
Persona (Bergman), 287
Peterson, Brian, 422
Petey and Johnny, 390
Petrov-Bytov, 145
Phantom (Murnau), 101
Phantom of Liberty, The (Buñuel), 514–515
Piccoli, Michel, 320
Pick, Lupu, 89, 109, 110, 172
Pilgrim, The (Chaplin), 172, 226
Pippa Passes (Griffith), 47, 48, 56
Pirandello, Luigi, 306
Plough and the Stars, The (Ford), 236
Polanski, Roman, 286

Pollack, Channing, 100
Pommer, Erich, 86, 89, 90, 91
Popeye, 248, 249
Porten, Henry, 88
Porter, Edwin S., 16, 18, 20–35, 36, 41, 43, 52
Potechina, Lydia, 88, 105
Potemkin (Eisenstein), 59, 86, 95, 122, 134, 136, 139, 140–141, 144, 147–155, 387. See also *Battleship Potemkin*.
Pour Construire Un Feu (Autant-Lara), 116–117
Pour la Suite du Monde (Brault and Perrault), 390
Powell, Dilys, 267
Powell, Eleanor, 178
Powell, Frank, 45
Préjean, André, 222
President McKinley's Inauguration (Porter), 21
Primary (Leacock), 389
Prince Cuckoo (Leni), 108
Prince of Avenue A, The (Ford), 234
Prisoner of Shark Island, The (Ford), 239, 240, 241
Prisoner of Zenda, The (Porter), 34
Private Property (Stevens), 408, 416
Private Worlds, 159
Proletcult, 138, 140
Proper Time, The (Laughlin), 408
Protozanov, Yakov, 138, 145
Pudovkin, Vsevolod Illarionovitch, 59, 78, 79, 122, 127, 128, 129, 131, 132, 133, 134, 135, 136–138, 142–144
Pull My Daisy (Frank-Leslie), 410, 411, 414–415, 418, 419

Queen Elizabeth, 54
Quiet One (Meyers), 409
Quo Vadis, 34, 55, 56, 59

Rahn, 110
Rail, The (Pick), 109
Rain (Ivens), 204
Rainbow Parade series, 71
Ramona (Griffith), 51

Range War, The (Ford), 234
Rashomon (Kurosawa), 330, 331–332
Raskolnikov (Wiene), 107, 109
Rasp, Fritz, 105, 106
Record of a Living Being, The (Kurosawa), 332–333. See also *Ikimono-no Kiroku*.
Record of a Tenement Gentleman (Ozu), 453
Red and the White, The (Jancsó), 459
Red Desert (Antonioni), 287
Red Man and the Child, The (Griffith), 41
Red Psalm (Jancsó), 459
Red Riding Hood (Méliès), 14
Regards sur la Folie (Ruspoli), 391
Reisman, 144
Réjane, Madame, 54
Remorques (Grémillon), 115
Renoir, Jean, 214, 268, 305, 308, 312, 317, 318, 325, 405, 408, 413
Report on the Party and the Guests (Němec), 496, 502
Resnais, Alain, 1, 286, 287, 289, 290, 338–342, 402, 404
Resurrection (Griffith), 45
Return of the Pilot, The (Rossellini), 277
Richardson, Tony, 317, 403
Rich Revenge, A (Griffith), 51
Richter, Hans, 415
Ride the High Country (Peckinpah), 323
Rien Que les Heures (Cavalcanti), 114, 115
Rifleman, The (Godard), 319, 320
Ritt, Martin, 408
Rittau, Gunther, 98
Rittner, Rudolph, 103, 104
River, The (Lorentz), 175
River and Death, The (Buñuel), 516
River Tragedy, A (Porter), 35
Robbe-Grillet, Alain, 341, 418, 426
Robber Band (Behrendt), 110
Robinson Crusoe (Buñuel), 507, 516
Robison, Arthur, 87, 88, 104–106, 108, 113
Rogers, Ginger, 178

Rogosin, Lionel, 410, 411, 416, 417, 418, 419
Röhrig, Walther, 88, 102, 103, 106
Roma, Città Aperta (Rossellini), 346
Romance of a Jewess (Griffith), 43
Romance of Happy Valley, A (Griffith), 61
Romance of the Western Hills, The (Griffith), 51
Rome, 11 o'Clock, 282, 283
Romeo and Juliet, 181
Rome Wants Caesar Back (Jancsó), 459
Room at the Top (Clayton), 404
Rooty Toot-Toot, 255, 256
Rosi, Francesco, 315
Rossellini, Roberto, 277, 279, 280, 317, 346, 367, 404, 405
Rossen, Robert, 262
Rossington, Norman, 374
Rotha, Paul, 235
Rothafel, S. L. ("Roxy"), 220
Rouch, Jean, 387, 391, 402, 404, 406
Round-Up, The (Jancsó), 459
Routledge, Robert, 170
Ruggles, Wesley, 59
Rules of the Game (Renoir), 307, 312. See also *La Règle du Jeu.*
Running, Jumping and Standing Still Film, The (Lester), 371, 373, 381
Ruspoli, 391, 392
Ruttman, Walther, 90, 99, 186, 214

Sagan, Françoise, 341, 406
St. Petersburg (Pudovkin), 134, 136, 137, 143, 144, 145. See also *The End of St. Petersburg.*
Sally of the Sawdust (Griffith), 84
Sanders, Brothers, 408, 411
Sands of Dee (Griffith), 37
Sanjuro Tsubake (Kurosawa), 335, 336
Sanshiro Sugata (Kurosawa), 331
Sarraute, 426
Sauvage, André, 115
Savage Eye, The (Meyers), 417–418, 419
Scalera, 279
Scherben (Pick), 110

Scherzo (McLaren), 258
Schinderhannes (Bernhardt), 91
Schorm, Evald, 495, 500, 505
Schwartz, Hans, 91
Scipio Africanus (Gallone), 276
Scorpio Rising (Anger), 329, 379, 435
Scrapper, The (Ford), 234
Secrets of the Soul (Pabst), 90, 92, 93–94, 96, 431
Seldes, Gilbert, 36, 409
Selections des Rhythmes (Gance), 113. See also *La Roue.*
Sennett, Mack, 376, 381
Sennwald, André, 164
Seven Deadly Sins, The (Méliès), 14
Seven Samurai (Kurosawa), 334–335. See also *Shichinin-no Samurai.*
Shadows, 409, 411–413, 418, 419
She Wore a Yellow Ribbon (Ford), 245
Shengelaia, Nikolai, 146
Shenson, Walter, 373
Shepherd, 390
Shichinin-no Samurai (Kurosawa), 334. See also *Seven Samurai.*
Shoeshine (De Sica), 161, 280, 282, 345
Shoot the Piano Player (Truffaut), 305, 308, 309–310
Shop on Main Street (Kadár, Klos), 502
Showman (Maysles Brothers), 392, 393
Shuker, Gregory, 388, 391
Siege of the Alcazar, The, 276
Siegfried (Lang), 88, 98, 99, 110
Sign of the Cross, The (DeMille), 82
Silence (Bergman), 287, 425
Silence and Cry (Jancsó), 459
Silly Symphonies series (Disney), 163, 250
Simon of the Desert (Buñuel), 509
Sins of the Fathers, The (Berger), 104
Sjöberg, Alf, 301
Skullduggery (Vanderbeek), 434
Smith, Jack, 424, 434
Snobs, The (Mocky), 376
Snyder, Don, 424

Soloman, Alan, 377
Something Different (Chytilová), 504–505
Song of Ceylon, 160
Song of the Shirt (Griffith), 37, 45
Sorrows of the Unfaithful, The (Griffith), 51
Sous les Toits de Paris (Clair), 113, 222, 223, 224, 227, 228
Spanish Earth (Ivens), 175
Spottiswoode, Aitken, 74
Spy, The (Lang), 90, 91, 98, 100
Stage Door, 159
Stage Rustler, The (Griffith), 39, 41
Stakeout on Dope Street (Kershner), 408
Stankiewicz, Richard, 413
Stars and Stripes (McLaren), 258
Statues Also Die, The (Resnais), 339
Steamboat Round the Bend (Ford), 236
Steinrück, Albert, 88
Stern, Bert, 411, 417
Stern, Gerd, 422, 424
Sternberg, Josef von, 125, 138, 325
Stevens, George, 375
Stevens, Leslie, 408
Stoker, Bram, 101
Stone Rider, The, 109
Storm Center (Aldrich), 385
Storm Over Asia (Pudovkin), 59, 78, 135, 136, 137, 138, 143, 144
Story of Floating Weeds, A (Ozu), 445, 453, 454
Strange Interlude, 159
Stranger, The (Welles), 274
Stray Dog (Kurosawa), 334. See also Nora Inu.
Street, The (Grune), 87, 88, 106, 107, 110
Stroheim, Erich von, 126, 138, 143, 325
Struggle, The (Griffith), 84
Student of Prague, The (Galeen), 85, 86, 87, 107
Sucksdorff, Arne, 114
Suicide Club (Griffith), 45
Summers, Elaine, 422
Sumurun (Lubitsch), 88
Sunday (Drasin), 434
Sunrise (Murnau), 103

Suvarov, 189
Sylvester (Pick), 109. See also New Year's Eve.

Taking Off (Forman), 504
Talbot, Daniel, 410
Tambellini, Aldo, 422, 424
Taming of the Shrew, The (Griffith), 37, 45
Tanner, Alain, 403
Taritsch, 145
Tartuffe (Murnau), 86, 88, 101–102, 103
Tashlin, Frank, 376
Tati, Jacques, 381
Taylor, Gilbert, 371, 373–374
Technique and Rite (Jancsó), 459
Tedesco, Jean, 115
Tell-Tale Heart, 255, 257
Temple, Shirley, 178
Ten Days That Shook the World (Eisenstein), 59, 134, 136, 138, 141–142, 144
Tess of the Storm Country (Porter), 34
That Obscure Object of Desire (Buñuel), 515, 516–517
That Royle Girl (Griffith), 84
Thérèse Raquin (Feyder), 118
There Was a Father (Ozu), 446–447, 453, 455
They Were Expendable (Ford), 230–234, 236, 240, 241, 242, 244, 245
Thief of Bagdad, The (Walsh), 59, 68, 70, 78
Thiele, Wilhelm, 223
Thieves' Gold (Ford), 234
Third Man, The, 245
Thirty-Nine Steps (Hitchcock), 160
This Strange Passion (Buñuel), 506
Those Who Tread on the Tiger's Tail (Kurosawa), 335
Thread of Destiny, The (Griffith), 49
Three Bad Men (Ford), 235
Three Forbidden Stories, 282, 283
Three Little Pigs, The (Disney), 163, 247, 250
Three Smart Girls Grow Up, 178–179
Throne of Blood (Kurosawa), 332

Tobacco Road (Ford), 240, 241, 243

Tokyo Story (Ozu), 447, 450, 452, 455

Tol'able David, 87

Toland, Gregg, 237, 242, 268

To Live (Kurosawa), 334. See also *Ikiru*.

To Live in Peace (Zampa), 280–281, 282

Tom Jones (Richardson), 317

Topkapi (Dassin), 317

Torgus (Kobe), 87, 109. See also *The Coffin Maker*.

Torment (Bergman), 301

Torre Nielsson, Leopoldo, 432

To the Shores of Tripoli, 245

Touch of Evil (Welles), 268, 274

Tour au Large (Grémillon), 114–115

Tourjanski, 91

Tracy, Spencer, 176

Tragic Chase (De Santis), 281

Tragic Hunt, 161

Trauberg, Ilya, 59, 138, 144, 145

Treasure, The (Pabst), 92

Trial, The (Welles), 268

Trip Through the Columbian Exposition, A (Porter), 21

Trip to the Moon, A (Méliès), 14–17

Tristana (Buñuel), 287, 513, 516

Trnka, Jiří, 496

Trotti, Lamar, 236, 240

Truffaut, François, 286, 305–314, 317, 341, 394, 395, 396, 402, 404, 412, 413, 432

Turin, Victor, 145

Turksib (Turin), 87, 145

12 Angry Men (Lumet), 408

Two Brothers, The (Griffith), 51

Two Brothers, The (Grune), 89, 106

Two Cents' Worth of Hope (Castellani), 283

Two Days (Stabavoi), 145

Two or Three Things I Know About Her (Godard), 470–473

Tyler, Parker, 409, 410

Ueberfall (Metzner), 98

Ufa, 94

Unchanging Sea, The (Griffith), 51

Uncle Tom's Cabin (Porter), 21, 26, 27, 189

Une Femme Douce (Bresson), 490–491, 492, 493

Une Femme est une Femme (Godard), 316, 318, 319, 471

Unexpected Help (Griffith), 51

Unicorn in the Garden, The, 255

United Productions of America (UPA), 254–257

Usurer, The (Griffith), 51

Vadim, Roger, 406

Vagabond King, The (Berger), 104

Valerie and Her Week of Wonders (Jireš), 502

Vampyr (Dreyer), 305

Vanderbeek, Stan, 424, 434

Vanina (Von Gerlach), 85, 89

Vanishing Lady, The (Méliès), 11

Vaquero's Vow, The (Griffith), 43

Vaudeville (Dupont and Pommer), 89, 110

Vedrés, Nicole, 115

Veidt, Conrad, 88, 106, 107, 108

V for Victory (McLaren), 259

Victor-Hugo, Jean, 119

Vidor, King, 59, 70, 125, 223

Vigo, Jean, 305, 405

Violinist of Florence, The (Bergner), 90

Virgin Spring, The (Bergman), 296

Viridiana (Buñuel), 287, 376, 509–510

Visconti, Luchino, 278, 281, 346

Vollbrecht, Karl, 88, 98

Voyage au Congo (Allegret and Gide), 115

Wagner, Fritz Arno, 95, 98, 100, 101, 105, 107

Walsh, Raoul, 59, 68, 70, 305

Walthall, Henry, 45

Walther, Hertha von, 97

Waltz Dream, The (Berger), 103, 104

War and Peace (Vidor), 59

Warm, Herman, 88, 107

Warning Shadows (Robison), 87, 88, 104, 105, 113
Waterloo (Grune), 59, 91, 107
Watkin, David, 374
Watt, Harry, 175
Waxworks (Leni), 87, 88, 102, 107, 108, 110
Way Down East (Griffith), 61
Way of a Man, The (Griffith), 46
Way of the World, The (Griffith), 51
Wead, Frank, 230
Weddings and Babies (Engel), 409, 411, 419
Wedekind, Frank, 97
Wegener, Paul, 89, 107
Weinberg, Herman G., 409
We Live in Peace, 161
We Live in Two Worlds, 160
Welles, Orson, 1, 161, 242, 263, 264, 265, 266, 267, 268, 269, 270, 271, 272, 273, 274, 325, 345, 413
Wendhausen, Fritz, 90
West Side Story (Wise), 385
What Did the Lady Forget (Ozu), 446
What Did You Do in the War, Daddy? (Edwards), 329
What the Daisy Said (Griffith), 51
White Caps (Porter), 21, 35
White Eagle, The (Protozanov), 145. See also *The Lash of the Czar.*
White Hell of Pitz Polü, The (Pabst), 92, 98, 109
White Rose, The (Griffith), 61
White Rose of the Wilds, The (Griffith), 52
White Sheik, The (Fellini), 351, 352. See also *Lo Sciecco Bianco.*
White Ship, The (Rossellini), 277
Who Killed Cock Robin? (Disney), 249
Wiene, Robert, 86, 87, 107, 431
Wild Angels, The, 329

Wild Duck, The (Pick), 89, 109
Wild in the Streets, 504
Wild Strawberries (Bergman), 262, 287
Willy the Kid, 255
Window Water Baby Moving (Brakhage), 435
Winninger, Charles, 178
Winterset, 177
Winter Wind (Jancsó), 459
Without Pity (Lattuada), 281
Wolff, Willi, 90
Woman of Paris, A (Chaplin), 452
Woman in the Moon, The (Lang), 98, 101
Woman Is a Woman, A (Godard), 318, 319. See also *Une Femme est une Femme.*
Women, The, 213
Wood, Charles, 370, 378
Woods, Frank, 43
Wrath of the Gods, The (Fanck), 98, 109
WR: Mysteries of the Organism (Makavejev), 440–442
Wyler, William, 241, 268

Yalkut, Jud, 422
Yellow Pass, The (Ozep), 144
Yojimbo (Kurosawa), 335, 336
Young and the Damned, The (Buñuel), 508, 509, 518
Young Mr. Lincoln (Ford), 236, 239, 240, 242
Young One, The (Buñuel), 516
Youth of Queen Louise (Grune), 107

Zampa, Luigi, 280, 281
Zavattini, Cesare, 279, 284, 345, 346, 354, 390
Zola, Émile, 118, 136, 345
Zone, La (Lacombe), 115
Zukor, Adolf, 34, 54, 56